PRINCELY EDUCATION IN EARLY MODERN BRITAIN

In the sixteenth century, Erasmus of Rotterdam led a humanist campaign to deter European princes from vainglorious warfare by giving them liberal educations. His prescriptions for the study of classical authors and scripture transformed the upbringing of Tudor and Stuart royal children. Rather than emphasising the sword, the educations of Henry VIII, James VI and I and their successors prioritised the pen. In a period of succession crises, female sovereignty and minority rulers, liberal education played a hitherto unappreciated role in reshaping the political and religious thought and culture of early modern Britain. This book explores how a humanist curriculum gave princes the rhetorical skills, biblical knowledge and political impetus to assert the royal supremacy over their subjects' souls. Liberal education was meant to prevent over-mighty monarchy, but in practice it taught kings and queens how to extend their authority over church and state.

AYSHA POLLNITZ is an Assistant Professor of History at Grinnell College.

Cambridge Studies in Early Modern British History

Series editors

This is a series of monographs and studies covering many aspects of the history of the British Isles between the late fifteenth century and the early eighteenth century. It includes the work of established scholars and pioneering work by a new generation of scholars. It includes both reviews and revisions of major topics and books which open up new historical terrain or which reveal startling new perspectives on familiar subjects. All the volumes set detailed research within broader perspectives, and the books are intended for the use of students as well as of their teachers.

For a list of titles in the series go to www.cambridge.org/earlymodernbritishhistory

PRINCELY EDUCATION IN EARLY MODERN BRITAIN

AYSHA POLLNITZ
Grinnell College

CAMBRIDGE
UNIVERSITY PRESS

CAMBRIDGE
UNIVERSITY PRESS

University Printing House, Cambridge CB2 8BS, United Kingdom

Cambridge University Press is part of the University of Cambridge.

It furthers the University's mission by disseminating knowledge in the pursuit of education, learning and research at the highest international levels of excellence.

www.cambridge.org
Information on this title: www.cambridge.org/9781107039520

First published 2015

Printed in the United Kingdom by Clays, St Ives plc

A catalogue record for this publication is available from the British Library

Library of Congress Cataloguing in Publication data
Pollnitz, Aysha, 1978–
Princely education in early modern Britain / Aysha Pollnitz.
pages cm. – (Cambridge studies in early modern British history)
Includes bibliographical references and index.
ISBN 978-1-107-03952-0 (hardback)
1. Education, Humanistic–Great Britain–History. 2. Education of princes–Great Britain–History. 3. Renaissance–Great Britain. I. Title.
LC1024.G7P65 2015
370.11′2–dc23
2014043733

ISBN 978-1-107-03952-0 Hardback

For my family

Contents

Acknowledgements

This is a book about teachers and one that has been planted, tended and pruned by some extraordinary educators and munificent institutions of learning. It has been shaped particularly powerfully by Richard Serjeantson, who supervised my graduate studies and who continues to read and question my work with lucidity and generosity. He is a truly princely pedagogue. Unlike the schoolmasters described in this study, however, Richard approaches his office without ideological or methodological blinkers. I am cognisant of the risk and intellectual burden he assumed in encouraging me to pursue a project of this chronological range and in giving me great latitude regarding the nature of the sources I examined and the manner in which I contextualised them. I was able to study under Richard, as well as Annabel Brett and Quentin Skinner in Cambridge, because of the generosity of Cambridge Australia Scholarships, the (now sadly defunded) Overseas Research Students Awards Scheme, the Faculty of History of the University of Cambridge, and Trinity College, Cambridge. My Ph.D. examiners, Stephen Alford and the late Eric Ives, saved me from a number of errors and have been subsequent sources of advice and support.

In October 2005 the master and fellows of Trinity College, Cambridge, elected me to a research fellowship that enabled me to develop an account of the relationship between the royal supremacy and liberal education in early modern Britain. The college's generosity was matched by the conviviality of its members past and present. I learnt a great deal from Coulter George, Sachiko Kusukawa, Jo Miles, Geraldine Parsons, Alisha Rankin, Andrew Taylor, Tessa Webber and other distinguished scholars there. I was especially fortunate that my elector at Trinity was Patrick Collinson, who first remarked on the historical ironies that contour this study. The volume of Pat's knowledge was equalled only by the sharpness of his wit. It is a great and continuing sadness to me that I failed to complete this book during his lifetime. He is survived by Alex Walsham, whose patience, kindness and perspicacious suggestions have helped to bring the book to a finished state in the end.

Clare Jackson invited me to present an early version of chapter six at the Cambridge Seminar for Early Modern British and Irish History. The questions that she and Mark Goldie asked me on that occasion were critical in catalysing its revision. I continue to benefit from their counsel and friendship and those of other Wednesday-night stalwarts, including Amy Blakeway, Thomas Freeman, Jacqueline Rose and Jessica Sharkey. The late István Hont encouraged me to present part of chapter four to the Cambridge Seminar for the History of Political Thought. I was particularly grateful to Richard Rex for his discerning comments on that paper and subsequent ones. At the Oxford Seminar for Literature and History in Early Modern England, Susan Brigden, Susan Doran and Paulina Kewes helped me to revise parts of chapter five. In 2007 the Centre for Research in the Arts, Social Sciences and Humanities in Cambridge and the British Academy supported a conference on 'Late Humanism, Politics, and Ideology' that enabled me to explore Prince Henry's rejection of James VI and I's political thought in august company. Malcolm Smuts and Anthony Grafton were particularly knowledgeable interlocutors on that occasion. Jacob Soll continues to be a bubbling brook of advice. I hope it will not be invidious of me to single out the learned contribution of Markku Peltonen, who subsequently invited me to talk about Renaissance education and translation to the polyglot members of the Helsinki Collegium for Advanced Studies. Chapter six owes its current form to John Marshall, Jamie Gianoutsos and the illustrious historians of the Monday Seminar at Johns Hopkins University. Other parts of this study have also benefitted immeasurably from the erudite interventions of scholars. George Bernard, Thomas Betteridge, James Carley, Conal Condren, Cathy Curtis, Andrew Fitzmaurice, Steven Gunn, John Guy, Janel Mueller, Geoffrey Parker, Jennifer Richards, Deirdre Serjeantson, Micheline White, Anna Whitelock and the late Kevin Sharp have been generous with their time and expertise.

In January 2009, the Folger Shakespeare Library became my intellectual home in the United States. I could not have completed this book without its rich collections, the generosity of its Fellowship Program, the knowledge of its curators Heather Wolfe and Georgianna Ziegler, and the care of Elizabeth Walsh and her Reading Room team. Carol Brobeck kindly invited me to discuss a version of chapter six with the diverse band of learned scholars assembled at the library in 2012. The community of readers at the Folger have been liberal with their wisdom and encouragement.

In particular I thank David Armitage, Elizabeth Hageman, Gerard Kilroy, John McDiarmid, Jason Rosenblatt, Alex Ryrie, David Trim and the inimitable Lois Schwoerer. Kathleen Lynch, J. G. A. Pocock, Gordon Schochet and Owen Williams offered me opportunities to participate in stimulating events organised by the Folger Institute. I am particularly grateful to David for encouraging me to articulate the approach to intellectual history that informs this monograph during conversations in Cambridge, Canberra, Washington, DC, and Houston.

Under the leadership of Lora Wildenthal the history department of Rice University proved an intellectually stimulating and supportive environment for research and teaching between 2010 and 2013. The first three chapters of this monograph benefitted enormously from Jack Zammito's sagacious and avuncular commentary. Its author continues to be indebted to his example as a scholar and teacher. The department's Monday Seminar offered valuable feedback on material that now appears in several chapters. Moramay Lopez-Alonso, Alida Metcalf and Kerry Ward are wise and warm sources of professional counsel. Lisa Balabanlilar, Katherine de Luna, Rebecca Goetz and Maya Soifer Irish have been incisive readers and remain inspiring friends. John Boles, Michael Maas, Rich Smith and Martin Wiener were generous with books and timely advice. Carl Caldwell's and Caleb McDaniel's incisive interventions helped me to articulate methodological and argumentative positions on several critical occasions. The members of Baker College continue to divert and educate me.

The faculty, students and staff of Grinnell College welcomed me with characteristic warmth in August 2014. The college generously supported the production of this manuscript in its final phase and sponsored the licence to reproduce Hans Holbein's magnificent and illuminating portrait of Prince Edward for the cover. The history department's workshop, under the leadership of Ed Cohn and Kelly Maynard, gave me the courage to make necessary cuts to chapter four. I have been especially fortunate in having Elizabeth Prevost as my department chair and mentor. My current students at Grinnell and my former students in Cambridge, in Georgetown and at Rice have impressed upon me something that humanist pedagogues rarely acknowledged: teachers learn rather more from their pupils than the other way around. I doubt I have the Socratian capacity to 'corrupt the young' but I have rejoiced in the powers that my students have derived from their liberal educations and the unexpected and compelling ways in which they use their learning.

The monograph's greatest debt is to the owners, custodians and curators of the manuscripts and rare books cited in its pages. I am especially anxious to acknowledge the librarians of the Bodleian Library, Oxford; the British Library; Cambridge University Library; the National Archives at Kew and in Edinburgh; the National Library of Scotland; and the Old Library of St John's College, Cambridge. It is a deep and absorbing pleasure to work in these and other collections. The industry and diligence of those who have digitised portions of their holdings, such as Hatfield House and the Matthew Parker Library of Corpus Christi College, Cambridge, have made research possible from afar. I am particularly grateful to David McKitterick and the librarians of the Wren Library of Trinity College, Cambridge, for sharing its treasures with me. It was David who alerted me to the presence of Prince Henry's schoolbooks a mere court away from my graduate rooms and who encouraged me to study a surviving fragment of Henry VIII's quarto Latin Bible.

The editors of the Early Modern British History series at Cambridge University Press have taught me a great deal about professional generosity as well as the framing of a historical argument. Alex Walsham, Ethan Shagan, John Morrill and Alexandra Shepard have read the entire manuscript on several occasions with inspiring efficiency and extraordinary erudition. At every stage they have encouraged me to make this the best book it could be. Their contribution has built on the learned and penetrating remarks of three early anonymous readers. The exemplary Elizabeth Friend-Smith of Cambridge University Press has managed the editorial and production process with patience, efficiency and unstinting kindness. With the able assistance of Rosalyn Scott, she has shown me why one cannot value editors too highly. Ashley Derr proofread the manuscript and assisted in the creation of the bibliography with a competence and cheerfulness that were priceless to me. Copy-editor Hazel Harris transformed the manuscript into an infinitely more elegant version of itself. I am grateful for her meticulous eye and patience with the determined irregularity of early modern printed books. I thank Jenny Slater for her flexibility, generosity and forbearance during the indexing and proofreading process. Chloé Harries has been similarly magnanimous and creative in marketing the book.

My first and most loving teachers were my parents, Lois and Christopher, and my sister, Emily. My mother's pedagogical expertise, my father's passion for literature and Emily's example of precocious determination have shaped the book and its author. In addition to many years of unflagging encouragement and support, they provided a study and library in Newcastle, Australia, and a month of evening seminars on chapter seven in January 2014. My beloved Nan supplied the occasion, Helen Oliver the champagne and Chris Willcox his knowledge of rhetoric. Stephen Bradshaw built two of the desks on which this monograph was written and gave me exclusive use of his on more occasions than I like to recall. He has travelled a long way with and for me and this book. It is to my family that this work is dedicated.

Abbreviations

ATS	*Accounts of the Treasurer of Scotland*, ed. C. T. McInnes, vols. XII–XIII (Edinburgh, 1978)
BL	British Library, London
BN	Bibliothèque Nationale, Paris
Bodleian	Bodleian Library, Oxford
Buchanan, *De iure regni*	George Buchanan, *A dialogue on the law of kingship among the Scots: A critical edition and translation of George Buchanan's 'De iure regni apud Scotos dialogus'*, eds. Roger A. Mason and Martin S. Smith (Aldershot, 2004)
CCR	*Calendar of the charter rolls preserved in the Public Record Office, 5 Henry VI–8 Henry VIII*, vol. VI: *1427–1516* (London, 1927)
CPR	*Calendar of the patent rolls preserved in the Public Record Office: Henry VI, Edward IV, Edward V, Richard III and Henry VII*, 11 vols. (London, 1897–1929)
CSPD James	*Calendar of state papers, domestic series, of the reign of James I: In the State Paper Department of Her Majesty's Public Record Office*, ed. Mary Anne Everett Green, 4 vols. (London, 1857–9)
CSP Milan	*Calendar of state papers and manuscripts in the archives and collections of Milan: 1385–1618*, ed. Allen B. Hinds (London, 1912)
CSP Scotland	*Calendar of state papers relating to Scotland and Mary Queen of Scots, 1547–1603*,

	ed. J. Bain *et al.*, 13 vols. (Edinburgh, 1898–1969)
CSP Spain	*Calendar of letters, despatches and state papers relating to the negotiations between England and Spain preserved in the archives of Simancas and elsewhere*, ed. G. A. Bergenroth *et al.*, 19 vols. (London, 1862–1954)
CSPV	*Calendar of state papers relating to English affairs in the archives of Venice*, eds. Rawdon Brown *et al.*, 38 vols. (London, 1864–1947)
CUL	Cambridge University Library
Edward, *CPP*	Edward VI, *The chronicle and political papers*, ed. W. K. Jordan (Ithaca, 1966)
Edward, *LR*	Edward VI, *Literary remains of King Edward the sixth, edited from his autograph manuscripts with historical notes and a biographical memoir*, ed. John Gough Nichols, 2 vols. (London, 1857)
EHR	*English Historical Review*
Elizabeth, *ACFL*	Elizabeth I, *Elizabeth I: Autograph compositions and foreign language originals*, eds. Janel Mueller and Leah Marcus (Chicago, 2003)
Elizabeth, *Translations*	Elizabeth I, *Elizabeth I: Translations, 1544–1589*, eds. Janel Mueller and Joshua Scodel (Chicago, 2009)
Ellis, *Letters*	*Original letters, illustrative of English history; including numerous royal letters; from autographs in the British Museum, and one or two other collections*, ed. Henry Ellis, 4 vols. (London, 1824–6)
Erasmus, *CWE*	Erasmus, *Collected works of Erasmus*, ed. James McConica *et al.*, 52 vols. (Toronto, 1974–)
Erasmus, *EECP*	Erasmus, *Education of a Christian prince with the Panegyric for Archduke Philip of Austria*, trans. Neil M. Cheshire and Michael J. Heath, ed. Lisa Jardine (Cambridge, 1997)
Erasmus, *OEDE*	Erasmus, *Opus epistolarum Desiderii Erasmi Roterodami: denuo recognitum et auctum*, P. S. Allen *et al.*, 12 vols. (Oxford, 1906–1958)
Erasmus, *Opera omnia*	Erasmus, *Opera omnia Desiderii Erasmi Roterdami: Recognita et adnotatione critica*

	instructa notisque illustrata, 9 ordines (Amsterdam, 1969–)
fol.	folio (fols. plural)
Foxe, *TAMO*	John Foxe, *The unabridged acts and monuments online* (Sheffield: HRI Online Publications, 2011), www.johnfoxe.org
FSL	Folger Shakespeare Library, Washington, DC
Haynes, *SP*	*Collection of state papers relating to affairs in the reigns of King Henry VIII, King Edward VI, Queen Mary and Queen Elizabeth, left by William Cecil*, eds. Samuel Haynes and William Murdin, 2 vols. (London, 1740–59)
HHCP	Hatfield House, Hertfordshire, Cecil Papers
HJ	*Historical Journal*
HMC Mar	*Report on the manuscripts of the Earl of Mar and Kellie preserved at Alloa house*, ed. H. Paton, 2 vols. (London, 1904–30)
HMC Salisbury	*Calendar of the manuscripts of the Most Honourable the Marquess of Salisbury, preserved at Hatfield House, Hertfordshire*, eds. R. A. Roberts *et al.*, 24 vols. (London, 1883–1976)
James, *BD*	James VI and I, 'Basilicon doron', in *James VI and I: Political writings*, ed. Johann P. Sommerville (Cambridge, 1994)
James, *Trew law*	James VI and I, *The trew law of free monarchies*, in *James VI and I: Political writings*, ed. Johann P. Sommerville (Cambridge, 1994)
LP	*Letters and papers, foreign and domestic, Henry VIII*, eds. J. S. Brewer *et al.*, 22 vols. (London, 1864–1932)
MS	manuscript (MSS plural)
NA	National Archives, Kew, London
NAS	National Archives of Scotland, Edinburgh
NLS	National Library of Scotland, Edinburgh
ODNB	*Oxford Dictionary of National Biography*
P&P	*Past and Present*
PPC	*Proceedings and ordinances of the Privy Council*, ed. Harris Nicolas, 7 vols. (London, 1834–7)
PPE	*Proceedings in the Parliaments of Elizabeth I*, ed. T. E. Hartley, 3 vols. (London, 1981–95)

RPCS	*Register of the Privy Council of Scotland*, eds. J. H. Burton *et al.*, 38 vols. (Edinburgh, 1877–1970)
RPS	*Records of the Parliaments of Scotland to 1707*, www.rps.ac.uk
sig.	signature (sigs. plural)
SCJ	*Sixteenth Century Journal*
SP	National Archives, Kew, State Papers
STC	*A short-title catalogue of books printed in England, Scotland, and Ireland and of English books printed abroad, 1475–1640*, first compiled by A. W. Pollard and G. R. Redgrave, revised and enlarged by W. A. Jackson, F. S. Ferguson and K. F. Pantzer, 3 vols. (London, 1986–91)
Warner	George F. Warner (ed.), 'The Library of James VI, 1573–1583: from a manuscript in the hand of Peter Young, his tutor', *Miscellany of the Scottish History Society* (Edinburgh, 1898)
WLTC	Wren Library, Trinity College, Cambridge

Introduction

In the early twenty-first century, the value of liberal education is publicly doubted by politicians, businesses, many schools, colleges and universities, and parents in liberal-democratic nations. Voices from both ends of the political spectrum question the utility of the skills it generates and they argue that the humanities turn their acolytes into rabid liberals. To some, liberal education is too left wing and secular. To others, it is too western, white, male, privileged and hetero-normative.[1] Its critics rarely acknowledge that they are making use of a discourse that is much older than the liberal-democratic state, or liberalism itself. Indeed, since the trial of Socrates at least, liberal education has been described by its detractors as good for nothing but corrupting the young.[2] Defences of the honour and utility of the liberal arts and sciences are similarly venerable. Since Aristotle's *Politics* (1337a–1342b) and Plato's *Republic* (377b, 401d–402a, 4454d, 473c–d, 531c–d, 540c) and *Apology for Socrates* (38a), champions of liberal education have focused on the way it teaches transferable discursive skills and critical thinking. Some argue, too, that it teaches citizenship and that it morally or even spiritually ameliorates its students to the general benefit of civil society.[3]

This study examines a high-stakes iteration of this debate, which was played out in the British isle between the accession of Henry VII (1457–1509) in 1485 and the wars of the three kingdoms. It aims to show

[1] K. Anthony Appiah, 'Liberal education: The United States example', in Kevin McDonough and Walter Feinberg (eds.), *Education and citizenship in liberal-democratic societies: Teaching for cosmopolitan values and collective identities* (Oxford, 2002); Janet M. Atwill, *Rhetoric reclaimed: Aristotle and the liberal arts tradition* (Ithaca, 1998); Alan Bloom, *The closing of the American mind: How higher education has failed democracy and impoverished the souls of today's students*, 2nd edn. (New York, 2008), pp. 356–79.

[2] Martha Nussbaum, *Cultivating humanity: A classical defense of reform in liberal education* (Cambridge, MA, 1997), pp. 1–2, 10, 26–7, 33.

[3] Yun Lee Too and Niall Livingstone (eds.), *Pedagogy and power: Rhetorics of classical learning* (Cambridge, 2000).

that liberal education, the study of classical languages, and literature that Renaissance pedagogues often referred to as the *bonae litterae*, transformed the upbringing of royal children and helped to reshape the political and religious culture of early modern Britain. More particularly, it considers a series of attempts made in the sixteenth and seventeenth centuries to use the liberal arts and sciences to teach Henry VIII (1491–1547), Henry Fitzroy, duke of Richmond (1519–36), Edward VI (1537–53), Mary I (1516–58), Elizabeth I (1533–1603), Lady Jane Grey (1537–54), Mary, Queen of Scots (1542–87), James VI and I (1566–1625) and his sons Prince Henry (1594–1612) and the future Charles I (1600–49) to espouse certain political and religious ideologies. I will ask whether its methods and curriculum were well suited to the task of indoctrination or whether the discursive skills princes acquired had a greater impact on the government of church and state.

To answer these questions, it is useful to engage with three existing conversations in early modern European history. The first is with intellectual historians and historians of education, who have examined what students learnt from their study of classical languages in the fifteenth, sixteenth and seventeenth centuries and debated its impact on pupils' identities and on the nature and form of civil and ecclesiastical polities.[4] I use household accounts, state papers, letters, library records and the comparatively well-preserved archive of royal school exercises to ask when, how and to what extent the Tudor and Stuart princes were educated liberally. Further, I investigate whether, in practice, the humanist iteration of liberal education cultivated a dynamic, even adversarial, outlook in its student princes or whether it encouraged a docile attitude towards authority.

The second discussion, conducted with historians of political and religious thought, explores competing theories of kingship in early modern Europe.[5] I examine manuscripts and printed treatises, sermons, speeches

[4] Including: T. W. Baldwin, *William Shakespere's smalle Latine and lesse Greeke*, 2 vols. (Urbana, 1944); Robert Black, 'Italian Renaissance education: Changing perspectives and continuing controversies', *Journal of the History of Ideas*, 52:2 (1991); Anthony Grafton and Lisa Jardine, *From humanism to the humanities: Education and the liberal arts in fifteenth- and sixteenth-century Europe* (Cambridge, MA, 1986); Paul Grendler (ed.), 'Forum: Education in the Renaissance and Reformation', *Renaissance Quarterly*, 43:4 (1990); Kenneth Gouwens, 'Perceiving the past: Renaissance humanism after the "cognitive turn"', *American Historical Review*, 103:1 (1998); Peter Mack, *Elizabethan rhetoric: Theory and practice* (Cambridge, 2002); Nicholas Orme, *Medieval schools: From Roman Britain to Renaissance England* (New Haven, 2006) and *From childhood to chivalry: The education of the English kings and aristocracy, 1066–1530* (London, 1984); Markku Peltonen, *Rhetoric, politics and popularity in pre-revolutionary England* (Cambridge, 2013); Quentin Skinner, *Reason and rhetoric in the philosophy of Hobbes* (Cambridge, 1996).

[5] Including Johan Huizinga, *Erasmus and the age of the Reformation*, trans. F. Hopman and B. Flower (New York, 1957); Peter Lake, 'The king (the queen) and the Jesuit: James Stuart's *True*

and letters to ask how princes learnt to describe the nature and extent of their authority. Finally, this study engages with historians of early modern Britain who have examined the ways that monarchs' personal piety, prejudices and priorities were formed, and how rulers shaped the political and religious culture of their realms in their turn.[6] I draw on princes' youthful writings and marginal annotations and on contemporaries' letters and accounts to ask how English and Scottish princes responded to the ideologies that their schoolmasters, preachers, governors and fathers, amongst others, tried to inculcate via their liberal educations.

It may be useful, at this point, to pause and explain more precisely what I mean by the phrase 'liberal education' in this monograph. The notion that schoolmasters might use it in a *deliberate* attempt to inculcate confessional or monarchical ideologies flies in the face of dominant modern understandings of this term. Even its toughest modern critics tend to argue that brain-washing is a perversion of the true mission of liberal education, or an unconscious if inevitable by-product of the process. Following John Locke's (1632–1704) *Some thoughts concerning education* (printed 1693), the study of the liberal arts and sciences has been associated increasingly with liberalism.[7] More specifically, liberal education has been described as the attempt to cultivate rational, free-thinking, even sceptical

law of free monarchies in context/s', *Transactions of the Royal Historical Society*, 6:14 (2004); Roger A. Mason, *Kingship and the commonweal: Political thought in Renaissance and Reformation Scotland* (East Lothian, 1998); James McConica, *English humanists and Reformation politics under Henry VIII and Edward VI* (Oxford, 1965); Richard Rex, 'The crisis of obedience: God's word and Henry's reformation', *HJ*, 39 (1996); Ethan Shagan, *Popular politics and the English Reformation* (Cambridge, 2003) and 'Beyond good and evil: Thinking with moderates in early modern England', *Journal of British Studies*, 49:3 (2010); Quentin Skinner, *The foundations of modern political thought*, 2 vols. (Cambridge, 1978); J. P. Sommerville, *Royalists and patriots: Politics and ideology in England, 1603–1640*, 2nd edn. (London, 1999); Richard Tuck, *Philosophy and government, 1572–1651* (Cambridge, 1993); Alexandra Walsham, *Providence in early modern England* (Oxford, 1999).

6 Including Stephen Alford, *Kingship and politics in the reign of Edward VI* (Cambridge, 2002); George Bernard, *The king's Reformation: Henry VIII and the remaking of the English church* (New Haven, 2005); Thomas Cogswell, Richard Cust and Peter Lake (eds.), *Politics, religion and popularity in early Stuart Britain: Essays in honour of Conrad Russell* (Cambridge, 2002); Richard Cust, *Charles I: A political life* (Harlow, 2005); John Guy (ed.), *The Tudor monarchy* (London, 1997); Ralph Houlbrooke (ed.), *James VI and I: Ideas, authority, and government* (Aldershot, 2006); Diarmaid MacCulloch, *Tudor church militant: Edward VI and the Protestant Reformation* (London, 1999); Peter E. McCullough, *Sermons at court: Politics and religion in Elizabethan and Jacobean preaching* (Cambridge, 1998); Anne McLaren, 'Challenging the monarchical republic: James I's articulation of kingship', in John McDiarmid (ed.), *The monarchical republic of early modern England: Essays in response to Patrick Collinson* (Aldershot, 2007); Kevin Sharpe, *Image wars: Promoting kings and commonwealths in England, 1603–1660* (New Haven, 2010) and *The personal rule of Charles I* (New Haven, 1992); David Starkey, *Henry: Virtuous prince* (London, 2008); Roy Strong, *Henry Prince of Wales and England's lost renaissance* (London, 1986).

7 Bruce Kimball, *Orators and philosophers: A history of the idea of liberal education*, rev. edn. (New York, 1995), pp. 115–56.

individuals whose minds are not hampered by desire, custom, authority or prejudice.[8] In the schoolroom, Locke and Jean-Jacques Rousseau encouraged play, self-directed learning and personal growth and discouraged corporal discipline.[9] In the political realm, Locke argued that men who had acquired sufficient reason to govern themselves neither required a state to impose arbitrary or absolute constraints on them nor could they rationally consent to such bondage.[10] With respect to religion, Locke's and David Hume's (1711-76) emphasis on reason and their distrust of custom, authority and even epistemological certainty rendered tolerance a virtue.[11] Thus subsequent thinkers who identify with various strands of liberalism have associated children's study of the liberal arts and sciences with citizenship, political rights and freedoms, and the democratic state. Martha Nussbaum has argued that this connection between pedagogy and politics may help explain 'why the idea of liberal arts education has flourished [in the modern United States] as it has not in Europe'.[12]

In this study, however, I hope to excavate a connection between liberal education and the politics of a European culture that preceded liberalism. Eugenio Garin has argued persuasively that there is a straight line between enlightenment thought and the study of the *studia liberalis* in the Renaissance.[13] When Locke referred to the 'liberal sciences' he meant the same study of classical languages and literature that Elizabeth I's schoolmaster, Roger Ascham (1515–68), had recommended when he, too, encouraged gentlemen to study the 'liberall sciences'.[14] When the Dutch humanist and pedagogue Desiderius Erasmus (1466–1536) wrote that the purpose of studying classical grammar and rhetoric was to make children (*liberi*) more *liberalis*, he was certainly discussing the need to cultivate reason and self-discipline, and to free students from psychological slavery to their passions and to corrupted customs, a Platonic and Aristotelian theme

[8] John Locke, *Some thoughts concerning education* (London, 1693), Wing L2762, pp. 39–41, 118–21, 221–3.

[9] Jean-Jacques Rousseau, *Émile; ou de l'éducation*, in *Oeuvres completes*, vol. IV, eds. Bernard Gagnebin and Marcel Raymond, 5 vols. (Paris, 1959–95), pp. 253–4, 310–12, 586–7; Locke, *Some thoughts*, pp. 66, 71, 83–4, 99–100.

[10] John Locke, *Two treatises of government*, ed. Peter Laslett (Cambridge, 1988), pp. 96–7, 323.

[11] John Locke, *Locke on toleration*, ed. Richard Vernon (Cambridge, 2010); David Hume, *Inquiry concerning human understanding*, ed. Stephen Buckle (Cambridge, 2007), pp. 8, 96, 106, 112–18.

[12] Martha Nussbaum, *Not for profit: Why democracy needs the humanities* (Princeton, 2010), p. 61.

[13] Eugenio Garin, *L'educazione in Europa, 1400–1600: Problemi e programmi*, rev. edn. (Rome, 1976), pp. 16–21, 259–81. See, too, Sheldon Rothlatt, *Tradition and change in English liberal education: An essay in history and culture* (London, 1976), pp. 23–31, 40–9.

[14] Locke, *Some thoughts*, pp. 212, 221–4; Roger Ascham, *The scholemaster or plaine and perfite way of teachyng children, to vnderstand, write, and speake, the Latin tong* (London, 1570), STC 832, sig. Sii^{r}.

that Locke would develop in *Some thoughts*.[15] For Erasmus, this freedom had an explicitly Christian dimension, too; God had created men with free will and then Christ had died for all men equally.[16] Locke might have quibbled about free will, but he would have endorsed Erasmus' account of the political consequences of Christian freedom: men could be governed by others only with their consent (*consensus*).[17] The object of a liberal education, then, was to learn to govern one's will and use one's freedom in an honourable manner. These significant discursive continuities in the curriculum and the ethical objectives of the course of studies I consider here make it reasonable, perhaps desirable, to use the phrase 'liberal education' to describe the humanist pedagogy of the fifteenth, sixteenth and early seventeenth centuries.

Nevertheless, Garin failed to note significant distinctions between sixteenth- and eighteenth-century understandings of the purpose and effect of liberal education. When Renaissance pedagogues, including Erasmus, used the word *liberalis* in educational and political contexts, they also intended to evoke a range of meanings that differed from, and sometimes outright contradicted, Locke's liberal discourse.[18] In particular, they were appealing to a Roman tradition of describing the *studia liberalia*, *ars liberalis* and *liberalis disciplinas* as well as the *studia humanitatis* and *bonae litterae* as those 'studies that were suitable to free-born men'.[19] In ancient Rome, neither slaves, beasts nor women were free-born men. This man's positive identity, however, revolved around his status as a person with enough leisure (*otium*, *libertas*) from paid employment to spend time reading and writing, and sufficient income to provide his son with tuition in these arts. The stoic philosopher Seneca was particularly keen to distinguish liberal education from learning how 'to make a living… These arts are our intellectual foundations, not our work'.[20] Yet they also provided the 'foundations' for men's future civic responsibilities as officeholders in the republic or empire. Serving as a lawyer, magistrate or military commander involved instructing and persuading others with eloquent speech.[21] Thus, when the orator Cicero argued that the liberal

[15] Erasmus, *De pueris instituendis*, in *CWE: Literary and educational writings IV*, p. 327.

[16] Erasmus, *EECP*, p. 41; Latin from Erasmus, *Institutio principis Christiani*, in *Opera omnia*, IV.i, p. 166.

[17] Erasmus, *EECP*, pp. 89, 105; Latin from Erasmus, *Institutio principis Christiani*, in *Opera omnia*, IV.i, pp. 203, 216.

[18] Kimball, *Orators and philosophers*, p. 115; Quentin Skinner, *Liberty before liberalism* (Cambridge, 1998).

[19] 'Quare liberalia studia dicta sint vides, quia homine libero digna sunt': Seneca, *Ad lucilium epistulae morales*, 88.2; see Skinner, *Reason and rhetoric*, pp. 22–3.

[20] 'Nullum in bonis numero, quod ad aes exit… [ars] si praeparant ingenium, non detinent… rudimenta sunt nostra, non opera': Seneca, *Ad lucilium epistulae morales*, 88.1–2.

[21] W. Martin Bloomer, *The school of Rome: Latin studies and the origins of liberal education* (Berkeley, 2011), pp. 2, 4.

arts and sciences were the means 'by which boys are shaped [*informari*] towards humanity [*humanitas*]', he assumed that being truly 'human' meant active participation in this highly verbal political culture.[22] After all, speech was the gift by which humans 'are most distinguished from brute animals'. It was, moreover, the power that 'assembled mankind' in cities, that 'brought them from wild and savage life to the present humane and civilized state of society' and that provided 'them [with] laws, judicial institutions, and rights'.[23] Rather than teaching its pupils how they might avoid the constraints of the state, reject traditional authorities and think independently, a Roman liberal education prepared students to take their place in the *res publica*.

In fifteenth-century Italy, strident defences of these Roman authorities on education were mounted by men who called themselves humanists (*humanista*), after Cicero's use of the phrase. They were similarly eager to equate the study of classical Latin and Greek languages and literature with persuasive speech and virtuous, public office-holding. Humanists argued that pre-professional training in logic at medieval universities should be replaced by the study of neo-classical grammar and rhetoric and of ancient histories, poetry and treatises of moral philosophy.[24] Beyond all other skills, humanists taught their students to speak and write eloquently, using the prescriptions and techniques of Isocrates, Demosthenes, Cicero and Quintilian.[25] Lucca della Robbia (1399/1400–82) depicted the resulting pedagogical clash between logic and rhetoric on a 1437 relief he chiselled for the Campanile of Florence's Duomo. Della Robbia fashioned the scholastic logician to show him reasoning calmly, with his finger pointing firmly to the authority of the text. His was contemplative learning by and for the book. The humanist orator, however, was formed to confront his interlocutor with the force of his delivery (*pronunciatio*). His toga flies out from his shoulder with the vigour of his movement and

[22] Cicero, *Pro Archia*, 11.3.

[23] 'Hoc enim uno praestamus vel maxime feris... Ut vero iam ad illa summa veniamus, quae vis alia potuit aut dispersos homines unum in locum congregare aut a fera agrestique vita ad hunc humanum cultum civilemque deducere aut iam constitutis civitatibus leges iudicia iura describere?': Cicero, *De oratore*, 1.8.32–4.

[24] John F. D'Amico, *Renaissance humanism in Papal Rome* (Baltimore, 1983), pp. 123–43; Eugenio Garin, *La disputa delle arti nel quattrocento* (Florence, 1947); Paul F. Grendler, *Schooling in Renaissance Italy: Literacy and learning, 1300–1600* (Baltimore, 1989), pp. 122–4, 171, 172, 212–29. Robert Black, *Education and society in Florentine Tuscany: Teachers, pupils, and schools, c. 1250–1450* (Leiden, 2007) points to significant continuities with medieval Latin education but underestimates the significance of the revival of Cicero.

[25] B. Kohl, 'The changing concept of the *studia humanitatis* in the early Renaissance', *Renaissance Studies*, 6 (1992); Robert Proctor, *Defining the humanities: How rediscovering a tradition can improve our schools* (Indiana, 1998), pp. 14–15; Skinner, *Reason and rhetoric*, pp. 5–6, 20–200.

his beseeching hands stretch out towards his adversary. Rhetoric's business was the affective persuasion of others. It was learning for public life. To this end, humanists argued that their curriculum was particularly well suited to those who were destined to govern the polity.[26] By improving the learning, virtue and speech of rulers, humanists claimed that their methods and curriculum would enhance the commonwealth.

This was, undoubtedly, an ideologically driven activity, but fifteenth-century humanists in Italian city-states were deliberately vague as to *how* their plans for the liberal education would ameliorate the polity.[27] They did not propose, for instance, that the *studia humanitatis* would prompt any kind of constitutional or political reform, or free them from dependence on the goodwill of a ruler or from the arbitrary or absolute government that later liberals criticised. In fact even so-called 'civic humanists', such as Leonardo Bruni (*c.* 1370–1444), who claimed to prefer republican to princely government, frequently advertised their willingness to serve a wide range of patrons and regimes.[28] Furthermore, Italian humanists in the fifteenth century did not argue that liberal education would reshape the social identity of its students in any way. As the humanist Baldassare Castiglione (1478–1529) confirmed in his *Book named the courtier*, 'the first and true profession of the courtier', or the republican aristocrat for that matter, must continue to 'be that of arms'.[29] Alongside the vast majority of fifteenth- and sixteenth-century humanists, Castiglione pointed to the examples of erudite Greek and Roman conquerors, such as Alexander the Great and Julius Caesar, to reassure aristocrats that a liberal education would not make them effeminate or unwarlike. Rather the *studia humanitatis* would lend a veneer of civility and eloquence to fifteenth-century soldiering. As Lauro Martines has demonstrated, the object of humanist education was not to challenge the political and military culture of the city-state any more than it was to

[26] For example Aeneas Silvius Piccolomini, 'The education of boys' (1450), in *Humanist educational treatises*, trans. and ed. Craig Kallendorf (Cambridge, MA, 2002), pp. 126–9; Brian Vickers, *In defence of rhetoric*, rev. edn. (Oxford, 1989), pp. 254–93.

[27] Grafton and Jardine, *Humanism to the humanities*, pp. 1–28.

[28] James Hankins, 'Rhetoric, history, and ideology: The civic panegyrics of Leonardo Bruni', in James Hankins (ed.), *Renaissance civic humanism: Reappraisals and reflections* (Cambridge, 2000), pp. 143–78; Nicolai Rubinstein, 'Italian political thought', in J. H. Burns and Mark Goldie (eds.), *Cambridge history of political thought, 1450–1700* (Cambridge, 1991), p. 33. For example, see the rededication of Il Platina to Lorenzo de' Medici, 'On the prince', trans. Nicholas Webb, in Jill Kraye (ed.), *Cambridge translations of Renaissance philosophical texts*, vol. II: *Political philosophy* (Cambridge, 1997).

[29] Baldesar Castiglione, *The book of the courtier*, ed. George Bull (London, 1967), p. 57.

insist on the desirability of a particular type of political constitution.[30] It was to teach noblemen to perform their existing political responsibilities well, and to secure patronage for the schoolmasters and men of letters who had educated them.

The self-interest of pedagogues was a constant but the royal schoolrooms of early modern Britain differed from their Italian predecessors in one significant way. They were the scenes of some of the first concerted attempts to use liberal education to effect political reform in Europe, albeit of a different tenor from the changes Locke proposed in his *Two treatises* and *Letters concerning toleration*. The critical event in radicalising a (small) circle of northern humanists took place in 1494, when Charles VIII of France invaded Naples. The subsequent fifty-five-year conflict between the Hapsburgs and Valois for control of the Italian peninsula sucked most of the European powers into its bloody vortex, prompted an alliance between the French and the Ottoman Turks and involved extensive use of increasingly powerful firearms. Erasmus of Rotterdam had been studying in Bologna in 1506 when fighting broke out in the ancient university town. The aged pontiff, Julius II (1443–1513), arrived at the head of a conquering army. Erasmus was disgusted that St Peter's successor was 'playing Julius [Caesar] to the life'.[31] Princes of church and state, he alleged, were putting their customary desire for military glory before their responsibilities to God or their free Christian subjects. Erasmus pointed out to Charles V of Spain and Henry VIII of England that, since they liked to claim that their powers derived from God, they should stop imitating Roman generals and take their pattern from the words and deeds of Christ, instead.[32] There was, he claimed, 'far more true glory' in Christ's peace 'than all those wars'.[33] Historians have tended to dismiss Erasmus' political writings as unctuous, unrealistic and even 'extremely primitive', but this study proposes that the northern humanist actually used classical and scriptural studies to make a courageous argument for radical change to the political culture of sixteenth-century Europe.[34]

Erasmus, moreover, argued that the most effective way to recalibrate royal priorities and rein in monarchical government was the liberal

[30] Lauro Martines, *Power and imagination: City-states in Renaissance Italy* (New York, 1979), pp. 191–219; Skinner, *Foundations of modern political thought*, vol. 1, p. 247.

[31] Erasmus, *CWE: Letters 142 to 297*, no. 205, p. 128.

[32] Erasmus, *EECP*, p. 46.

[33] Erasmus, *Dulce bellum inexpertis*, in *CWE: Adages iii iv 1 to iv ii 100*, p. 440.

[34] Alistair Fox, 'English humanism and the body politic', in Alistair Fox and John Guy (eds.), *Reassessing the Henrician age: Humanism, politics and reform, 1500–1550* (London, 1986), p. 39; Huizinga, *Erasmus and the age of the Reformation*, p. 153; James D. Tracy, *The politics of Erasmus: A pacifist intellectual and his political milieu* (Toronto, 1978), pp. 33, 126–7.

education of princes. Not only would the *bonae litterae*, or good letters, teach them to govern their own wills honourably but they could also teach them to govern other free Christian men in an honourable manner. As the humanist explained in the treatise *The education of a Christian prince* (1516), 'when a prince is born to office, not elected… then the main hope of getting a good ruler hangs on his proper education', since other mechanisms for checking monarchy had been 'lost with the right to vote'.[35] Chapter two of this monograph argues that Erasmus and his circle made it clear to aristocrats that 'proper education' did not involve military training. Unlike the Italian humanists, he argued for letters *instead* of arms. More specifically, Erasmus proposed that the princely study of *bonae litterae* could be used to reform monarchical government. Training in classical Latin and Greek grammar and rhetoric would give students a 'knowledge of words', which Erasmus argued was the only working gateway to reason and the proper understanding of public duties.[36] Reason alone, though, would not suffice. The most important words that princes would read were contained in scripture. It was the royal schoolmaster's job, Erasmus argued, to see that Christ's words and deeds, especially regarding 'those things which are particularly relevant to the prince's role', struck the prince in the heart and transfigured his emotional and spiritual life.[37] When managed correctly, Erasmus argued, a liberal education *could* wean student princes off bellicosity and tyranny and refocus their office on Christian charity and the propagation of scripture. Erasmus put his faith in the power of liberal education not merely to teach eloquence and the capacity to discharge a public office but also to inculcate an alternative political and religious ideology in its princely students.

Scholars have shown that Erasmus' pedagogical prescriptions had a significant impact on early modern European reading practices; the statutes of schools, colleges and universities; discussions about vernacular Bibles; and Protestant and Catholic reform movements.[38] This study argues, however, that Erasmus' methods and curriculum for the liberal arts and sciences had particularly strong traction in English royal schoolrooms after 1499, when

[35] Erasmus, *EECP*, p. 5.

[36] Erasmus, *De ratione studii*, in *CWE: Literary and educational writings II*, p. 667.

[37] Erasmus, *EECP*, p. 61.

[38] Baldwin, *William Shakespere's smalle Latine*; Marcel Bataillon, *Erasme et l'Espagne*, eds. Charles Amiel and Daniel Devoto, 3 vols. (Geneva, 1991); Grafton and Jardine, *Humanism to the humanities*, pp. 122–60; Elizabeth Leedham-Green, *Books in Cambridge inventories: Book-lists from vice-chancellor's court probate inventories in the Tudor and Stuart periods*, 2 vols. (Cambridge, 1986); Mack, *Elizabethan rhetoric*; John O'Malley, *The first Jesuits* (Cambridge, MA, 1993), pp. 23–36, 200–42; Hugh Trevor-Roper, 'Desiderius Erasmus', in *Historical essays* (London, 1957), pp. 35–61.

the humanist brought himself to the attention of the future Henry VIII. Neither Henry VII nor any other court Maecenas had invited Erasmus and his fellow *Graecistes* into Prince Henry's orbit. Rather, the thrusting, pecking flock of humanists who circled the court, hoping for crumbs, had seized on an opportunity to attach themselves to the king's second son, and they clung on as his dynastic star rose.[39] Chapter one examines letters, household orders and accounts, treatises and neglected literary gift manuscripts of poems and classical translations to show how Erasmus' circle shaped Henry's education in ways that broke with Yorkist precedent and ensured that he came to the throne as the most learned monarch to rule England hitherto. Subsequent chapters demonstrate the extent of Erasmus' influence on the schoolrooms of Henry's children and, later, on the curricula studied by Stuart princes. While Erasmus never managed to deter English or Scottish royal boys from military training, he did succeed in tipping the scales in letters' favour: between 1534 in England, 1566 in Scotland and the outbreak of the Bishops' Wars in 1639, princes male and female spent more time learning to wield pens than swords or guns.

Even in an era noted for its enthusiasm for reviving classical literature, British princes were notably bookish. Amongst the Spanish Hapsburgs, for instance, fifteenth-century tradition, which focused on bureaucratic skills, handling weapons and orthodox piety, remained much more significant than humanists' prescriptions in shaping royal education. Charles V and Philip II had high-powered humanists in their schoolrooms at times, but they became bureaucratic wizards rather than perfect orators.[40] In France, it was only the demands of managing a highly centralised, militarised and absolutist state that drove princes indoors in the middle of the seventeenth century. Even then, it was to study methods of accounting, military logistics and information management rather than to immerse themselves in the liberal arts and sciences.[41] In the chapters that follow, we will see that Edward VI and James VI, in particular, remained engrossed in their study of *bonae litterae* despite rebellions, assaults on their persons and the demands of minority rule. In early modern Britain, getting a liberal education was a serious business for princes.

[39] David Carlson, 'Royal tutors in the reign of Henry VII', *SCJ*, 22:2 (1991).

[40] Martha Hoffman, *Raised to rule: Educating royalty at the court of the Spanish Habsburghs, 1601–1634* (Baton Rouge, 2011), pp. 25–110; Jose Luis Gonzalo Sanchez-Molero, *Felipe II: La educación de un 'felicísimo princípe' 1527–1545* (Madrid, 2014).

[41] Jean Meyer, *L'Éducation des princes en Europe: du XVe au XIXe siècle* (Paris, 2004); Jacob Soll, *The information master: Jean-Baptiste Colbert's secret state intelligence system* (Ann Arbor, 2009), esp. pp. 58–65.

Female princes' opportunity to study classical languages, however, was more contingent. Fifteenth- and sixteenth-century humanists had mounted strong arguments for the liberal education of royal and aristocratic women but neither pedagogical theorists nor the women they taught expected that their learning would disrupt existing power dynamics within elite families. The *bonae litterae* might help wives and daughters limit the dynastic damage of failures of primogeniture, but it would not be used to teach sisters to challenge their brothers' superiority. As such, the Lady Jane Grey, who had no brothers or royal fiancé, received a much better humanist education than Mary, Queen of Scots or Elizabeth Stuart (1596–1662), despite their proximity to the throne. The complications of royal half-brothers also affected the provisions made for Mary I's and Elizabeth I's schooling. Despite the confessional orientations of Elizabeth and Edward VI, Elizabeth's education had more in common with Mary's studies than with Edward's. In particular, neither Tudor princess was encouraged to develop the skills in dialectic and theological argument that the young king practised from 1547. Elizabeth, who strove to govern her church as well as the state, found it difficult to overcome this deficit in the cut and thrust of parliamentary debates about further ecclesiastical and doctrinal reform in England. To the end of her life, she preferred to rely on appeals to *ethos* and the literary genres she had studied in her youth to direct her subjects' worship. Nevertheless, the classical learning of both Tudor queens certainly exceeded that of fifteenth-century royal women in England and demonstrated close engagement with Erasmus' pedagogical and spiritual writings. Ultimately both Mary and Elizabeth became impressive orators and formidable interlocutors, and they cultivated their reputations for learning. It is no exaggeration, then, to say that Erasmus' pedagogy revolutionised the activities of royal schoolrooms in England and Scotland, for both male and female princes.

The enthusiastic royal take-up of Erasmus' prescriptions for liberal education sharpens the question of his ideological influence in early modern Britain. James McConica has argued that Erasmus prompted real spiritual transformation in the court of Henry VIII. This 'remarkable enterprise' for the purging of 'decay and corruption' and propagation of 'reform in church and state' allegedly culminated in the king's decision to sever the English church from Rome. Subsequently, McConica claimed, the humanist's writings and ideas animated the government of Edward VI.[42] In McConica's eyes, Erasmus hatched the spirit of the

[42] McConica, *English humanists and Reformation politics*, p. 124; see too pp. 109–10.

Reformation in early modern England. More recently, and with much closer attention to English religious doctrine after 1534, George Bernard has described Henry's personal piety and the church he instituted in England as 'Erasmian'.[43] Chapters one and three of this study argue that Henry VIII's immersion in the *bonae litterae* was critical in teaching the king to fight Rome with his pen and to govern his church in the 1530s and 1540s. Nevertheless I suspect that historians have been too generous in attributing a sincere desire to affect Erasmian religious reform to the English prince.[44] Erasmus' spiritual works were frequently translated and printed in this period, and his description of the true Christian prince was rarely off Henry's lips, but this study asks whether the king and his apologists were hijacking the humanist's writings to fabricate an argument for the royal supremacy in England. Could Erasmus' attempt to use liberal education to put the brake on over-mighty monarchy have contributed, inadvertently, to one of the more audacious power-grabs in early modern European history?

When Henry VIII came to arrange for the education of his own son and heir, he certainly turned to Erasmus' pedagogy and those schoolmasters he believed would use it to prepare Prince Edward to govern a church as well as a state. I argue in chapters two, four and five that it was the royal supremacy in England, and anxiety concerning the role of the prince in the Scottish kirk, that led Tudor and Stuart princes to take liberal education more seriously than most of their continental contemporaries. Henry's own dipping in the font of the muses had been a mix of serendipity and Erasmus' self-promotion but his children's schooling would be more carefully planned. A temporal ruler could get away with a strong sword arm, a taste for demonstrations of orthodox piety, sufficient literacy and numeracy to oversee bureaucracy and advanced enough social skills to avoid alienating his or her nobility. Thus, the failure of Henry VIII's illegitimate son, Henry Fitzroy, duke of Richmond, to make much progress in the *bonae litterae* between 1525 and 1529 was of little matter. He was still perfectly capable of discharging a number of military and political offices during his short life. But things would be different by the time his half-brother, Edward, was born in 1537. The supreme head of the church in England would require 'clerkish' skills and knowledge to defend her or his faith and govern the ecclesiastical polity.

[43] Bernard, *King's Reformation*, pp. 233–47.

[44] Richard Rex, 'The religion of Henry VIII', *HJ*, 57:1 (2014).

The extraordinary archive of Edward VI's school exercises examined in chapter four is testimony to the capacity of an Erasmian education to teach its pupils to make precocious and persuasive interventions in contemporary controversies. Even when Edward's schoolmasters took a sharp turn towards further religious reform in 1547, the techniques of his liberal education enabled him to comprehend and advocate for the doctrinal changes being made in his name. Eventually his zeal outflanked most of his counsellors' and his argumentative persistence exhausted their patience. The president of Edward's council, John Dudley, duke of Northumberland (1504–54) and his client, William Thomas (d. 1554), concocted an innovative strategy to re-educate their godly monarch.

After the deposition of Mary, Queen of Scots and her flight to England, British princes needed considerable reserves of eloquence to defend their vision of church and state from increasingly fractious councils, parliaments, estates, kirks and churches. Historians have begun to revive the notion that confessional discord and the participatory character of government in England and Scotland were making these institutions more adversarial.[45] As Ethan Shagan has argued, the revisionists' account of pre-war politics as largely consensual has been replaced by a picture of 'a culture in which division rather than unity was acknowledged as the fundamental wellspring' of affairs of state.[46] The issues that polarised subjects were typically confessional, but Peter Mack, Markku Peltonen and Quentin Skinner have made a persuasive case that grammar school and university education amplified the contentious utterances that issued

[45] Patrick Collinson, 'The monarchical republic of Queen Elizabeth I', *Bulletin of the John Rylands Library*, 62 (1987) and *De republica Anglorum: Or history with the politics put back* (Cambridge, 1990); Mark Goldie, 'The unacknowledged republic: Office-holding in early modern England', in Tim Harris (ed.), *The politics of the excluded, c. 1500–1850* (Basingstoke, 2001); Steve Hindle, *The state and social change in early modern England, c. 1550–1640* (Basingstoke, 2002); Peter Lake, 'The politics of "popularity" and the public sphere: The "monarchical republic" of Elizabeth I defends itself', in Peter Lake and Steven Pincus (eds.), *The politics of the public sphere in early modern England* (Manchester, 2007); John McDiarmid (ed.), *The monarchical republic of early modern England: Essays in response to Patrick Collinson* (Aldershot, 2007); Natalie Mears, *Queenship and political discourse in the Elizabethan realms* (Cambridge, 2005); Markku Peltonen, *Classical humanism and republicanism in English political thought, 1570–1640* (Cambridge, 1995); Phil Withington, 'Public discourse, corporate citizenship, and state formation in early modern England', *American Historical Review*, 112 (2007).

[46] Shagan, *Popular politics and the English Reformation*, p. 199. See also Thomas Cogswell, *The blessed revolution: English politics and the coming of war, 1621–1624* (Cambridge, 1989); David Colclough, *Freedom of speech in early Stuart England, 1603–1628* (Cambridge, 2005); Richard Cust, 'News and politics in early seventeenth-century England', *P&P*, 112 (1986) and 'Was there an alternative to the personal rule? Charles I, the Privy Council and the parliament of 1629', *History* 90:299 (2005); Chris Kyle, *Theater of state: Parliament and political culture in early Stuart England* (Stanford, CA, 2012); Mack, *Elizabethan rhetoric*, pp. 176–92.

forth from pulpits, printing presses and parliaments.[47] After the wreckage of the wars in the three kingdoms, Thomas Hobbes (1588–1679) blamed liberal education for introducing its students to Athenian democracy and the Roman republic and for encouraging them to indulge their taste for speech-making. In his eyes, the legacy of Socrates had corrupted the young and dissolved the state. As David Norbrook has put it, the 'general pressure towards wider debate and discussion' exerted by humanists' *ars rhetorica* taught these men to imagine that true citizens lurked inside their subject bodies.[48]

In 1603 Elizabeth's frustration and articulate circumlocution in the face of their demands gave way to Stuart kingship. The penultimate and final chapters of this study consider the response of James VI and I and of his sons, Henry and Charles, to outbreaks of this more aggressively anti-monarchical ideology in Scotland and England. In fact, James had confronted a stridently republican and Presbyterian discourse in his own schoolroom. In 1570, the four-year-old king was placed under the tutelage of the humanist George Buchanan (1506–82) and his Calvinist assistant, Peter Young (1544–1628). Both men were tasked with teaching James to accept the justice of his mother's deposition and the strictly limited monarchy and Presbyterian kirk that a cabal of noblemen had erected in Scotland in his name. Chapter five asks how the king managed to emerge from Buchanan's schoolroom as one of the foremost proponents of episcopacy and the divine right of kings in early modern Europe. Not only had Buchanan's liberal education (and liberally administered beatings) failed to indoctrinate James but the king actually used the rhetorical skills and expertise in biblical exegesis that his schoolmasters had taught him to refute Buchanan's writings. When it came time to educate his own sons, however, James VI and I preceded Hobbes in cautioning Henry and Charles against over-zealous immersion in the liberal arts and sciences, particularly the study of rhetoric. Did the king deny his successor his own best weapon against the swelling tide of popular libelling, puritan preaching, Presbyterian covenanting and political speech-making? Or was Kevin Sharpe right to argue that 'no monarch' in the British isle 'succeeded to the throne better briefed in the responsibilities of office than Charles I'?[49]

[47] Mack, *Elizabethan rhetoric*; Peltonen, *Rhetoric, politics and popularity*; Skinner, *Reason and rhetoric*.

[48] Thomas Hobbes, *Behemoth or The Long Parliament*, ed. Ferdinand Tönnies (London, 1889), pp. 2–3, 33, 46, 109 and *The leviathan*, ed. Richard Tuck (Cambridge, 1996), pp. 181, 483–4; David Norbrook, 'Rhetoric, ideology and the Elizabethan world picture', in Peter Mack (ed.), *Renaissance rhetoric* (New York, 1994), p. 141.

[49] Kevin Sharpe, 'Private conscience and public duty in the writings of Charles I', *HJ*, 40.3 (1997), p. 642 (quotation) and *Personal rule of Charles I*, pp. 179–208.

Sharpe has certainly made a persuasive argument that Charles I's theory of kingship reiterated the script that had been written by his father. This would not surprise Anthony Grafton or Lisa Jardine. They have argued that, despite humanists' elevated claims to teach *liberi* to become more *liberalis*, the repetitive drilling, rote learning exercises and limited texts that they set for their pupils 'fostered in all its [liberal education's] initiates a properly docile attitude towards authority'.[50] Grafton and Jardine are wise to direct our attention to the gap between pedagogical theory and the social practices of teaching and learning. In the course of this study I have found that this is the space in which royal students' ideological transformations took place. Yet I have also found that these metamorphoses rarely followed schoolmasterly prescriptions. With the exception of Charles I, perhaps, early modern British princes were not made more docile, obedient or receptive to the ideology of their instructors by the study of the *bonae litterae*.

There is a danger that, whenever teachers try to transmit or translate a nominally authoritative idea across a cultural gap, students will misunderstand, misuse or mock this attempt.[51] Here, however, the discursive skills taught by humanist schoolmasters worked actively against their attempts to inculcate political or religious dogma. The capacity to create and organise an argument (*inventio* and *dispositio*), to seek out authorities (*loci*) from scripture and ancient texts to evidence a claim, and to see both sides of a case (*in utramque partem*) did not foster liberal 'free-thinking', but it did encourage intellectual independence – in certain instances, arrogant bloody-mindedness – in student princes. Despite the intentions of northern humanists and religious reformers to use letters to moderate monarchy in early modern Britain, Tudor and Stuart rulers used their discursive skills, wide reading and biblical knowledge to articulate increasingly absolute accounts of their authority over church and state. Prior to the outbreak of wars in the three kingdoms, Erasmus had succeeded in encouraging English and Scottish princes to prioritise letters over arms, but his methods and curriculum also taught rulers to wield their pens like swords.

50 Grafton and Jardine, *Humanism to the humanities*, pp. xiv, 23–4, 138–45, 148.

51 Homi Bhabha, 'Of mimicry and man: The ambivalence of colonial discourse', *October*, 28 (1984), 125–33.

CHAPTER 1

'Thys boke is myne': how humanism changed the English royal schoolroom, 1422–1509

After Henry VII (1457–1509) had triumphed at the battle of Bosworth in August 1485, he was anxious to buttress his weak genealogical claim to the throne. The first step was to establish a viable line of succession with his bride, Elizabeth of York (1466–1503). The second step, according to the classic account told with clarity and conviction by Nicholas Orme, was to make the new royal family look as much like the old as possible. Consequently, Orme argues that Henry VII's sons, Prince Arthur (1486–1502) and Prince Henry (1491–1547), were brought up according to a pattern established in the fifteenth century for the education of the Lancastrian King Henry VI (1421–71) and the Yorkist Edward V (1470–83).[1] If the Tudor dynasty wrought change on sixteenth-century England, Orme implied, this change had little or nothing to do with what had gone on in their thoroughly traditional schoolrooms.

Orme explained that English arrangements for the education of the king's eldest son had been largely static from the Norman conquest until the early years of the fifteenth century. The prince was typically entrusted to a knightly *pedagogus* (subsequently known as a *magister* or *meistre*) to be brought up in manners, noble accomplishments and knightly arts. Sometimes the knight might also instruct the prince in Latin and French, but this role was more frequently passed on to a relatively lowly *doctor* or grammar master.[2] It was in the fifteenth century that the dramatic 'changes… in the traditional system' of royal education had taken place and a new 'educational consciousness' had emerged.[3] Orme argued that the model for princely education established for Henry VI and Edward V

[1] Nicholas Orme, *From childhood to chivalry: The education of English kings and aristocracy 1066–1530* (London, 1984), pp. 21–5, 48–55 and *Education and society in medieval and Renaissance England* (London, 1989), pp. 177–88.

[2] Orme, *From childhood to chivalry*, pp. 18–21.

[3] Nicholas Orme, *From childhood to chivalry*, p. 21 and 'The education of Edward V', *Bulletin of the Institute of Historical Research* 52:136 (1984), p. 28, respectively.

set the pattern for royal and aristocratic schoolrooms well into the seventeenth century. As a medieval historian, he was aiming his longbow firmly at the bloated claims made by some of his colleagues for the wide-ranging impact of 'the English Renaissance' of the sixteenth century on the idea and experience of childhood.[4] In Orme's view, the only pedagogical innovation of the Renaissance was a relatively cosmetic change in the way small boys learnt Latin. 'We should be cautious', he wrote, about 'exalting [this period] over the others'.[5]

When one reviews the household accounts, patent rolls, close rolls, chronicles, diplomatic letters and princely *specula* that issued forth from royal schoolrooms between 1422 and 1509, these sources confirm aspects of Orme's account. Certain fifteenth-century practices of princely education continued well into the seventeenth century: professional schoolmasters were appointed; princes were expected to hold offices of state precociously to learn how to perform them; royal children received literary dedications, nominally for their education but usually as part of a bid to secure patronage; the eldest son frequently lived in an independent household that functioned as a courtly college, while his younger brothers and sisters often remained together with the queen; rulers and councils set out decrees regarding the cultivation of royal children's bodies, minds, manners and souls; and future princes were supposed to acquire some knowledge of letters, manners and military matters before ascending to the throne. Orme is wise to remind historians of these continuities between the medieval and early modern worlds.

Occasionally, however, the search for continuities may obscure our view of change. The same sources, and a few that have been hitherto neglected, suggest that sixteenth-century humanists' emphasis on liberal education transformed the upbringing of royal children and reshaped the political and religious culture of the British isle. This chapter locates the serendipitous inauguration of this new method of princely education in the juvenile household of Henry VII's second son, Henry, duke of York. The first section re-examines the fifteenth-century arrangements for Henry VI's and Edward V's upbringing, particularly the priority given to arms and vocational training in their schooling. The remainder of the chapter considers manuscripts, letters and early modern printed books associated with the

[4] Orme, *From childhood to chivalry*, p. 223 cited Kenneth Charlton, *Education in Renaissance England* (London, 1965) and Joan Simon, *Education and society in Tudor England* (Cambridge, 1966). See also Lawrence Stone, 'The educational revolution in England, 1560–1640', *P&P*, 28 (1964).

[5] Nicholas Orme, *Medieval schools: From Roman Britain to Renaissance England* (New Haven, 2006), p. 127.

education of Henry VII's sons, Arthur and Henry. Henry VII took pains to ensure that his son and heir, Prince Arthur, would have a traditional, deluxe upbringing in the Welsh Marches in the manner of Edward V. His education in new, that is to say antique, Latin grammar simply added some continental gloss to his epistolary style. After Arthur's premature demise, however, the king kept his second son closer to home and left him with the tutors who had attached themselves to his ducal household. The result was that the future Henry VIII benefitted from long and deep immersion in *bonae litterae* ('good letters'), a phrase that the humanist Erasmus of Rotterdam used to describe his methods for liberal education. Henry VIII's introduction to the latest currents of neo-Latin learning was nothing short of a revolution of the pen in royal and aristocratic schoolrooms. Moreover, this change in the way that one small boy studied Latin would have significant consequences for the political and religious culture of the British isle.

ROYAL EDUCATION IN THE FIFTEENTH CENTURY: HENRY VI AND EDWARD V

According to Orme's meticulous account, the dawn of a new 'educational consciousness' broke on 26 August 1422 in France. Henry V (1386–1422), lying in the throws of dysentery in the castle of Bois de Vicennes, made two codicils to his will. His youngest brother, Humphrey, duke of Gloucester (1390–1447), then serving as regent in England, was named *tutela et defensio… principales* (principal custodian and protector) of the infant Henry VI. Henry V's uncle, Thomas Beaufort, duke of Exeter, was declared *person[a]e su[a]e [regimen] et gubernatio* (guardian and governor of [Henry VI's] person) and given the responsibility for selecting the prince's servants. This was the first time peers had been explicitly appointed to protect and govern a baby. Two Knights of the Garter, Walter, Lord Hungerford (1378–1449), and Henry, Lord Fitzhugh (1363?–1425), were designated to assist Exeter in managing the royal household.[6] Henry V died five days later. The final legacy of the great warrior king was to create 'more elaborate and formal arrangements' for royal childhood in England.[7] But did Henry V's plan ever come to fruition?

[6] Patrick Strong and Felicity Strong, 'The Last will and codicil of Henry V', *EHR*, 96 (1981), pp. 84, 99–100.

[7] Orme, *From childhood to chivalry*, p. 21.

The codicils were a laudable attempt to secure the throne for the infant Henry VI but they were (perhaps predictably) frustrated by the political wrangling that accompanied the royal minority. A long struggle ensued between Gloucester, John, duke of Bedford (1389–1435), and Henry Beaufort, Bishop of Winchester (1375?–1447), for control of the realms of England and France.[8] During this conflict, few of the men mentioned in the codicil showed any interest in 'nurturing' the young king's person.[9] Only Hungerford and Fitzhugh attended Henry VI at all, as steward and chamberlain of his household. From 1422 to 1428 Queen Katherine (1401–37) was left to direct her son's establishment and prop it up financially. Despite her contributions, the king's retinue was dogged by poverty.[10] On 1 June 1428, when Henry was six years old and of age to move from the care of women, Gloucester might have been expected to step in. As president of the regency council, however, the duke ceded this office to Richard Beauchamp, earl of Warwick (1382–1439), and Henry VI's *magister* or 'master'.[11]

Not only were Henry V's 'elaborate and formal arrangements' for his son's upbringing largely ignored but also the content of Henry VI's education reflected the practice of previous centuries. Warwick's foremost charge was to teach the king to fight, and he took it seriously. He made 'a litel harneys' for Henry VI and obtained two 'lytill cote armurs' for him, one of which was made when the king was scarcely seven years of age. He was also given 'viii swerdis and a long blade of a swerde… for to lerne… to play'.[12] This young ruler would need to defend not only his English realm but also the territories that his father had won in France. Even the relatively pacific author of *Tractatus de regimine principum ad regem Henricum Sextum* (1436/7?), which was dedicated to Henry VI, emphasised that a fifteenth-century 'king must be strong in war' to maintain his title across the channel.[13]

[8] Charles T. Wood, *Joan of Arc and Richard III: Sex, saints, and government in the middle ages* (New York, 1988), p. 39.

[9] S. B. Chrimes, 'The pretension of the duke of Gloucester in 1422', *EHR*, 45 (1930); Ralph A. Griffiths, *The reign of King Henry VI: The exercise of royal authority*, 2nd edn. (Stroud, 1996), pp. 15–23; David Rundle, 'Was there a Renaissance style of politics in fifteenth-century England?', in George Bernard and Steven Gunn (eds.), *Authority and consent in Tudor England: Essays presented to C. S. L. Davis* (Aldershot, 2002), pp. 22–3; Bertram Wolffe, *Henry VI* (New Haven, 2001), p. 29–31, 37.

[10] *PPC*, vol. III, pp. 143, 191, 284–5; Griffiths, *Reign of King Henry VI*, pp. 51, 52, 54, 56; Wolffe, *Henry VI*, p. 36.

[11] Griffiths, *Reign of King Henry VI*, p. 52; Wolffe, *Henry VI*, pp. 45–7.

[12] *CPR 1452–61*, p. 247.

[13] 'Rex erit in bello fortis': [Anonymous] 'Tractatus de regimine principum ad regem Henricum Sextum' in Jean-Philippe Genêt (ed.), *Four English political tracts of the later middle ages*, vol. XVIII (London, 1977), p. 78.

To cultivate Henry VI's skills as a military leader and give him peers with whom he could parry swords, the council decreed on 28 June 1425 that the minor heirs of the crown's tenants-in-chief (barons and above) should be brought up in the royal household.[14] John Fortescue (*c.* 1397–1479), writing for Henry VI's son Edward, claimed that this measure had provided 'a school of vigour, probity and manners' for young noblemen.[15] At the time, however, Warwick had not been impressed. In November 1432 he complained to the Privy Council that certain youths had 'sturred' the king 'frome his lernyng' and corrupted him with 'matiers not behovefull'. Warwick wanted the troublemakers removed and the king formally reprimanded.[16] After the testimony of John Mowbray (1415–61), duke of Norfolk, to the council, a number of the young men were dismissed and the king was required to conform to a strict new code of conduct.[17] Fortescue insisted that educating aristocratic youths at court would keep England 'secured against invaders, and… formidable to [its] enemies'.[18] It must have been on these military grounds that the arrangement was continued despite its cost and moral disadvantages.

Compared to military prowess, book-learning was of small account. The council did instruct Warwick to 'teche the kyng… nurture [manners] lettrure [litterature] langage and other mannere of cunnyng [learning]'.[19] The early years that the king spent with his mother's household gave him excellent French.[20] By March 1428 he had learnt to say the services from a Latin primer.[21] Then in June that year the great council required Warwick to acquaint his charge with *specula principis* literature, to 'drawe [Henry] to vertues and the eschewyng of vices' and to teach him to 'love, worship and drede God'.[22] This task Warwick seems to have passed off to John Somerset (d. 1454), an Oxford and Cambridge graduate and former schoolmaster at Bury St Edmunds. At Easter 1427 Somerset had joined Henry's household as its physician and by January 1428 he was earning £40 per annum.[23] Between 1429 and 1432, however, when he doubled up as 'the king's master in medicine' as well as 'learning', his salary actually shrank to forty marks, or £26.13s.4d., a year.[24] He seems to have been

[14] *PPC*, vol. III, p. 170; Wolffe, *King Henry VI*, pp. 36–7.
[15] John Fortescue, 'In praise of the laws of England', in *On the laws and governance of England*, ed. Shelley Lockwood (Cambridge, 1997), p. 64.
[16] *PPC*, vol. IV, p. 135–6. [17] Orme, 'Education of Edward V', p. 122.
[18] Fortescue, 'In praise of the laws of England', p. 64.
[19] *PPC*, vol. III, p. 299. [20] Griffiths, *Reign of King Henry VI*, p. 241.
[21] Griffiths, *Reign of King Henry VI*, p. 53. [22] *PPC*, vol. III, p. 299.
[23] *PPC*, vol. III, p. 282; Carole Rawcliffe, 'Somerset, John (d. 1454)', *ODNB*.
[24] 'Magistro in medicina et doctori Regis': *PPC*, vol. IV, p. 30.

well liked by his charge, who rewarded him handsomely after 1439: he was made chancellor of the exchequer and warden of the royal mint, and he presided over Henry VI's patronage of Cambridge colleges and Eton school.[25] Yet as a fifteenth-century royal grammar master his skills had been valued slightly. Teaching the king 'lettrure' was a part-time job.

Scholars who emphasise the weight placed on literature in Henry VI's education argue that, in 1428, the council's directions to Warwick about his reading matter and its political benefits were specific and detailed. The king was to examine princely 'mirrours and examples of tymes passed of the good grace and sure prosperite and wele that have fallen to vertuous Kyngis... and of that contrair fortune that hath ensued to the Kyngis and to here landes and subgittes of the contrarie disposicion'.[26] Henry VI's council was probably thinking of treatises such as Thomas Hoccleve's *Regement of princes* (*c.* 1411), Giles of Rome's *De regimine principum* (*c.* 1280) and the Pseudo-Aristotelian *Secretum secretorum*. John Watts insists that Henry VI was one of the nobles who owned this sort of didactic literature and took it seriously.[27] Further still C. W. T. Blackwell and Susanne Saygin have suggested that Gloucester commissioned didactic literature such as Thomas Lydgate's *Fall of princes* in 1431, Leonardo Bruni's Latin translation of Aristotle's *Politics* in 1433 and Tito Livio Frulovisi's (fl. 1429–56) *Vita Henrici quinti* in 1436, to serve as 'instructional treatises' for Henry VI.[28] By their accounts the young king benefitted from both traditional medieval advice literature and the new currents of Italian humanist political thought.

Yet these scholars have overestimated the extent to which Henry VI or his supposed *tutela et defensio*, Humphrey, duke of Gloucester, engaged intellectually with texts they owned. It is doubtful, for instance, that either royal patron had great proficiency in Latin. On the rare occasion that they wrote, they did so in French. Would either have known whether Bruni's Latin translation of *Politics* was superior to William Moerbeke's

[25] *CCR*, pp. 74–5; Rawcliffe, 'Somerset, John (d. 1454)'.

[26] *PPC*, vol. III, p. 299.

[27] John Watts, *Henry VI and the politics of kingship* (Cambridge, 1996), pp. 15, 54–6. See similarly Richard F. Green, *Poets and prince pleasers: Literature and the English court in the late middle ages* (Toronto, 1980), pp. 75, 76, 78, 140–2.

[28] C. W. T. Blackwell, 'Humanism and politics in English royal biography: The use of Cicero, Plutarch and Sallust in the *Vita Henrici quinti* (1438) by Titus Livius de Frulovisi and the *Vita Henrici septimi* (1500–1503) by Bernard André', in I. D. McFarlane (ed.), *Acta conventus neo-Latini sanctandreani: Proceedings of the fifth international congress of neo-Latin studies* (Binghamton, 1986), p. 432; Susanne Saygin, *Humphrey, duke of Gloucester (1390–1447) and the Italian humanists* (Leiden, 2002), pp. 59 (quotation), 73–4.

version from the 1260s?[29] Frulovisi himself seems to have been aware that their literary interest in his work was limited. Having been a student of the great Renaissance pedagogue Guarino of Verona, he generated a plan for educating princes in neo-Latin oratory but he made no attempt to use it for the instruction of Gloucester or his royal nephew.[30] As David Rundle has pointed out, moreover, Frulovisi had had to 'request and opportune' his patron extensively to convince him to commission works at all.[31] The *Vita* was not a work generated by Gloucester to educate his nephew or to further any particular political agenda at court. His patronage of humanists was little more than a general statement of his princely liberality. Ultimately, then, the case for regarding Henry VI's childhood as the dawning of a new era in royal education is slight. In keeping with the dominant medieval pattern of royal cultivation in England, he was brought up to be a chivalrous knight, a pious ruler and a politely disinterested patron of clerics and scholars.

Orme's claims for the fifteenth century rest more securely on the slight shoulders of Edward V.[32] Edward IV's (1442–83) careful arrangements for his son's upbringing suggest its political import. As a baby Edward was entrusted to the care of a 'lady mistress', Elizabeth Darcy, who was assisted by a staff of nurses and rockers.[33] Then in September 1473 Edward IV established a set of ordinances 'for the vertuous guyding of the person of our deerest first begotten sonne' and 'the pollytique, sadde [grave], and good rule of his householde'.[34] The king's impetus to codify these arrangements coincided with his desire to consolidate royal authority in Wales.[35] In the spring of 1473 Queen Elizabeth (*c.* 1437–92) took her son to Ludlow with some of the twenty-two 'tutors and councillors' who had been given

[29] Carol M. Meale, 'Patrons, buyers and owners: Book production and social status', in J. Griffiths and D. Pearsall (eds.), *Book production and publishing in Britain, 1375–1475* (Cambridge, 1989), p. 204; Griffiths, *Reign of King Henry VI*, p. 241.

[30] Titus Livius de Fulovisi, *Opera hactenus inedita T. Livii de Frulovisiis de Ferraria*, ed. C. W. Previté-Orton (Cambridge, 1932), pp. 352–3.

[31] Cited by David Rundle, 'Humanism before the Tudors: On nobility and the reception of the *studia humanitatis* in fifteenth-century England', in Jonathan Woolfson (ed.), *Reassessing Tudor humanism* (London, 2002), p. 27.

[32] Orme, *From childhood to chivalry*, pp. 21–2 and 'Education of Edward V', pp. 119–30.

[33] *CPR 1467–77*, p. 358; *CPR 1477–85*, pp. 241, 259; *Calendar of the close rolls preserved in the Public Record Office: Edward IV, Edward V, and Richard III, 1476–1485*, ed. K. H. Ledward (London, 1949–54), no. 855, p. 254.

[34] 'Ordinances for the government of Prince Edward son of King Edward IV', in John Gough Nichols (ed.), *A collection of ordinances and regulations for the government of the royal household made in divers reigns* (London, 1790), p. 27.

[35] *CPR 1467–77*, p. 283; David E. Lowe, 'Patronage and politics: Edward IV, the Wydevills and the council of the Prince of Wales, 1471–83', *Bulletin of the Board of Celtic Studies* 29:3 (1981); Charles Ross, *Edward IV*, 2nd edn. (New Haven, 1997), pp. 193–4, 196.

responsibility for the prince's estates in Wales until his fourteenth birthday, an age he never attained. On 10 November 1473, the council was enlarged to twenty-five members, dominated by the queen and her family, and placed under the presidency of John Alcock, Bishop of Rochester (1430–1500). Its responsibility was to regulate Wales judicially and financially in the prince's name.[36]

As such Edward V's childhood was caught between his political utility as an emissary of royal power in the principality and his parents' concern for their son's education. Alcock was also named as Edward's 'teacher' and responsible for bringing the prince up 'in virtue and cunning [learning]'. He shared his authority with the queen's brother, Anthony Woodville, Earl Rivers (*c.* 1440–83), Edward's 'governor and ruler', who was responsible for the prince's 'person' and for bringing him up 'virtuously, cunningly and [to be] knightly'.[37] Unlike Exeter in 1422, Rivers took attendance on Prince Edward seriously and his appointment arguably raised the prestige of holding office in a royal child's household.[38] The practice of appointing a high-ranking royal governor, however, would prove short lived in England. As Orme himself acknowledged, Edward IV's plan had the unintended effect of affiliating his son with 'one unpopular group of courtiers', the Woodvilles.[39] Following Edward IV's death in 1483, Edward V may have seemed too much Woodville's creature to survive the protectorate of Richard, duke of Gloucester.[40] Following the demise of both Edward and his brother, the duke of York (1473–83), neither Henry VII nor Henry VIII appointed high-ranking *magistri* or 'governors' for their sons.

Edward IV's more durable pedagogical innovation was to issue a daily timetable for his son's education. He instructed Rivers that the prince was to rise at the same time every day (probably about seven o'clock).[41] Attended only by Rivers, his chamberlain and a chaplain, Prince Edward was to ready himself and hear matins. He would go on to his chapel or closet to hear a mass. Next was breakfast. Then for about two hours each morning the prince would be occupied with 'such vertuous learning as his adge shall now suffyce to receave'. The day's main meal was probably taken at ten or eleven on fast days. During the meal someone was to read out aloud 'noble storyes as

[36] *CPR 1467–77*, pp. 283, 366; J. L. Laynesmith, *The last medieval queens: English queenship, 1445–1503* (Oxford, 2004), pp. 152–5; Lowe, 'Patronage and politics', pp. 545, 551.
[37] *CPR 1467–77*, pp. 401, 417; 'Ordinances for the government of Prince Edward', in Nichols, *Collection of ordinances*, p. 27.
[38] Orme, 'Education of Edward V', p. 120.
[39] BL, Sloane MS 3479, fols. 54^{v}–55^{r} printed in Orme, 'Education of Edward V', p. 130.
[40] Orme, *From childhood to chivalry*, p. 22.
[41] 'Ordinances for the government of Prince Edward', in Nichols, *Collection of ordinances*, p. 28.

behoveth to a Prynce to understande'. Subsequent dinner conversation was to be 'of vertu, honor, cunynge, wisdom, and deedes of worshippe'. Then, in the name of 'eschewinge… idlenes', the prince would return briefly to his books before going outside to practise those military skills and courtly 'disportes and exercyses as behoveth his estate to have experience in'.[42] After knightly training came evensong, supper and some 'recreation' that may have involved music, dancing, or chess. The prince went to bed at eight o'clock.[43] The timetable attempted to cultivate desirable qualities and skills in the future king: orthodox piety, good manners and civil conversation, self-discipline, military prowess, courtly accomplishments and, for two to three hours each day, book 'learning'.

This timetable does suggest what Orme called a heightened 'educational consciousness'.[44] The ordinances recognised that a prince was also a child who still required mental, physical and spiritual nurture, sentiments that found a shrill echo in Elizabeth Woodville's 'pitefull screeches' upon Edward's death in 1483.[45] The ordinances also emphasised that a child was more mutable or, perhaps, corruptible than an adult: opportunities for loafing about in 'idlenes' were curtailed; Edward's chamberlain, Thomas Vaughan, was instructioned to ration access to the prince's person; Edward was spared public responsibility.[46] Revisions to the ordinances in 1483 suggest that, as Edward came to the cusp of his majority, the king and queen regarded his burgeoning sense of authority to be the main threat to his character. Prince Edward was forbidden from issuing orders without taking counsel from Rivers or Alcock, who retained the right to discipline him.[47]

Nevertheless the protective wall of the royal ordinance was breached regularly by ceremonies, events and duties that celebrated Edward's princely authority. On 11 June 1471, he was made Prince of Wales, duke of Cornwall and earl of Chester. He received homage from the peerage on at least two subsequent occasions.[48] Having been invested as a Knight of the Garter in 1472, he subsequently attended a number of the Order's chapters. In 1474 the prince participated in a formal entry to Coventry, where he heard poems and speeches in his honour, received the allegiance of the

[42] 'Ordinances for the government of Prince Edward', in Nichols, *Collection of ordinances*, p. 28.

[43] 'Ordinances for the government of Prince Edward', in Nichols, *Collection of ordinances*, p. 28.

[44] Orme, 'Education of Edward V', p. 122. See similarly Wood, *Joan of Arc and Richard III*, p. 32.

[45] Edward Hall, *Hall's chronicle; containing the history of England*, ed. Henry Ellis (London, 1809), p. 379.

[46] 'Ordinances for the government of Prince Edward', in Nichols, *Collection of ordinances*, p. 29.

[47] BL, Sloane MS 3479, fols. 54^v–55^r printed in Orme, 'Education of Edward V', p. 130.

[48] *Rotuli Parliamentorum; ut et petitiones, et placita in Parliamento*, ed. John Strachey, 6 vols. (London, 1767–77), vol. VI, pp. 9–14; *CPR 1467–77*, pp. 273, 365; Michael Hicks, *Edward V: The prince in the Tower* (Stroud, 2003), pp. 57–9.

mayor and corporation, and was given gifts of a gilt cup and handkerchief. Aristocrats were usually knighted at twenty-one; Edward was five when he was honoured in April 1475.[49] These ceremonies had an important political function. Edward's precociously perfect political body emphasised Yorkist dynastic strength in the localities and his liberality and magnificence established a patronage network in Wales, Cornwall and Chester. Yet these duties kept the prince 'on the road'.[50] He probably learnt a great deal about the geography of his kingdom but his timetable – the daily routine that acknowledged his childhood and his need for education – was also frequently and seriously disrupted.

Precocious office-holding could be pedagogical in a vocational sense. It gave Edward an apprenticeship in the bureaucratic and ceremonial aspects of princely government. In the summer of 1475, for instance, he travelled to Westminster to serve as keeper of the realm and lieutenant during Edward IV's thirteen-week invasion of France.[51] At the beginning and end of 1476 he was appointed general commission of oyer and terminer in Salisbury, Hereford, Gloucester, Worcester, Wales and the Marches.[52] In November 1477 he attended the great council at Westminster. In December he was granted a permit to make 'all manner of charters, letters patent and writs… in the chancery and any other courts'.[53] Prince Edward's signet warrants place him in Shrewsbury for part of 1478–9 and 1480, a visit probably relating to his new title as earl of March and Pembroke.[54] In January 1479 he witnessed the foundation charter of a chapel of St Erasmus in St Peter's Westminster.[55] This introduction to the technical and ritual aspects of government was given priority in his education; it was accepted that it should interrupt his 'vertuous learning' at Ludlow.

When Edward was following his timetable he learnt 'to ryde clenely and surely… to j[o]uste[,] to learne… [to] were… harneys'.[56] These were activities that he shared with his 'henchmen', the noble and gentle youth educated in his household, who seem to have behaved rather better than their Lancastrian predecessors.[57] The Italian-born chronicler Domenico Mancini (b. before 1434, d. 1494x1514), who was probably drawing on the

[49] Hicks, *Edward V*, pp. 57–8. [50] Hicks, *Edward V*, pp. 57–8, 64–6 (quotation).
[51] *CPR 1467–77*, pp. 499, 534–5; Hicks, *Edward V*, pp. 68–9.
[52] *CPR 1467–77*, pp. 574, 605; *CPR 1477–85*, p. 5.
[53] *CCR*, no. 164, p. 49; *CPR 1477–85*, pp. 59–60.
[54] Hicks, *Edward V*, p. 65. [55] *CPR 1477–85*, pp. 133–4.
[56] 'Liber niger domus regis angliae id est domus regiae sive aulae Angliae regis Ed. IV' and 'Ordinances for the government of Prince Edward', in Nichols, *Collection of ordinances*, pp. 29, 45.
[57] Bodleian, MS Ashmole 1137, fol. 152^{v} cited by Orme, 'Education of Edward V', p. 123.

testimony of Edward's physician, John Argentine (d. 1508), reported that the prince enjoyed strenuous exercise. While in Wales he had 'devoted himself to horses and dogs and other youthful exercises to invigorate his body'.[58] Later, when Edward was incarcerated in the Tower of London, he and his brother were seen playing with bows and arrows in the garden.[59] A refurbished copy of *The boke of noblesse* (1475), compiled by William Worcester's son, urged Edward V to prioritise his military training so that he could renew the English war against France.[60] In fact, the prince's education was also devised to hedge against local challenges to his crown. Edward IV had won his throne with victories at Barnet and Tewkesbury. His son needed to be ready to defend it.

Orme claimed that, despite the importance ceded to military training and the continual interruptions to his timetable, Edward V excelled in the liberal arts. Yet the evidence Orme cites for Edward's attainments is second hand or from the pen of indiscriminately unctuous men such as Pietro Carmeliano, a Brescian-born humanist, whom Edward encountered in London in 1483.[61] There is another reason for doubting that Edward V made extensive progress in letters: the man responsible for teaching him was part time, as Henry VI's tutor had been. John Giles, a professional grammar 'enformor', joined Edward's service in 1473.[62] On 1 May 1476, however, he was given a grant for life for having instructed not Edward but his younger brother, Richard, in grammar.[63] Richard lived with his mother's household, which tended to be based in the Thames valley. Giles could not have been teaching the two boys together.[64] Were the ordinances for the Prince of Wales's 'vertuous learning' only enforced for the three years between 1473 and 1476 or did Giles shuttle between the two households on a pony? Regardless, it seems that he must have been absent for long periods. For educating *both* the king's sons, moreover, the

58 'Ibi equis et canibus aliisque iuvenilibus studiis ad corpus confirmandum indulgebat': Dominicus Mancinus, *The usurpation of Richard the third*, ed. C. A. J. Armstrong, 2nd edn. (Oxford, 1969), pp. 70, 71.

59 A. H. Thomas and I. D. Thornley (eds.), *The great chronicle of London*, eds. (London, 1938), p. 234.

60 Edward IV's copy is BL, Royal MS 18 B XXII; Lambeth Palace MS 506 is dedicated by Worcester's son to Edward V and then Richard III.

61 Orme, 'Education of Edward V', pp. 123–4; J. B. Trapp, 'Carmeliano, Pietro (c. 1451–1527)', *ODNB*.

62 *Calendar of the close rolls… for Edward IV, Edward V, and Richard III*, no. 1, p. 1; *CPR 1461–76*, p. 456 yet see *CPR 1467–77*, p. 295.

63 *CPR 1467–77*, p. 592.

64 *British Library Harleian manuscript 433*, eds. Rosemary Horrox and P. W. Hammond, 4 vols. (Gloucester, 1978), vol. I, p. 93 and vol. III, p. 194; *CPR 1467–77*, p. 592; *Calendar close rolls… for Edward IV, Edward V, and Richard III*, no. 1, p. 1; Mancinus, *Usurpation of Richard the third*, pp. 70, 71; A. R. Myers (ed.), *The household of Edward IV: The black book and the ordinance of 1478* (Manchester, 1959), p. 223; Orme, *From childhood to chivalry*, p. 22.

schoolmaster was granted only £20 a year during Edward IV's lifetime.[65] Latin grammar was not, perhaps, given as high a priority in Edward V's education as Orme has supposed.

When Edward did read, moreover, his tastes were traditional. He owned epic tales in French, Burgundian stories of chivalry and anti-French literature. One would expect no less of a Yorkist prince. Edward IV had spent much of his 1470–1 exile at the Hague and subsequently in Bruges with Louis de Gruuthuse (1422–92), the *stad holder* of Holland.[66] Upon return to England, the king built up his own library in imitation of de Gruuthuse's. He bought enormous, illustrated copies of works such as *Le fait de Julius Caesar* (1479) and the fourth book of Jean Froissart's *Chroniques de France et d'Angleterre* (1460–80).[67] The king had their borders embellished with Yorkist coats of arms and sent them for 'gilding and dressing', 'coveryng and garnysshing' in crimson velvet. The volumes were bound with clasps, buttons and nails of copper and gilt, and tied with 'laces and tassels of silk'. Chests lined with fur were built to transport them to Eltham, the planned location for the royal library.[68] They were sized and ornamented to be read from a lectern and admired by auditors during a meal, rather than perused in private. There is evidence that Edward passed his literary preference for chivalric tales and chronicles onto his son.

When William Caxton (1415x24–1492), who had been the governor of the English Merchant Adventurers in Bruges, established his printing press, he reeled off Burgundian titles that would appeal to the royal ear and eye.[69] In 1477, for instance, he offered Prince Edward a translation of

[65] Hicks, *Edward V*, p. 69; *CPR 1477–85*, p. 258. Richard III raised Giles's annuity to £40 per annum in November 1483 then halved it again in July 1484: *British Library Harleian manuscript 433*, vol. III, p. 94; *CPR 1477–85*, pp. 373, 481.

[66] Gordon Kipling, *The triumph of honour: Burgundian origins of the Elizabethan Renaissance* (Leiden, 1977), p. 31 may overstate de Gruuthuse's direct involvement; Marina Belozerskaya, *Rethinking the Renaissance: Burgundian arts across Europe* (Cambridge, 2002), pp. 146–7.

[67] BL, Royal MS 17 F II and BL, Royal MS 18 E II; Janet Backhouse, 'Founders of the royal library: Edward IV and Henry VII as collectors of illuminated manuscripts', in Daniel Williams (ed.), *England in the fifteenth century: Proceedings of the 1986 Harlaxton symposium* (Woodbridge, 1987), p. 24; Scot McKendrick, '*La Grande Histoire Cesar* and the manuscripts of Edward IV', *English Manuscript Studies* 2 (1990), 'Lodewijk van Gruuthuse en de Librije van Edward IV', in M. P. J. Marten (ed.), *Lodewijk van Gruuthuse, Mecenas en Europees Diplomaat, ca. 1427–1492* (Bruges, 1992), p. 154 and 'The Romuléon and the manuscripts of Edward IV', in Nicholas Rogers (ed.), *England in the fifteenth century: Proceedings of the 1992 Harlaxton Symposium* (Stamford, 1994), p. 161.

[68] 'The wardrobe accounts of King Edward the fourth', in Nicholas Harris Nicolas (ed.), *Privy purse expenses of Elizabeth of York* (London, 1830), pp. 125–6, 152; Backhouse, 'Founders of the royal library', pp. 28–9, 39–41.

[69] Belozerskaya, *Rethinking the Renaissance*, pp. 70–2, 147–9; Margaret Kekewich, 'Edward IV, William Caxton, and literary patronage in Yorkist England', *Modern Language Review* 66:3 (1971), 481–7.

Raoul Lefèvre's *The history of Jason*, the hero who had 'conquerd the Flees of Golde'. The Order of the Golden Fleece was, of course, the highest association of chivalry in Burgundy. Caxton wrote in his letter dedicatory that he assumed that Edward IV, a member of the order, owned the work in French but he hoped that his son would 'begynne to lerne to rede Englissh' from the printed translation.[70] Caxton was not the only client to pander to Prince Edward's taste for chivalry. A few years later, the prince received a manuscript copy of Jean de Waurin's *Anciennes et nouvelles chroniques d'Angleterre* (produced 1470–80). It emphasised the Burgundian support for the Yorkist restoration in 1471 and featured a miniature that depicted de Waurin presenting his work to Edward IV, who was wearing the Order of the Golden Fleece.[71] Prince Edward patronised works that celebrated Yorkist military victories as well as England's alliance with Burgundy and her ambitions in France. Like the Lancastrians before him, he favoured literature that glamorised the chivalric culture of the court and exhorted courage in battle and pious service to the church.

We may see the shoots of a new 'educational consciousness' in aspects of Edward V's upbringing, most notably in the timetable that attempted to carve out a period of mental, moral and physical cultivation for the prince. Yet many of the Yorkist pedagogical buds failed to bloom. Edward V's institution was constantly interrupted in the name of his political apprenticeship. His schoolmaster was poorly paid and frequently absent. The focus of his training was military and his study of literature looked nostalgically to Burgundy rather than towards the new humanist editions of ancient authors that were finding their way to London and Oxford from Italy. Ultimately, Henry VI and Edward V were brought up in the same manner as their fathers and royal predecessors. They were encouraged to practise conventional piety and to demonstrate courteous manners and courage on the battlefield. Through a royal apprenticeship and precocious office-holding they were supposed to learn to manage their estates, administer justice and develop patronage networks in the localities. They acquired sufficient grammatical skills to oversee governmental bureaucracy and patronise chivalric literature. Yet both were brought up to regard the sword, rather than the pen, as the greatest weapon of kingship. Tudor royal schoolrooms would eventually teach princes differently; the circumstances that brought about this reversal were not entirely planned.

[70] Raoul Lefèvre, *The history of Jason (1477)*, trans. William Caxton, ed. John Munro (London, 1913), pp. 3, 2 respectively.
[71] BL, Royal MS 15 E IV, fol. 14^r.

THE EDUCATION OF PRINCE ARTHUR

Having spent his iconoclastic energy bringing down a reigning monarch, Henry VII's instinct was to educate his eldest son, Prince Arthur, conservatively. His own haphazard upbringing, which began in the house of his dynastic enemy, William Herbert, earl of Pembroke (*c.* 1423–69), and which was disrupted by war and exile in Brittany, did not provide a desirable model for his heir.[72] Instead, as Orme has rightly pointed out, the first Tudor king turned to his adolescent tormentor Edward IV for inspiration.[73] Henry VII's 1493 regulations for royal ceremonies rested on the edifice of Edward IV's ordinances, and Prince Arthur's education took its cues from Edward V's.[74]

There were many consciously created parallels between the *primogeniti*. Patent rolls show that Arthur's independent household was overseen by Lady Elizabeth Darcy, who had also presided over Edward V's nursery.[75] He was created Prince of Wales and earl of Chester on 29 November 1489.[76] A council was established to administer Wales and the Marches in Arthur's name, initially under the presidency of Edward's former 'teacher', John Alcock, now bishop of Ely.[77] Other members of Edward's household who served Arthur included John Argentine, the prince's physician and dean of chapel until 1501, and John Burton, his former chaplain and counsellor.[78] Arthur had no royal governor but, like Edward, he was attended by members of the royal family: his chamberlain, from 6 March 1490, was Richard Pole (1458/9–1504), Henry's first cousin of the half blood. Pole's wife, Margaret, was also the first cousin of Elizabeth of York.[79] Like Edward, Arthur was deemed to have a precociously perfect political body. During his father's campaign in France in 1492, the prince was brought

[72] Ralph A. Griffiths and Roger S. Thomas, *The making of the Tudor dynasty* (New York, 1985), pp. 55, 58–60, 75–88. He did reward his former grammar master, Edward Haseley, upon his accession: *CPR 1485–1494*, pp. 332, 346.

[73] Orme, *From childhood to chivalry*, p. 23

[74] 'King Henry VII for the regulation of his household', in Nichols, *Collection of ordinances*, pp. 109–33.

[75] NA, SC 6/Henry VII/1087; *CPR 1477–85*, pp. 181, 203, 241; *CPR 1485–94*, pp. 152, 256, 306; *CPR 1494–1509*, p. 5.

[76] *CPR 1485–94*, pp. 438–9, 441.

[77] J. Beverley Smith, 'Crown and community in the principality of north Wales in the reign of Henry Tudor', *Welsh History Review*, 3:2 (1966).

[78] For Argentine see Bodleian, MS Rawlinson B 274, fol. 10^r; *CPR 1485–94*, p. 158. For Burton, see BN, Arsenal MS 360, fol. 347^v; *CPR 1494–1509*, p. 4. I thank Professor Daniel Hobbins for his generosity in sharing his transcription of this section of the manuscript with me.

[79] NA, SC 6/Henry VII/1594; Hazel Pierce, 'The king's cousin: The life, career and Welsh connection of Sir Richard Pole, 1485–1504', *Welsh History Review*, 19:2 (1998).

to Westminster to preside as figurehead 'keeper of England and the king's lieutenant'.[80]

Like Edward, Arthur's most important office was to help hold Wales for his father. David Loades has contended that he did not live in the principality until after his marriage.[81] Yet his presence prior to 1502 is evidenced by use of his signet on documents relating to the county palatine of Chester, the messages Henry VII sent 'to my lorde p[re]sident w[ith] my lorde prynce' in the Marches, and even his own letters, which were signed from his house at Ludlow.[82] In fact Arthur probably went to live in the principality the year he turned seven, following an extensive reorganisation of his household, lands and council.[83] The Tudors followed the Yorkists in making Ludlow the Prince of Wales's main residence.[84] Arthur left his seat occasionally to meet the king at Woodstock, Windsor, Richmond and Westminster, but he did not travel as frequently or as far as Prince Edward.[85]

As Steven Gunn has shown, Arthur's residency in Wales was arranged to teach him the mechanics of fifteenth-century kingship. His household fostered regional loyalties in Wales, Chester and Cornwall, as Edward's had.[86] The prince was served by former adherents of Lancaster and York, all the better to unite a divided aristocracy when he came to the throne. He learnt to supervise his estate managers, whether they were conscientious, officious or lax. Arthur demonstrated magnificence in his wardrobe, minstrels, organist, trumpeters and company of players, who toured the provinces regularly from 1495.[87] In August and September 1499 he formally entered Chester, as Edward had done before him.[88] Arthur levied troops in 1495–6 and was given power to appoint the king's officers of oyer and terminer in Wales and the Marches. His officeholders came

80 *CPR 1485–94*, p. 407–8; he attested writs 619a, 621 and 623 in *Calendar of the close rolls... for Edward IV, Edward V, and Richard III*, pp. 182–93.

81 David Loades, *Princes of Wales: Heirs in waiting* (Kew, 2008), p. 82.

82 NA, SC 6/Henry VII/1617; National Library of Wales, Aberystwyth, MS 6620, no. 66; NA, E 101/414/6, fol. 53^r; BL, Egerton MS 616, fols. 14, 16 and 17.

83 BL, Royal MS 18 A LXXVII, fols. 15, 17; *CPR 1485–94*, pp. 434, 438–9, 441, 453–4. Their authority was extended further geographically after the attainder of Sir William Stanley for treason in 1495 (*CPR 1494–1509*, p. 29). On 5 November 1493 Arthur succeeded to Prince Edward's estates in Wales: *CPR 1485–94*, p. 453.

84 W. R. B. Robinson, 'Prince Arthur in the Marches of Wales, 1493–1502', *Studia Celtica*, 36 (2002).

85 Pierce, 'The king's cousin', p. 207.

86 Steven Gunn, 'Prince Arthur's preparation for kingship', in Steven Gunn and Linda Monckton (eds.), *Arthur Tudor, Prince of Wales: Life, death and commemoration* (Woodbridge, 2009), esp. pp. 10–15. I am grateful to Dr Gunn for allowing me to consult his chapter prior to its publication.

87 NA, E 101/414/6, fols. 47^r, 90^r.

88 Robinson, 'Prince Arthur in the Marches of Wales', p. 95.

to dominate lists of justices of the peace appointed in the area. Arthur may even have presided over tribunals in Hereford in 1493 and 1498 himself. On at least one occasion in 1498, he sat at a meeting of his father's council and was subsequently received by the city of London.[89] Before his death in April 1502, therefore, Arthur had had a traditional apprenticeship in the political, administrative, judicial and geographical aspects of English kingship.

Beyond the fact that Prince Arthur acquired an expensive bow at the age of five, we know little of his training in arms.[90] Like the Yorkist kings, however, Arthur's performance in princely rites of passage was designed to emphasise his chivalric virtues. His name, birth and christening at Winchester associated him with the mythical King Arthur.[91] From birth, poets called him Arturus Secundus and urged him to 'surpass the deeds of his ancestors in piety and arms'.[92] In May 1491 he was installed as a Knight of the Garter in the St George's Chapel, Windsor, in the stall of Edward the Black Prince. Thereafter Garter ceremonies became central to his princely identity. In 1499 he hosted the order's observance of the feast of St George in Hereford.[93] In 1502 St George was depicted on the fourth banner supporting the canopy in Arthur's funeral procession, a position that suggests that he had taken the knight as his patron saint.[94] On that sad day the 'baner of the Princes owne armes' was carried by Gruffydd ap Sir Rhys, a young man from his Welsh household. The two may have practised feats of arms together.[95]

The ceremonies attending Arthur's marriage to Catherine of Aragon (1485–1536) on 14 November 1501 may also provide evidence of his military training and courtly recreations. The ceremony was followed by a week of

89 Robinson, 'Prince Arthur in the Marches of Wales', p. 94.

90 Nicholas Harris Nicolas (ed.), *Extracts from the privy purse expenses of King Henry VII, from December 7, 1491, to March 20, 1505* (London, 1831), p. 88.

91 David Carlson, 'King Arthur and court poems for the birth of Arthur Tudor in 1486', *Humanistica Lovaniensia*, 36 (1987).

92 'Proavos vincat pietate vel armis': Bernard André, 'Vita Henrici VII' in *Historia regis Henrici septimi, a Bernardo Andrea Tholosate conscripta: Necnon alia quaedam ad eundem regem spectanti*, ed. James Gardiner (London, 1858), pp. 10, 42; Daniel Hobbins, 'Arsenal MS 360 as a witness to the career and writings of Bernard André', *Humanistica Lovaniensia*, 50 (2001), p. 168n.19.

93 John Anstis (ed.), *The register of the most noble Order of the Garter, from its cover in black velvet, usually called the Black book*, 2 vols. (London, 1724), vol. 1, p. 240.

94 [Stephen Hawes?], *The receyt of the Ladie Kateryne*, ed. Gordon Kipling (Oxford, 1990), p. 83; 'Articles ordained by King Henry VII', in Nichols, *Collection of ordinances*, p. 130; Ralph Houlbrooke, 'Prince Arthur's funeral', in Steven Gunn and Linda Monckton (eds.), *Arthur Tudor, Prince of Wales: Life, death, and commemoration* (Woodbridge, 2009), p. 68.

95 John Morgan-Guy, 'Arthur, Harri Tudor and the iconography of loyalty in Wales', in Steven Gunn and Linda Monckton (eds.), *Arthur Tudor, Prince of Wales: Life, death, and commemoration* (Woodbridge, 2009), p. 51.

'justes', 'noble runnynges' with 'sharp sperys' and a 'turney with armyng swordes', at Westminster. The prince was an eager player in the celebratory 'diguysing', dancing and banquets that followed.[96] His performance in these entertainments probably benefitted from Robert Fayrfax's musical instruction on courtly love songs, devotional music and rustic ayres.[97] Before Arthur was struck down in April 1502, he was described by the Milanese ambassador as a tall and vigorous youth.[98] It seems likely that, like Edward V, he was carefully trained in the full complement of chivalric and courtly exercises.

The Yorkist model for Arthur's schooling extended to the *specula principis* that were directed towards him. Indeed one of the most beautiful examples in his possession had been purchased by Edward IV.[99] It was subsequently refurbished by the Flemish craftsman Quentin Poulet (fl. 1477–1506), Henry VII's royal librarian at Richmond, for the Tudor dynasty.[100] In 1500, Poulet had the decorative borders of certain folios altered to incorporate the new king's arms. Poulet also commissioned four more miniatures, probably from the artist known as the Master of the Prayerbooks, to convert the manuscript for Prince Arthur's use.[101] One of them depicts the prince himself: the coronet, robes and armorial ostrich feather bearing the motto 'Ic dien' in the border signify the Prince of Wales; the Beaufort greyhound in the foreground indicates his Tudor lineage; the date of 1500 inscribed below identifies the figure as Arthur. In the left foreground of the illumination, the prince stands beneath a canopy of state, taking advice from clerics and grave counsellors as he consults a roll of business. Through an open doorway we glimpse the prince again. This time he kneels, praying at the canon of the mass in the period following consecration.[102]

96 [Hawes?], *The receyt*, pp. 52–74, quotation from 52, 61.

97 Roger Bowers, 'Early Tudor courtly song: An evaluation of the Fayrfax book (BL, Additional MS 5465)', in Benjamin Thompson (ed.), *Reign of Henry VII: Proceedings of the 1993 Harlaxton symposium* (Stamford, 1995), p. 195.

98 *CSP Milan*, p. 322, no. 539.

99 Edward's prior ownership is signified by the white roses within suns in splendour: BL, Royal MS 16 F II, see fols. 1^r, 78^r.

100 Backhouse, 'Founders of the royal library', p. 36. For Poulet, see Belozerskaya, *Rethinking the Renaissance*, p. 158; *CPR 1485–94*, pp. 378, 456; Jayne R. Sears and Francis R. Johnson (eds.), *The Lumley Library: The catalogue of 1609* (London, 1956), p. 292. For the library at Richmond see [Hawes?], *The receyt*, p. 77; Kipling, *Triumph of honour*, pp. 3–10, 42–8.

101 Janet Backhouse, 'Illuminated manuscripts associated with Henry VII and members of his immediate family', in Benjamin Thompson (ed.), *The reign of Henry VII: Proceedings of the 1993 Harlaxton Symposium* (Stamford, 1995), pp. 175–6. On dating the tract 'lan de septante & trente quatorze cens de sente': BL, Royal MS 16 F II, fol. 210^v.

102 BL, Royal MS 16 F II, fol. 210^v. I thank Dr Gerard Kilroy for identifying this moment with precision.

The illumination illustrates themes of the French *speculum* that follows, *Le livre dit grace entiere*.[103] This popular advice-treatise echoes the argument of Giles of Rome, in *De regimine principum* (*c.* 1280), that the prince should be a humble, virtuous and pious man, the charitable master of an estate, and a wise, just, prudent and merciful king.[104] The advice reinforced the practical lessons Arthur received in Wales. He was told to keep account of his rents and to use them prudently; to heed wise old counsellors; to choose honest servants;[105] and to ensure that justice be 'kept through his lande and alle his obeisaunce'. If he failed he would 'soone be with oute lordship'.[106] The author echoed Thomas Aquinas's (1225–74) lesson in *De regno* (*c.* 1271), that a prince should act for the common good instead of private profit.[107] If a ruler had just cause to make war he should 'knyghtly and corageously undirtake and systeyne his werres... praying God continuelly'.[108] The *Livre* recommended reading Flavius Vegetius Renatus' *De re militari* (*c.* 390) to develop martial judgement.[109] In order to preserve dynastic property, Arthur was advised to ensure that his own son was 'well noryshed and well induced in good thewes [customs], in faire langage... and faire maners'. Otherwise his possessions would be left 'unto a foole succesoure'.[110] Like other *specula* popular between the thirteenth and sixteenth centuries in northern Europe, *Le livre dit grace* described a good king as a warrior, an administrator, a landowner and a judge who loved and feared God.[111] Like other

103 The treatise was written *c.* 1347 for John duke of Normandy. See Genêt (ed.), *Four English political tracts*, pp. 180n.27, 181n.28. There is a mistaken tradition of attributing this text to Bernard André: David Carlson, 'Royal tutors in the reign of Henry VII', *SCJ*, 22:2 (1991), corrected in his 'Writings of Bernard André (c. 1450—c. 1522)', *Renaissance Studies*, 2:2 (1998).

104 Edward IV owned *De regimine* in French: 'The wardrobe accounts of King Edward the fourth', in Nicolas (ed.), *Privy purse expenses of Elizabeth of York*, p. 126. For *Le livre*'s popularity, see Genêt (ed.), *Four English political tracts*, pp. 174–6.

105 BL, Royal MS 16 F II, fols. 217^{v}–222^{v}, 226^{v}–230^{v}, 234^{v}, 238^{r}–239^{r} respectively.

106 'De faire garder sa terre par iustice et que par les officieus de sa terre iustice ait cours' or 'par raison estre sans seigneurie': BL, Royal MS 16 F II, fol. 232^{r-v}, trans. Genêt (ed.), *Four English political tracts*, p. 197.

107 BL, Royal MS 16 F II, fols. 232^{v}–234^{r}. See Thomas Aquinas, *On kingship to the King of Cyprus*, trans. G. B. Phelan, ed. I. T. Eschmann (Toronto, 1982), p. 7.

108 'Il doit mettre grant paine anicois que a la guerre se meite... pryer continuellement: BL, Royal MS 16 F II, fol. 242^{v}, trans. Genêt (ed.), *Four English political tracts*, p. 207.

109 BL, Royal MS 16 F II, fol. 244^{r-v}.

110 'Soyent bien nourriz et bien introduitz en bonnes meurs en belles parolles bonnes et saiges et en bonne mainere et contenance' in order that 'les biens et les possessions ni ferent pas apres la mort a fol successeur': BL, Royal MS 16 F II, fols. 240^{r} and 240^{r-v}, trans. Genêt (ed.), *Four English political tracts*, p. 205. See Proverbs 10:1.

111 Watts, *Henry VI and the politics of kingship*, pp. 18–19, 21, 24–6, 37.

works favoured by fifteenth-century English kings, it was in French, still the modish literary language of the court.[112]

The *Livre dit grace* prescribed the same sorts of conduct, manners and expertise that Arthur was studying in Wales. Like Edward V before him, he was learning to be conventionally devout, courteous of manner, well trained in feats of arms and capable of managing his estates, developing client networks and administering justice in the locality.

SOME HUMANIST GLOSS: ARTHUR AND THE *STUDIA LITTERARUM*

The refurbishment of *Le livre dit grace entiere* in 1500, however, coincided with the end of the part of Arthur's education that had departed from the Yorkist tradition. After Arthur's fourteenth birthday on 20 September 1500, Bernard André (*c.* 1450–*c.* 1522), Henry VII's 'blynde poet', reported that the prince's 'study of Latin letters', or *studia litterarum*, had been discontinued as he was of an age to marry.[113] The phrase *studia litterarum* is telling. It had been drawn from Cicero's *Pro Archia* (62 BC), an oration in defence of a teacher of the *studia humanitatis ac litterarum* in Rome, and was used by fifteenth-century humanists to describe their approach to studying classical Latin and Greek authors.[114] We have seen that earlier royal patrons such as Humphrey, duke of Gloucester, were accredited with demonstrating 'care and love' of classical literature, despite their evident preference for writing in French.[115] Arthur's intellectual engagement with the *studia litterarum* ran a little deeper and left clear textual traces.

Humanists did not invent the practice of reading classical authors, yet the way that they approached the ancients differed significantly from the method of others. Burgundian poets such as Jean Molinet and Jean Lemaire de Belges mined classical texts for well-known myths and stories that they turned into romantic French literature.[116] Humanists, however,

[112] *CSP Spain*, vol. 1, no. 294, p. 255.

[113] For André see NA, E 101/414/6, fols. 47^{r}, 87^{r}; E 101/414, fols. 16^{v}, 69^{r}; E 101/415/3, fols. 13^{r-v}. For the conclusion of his education, see BN, Arsenal MS 360, fol. 467^{r-v} cited by Hobbins, 'Arsenal MS 360'.

[114] Petrarch recovered the speech in 1333 and Coluccio Salutati cited it regularly: Michael D. Reeve, 'Classical scholarship', in Jill Kraye (ed.), *The Cambridge companion to Renaissance humanism* (Cambridge, 1996), pp. 21–2. For use of the phrase in England, see Pietro Candido Decembrio's flattery of Duke Humphrey, *CSP Milan*, p. 7.

[115] 'Diligentiam et amorem *tuae claritatis* erga studia litterarum': from *CSP Milan*, p. 7. For praise of Henry VII's erudition, see *Letters and papers illustrative of the reigns of Richard III and Henry VII*, ed. James Gairdner, 2 vols. (London, 1861), vol. 1, pp. 126–8. More generally, see Rundle, 'Humanism before the Tudors', pp. 22–42.

[116] Kipling, *Triumph of honour*, pp. 11–30.

proclaimed themselves anxious to recover, edit and circulate seemingly lost texts.[117] Burgundian poets focused on the narrative and moral lessons conveyed by Roman poetry and history. In addition to these aspects, humanists examined the grammatical and rhetorical features of the language in which classical letters, oratory, poetry, philosophy and history were written. They were conscious of historical differences in the way ancient authors used Latin, and were also eager to revive Greek and keenly aware that these writers were from a world that was cut off from their own.[118] Their philological interests and sense of the past shaped their editions and interpretations of classical texts. They also conditioned their attempts to imitate the prose styles of Latin authors and to translate Greek writers.[119] Towards the end of the fourteenth century, Italian humanists started writing in a script they fancied imitated ancient Roman hands, the *littera antiqua* or *italica*.[120] The European exchange of ambassadors, papal collectors and university students had given humanism a toe-hold at the English court and the University of Oxford in the fifteenth century.[121]

In the reign of Henry VII, however, humanism began to gain political and diplomatic traction in London. The sermons that opened the first Tudor parliaments, for instance, justified crown policies by using classical *loci*.[122] In 1485 John Alcock, who would become the leader of Arthur's council, urged all three estates present to strive for prosperity and harmony after civil war by drawing on Livy's account of Menenius Agrippa's fable of the belly, Seneca's description of the good ruler as a king bee with no sting, Ovid's account of the golden age, and Virgil's appeal for

117 I. D. Reynolds and N. G. Wilson, *Scribes and scholars: A guide to the transmission of Greek and Latin literature*, 3rd edn. (Oxford, 1991), pp. 128–49; Remigio Sabbadini, *Storia e critica di testi Latini*, 2nd edn. (Padua, 1971);.

118 W. K. Ferguson, *The Renaissance in historical thought: Five centuries of interpretation* (Boston, 1948), pp. 1–28; Peter Burke, *The Renaissance sense of the past* (New York, 1969), esp. pp. 21–7, 39, 50–69.

119 Anthony Grafton, 'On the scholarship of Politian and its context', *Journal of the Warburg and Courtauld Institutes*, 45 (1977).

120 A. C. De la Mare, 'Humanistic script: The first ten years', in F. Krafft and D. Wuttke (eds.), *Das Verhältnis der humanisten zum Buch* (Boppard, 1977); B. L. Ullmans, *The origin and development of humanistic script* (Rome, 1960), esp. pp. 14, 16–17, 59, 91.

121 Denys Hay, 'England and the humanities in the fifteenth century', in H. A. Oberman and T. A. Brady Jr (eds.), *Itinerarum Italicum: The profile of the Italian Renaissance in the mirror of its European transformations* (Leiden, 1975); P. O. Kristeller, 'The European diffusion of Italian humanism', in *Renaissance thought II: Papers on humanism and the arts* (New York, 1965); Richard J. Schoeck, 'Humanism in England', in Albert Rabil Jr (ed.), *Renaissance humanism: Foundations, forms, and legacy* (Philadelphia, 1988), p. 6; Roberto Weiss, *Humanism in England during the fifteenth century*, 2nd edn. (Oxford, 1957), p. 2.

122 P. R. Cavill, *The English parliaments of Henry VII, 1485–1504* (Oxford, 2009), pp. 22–3.

its return through the ministrations of justice and godly rule.[123] His allusions were lost on a number of those present, which may have provoked Alcock to insist that Prince Arthur required a more careful introduction to classical letters than his predecessors.[124] For the virgin to return to earth, Arthur would need to return *ad fontes*.

Arthur's relatively settled life in Wales would have facilitated the regular hours of study needed to digest neo-classical Latin grammar and rhetoric. Bernard André reported that, once the prince 'had mastered the rudiments of letters with the greatest speed, he was introduced to the higher branches of knowledge by the greatest and most learned teacher [*praeceptor*] his schoolmaster [*magister*] John Rede, without wearisome labour by either of them'.[125] As David Carlson's pioneering work on royal tutors has shown, John Rede was one of the new breed of professional schoolmaster. He had taught at Winchester College and was a former fellow of New College, Oxford.[126] Rede may well have been the party who helped Margaret Beaufort (1443–1509) to obtain an illuminated, printed copy of Cicero's works (Mainz, 1465) for Arthur. The manuscript is decorated with a historiated initial of a schoolroom scene in which a young boy dressed in ermine says his lesson to a man in a doctoral bonnet.[127]

By October 1499, Rede had taught Arthur sufficient Latin grammar and rhetoric that he was able to write neo-Latin love letters to Catherine of Aragon.[128] The two extant epistles constitute the first surviving attempt made by a British prince to speak or write in the antique Latin style. Indeed the central romantic conceit of the letters is the capacity of a script to represent the person of its author. In a chaste echo of Pliny the Younger's second letter to Calpurnia (VI.6), or perhaps even Ovid's *Heroides* (XVIII, lns. 5–12), Arthur wrote to say how Catherine's letters to him, 'written by [her] very own hand', evoked the princess's presence and

[123] *Rotuli Parliamentorum*, vol. VI, p. 267. See Livy, *Ab urbe condita*, II.32; Ovid, *Metamorphoses*, I, lns. 89–110; Seneca, *De clementia*, I.19; Virgil, *Eclogues*, IV, lns. 6–17.

[124] John Watts, 'The policie in Christen remes: Bishop Russell's parliamentary sermons of 1483–84', in George Bernard and Steven Gunn (eds.), *Authority and consent in Tudor England: Essays presented to C. S. L. Davis* (Aldershot, 2002), p. 33.

[125] 'Postquam enim velocissime prima litterarum elementa pernovisset, ad altiorem scientiae cognitionem ab optimo et doctissimo praeceptore suo magistro Johanne Rede sine magno utriusvis labore perductus est': Bernard André, 'Vita Henrici VII', p. 43.

[126] Carlson, 'Royal tutors', pp. 260–1.

[127] Emmanuel College, Cambridge, MS 5 3 11, fol. 1r; J. J. G. Alexander, 'Foreign illuminators and illuminated manuscripts', in Lotte Hellinga and J. B. Trapp (eds.), *The Cambridge history of the book in Britain*: vol. III: *1400–1557* (Cambridge, 1999), p. 63.

[128] BL, Egerton MS 616, fols. 14r, 16r, 17r (variant). I thank Dr Steven Gunn for sharing his transcriptions with me.

even embrace (*amplectus*).[129] Arthur stuffed his next letter with phrases cut raw and bleeding from the fifth book of Cicero's *Ad familiares*: Catherine's reply 'showed the greatest favour to [Arthur] joined with her prudence'; he hoped that they would soon be united. He wished to 'convince [her] that in this matter and in all others [his] devotion to [her] is eternal'.[130] The surviving letters were the first of a series that Arthur wrote to confirm the ratification of the marriage treaty and to urge Catherine's departure for England.[131] For Arthur, the study of Latin grammar and rhetoric had courtly and diplomatic utility. It enabled him to pursue a dynastically advantageous alliance by demonstrating that, when it came to good letters, England was no cultural backwater. Humanist pedagogical practice had begun to infiltrate the royal schoolroom.

André explained that, after Rede, he had tutored Arthur himself. The Augustinian friar and doctor of civil and canon law had arrived in England shortly after the battle of Bosworth and spent the next thirty-six years praising the achievements of Henry VII and Henry VIII, their families and partisans like an 'early Tudor Choerilus'.[132] For this he was paid the relatively modest sum of £10 per annum from November 1486, supplemented by sporadic royal gifts. In 1501 this was translated into a benefice and then into an annual pension worth £24 in 1515.[133] From around 1496 until 1501 André claimed that he was 'of use' to the prince. 'Apollo planted, I watered but the Lord made it grow', he declared.[134] It is difficult to confirm, however, that André actually resided with Arthur at Ludlow. He was with the prince at the time of his proxy wedding on 19 May 1499 and again in June 1500 at Beaulieu Abbey in the New Forest.[135] Yet marginal annotations on his commentary on Saint Augustine's *City of God* suggest that the poet's main residence was in London. As Daniel Hobbins has discovered, André passed the manuscript of his commentary

[129] 'Ita nempe me recrearunt ipse littere vestre propria uestra manu exscripte itaque hylarem et iucundum rediddеrunt ut et vestram celsitudinem viderer intueri et preclarissimam meam sponsam affari et amplecti': BL, Egerton MS 616, fol. 14r.

[130] 'Declarant enim vestram in nos summam benevolentiam coniuctam pari prudencia' [sic] and 'Respondeat in quo rem nobis acceptissimam facietis sibique persuadeat esse in vos in ea re ceterisque omnibus pari studio erga vos et eadem voluntate': BL, Egerton MS 616, fols. 16r and 17r; Cicero, *Ad familiares*, v.13.1 and v.11.1, respectively.

[131] *CSP Spain*, vol. 1, no. 280, p. 234.

[132] Carlson, 'Writings of Bernard André', pp. 229–50.

[133] NA, E 101/414/6, fol. 47r and E 101/415/3, fol. 41r.

[134] 'Nos… nonnihil adiumenti attulimus; estque de nobis illud apostolicum verificatum, "Apollo plantauit, ego regaui, dominus autem incrementum dedit" ': André, 'Vita Henrici VII', p. 43 citing 1 Corinthians 3:6.

[135] *CSP Spain*, vol. 1, no. 241, p. 209; BN, Arsenal MS 360, as cited by Hobbins, 'Arsenal MS 360', pp. 182, 185.

regularly to Burton, who had been Prince Edward's and Arthur's 'chaplain and counsellor' but who subsequently resided 'in the city of London'.[136] It seems likely, then, that André lived primarily at his order's house in Austin Friars so that he could attend his friends, and his ultimate patron, the king.

André's physical distance from the prince is one reason to doubt his oft-cited claim that, under his guidance, Arthur had absorbed the works of twenty-four classical and humanist authors before his sixteenth birthday:

> in grammar Guarino, Perotti, Pomponius, Sulpicius, Aulus Gellius and Lorenzo Valla; in poetry Homer, Virgil, Lucan, Ovid, Silius, Plautum and Terence; in rhetoric Cicero's *de Officiis, Epistolae* and *Paradoxa* and Quintilian; in history Thucydides, Titus Livius, Caesar's *Commentarii de bello gallico* and *de Bello civili*, Suetonius, Cornelius Tacitus, Pliny, Valerius Maximus, Sallust, and Eusebius.[137]

The other reason to doubt André's list is its sheer Italianate modishness. Carlson acknowledges as much but even he underestimates the difficulties that Arthur would have had to overcome to 'turn' the pages of these authors 'with his own hands or read [them] with his eyes', let alone commit 'the greater part' of their works 'to memory'.[138] In 1500, for instance, manuscripts of Homer in Latin were rare and his Greek defeated all but the most expert Hellenist. The prodigy Angelo Politian (1454–94) was the only known fifteen-year-old to read it. Even those with the capacity to translate the *Iliad* Latinised it as prose. Only two editions of Lorenzo Valla's (1407–57) and Francesco Griffolini's *Iliad* had been printed in Brescia (1474 and 1497) and one incomplete version in Rome (1474).[139] André's acquisition of one such work, let alone copies of all the listed authors, is likely to have merited comment. Perhaps Prince Arthur simply cribbed his account of the Trojan wars from the *Aeneid*, like everyone else. By the time André penned his account of the prince's learning, moreover,

[136] Hobbins, 'Arsenal MS 360', p. 170. I am grateful to Professor Hobbins for describing Burton's marginal annotations on the manuscript and for sending me his transcription of André's eulogy of the chaplain.

[137] 'Hoc unum audacter affirmarim, illa aetate qua sextum decimum nondum attigerat annum in grammatica Garinum, Perotum, Pomponium, Sulpicium, Aulum Gellium, Vallam; in poetica Homerum, Virgilium, Lucanum, Ovidium, Silium, Plautum, Terentium; In oratoria Ciceronis Officia, Epistolas, Paradoxa Quintilianum; in historia Thucydidem, Titum Livium, Caesaris Commentaria, Suetonium, Cornelium Tacitum, Plinium, Valerium Maximum, Sallustium, Eusebium ipsum, André, 'Vita Henrici VII', p. 43.

[138] 'Vel memoriae partim commendasse, vel certe propriis manibus oculisque tum volutasse tum lectasse': André, 'Vita Henrici VII', p. 43; Carlson, 'Royal tutors', p. 257.

[139] Philip Ford, 'Homer in the French Renaissance', *Renaissance Quarterly*, 59:1 (2006); Robin Sowerby, 'Early humanist failure with Homer (I)', *International Journal of the Classical Tradition*, 4:1 (1997) and 'Early humanist failure with Homer (II)', *International Journal of the Classical Tradition*, 4:2 (1997).

Arthur was not alive to confirm or deny his knowledge of Homer, or any other classical author. Besides, as André explained in his *Vita Henrici septimi*, the object of writing history was not necessarily to recount a prince's deeds accurately.[140] Instead, the historian should 'briefly' relate those feats that came 'freely to his mind' in order to provide his reader with persuasive moral instruction.[141] Here, the lesson André attempted to convey was that it was important for princes to read classical authors and that he, Bernard André, had proved masterful in introducing a prince to the best of antiquity. Pedantic attention to detail might have got in the way of a good story.

Not only did André exaggerate the prince's knowledge of classical authors but also he may have blocked Arthur's opportunity for advanced humanistic studies. Self-promotion is hardly unknown amongst courtiers but André guarded his pre-eminence amongst Henry VII's 'flock of poets' (*grex poetarum*) with particular vigilance. Despite his poor eyesight, André had managed to acquire a little Greek and was proud of his efforts, as his quotations from Plutarch in the Arsenal Manuscript at the Bibliothèque Nationale attest.[142] Yet the turn of the century witnessed an influx of highly competent Greek scholars to England.[143] There was William Grocyn (1449?–1519), who had studied ancient Greek in Florence under Politian and Demetrius Chalcondylas and who returned to Oxford to teach it in 1492. Grocyn's godson, William Lily (1468?–1522/3), followed him east and studied under Byzantinian exiles in Rhodes. Thomas Linacre (*c.* 1460–1524) had been a fellow student of Grocyn's in Florence. Linacre travelled on to Rome and Padua, where he studied medicine, and Venice, where he befriended Aldus Manutius and his *Neakadēmia*. Linacre returned to England in 1499, with a trunk stuffed with manuscripts of Galen, the editing and translation of which would earn him European celebrity. Thomas More (1478–1535), then a student at Lincoln's Inn, began to study under Grocyn and Linacre. In 1499 this circle, dubbed the *Graecistes* by More, encouraged Erasmus of Rotterdam, the future editor and translator of the New Testament, to devote himself to the tongue. Bernard André was immediately hostile to these thrusting, fashionable upstarts at Henry VII's court.

[140] Blackwell, 'Humanism and politics', pp. 436–7.

[141] 'Statui res gestas… carptim, ut quaeque memoriae mihi occurrentia,… eo magis quod mihi animus liberimus tunc erat. Quapropter de vita atque gestis ipsius quam verissime potero paucis absolvam': André, 'Vita Henrici VII', pp. 7–8.

[142] BN, Arsenal MS 360, fols. 96^{v}–97^{v}; see Hobbins, 'Arsenal MS 360', p. 162n.1.

[143] Eric Nelson, *The Greek tradition in republican thought* (Cambridge, 2004), pp. 24–5.

On 27 August 1499, Linacre, who was then the most accomplished of the Greek scholars, made a bid to enter Prince Arthur's service. He presented Arthur with a manuscript version of his Latin translation of *De sphaera*, which Aldus had recently printed in Venice. Linacre attributed *De sphaera* to the fourth-century Neo-Platonist Proclus. It purported to explain the axis of the cosmos, its constellations and the terrestrial zones on the earth.[144] Linacre's prefatory letter praised Arthur's zeal in tackling the 'reading of poets' and emphasised that his translation had particular relevance for one who was 'named for the star' Arcturus.[145] It contained information that Arthur could not derive from personal observation or exploration. Kings 'are not permitted to scour the globe', Linacre pointed out, so 'without knowledge of the sphere from these books, they would be utterly unable to understand it'.[146] He urged Arthur to study Greek, the original language of *De sphaera* and one 'in which all monuments of civilisation have been preserved'.[147] It was the tongue, moreover, in which Linacre had especial expertise.

Linacre's gift was a job application and it was good enough to have convinced a number of historians that he was appointed Prince Arthur's schoolmaster.[148] In fact Erasmus recorded how Bernard André actually saw the upstart Linacre off his royal patch:

> [The presentation of the manuscript] went very badly for Thomas Linacre... André of Toulouse, preceptor to Prince Arthur... a blind flatterer, not only a flatterer but the most evil accuser, informed the king that the little book had already been translated by an unknown man. It had been, but poorly. On this account, the king both rejected the gift and developed an undying hatred for Linacre, as if [he was] an impostor.[149]

144 WLTC, MS R 15 19. It was actually four chapters (4, 5, 15 and 3) of Geminus' *Elementa astronomiae*, written in the first century BC. Various Greek manuscripts of Geminus, which were discovered in the fifteenth century, contained only these chapters, leading to the belief that they constituted an independent treatise. It was only in 1585 that Frances Barozzi recognised that *De sphaera* was by Geminus: Robert B. Todd, 'Geminus Rhodius/ Ps. Proclus', in Virginia Brown (ed.), *Catalogus translationum et commentariorum: Mediaeval and Renaissance Latin translations and commentaries: Annotated lists and guides*, 8 vols. (Washington, DC, 2003), vol. VIII, p. 14.

145 'Quippe qui... syderis nomine vocarere: huc accedit quod non parum adiumenti praestabit... ad poetarum lectionem (cui te incumbere miro iam successu coepisse intelligo)': WLTC, MS R 15 19, fol. 1r.

146 'Cui per occupationes Regni peragrare orbem minime licebit quam ex iis libris qui prorsus intelligi sine sphaerae notitia non possunt': WLTC, MS R 15 19, fol. 1v.

147 'Ex ea lingua... in qua omnis humanitatis monumenta sunt condita': WLTC, MS R 15 19, fol. 2r.

148 See for instance Loades, *Princes of Wales*, p. 85; Vivian Nutton, 'Linacre, Thomas (c. 1460–1524)', *ODNB*. The error is corrected in Carlson, 'Royal tutors', pp. 262–3.

149 'Thomae Linacro pessime cessit... Andreas quidam Tolasates, praeceptor Arcturi Principis... caecus adulator, nec adulator tantum sed et delator pessimus, Regem admonuit hoc libelli iam

Indeed, André managed to offend all the *Graecistes* one way or another. Erasmus wrote on another occasion that Arthur was 'the best of princes' yet André was 'not the best of preceptors'.[150] One of Thomas More's *Epigrammata* (1518) sneered at André's poetic pretensions: the blind friar 'wrote in haste, but even so with all the time in the world he could not have written better'.[151] As Dudley Carlson has pointed out, More's malicious irony went further still. The councillor had previously sent the same epigram to André for inclusion as a genuine, laudatory verse advertising the latter's *Hymni Christiani* (1517).[152] Erasmus and More might have forgiven André's metrical laxity in 1517 if he had not wielded his pre-eminence at court like a blunt axe in 1499. Through André's intervention Arthur was protected from the *Graecistes*. He was also protected from the latest currents of humanist learning available in England.

As Orme has pointed out, Henry VII had refused to place his sons under the governorship of a senior nobleman. He did not want his heir to be tied exclusively to one of the realm's great, fractious families.[153] His policy had the unintended effect of making Arthur's schoolmaster one of the most powerful men in his affinity. André's attempts to guard his pre-eminence against *Graecistes* intruders were assisted by geography. Arthur's location in Wales may have given him the time and steady routine necessary to master Ciceronian epistolary style but it also secluded him from cosmopolitan Londoners and Oxonians. Erasmus would cross the Alps but he would never make it to Wales. These factors prevented Arthur from taking more than a sip of the newly fashionable study of old letters. Arthur was protected from novelty by his father, his preceptor and his location, and as such his education was shaped firmly by his parents' plan to make him a second Edward V. They succeeded on several counts. Arthur's regional apprenticeship in government imitated Edward's. He shared his predecessor's taste for Burgundian princely literature. Finally

olim fuisse versum a nescio quo; et erat, sed misere. Hanc ob causam Rex et munus aspernatur est, et in Linacrum velut in impostorem inexpiabile concepit odium': Erasmus, *OEDE*, vol. IX, no. 2422, p. 108. Erasmus is probably referring to Giorgio Valla's partial translation made prior to 1491: Virginia Brown, James Hankins and Robert Kaster (eds.), *Catalogus translationum et commentariorum: Mediaeval and Renaissance Latin translations and commentaries* (Washington, DC, 2003), p. 12.

150 Erasmus, *OEDE*, vol. V, no. 1490, p. 539.

151 'Non subito scripsit, sed sic ut scribere posset / Quantumuis longo tempore non melius': Thomas More, *The complete works of Saint Thomas More*, vol. III, part 2: *Latin poems*, eds. Clarence H. Miller *et al.* (New Haven, 1984), pp. 196–7, no. 148, lns. 11–12.

152 David R. Carlson, 'Reputation and duplicity: The texts and contexts of Thomas More's Epigram on Bernard André', *ELH*, 58:2 (1991).

153 Orme, *From childhood to chivalry*, pp. 22–3.

and most unfortunately the lamentations at the demise of one 'faire, goodly, and towardly yong prince' of Wales were echoed in the mourning for another when Arthur died at Ludlow in April 1502.[154]

THE EDUCATION OF HENRY, DUKE OF YORK: JOHN SKELTON AND THE *GRAECISTES*

The education of Prince Henry, the second son of the new Tudor line, mirrored his brother's upbringing in a number of ways. Henry studied Latin, French, the chivalric arts and courtly accomplishments. His father gave him a lute in 1498 and employed the Flemish musician Giles du Wés (d. 1535) to teach him music.[155] Yet, as might be expected, the second son's upbringing lacked something of the glamour (and much of the expense) of his elder brother's schooling. Where 'my lorde prince' had minstrels, organists and trumpeters, 'my lorde of York' just had minstrels.[156] Henry's household was less well established and his schoolmasters were more obscure than Arthur's. By comparison, Henry's education also lacked vocational rigour. There is evidence that he witnessed the occasional charter and received summons to Parliament, but he was not apprenticed to estate management or government business as his brother had been.[157] As the duke of York, Henry was brought up to be the stalwart sword arm of Arthur's future regime.

David Starkey has seen the portents of marital adventure in the fact that the young Prince Henry was raised in a household at Eltham with his sisters Margaret (1489–1541) and Mary (1496–1533).[158] In fact, it was typical for cadet royals to spend longer in the queen's household than the *primogenitus*. Elizabeth Woodville had been given £400 *per annum* to maintain her younger offspring and they even accompanied her to sanctuary in Westminster Abbey in 1470 and 1483.[159] Similarly Elizabeth of York presided over the gaggle of gentlewomen, nurses and rockers who attended

[154] [Hawes?], *The receyt*, p. 81.

[155] Dietrich Helms, 'Henry VIII's book: Teaching music to royal children', *Musical Quarterly*, 92:1–2 (2009); Nicolas (ed.), *Privy purse expenses of Elizabeth of York*, p. cxxxviii.

[156] NA, E 101/414/6, fols. 47^r, 49^v, 90^r. The context of references to 'my lord of York' in Henry VII's chamber accounts help in determining whether Henry, duke of York, or Thomas Rotherham (1423–1500), archbishop of York, was intended. It seems probable that the king would pay for minstrels for his son rather than for the aged archbishop.

[157] *Calendar of the close rolls preserved in the Public Record Office for the reign of Henry VII*, eds. K. H. Ledward and R. E. Latham, 2 vols. (London, 1955–63), vol. 1 (1485–1500), no. 845, p. 248 and no. 969, p. 287; *CPR 1485–1494*, p. 72.

[158] David Starkey, *Henry: Virtuous prince* (London, 2008), pp. 52, 62–4, 66–71, 118–20.

[159] *CPR 1467–77*, p. 110; Laynesmith, *Last medieval queens*, p. 148.

her younger children collectively.[160] During the Cornish rebellion of June 1497, she took Henry and his sisters with her to Lady Margaret Beaufort's house in London, then to the Tower, and on to Woodstock.[161] Nevertheless, by 1497, patent rolls demonstrate that Henry, duke of York, had his own household supported by revenue from the estates of Jasper Tudor, earl of Bedford.[162] Henry's chaplain, Christopher Tenant, was appointed in March 1496 and then his nurse, Anne Uxbridge, was pensioned off in May.[163] In December John Redying was made Henry's treasurer.[164] Even more decisively, in January 1497 Redying and other named individuals were commissioned to purvey victuals, fuel and wheat to the duke's household.[165] Henry's establishment may have been housed at Eltham with his sisters for much of the time, but these provisions demonstrate that it operated independently on occasion.

Henry was undoubtedly close to his mother but she was not the only adult involved in his upbringing. He had a fool and a schoolmaster.[166] Indeed the man who claimed to have provided Henry with his 'lernyng primordiall' was adept at playing both.[167] John Skelton (*c.* 1460–1529) was a priest, a ribald balladeer, a sycophant and a scourge of court life. Skelton recommended himself as a royal tutor, or 'creaunser', by imitating Bernard André's statist Latin verses with statist vernacular offerings that commemorated events such as Prince Arthur's birth.[168] In 1490 he dedicated a translation of Virgil's *Aeneid* to Prince Arthur. At the end of 1494, Skelton wrote a Latin poem honouring Henry's creation as duke of York.[169] In 1495 the son of his patron, Thomas Howard, second duke of Norfolk (1443–1524), married Anne of York, sister to the queen.[170] The poet came into service as a royal tutor afterwards. Mid-1496 seems a likely moment: Henry was five years old and moving from the care of women. His father presented him with a book to mark the occasion.[171] The duke's study of French and Latin grammar had begun.

160 NA, E 404/81/1, 404/81/3, 404/81/4.

161 *CSPV*, vol. 1, no. 754, pp. 252–66; Starkey, *Henry*, pp. 114–15.

162 *Calendar of the close rolls... for Henry VII*, vol. 1 (1485–1500), no. 1071, p. 316 and no. 1080, p. 319; *CPR 1494–1509*, p. 303.

163 *CPR 1494–1509*, p. 39.

164 *CPR 1494–1509*, p. 92.

165 *CPR 1494–1509*, pp. 126–7.

166 Nicolas (ed.), *Privy purse expenses of Elizabeth of York*, p. 2.

167 John Skelton, *Agenst Garnesche* (1514), 5, ln. 105 cited by Carlson, 'Royal tutors', p. 264.

168 Skelton, *Garland of Laurel* (1523) ln. 1226 cited by Carlson, 'Royal tutors', pp. 264, 265.

169 John Skelton, 'Epigramma ad sancti principis maiestatem', in 'The Latin writings of John Skelton', ed. David R. Carlson, *Studies in Philology*, 88:4 (1991), pp. 42–3.

170 Thomas Penn, *Winter king: Henry VII and the dawn of Tudor England* (New York, 2012), p. 104.

171 NA, 101/414/6, fol. 5^r^.

Skelton is better known as a vernacular poet than a pedagogue but his time in Cambridge, where he claimed to have studied, and in Oxford, where he took his degree, gave him a taste for antiquity.[172] In his autobiographical poem, *Garland of Laurel*, Skelton listed the treatises he claimed to have authored for Henry.[173] Only one of these works survives, a *Speculum principis* (1501).[174] The text drew heavily on *Disticha Catonis* (*c.* 200–399), a collection of moral sentences written in elementary classical Latin, and Valerius Maximus' *Dicta et facta memorabilia* (*c.* 30 AD), which epitomised the deeds of figures described by Livy and Cicero. The *Disticha* and *Dicta* were popular in the middle ages but humanist pedagogues in Italy and beyond continued to use them.[175] The works introduced students to classical Latin grammar and vocabulary while inculcating manners and moral principles. The sentences that Skelton selected for Henry's edification were stoical – he warned him against succumbing to gluttony, drunkenness, loquaciousness or anger – and encouraged courage, piety, chivalrous conduct towards women and generosity to poets.[176]

The model for royal conduct prescribed in the *Speculum* echoed the chivalric ideal of nobility contained in the Burgundian romances and chronicles that Skelton typically used to teach Henry.[177] In 1497 Henry VII had acquired a glorious illuminated copy of *L'Enseignement de vraie noblesse* (*c.* 1440) that Skelton translated into English for his pupil. It told the story of a pilgrim who encountered a vision of a dazzling lady called Imagination outside the city of Hal. Imagination persuaded the pilgrim that piety and the common good depend on princes and knights cultivating the true nobility of virtue rather than relying on their wealth or birth for pre-eminence.[178] To define 'virtue', Skelton may have turned to a fifteenth-century manuscript copy of a French chronicle of the third crusade, *Le Récit d'un ménestrel de Reims*, which he used to teach Henry history. Skelton's annotations on the manuscript drew the duke's attention to memorable events in Richard I's life and emphasised the moral lessons to be drawn from his experiences. In a dedicatory verse that Skelton added in December 1511, he urged Henry to

172 John Scattergood, 'Skelton, John (c.1460–1529)', *ODNB*.
173 Skelton, *Garland of Laurel* (1523) lns. 1175, 1182 cited by Carlson, 'Royal tutors', p. 268.
174 Skelton, 'Speculum principis', in *The Latin writings of John Skelton*, ed. David R. Carlson (Chapel Hill, 1991).
175 Paul F. Grendler, *Schooling in Renaissance Italy: Literacy and learning 1300–1600* (Baltimore, 1989), pp. 197–9, 262–3.
176 Skelton, 'Speculum principis', in *Latin writings of John Skelton*, pp. 27–8.
177 Gordon Kipling, 'John Skelton and Burgundian letters', in Jan van Dorsten (ed.), *Ten studies in Anglo–Dutch relations* (Leiden, 1974), pp. 1–29.
178 BL, Royal MS 19 C VIII; Skelton, *Garland of Laurel*, ln. 1180 cited by Kipling, 'John Skelton and Burgundian letters', p. 7.

imitate Richard, 'the greatest hero of the English… like a fearless Hector against the Sacarens'.[179] As this comparison suggests, Skelton daubed a traditional chivalric model of princely conduct with neo-classical varnish. Indeed, in Skelton's hands, English knights and Greek warriors became largely interchangeable models of Christian piety, fortitude and moral rectitude.

Skelton's glorification of chivalry was well suited to the loyal, military future that Henry VII envisioned for his second son. In his *Life and reign of Henry VIII* (1649), Herbert of Cherbury elaborated on Paolo Sarpi's salty fiction that the 'prudent' Henry VII had destined his son 'to the Archbishoprick of Canterbury' because he considered the vocation 'the most cheap and glorious' office for a cadet royal.[180] In fact Henry VII honoured his son with a series of titles that indicated otherwise. On 5 April 1493 'lord Harry' was made Constable of the Cinque Ports and Warden of Dover Castle and subsequently Earl Marshall of England. On 12 September 1494 he became Lord Lieutenant of Ireland.[181] On 30 October 1494 Henry was admitted to the Order of the Bath and the next day he was created duke of York.[182] It was a blast of the trumpet against the pretensions of Perkin Warbeck (1474–99), who had just been received as Richard, duke of York, by the Holy Roman Emperor Maximilian I (1459–1519).[183] Then in December 1494, when evidence emerged that Sir William Stanley (*c.* 1435–95) was in conspiracy with Warbeck and England's north-west had been left vulnerable to attack, the young duke was appointed warden of the Scottish Marches.[184] To cement Henry's status as the premier soldier of his father's court, the duke was elected to the chivalric Order of the Garter on 17 May 1495.[185] In the 1490s the actual work of these offices was performed by gentleman deputies but Henry's juvenile appointment kept the posts in Henry VII's affinity. Such titles also foretold a time when the adult duke of York would hold the north, Ireland and the ports for his brother, King Arthur.

179 Matthew Parker Library, Corpus Christi Cambridge, MS 432 in Skelton, *Latin writings of John Skelton*, p. 45.

180 Edward Herbert of Cherbury, *Life and raigne of King Henry the eighth* (London, 1649), Wing H1504, p. 2 drawing upon Paolo Sarpi, *The historie of the Councel of Trent conteining eight books*, trans. Nathanael Brent (London, 1620), STC 21761, p. 16.

181 *CPR 1485–1494*, p. 423; *CPR 1494–1509*, pp. 26, 62; *Letters and papers illustrative of the reigns of Richard III and Henry VII*, vol. II, p. 374.

182 *Calendar of the close rolls… for Henry VII*, vol. I (1485–1500), no. 97, p. 236; *CPR 1494–1509*, pp. 26, 62, 67; *Letters and papers illustrative of the reigns of Richard III and Henry VII*, vol. I, pp. 388, 403; NA, E 404/81/4.

183 Frank A. Mumby, *The youth of Henry VIII: A narrative in contemporary letters* (London, 1913), p. 2; Starkey, *Henry*, pp. 74–82.

184 *CPR 1494–1509*, pp. 29, 67, 202; Sean Cunningham, *Henry VII* (London, 2007), pp. 180–2.

185 *Letters and papers illustrative of the reigns of Richard III and Henry VII*, vol. II, p. 57; Nicolas (ed.), *Extracts from the privy purse expenses of King Henry VII*, p. 103.

By encouraging Prince Henry to think of himself as a knight of the round table, Skelton was doing an admirable job of shaping his pupil for his supposed future responsibilities. Unlike André, however, the cadet poet and pedagogue also craved the approval of the learned *Graecistes*. According to the grammar master William Lily, Skelton was anxious 'to procure a reputation for learning and to seem a learned poet' despite this modest acquaintance with the classics.[186] It was probably in 1499 that he made his deal: Skelton agreed to trade access to his royal charge in return for the symbolic capital of praise of his erudition from other men of letters. When Henry was staying with his sisters at Eltham Palace that summer, Skelton welcomed a learned young nobleman, William Blount, Lord Mountjoy (*c.* 1478–1534), to the duke's presence. Mountjoy lived just a few miles from Greenwich and Eltham. His estate at Cornbury, Oxfordshire, lay near Queen Elizabeth's favoured palace at Woodstock, and his stepfather, Thomas Butler, seventh earl of Ormond, was the queen's chamberlain.[187] Just as significantly for Skelton, Mountjoy introduced the duke to a Dutch humanist, Erasmus of Rotterdam, who had been his tutor in Paris, and Erasmus' English friend, Thomas More. Erasmus' report of his first encounter with Prince Henry was written with the benefit of twenty-four years' hindsight so he was able to pronounce confidently that the child 'already looked somehow like a natural king, displaying a noble spirit combined with peculiar courtesy [*singularis humanitas*]'.[188] More, Erasmus complained, had arrived bearing a literary gift but had not forewarned his guest, who had nothing to hand. Thus, over dinner, Prince Henry passed Erasmus a note challenging his pen. For the next three days, Erasmus claimed, he laboured to produce suitable verses.

Erasmus sent the prince a hastily copied manuscript of poems, two of which were in apparent praise of John Skelton.[189] Erasmus described Skelton as 'the light and ornament of English letters', the Homer and Virgil of *terra Britannia*, the

first to bring the Muses
hither from the world of Rome

[186] 'Doctrinae tibi dum parare fama / Et doctus fieri studes poeta': cited in Skelton, *Latin writings of John Skelton*, p. 8.

[187] Nicolas (ed.), *Privy purse expenses of Elizabeth of York*, pp. 28–9; Penn, *Winter king*, p. 106; Starkey, *Henry*, p. 176.

[188] Erasmus, *OEDE*, vol. 1, no. 1, p. 6; *CWE: Letters 1252 to 1355*, no. 1341A, p. 299–300.

[189] BL, Egerton MS 1651, fols. 6^v–7^r; Starkey, *Henry*, p. 130 mistakenly described it as illuminated.

and make them speak English.[190] Such effusive praise would have delighted the poet until he recalled that Erasmus did not understand a word of English.[191] Indeed, a quick glance at the manuscript also reveals that Erasmus was not even sure of Henry's schoolmaster's name. Was it 'Stelkon' or 'Skelton' he was supposed to be honouring?[192] It is little wonder that Erasmus did not trouble to have this verse congratulating Henry's tutor printed. It was merely payment for a service rendered, and relatively poor payment at that.

Erasmus put a bit more effort into a subsequent poem lauding the Tudor dynasty, his *Prosopopoeia Britanni[a]e maioris*. He committed it to print in 1500, alongside the dedicatory letter with which he had prefaced his earlier, scribbled verses for Henry.[193] Erasmus stitched a complex web of classical allusions into the poem, but its central conceit is indicated by its metre: dactylic hexametre with iambic trimetre. Horace had adopted this scheme in his sixteenth epode, which lamented the horror of the Sicilian revolt against the second Triumvirate (44–36 BC). To avoid future civil war, Horace proposed that Rome's inhabitants set sail for a blessed isle elsewhere. Erasmus figured that isle as Britain, a land of plenty and (allegedly) pleasant weather.[194] The other bit of flattery lay in the title. A *prosopopoeia* is a poem in which a personified country praises itself and its royal house. Here 'Britannia' declares that Henry VII 'will be my Apollo, the father of the golden age'.[195] Erasmus portrayed the duke of York as a heroic son from the *Aeneid* or *Iliad*, ready to protect his father's realm:

> How much of his father shines forth in his
> countenance! So in shone the image
> of Aeneas; so the face of Achilles reflected the
> beauty of Thetis.[196]

In his dedicatory letter, moreover, Erasmus urged Henry to imitate the achievements and literary patronage of ancient princely warriors such as Julius Caesar, Alexander and Achilles. He used Cicero's claim in the *Pro*

[190] 'Unum Britannicarum literarum lumen et decus', 'Grecia Meonio quantum debebat Homero, / Mantua Virgilio, / Tantum Skeltono iam se debere fatetur/ Terra Britanna suo': Erasmus, BL, Egerton MS 1651, fols. 1^{v}, 7^{r}.

[191] Maurice Pollet, *John Skelton: Poet of Tudor England*, trans. John Warrington (London, 1971), pp. 39–40.

[192] See the correction on BL, Egerton MS 1651, fol. 6^{v}.

[193] Erasmus, *Adagiorum collectanea* (Paris, 1500); Erasmus, *CWE: Poems ii*, pp. 442, 445.

[194] Erasmus, *CWE: Poems I*, pp. 32, 33.

[195] Erasmus, *CWE: Poems I*, pp. 34, 35, ln. 52 alluding to Virgil, *Aeneid*, VI, lns. 792–3 and *Eclogues*, IV, lns. 6–10.

[196] Erasmus, *CWE: Poems I*, pp. 38, 39, lns. 132–4. For Henry see Virgil, *Aeneid*, IV, lns. 328–9 and XII, ln. 348.

Archia that Alexander 'envied Achilles' who was 'blessed… in having such a one as Homer to sing his praises'.[197] Writing in 1499, Erasmus petitioned to become the poet of Henry's future military glory. As we shall see in chapter two, it was an offer that he would come to regret.

Before 1502, then, it seemed as though Skelton's willingness to barter access to his charge in return for poetic praise had not disrupted Henry VII's plans for his second son. Both Skelton and humanist interlopers such as Erasmus were encouraging Henry to become a loyal knight in the second Arthurian court. Henry played his role beautifully in November 1501 when he met Catherine of Aragon, his brother's betrothed, at the head of four hundred gentlemen-at-arms and escorted her triumphal entry into the city of London.[198] As an adult Henry VIII would demand pre-eminence in all things but as a child he played his supporting role with good grace.

After Arthur's death in April 1502, Henry continued to study music and French under Giles du Wés. By 1503 Prince Henry was playing the pipes as well as his lute.[199] He learnt to hawk, to ride, to shoot a bow and to bear arms under Thomas Simpson, his 'master at Axes'.[200] Lady Margaret Beaufort encouraged her grandson's chivalric exercises with the gift of a saddle and harness.[201] Henry practised even more tenaciously in the ring after Philip of Burgundy (1478–1506) washed up on English shores in January 1506. Philip and his wife Juana, the sister of Catherine of Aragon, had been blown off course en route to Castile. The archduke was a keen jouster whose gallant style offered Henry a living model of Skelton's lessons.[202] Philip was made a Knight of the Garter and then he inducted Prince Henry into the Order of the Golden Fleece in return.[203] The archduke impressed Henry sufficiently to become the recipient of his first surviving letter, a courtesy note in French, dated 9 April 1506.[204] Moreover Bernard André's *Annales* revealed that following Philip's visit the prince began 'to march out and fight daily with his companions in arms

[197] Erasmus, *CWE: Poems I*, pp. 28, 29, lns. 28–30; Cicero, *Pro Archia*, x.29.

[198] [Hawes?] *The receyt*, pp. 40–53; Thomas More, *The correspondence of Sir Thomas More*, ed. Elizabeth F. Rogers (Princeton, 1947), pp. 3–5.

[199] Helms, 'Henry VIII's book', pp. 118–35; Nicolas (ed.), *Privy purse expenses of Elizabeth of York*, p. cxxxviii; NA, LC 2/1/1, fol. 73v.

[200] Nicolas (ed.), *Extracts from the privy purse expenses of King Henry VII*, p. 123; NA, LC 2/1/1, fol. 73v.

[201] Michael K. Jones and Malcolm G. Underwood, *The king's mother: Lady Margaret Beaufort, Countess of Richmond and Derby* (Cambridge, 1992), p. 79.

[202] *CSPV*, vol. 1, no. 854, p. 306. [203] *CSPV*, vol. 1, no. 867, p. 320.

[204] BL, Additional MS 21404, fol. 9r.

at games of war'.[205] In this he received encouragement from Baldassare Castiglione, who arrived in England on embassy in October 1506. After meeting Henry at the November meeting of the Order of the Garter, he reported that the prince was advancing sufficiently in his studies at arms to lead a crusade. Nature, Castiglione claimed, had brought 'together in [his] single body enough virtues for a host of men'.[206]

While the crusade would not eventuate, Henry's practice at arms would pay off. In tourneys at Greenwich in June 1508, the *adolescens* distinguished himself in 'running at ring' (*ad annulum hastis*), a sport that involved using a lance to spear a suspended hoop.[207] It was a relatively safe exercise for the sole surviving son of the first Tudor king. Safety was less of a concern to the vainglorious Prince of Wales himself, who managed to break the arm of Richard Grey, earl of Kent, in combat the following month.[208] Prior to his accession Henry demonstrated his princely potential by playing the knight at every opportunity.

'THYS BOKE IS MYNE': PRINCE HENRY AND THE ERASMIAN TURN

Nevertheless, this chivalric model of kingship would not be the only suit in Henry's royal hand. After Arthur's death, Henry did not begin a princely apprenticeship at Ludlow or start to shadow his father at court. His first progress with the king was delayed until 1504, 'so as not to interrupt his studies'.[209] Even after this, the journeys he took were limited; prior to his accession in 1509 Henry VIII had scarcely left the Thames valley.[210] Nor were men of business or diplomats encouraged to come to him. As late as 1508 the Spanish diplomat Gutierre Gómez de Fuensalida claimed that Henry VII was restricting foreigners' access to his son.[211] Instead of thrusting the new Prince of Wales into the training ring of regional government and estate management, Henry VII broke with Yorkist precedent and left Prince Henry to continue his liberal education.

The king's reasons for doing so had more to do with the desire to protect his surviving son than a wish to make a stand for the princely utility

205 'Cum suis commilitonibus belli praeludia tentans sese exercuit exercetque indies': André, 'Annales', p. 116.

206 Baldesar Castiglione, *The book of the courtier*, trans. and ed. George Bull (London, 1967), pp. 312–13.

207 André, 'Annales', p. 120. 208 André, 'Annales', p. 122.

209 *CSP Spain*, vol. 1, no. 398, pp. 329–30.

210 Gunn, 'Prince Arthur's preparation for kingship', p. 15.

211 Gutierre Gómez de Fuensalida, *Correspondencia de Gutierre Gómez de Fuensalida, embajador en Alemania, Flandes é Inglaterra (1496–1509)*, ed. Jacobo Fitz-James Stuart y Falcó (Madrid, 1907), p. 449.

of the *bonae litterae*. Threats to Henry's health were taken even more seriously after the death in childbed of Queen Elizabeth on 11 February 1503. Some thought that Ludlow provided an 'unhealthy situation' for young princes.[212] More pressingly, the rebellious Edmund de la Pole, earl of Suffolk (1471/2–1513), was whispering in Maximilian I's ear that 'there should be no doubt of [Pole's] claim, should Henry [VII]'s second son happen to die'.[213] De la Pole's activities also impeded the king's capacity to finance an establishment for Henry in Wales. The hefty loans he was sending to Maximilian I to banish the earl of Suffolk from the empire were draining his coffers in 1503.[214] The king even dismembered his Welsh council that year to save money.[215] Keeping Prince Henry cooped up in his schoolroom was an effective, convenient and inexpensive method of protecting the surviving heir, especially as Henry VII's own health had begun to deteriorate.[216] This decision left the future Tudor king with a poor sense of the geography of his realm and the mechanisms of government business.[217] It did mean, however, that Henry VIII would come to the throne more learned in neo-classical Latin grammar and rhetoric than any English ruler before him.

After 1499, the *Graecistes* had continued to flock about the court, fighting for any crusts that came their way. When it became clear that the new Prince of Wales would remain in the schoolroom, they swooped to reorganise its personnel. It was probably Mountjoy who put the case to Queen Elizabeth before her death. The detested André was excluded and Skelton was rusticated to a parish at Diss in Norfolk in Margaret Beaufort's gift. A crown payment of forty shillings to 'the duc of york Scolemaster' on 29 April may well have been his salary in arrears.[218] Also departing in July 1503 was a mysterious 'Scottisheman scole maister'.[219] In their places, a new tutor to 'my lorde prince' was paid £4, apparently in advance.[220] A list of Prince Henry's householders made after Queen Elizabeth's death in February 1503 reveals that his new pedagogue was John Holt (d. 1504).[221] Holt had close connections to the *Graecistes*. From around 1494 he had been an usher at the Magdalen School,

[212] *CSP Spain*, vol. 1, no. 322, p. 269.
[213] 'Quod si secundus Henrici filius esset mortuus, nullum esset dubium de titulo domini mei': *Letters and papers illustrative of the reigns of Richard III and Henry VII*, vol. 1, p. 180.
[214] Cunningham, *Henry VII*, p.112; *Letters and papers illustrative of the reigns of Richard III and Henry VII*, vol. 1, pp. 220–5; Penn, *Winter king*, p. 89.
[215] *Pace* Cunningham, *Henry VII*, p. 272. See Smith, 'Crown and community', p. 168.
[216] Cunningham, *Henry VII*, p. 107.
[217] Geoffrey Elton, *Reform and reformation: England, 1509–1558* (Cambridge, MA, 1977), p. 17.
[218] NA, E 101/414/6.
[219] Nicolas (ed.), *Privy purse expenses of Elizabeth of York*, p. 28.
[220] NA, E 101/414/6. [221] NA, LC 2/1, fol. 73r.

Oxford, William Lily's *alma mater* and the first school in England to adopt a humanist curriculum.[222] At Easter 1496 Holt became grammar master to the youths in the household of Cardinal Morton, archbishop of Canterbury.[223] There he befriended Morton's former page, Thomas More. Indeed Holt is the recipient of More's first surviving letter of 1501, which discusses his progress in Greek.[224] Through More and Mountjoy, Holt had almost certainly met Erasmus as well.[225] Indeed it was John Holt who made Henry's education Erasmian.

Alistair Fox has complained that scholars have played fast and loose with the term 'Erasmian' in Tudor England.[226] I use it here in two senses. The first is a narrow one: Henry's studies followed the Dutch educator's prescriptions for *bonae litterae* closely. Holt's admiration for Erasmus' curriculum is apparent in his elementary grammar, the *Lac puerorum* or *Milk for children* (written 1498/9).[227] As Nicholas Orme has noted, Holt included three unusual pedagogical woodcuts in his tract to explain the declension of nouns and pronouns.[228] To remember the demonstrative pronoun, for instance, Holt assigned the nominative to the thumb, the genitive to the index finger, the dative to the middle finger, the accusative to the ring finger, the vocative to the little finger and the ablative to the ball of the thumb.[229] Henry was probably past *hic, haec, hoc*-ing in 1502 but Holt's grammar may still shed light on the way he taught Henry Latin. In his verse epilogue to the treatise, More explained that the *Lac puerorum* was intended to prepare childish palates for the stronger meat of humanist grammarians Niccolò Perotti and Giovanni Sulpizio, whose

[222] Nicholas Orme, *Education in early Tudor England: Magdalen College Oxford and its school, 1480–1540* (Oxford, 1998), 'John Holt (d.1504), Tudor schoolmaster and grammarian', *The Library*, 18:4 (1996) and 'Schools and school-books', in Lotte Hellinga and J. B. Trapp (eds.), *The Cambridge history of the book in Britain*, vol. III: *1400–1557* (Cambridge, 1999), pp. 302–3, 310, 459–63, 468–9; J. B. Trapp, 'The humanist book', in Lotte Hellinga and J. B. Trapp (eds.), *The Cambridge history of the book in Britain*, vol. III: *1400–1557* (Cambridge, 1999).

[223] Orme, 'John Holt', p. 287.

[224] More, *Correspondence of Sir Thomas More*, pp. 3–5.

[225] Peter G. Bietenholz and Thomas B. Deutsche (eds.), *Contemporaries of Erasmus: A biographical register of the Renaissance and Reformation*, 3 vols. (Toronto, 1985–7), vol. II, p. 198.

[226] Alistair Fox, 'Facts and fallacies: Interpreting English humanism' and 'English humanism and the body politic', in Alistair Fox and John Guy (eds.), *Reassessing the Henrician age: Humanism, politics and reform 1500–1550* (Oxford, 1986), pp. 10, 17–18, 21–5, 28, 34–5, 50–1, regarding Arthur B. Ferguson, *The articulate citizen and the English Renaissance* (Durham, NC, 1965) and James McConica, *English humanists and Reformation politics under Henry VIII and Edward VI* (Oxford, 1965).

[227] John Holt, *Lac puerorum* (London, 1508), STC 13604, sigs. aIII^{r}, hv^{r}.

[228] Holt, *Lac puerorum*, sigs. aIII^{v}, av^{r} and aIII^{v}.

[229] Holt, *Lac puerorum*, sig. aIII^{v}.

works Erasmus also recommended for young men.[230] Like Holt, they tried to use classical vocabulary, constructions and syntax and they illustrated their precepts with excerpts drawn from ancient authors.[231] The humanist practices of philological investigation, locating authorities and sourcing *loci* and *exempla* for propositions in antique texts would stay with Henry throughout his life.[232]

The prince's education was Erasmian in a broader sense too. In keeping with Erasmus' prescriptions, Henry's studies associated the grammatical and rhetorical understanding of words with the pursuit of philosophical wisdom and Christian piety.[233] In Erasmus' *Handbook of the Christian soldier* (1503), the humanist claimed that the two weapons of the Christian soldier were prayer and knowledge. To acquire knowledge, one needed to read edifying authors, suppress the passions through reason and live justly. This, Erasmus said, was the equivalent of Paul's command to 'walk in the spirit' rather than succumb to the flesh.[234] For Erasmus, then, reason was a precondition for the pursuit of revelation. In 1516, Erasmus would claim that a philosopher-king 'rejects illusory appearance and undauntedly seeks out and follows what is true and good. Being a philosopher is in practice the same as being a Christian; only the terminology is different'.[235] The idea that a liberal education could promote virtuous conduct and even piety explained why Erasmus described his curriculum for schoolboys as *bonae* or occasionally *honestae litterae*.[236] The study of apparently pagan letters could make one more truly Christian.

This aspect of Erasmus' pedagogy influenced Holt's decision to read Cicero's *De officiis* with his royal student. We know Henry tackled this text because he tells us on the first folio of his copy, printed in April 1502,

[230] Holt, *Lac puerorum*, sig. hv^r; Erasmus, *Ratio studii ac legendi interpretantique aucthores*, in *CWE: Literary and educational writings II*, p. 667.

[231] Kristian Jensen, 'Humanist reform of Latin and Latin teaching', in Jill Kraye (ed.), *Cambridge translations of Renaissance philosophical texts*, vol. II: *Political philosophy* (Cambridge, 1997), pp. 70–2.

[232] James P. Carley, *The books of King Henry VIII and his wives* (London, 2004), pp. 55–8 and 'Marks in the books and the libraries of Henry VIII', *Papers of the Bibliographical Society of America*, 91 (1997).

[233] Erasmus, *Antibarbari*, in *CWE: Literary and educational writings I*, p. 30; Brendan Bradshaw, 'The Christian humanism of Erasmus', *Journal of Theological Studies*, 33:2 (1982).

[234] Erasmus, *Handbook of the Christian soldier*, in *CWE: Spiritualia and pastoralia I*, p. 47, regarding Galatians 5:16.

[235] Erasmus, *EECP*, p. 15;

[236] For example Erasmus, *Institutio principis Christiani*, in *Opera omnia*, IV.i, p. 188. More generally, see James McConica, 'The fate of Erasmian humanism', in N. Phillipson (ed.), *Universities, society and the future* (Edinburgh, 1983), pp. 41–2.

'Thys boke is Myne'.[237] As we have seen, Arthur owned a decorative, illuminated manuscript of the Roman orator and philosopher to 'turn with his own hands', but Henry attacked his Cicero with his pen. Indeed he may have been one of the first English schoolboys to do so. Prior to the sixteenth century, *De officiis* played a significant role in the political thought of the Renaissance but it was rarely taught in schools. Humanist pedagogues before Erasmus had tended to follow Guarino of Verona's lead: they taught Cicero's orations and epistles, which offered school students directly applicable compositional models for sharpening their Ciceronian style of speaking and writing.[238] Erasmus, on the other hand, railed against pedantic imitation of Cicero's prose but praised *De officiis* as a handbook or weapon (*enchiridion*) for ethical Christian conduct. It was a 'tiny dagger' of morality to keep close to one's breast.[239] In dedicating his 1501 edition of *De officiis* to schoolmaster Jacob Voogd, Erasmus argued that 'neither Homer's Achilles nor Virgil's Aeneas was better equipped' for public life than the young man bearing Cicero as a guide, 'for it is more heroic to tackle faults than foemen'.[240] Erasmus' editions of *De officiis* and his pedagogical defence of the work made it a classroom staple for fourth- and fifth-form boys in England and northern Europe.[241] Thus Robert Whittington's 1534 facing-page English translation of Cicero is dedicated aptly to Henry VIII.[242] Through Holt's ministrations in 1502, the prince had been at the vanguard of a distinctly Erasmian direction in humanist pedagogy.

[237] FSL, PA 6295 A3 1502 Cage: Cicero, *Commentu[m] familiar in Ciceronis Officia*, ed. Petrus Marsus (Lyon, 1502), fol. 1^r^. Folger's Hamnet catalogue associates this work with John Skelton but the date of printing demonstrates that Henry did not study it on the poet's watch.

[238] Grendler, *Schooling in Renaissance Italy*, pp. 121–4, 216–17.

[239] Erasmus, *OEDE*, vol. 1, no. 152, p. 357, translation from *CWE: Letters 142 to 297*, no. 152, p. 31. On Erasmus' rejection of Italian Ciceronianism see Judith Rice Henderson, 'Despauterius' *Syntaxis* (1509): The earliest publication of Erasmus' *De conscribendis epistolis*', *Humanistica Lovaniensia*, 37 (1988). On his belief that the Roman author could encourage Christian conduct, see Charles Béné, 'Erasme et Cicéron', *Colloquia Erasmiana Turonensis*, 2 vols. (Paris, 1972), vol. 11, pp. 571–9.

[240] Erasmus, *CWE: Letters 142 to 297*, no. 152, p. 31.

[241] In addition to his school-friendly 1501 and 1520 editions of Cicero, Erasmus' annotations on the author were used in many early modern textbooks. Erasmus promoted *De officiis* in his popular *De copia*; in *CWE: Literary and educational writings II*, p. 415; and in *CWE: Colloquies I*, pp. 184, 192. For the *De officiis* in English schools, see T. W. Baldwin, *William Shakespere's smalle Latine and lesse Greeke*, 2 vols. (Urbana, 1944), vol. 1, pp. 310, 342–4, 345–51; Simon, *Education and society*, pp. 79, 144n.2, 189, 378. For one of the many editions to use Erasmus' notes, see Cicero, *Officia diligenter restituta*, eds. Desiderius Erasmus, Philip Melanchthon and Barthow Latomus (Paris, 1541).

[242] Cicero, *The thre bookes of Tyllyes offyces both in latyne tonge [et] in englysshe*, trans. Robert Whittington (London, 1534), STC 5278, sigs. a.1^v^–a.3^r^.

So how did Henry VIII read his Cicero? Many hands have annotated his copy over the years but one of the earliest secretary scripts bears some resemblance to Henry's: its 'd's lack definition and splay towards the left; the limbs on its 'H' descenders are exaggerated and either curve back on themselves or kick forward; its 'y' limb descenders curve to kick right; it prefers the z-shaped 'r' and extends the head strokes on 'g'. Yet Henry's 'e' is typically italic, while this hand alternates between secretary forms of the letter.[243] It is worth noting that this reader and the other early sixteenth-century hands marking this copy of *De officiis* (belonging, perhaps, to other young men in Henry's household) were studying the text for pedagogical purposes. In fact they were reading the text as Erasmus had recommended: they ignored Pietro Marso's 'exhaustive' commentary and focused instead on translating key phrases of the text and noting ethical points.[244]

If Henry was one of these readers, which parts of this *enchiridion* was he taught to keep by his breast? The relevant secretary-hand annotations occur only in the first book, which focused on the virtues and the need to control emotional impulses in public life.[245] One early reader studied Cicero's account of justice with particular care. He inserted English translations for *ortus* and *praeclare* to parse the line, 'We are not born for ourselves alone, to use Plato's excellent phrase'.[246] Erasmus, too, argued for this sentiment's excellence. In his *Handbook of the Christian soldier* he described it as the first belief worthy of a Christian man. Christ had bestowed his charity on men so that they might share it with other Christians, he argued.[247] From a young age, Henry read classical works that urged him to practice communitarian *pietas* and assumed his ability, indeed duty, to do good works.

Erasmus had translated Cicero's civic ethos in *De officiis* for a Christian context but how were the Roman orator's lessons in republican citizenship interpreted for a future monarch? A prince tackling only the first book of *De officiis* would not have been troubled by Cicero's justification for Caesar's assassination in books two or three.[248] If Henry read merely

243 FSL, PA 6295 A3 1502 Cage, fols. 12^r, 13^{r-v} and 16^r cf. BL, Additional MS 21404, fol. 9^r; BL, Cotton MS Caligula D VI, fol. 121^v. James Carley, '*Rex noster est inconstans*: Henry VIII's reading practices', in *King Henry's prayer book*, ed. James Carley (London, 2009), p. 14 deemed the script to be 'Henry's unpractised hand' but additional contemporary samples would be necessary to confirm his claim.

244 Erasmus, *CWE: Letters 142 to 297*, no. 152, pp. 130–1.

245 Cicero, *De officiis*, 1.6–70.

246 Cicero, *De officiis*, 1.22; FSL, PA 6295 A3 1502 Cage, fol. 22^r.

247 Erasmus, *Handbook of the Christian soldier*, in *CWE: Spiritualia and pastoralia I*, pp. 93–4.

248 Cicero, *De officiis*, II.23–4, III.19 and 32.

the first thirty folios of his edition, however, he would have encountered Cicero's meditation on the tendency of kings, including Julius Caesar, to 'overturn the law of God and men for the sake of pre-eminence'.[249] As Erasmus cautioned in his *Handbook*, Christian princes should never believe themselves to be 'above the law' temporal or divine.[250] It seems likely, therefore, that Holt offered up Cicero to caution him against over-mighty monarchy.[251] Henry's study of Cicero's treatise was intended to inculcate Latin vocabulary, grammar and rhetoric and to teach him to rule himself before he ruled others.

Skelton, in his vanity, had opened the door of Henry's schoolroom to Erasmus and his friends in 1499 and they refused to leave. After Holt's death in mid-1504, Henry came to court in order to be furnished with 'good habits' but, even then, his liberal education continued.[252] Holt was replaced by William Hone (d. 1522), who had previously been his successor as master of Chichester Prebendal School. Hone probably followed Holt's methods, too.[253] At court, according to Erasmus, Mountjoy continued to serve as Henry's *socius studiorum*: the two 'immersed themselves completely' in Livy's *Ab urbe condita* with Henry VII's blessing. In addition, Mountjoy may have continued Henry's instruction in letter-writing using an early version of Erasmus' *De conscribendis epistolis*.[254] The Spanish ambassador, Gómez de Fuensalida, confirmed that the prince was still surrounded by tutors in 1508.[255] Ultimately Prince Henry's study of *bonae litterae* continued for around nine years compared to Prince Arthur's four or five.

RELIGION AND POLITICS IN PRINCE HENRY'S EDUCATION

There was a further consequence of Henry VII's decision to allow his surviving son to continue his liberal education under northern humanists that has been insufficiently appreciated by historians: prior to his accession, Henry VIII was immersed in Erasmus' political and religious thought. As we will see in the next two chapters, this knowledge did not

[249] Cicero, *De officiis*, 1.27.
[250] Erasmus, *Handbook of the Christian soldier*, in *CWE: Spiritualia and pastoralia I*, p. 99.
[251] See similarly Erasmus, *EECP*, p. 62.
[252] *CSP Spain*, vol. 1, no. 398, pp. 329–30.
[253] Orme, 'John Holt', pp. 290, 298; William George Searle (ed.), *Grace book Gamma: Containing the records of the University of Cambridge for the years 1501–1542* (Cambridge, 1908), p. 37.
[254] Erasmus, *OEDE*, vol. IX, no. 2435, p. 145; Henderson, 'Despauterius' *Syntaxis* (1509)', p. 177 but see Jacques Chomarat, *Grammaire et rhétorique chez Erasme*, 2 vols. (Paris, 1981), vol. II, p. 1006n. 16.
[255] Fuensalida, *Correspondencia de Gutierre Gómez de Fuensalida*, p. 449.

shape the king's thinking or conduct in the ways Erasmus would have wished, but it certainly left its mark.

Prince Henry's liberal education may have influenced his youthful personal piety. Certainly, his religious upbringing was generally conventional. In 1503, for instance, Henry's Richmond household contained five chaplains and was located between the Bridgettine sisters and brothers of Syon and the Carthusian monks of Sheen.[256] His father and grandmother, Lady Margaret Beaufort, who were key figures in his childhood, went to great expense to minimise their time in purgatory.[257] Despite her largely traditional outlook, however, Beaufort also took spiritual direction from John Fisher (*c.* 1469–1535), whose sacramental, Christocentric theology and exegetical sermonising Erasmus had praised.[258] She and her son took Henry to hear the bishop of Rochester preach in Cambridge in July 1507.[259] Indeed it is worth noting that many of Henry VIII's earliest *exempla* of godly learning were men like the bishop: they were of the university and the world rather than the monasteries; they had mixed social origins; they favoured church renewal. Amongst his pious tutors, Holt and Hone were professional schoolmasters, Mountjoy was a nobleman and More was a lawyer. Erasmus had taken holy orders but he avoided cloisters. Henry VIII's adult preference for intellectually agile counsellors, his comparative lack of concern for the circumstances of their birth and his special patronage of university colleges may owe something to these circumstances. Through his contacts with northern humanists and Fisher, moreover, Henry was exposed to reformist currents within the church in England.

For evidence that Henry was influenced by these currents, we might turn to the prince's illuminated 'Bede' or prayer roll, preserved at Ushaw College, Durham. David Starkey and Don Skemer have made strong arguments that the Bede roll shows that Henry's juvenile religiosity was firmly rooted in the 'magical, mysterious, many-coloured world of late medieval piety'. Certainly, the roll *could* be carried as a protective amulet. Alongside classic devotional prayer texts, it contained a depiction of

256 NA, LC 2/1/1, fol. 73r; Diarmaid MacCulloch, 'Henry VIII and the reform of the church', in Diarmaid MacCulloch (ed.), *The reign of Henry VIII: Politics, policy and piety* (Basingstoke, 1995), pp. 164–5.

257 Eamon Duffy, *The stripping of the altars: Traditional religion in England, c. 1400–c. 1580* (New Haven, 1992), pp. 328–9, 338–76; MacCulloch, 'Henry VIII and the reform of the church', pp. 164–5; Cunningham, *Henry VII*, p. 117.

258 Jones and Underwood, *The king's mother*, pp. 208–10.

259 Carlson, 'Royal tutors', p. 272; Bodleian, MS Bodley 13, fols. 22r–31v as cited and dated by M. Underwood, 'John Fisher and the promotion of learning', in Brendan Bradshaw and Eamon Duffy (eds.), *Humanism, reform and Reformation: The career of Bishop John Fisher* (Cambridge, 1989), p. 42.

the nails of the crucifixion and a version of the 'Charlemagne' legend that promised its bearer remissions from purgatory, material prosperity and safe delivery for mothers in labour.[260] Yet there is no positive evidence that Henry had faith in the roll's supposedly talismanic properties. His suspicions may have been aroused when it failed to protect his mother, Queen Elizabeth, during her final, fatal pregnancy. Perhaps there was something to be said for Erasmus' critiques of 'superstitious' charms and barren rituals.[261] Even if Henry displayed conventional respect towards shrines and monastic houses during his reign, he did not hear about their tendencies towards corruption, dishonesty, hypocrisy and greed for the first time in 1536.[262] In fact, rather than seeing his Bede roll as an amulet, there is evidence that Prince Henry used it differently. Before his accession, he presented the roll to one William Thomas (d. 1543), his groom of the chamber. 'I pray you pray for me your loving master Prynce Henry', he wrote below the *Ave Maria, gratia tecum* and above an image of Christ with his wounds pouring blood into a well.[263] The inscription suggests that he may have prayed while holding the scroll before him and meditating on this affective representation of Christ's passion. Was the roll primarily a spur to help him to intensify his devotions during prayer? By making a gift of it to another young man in his household, he suggested that there was a charitable, Christian bond between them, despite the difference in their ranks. This was the sort of intense, personal and communitarian piety that Erasmus' *Handbook of the Christian soldier* had endorsed.

Henry would subsequently testify to the extent to which he used the image of Christ's passion to interpret his own youthful sufferings. He probably met with Erasmus again in the winter of 1506. The humanist was staying with Mountjoy, who was assisting with the courtly entertainment of the Archduke Philip.[264] Prince Henry instantly adored the dashing, chivalrous archduke but Erasmus knew Philip of old. As a citizen of the Low Countries, he had delivered a *Panegyric* to welcome Philip on his return from Spain in January 1604. Erasmus used this oration of praise

260 Durham, Ushaw College Library, MS 29. Quotation from Starkey, *Henry*, p. 198. See also Don C. Skemer, *Binding words: Textual amulets in the middle ages* (University Park, PA, 2006), pp. 265–6; Duffy, *Stripping of the altars*, p. 273.

261 Erasmus, *Handbook of a Christian soldier*, in *CWE: Spiritualia and pastoralia I*, pp. 71–4.

262 George Bernard, 'The piety of Henry VIII', in Scott Amos, Andrew Pettegree and Henk van Nierop (eds.), *The education of the Christian Society: Humanism and the Reformation in Britain and the Netherlands* (Aldershot, 1999), p. 75 but see Richard Rex, 'The religion of Henry VIII', *HJ*, 57:1 (2014).

263 Durham, Ushaw College Library, MS 29.

264 Erasmus, *CWE: Letters 142 to 297*, no. 189, p. 110.

to sting Philip with a number of precepts regarding good kingship.[265] He urged Philip to keep the peace terms of the Treaty of Blois (1501) and retracted his 1499 recommendation that princes pattern their life on the bellicose examples of Julius Caesar, Alexander or Achilles. Erasmus urged Philip to recall that Caesar spent his last years 'tormented by the knowledge of his crimes [in war] and by the shades of those whom he had killed'.[266] A prince, Erasmus argued, was not granted supreme power (*imperium*) over subjects in order to fight wars, 'keep lives in chaos and collect taxes'. Instead he possessed the power of 'public administration' (*publicum administrandum*), a much milder form of authority that he exercised for the common good.[267] Erasmus described an alternative set of stoical qualities that would provide the foundation for good government. Philip needed 'to control [his] impulses [*affectiones*], and first to be a ruler over [himself], then a father rather than a master to his people'.[268] Erasmus' *Panegyric* failed to persuade Philip of the wisdom of peace with Guelders: the archduke understood neither Erasmus' Latin nor his growing exasperation at vainglorious militarism.[269] Yet Erasmus' experience with Philip shaped his subsequent plans for the archduke's disciple, Henry, Prince of Wales.

It was Philip's death in September 1506 that prompted an exchange of letters between Erasmus and Henry. By this stage, Erasmus had left England. His first stop had been Paris, where he oversaw the printing of the translations of Lucian that he and Thomas More had been working on in 1505–6. Then he accompanied the two sons of Henry VII's Genoan physician, Giovanni Battista Boerio (d. 1520), to university in Bologna, only to find the city besieged.[270] Writing from war-torn Tuscany in November 1506, Erasmus informed Prince Henry of the report 'that is too sad for anyone willingly to believe... to the effect that Prince Philip has departed life'.[271] Henry replied on 17 January 1507, in the second of his

[265] Erasmus, *Panegyricus ad Philippum Austriae ducem*, in *Opera omnia*, IV.i, pp. 22–93, translation from *Panegyric for Archduke Philip of Austria*, in *CWE: Literary and educational writings V*, pp. 1–76.

[266] Erasmus, *Panegyricus ad Philippum*, in *Opera omnia*, IV.i, p. 75; *CWE: Literary and educational writings V*, p. 56; James D. Tracy, *The politics of Erasmus: A pacifist intellectual and his political milieu* (Toronto, 1978), pp. 13–14, 20–1.

[267] Erasmus, *Panegyricus ad Philippum*, in *Opera omnia*, IV.i, p. 64; *CWE: Literary and educational writings V*, p. 44.

[268] Erasmus, *Panegyricus ad Philippum*, in *Opera omnia*, IV.i, p. 63; *CWE: Literary and educational writings V*, p. 43. See also Erasmus, *CWE: Adages I i 1 to I v 100*, pp. 50–1; Seneca, *De clementia*, I.II.2, I.14.2 and *De ira*, III.7.

[269] Tracy, *Politics of Erasmus*, p. 16.

[270] Erika Rummel, *Erasmus as a translator of the classics* (Toronto, 1985), pp. 51–2.

[271] Erasmus, *CWE: Letters 142 to 297*, no. 204, p. 126.

surviving pre-accession letters, that 'no less welcome news has ever come here since the death of my very dear [*charissima*] mother... it seemed to re-open a wound [*cicatrix*] that time had healed'.[272] Erasmus apparently kept this letter with him in a little box, 'like hidden treasure'.[273] As we will see in subsequent chapters, he noticed the depth of Henry's grief for Philip and his mother and the metaphor, redolent of Christ's wounds and his passion, that the prince used to describe his feelings.

What also excited Erasmus about Henry's letter was that it was 'written in [his] own hand' and 'savoured of nothing but the most pure Latin'.[274] Indeed Henry's grammatical and rhetorical proficiency was sufficient for Erasmus to doubt that the fifteen-year-old had composed the letter himself. It was only later, when Mountjoy showed Erasmus a copy of another heavily corrected draft epistle by Henry, that Erasmus was convinced.[275] He had found a prince who 'read nothing more diligently than [his own] writings'! He had found a prince whose Latin style imitated his own![276] On the basis of Henry's knowledge of words, Erasmus determined that he was ready for the moral, political and spiritual knowledge that Philip had eschewed.

A neglected manuscript in the British Library confirms that the letter exchange convinced the humanist to take a direct hand in the final stage of Henry's princely education. In the early months of 1507, Erasmus had his pupil Giovanni Boerio, the elder son of the physician, send an instructive set of translations to Henry.[277] As a gift, Boerio's volume was sumptuous: a quarto on vellum, bound in silk and elegantly penned by Pierantonio Sallando of Reggio Emilia.[278] Equally impressively, it contained translations of Lucian and Isocrates from Greek into Latin, which was no mean feat in 1507. Erasmus had taught Boerio well.[279] We can see

[272] Erasmus, *OEDE*, vol. I, no. 206, p. 436; Erasmus, *CWE: Letters 142 to 297*, no. 206, p. 129.

[273] Richard Pace, *De fructu qui ex doctrina percipitur: The benefit of a liberal education*, trans. and eds. Frank Manley and Richard S. Sylvester (New York, 1967), pp. 140–1.

[274] Pace, *De fructu*, pp. 140–1. See also Erasmus, *CWE: Letters 142 to 297*, no. 296, p. 298.

[275] Erasmus, *OEDE*, vol. VIII, no. 2143, pp. 129–30.

[276] Erasmus, *CWE: Letters 1252 to 1355*, no. 1275, p. 68 and no. 1313, pp. 181–2.

[277] BL, Additional MS 19553. For Boerio, see Bietenholz and Deutsche (eds.), *Contemporaries of Erasmus*, vol. II, p. 159.

[278] Alexander, 'Foreign illuminators and illuminated manuscripts', p. 55. This is the same hand that penned Filippo Alberici's *De homine condito*, which the poet presented to Henry VII. David Rundle, 'Filippo Alberici, Henry VII and Richard Fox: The English fortunes of a little-known Italian humanist', *Journal of the Warburg and Courtauld Institutes*, 68 (2005), 137–55 argues that Queen's College MS 298 was made in Paris for Henry VII in 1508. Given that Alberici was a friend of Giovanni Battista Boerio, it seems likely that Pierantonio Sallando also penned *De homine condito*, in Italy in 1507.

[279] Erasmus, *CWE: Letters 142 to 297*, no. 205, pp. 126–7.

the humanist hovering over Giovanni's shoulder as he describes himself in his dedicatory letter as a 'beginner' in the '*bonae litterae*', Erasmus' preferred term for classical literature.[280] Boerio also followed Erasmus' translation practice of offering two Latin adjectives to draw out the nuances of a single Greek term. He rendered Isocrates' *πραοτέρας*, for instance, as *mitiorem, faciliorem q[ue]* or 'milder and easier'.[281] Finally Boerio praised Henry for possessing a *singularis humanitas*, or 'a peculiar civility'.[282] It was precisely the phrase that Erasmus used to praise Henry's kingly demeanour at Eltham in 1499.

We can also see Erasmus' hand in selecting the texts that Boerio translated for Henry. The first was Lucian's essay *De calumnia*. The choice was intended to complement the translations of Lucian that Erasmus presented to Henry VII's counsellors in 1506: *Toxaris* to Richard Foxe, *Tyrannicida* to Richard Whitford, *Timon* to Thomas Ruthall and *Gallus* to Christopher Urswick.[283] Erasmus frequently claimed that Lucian's satirical style was particularly appropriate for court life. It could puncture unthinking custom, passions and hypocrisy without betraying indecorous rage.[284] In *De calumnia* Lucian criticised court slanderers but the real object of his satire was the prince who listened to them. Rulers such as Alexander the Great were too ignorant, too used to 'the royal diet of flattery', too emotional and too inclined to think of themselves as 'not only a God's son, but a God-maker' to hear the truth behind the calumny. It would take a true God, Lucian concluded, to 'lay bare our lives for us. Then fleeing slander would disappear down into the abyss... All would be illuminated by truth'.[285] Erasmus would subsequently claim that these words echoed Christ's instructions to the Apostles (Matthew 10:26) and his parable of the lamp (Mark 4:11, Luke 8:17): the light of truth in the world would be spread by scripture.[286]

280 Giovanni Boerio, BL, Additional MS 19553, fol. 1^v.

281 Isocrates, *Ad Nicocles*, trans. Boerio, BL, Additional MS 19553, fol. 5^r; Rummel, *Erasmus as a translator of the classics*, p. 60.

282 Boerio, BL, Additional MS 19553, fol. 1^v.

283 Dominic Baker-Smith, '"Inglorious glory": 1513 and the humanist attack on chivalry', in Sydney Anglo (ed.), *Chivalry in the Renaissance* (Woodbridge, 1990), p. 133; Rummel, *Erasmus as a translator of the classics*, p. 51; Tracy, *Politics of Erasmus*, p. 32.

284 Erasmus, *CWE: Letters 142 to 297*, nos. 187, 191, 192, 193, pp. 112–13, 113–14, 114–17.

285 'Si deorum aliquis, unius cuiusq[ue] n[os]tr[a]m uitam retegat, aufugiens calumnia in barathrum abierit: quum nullus illi locus relictus esset: puta rebus a ueritate illustratis': Lucian, 'Non facile credendum esse calumniae', trans. Boerio, BL, Additional MS 19553, fol. 35^r.

286 See the frontispiece of Erasmus' 1519 *Novum Testamentum*, featuring Ambrosius Holbein's woodcut of Lucian's *De calumnia*. On its verso, a letter from Pope Leo X refuted the conservative calumny made of Erasmus' 1516 edition by conservative clergymen: Erasmus (ed.), *In Novum Testamentum* (Basel, 1519), frontispiece recto and verso on BL, D-3225.f.6.

The other text that Erasmus thought Prince Henry could use in 1507 was Isocrates' *Ad Nicocles*. Since at least 1501 Erasmus had been interested in the political lesson Isocrates had offered the young king of Cyprus on the death of his father. He regarded Isocrates' style of epideictic rhetoric as particularly useful for exhorting young royals to conduct themselves virtuously.[287] In his translation Boerio forcefully conveyed Isocrates' argument that Henry should study to make his rule 'milder and easier' on his subjects: not only was moderate government intrinsically virtuous but it would also give Henry 'greater security in office'.[288] He must learn to govern his conduct and to 'regard [himself] the greatest prince only when [he is] no slave to pleasure but rules over [his] desires more firmly than over the citizens themselves'.[289] He should try 'making peace by negotiation' rather than engaging in unjust aggression. He should emulate 'not those who have most widely extended their dominion, but those who have made best use of the power they already possess'.[290] In short, Erasmus and Boerio selected translations for Prince Henry that echoed the account of good kingship Erasmus had offered Archduke Philip in his *Panegyricus*. Good government depended on a prince's learning, reason and control of his passions. It required him to show piety in all his actions, to moderate his authority and to avoid vainglorious militarism. This was the advice of a theologian whose fury had been roused by the sight of Pope Julius II marching into Bologna on 11 November 1506 at the head of an army, violating Christ's injunction for peace and 'in fact playing Julius to the life'.[291] It was the advice of a pedagogue who regretted his bellicose letter and poem to Prince Henry in 1499.

What Prince Henry made of Boerio and Erasmus' gift is unclear but Erasmus and his circle greeted his accession in 1509 with self-congratulating raptures. Afterwards, the *Graecistes* quickly discovered that the prince's exposure to Isocrates' account of moderate kingship would not diminish

[287] Rummel, *Erasmus as a translator of the classics*, pp. 103–5. See his preface to his *Apophthegmatum sive scite dictorum* (Basel, 1531), sig. a2^{v}.

[288] 'Uero politicam uitam mitiorem, facilioremq[ue], efficiet': Isocrates, *Ad Nicocles*, trans. Boerio, BL, Additional MS 19553, fol. 5^{r}.

[289] 'Maxime rege dignu[m] putes, si nulli voluptati seruias: sed si magis tuis affectibus imperes, quam ciuibus ipsis': Isocrates, *Ad Nicocles*, trans. Boerio, BL, Additional MS 19553, fol. 11^{r}.

[290] 'Pacificus vero hoc pacto', 'Non eos admiratione dignos existimes, qui qua maximu[m] possident imperium: Sed qui pr[a]esens imperium quam optime administrauerint': Isocrates, *Ad Nicocles*, trans. Boerio, BL, Additional MS 19553, fols. 9^{v}, 10^{r}. See similarly Thomas More, 'De cupiditate regnandi', in *The complete works of Saint Thomas More*, vol. III, part 2, no. 243, pp. 256–7.

[291] Erasmus, *CWE: Letters 142 to 297*, no. 205, p. 128. See too Baker-Smith, 'Inglorious glory', p. 134; Tracy, *Politics of Erasmus*, pp. 24–32.

his enthusiasm for Philip's chivalric example or for war. This would not be the last complaint of peace that Erasmus sent to his student prince.

CONCLUSION

Despite Henry's mixed response to the northern humanists' political and religious writings, their intervention in his education had been decisive. Henry VIII's education had broken firmly with the Yorkist model for cultivating kings. Erasmus and his circle's emphasis on reason as part of the search for revelation, on peace rather than war and on the moderation of royal authority differed from the prescriptions of *Le livre dit grace* for Arthur, Skelton's counsel to Henry or indeed the example of the Archduke Philip. As far as Erasmus was concerned, his prescriptions for princely education did not merely add some Renaissance gloss to traditional royal pedagogy. He was trying to root out the dominant tradition of aristocratic education in northern Europe and replace it with good letters. Fifteenth-century princes were trained vocationally but Henry's studies were predominantly liberal. Their upbringings had emphasised the sword but Henry's had given substantial weight to the pen. Erasmus and his circle would have been surprised by Nicholas Orme's claim that all he and his friends sought to accomplish in the royal schoolroom was an apparently superficial shift in the way princes studied Latin.[292]

This is not to deny that the northern humanists' first object was curriculum change, nor that this curriculum change began with Latin grammar. It is important to acknowledge, however, that teaching princes to imitate classical Latin authors had significant consequences for their upbringing. Erasmus, John Holt and William Hone attempted to convey literary knowledge and skills that could only be learnt if a prince spent longer in the schoolroom than traditional models of royal education allowed. Giving the prince a liberal education had necessitated the regular attendance of a number of professional schoolmasters and learned friends, such as Lord Mountjoy. The time and money spent on Henry's *institutio* and *disciplina* – book-learning and intellectual knowledge – gave liberal education a higher status in Henry's education than it had won in previous royal schoolrooms. Indeed, as we will see in subsequent chapters, the humanist education that Henry would provide for his own sons and, eventually, his daughters would raise the standing of *bonae litterae* in England and Scotland in the sixteenth century.

[292] Orme, *Medieval schools*, p. 127.

Henry's youthful studies in *bonae litterae* also had consequences for the sort of king he became. His education did not encourage him to be a diligent account keeper, or give him expertise in the mechanics of royal government; his dependence on Thomas Wolsey (1473–1530) and Thomas Cromwell (*c.* 1485–1540) for these things is well known. Yet, as we will see in chapter three, Henry's education did give him the skills and confidence to tackle questions that had been the preserve of the clergy in England. The king learnt the value of fighting with his pen during his Great Matter. Henry commissioned scholars to gather up chronicles and theological works from monasteries in England and beyond. Some were digested into the *Collectanea satis copiosa* (1530) and others were placed in the king's working library.[293] As James Carley's pioneering work has shown, Henry gutted these treatises to locate *loci* and *exempla* that supported arguments against papal jurisdiction and for divorce and royal authority over the clergy. Even unlikely material, such as Augustinus Triumphus' early fourteenth-century defence of papal monarchy, *Summa de potestate ecclesiastica*, was squeezed until it yielded nectar. In the time of the patriarchs, was it considered against the law of nature to have multiple wives? No, it was not. 'Therefore neither in ours', Henry exalted.[294] Henry's marginal annotations show a king using his humanist education as a tool for statecraft and enjoying himself tremendously.

Indeed Henry's grammatical facility and theological readiness compared favourably to the literary skills of contemporary rulers Francis I of France (1494–1547) and Charles V of Spain (1500–58).[295] The humanist Guillaume Budé (1467–1540) urged the French king to read classical histories but he had to write his appeal in the vernacular so that Francis could understand it. Budé confessed to Erasmus in February 1517 that his ruler knew 'nothing of literature'.[296] Charles V fared significantly better. Erasmus' interventions

[293] John Guy, 'Thomas Cromwell and the intellectual origins of the Henrician revolution', in Fox and Guy (eds.), *Reassessing the Henrician age*, pp. 151–78.

[294] Carley, *Books of King Henry VIII and his wives*, pp. 55–8 and '*Rex noster est inconstans*: Henry VIII's reading practices', pp. 30–1. See also T. A. Birrell, *English monarchs and their books: From Henry VII to Charles II* (London, 1987), pp. 8–10.

[295] Glen Richardson, *Renaissance monarchy: The reigns of Henry VIII, Francis I and Charles V* (New York, 2002), pp. 11–16.

[296] Guillaume Budé, *De l'institution du prince. Livre contenant plusieurs histoires, enseignements, and saiges dicts des anciens tant Grecs que Latins* (Paris, 1547), sigs. A5^{r-v}; Erasmus, *CWE: Letters 446 to 593*, no. 522, p. 207. See Pierre du Chastel, *Deux sermons funebres prononcez es obseques de François Premier de ce nom*, ed. Pascale Chiron (Geneva, 1999), pp. 7, 12, 15, 32; Michael Heath, 'The education of a Christian prince: Erasmus, Budé, Rabelais – and Ogier le Danois', in Philip Ford and Gillian Jondorf (eds.), *Humanism and letters in the age of François Ier* (Cambridge, 1996); R. J. Knecht, *The French renaissance court, 1483–1589* (New Haven, 2008), pp. 199–205 and *Renaissance warrior and patron: The reign of Francis I* (Cambridge, 1994), pp. 6–8; Robert de la Marck, *Nouvelle*

and the work of a tutor, Adrian of Utrecht, future Pope Adrian VI, ensured that Charles acquired enough Latin to sign his correspondence in good faith.[297] Indeed, he became a master of political information systems. Yet the tempting distractions of hunting and Burgundian chivalric literature (in French), alongside his early governmental responsibilities, meant that he grew up without much of an entry into rhetoric. Sir Richard Wingfield reported to Wolsey in June 1521 that when Charles received Latin epistles from Henry VIII, which dealt with Martin Luther's (1483–1546) theological errors, he had to refer them to his chancellor.[298] As Holy Roman Emperor, Charles would explain that he had refused to listen to the exculpatory claims of heretics because he 'knew little grammar' and suspected that they would try to bamboozle him with their subtle turns of Latiny.[299] He certainly insisted that his son, Philip II (1527–98), should drink more deeply from the font of the muses.[300] Like Prince Arthur, Charles and Francis had been given a bit of Renaissance gloss by their humanist schoolmasters. Yet their educations had continued to prioritise traditional accomplishments. This was not the only reason that these kings were alternately hesitant and recalcitrant in dealing with the theological controversies of the age, but it may well have inhibited them.

In contrast, Henry revelled in religious debate. Following the Act of Supremacy (1534) he engaged enthusiastically, if sometimes naively, in interlinear discussions with his bishops on the doctrines of his church. He waded in on the issues of justification, purgatory, auricular confession and on the revision of the *Bishops' book* (1537), the wording of the Act of Six Articles (1539) and *The king's book* (1543).[301] Henry was equally ready to engage in public disputation. He intervened personally at the trial of a former Cambridge fellow, John Lambert, at York Palace, London, in

collection des mémoires relatifs à l'histoire de France (Paris, 1854), pp. 5–7; Paulin Paris, *Études sur François premier roi de France*, 2 vols. (Paris, 1885), vol. I, pp. 31–3, 38–41.

297 William Blockmans, *Emperor Charles V, 1500–1558*, trans. Isola van den Hoven-Vardon (New York, 2002), p. 16; Karl Brandi, *The emperor Charles V: The growth and destiny of a man and of a world-empire*, trans. C. V. Wedgewood (London, 1939), pp. 47–8; Otto von Habsburg, *Charles V*, trans. Michael Ross (New York, 1970), pp. 30–1.

298 *LP*, vol. III, no. 1328, p. 531.

299 Tracy, *Politics of Erasmus*, pp. 59–69; Royall Tyler, *The Emperor Charles the fifth* (Liverpool, 1956), pp. 28, 101.

300 Jose Luis Gonzalo Sanchez-Molero, *Felipe II: La educación de un 'felicísimo princípe' 1527–1545* (Madrid, 2014).

301 George Bernard, *The king's Reformation: Henry VIII and the remaking of the English church* (New Haven, 2005), pp. 49–50, 475–512, 583–9; Diarmaid MacCulloch, *Thomas Cranmer: A life* (New Haven, 1996), esp. pp. 208–13; Rex, 'The religion of Henry VIII', p. 6; Alec Ryrie, 'Divine kingship and royal theology in Henry VIII's reformation', *Reformation*, 7 (2002).

November 1538, citing scripture at him to insist on the real presence of Christ in the sacrament of the altar.[302] The hours the prince spent studying *bonae litterae* gave Henry VIII the confidence to defend his faith. The king embraced the grammatical and rhetorical skills his schoolmasters had taught him, but what about the moral and political dimension of Erasmus' lessons? The next chapters will consider the king's engagement with the humanists' account of pacific and self-disciplined royal government.

[302] Foxe, *TAMO* [1563], pp. 531–7; Richard Rex, *Henry VIII and the English Reformation*, 2nd edn. (Basingstoke, 2006), pp. 123–4, 169.

CHAPTER 2

Chivalry, ambition and bonae litterae, *1509–1533*

At the beginning of Henry VIII's (1491–1547) reign in 1509, northern humanists rejoiced in the prospect of an English philosopher-king. They trusted that, in addition to grammatical and rhetorical skills, the king's liberal education had taught him reason and self-discipline and had encouraged him to rule moderately, justly, pacifically and with wisdom. The early years of Henry's kingship did not reward their confidence. Like other sixteenth-century princes, Henry seemed determined to fill his days and empty his coffers with war. Northern humanists were horrified. They could find no honour or utility in conflicts motivated by the desire for glory or ancient ancestral claims to territory. Erasmus, Thomas More, Richard Pace (1483?–1536) and Guillaume Budé began to blame Henry's bellicosity, and that of other European powers, on those military exercises that, as we have seen, traditionally dominated aristocratic education. The humanists claimed that Henry and his contemporaries had failed to ingest the moral and political implications of their study of *bonae litterae* because they had been corrupted by their training in martial exercises, recreations such as hawking and hunting, and chivalric literature that glorified war.

Twentieth-century historians have argued that the humanists' complaints of peace were insincere or unrealistic.[1] It is certainly true that this generation of transalpine humanists found vainglory a convenient charge to level against a rival pedagogical tradition in European courts. Yet Erasmus' critique of Henry VIII's early wars with France, which argued that they originated from unthinking custom and unchecked ambition, may have been sharper and more perspicacious than historians have acknowledged. Henry may have known that this 'old obsolete claim to sovereignty [of France was] not very important', yet nostalgia and the

[1] Discussed in Bruce Mansfield, *Erasmus in the twentieth century: Interpretations c. 1920–2000* (Toronto, 2003), pp. 22–3.

desire for military glory drove his attempts to imitate Henry V.[2] For the *bonae litterae* to have any chance of shaping a prince's view of his office, changes would need to be made.

Erasmus' response to his pedagogical failure with Henry VIII was swift and robust. Between 1512 and 1516 he revised his earlier assumption that grammatical and rhetorical knowledge would naturally produce moral wisdom in a ruler. He devised a skeleton curriculum that showed schoolmasters how they could teach royal pupils to move from the knowledge of words to pacific and just rule. He emphasised that ancient authors and scripture needed to be made emotionally compelling, exciting even, for student consumption. Then he bombarded potentially sympathetic patrons and pedagogues, including Henry's pre-eminent counsellor, Thomas Wolsey, with accounts of his revised method. Erasmus' prescriptions in *The education of a Christian prince* and *De ratio studii*, amongst other works, would prove extraordinarily influential in the sixteenth century. They provided the foundation for the educational writings of other transalpine humanists and shaped the activities of many royal schoolrooms.

One such schoolroom was established for the education of Henry VIII's eldest son, the royal bastard Henry Fitzroy, duke of Richmond and Somerset. As the final sections of this chapter will show, the *bonae litterae* influenced Henry VIII's and Wolsey's arrangements for Richmond. They also divided his household. It became clear to Richmond's schoolmasters that the tension that northern humanists had identified between arms and letters was not confined to the page. Indeed, despite making a number of theoretical advances, the future of humanist learning in royal and aristocratic schoolrooms looked uncertain or, at the very least, embattled between 1509 and 1533.

'AMBITIOUS AND IMMODERATE': HENRY VIII'S WARS WITH FRANCE

In 1509 the humanists' faith in Henry VIII was indistinguishable from their hope that he would reward those who had contributed to his education. Such hopes seem self-interested and naïve but, as we may discern from the cheering crowds that welcome each and every modern president-elect to Washington, DC, hopes need be no less genuine for that. Erasmus, Thomas More and William Blount, Lord Mountjoy, the

[2] Erasmus, *Aut regem aut fatuum nasci oportere*, in *Opera omnia*, vol. II.i, p. 308, trans. from *CWE: Adages, I i 1 to I v 100*, pp. 230–1.

northern humanists who had guided Henry's studies of *bonae litterae*, insisted that his grammatical and rhetorical skills and his reading of good authors under their guidance would manifest themselves in his good government. One may imagine their horror when he ignored their counsel and set about invading France instead.

In May 1509, Mountjoy wrote to Erasmus to proclaim that Henry was acting as 'wisely' as Erasmus could hope in his new office. With some assistance from the Latin secretary, Andreas Ammonius, Mountjoy claimed the king's manifold virtues were a direct result of his studies:

> What a passion he has for justice and honesty… Tight-fistedness is well and truly banished… Our king's heart is not set upon gold or jewels or mines of ore, but upon virtue, reputation, and eternal renown… a few days ago, when he said that he longed to be a more accomplished scholar, I remarked 'We do not expect this of you; what we do expect is that you should foster and encourage those who are scholars'. 'Of course', he replied, 'for without them we could scarcely exist'. What better remark could be made by any king?[3]

In November 1509, the king acquired a new almoner, Thomas Wolsey, who continued his liberal education.[4] Wolsey may have also encouraged him to reward his former pedagogues and fellow students. On the eve of Henry's coronation, Mountjoy was made a knight of the Bath. On 9 July he gained the lucrative office of master of the royal mint. By the end of the same month he had made an advantageous marriage to Inez de Venegas, one of Catherine of Aragon's attendants. In October 1509 Mountjoy was appointed lieutenant of the castle of Hammes, near Calais, and in November Henry VIII cancelled the recognisance that Henry VII had levied against his family. As icing on this well-risen cake, Henry made Mountjoy the chamberlain of the queen's household in 1512.[5] The king rewarded his former *socius studiorum* swiftly and generously.

Mountjoy was not the only northern humanist who placed high hopes in Henry VIII and his liberal education. Thomas More wrote a poem to celebrate the new king's coronation, which took place on 24 June, a few days before his eighteenth birthday.[6] More lauded Henry's decision to break with his father's government by arresting Henry VII's officers,

[3] Mountjoy [or Andreas Ammonius, his secretary], in Erasmus, *OEDE*, vol. I, no. 215, p. 450; Erasmus, *CWE: Letters 142 to 297*, no. 215, pp. 147–8; *LP*, vol. I, no. 257/5, p. 122 and 80, p. 126.

[4] Polydore Vergil, *Anglica historia: The Anglica historia,* A.D. *1485–1537*, ed. Denys Hay (London, 1950), p. 196.

[5] J. P. Carley, 'Blount, William, fourth Baron Mountjoy (c. 1478–1534)', *ODNB*; David Starkey, *Henry: Virtuous prince* (London, 2008), p. 304.

[6] Thomas More, 'On the coronation day of Henry VIII', in *The complete works of Thomas More*, vol. III, part 2: *Latin poems*, eds. C. H. Miller *et al.* (New Haven, 1984), pp. 104, 105.

Richard Empson and Edmund Dudley, and by overturning certain bonds, recognisances and mercantile impositions. The humanist suggested that all these decisions proceeded directly from Henry's studies. Cicero had taught the king to weigh his duties: 'he placed his country, as he should, before his father. This preference does not surprise me.' More continued: 'What could lie beyond the powers of a prince whose wit has been enhanced by the arts [*ingenuae artes*], a prince bathed by the nine sisters in the Castalian fount and steeped in philosophy's own precepts?'[7] Of course, More was writing in the hope of advancement and patronage. Like Mountjoy, he was eager to connect Henry's liberal education, in which he had played a role, with the liberality and justice of his government.

In response to his friends' raptures, Erasmus hurried back from the continent, hoping to share in the king's bounty. Surely the pedagogical offices of Holt, Hone and Giovanni Boerio had inoculated Henry from the corrupting effects of bad advice, the passions and vainglorious militarism? Erasmus was eager to believe that this king would be an ideal prince and patron. While Erasmus waited at Thomas More's house in Chelsea and later in Cambridge for his hoped-for benefice, Henry VIII set about invading France. The scales fell from the humanists' eyes. Their carefully educated prince had turned out to be as ambitious, foolish and mad for war as the rest of his sort.

In his initial assessment of the new English king, Andrea Badoer, the Venetian ambassador, pronounced him to be 'magnificent, liberal… and a great enemy of the French'.[8] Apart from a few strategic moments in Henry VIII's reign, so he proved to be. In November 1511 Henry joined the 'Holy League' of powers against Louis XII. Failed sallies in Brittany and Gascony in 1512 and 1513 cost the king ships, his admiral Sir Edward Howard and much military honour. In the summer of 1513 he spent his inheritance on an invading force of well over thirty thousand English troops, whom he led across the channel himself, to capture Thérouanne and Tournai. In his absence, France's ally James IV of Scotland (1473–1513) invaded Northumberland. The fighting on Flodden field on 9 September 1513 was brutal. The English won the day convincingly, losing a mere four thousand men to Scotland's ten thousand. In 1516 Henry used extraordinary parliamentary taxation to pay the Holy Roman Emperor Maximilian

[7] Adapted from More, 'On the coronation day of Henry VIII', in *Complete works*, pp. 106, 107. The phrase *artis elegantes et ingenuas* is from Cicero, *De finibus*, III.4. Lorenzo de Medici had been praised in similar terms: Poggio Bracciolini, 'Oration in funere Laurentii de Medicis', in Erasmus, *Opera omnia*, vol. I, pp. 282, 284.

[8] *CSPV*, vol. I, no. 942, p. 346.

I and the Swiss to eject the French from Italy.[9] In 1523 the English army exhausted a special parliamentary grant before they reached Paris. A 1525 invasion was shelved when an exhausted English commonwealth pleaded poverty. From 1543 to 1546 loans, benevolences and the dissolution of the monasteries paid for Henry's dogged pursuit of Boulogne.[10] Henry's subjects were typically generous when their king announced his intention to venture forth into France yet their acquiescence was tested as costs mounted and the Scots threatened. His wars yielded 'greate pouertie'[11] but, as one contemporary parliamentarian noted, little territorial gain beyond a few 'ungracious dogholes' in France,[12] such as Thérouanne.

As early as September 1511, Thomas Wolsey, then the royal almoner, had warned Robert Fox, Bishop of Winchester, that the king was 'more disposed to war than peace' and that steps needed to be taken to 'repress this appetite'.[13] No one would ever succeed on this score. Indeed Wolsey himself proved an inconstant friend to peace. His willingness 'to avaunce the kynges oonly wyll & pleasure' and his efficient provisioning of Henry's early campaigns brought him his master's favour and rapid advancement.[14] He became archbishop of York in 1514, a cardinal in 1515 and Henry VIII's chancellor the following year. As he accreted offices and influence, Wolsey's foreign-policy objectives solidified: he wanted to maintain a high profile in European affairs and win glory for his master and himself. The cardinal was ready to use war, balance-of-power politics or peace – whatever seemed most honourable and expedient at the time.[15] Ultimately it was Erasmus and his humanist circle, rather than any one counsellor or faction of Henry's council, who worked consistently to deter the king and his advisers from the path of militaristic vainglory.[16] Indeed

[9] S. J. Gunn, 'The French wars of Henry VIII', in J. Black (ed.), *The origins of war in early modern Europe* (Edinburgh, 1987); J. J. Scarisbrick, *Henry VIII* (Berkeley, 1968), pp. 21–96.

[10] George Bernard, *War, taxation and rebellion in early Tudor England: Henry VIII, Wolsey and the amicable grant of 1525* (Brighton, 1986), pp. 152–7.

[11] BL, Cotton MS Cleopatra F VI, fol. 337[r].

[12] *LP*, vol. III, no. 2956, p. 1248 cited in Bernard, *War, taxation and rebellion*, p. 6 and Gunn, 'French wars of Henry VIII', p. 47.

[13] *LP*, vol. I, no. 880, p. 463.

[14] George Cavendish, *The life and death of Cardinal Wolsey*, ed. Richard S. Sylvester (London, 1959), p. 11; Gunn, 'French wars of Henry VIII', pp. 28–47; A. F. Pollard, *Wolsey* (London, 1929), pp. 18–20.

[15] Bernard, *War, taxation and rebellion*; S. J. Gunn, 'Wolsey's foreign policy and the domestic crisis of 1527–28', in Steven Gunn and Phillip Lindley (eds.), *Cardinal Wolsey: Church, state and art* (Cambridge, 1991), pp. 150–2; Peter Gwyn, *The king's cardinal: The rise and fall of Thomas Wolsey* (London, 1990), pp. 147–58 and 'Wolsey's foreign policy: The conferences at Calais and Bruges reconsidered', *HJ*, 23:4 (1980).

[16] Dominic Baker-Smith, '"Inglorious glory": 1513 and the humanist attack on chivalry', in Sydney Anglo (ed.), *Chivalry in the Renaissance* (Woodbridge, 1990), p. 131.

the ditties of peace that Erasmus had sung to Philip of Burgundy in 1504 and against Julius II in 1506 now became a full-throated aria. John Colet's (1467–1519) Good Friday sermon, preached at court on 27 March 1513, rebuked Henry's intention to follow 'the example... of a Julius Caesar or an Alexander', or indeed a Pope Julius II, rather than Christ.[17] In the dialogue *Julius, excluded from heaven* (written *c.* 1513, printed *c.* 1517), the persona of Pope Julius II explained to an unimpressed St Peter at the (firmly closed) pearly gates that Henry VIII was 'restless and warlike... ambitious and immoderate'. The incorrigible pope credited the chivalric strain in Henry's education with goading him to attack the French 'from his earliest years'.[18] In Erasmus' *Complaint of peace* (1517), Henry figured as the blasphemous ruler who had christened his twelve siege canons after the Apostles. 'A cruel mockery!' cried Erasmus. 'Is Paul, the unfailing preacher of peace, to aim a hellish engine of war at a Christian?'[19] In his 1515 edition of the adage *A dung-beetle hunting an eagle*, Erasmus compared the blood-thirsty 'hare-hunter' eagles to emperors, for whom the title of 'king' was insufficient. In his eyes, two particularly imperious birds merited naming and shaming. There was 'Germanicus', a reference to the Holy Roman Emperor Charles V, and 'Britannicus', the brutal would-be emperor Henry VIII.[20] James Tracy has claimed that Erasmus excused Henry VIII's bellicosity on the grounds that the king had had a humanist education.[21] In fact, Henry's failure to ingest the moral and political

[17] 'Addidit ut Christum Principem suum imitarentur potius quam Iulios et Alexandros': Erasmus, *OEDE*, vol. IV, no. 1211 p. 525.

[18] [Erasmus], *Julius excluded*, in *CWE: Literary and educational writings V*, p. 189; *Erasmi opuscula: A supplement to the Opera omnia*, ed. W. K. Fergusson (The Hague, 1933), pp. 111–12. Catherine Curtis has made a provocative case for ascribing this treatise to Richard Pace: 'Richard Pace on pedagogy, counsel and satire' (Ph.D. dissertation, University of Cambridge, 1996), pp. 184–261. Nevertheless Erasmus' letters, his *Praise of folly* and his epigrams show that he had been comparing the bellicose ambitions of Julius II and Julius Caesar since 1507. In previous works Erasmus had also repeatedly referred to the Pope's tyranny, his hatred of the French and his alleged alcoholism and epilepsy, specific charges that were levied in *Julius excluded.* It was Erasmus, not Pace, who published the classical text on which the *Julius exclusus* was modelled, *Ludus de morte Claudii*, in his 1515 edition of Seneca and referred to it extensively in his 1515 *Adages*. Erasmus' *Colloquies* demonstrate close stylistic parallels to the conversational style of *Julius excluded.* Letters edited by P. S. Allen demonstrate the existence of a manuscript in Erasmus' script entitled *Julii genius* (1515 to 1517), and this title approximated the first English translation of *Julius exclusus* as *The dialoge between Julius the seconde, Genius and saynte Peter* (London, 1534), STC 14841.5 and STC 14842. See Michael J. Heath, 'Introductory note: *Julius excluded*', in Erasmus, *CWE: Literary and educational writings V*, pp. 156–67.

[19] Erasmus, *Complaint of peace*, in *CWE: Literary and educational writings V*, p. 319 and *Opera omnia*, IV.ii, p. 96.

[20] T. F. Mayer 'Tournai and tyranny: Imperial kingship and critical humanism', *HJ*, 34:2 (1991). See Erasmus, *Dung-beetle hunting an eagle*, in *CWE: Adages III iv 1 to IV ii 100*, p. 192.

[21] James D. Tracy, *The politics of Erasmus: A pacifist intellectual and his political milieu* (Toronto, 1978), pp. 33, 126–7.

lessons of his study of *bonae litterae* enraged Erasmus, who attempted to recall him to the path of peace and moderate government.

Tracy is not the only historian to question whether the critiques of war mounted by Erasmus, by Thomas More in *Utopia* (1516) and *Epigrammata* (1518), by Guillaume Budé in *De asse et partibus eius* (1515) and by Juan Luis Vives (1492/3–1540) in *De pace inter Caesarem et Franciscum* (1525), *De Europae dissidiis et bello Turcico* (1526) and *De concordia et discordia in humano genere* (1529) were realistic.[22] In particular, Johan Huizinga lamented Erasmus' ignorance of 'the difficulties and necessities of government' and argued that his pacific advice was 'extremely primitive'.[23] To Huizinga, Erasmus had missed a development that was self-evident to his Florentine contemporary, Niccolò Machiavelli (1469–1527); the traditional chivalric impulse to win honour through 'great campaigns' was actually critical to maintaining princely authority in the early modern world.[24] Yet Erasmus lived in northern Europe, not war-ravaged Italy. He advised the 'barbarian' aggressors in the struggle for the peninsular – Charles V and Francis I – rather than the Medici, whom Machiavelli saw as Florence's last hope for independence. From where Erasmus was sitting, preserving one's throne meant restraining the impulse to overtax subjects' property and lives in pursuit of foreign dominions. In his view, the imperial ambitions of northern European monarchs could prompt their subjects to withdraw their consent to be ruled.[25]

In addition to potentially threatening a prince's hold on his crown, northern humanists argued that Francis I's, Charles V's and Henry VIII's military commitments produced manifold incommodities for the commonwealth. In 1519 Guillaume Budé complained that war caused 'the liberal arts and sciences, together with politics, and those things called the humanities [*humaines*], [to be] lost, or put down'.[26] Budé and his humanist correspondents regarded their personal disadvantage as consistent with the cost to the polity as a whole. As 'Raphael Hythloday'

[22] See Mansfield, *Erasmus in the twentieth century*, pp. 22–3 and, in addition, C. S. L. Davies, *Peace, print and Protestantism, 1450–1558* (London, 1976), pp. 160–4; Alistair Fox, 'English humanism and the body politic', in Alistair Fox and John Guy, *Reassessing the Henrician age: Humanism, politics and reform, 1500–1550* (London, 1986), p. 39; Scarisbrick, *Henry VIII*, pp. 21–4.

[23] Johan Huizinga, *Erasmus and the age of the Reformation*, trans. F. Hopman and B. Flower (New York, 1957), p. 153.

[24] Niccolò Machiavelli, *The prince*, eds. Quentin Skinner and Russell Price (Cambridge, 1988), p. 76.

[25] Erasmus, *EECP*, pp. 17, 19, 33–6, 103–9.

[26] 'Mais pour le iourdhuy (sans vostre ayde, & secours) le pris des sciences et arts liberaulz, ensemble des politicques, & qui s'appellent humaines, est ou perdu': Guillaume Budé, *De l'institution du prince. Livre contenant plusieurs histoires, enseignements, and saiges dicts des anciens tant Grecs que Latins* (Paris, 1547) p. 49.

warned in 1516, war would 'exhaust [the French king's] treasury and demoralise his people, yet in the end come to nothing' or worse.[27] War robbed the commonwealth of justice (since the rule of law was no longer sovereign), humanity (since men were behaving like beasts) and wealth (as war taxation was bleeding subjects dry).[28] Only concord, Vives wrote, would 'reinstate the fallen, retain what is now fleeing from us, and restore what has already been lost'.[29] If princes could but learn to rein in their bestial impulses, justice, moral rectitude and prosperity would return to the commonwealth and rulers would sit securely on their thrones.[30]

Princes, they complained, defined their honour according to a knightly code of conduct. 'True nobility' was the demonstration of courage, constancy, loyalty and enterprise in battle, despite the discommodity that fighting caused to their subjects.[31] This definition of honour had regained prominence in northern courts of the late fifteenth century thanks to a chivalric revival underway in Burgundy.[32] As we saw in chapter one, works such as William Worcester's *The boke of noblesse* (1475) and William Caxton's translation of Ramón Lull's *Book of the ordre of chiualry or knyghthode* (1484) had found a ready audience in England. Further, chivalric understandings of honour reminded fifteenth- and sixteenth-century Italian court humanists, such as Francesco Patrizi, Giovanni Pontano (1429–1503) and Baldassare Castiglione, of the Greek and Roman search for glory. Castiglione insisted that, despite humanists' pedagogical emphasis on letters, 'the first and true profession of the courtier', or indeed the prince, must 'be that of arms'. Pontano urged princes to recognise that the study of ancient generals such as Cyrus and Scipio Africanus would frame this quest in grander terms.[33] Italian humanists had tried to

[27] Thomas More, *Utopia*, eds. George M. Logan and Robert M. Adams, rev. edn. (Cambridge, 2003), p. 30.

[28] Juan Luis Vives, *De concordia et discordia in humano genere* (1529), in *Opera omnia*, vol. v, pp. 233, 281, 288, 314; Erasmus, *EECP*, p. 104.

[29] Vives, *De concordia*, in *Opera omnia*, vol. v, p. 187.

[30] More, *Utopia*, pp. 32–3.

[31] Ramón Lull, *Here begynneth the table of this present booke intytuled the book of the ordre of chiualry or knyghthode*, trans. William Caxton (London, 1484), STC 3356.7; William Worcester, *The boke of noblesse: Addressed to Edward IV on his invasion of France in 1475*, ed. J. G. Nichols (London, 1860); Mervyn James, 'English politics and the concept of honour, 1485–1642', *P&P*, suppl. 3 (1978), pp. 3, 10.

[32] Marina Belozerskaya, *Rethinking the Renaissance: Burgundian arts across Europe* (Cambridge, 2002).

[33] Baldesar Castiglione, *The book of the courtier*, ed. George Bull (London, 1967), p. 57; Giovanni Pontano, *De principe*, in *Prosatori Latini del quattrocento*, ed. E. Garin (Turin, 1977), vol. viii, p. 1036. See also Francesco Patrizi, *De regno et regis institutione* (Paris, 1567), fols. 320^{v}–328^{r}; Quentin Skinner, *The foundations of modern political thought*, 2 vols. (Cambridge, 1978), vol. i, p. 247.

capitalise on the appeal of chivalry in their attempts to win aristocratic and royal patrons.

In contrast, northern humanists attempted to tackle the knightly honour code head on. They attempted to redefine honour as having nothing to do with warfare. The rational citizens of Thomas More's *Utopia* regarded 'nothing so inglorious as the glory won in battle'.[34] Indeed they were 'ashamed' of martial success that depended on the possession of superior physical 'strength and ferocity'; these were the virtues of 'wild beasts' rather than men. More and Erasmus attempted to redefine 'honour' as pertaining to the peculiarly human qualities of self-control, 'intelligence and rationality'.[35] For Erasmus, the ultimate example of an honourable man was not King Arthur, Scipio Africanus or Cyrus. It was Christ, whose life was nothing 'but a lesson in concord and mutual love'.[36] There was, he argued, 'far more true glory' in Christ's peace 'than all those wars'.[37] For princes, true honour depended on preserving the welfare of their subjects. In a poem that slyly criticised Henry VIII's 1514 victory in Tournai, More wrote that, though the king 'felt that he had gained honour by taking' the city, his true honour (*honorificus*) was 'no less' (and evidently no more) than the benefit Tournai derived from having been conquered by him.[38] A really honourable prince, More concluded in his preceding epigram, would 'rule one kingdom well' rather than fight in order to govern more than one kingdom badly.[39]

To certain twentieth-century historians of political thought, the humanists' critique of war missed the point. According to Ferdinand Geldner, Erasmus was anachronistically resistant to the centralising policies of the Burgundian dukes and Habsburg princes.[40] J. A. Fernández-Santamaria reckoned that northern humanists failed to appreciate that these conflicts heralded 'the appearance of the modern state'.[41] Yet it is becoming increasingly apparent to historians of early modern Europe that

[34] More, *Utopia*, p. 85. [35] More, *Utopia*, p. 86.

[36] Erasmus, *Complaint of peace*, in *CWE: Literary and educational writings V*, p. 299.

[37] Erasmus, *Dulce bellum inexpertis*, in *CWE: Adages III iv 1 to IV ii 100*, p. 440.

[38] Thomas More, 'De deditione nerviae Henrico VIII Angliae regi', in *The complete works of Thomas More*, vol. III, part 2: *Latin poems*, eds. C. H. Miller *et al.* (New Haven, 1984), no. 244, pp. 257–8.

[39] Thomas More, 'De cupiditate regnandi', in *The complete works of Thomas More*, vol. III, part 2: *Latin poems*, eds. C. H. Miller *et al.* (New Haven, 1984), no. 243, p. 257; see too More, *Utopia*, pp. 30–1.

[40] F. Geldner, *Die Staatsauffassung und Fürstenlehre des Erasmus von Rotterdam* (Berlin, 1930), pp. 142–5.

[41] J. A. Fernández-Santamaria, *The state, war and peace: Spanish political thought in the Renaissance, 1516–1559* (Cambridge, 1977), p. 130.

sixteenth-century princes were not attempting to 'centralise', 'build' or 'defend' their realms when they invaded neighbouring countries. These were neither their intentions nor the effects of their activities.[42] Henry VIII, for instance, was certainly not trying to create a 'modern state' when he invaded France. His plan was quite the opposite: it was a nostalgic attempt to recapture the feudal dues that Henry V had won from Charles VI.[43] The king's justifications to Parliament for war subsidies appealed to the very Augustinian defence of just war that Erasmus had dismissed as a ruse.[44] Moreover Henry VIII's increasingly frenetic tourneying and the literary dedications he received in the early years of his reign demonstrated an 'almost ritualistic imitation' of the victor of Agincourt, Henry V.[45] The Tudor prince wanted to revive Lancastrian glory and he was prepared to empty his coffers and drive up taxes to do it.[46] Far from 'modernising' the realm, Henry VIII's French wars actually threatened his father's centralising financial reforms in the name of tradition. 'Custom', Erasmus argued, was being used to lend 'this obvious madness… its own code of honour'.[47] The so-called 'primitive' northern humanists seem to have understood Henry VIII's ambition and the language he used to cloak it very clearly indeed.

Ultimately, of course, the humanists did not succeed in teaching Henry VIII to relinquish military vainglory for the true glory of Christian concord. Nevertheless there is some evidence that their complaint of peace did not go unheard – indeed that it was used by the king and his chancellor to further their own ends. In October 1518 Henry VIII's ambassadors signed the Treaty of London. It was described by its signatories as the first step towards a collectively enforced universal peace of the kind that Erasmus had advocated.[48] The treaty was orchestrated by Wolsey, one of Erasmus' English patrons, and it was signed by Erasmus' friends including

[42] Glenn Richardson, *Renaissance monarchy: The reigns of Henry VIII, Francis I and Charles V* (London, 2001), pp. 36–8.

[43] Bernard, *War, taxation and rebellion*, p. 7; Gunn, 'French wars of Henry VIII', pp. 28–51 and 'Chivalry and the politics of the early Tudor court', in Sydney Anglo (ed.), *Chivalry in the Renaissance* (Woodbridge, 1990), pp. 107–28.

[44] *LP*, vol. III, no. 2957, p. 1246; Geoffrey Elton, 'War and the English in the reign of Henry VIII', in L. Freeman, P. Hayes and R. O'Neill (eds.), *War, strategy and international politics: Essays in honour of Sir Michael Howard* (Oxford, 1992), p. 4.

[45] Gunn, 'French wars of Henry VIII', p. 37. See Anonymous, 'Proem', in *The first English life of King Henry the Fifth written in 1513*, ed. C. L. Kingsford (Oxford, 1911), p. 4.

[46] Baker-Smith, 'Inglorious glory', p. 135; Bernard, *War, taxation and rebellion*, pp. 7, 155–6; Gunn, 'French wars of Henry VIII', pp. 37, 47.

[47] Erasmus, *Dulce bellum inexpertis*, in *CWE: Adages: III iv 1 to IV ii 100*, pp. 408, 409.

[48] Erasmus, *EECP*, p. 97.

More, Cuthbert Tunstall and Lord Mountjoy. It was formally celebrated in an oration by his correspondent, the royal secretary and pedagogical writer Richard Pace.[49] Like Vives's, More's and Erasmus' treatises, Pace's oration at St Paul's celebrated peace for turning men from ambition, avarice and vainglory to 'right, just, pious and honourable' amity.[50] Men, Pace said, were 'endowed with reason'. If a reasonable man considered 'the life of our redeemer Christ in its entirety', Pace proclaimed, 'he would find that it was nothing but a lesson in concord, charity and peace'.[51] Northern humanists would never convince Henry VIII that there was no honour in war, but they had shown him how peace could also be cloaked in honourable garb.

In May 1519, Erasmus wrote to Henry VIII and exhorted the king to keep faith with the treaty. He used praise to deliver a precept to the prince: Henry showed 'a spirit truly royal… a lofty mind worthy… of a Christian monarch' in securing amity in Christendom.[52] By making the concord truly perpetual, he argued, Henry would become 'a pattern' (*praestas ipse*) of Christian conduct for his subjects' imitation.[53] Erasmus urged Henry to reflect on the benefits of his liberal education for his (temporary) role as European peace-maker: 'Among princes with no learning was there ever one more skilled than you in every office of kingship?' Erasmus asked.[54] In the same month he praised Wolsey for negotiating the treaty and for his generosity as the benefactor of public lectureships at Oxford in *bonae litterae*. Wolsey was the champion of the liberal arts and of peace. 'I see a kind of golden age arising', Erasmus predicted, if 'that spirit of yours enters a certain number of princes'.[55] Northern humanists had taught Henry and Wolsey how to describe Christ's peace as more glorious than war, particularly when a shortage of men and money meant that there was no war to be had.

[49] *LP*, vol. II, nos. 4468 and 4469, pp. 1372–3.

[50] 'Ad ea recta iusta sancta sunt et honesta: conuertit': Richard Pace, *Oratio… in pace nuperime composita et foedere percusso: inter inuictissimum Angliae regem et Francorum regem christianissimum in aede diui Pauli Londini habita* (London, 1518), STC 19081a, sig. A3r.

[51] 'Si quis Christi redemptoris nostri uniuersam vitam… nihil aliud eam fuisse comperiet: q[ue] co[n]cordi[a]e charitatis / pacisq[ue] doctrinam': Pace, *Oratio… in pace*, sig. A3v.

[52] Erasmus, *OEDE*, vol. III, no. 964, p. 580; *CWE: Letters 594 to 841*, no. 964, pp. 357–8; Scarisbrick, *Henry VIII*, p. 73.

[53] Erasmus, *OEDE*, vol. III, no. 964, p. 581; *CWE: Letters 594 to 841*, no. 964, p. 359.

[54] Erasmus, *OEDE*, vol. III, no. 964, p. 581; *CWE: Letters 594 to 841*, no. 964, p. 360.

[55] Erasmus, *CWE: Letters 842 to 992*, no. 967, pp. 366–7.

CHIVALRIC EDUCATION AND PRINCELY VAINGLORY

Of course, Erasmus' circle was not the first to mount stoic and Christian critiques of war-mongering.[56] Nevertheless they were the first to connect princely vainglory to what was, at the time, the dominant mode of aristocratic schooling in Europe: training-at-arms; instruction in militaristic recreations such as hawking and hunting; and reading literature that glorified chivalry.

Given their own pedagogical interests, it is unsurprising that humanists blamed faulty education for the woes of war. Northern humanists tended to regard children's upbringing, rather than a polity's laws, as the key to unlocking political problems.[57] Even Thomas More, who imagined a constitutional alternative to the English commonwealth, made education the central ordering force in *Utopia*.[58] His ideal citizens had 'very few laws, for their training is such that very few suffice'.[59] If humanists perceived contemporary political culture to be overly bellicose, they were likely to seek the source of the poison in elite schooling. J. H. Hexter has gone so far as to suggest that they were blinkered by their pedagogical prejudice. After all, he argued, by the sixteenth century European rulers were far from ignorant; humanists' complaints were little more than literary commonplaces.[60] Yet Hexter declared the victory of liberal education prematurely. As we saw in chapter one, before Henry VIII, English princely schooling *was* dominated by training-at-arms. In the early sixteenth century, northern humanists' rhetorical strike against military education was an attack against the dominant educational culture of the court. It was as just and useful to attack chivalry at court as it was to complain about scholasticism in the universities.

Moreover, Erasmus' experience with Henry VIII suggests that the humanists were pointing their manicules with some cause. Though they

[56] Catherine Curtis, 'The social and political thought of Juan Luis Vives: Concord and counsel in the Christian commonwealth', in Charles Fantazzi (ed.), *A companion to Juan Luis Vives* (Leiden, 2008), p. 119; Ben Lowe, 'Peace discourse and mid-Tudor foreign policy', in Paul A. Fideler and Thomas F. Mayer (eds.), *Political thought and the Tudor commonwealth: Deep structure, discourse and disguise* (London, 1992), pp. 110–12; J. McManoman, *Funeral oratory and the cultural ideals of Italian humanism* (Chapel Hill, 1989), pp. 80, 93, 103, 107.

[57] I thank Dr Richard Serjeantson for this insight; Richard Pace, *De fructu qui ex doctrina percipitur: The benefit of a liberal education*, trans. and eds. Frank Manley and Richard S. Sylvester (New York, 1967), pp. 112, 113; Erasmus, *EECP*, p. 72.

[58] More, *Utopia*, p. 99.

[59] More, *Utopia*, p. 82.

[60] J. H. Hexter, 'The education of the aristocracy in the Renaissance', *Journal of Modern History*, 22:1 (1950).

had succeeded in training Henry to imitate Erasmus' Latin prose, chivalry dominated his idea of kingship. Other princes on whom northern humanists had lavished pedagogical care also leapt eagerly from their books at the first blast of the trumpet.[61] At least one of Erasmus' aristocratic pupils was killed in battle. During his trip to Italy in 1506–7, the humanist had taught Greek grammar and rhetoric to Alexander Stewart (*c.* 1493–1513), the illegitimate son of James IV and archbishop-designate of St Andrew's. In return, Stewart had presented his master with a cameo of the Roman god Terminus. Erasmus took it as his emblem.[62] When Stewart was slain by the English at Flodden field in 1513, Erasmus mourned his fallen pupil: 'Those gifts of nature, those high qualities, those splendid hopes… the pains I had devoted to teaching you' were all lost, Erasmus wrote, 'to a single fight'.[63] Would Henry be next, or would he merely lead his subjects to their deaths and financial ruin? Thus far, the study of *bonae litterae* had not taught European princes to live or rule with justice, moderation or self-control.

In response, Erasmus and his circle began an intensive literary campaign to re-educate Europe's Christian princes and their advisers. In July 1513, days after Henry had arrived in France, Erasmus tried to dissuade his former student from war. Via Wolsey, he sent him a manuscript presentation copy of his Latin translation of Plutarch's essay *How to tell a friend from a flatterer*. Erasmus prefaced his translation with a slew of bellicose rulers who failed to heed honest counsellors: Xerxes ignored Demaratus' advice against taking on Sparta in 480 BC and suffered an ignominious defeat; Nero rejected Seneca's stoical counsel and became an infamous tyrant.[64] How could Henry VIII forget Erasmus' instructions to him, 'in times past' when he was 'a boy of the greatest hope'?[65] Why had he ignored the way of self-discipline, justice and moderation? To this gift, pregnant with implicit questions, Erasmus received no reply. Henry, Erasmus concluded, was too busy fighting to trouble with letters.[66]

As Erasmus reflected on these questions, he determined that at least part of the cause of his failure with Henry was the successful intervention of his pedagogical rivals. In his 1515 adage *Dulce bellum inexpertis*, Erasmus described the English king as one of those stupid 'youths, with

[61] Tracy, *Politics of Erasmus*, pp. 49–69.
[62] Baker-Smith, 'Inglorious glory', pp. 134, 139.
[63] Erasmus, *Spartam nactus es, hanc orna*, in *CWE: Adages II i 1 to II vi 100*, p. 242.
[64] CUL, Additional MS 6858, fol. 3^{v}.
[65] 'Olim amplissime spei puero': CUL, Additional MS 6858, fol. 4^{v}.
[66] Erasmus, *OEDE*, vol. III, nos. 657 and 658, pp. 78, 80; *CWE: Letters 594 to 841*, nos. 657 and 658, pp. 112, 114.

no experience' who were 'inflamed (*inflammati*) by the bad example of their forbears', such as Henry V and Archduke Philip, 'and by the records of the histories that fools have spread about fools'. The king had 'been encouraged by flatterers, goaded by lawyers and theologians, with the consent or connivance of bishops' to go to war.[67] The 'flatterers' Erasmus was referring to probably included royal tutors such as John Skelton, who instructed Prince Henry using Burgundian chronicles and epic poems, 'histories that fools have spread about fools'.[68] Future rulers needed to be protected from these bad influences.

Erasmus insisted that such tales be banned from all princely schoolrooms. The stories of King Arthur, he proclaimed, were 'not only tyrannical but also utterly illiterate' (*ineruditis*).[69] Juan Luis Vives agreed that tales of Tristan, Lancelot du Lac and Pyramus and Thisbe were 'written by idle, unoccupied, ignorant men, the slaves of vice and filth' and treated 'of no other material than sex and war'.[70] They glamorised the so-called 'hero' who 'killed twenty single-handed'. Having been 'left for dead', the vainglorious protagonist rose 'to his feet and… [laid] two giants low in a single battle' before continuing 'on his way, laden with gold, silver, silks and jewels'.[71] The purveyors of these stories were no better than 'those who contaminate the public fountains with poison'.[72] As Vives's comparison of Lancelot-loving schoolmasters and mass murderers suggests, the northern humanist critique of Burgundian literature involved some invective, caricature and self-interest.[73] Nevertheless Erasmus and Vives were perceptive in identifying a connection between the fictional glamourisation of violence and its centrality to the aristocratic honour code.

The sincerity of Erasmus' desire to expunge tales of war from the schoolroom is confirmed by his new-found willingness to extend the prohibition to bellicose classical texts. Typically, humanists in courts had pandered to their patrons' martial interests by prescribing works such as

67 Erasmus, *Dulce bellum inexpertis*, in *CWE: Adages III iv 1 to IV ii 100*, pp. 435–6; Erasmus, *Opera omnia*, II.vii, p. 41.

68 Erasmus, *Dulce bellum inexpertis*, in *CWE: Adages III iv 1 to IV ii 100*, pp. 435–6; Erasmus, *Opera omnia*, II.vii, p. 41.

69 Erasmus, *EECP*, p. 61.

70 Juan Luis Vives, *De institutione feminae Christianae: Introduction, critical edition, translation and notes*, trans. C. Fantazzi, eds. C. Fantazzi and C. Matheeussen, 2 vols. (Leiden, 1996), vol. 1, pp. 42, 43, 46, 47 and *De disciplinis libri XX* (Frankfurt, 1532), p. 82.

71 Vives, *De institutione feminae Christianae*, vol. 1, pp. 46, 47.

72 Vives, *De institutione feminae Christianae*, vol. 1, pp. 44, 45.

73 Michael Heath, 'The education of a Christian prince: Erasmus, Budé, Rabelais – and Ogier le Danois', in Philip Ford and Gillian Jondorf (eds.), *Humanism and letters in the age of François Ier* (Cambridge, 1996), pp. 52–4.

Julius Caesar's *Gallic wars*.[74] In 1499 Erasmus had done this himself when he offered to play Homer to Prince Henry's Achilles in the *Prosopopoeia Britanni[a]e maioris*.[75] A decade later, however, the humanist had come to view the power of ancient history and epic poetry rather differently. He acknowledged in *Dulce bellum inexpertis* that Homer's *Iliad* had goaded 'stupid kings and peoples' into battle.[76] In *The education of a Christian prince* (1516), he warned Prince Charles and Henry VIII that, while some prudential *exempla* could be culled from ancient historians, a prince might 'also take in the most destructive ideas' from Herodotus, Xenophon, Livy and Sallust.[77] 'What greater madness could there be than for a man who has received the Christian sacraments to model himself on Alexander, Julius Caesar, or Xerxes?' Erasmus asked.[78] Seneca had been right to call these warriors 'great raging bandits'.[79] Trying to find an example of honourable princely conduct in ancient history was like looking for 'a jewel in a dung-heap' (*gemma e sterquilinio*).[80] Erasmus did not propose a blanket ban on ancient histories but he insisted that royal pedagogues edit them wisely if they wished to avoid goading their princely charges to war.

According to Erasmus' circle, military training was even worse for princes. As 'Raphael Hythloday' put it in *Utopia*, the emphasis on learning to fight in royal and aristocratic schooling left princes 'deeply immersed… and infected with false values from boyhood on'.[81] Exercises such as hunting also earned More's and Erasmus' disapprobation. The sport taught boys 'to find cruel amusement in bitter slaughter' and made them 'more savage [*truculentius*] than any beast'.[82] Humanists adopted similar reasoning when they cautioned schoolmasters against striking their pupils. Beatings corrupted the schoolmaster and encouraged slavishness and animal-like aggression, rather than humanity and self-discipline, in 'free-born' (*e natura liberi*) children.[83] As far as More and Erasmus were

[74] Budé, *De l'institution du prince*, p. 45; Castiglione, *Book of the courtier*, p. 92.

[75] Erasmus, *CWE: Poems I*, pp. 26–9.

[76] Erasmus, *Dulce bellum inexpertis*, in *CWE: Adages III iv 1 to IV ii 100*, p. 436.

[77] Erasmus, *EECP*, p. 62. [78] Erasmus, *EECP*, p. 64.

[79] Erasmus, *EECP*, p. 62. [80] Erasmus, *EECP*, p. 62.

[81] More, *Utopia*, p. 28.

[82] Thomas More, 'Comments of a rabbit which, after eluding a weasel, fell into nets spread by hunters', in *The complete works of Thomas More*, vol. III, part 2: *Latin poems*, eds. C. H. Miller *et al.* (New Haven, 1984), pp. 122, 123 and *Utopia*, p. 71. See similarly Erasmus, *Praise of folly*, in *CWE: Literary and educational writings V*, pp. 112–13.

[83] Erasmus, *De pueris instituendis*, in *CWE: Literary and educational writings IV*, p. 327; Juan Luis Vives, *De tradendis disciplinis* (1531), in *Opera omnia*, ed. Gregorius Majansius, 8 vols. (London, [1745] 1964), vol. VI, p. 282; Rebecca Bushnell, *A culture of teaching: Early modern humanism in theory and practice* (Ithaca, 1996), pp. 27–37.

concerned, the point of education was to make children (*liberi*) more humane and civilised (*liberalis*), not more bestial or servile.[84]

Erasmus' circle was unusual amongst European humanists in complaining about martial training for future governors. Castiglione and other Italian men of letters regarded it as the courtier's 'first duty… to know how to handle expertly every kind of weapon'.[85] He should be able to wrestle, 'be an accomplished and versatile horseman' and excel at the 'tilt and joust'.[86] In England Thomas Elyot (1490–1546) was an enthusiastic proponent of recreations that made one apt for battle. In *The boke named the gouernour* (1531), he praised wrestling, swimming, weapons' handling, riding and 'vauntynge of a horse', hunting and hawking for future governors.[87] In his *Dialogue between Pole and Lupset* (drafted 1529–32 and then revised for royal presentation on Starkey's return from Italy in 1534), Thomas Starkey's (*c.* 1498–1538) 'Mastur Pole' proposed that, in addition to 'lernyng & lettyrs', aristocratic youths be brought up 'in al featys of chyvalry'.[88] Most humanists beyond Erasmus' circle conceded that training-at-arms should remain central to princely education.

For Erasmus, More, Pace and Budé, however, this concession fatally weakened the cause of liberal education in northern European courts. They doubted that *bonae litterae* would get a fair hearing while arms dominated royal education.[89] Budé protested to Richard Pace in 1518 that 'our kings and princes… drive anyone of learning far away from their courts' in order to continue fighting, hunting and hawking without reproach.[90] The 'foremost nobility', he claimed in *De asse et partibus* (1514), 'revel in their ignorance of letters and think none of their duty lies in the arts of peace'.[91] Budé may have been exaggerating the extent of noble distaste for letters but he did so to make a fair point: the hierarchy of arms over letters encouraged rulers to regard their military duties as more significant than their civil responsibilities.[92] Pace's *De fructu qui ex doctrina percipitur* (1517) famously opened with a dialogue between the secretary and a rustic

[84] Erasmus, *De pueris instituendis*, in *CWE: Literary and educational writings IV*, p. 327.
[85] Castiglione, *Book of the courtier*, p. 61.
[86] Castiglione, *Book of the courtier*, pp. 62, 63.
[87] Thomas Elyot, *Boke named the gouernour*, ed. H. H. S. Croft, 2 vols. (London, 1883), vol. I, pp. 173–202.
[88] Thomas Starkey, *A dialogue between Pole and Lupset*, ed. T. F. Mayer (London, 1989), p. 126.
[89] Erasmus, *De pueris instituendis*, in *CWE: Literary and educational writings IV*, p. 308.
[90] 'Regum nostorum principiumque… semetipsi ab aula docti utro procul submoverent': Guillaume Budé, *Opera omnia Gulielmi Budaei*, 4 vols. (Basle, 1557), vol. I, p. 242.
[91] 'Primores procerum, ignorantiam literarum percupide sibi vendicent, ac nihil sui muneris esse in pacis artibus credant': Budé, *Opera omnia Gulielmi Budaei*, vol. II, p. 23.
[92] Budé, *Opera omnia Gulielmi Budaei*, vol. II, p. 25.

aristocrat, who insisted that the best education for young noblemen was to learn to 'blow the horn properly, hunt like experts and train and carry a hawk gracefully'. 'Pace' retorted that this would leave this youth unable to address ambassadors or participate in government. 'Learned country boys would be called upon' to replace him in office.[93] When it came to princes, however, ignorance was not merely inconvenient 'but disaster in our time'. Soldier-rulers were susceptible to evil counsellors but flatterers 'would not go about freely attempting to fool princely eyes with their apish deceptions' if kings were learned.[94] It was only by placing a higher priority on *bonae litterae* and reducing military training that rulers would become proficient in the arts of peace.

The disappointment of the first decade of Henry VIII's bellicose government did not cause northern humanists to doubt the potential benefits of letters for future rulers. Indeed they redoubled their efforts to persuade princes to peace, a stand that prompted them to sharpen their critique of traditional aristocratic education. It also encouraged them to explain their account of the way in which the study of ancient literature could shape the moral and political conduct of kings more carefully, and to develop a curriculum that they hoped would cultivate truly Christian princes in sixteenth-century Europe.

CULTIVATING THE TRULY CHRISTIAN PRINCE: UNDERSTANDING WORDS, THINGS AND FEELINGS

In *The education of a Christian prince*, Erasmus proposed that, in addition to stripping out training-at-arms, hunting, riding and chivalric literature from the education of future princes, schoolmasters should immerse royal children in the same course of studies he had prescribed for future clergymen. Being a philosopher-king, Erasmus pronounced, was 'in practice the same as being a Christian; only the terminology is different'.[95] In addition to setting out a curriculum for royal education, Erasmus explained in his *Education of a Christian prince*, *De ratione studii* (1512) and *Ratio seu methodus* (1516) how, in the hands of a talented schoolmaster, a pupil's knowledge of grammar and rhetoric *could* be translated into moral virtue

[93] Pace, *De fructu*, pp. 22, 23. See also Elyot, *Boke named the gouernour*, vol. I, pp. 99, 104–5; Starkey, *Dialogue between Pole and Lupset*, p. 124.

[94] 'Illa extitit indignitas, non tantum incommoda, sed memoria nostra etiam fere dira, quod principes natura boni, sed blandimentis incuriae capti atq[ue] immunitatis, cui a pueris insueuerunt, auctoritatem regiam... accommodant, quando semel omnia amicis permisere [sic]... ob oculos principales cercopum praestigiae ludisicari pergerent': Budé, *Opera omnia Gulielmi Budaei*, vol. II, p. 24.

[95] Erasmus, *EECP*, p. 15.

and political wisdom. Some scholars have been sceptical about the efficacy of Erasmus' pedagogy on this point.[96] Yet Erasmus' disappointment in the initial fruits of his attempts to educate princes led him to set out the process carefully.

In his *Education of a Christian prince*, Erasmus continued to argue that those born for the state should study good letters. The heart of this curriculum was Latin and Greek grammar and rhetoric, and scripture. It was virtually identical to the course of study that he had prescribed for John Colet's schoolboys at St Paul's, young men of gentle birth who were destined for the clergy, in his *De ratione studii* and *De copia* (1512, enlarged in 1514, 1526 and 1534).[97] As the prince gained a surer grasp of language and literature, Erasmus claimed, his moral and spiritual judgement could sharpen. In fact he encouraged princes to use his general textbook *De copia*, a digest of commonplaces and phrases and compendium of techniques for enriching Latin discourse, with this end in view.[98]

It was Erasmus' eagerness to get princes reading *De copia* that confirmed, for Lisa Jardine and Anthony Grafton, that his real concern throughout *The education of a Christian prince* was not moral or political preparation for leadership but fluent Latin.[99] They argued that Erasmus was 'deliberately vague' as to how his 'meticulous training in eloquence' actually contributed to the 'preparation of the "Christian soldier"'.[100] A leap of faith was required to 'make the crucial equivalence between humanistic discipline… and moral probity'.[101] Sixteenth-century readers, Jardine and Grafton explained, were willing to jump because of Erasmus' carefully cultivated 'public personality' and reputation for piety.[102] Yet their faith was misplaced. Erasmus sold them his textbooks, methods and curricula on the fantasy 'that successful drilling in *copia* and *methodus* [would] guarantee a classroom product of moral uprightness and good character'.[103] At best, Grafton and Jardine reckoned that Erasmus' reasoning was woolly. At worst, they suggested, he was a charismatic charlatan.

96 Anthony Grafton and Lisa Jardine, *From humanism to the humanities: Education and the liberal arts in fifteenth- and sixteenth-century Europe* (Cambridge, MA, 1986), pp. 23–4, 138–45, 148.

97 Erasmus, *De duplici copia verborum ac rerum commentarii duo* and *De ratione studii*, in *CWE: Literary and educational writings II*, p. 286; Erasmus, *EECP*, pp. 12–13, 61–2.

98 Erasmus, *EECP*, p. 63.

99 Jardine's editorial note in Erasmus, *EECP*, p. 63n.105; Grafton and Jardine, *Humanism to the humanities*, pp. 23–4, 138–45, 148.

100 Grafton and Jardine, *Humanism to the humanities*, pp. 137, 138.

101 Grafton and Jardine, *Humanism to the humanities*, p. 142.

102 Grafton and Jardine, *Humanism to the humanities*, p. 139.

103 Grafton and Jardine, *Humanism to the humanities*, p. 139.

In fact, Erasmus' pedagogy in both *De copia* and *Ratio seu methodus*, a treatise in which he explained how the tools of humanist textual exegesis could be applied to scripture, promised less than Grafton and Jardine have implied, and delivered rather more. As he wrote in *De ratione studii*, the study of discourse was not equivalent to moral training, nor were grammar and rhetoric silver bullets that could be used to bring down the morally depraved. Instead, he proposed that these disciplines contributed first to the 'knowledge of words'. As Erasmus cheerfully admitted, the study of words was much less valuable than the understanding of 'things', by which he meant objects of thought and experience. Nevertheless, as the full title of *De... copia verborum ac rerum* indicated,[104] Erasmus thought that it was impossible to comprehend things accurately or thoroughly *without* first concerning oneself with the words. Things were truly known only to those who had the language to describe them. Conversely, 'a person who is not skilled in the force of language is, of necessity, short-sighted, deluded, and unbalanced in his judgment of all things'.[105] To study grammar and rhetoric was not to acquire wisdom, sound moral judgement or Christian piety perfectly. In Erasmus' opinion, however, the *bonae litterae* were the only working doorways to the cultivation of these qualities on earth.

At the same time as Erasmus was composing his *Education of a Christian prince*, he explained in his *Methodus* (1516) how this theory of words and things could be applied to glean knowledge of the New Testament. Erasmus argued that, just as one had to understand ancient Latin and Greek words to comprehend pagan philosophy, so one had to understand God's word as revealed in scripture before one could set about understanding and imitating Christ's life. Scholastic theologians, who lacked knowledge of words (*vocabula*), 'abused divine scripture'. They interpreted ' "church" to mean "priests", and "the world", a word they use[d] to deem things evil, to mean "lay Christians", as if these men and women did not belong to the church'. 'Where the bible refers to "all Christians" ', Erasmus concluded, 'their interpretation considers only monks'.[106] Clerics' failure to understand words had brought 'the power of sacred letters...

[104] Erasmus, *De ratione studii*, in *CWE: Literary and educational writings II*, p. 666; Jacques Chomarat, *Grammaire et rhétorique chez Erasme*, 2 vols. (Paris, 1982), vol. 1, pp. 25, 29, 73–4, 407.

[105] Erasmus, *De ratione studii*, in *CWE: Literary and educational writings II*, p. 667 and *De pueris instituendis*, in *CWE: Literary and educational writings IV*, pp. 295, 297.

[106] 'Abutentes divinae scripturae vocabulis ecclesiam interpretamur sacerdotes, mundum, quo vocabulo mali affectus designantur, interpretamur laicos Christianos, perinde quasi hi ad ecclesiam non pertineant, interim quod de Christianis omnibus est dictum, proprie monachis accomodantes': Erasmus, *Ratio seu methodus compendio perveniendi ad veram theologiam*, in *Ausgewählte werke*, eds. A. Holborn and H. Holborn (Munich, 1933), p. 285.

to total destruction'. It had built 'the great edifice [of faith]... on rotting foundations'.[107] Erasmus argued instead for an account of faith that began with the grammatical study of God's word. It was critical to consider 'the origin of what is said, to whom it is said, the time, the occasion, in what words, in what spirit, what precedes it, what follows it' if one was to interpret 'the meaning of a given utterance' in scripture.[108] Grafton and Jardine complained that Erasmus failed to explain in his *Methodus* 'how the right reading will produce the right doctrine'.[109] Yet this was not his contention. Understanding the meaning of scripture was not enough to make one live as a true Christian. Yet it was not possible to take those next moral and spiritual steps unless one began with the word properly discerned.

In *The education of a Christian prince*, Erasmus attempted to teach schoolmasters how to cultivate princes' knowledge of words so that they acted as a spur to virtue. A future ruler was to learn grammar through reading morally improving tales such as Aesop's fables and other pagan myths with his tutor.[110] He should begin with the grammar and diction of each story. Then Erasmus instructed the schoolmaster to draw his charge's attention to its moral and political lesson: the fable of the lion and the mouse taught the prince to court the humble; the tale of the eagle and beetle cautioned rulers against provoking the lowliest of his enemies; the story of Phaethon showed that 'the headstrong enthusiasm of youth' required tempering wisdom; Homer's account of the Cyclops showed how 'great physical, but not mental, strength' was an inadequate basis for kingship; Pliny's and Seneca's descriptions of the government of the bees reminded a monarch to seek fame for his clemency rather than his military valour.[111] To take the final step – of encouraging the young prince to conduct himself virtuously – the schoolmaster should play up the dramatic quality of the stories to deter princes from un-Christian conduct.

Next came the teachings of Christ, by which Erasmus probably meant the parables, 'gathered together in some convenient form'. The humanist composed a sermon on the parables for the students at Colet's school; it was published alongside his *De ratione studii* in its early editions. It modelled the way in which Christ's stories could be explicated to take young

[107] 'Interim tota dissertione vis fit sacris litteris, et putribus fundamentis inanis aedificii moles imponitur': Erasmus, *Ratio seu methodus*, p. 285.

[108] 'Perpendat, a quo dicatur, cui dicatur, quo tempore, qua occasione, quibus verbis, quo animo, quid praecesserit, quod consequatur. Quandoquidem ex hisce rebus expensis collectisque deprehenditur, quid sibi velit quid dictum est': Erasmus, *Ratio seu methodus*, p. 285.

[109] Grafton and Jardine, *Humanism to the humanities*, p. 148.

[110] Erasmus, *EECP*, p. 12.

[111] Erasmus, *EECP*, pp. 12–13; see also Erasmus, *CWE: Adages, III iv 1 to IV ii 100*, pp. 178–214.

boys from comprehending his words to understanding the moral of his tales to appreciating the spiritual force of God's message.[112] Next Erasmus recommended that the prince be offered relevant sections of the proverbs of Solomon, Ecclesiastes and the Book of Wisdom, followed by the Gospels. Erasmus was emphatic that the teacher must use concise and straightforward narratives to explicate scripture, as he would do in his own *Paraphases on the New Testament*. Most importantly, Erasmus insisted, the royal tutor must 'kindle a love of the [divine] author' of the Gospels 'and the work in the boy's mind' by showing him clearly and 'even excitingly… those things that are particularly relevant to the prince's role' in scripture.[113] It was through words that the earthly ruler would meet his divine *exemplum* for the first time. It was critical that his schoolmaster made him excited about the encounter.

Once a prince had understood 'the standard of Christ' (*ad Christi regulam*), he had a measure against which to test his subsequent readings drawn from the ancient stoa.[114] First, Erasmus recommended Plutarch's *Apophthegms* and *Moralia*, many of which he had translated in his *Opuscula Plutarchi* (1514) and *Parabolae* (1514). He praised the *Moralia*, particularly, for its 'Christian-like notions'.[115] Indeed the letters on 'How to distinguish between flatterers and friends', 'Learning is necessary to the prince' and 'With princes one ought especially to discuss philosophically' were all reissued with the 1516 edition of his *Education of a Christian prince* printed by Johann Froben (1460–1527) in Basel. Erasmus also recommended Plutarch's *Lives* for 'the examples set by famous men' that 'vividly inspire a noble youth's imagination' and goad him towards good conduct.[116] Such exciting stories were especially powerful tools for 'transforming conduct and feelings' (*in mores et in affectus mutae*).[117] Erasmus showed a professional respect for schoolmasters' ability to filter out material that might corrupt a prince and to heighten the appeal of literary 'antidotes' to vice.[118]

Moral philosophy was more reliable than history for instructing princes in just and pacific conduct but it tended to be less thrilling. Thus Erasmus made it a tertiary discipline. It helped if a prince was well disposed to its lessons *before* he took such books in hand. If a prince was intending to 'get up from his reading a better man',[119] the works of Seneca could 'excite

112 Erasmus, *EECP*, pp. 12, 13.
113 Erasmus, *EECP*, p. 61.
114 Erasmus, *Institutio principis Christiani*, in *Opera omnia*, IV.i, p. 179; Erasmus, *EECP*, p. 60.
115 Erasmus, 'The godly feast', in *CWE: Colloquies I*, p. 204.
116 Erasmus, *EECP*, p. 10.
117 Erasmus, *Institutio principis Christiani*, in *Opera omnia*, IV.i, p. 179, trans. from *EECP*, p. 61.
118 Erasmus, *EECP*, p. 61.
119 Erasmus, *EECP*, p. 64.

and inspire the reader... to cultivate integrity and lift his spirit high above worldly concerns, especially in their repeated denunciation of tyranny'.[120] Extracts from Aristotle's *Politics* and Cicero's *De officiis* and *De legibus* were also recommended, though Erasmus thought that Plato's *Republic* had the 'more divine' (*sanctius*) message on the duties of the philosopher-king.[121] 'A considerable part of goodness is the wish to achieve it', and good literature would show a prince how.[122] Subsequently the authors a prince read as a child, Erasmus theorised, would serve him as his honest counsellors in government.

The study of grammar and rhetoric *could* serve as a portal to the understanding of things and the subsequent cultivation of moral probity and piety. Erasmus openly acknowledged that, for his prescriptions to carry the student prince to Christian kingship, the prince would be relying on charismatic schoolmasters to explain grammar clearly, to tell stories persuasively, to convey moral precepts powerfully, to maintain discipline gently and to encourage palliative classroom rivalries, amongst other things. To trust in teachers is to accept that one's pedagogical method is imperfect, but the western world has yet to discover a better approach.

Erasmus' disappointment with Henry VIII did not cause him to lose faith in letters but it did encourage him to explain their relationship to virtuous political conduct more carefully. His literary friends professed themselves persuaded. In 1519 Guillaume Budé put the case bombastically: a humanist education could leave princes 'so perfectly prudent, so eminently and outstandingly noble, so imbued and proved in Justice and Equity, that it [would] not [be] necessary to use law or regulation to restrain them'.[123] Erasmus was more pragmatic. In hereditary monarchies such as England, Scotland, France and Spain, as opposed to his native Netherlands, there were no laws or elections to restrain princes effectively. Thus the *bonae litterae* was one of the few viable brakes on over-mighty monarchy. What had been 'lost with the right to vote could be made up for in the care given to [a prince's] upbringing'.[124]

[120] Erasmus, *EECP*, p. 62.

[121] Erasmus, *Institutio principis Christiani*, *Opera omnia*, IV.i, p. 180, trans. from *EECP*, p. 62.

[122] Erasmus, *EECP*, p. 64.

[123] 'Car il est presumer, qu'ilz sont si perfaicts en prudence, si eminens & eleues par noblesse, si imbues, si imbuts & proueus de Iustice & de Equité, qu'il ne leur faut point de reigle': Budé, *De l'institution du prince*, p. 20.

[124] Erasmus, *EECP*, p. 5.

ERASMUS' INFLUENCE IN ENGLAND: THOMAS ELYOT'S *BOKE NAMED THE GOUERNOUR* (1531)

Erasmus' *Education of a Christian prince*, when used alongside *De ratione studii* and *De copia*, became one of the most influential curricula in early modern Europe. Johann Sturm (1507–1589) amplified Erasmus' prescriptions in *De educatione principis* (1551). Conrad Heresbach, Prince William of Cleves's tutor from 1522, elaborated on Erasmus' synoptic outline in his *De educandis erudiendisque principum liberis, reipublicae gubernandae destinatis* (printed 1570).[125] Catherine de Medici commissioned a French paraphrase for her sons. Sebastian Coccius used it to educate Prince Christoph of Württemberg.[126] Felipe de la Torre drew heavily upon it in composing his *Institución de un rey Christiano* (1556) for Philip II.[127] In England, Juan Luis Vives and Henry Peacham recommended Erasmus' *Education of a Christian prince* to future governors in their popular pedagogical treatises.[128] Grafton and Jardine were certainly right to suggest that these pedagogues' enthusiasm was heightened by Erasmus' 'public personality',[129] but close examination of their writings suggests that some were also persuaded that his *methodus* had potential. Erasmus' prescriptions were translated for an English-speaking audience by Thomas Elyot, a client of Wolsey's and senior clerk of the Privy Council prior to the cardinal's fall in 1529.[130]

Elyot's *Boke named the gouernour* (1531) was an attempt to revive his fortunes in the wake of Wolsey's disgrace. He may well have chosen to flesh out Erasmus' efforts, 'in our vulgare tunge', because he thought Henry would not dislike a work that imitated the Dutch humanist's. In fact, not only was Elyot's next office, that of English ambassador to Charles V, a mark of favour but the *Boke* became a pedagogical hit in its own right; it

[125] Conrad Heresbach, *De educandis erudiendisque principum liberis, reipublicae gubernandae destinatis, deque republica christiana administranda* (Frankfurt, 1570); Johann Sturm, *De educatione principis* (Frankfurt, 1570).

[126] Lester K. Born, 'Introduction', in *The education of a Christian prince*, ed. Lester K. Born (New York, 1968), pp. 28–9; Lewis W. Spitz, 'Further lines of enquiry for the study of "Reformation and Pedagogy"', in C. Trinkaus and H. A. Oberman (eds.), *The pursuit of holiness in late medieval and Renaissance religion* (Leiden, 1974), pp. 303–4.

[127] Marcel Bataillon, *Erasme et l'Espagne*, eds. Charles Amiel and Daniel Devoto, 3 vols. (Geneva, 1991), vol. II, pp. 252–3; Ronald W. Truman, *Spanish treatises on government, society and religion in the time of Philipp II* (Leiden, 1999), pp. 86–7.

[128] Elyot, *Boke named the gouernour*, vol. I, p. 95; BL, Royal MS 17 A XLIX; Juan Luis Vives, *Epistola I de ratione studii puerilis* (1524), in *Opera omnia*, ed. G. Mayans, 8 vols. (London, [1782–90] 1964), vol. I, p. 269; Henry Peacham, *The compleat gentleman fashioning him absolute in the most necessary and commendable qualities concerning minde or bodie* (London, 1622), STC 19502, sig. B1r.

[129] Grafton and Jardine, *Humanism to the humanities*, p. 139.

[130] Stanford Lehmberg, 'Elyot, Sir Thomas (*c.* 1490–1546)', *ODNB*.

was reprinted five times in the sixteenth century alone. Alongside copies of Erasmus' works, it was present in English and Scottish royal libraries. In his dedicatory letter to Henry VIII, Elyot claimed that his *Boke* was for 'the education of them that hereafter may be demed worthy to be gouernours of the publike weale'. It was a tactful formula that sidestepped the fraught question of Henry's heir in 1531 while simultaneously urging him to consider his counsellors as fellow rulers.[131]

The boke named the gouernour echoed Erasmus' insistence that the proper understanding of words was the foundation of the correct interpretation of things. In order to have any chance at developing either, English boys would need to begin their formal schooling in Latin and Greek earlier than the seven years that had been recommended by Quintilian in his *Institutio oratoria*, for these were not their 'maternall tonges'.[132] The tender age of pupils was, for Elyot, an additional argument in favour of Erasmus' prescription that learning should be pleasant and discipline gentle. Very young boys, Elyot proposed, could be tempted to study 'painted or limned' alphabets and 'allured' to learning 'with praises and… praty gyftes'. Like Erasmus, he abhorred corporal punishment, arguing that it would foster servility and brutishness in young boys, not nobility or self-government.[133] Once boys were 'taken from the company of women' and placed formally under the care of a schoolmaster, he was to address them with 'moch gentilnes, mixte with grauitie'.[134] Even when boys grew older, Elyot proposed that the schoolmaster should appeal to the boys' sense of honour, rather than turning to the birch rod, to 'bridell' their pupils and 'sharpe spurre' them 'towarde lernyng and vertue'.[135] Elyot also agreed with Erasmus that future governors would travel all the more speedily if they were competing with schoolfellows for pre-eminent 'place and soueraintie' in their lessons.[136] To master language was to learn to rule one's peers as well as oneself.

Elyot's prescriptions for the study of ancient tongues cleaved to Erasmus' detailed curriculum in *De ratione studii*, especially its emphasis on Greek.[137] Like Erasmus, Elyot pointed out that there were several

131 Elyot, *Boke named the gouernour*, vol. 1, p. cxcii.

132 Elyot, *Boke named the gouernour*, vol. 1, pp. 31–2; Quintilian, *Institutio oratoria*, 1.1.15.

133 Elyot, *Boke named the gouernour*, vol. 1, p. 32.

134 Elyot, *Boke named the gouernour*, vol. 1, pp. 36, 50.

135 Elyot, *Boke named the gouernour*, vol. 1, pp. 50, 51; Erasmus, *De pueris instituendis*, in *CWE: Literary and educational writings IV*, pp. 324–7; Erasmus, *EECP*, pp. 7, 54.

136 Elyot, *Boke named the gouernour*, vol. 1, pp. 36; Erasmus, *EECP*, p. 55.

137 Elyot, *Boke named the gouernour*, p. 53; Erasmus, *De ratione studii*, in *CWE: Literary and educational writings II*, p. 667; Quintilian, *Institutio oratoria*, 1.1.12.

authoritative grammars in print but he urged schoolmasters to move swiftly to the 'swete and pleasant redinge of olde autours'.[138] Like Erasmus, Elyot recommended beginning with Aesop's fables 'in greke'. They would teach 'plentie of the tonges' or 'Copie' and could then be mined for 'moche morall and politike wisedome'. Next, for 'eloquence, ciuile policie, and exhortation to vertue', came Lucian and Aristophanes.[139] With respect to Latin authors, Elyot left out Terence, Erasmus' favourite playwright, but he seconded his inclusion of Virgil, Horace and Cicero.[140] Elyot imitated Italian humanists in favouring military training for future governors, so he recommended Roman historians unreservedly: Livy would show royal boys the vices that undid monarchies and Julius Caesar's *Gallic wars* provided English princes with a storehouse of tactics for fighting the modern Scots and Irish.[141] Like Erasmus, however, Elyot saw the real pedagogical benefit of Roman history as its capacity to excite the student prince to emulation.

Elyot recommended that, at the age of fourteen, the future governor make a brief rest stop at logic and dialectic, using Rudolphus Agricola's *De inventione dialectica* (written *c.* 1480).[142] Next was the study of rhetoric, which would give a prince sufficient mastery of words to begin to comprehend things and pursue virtue. Some students might content themselves with Latin textbooks, namely Quintilian, Cicero's *De oratore* and Erasmus' own *De copia*.[143] The more ambitious would continue to the orations of Cicero, Demosthenes and Isocrates. Where Erasmus had translated Isocrates' *Ad Nicocles* into Latin, Elyot rendered it in English and presented it to the king. He argued that it was particularly well suited for 'persuading, as well a prince, as a priuate persone, to vertue'.[144] For both

138 Elyot, *Boke named the gouernour*, vol. 1, p. 55; Erasmus, *De ratione studii*, in *CWE: Literary and educational writings II*, pp. 667, 678.

139 Elyot, *Boke named the gouernour*, vol. 1, pp. 57–9, 67; Erasmus, *De ratione studii*, in *CWE: Literary and educational writings II*, pp. 669, 673.

140 Elyot, *Boke named the gouernour*, vol. 1, pp. 60–1, 68, 83–5; Erasmus, *De ratione studii*, in *CWE: Literary and educational writings II*, p. 669.

141 Elyot, *Boke named the gouernour*, vol. 1, pp. 83, 88.

142 Elyot, *Boke named the gouernour*, vol. 1, p. 72; Erasmus, *De copia*, in *CWE: Literary and educational writings II*, p. 289.

143 Elyot, *Boke named the gouernour*, vol. 1, pp. 72–4; Erasmus, *De ratione studii*, in *CWE: Literary and educational writings II*, pp. 672–3, 675.

144 Elyot, *Boke named the gouernour*, vol. 1, pp. 74–5. Erasmus' Latin *Ad Nicocles* was printed with the 1516 edition of the *Institutio principis Christiani* and the 1517 illuminated presentation copy for Henry VIII: C. H. Clough, 'A presentation volume for Henry VIII: The Charlecote Park copy of Erasmus's *Institutio principis christiani*', *Journal of the Warburg and Courtauld Institutes*, 44 (1981). For Elyot's translation, see Thomas Elyot, *The doctrinall of princis* (London, [1533?]), STC 14278, reprinted in 1550, STC 14279.

sixteenth-century humanists, the study of rhetoric was less about giving princes a golden tongue to enchain their subjects' passions and more about exhorting them to understand their own obligations.

Elyot may have been willing to countenance military training for youthful aristocrats, yet he shared Erasmus' eagerness that princes' youthful 'courage be bridled with reason' through the study of moral philosophy.[145] Like Erasmus, he recommended the first two books of Aristotle's *Nicomachean ethics*, Cicero's *De officiis* and the works of Plato 'above all others'. Once again, well-chosen words were the entry to an understanding of things: these authors combined 'excellent wysedome with diuine eloquence' and 'profitable counsaile, ioyned with honestie'.[146] *The boke named the gouernour* also followed Erasmus in insisting that scripture was an essential guide for Christian morals and politics. Elyot recommended 'the proverbes of Salomon with the bokes of Ecclesiastes and Ecclesiasticus' as 'very good lessons' for future rulers yet he preferred the 'historicall parts of the bible' to the doctrinal, and suggested that the New Testament 'be reuerently touched, as a celestiall iewell or relike', rather than thoroughly digested by royal pupils. Elyot also reserved Bible study for 'after [the governor] is mature in yeres'.[147] His caution was a sign of the times. In 1531, scripture-reading was liable to signal one's support for Martin Luther and William Tyndale (*c.* 1494–1536), rather than Erasmian piety.[148] Elyot was no fan of evangelicalism but he tied his colours firmly to Erasmus' mast in *The boke named the gouernour*. 'Wolde [the humanist's *Education of a Christian prince*] be as family are alwaye with gentilmen, at all tymes, and in euery age. As was Homere with the great king Alexander, or Xenophon with Scipio', he wrote.[149] Elyot promised that Erasmus' curriculum would provide 'noble men' with the 'lernynge and studie… to be worthy to haue autorite in a publike weale'.[150]

Elyot's popular treatise demonstrated Erasmus' influence in reshaping the theory of elite education in England. Admittedly Elyot allowed 'actes martiall' a berth in princely pedagogy but he took Erasmus' point that 'letters' and 'liberal sciences' deserved pre-eminence.[151] *The boke named the gouernour* also suggests that Elyot had made a serious study of Erasmus'

[145] Elyot, *Boke named the gouernour*, vol. 1, p. 91.
[146] Elyot, *Boke named the gouernour*, vol. 1, p. 94.
[147] Elyot, *Boke named the gouernour*, vol. 1, p. 94.
[148] Alan Stewart, 'The trouble with English humanism: Tyndale, More and Darling Erasmus', in Jonathan Woolfson (ed.), *Reassessing Tudor humanism* (Basingstoke, 2002).
[149] Elyot, *Boke named the gouernour*, vol. 1, p. 95.
[150] Elyot, *Boke named the gouernour*, vol. 1, p. 96.
[151] Elyot, *Boke named the gouernour*, vol. 1, p. 37.

method for making the study of words an entry to the understanding of things. On the level of pedagogical theory at least, Erasmus' reinforced defence of *bonae litterae* was winning adherents in England.

THE INFLUENCE OF THE *BONAE LITTERAE*: HENRY FITZROY, DUKE OF RICHMOND AND SOMERSET

The most important measure of success for Erasmus' princely curriculum, however, was his impact on royal schoolrooms. As we have seen, the depth of Henry VIII's childhood immersion in the *bonae litterae* was the result of serendipity and the humanists' ambition and persistence, rather than the outcome of deliberate royal policy. It is a measure of Erasmus' success that Henry VIII's children were liberally educated by design. Yet some Tudor children were submerged more completely in the font of good letters than others. The first to be considered here is Henry VIII's illegitimate son, Henry Fitzroy, duke of Richmond and Somerset, whose education reveals both the influence of Erasmian pedagogy in England and its limits prior to the king's break with Rome.

Henry shared responsibility for orchestrating his first surviving son's education with Wolsey, Fitzroy's godfather, who was simultaneously establishing Cardinal College, Oxford, and a feeder grammar school in Ipswich, the town of his birth.[152] As Erasmus noted later, Wolsey had gone 'from being a schoolmaster to mastering a kingdom' and his pedagogical activities were not insignificant in facilitating his promotion.[153] In planning the education of Henry's first male child to survive infancy, the king and Wolsey selected protégées of Erasmus and More to be Richmond's schoolmasters: John Palsgrave (d. 1554) in July 1525 and later Richard Croke (1489–1558). Both men made conscientious attempts to educate their pupil in *bonae litterae*. Yet both found it difficult to guide Richmond from an understanding of words to any observable sign that he enjoyed learning, let alone that he had acquired moral or political wisdom from it. Amongst other things, their efforts were thwarted by members of the duke's household at Sheriff Hutton who paraded the same aristocratic prejudices against liberal education that Erasmus, More, Pace and Vives had lampooned in their pedagogical treatises.

152 John Newman, 'Cardinal Wolsey's collegiate foundations', in Steven Gunn and Phillip Lindley (eds.), *Cardinal Wolsey: Church, state and art* (Cambridge, 1991), pp. 103–15.

153 'Ex ludimagistro subvectus est ad regnum': Erasmus, *OEDE*, vol. VIII, no. 2253, p. 322; Starkey, *Henry*, pp. 364, 367.

Henry Fitzroy was born in 1519, probably on 18 June, to Elizabeth Blount (*c.* 1500–39x41), a gentlewoman of Catherine of Aragon's chamber.[154] According to the chronicler Edward Hall, when this 'faire damosell' had come to court, her dancing 'wan the kynges harte'. 'By hym she bare a godly manne child', whom Henry recognised as his son.[155] In 1525, the boy's godfather, Cardinal Wolsey, asked the king to approve a coat of arms, 'as Your Highnes hath divised… for your entierly biloved sonne'.[156] They included the arms of France and England but were crossed with the baton sinister argent to denote that Fitzroy was illegitimate. As the arms suggested, the king's decision to recognise Fitzroy was not merely a matter of sexual pride. On 7 June 1525 Fitzroy was unanimously elected to the Order of the Garter, the realm's highest chivalric honour.[157] Nine days later the six-year-old was taken from Wolsey's house at Durham Place and created duke of Richmond and Somerset and earl of Nottingham. He was to have pre-eminence over all nobles in the kingdom, excepting the king's legitimate issue, Princess Mary. Thomas More read the patents.[158] The duke was marked out by his father as a future governor whose royal blood would be used to support the Tudor dynasty, even if it was unclear what role the bastard would play in the succession.[159]

The ambiguity regarding Richmond's future was evident in his most important new office, that of Warden Generalship of the Scottish Marches. The title had been relinquished by that great northern magnate Thomas Howard, third duke of Norfolk (1473–1554), but it had previously been held by Henry VIII in 1494.[160] Unlike his father, however, Richmond was actually sent north to the castle of Sheriff Hutton with an independent household of 245 people in August 1525. He was to preside, nominally, over lands, fees and revenues worth £4,000 per annum, and a Council of the North to govern the borderlands.[161] Yet, while Henry VII had expected his son Arthur to learn his office by plying it in the provinces, there is

154 Beverly A. Murphy, 'Blount, Elizabeth (c. 1500–1539x41)', *ODNB*.

155 Edward Hall, *The vnion of the two noble and illustrate famelies of Lancastre [and] Yorke* (London, 1548), STC 12721, fol. 143[v]; BL, Harleian MS 252, fol. 26[r].

156 SP 1/34, fol. 227[v].

157 SP 1/34, fol. 227[v]; BL, Additional MS 6113, fol. 61[r].

158 John Gough Nichols (ed.), *Inventories of the wardrobes, plate, chapel stuff, etc. of Henry Fitzroy, duke of Richmond, and of the wardrobe stuff at Baynard's Castle of Katharine, Princess Dowager with a memoir and letters of the duke of Richmond* (London, 1855), pp. lxxiv–lxxxiv.

159 Beverly A. Murphy, *Bastard prince: Henry VIII's lost son* (Stroud, 2003), pp. 53–4; SP 1/34, fol. 227[v]; *LP*, vol. IV, no. 1500, p. 673.

160 *LP*, vol. IV, no. 1510, p. 676.

161 *LP*, vol. IV, nos. 1512–15, pp. 676–80; Nichols (ed.), *Inventories of… Henry Fitzroy*, pp. xxii–xxvi; SP 1/235, fol. 1.

no record of Richmond personally sitting in commissions for the peace, or oyer and terminer, or regularly signing council correspondence.[162] The mere presence of royal blood, backed up by Wolsey's obedient clerics and lawyers on the council, was supposed to subdue the 'debatable lands'.[163] The doughty duke of Norfolk, left to fust unused on his estates, must have taken savage pleasure in watching the new council flail and flounder.[164] While this political drama was unfolding, however, Henry VIII and Wolsey expected that Richmond would be getting on with his liberal education.

It has been suggested that the 'magnificent style' of the 'ducal household made no concession to Richmond's tender age'.[165] In fact, the first known officer appointed to Richmond's prospective establishment in April 1525 was his schoolmaster, John Palsgrave.[166] The tutor had not been favoured by Wolsey in the past so it seems likely that he was the king's own choice.[167] Henry VIII sent Palsgrave off from Hampton Court personally with instructions to bring up his 'worldly iuell… in vertu and lerning'. The king canvassed Thomas More and Stephen Gardiner (*c.* 1495×8–1555), one of Wolsey's secretaries, on whether Richmond should begin Greek and Latin simultaneously.[168] Despite losing out on the pick of Richmond's schoolmaster, Wolsey took it upon himself to plan his godson's routine so as to emphasise adequate rest, religious worship and study.[169] The king and cardinal may not have seen eye to eye about Palsgrave but they agreed that Richmond required a liberal education.

John Palsgrave graduated from Cambridge in 1504 and probably took holy orders prior to his April 1514 appointment as schoolmaster to the Princess Mary, sister of Henry VIII and future queen of France.[170] He was a correspondent of Thomas More and Erasmus and shared their

[162] Murphy, *Bastard prince*, pp. 60–1; SP 1/84, fol. 51. In addition, see the council's defiant haste in claiming vacant stewardships for two of their number, Sir William Parr and George Cotton, in July 1528: SP 1/49, fol. 124.

[163] Nichols (ed.), *Inventories of… Henry Fitzroy*, p. xxii.

[164] SP 1/44, fol. 1; BL, Cotton MS Caligula B III, fol. 211; Murphy, *Bastard prince*, pp. 96–104.

[165] Murphy, *Bastard prince*, p. 97.

[166] P. L. Carver in William Fullonius, *The comedy of Acolastus by [William] Fullonius*, trans. J. Palsgrave, ed. P. L. Carver (London, 1937), p. xxvii; Nichols (ed.), *Inventories of… Henry Fitzroy*, pp. xxiii, xxiv.

[167] SP 1/10, fol. 114. Palsgrave had previously served Henry VIII as a secretary: *LP*, vol. I, no. 3348, p. 1408; Carver in Fullonius, *Comedy of Acolastus*, p. xxvii; *LP*, vol. III, no. 907, p. 327.

[168] *LP*, vol. IV, no. 5806, p. 2593 and no. 5807, p. 2594; John Palsgrave in *The correspondence of Sir Thomas More*, ed. Elizabeth F. Rogers (Princeton, 1974), p. 403.

[169] SP 1/42, fol. 26^{r}.

[170] *LP*, vol. II, p. 1459; Gabriel Stein, *John Palsgrave as Renaissance linguist: A pioneer in vernacular language description* (Oxford, 1997), p. 4.

study of Latin and Greek.[171] When Mary's English retinue were cut loose in Paris, Palsgrave took the opportunity to study at the Sorbonne before reading law in Louvain and renewing his acquaintance with Erasmus.[172] Upon his return to England, Thomas More ensured that he received sufficient church livings to support his scholarship.[173] In addition to these personal connections, Palsgrave's lexicographical and grammatical works demonstrate his enthusiasm for Erasmian pedagogy, or 'good letters'.[174] The third book of his *Lesclarcissement de la langue francoyse* (1530) mimicked Erasmus' *Adagia* by offering a key to idiomatic French commonplaces, 'darke sente[n]ces comprehe[n]dyng great wydsome'.[175] Richmond's first schoolmaster extended Erasmus' pedagogical method to the French tongue.

Palsgrave was similarly Erasmian in his approach to the study of Latin. His edition of William Fullonius' *Comedy of Acolastus* (1529, English version printed 1540) was intended to offer schoolboys a neo-Latin play in the style of Terence that told a version of the story of the prodigal son. The *Comedy* suggests that Palsgrave was keenly aware of the emotional appeal of a lively story to small boys, who would better remember Latin commonplaces when their interest was engaged by a tale of gambling and lascivious living. In order to develop a knowledge of words, Palsgrave proposed that schoolmasters begin by translating the Latin 'into oure englysshe tongue', 'first worde for worde, as the latyne lyeth'. 'Afterward', teacher and student should parse it again, 'accordynge to the sence and meanynge'.[176] Once students had comprehended the meaning, Palsgrave insisted on an additional step. If they were to 'do any seruice in the co[m]mon welth, eyther to preach in open audience, or to haue other administration… to instructe any of your graces noble mennes chyldren', his pupils would also need to learn to communicate their understanding in elegant English.[177] Palsgrave's pedagogy sought to adapt Erasmus' method to the British isle.

Before taking up his post at Sheriff Hutton, Palsgrave surveyed works by humanists including Maffeo Vegio, Baptista Guarino, Otto Brunfels

[171] *LP*, vol. I, no. 3348, p. 1409.

[172] Erasmus, *OEDE*, vol. III, no. 607, p. 20; More in *OEDE*, vol. II, no. 499, pp. 412–13.

[173] Carver in Fullonius, *Comedy of Acolastus*, p. xxvii.

[174] John Palsgrave, *Ecphrasis Anglica in comoediam Acolasti: The comedye of Acolastus translated into oure englysshe tongue* (London, 1540), STC 11470.

[175] John Palsgrave, *Lesclarcissement de la langue francoyse* ([London?], 1530), STC 19166, sig. Aiii^{r}, fol. cccclxxiii^{v}.

[176] Palsgrave, *Comedye of Acolastus*, sigs. Bi^{v}, Ai^{r}.

[177] Palsgrave, *Comedye of Acolastus*, sig. Aiv^{v}.

and 'especially' Erasmus in an effort 'to make the chylde loue lernyng'. He claimed he never put Richmond 'in fere off any maner [of] correction' or wearied him but devised ways 'to make lernyng playsant to hym', just as Erasmus instructed. He even anticipated Elyot in proposing that they locate a painter to decorate Richmond's letters. Upon arrival Palsgrave claimed that his methods were starting to bear fruit: the duke knew the basic parts of speech and Virgil's *First eclogue*. To excite his pupil's interest further, the schoolmaster set Richmond Terence's *Adelphoe* so that he could laugh at the dire results of both overly strict and overly permissive styles of aristocratic education.[178] Palsgrave's pedagogical compass pointed straight to Rotterdam.

Despite his conscientious efforts, however, Palsgrave grew frustrated. He claimed that members of Richmond's household were throwing obstacles in his path. The 'shaven' or tonsured clerics on the Northern Council allegedly shook their heads and murmured that 'lernyng ys a great hyndrance and displeasur to a nobyll man'. Householders permitted a constant stream of visitors 'to bring [Richmond's] mynde from lernyng'. The blow-ins would not depart Sheriff Hutton, Palsgrave huffed, until they had seen Richmond 'crye at a hare… kyll a bucke with hys bow, sometime with grayhowndes, and somtyme with buckehow(n)des' or make 'a flyght with a hawke' or 'ryde a hors'.[179] Like the nobleman Pace had railed against in *De fructu*, these 'sondry callers' measured the child's princely potential by his progress in military exercises and sports rather than *bonae litterae*. Palsgrave, however, feared that Richmond's 'singular wytt' was being dulled by continuous rounds of sports. He urged Thomas More to remind the king of the value of Richmond's liberal education.[180] Indeed he pleaded with More, Elizabeth Blount and the king to come to Yorkshire and evaluate the situation for themselves.[181]

Far from being a mere literary commonplace, the standoff between pens and swords, and peace and war was made manifest at Sheriff Hutton. One might conclude that it was the humanists' self-pitying, literary laments that had inspired Palsgrave to imagine his grievances or use this conventional trope to excuse his failures as a teacher.[182] Yet Palsgrave's successor at Sheriff Hutton ran into the same set of problems. Between February and

178 Palsgrave, in *Correspondence of Sir Thomas More*, p. 405; *LP*, vol. IV, no. 5806, p. 2593 and no. 5807, p. 2594. This letter has been dated to 1529 but it must have been written during Palsgrave's stint at Sheriff Hutton.

179 Palsgrave, in *Correspondence of Sir Thomas More*, pp. 404–5.

180 Palsgrave, in *Correspondence of Sir Thomas More*, pp. 404–5.

181 *LP*, vol. IV, no. 5807, p. 2594.

182 Hexter, 'Education of the aristocracy in the Renaissance', pp. 1–20.

June 1526, after less than a year as Richmond's schoolmaster, Palsgrave was recalled to London.[183] Perhaps he was deemed to be an ineffective teacher. Perhaps other council members resented him. Perhaps Wolsey simply dismissed him in favour of his long-preferred candidate.[184] The fact remains that Richmond's new schoolmaster, Richard Croke, had no more success than his predecessor.

Croke was Wolsey's 'orator and daylie bedeman'.[185] He was also one of the prickliest and most accomplished Greek scholars that Cambridge produced in a century when its university turned out *Graecistes* and cranks in abundance. Croke's capacity to alienate men developed with age.[186] In 1526, however, when he took up his post in Yorkshire, Richmond's second schoolmaster was better known for his eloquence than his paranoia. Croke had taken his BA from Cambridge in *c.* 1510. His proficiency in Greek had already brought him to the attention of Erasmus, William Grocyn, Budé and the Parisian printer Gilles de Gourmont, with whom he produced the 1511 edition of Erasmus' *Praise of folly*. After Paris, Croke travelled to Louvain and to the University of Cologne, where he matriculated on 20 March 1515. That year he became one of the first Greek scholars at the University of Leipzig, where he published a popular set of tables of Greek grammar (1516, 1521) and a Latin edition of the last book of Theodore Gaza's Greek grammar (1516). Croke returned to England in November 1517 and a few months later Erasmus congratulated him on having secured a readership in Greek at Cambridge.[187] Croke's deliberative orations in favour of Greek studies at Cambridge may have encouraged Henry VIII to undertake a few declensions under his guidance in 1519.[188] From 1521 to 1523 he was the university's orator and took his doctorate in theology.[189] In June 1526 he was granted a pension at the king's request and journeyed north to become Richmond's singularly overqualified schoolmaster.[190] Unlike Palsgrave, Croke was Wolsey's man, through and through. Unlike Palsgrave, he did not sit on the duke's council. Like Palsgrave, however,

183 Jonathan Woolfson, 'Croke, Richard (1489–1558)', *ODNB*.

184 Gwyn, King's cardinal, p. 614.

185 SP 1/37, fol. 115r.

186 Diarmaid MacCulloch, *Thomas Cranmer: A life* (New Haven, 1996), p. 51; Scarisbrick, *Henry VIII*, pp. 256–7.

187 Erasmus, *OEDE*, vol. III, no. 827, pp. 293–4.

188 Scarisbrick, *Henry VIII*, p. 15.

189 Richard Croke, *Orationes… duae, altera a cura, qua vtilitatem laudem que Græcæ linguae tractat, altera a tempore, qua hortatus est Cantabrigiensis, ne desertores essent eiusdem* (Paris, 1520). That year also saw the printing of his *Introductiones in rudimenta Graeca* (Cologne, 1520), STC 6044a.5.

190 Woolfson, 'Croke, Richard (1489–1558)'.

Croke was a cleric, a zealous student of the *bonae litterae*, an experienced teacher, a correspondent of Erasmus and a failure at Sheriff Hutton.

Between May 1527 and February 1528, Croke sent a series of letters to Wolsey and the king in which he complained about the household's disdain for liberal education and his schoolmasterly authority.[191] The first diatribe, addressed to Wolsey on 25 May 1527 from the Castle of Pontefract, was a fugue with variations on Palsgrave's lament: the duke's studies were being constantly and purposely derailed in favour of traditional aristocratic pursuits and entertainments. The ringleader, Croke claimed, was Richmond's gentleman usher George Cotton, who strove 'daily to incite animosity towards letters and clerics alike in the tender souls of the prince and his school-fellows by means of the most cunning fabrications'.[192] Cotton was charged with limiting Croke's access to the prince and admitting 'fools and players who sang songs worthy of a brothel' in Richmond's presence.[193] Without the schoolmaster's leave 'and often against [his] will, [Cotton] would take some of [the boys] off to hunt, to wander abroad, or to feast with him'.[194] In February 1528, Croke alleged that Cotton was being supported by Sir William Parr (*c*. 1483–1547), the duke's chamberlain. Croke charged Sir William with fiddling the books, sixty-six weeks of delinquency from Sheriff Hutton and idling away his days hawking and hunting.[195]

Croke argued that advancing Richmond's studies was impossible in this environment. Wolsey's schedule was still being 'interuptid for every tryefull, or reasorte of every stranger' who arrived at the castle. Moreover, Croke alleged that such visitors continued to expect Richmond to entertain them with chivalric and sporting 'pastymes'.[196] The cardinal's schedule was also challenged by George Cotton, who objected to the boys rising before six or studying with Croke after dinner.[197] Instead, Croke claimed, Cotton would tire Richmond with archery practice or by having him write letters, 'for Cotton's profit and advantage, without the knowledge of the Council... mainly to abbots and others in the locality for gifts of hawks and other trifles'. It was nothing short of 'prostituting [Richmond's] princely

[191] Croke's first letter describes the duke as being eight years old, dating its composition to May 1527: SP 1/42, fols. 26^{r}–29^{r}.

[192] 'Qui et principis et teneros condiscipulo[rum] animos astutissimis co[m]mentis in l[i]t[e]ra[rum] pariter ac sacerdotu[m] odiu[m] quottidie impellere moliu[n]tur': SP 1/42, fol. 26^{r}.

[193] 'Scias te nunquam q[uam] ad docendi tempora ad principe[m] ingressu[rum]. At hic tam in Preceptore arcendo diligens, libenter patitur scurras & mimos (qui digna lupanari in sacro cubiculo coram principe cantillent) admitti': SP 1/42, fol. 26^{v}.

[194] 'Interim nulla mea venia, sed pleru[m]q[ue] etia[m] me invito, abducere quoslibet, venatu[m], expatiatu[m], co[m]messatu[m] secu[m]': SP 1/42, fol. 27^{v}.

[195] SP 1/37, fol. 124^{r}. [196] SP 1/37, fol. 115^{r}. [197] SP 1/42, fol. 27^{v}.

dignity'.[198] Still worse, Cotton had Richmond pen these letters in a base secretary script rather than the italic hand Croke was teaching him.[199] In early 1528 the schoolmaster again urged Wolsey to send directions to the duke's council regarding the times Richmond was to be at his book to forbid any but Croke to supervise his 'hande and stile in bothe the tonges'.[200]

From Cotton's perspective, insofar as it can be discerned from Croke's hostile testimony, the gentleman usher was encouraging the duke in those pastimes that befitted a nobleman. When Croke challenged Cotton with Wolsey's prescriptions, the usher allegedly responded that 'the Cardinal will not dare to maintain those orders if the king wishes to dispute them'.[201] Cotton had confidence that Henry VIII and others would back him on the value of sports for a future governor. In February 1527, for instance, Dr Thomas Magnus (1463/4–1550), the surveyor and receiver general of Richmond's household, wrote to Wolsey to gloat that, upon the request of the fifteen-year-old James V (1512–42), Richmond had 'sent to the said king tenne couple of his oune houndes' and a suitably unctuous letter. Magnus trusted that this overture would ensure 'myche goodnes, perfite love, and favour… betwene booth the young princes' and might even accelerate the handover of certain English fugitives.[202] To certain householders, Richmond's chivalric interests had more diplomatic value than a piece of well-turned Latin.

Croke contended, however, that the duke's princely dignity and character were being corrupted by 'masters, who measure everything for their own pleasure and benefit, and nothing by its advantage of their lord'.[203] For Croke, the most obvious sign of Richmond's degeneration under Cotton and Parr's regimen was his diminishing respect for schoolmasterly authority. Thanks to Cotton's example, Richmond 'never attends to learning and contemns all my threats and praises'.[204] Whenever the schoolmaster chided his pupil, Cotton would castigate Croke: 'Why do you keep scolding him? My Lord has done well. That place [in his book] was

198 'Volent ad quoslibet in Cotoni co[m]modu[m] aut fauorem: principis autographae, et ignaris consiliariis et me invito puta ad abbates pro accipitribus et id genus nugis, co[n]tra quod tua Celsitudo iusserat, prostituta principis dignitate': SP 1/42, fol. 28^{v}.

199 SP 1/42, fol. 28^{r-v}.

200 SP 1/37, fol. 115^{r}.

201 'Non audebit inquit ista asserere D. Cardinalis, si his de rebus rex cu[m] illo velit disputare': SP 1/42, fol. 26^{r}.

202 T. Magnus, 'Letter to Cardinal Wolsey', in Nichols (ed.), *Inventories of… Henry Fitzroy*, p. xxxii.

203 'Ingenium longe optimum… perierit tandem, his magistris, qui sua voluptate utilitateque omnia, nihil domini commodo metiuntur': SP 1/37, fol. 124^{v}.

204 'Planeq[ue] eo p[er]duxit principe[m] ut… doctus nihil quidq[uam] advertat, laudes iuxta ac minas o[m]nes meas co[n]te[m]nat, ut nisi tua prudentia saluberrimas istas manus tuas, ocyus admouerit huic malo': SP 1/42, fol. 26^{v}.

too difficult'. Then the usher would break off Richmond's lesson and take him out to play.[205] Desperate to restore order, Croke had attempted corporal punishment but his efforts were derided by the tiny, imperious duke, who warned his low-born schoolmaster, 'Preceptor, if you strike me, I will strike you.'[206] For those eager to use education to bridle over-mighty monarchy, Richmond's recalcitrance must have been a cruel blow. Richmond's capacity for self-government was being eroded, rather than enhanced, by his upbringing.

Nor did the duke strive to achieve intellectual and moral 'sovereignty' over his schoolfellows, as they had hoped. Wolsey had arranged for Richmond to be educated at Sheriff Hutton alongside several noble and gentle youths, including William Parr, the nephew of his chamberlain, and George and Henry Blount, his mother's younger brothers.[207] Yet Croke claimed that these youths encouraged the duke's insubordination. 'Why would [Richmond] not reckon to render [such impertinences] and to speak with impunity to me,' Croke asked, 'when he hears boys greatly inferior to him – his schoolfellows and his servants of the privy chamber – address me with mocks and jeers?'[208] The youthful ringleader was 'a certain Scrope', perhaps John le Scrope, later Baron Scrope of Bolton (*c.* 1510–49). Croke claimed that he had 'often taught [Scrope] Latin... and with the greatest gentleness' but that the boy had proved 'impervious to the merits of princely studies'. Scrope now lived to 'corrupt the others with his bad example and provoke the duke's disdain' for his schoolmaster.[209] At Cotton's urging, Scrope had begun to 'disparage monstrously the Latin tongue and its literature'. In the prince's very chapel Scrope called Croke a 'Bastard, Slave, Rogue, Sad-Sack and a thousand other rude names... in the shrill and strident tones of a barbarian and savage woman'.[210] He had beaten a new boy 'of good quality, who had been

205 'Quo tempore si quid ego increpui, statim occurrere castigationi Cotonus, "Quid adeo increpitas? Bene fecit d[o]m[i]n[us], Nimis difficilis locus est"... ludos p[er]mittere principi, scilicet': SP 1/42, fol. 28ᵛ.

206 'Preceptor, sit tu me verberes ego te verberabo': SP 1/42, fol. 26ᵛ.

207 Murphy, *Bastard prince*, p. 77.

208 'Et cur no[n] putet se debere mihi impune ista dicere, cu[m] pu[er]os se multis gradibus inferiors, suos condiscipulos, suos ministros arridentibus et confirmantibus illos ad hoc (qui a sacros principis cubiculo su[n]t) audiat. Non modo a tergo lacerare me, sed etiam in os mihi convitiari': SP 1/42, fol. 27ʳ.

209 'Est hic Scropus quida[m], puer ineptus ad o[mn]ia digna principe studia, olim a me Rhomanam literarum doctus, su[m]ma cleme[n]tia, sed ne amplius a me disceret in hoc a Cotono et aliis vetitus [est], ut exe[m]plo malo et p[ue]ros ceteros corru[m]peret et dominum ad me co[n]temne[n] du[m] provocaret': SP 1/42, fol. 27ʳ.

210 'Na[m] et apud alios pu[e]ros Rhomana[m] l[ite]ra[rum] atque linguam mirifoce vituperat... herens in ecclesia principis velo, mihi co[n]vitiatus est... vocav[er]at en[im] me altissimo et

sent [to Richmond's household] by the king'.[211] Rather than learning to rule himself and others, the duke was acquiring the techniques of petty tyranny. If even half of what Croke reported to Wolsey was true, the duke was becoming a northern Lord of the Flies.

Croke did have some small success at Sheriff Hutton, though its nature seems to confirm Grafton and Jardine's worst fears about the degeneration of Erasmian theory in classroom practice. Alongside capitulating to the brutish discipline of the birch rod, Croke gave up trying to make the *bonae litterae* an alternative to traditional forms of aristocratic education. In January 1528 he agreed that, when Richmond finished his study of Julius Caesar's *Gallic wars*, he should have 'an harnes', the defensive armour worn by a knight and horse, to 'exercyse [him]self yn armys according to [his] erudition in the commentaryes off Caesar'.[212] By the end of July Richmond had received this and some 'riche and goodly Apparell' from his father, on the condition that he would continue to 'applie and incline me to my lerny[n]g'.[213] With Henry VIII's and Wolsey's connivance, Croke managed to bribe his charge to 'the diligent appliance off… sciences and feates of lernig'.[214]

In Richmond's childhood letters to his father and godfather, he claims that Croke had taught him 'most highly to esteme his boke of all his other studies'.[215] Yet the nature of the duke's letters suggests that Croke actually drilled Richmond in a narrow range of skills and authors. The schoolmaster reported to Henry and Wolsey that Richmond could translate by rote any place in Caesar's *Gallic wars* 'both precisely according to the rules of grammar and with style'.[216] Yet Croke gave no indication that this study would proceed to an examination of the political dimensions of Caesar's history, or indeed other authors' works. There is no evidence that the duke continued with Greek under Croke, despite the schoolmaster's expertise in the tongue. Instead, Croke drilled Richmond's hand until he produced a regular and fine italic script, that highly visible sign of humanistic training.[217] Croke also urged Wolsey that, rather than ride or hunt for his visitors' entertainment, Richmond should 'exhibit and make som[e] shew of his lernyng' for his guests.[218] On the one hand, making learning

barbara[m] qua[n]da[m] sevitia[m] spira[n]te, voce: Nothu[m], Nebulone[m], Improbum, Melancholicum, et mille alia id genus scelerata no[m]i[n]a': SP 1/42, fol. 27r.

211 'Ut puerum bona indole a rege huc recens missum cedat pulsetque indigne': SP 1/42, fol. 27v.

212 SP 1/37, fol. 150r.

213 SP 1/49, fol. 123r.

214 SP 1/37, fol. 150r.

215 SP 1/37, fol. 115r.

216 'Octen[n]em ia[m] pu[er]um ubivis loc[orum] Caesare[m] posse An[g]lice interpretari, structur[a] e lege pariter ac arte ad u[n]guem servata': SP 1/42, fol. 29r.

217 SP 1/37, fol. 115r.

218 SP 1/37, fol. 115r.

a performance had the potential to make letters seem more valuable to court culture. On the other, Croke's narrow focus on keeping up appearances suggests that he had thrown over Erasmus' method in a desperate attempt to keep his office.

Richmond's letters to the king and Wolsey may be seen in this light. Of course epistolary composition was not a facile or superficial skill. Humanists' capacity to write elegant letters was central to their political utility in early modern Europe. Cicero's familial letters provided the pre-eminent classroom model and Erasmus' *De conscribendis epistolis* (1499, printed 1521) was increasingly regarded as offering authoritative instructions for letter-writing.[219] When Croke had Richmond 'make a demonstration' of his 'procedinge in writinge' to Henry and Wolsey, the schoolmaster was trying to show that the duke was acquiring the covetable capacity to write elegant letters, despite the trying circumstances at Sheriff Hutton.[220] As demonstrations of learning went, however, Richmond's letters were a mixed bag. The duke's italic hand was fine but his letters were in English. Had the duke not made sufficient 'proceedinge' in Latin to risk writing in that 'tonge'? The only surviving piece of Latin from Richmond's pen was a short commendation to the king of his former servant Matthew Boynton. It was admirably ornamented with phrases of gratitude and obligation culled from the letters of Pliny the Younger, but Richmond was nearly thirteen when he wrote it, an age when grammar-school contemporaries would have been writing themes or even orations in Latin.[221] The epistles actually suggest that Croke may have focused on developing Richmond's italic hand to distract attention from the duke's slow progress in Latin.

It is ironic, then, that Richmond's handwriting exercises ventriloquised Erasmus' lofty claims for the moral, spiritual and political value of learning. The duke wrote to Wolsey and his father that he would 'endevoure my self… to thattaynge off lernynge virtue and conyng corespondente'.[222] In July he pledged to 'applie and incline me to lerni[n]g, and to procede in virtue w[ith] the helpe off God in the best tha[t] I canne'.[223] On 5 November,

[219] J. R. Henderson, 'Erasmian Ciceronians: Reformation teachers of letter-writing', *Rhetorica*, 10:3 (1992); Peter Mack, *Elizabethan rhetoric: Theory and practice* (Cambridge, 2002), pp. 24–6; *pace* Murphy, *Bastard prince*, p. 78.

[220] BL, Cotton MS Vespasian F III, fol. 18^{v}; SP 1/37, fol. 166^{r}.

[221] 'Et tu clarissime princeps occasiones obligandi me avidissime amplecteris, & ego nemini libentius debeam' is adapted from Pliny, *Letters*, II.13, lns. 1–2 and 'habebis me habebis ipsum gratissimum debitorem' is from Pliny, *Letters*, II.2, lns. 7–8: SP 1/69, fol. 98^{r}.

[222] BL, Cotton MS Vespasian F III, fol. 18^{v}; SP 1/37, fol. 166^{r}.

[223] SP 1/49, fol. 123^{r}.

he praised the departing Croke to Henry VIII for his 'payne Labour and diligence tenduce me in Lerninge', since it would enable Richmond 'to be more able to serue youre said highnes'.[224] While Croke was drilling Richmond in English dictation and handwriting exercises, he had the duke parrot Erasmus' claims for the relationship between learning, virtue and governorship for the benefit of his schoolmasterly reputation. These were not ideas that Richmond internalised. When left to his own devices, the duke's correspondence consisted of petulant complaints to Thomas Cromwell about the lack of game parks in Sheffield. The gifts he received during his life and those items bequeathed at his death similarly confirm his proficiency in handling a bow, lute, horn and bridle, and his disinterest in letters.[225]

Richmond's education confirms much of what Grafton and Jardine allege bedevilled humanists' pedagogical practice. Croke was evidently ill-suited to tutoring reluctant pupils and to living in an aristocratic household yet his abrasive personality was not the only factor to limit his success at Sheriff Hutton. Ultimately neither Palsgrave nor Croke managed to translate Erasmus' pedagogical method to Richmond's princely schoolroom. In part, they failed because few people beyond Erasmus' humanist circle thought it was important for them to succeed. For Richmond's political offices in the 1530s – the Lord Lieutenancy of Ireland, the landed magnate, even his quasi-diplomatic role as a hostage at the French court – the smattering of learning he had was a sufficient complement to his military vigour. After October 1528, the duke's subsequent tutors, who may have included Cambridge graduate George Folbury, did not challenge his natural inclinations or the pre-eminence of sports in his daily routine, whether because they 'had fewer illusions about [their] proper place',[226] as Murphy claimed, or because they themselves saw little point in making the prince genuinely learned. From 1530 onward, Richmond had the noble youth and poet Henry Howard, earl of Surrey (1516/17–47), as his 'preceptor and guide' (*incitateur*).[227] Surrey positively encouraged the younger boy's chivalric inclinations. His 'lust and joye' for Richmond depended more on their shared passion for tennis, riding 'fomynge horse with swordes' and the 'crye of houndes' than any mutual delight

224 SP 1/44, fol. 180r.

225 Nicholas Harris Nicolas (ed.), *Privy purse expenses of Henry VIII from November 1529 to December 1532* (London, 1827), pp. 40, 131; Nichols (ed.), *Inventories of… Henry Fitzroy*, pp. 3, 4, 20–1; Murphy, *Bastard prince*, pp. 121–2.

226 Murphy, *Bastard prince*, p. 78 and 'Folbury, George (d. 1540)', *ODNB*.

227 *CSP Spain*, vol. IV.i, no. 228, pp. 160–3.

in Petrarchan metre.[228] Yet Richmond's comparative ignorance of letters did not hinder their passionate friendship. Nor was he passed over at his father's court in favour of learned country boys. His royal blood, military skills, physical prowess and chivalric training made him perfectly suited to discharging his responsibilities as an English governor in the 1530s.

Erasmus had argued, of course, that *bonae litterae* were a critical first step in cultivating the deep personal piety that was the hallmark of a truly Christian prince. There is no sign that Richmond regarded his passing acquaintance with letters as significant to his religious life. The only books recorded in the inventory of his belongings taken after his death in 1536 were 'Masse bookes', missals or books of hours, of his chapel.[229] There is no evidence that he possessed a Bible, Vulgate or otherwise. In fact, Richmond's large collection of gilt images of saints (including Dorothy, Andrew, Margaret and, of course, George) suggests that he was no adherent of the *philosophia Christi*.[230] The duke's confessional life was thoroughly orthodox and largely unconnected to his self-image as a governor, or to his liberal education. Prior to and immediately following Henry VIII's break with Rome, a prince like Richmond had no responsibility for the care of religion in England and comparatively little political use for literary studies.

CONCLUSION

Northern humanism had some significant political and pedagogical successes in England between 1509 and 1534. Erasmus and his circle responded quickly and intelligently to the continued dominance of martial exercises and chivalry in aristocratic education. Their critique of vainglorious glory influenced the peace-making rhetoric, if not the long-term conduct, of English government under Erasmus' former pupil, Henry VIII. Indeed, contemplating Henry's largely futile and nostalgic attacks on France had encouraged Erasmus to spell out his own pedagogical methods in greater detail. He explained how a talented teacher could propel the student prince from the knowledge of words to the understanding of things and to ruling with charity, wisdom, justice and moderation. Far from being regarded by contemporaries as naïve or static, Erasmus' curriculum

[228] Henry Howard, 'So crewell prison', in *Henry Howard, Earl of Surrey: Poems*, ed. E. Jones (Oxford, 1964), lns. 2, 17, 31. On the friendship between the young men, see W. A. Sessions, *Henry Howard: The poet earl of Surrey, a life* (Oxford, 1999), pp. 69–85, 187.

[229] Nichols (ed.), *Inventories of… Henry Fitzroy*, p. 14.

[230] Nichols (ed.), *Inventories of… Henry Fitzroy*, p. 7.

for princely education was tremendously influential in early modern Europe. Contemporaries, not least Thomas Elyot in England, adopted his *Education of a Christian prince* and translated its principles for a wider audience. A lawyer and royal counsellor like Elyot, who lacked Erasmus' pacifism, could see the humanist's pedagogy as one of the few potential brakes on over-mighty monarchy in England.

Erasmus and his circle had one further success on the ground. Their men – John Palsgrave and Richard Croke – were appointed to Richmond's schoolroom by Wolsey and Henry VIII. The preceptors' failure to teach the duke much Latin, let alone self-government, was largely on account of their contemporaries' conviction that chivalric training and military skills were more useful and honourable to a future ruler than letters. Under pressure from Richmond's household Croke, in particular, seems to have crumbled. He turned to corporal punishment and blatant bribery to keep order and he narrowed Richmond's curriculum to the superficial skills that the duke could 'shew' to a court audience to keep his office. The fact that the duke's utility as a governor, courtier, magnate and quasi-diplomat was not impaired by his lack of learning was even more damaging to the cause of Erasmus' pedagogy in England. Before Henry VIII's break with Rome, the consensus amongst political sorts seems to have been that a smattering of letters gave a royal child some Renaissance polish but that the realm had no need of philosopher kings. The pen was still the weapon of clerks rather than princes. It was only when the king became responsible for his subjects' souls as well as their bodies that cultivating a truly learned Christian prince would become imperative in early modern England.

CHAPTER 3

Erasmus' Christian prince and Henry VIII's royal supremacy

Despite humanists' success in infiltrating Henry VIII's (1491–1547) schoolroom and Erasmus' efforts to improve and explicate his pedagogical methods in the 1510s, the critical event in establishing *bonae litterae* as the pre-eminent component of princely education in England was the royal supremacy. While princes were merely responsible for temporal and military matters, a royal son, such as Henry Fitzroy (1519–36), duke of Richmond, was able to get away with a strong sword arm and a pretty italic hand. When the English king took ultimate responsibility for the spiritual leadership of his church, however, the game changed. Henry VIII took great delight in displaying his scholarly prowess during the Great Matter; indeed, his battle with Rome was fought with the pen. After 1534, moreover, he found that the literary skills he had acquired during his Erasmian education were critical in enabling him to govern his church. Further, this chapter will propose that, in the 1530s, the king and Thomas Cromwell found that Erasmus' writings could be used to justify the royal supremacy to English readers. This is not to suggest, as James McConica does at points in his survey of Erasmus' influence on Tudor England, that the humanist had provoked an ethical or spiritual transformation in this vainglorious, grasping and belligerent prince.[1] Nor is it to insist that Henry's personal piety or the church he attempted to create were consistently Erasmian.[2] Yet, during the 1520s and 1530s, Henry VIII had come to find that his former preceptor's works could help him defend his authority over the church in England.

In particular, Henry and his apologists drew on an account of kingship set out in the humanists' *Education of a Christian prince*, which he presented to Henry in 1517, and his *Paraphrases on the New Testament*

[1] James McConica, *English humanists and Reformation politics under Henry VIII and Edward VI* (Oxford, 1965), pp. 107–11, 151.

[2] George Bernard, *The king's Reformation: Henry VIII and the remaking of the English church* (New Haven, 2005); see also Richard Rex, 'The religion of Henry VIII', *HJ*, 57:1 (2014).

(1517–24), one of which was dedicated to the English ruler. As this chapter will show, Henry and his apologists hijacked Erasmus' account of the Christian prince to advance his own discursive ends. Ironically, Erasmus' argument against imperial monarchy proved particularly well suited to justifying Henry VIII's radical expansion of royal authority over the church in sixteenth-century England.

ERASMUS' ACCOUNT OF THE CHRISTIAN PRINCE

As we saw in chapter two, Erasmus was shocked and dismayed when he realised that Henry VIII had gleaned grammatical and rhetorical skills from his education but had failed to digest his lessons on moderate, pacific and just kingship. In response Erasmus revised his pedagogical method. In order to take pupils from the knowledge of words to the proper judgement of things, he argued that it was necessary to appeal to their emotions as well as their reason. In the wake of Henry VIII's seduction by vainglorious glory, Erasmus also revised his account of the good prince. Rather than continuing to praise stoical Greek and Roman model rulers unequivocally, Erasmus began to argue that feelings of compassion, mutual affection and charity were critical for truly Christian kingship.

One of the last things Erasmus wrote before he departed war-mad England for the Low Countries in 1514 was an adage taken from a line in a recently recovered Senecan manuscript of *Ludus de morte Claudii*: 'One should be born a king or a fool.'[3] Erasmus began the adage by reasserting the stoical argument he had made in his *Panegyricus* of 1504: kings need to be philosophers, to shun custom in favour of reason and to master their passions. Yet, by Erasmus' more recent reckoning, the most dangerous of the passions was not lust but ambition, anger and cruelty.[4] The humanist was beginning to wonder whether reason alone was an effective antidote to royal ambition, and the case of his erstwhile favourite, Henry VIII, was on his mind. 'You may well find among rulers', he mused in the adage, 'one who can see that it is not possible to go to war without grave disaster to human affairs, and that an old obsolete claim to sovereignty is

[3] Erasmus, *CWE: Letters 298 to 445*, p. 66.

[4] Erasmus, *Aut regem aut fatuum nasci oportere*, in *CWE: Adages I i 1 to I v 100*, p. 228. Jacques Chomarat identifies Erasmus' view of the most dangerous sin as shifting from sensuality to ambition sometime between *Handbook of the Christian soldier* (1503) and *De lingua* (1525) but this adage pinpoints the turn more precisely: Jacques Chomarat, *Grammaire et rhétorique chez Erasme*, 2 vols. (Paris, 1981), vol. 1, pp. 71–3.

not very important'. This was a reference, none too subtle, to the English claim on France. Nevertheless this apparently learned ruler might yet 'plunge everything into war merely out of ambition'. A prince like this had to learn 'to recoil from evil and to be led towards good. For true wisdom consists not only in the knowledge of truth, but in the love and zeal for honourable conduct [*studium et amorem honesti*]'.[5] A prince like Henry VIII may have been learned enough to discern the right path but Erasmus had realised that the king also needed to *feel* that it was imperative to take it. Pagan literature could take one only so far in that direction. Ancient warrior princes and even Israelite kings could prove faulty models for princely behaviour. Even the 'double-dyed stoic Seneca', who stripped his ideal ruler 'of every emotion', could not be relied upon absolutely. Seneca left 'nothing at all of the man... What he created was a kind of marble statue... devoid of sense and any sort of human feeling [*humanus sensus*]'. A prince who remained unmoved by 'natural feeling [*naturae sensus*]... love, or pity' would lack the compassion to act honourably.[6] Instead, Erasmus proposed that the only sure guide to good government was Christ himself.

For that spur towards truly honourable and beneficial conduct, then, Erasmus turned to his contemporary work on the Greek New Testament. God, in the person of Christ, was no marble statue of reason but 'truly human, subject alike to the affections of the body and the mind'.[7] Since Erasmus' 1499 debate with John Colet on the cause of Christ's agony in the garden of Gethsemane, the humanist had argued that it was the Lord's natural, human feelings that gave rise to his compassion and self-sacrifice. Christ 'set us an example of charity and gentleness'.[8] This emphasis on Christian love had long been at the centre of Erasmus' moral thought.[9] From 1515 onwards, however, Erasmus' political writings became more explicitly indebted to the tenet that an honourable prince was, first and foremost, a charitable Christian.[10] Christ was 'all-seeing, all-feeling [*nihil non sensit*], and [yet] swayed by no passions', such as ambition or anger.

[5] Erasmus, *Aut regem aut fatuum nasci oportere*, in *Opera omnia*, II.i, p. 308, trans. from *CWE: Adages, I i 1 to I v 100*, pp. 230–1.

[6] Erasmus, *Moriae encomium*, in *Opera omnia*, IV.iii, p. 106, trans. from *CWE: Literary and educational writings V*, p. 104.

[7] Erasmus, *CWE: Paraphrases on Matthew*, p. 254.

[8] Erasmus, *Disputatiuncula de taedio, pavore, tristicia Iesu*, in *CWE: Spiritualia and pastoralia V*, pp. 65–6; Erasmus' letters to Colet in October 1499, in *CWE: Letters 1 to 141*, no. 108, pp. 202–6, no. 109, pp. 206–11, no. 110, pp. 211–19 and Colet's reply, no. 110, pp. 211–12. He retained this reading in his paraphrases on Matthew (26:37–40), Mark (14:31–6) and Luke (22:42–4).

[9] Erasmus, *Handbook of the Christian soldier*, in *CWE: Spiritualia and pastoralia I*, esp. pp. 84–93.

[10] Erasmus, *EECP*, p. 51.

Christ was 'greatest in power, but at the same time greatest in goodness'.[11] The key to cultivating morally and politically honourable conduct in princes was not to attempt to suppress their emotions entirely but to cultivate those natural feelings that taught them to love and care for their subjects. Erasmus set out to do just that with his former pupil, Henry VIII.

In 1517 Erasmus gave a presentation copy of his *Education of a Christian prince*, dedicated to Prince Charles of Spain (soon to be Charles V), to the English king and arranged his literary gift to appeal to Henry's natural Christian emotion.[12] Erasmus bound a number of other works and translations together with the new treatise to gesture to his long-standing pedagogical relationship with the English king.[13] There was Erasmus' own translation of Isocrates' oration *Ad Nicocles*, the very speech that Erasmus and Giovanni Boerio had sent to Prince Henry in 1507. There was a printed edition of Erasmus' translation of Plutarch's essay on friends and flatterers, which he had sent to the king in manuscript form in 1513. Even more powerfully, Erasmus included a revised version of his 1504 *Panegyricus* to Archduke Philip. Henry had told Erasmus in 1506 that the archduke's death had reopened the wound left by the death of his own mother.[14] Erasmus confessed to Thomas Wolsey, whom he hoped would be sympathetic to his moderating enterprise, that the king 'loved [Philip] as a brother'.[15] By appealing to the memory of Henry's filial affections, Erasmus tried to spur the king away from his military ambitions and towards the loving embrace of Christ. By replacing the real, bellicose Philip with an image of an ideal prince in Henry's mind, he attempted to draw the king back to his books, 'for which [the king] had a not unpromising taste as a boy', and return his attention to his subjects' welfare.[16]

Once Henry's natural Christian feelings had been excited, Erasmus hit him with a pattern of monarchy that departed from the stoical form of his previous offerings. As Erasmus explained in his 9 September 1517 dedication

[11] Erasmus, *Aut regem aut fatuum nasci oportere*, in *Opera omnia*, II.i, p. 309, trans. from *CWE: Adages, I i 1 to I v 100*, p. 231.

[12] C. H. Clough, 'A presentation volume for Henry VIII: The Charlecote Park copy of Erasmus's *Institutio principis christiani*', *Journal of the Warburg and Courtauld Institutes*, 44 (1981).

[13] Henry received Erasmus' *Institutio principis Christiani saluberrimis referta praeceptis* (Basel, 1516), which also contained *Ad Carolum praefatio* and *Ad Philippum panegyricus*. It was bound with his translations of Isocrates, *De regno adminstrando* and Plutarch, *De discrimine adulatoris et amici*, *De utilitate capienda ab amicis*, *De utilitate capienda ab inimicis*, *De doctrina principum* and *Cum principibus maxime philosophum debere disputare*.

[14] Erasmus, *CWE: Letters 142 to 297*, no. 206, p. 129. For these earlier literary gifts, see chapter one.

[15] Erasmus, *CWE: Letters 594 to 841*, no. 658, p.113.

[16] Erasmus, *OEDE*, vol. III, no. 658, p. 80, trans. adapted from *CWE: Letters 594 to 841*, no. 658, p. 114.

to Henry, 'a king is something special in the world of men, and almost like a god; but none the less he is a man' and alive to human frailty and suffering.[17] The treatise that followed urged princes to take their 'model for government... from God himself, and from Christ who is both God and man'.[18] The first step was for a prince to receive 'Christ with the deepest emotion'. This spiritual embrace would refigure the prince's affective spurs or goads. He would see no glory in winning back a few ancestral dogholes in France. 'Having sworn the oath of Christ, will you turn aside to the behaviour of Julius or Alexander the Great?',[19] the theologian asked his princely reader.

Erasmus proposed that a truly Christian prince would feel emotionally bound to his subjects. He would be as ready to 'sacrifice' (*cruciare)* himself for the commonweal as Christ had been. A true Christian prince is he:

> Who holds the life of each individual dearer [*charior*] than his own; who works and strives night and day for nothing else than that conditions should be the best possible for everyone; ... he wants so much to do well by his people [*ciuis*] of his own free will that if necessary he would not hesitate to attend to their well-being at great risk to himself; who considers that his own wealth consists in the welfare of his country; who is always on the watch so that everyone else may sleep soundly; who leaves himself no leisure so that his country has the chance to live in peace; who torments himself [*se discruciet*] with constant anxieties so that his subjects may enjoy peace of mind.[20]

When such self-torment was undertaken out of love for others, Erasmus argued, it would produce feelings of pleasure [*sentire voluptatem*].[21] A prince would derive genuine satisfaction from self-sacrifice on his subjects' behalf.

Erasmus' greater emphasis on Christian love in his political writing had consequences for the way in which he justified moderate, pacific rule. God created men with free will, he explained, and Christ had died for all men equally.[22] Since Christian men had liberty (*libertas*) they could only be governed by their consent (*consensus*).[23] They formed commonwealths (*respublicae*) independently and if they took a prince – and Erasmus emphasised that they had other options – the allegiance they swore to him

[17] Erasmus, *CWE: Letters 594 to 841*, no. 657, p. 109.
[18] Erasmus, *EECP*, p. 46. [19] Erasmus, *EECP*, p. 18.
[20] Erasmus, *EECP*, p. 27; Latin from Erasmus, *Institutio principis Christiani*, in *Opera omnia*, IV.i, p. 154.
[21] Erasmus, *EECP*, pp. 47–8; Latin from Erasmus, *Institutio principis Christiani*, in *Opera omnia*, IV.i, p. 170.
[22] Erasmus, *EECP*, p. 41; Latin from Erasmus, *Institutio principis Christiani*, in *Opera omnia*, IV.i, p. 166.
[23] Erasmus, *EECP*, pp. 89, 105; Latin from Erasmus, *Institutio principis Christiani*, in *Opera omnia*, IV.i, pp. 203, 216.

at his coronation was conditional.[24] The prince was required to behave 'like a father to the state' rather than a master over slaves. It was tyrannical, Erasmus wrote, to 'regard as slaves those whom Christ redeemed with the same blood as he redeemed you'.[25] A tyrant was one who extorted heavy taxation, revoked his subjects' customary rights and privileges, or pursued vainglorious wars.[26] Christ had distinguished between the political order amongst gentiles, which permitted such behaviour, and the charitable conduct he commended to his followers in Matthew 20:25–6. 'Pagan princes... dominate' (*dominor*) their subjects, Erasmus wrote, but 'the office of [a Christian] prince means orderly control [*administratio*], not imperial power [*imperium*], and kingship means helpful supervision [*regnum beneficium*], not tyranny'.[27] Ultimately, rulers must remember that it is 'Christian charity' that 'binds prince and people together'.[28] God would judge harshly those princes who broke a bond sealed with Christ's sacrifice.

Erasmus did not condone *active* resistance to a tyrannous prince. In keeping with his general espousal of peace, he argued in his *Education of a Christian prince*, *Paraphrases on Romans* (November 1517) and *Paraphrases on Matthew* (March 1522) that subjects owed their temporal rulers obedience. Magistrates 'bear a sort of image of God'.[29] Indeed, even after Martin Luther's break with Rome had made it clear that showing obedience to civil rulers could mean disobeying the Catholic church, Erasmus held his line (though he added the caveat that Christian magistrates would not order their subjects to live in an ungodly manner).[30] Nevertheless, Erasmus also warned princes that subjects were *likely* to withdraw their consent to being governed if a monarch was over-mighty. If the prince was pious, just, temperate, honest, wise and law-abiding, this would encourage his subjects to live virtuously and obediently. If he

[24] *Pace* Alistair Fox, 'English humanism and the body politic', in Alistair Fox and John Guy, *Reassessing the Henrician age* (Oxford, 1986), pp. 43, 51.

[25] Erasmus, *EECP*, p. 40.

[26] Erasmus, *EECP*, pp. 17, 19, 33–6, 103–9.

[27] Erasmus, *EECP*, p. 32, Latin from Erasmus, *Institutio principis Christiani*, in *Opera omnia*, IV.i, p. 159.

[28] Erasmus, *EECP*, p. 43.

[29] Erasmus, *CWE: Paraphrases on Romans and Galatians*, p. 74. See also Erasmus, *CWE: Annotations on Romans*, p. 247; Erasmus, *CWE: Paraphrases on Matthew*, pp. 306–7; Erasmus, *EECP*, p. 41.

[30] Erasmus, *Dilucida et pia explanation Symboli quod Apostolorum dicitur, decalogi praeceptorum, & dominicae precationis* (Antwerp, 1533), sig. K3r. Erasmus, *CWE: Spiritualia and pastoralia V*, p. 377 translates *magistratus* unhelpfully as 'public functionaries'. William Marshall rendered it more accurately as 'offycers and rulers': Erasmus, *A playne and godly exposytion or declaratio[n] of the co[m] mune crede (which in the Latin tonge is called Symbolum Apostolorum) and of the x co[m]maundementes of goddes law*, trans. William Marshall (London, 1534), STC 10504, fol. 165r.

behaved viciously or arbitrarily, he could expect them to imitate his disorderly, impious conduct.[31]

In his literary gift to the prince in 1517, Erasmus dressed up precept as praise, broke his reasoning into easily digestible adages and plucked at Henry's heartstrings in an attempt to check the prince's burgeoning sense of royal authority.[32] His revised explanation of the relationship between Christian charity and a prince's political duties moved beyond the commonplaces of the *speculum principis* genre, insofar as it was known in the British isle at the time.[33] In addition to having a significant influence on pedagogical theory in the sixteenth century, it will become apparent in subsequent chapters that Erasmus' account of the responsibilities and limits of monarchical government would shape sixteenth- and seventeenth-century understandings of kingship in Britain.

Of course, *Education of a Christian prince* did not effect a radical moral or spiritual turn in Henry VIII or his government. It is doubtful that Erasmus expected a political miracle. Like the character of 'Morus' in *Utopia*, he had counselled the king in order that 'what cannot be made good, can at least be made as little bad as possible'.[34] When Henry VIII responded to Erasmus' gift in April 1518 with £20 and hints of a benefice, Erasmus was politic enough to praise the king's manifest 'goodwill towards good letters' (*bonae litterae*) and to describe his court as 'a model of Christian learning' (*Christiana disciplina*).[35] Over time, however, it would become apparent that Henry VIII paid closer attention to Erasmus' treatises than his initial response had suggested. In fact, Henry would find them very useful rhetorically. It was a cruel irony that Erasmus' emotionally charged attempts to deter Henry VIII from over-mighty monarchy gave the king a discourse he would use to justify enlarging his authority. By emphasising the Christian responsibilities of temporal rulers, Erasmus inadvertently contributed to one of the more audacious power-grabs in early modern European history.

31 Erasmus, *EECP*, p. 21.

32 Richard F. Hardin, 'The Literary conventions of Erasmus' *Education of a Christian prince*: Advice and aphorism', *Renaissance Quarterly*, 35:2 (1982); David Rundle, '"Not so much praise as precept": Erasmus, panegyric and the renaissance art of teaching princes', in Yun Lee Too and Niall Livingstone (eds.), *Pedagogy and power: Rhetorics of classical learning* (Cambridge, 1998).

33 Otto Herding, 'Isokrates, Erasmus und die *Institutio principis Christiani*', in Rudolf Vierhaus and Manfred Botzenhauf (eds.), *Dauer und wandel der geschichte: Aspekte europäischer vergangenheit, festgabe für Kurt von Raumer* (Munster, 1966).

34 Thomas More, *Utopia*, eds. George M. Logan and Robert M. Adams, rev. edn. (Cambridge, 2003), p. 36.

35 Erasmus, *OEDE*, vol. III, no. 834, pp. 304–5; Erasmus, *CWE: Letters 594 to 841*, no. 834, p. 411.

THE PARAPHRASING PRINCE

This enlargement of monarchical authority was created by the parliamentary acts that proclaimed Henry VIII supreme head of the English church in 1533 and 1534. The royal supremacy made the church, formerly an effective counterweight to temporal government in England, a buttress of the crown. It made the king the arbiter of true religion. It made obedience to Henry VIII a spiritual, as well as civic, duty. The birth pangs of the legal aspect of Henry VIII's claim to have 'no superior but God alone' had been growing slowly and steadily for years before the proclamation of the supremacy.[36] The theological aspect of the king's claim – his assertion of spiritual supremacy over the church in England – may be historicised, too. In explaining the development of Henry's religious authority, the king's use of Erasmus' writings in the 1520s and early 1530s is significant.

Historians have argued for Erasmus' influence on Henry VIII's religiosity and the form of the English church under Cardinal Wolsey and vice-gerent Thomas Cromwell. George Bernard has hazarded to call Henry's lack of enthusiasm for 'superstition', saints' shrines and pilgrimages; his anti-clericalism; his support for a vernacular Bible; and his traditional commitment to the sacrament of the mass and the efficacy of good works 'Erasmian'.[37] James McConica went further still, arguing that Erasmus inspired the king and his court to undertake 'a remarkable enterprise' for the purging of 'decay and corruption' and the 'reform in Church and State' in England between 1529 and 1534.[38] The historians may have been too ready to conflate Henry's pious utterances and attacks on the monasteries after 1536 with his enduring personal convictions. There was plenty of grubby dynastic politics driving Henry's break from Rome and a great deal of political expediency and doctrinal compromise that went into establishing the theologically unstable form of the Henrician church. Henry was certainly persuaded by conversations and doctrinal arguments in treatises, but neither Erasmus nor any other royal counsellor managed

[36] Huntington Library, Ellesmere MS 6109 as cited by John Guy, 'Henry VIII and the *praemunire* manoeuvres of 1530–1531', *English Historical Review*, 97 (1982), p. 498. See too John Guy, 'Thomas Cromwell and the intellectual origins of the Henrician revolution', in Alistair Fox and John Guy (eds.), *Reassessing the Henrician age: Humanism, politics and reform, 1500–1550* (London, 1986), pp. 151–78 and *Tudor England* (Oxford, 1988), pp. 110–11; Peter Marshall, *Reformation England 1480–1642* (London, 2003), pp. 23–4; Walter Ullmann, 'This realm of England is an empire', *Journal of Ecclesiastical History*, 30 (1979).

[37] Bernard, *King's Reformation*, pp. 233–47 and 'The piety of Henry VIII', in Scott Amos, Andrew Pettegree and Henk van Nierop (eds.), *The education of a Christian Society: Humanism and the Reformation in Britain and the Netherlands* (Aldershot, 1999), pp. 62–88.

[38] McConica, *English humanists and Reformation politics*, p. 124, see too pp. 109–10.

to shape the king's spirituality in a thorough, theologically consistent manner.[39]

Nevertheless Henry VIII and his tame advisers used Erasmus' writings in their defence of the king's spiritual supremacy. First, Erasmus' account of kingship in his *Education of a Christian prince* and his *Paraphrases on the New Testament* (1522–24) contributed to Henry VIII's and Cardinal Wolsey's increasing readiness in the 1520s to assert the king's 'pastoral duty for the souls of his subjects'.[40] In these early years, Henry and Wolsey claimed that the former's intervention was to protect the English from Martin Luther's Protestant heresies and William Tyndale's corrupting vernacular Bible. As the Great Matter gathered steam, however, the king and his counsellors began to use Erasmus' writings to mount a critique of the traditional church. They claimed that Henry was acting to reform clerical ignorance and correct papal neglect of divine law on his subjects' behalf.

Between 1522 and 1524 Erasmus dedicated his *Paraphrases on Matthew, Mark, Luke* and *John* to European princes Charles V, Francis I, Henry VIII and Ferdinand, archduke of Austria.[41] It was an obvious play for royal patronage but Erasmus also intended to emphasise the spiritual duties of civic leaders. In presenting his *Paraphrases on Luke* to Henry in 1523, for instance, Erasmus described scripture as a powerful 'medicine' prescribed by Christ and distributed by the physician Luke. Scripture served as an antidote to sin and vice and an entry way to the path to salvation. It was 'a necessity for everyone'.[42] 'The farmer, the smith, the stone-cutter will read [Christ's words], prostitutes and pimps will read him, even the Turks will read him', Erasmus insisted.[43] Not only was knowledge of the Gospels critical for every soul but also Erasmus emphasised that they would remedy the moral diseases that afflicted the body of the commonwealth as a whole.[44] Erasmus noted that Henry VIII's own writings against Martin

[39] Geoffrey Elton, 'Humanism in England', in A. Goodman and A. MacKay (eds.), *The impact of humanism on western Europe* (London, 1990), pp. 276–7 and 'Review of *English humanists and Reformation politics under Henry VIII and Edward VI* by James K. McConica', *HJ*, 10:1 (1967), pp. 137–8; Fox, 'English humanism and the body politic', pp. 34–51; Richard Rex, 'The crisis of obedience: God's word and Henry's reformation', *HJ*, 39:4 (1996), p. 894; Alec Ryrie, 'Divine kingship and royal theology in Henry VIII's reformation', *Reformation*, 7 (2002), pp. 55–6.

[40] Bernard, *King's Reformation*, pp. 1–72; Geoffrey Elton, *Reform and reformation: England, 1509–1558* (Cambridge, MA, 1977), p. 133. See also J. J. Scarisbrick, *Henry VIII* (Berkeley, 1968), pp. 245–6, 252–4, 273, 398.

[41] Erasmus, *CWE: Letters 1252 to 1355*, pp. 6–11, 231–45; *Letters 1356 to 1534*, pp. 59–74, 113–26, 131–3.

[42] Erasmus, *CWE: Letters 1356 to 1534*, p. 73.

[43] Erasmus, 'Pio lectori', in Erasmus (ed.), *Novum Testamentum paraphrases*, 2 vols. (Basel, 1524), vol. 1, sig. a4^{r-v}, trans. from Erasmus, 'Letter to the pious reader', in *CWE: Paraphrases on Matthew*, p. 11.

[44] Erasmus, *CWE: Letters 1356 to 1534*, p. 68.

Luther had indicated that he suffered no 'distaste for sacred literature'.[45] As such, Erasmus suggested to Henry that he should become a 'champion' (*propugnator*) of the gospel in his kingdom.[46] Erasmus distinguished the spiritual responsibilities of magistrates, who defended scripture, from the duties of clerics, whose job it was to teach the Bible and arbitrate on doctrine. In his 1520 dedication of his *Paraphrases on the two letters of Saint Peter* to Wolsey, for instance, he charged the cardinal (and alleged papal candidate) with restoring the 'true and genuine philosophy of the Gospel'.[47] Nevertheless Erasmus also encouraged Europe's kings to extend their oversight into the care of scripture and religion in their territories, a responsibility that he acknowledged had traditionally been the preserve of 'abbots and bishops'.[48] Princes could contribute to their peoples' spiritual welfare by supporting Bible-reading and serving as pious examples for their subjects' imitation.[49]

Henry VIII found this aspect of Erasmus' thought more congenial and infinitely more useful than his pacifism. He studied his 1524 Froben edition of Erasmus' *Paraphrases* carefully and made marginal annotations on the author's letter to Charles V, his letter to the pious reader, his commentary on Paul's letter to Romans and his paraphrases of the gospels of Matthew and John.[50] The reading techniques that the king had honed on his schoolroom copy of *De officiis* are evident. Henry inserted English translations of unfamiliar words, corrected printing errors and planted his initials boldly on the title page. When it came to marginal annotation Henry VIII was no Gabriel Harvey. His markings are largely pistol-shaped manicules, wavy lines, crosses, tadpole-shaped arrangements of three dots and a curved tail, approving reminders to *nota bene* and several long-beaked birds.[51] Yet from them we may deduce his interest in certain passages. He marked Erasmus' repeated warnings against 'twisting scripture to your own desires and resolutions' rather than tempering 'your opinions and way of life to its rule'.[52] Was this a prognostic to the pricking

45 Erasmus, *CWE: Letters 1356 to 1534*, p. 61.

46 Erasmus, *CWE: Paraphrases on Matthew*, pp. 5–6; Erasmus, *OEDE*, vol. v, no. 1255, p. 7.

47 Erasmus, *CWE: Letters 993 to 1121*, p. 310

48 Erasmus, *OEDE*, vol. v, no. 1255, p. 7, trans. from Erasmus, *CWE: Paraphrases on Matthew*, p. 5.

49 Erasmus, *CWE: Paraphrases on Matthew*, p. 5. See too Erasmus, *EECP*, p. 73.

50 Erasmus (ed.), *Novum Testamentum paraphrases*. Henry's copy is BL, 3913 k. 4. He also owned and marked his initials on the title page of Erasmus' *In primum et secundum psalmum exactissimae enarrationes, in tertium paraphrasis* (Basel, 1525), BL, 689.a.3. See James Carley, '*Rex noster est inconstans*: Henry VIII's reading practices', in *King Henry's prayer book*, ed. James Carley (London, 2009).

51 For example Erasmus (ed.), *Novum Testamentum paraphrases*, BL, 3913 k.4, vol. I, pp. 2, 4, 11 (each section in the volume is paginated separately) and vol. II, pp. 9, 11, 16.

52 For example Erasmus (ed.), *Novum Testamentum paraphrases*, BL, 3913 k.4, vol. I, sigs. A3^{r}, a5^{v}.

that Henry claimed Leviticus 18:16 and 20:21 gave his conscience in 1527? Overall, the pattern of notation testifies to the king's intellectual engagement with Erasmus' argument that holy writ was the foundation of divine law. Moreover his interest suggests that he considered this claim relevant to his royal office.

Henry's attention to scripture and Erasmus' writings developed apace with his revulsion at the works of Martin Luther. To this extent at least, Erasmus' compliment in the *Paraphrases on Luke*, that Henry was 'free from any distaste for sacred literature... as your own writings bear witness', was not empty praise.[53] The king was probably propelled into his pamphlet campaign against Luther by the same hunger for glory that had thrust him across the channel in 1513. After all, writing against Luther was a much cheaper way of winning renown than fighting the Holy League, getting himself elected Holy Roman Emperor or obtaining the papacy for Wolsey. Indeed it was the latter who suggested to the king that he should attack Luther's *The Babylonian captivity of the church* with his pen in 1520.

Historians have tended to view the result, *The defence of the seven sacraments* (1521), as demonstrating Henry's traditional religious beliefs; it certainly is true that *The defence* asserted the pope's supremacy and the inviolable sacrament of marriage.[54] Yet composing a theological argument against heresy and explaining the true path to salvation was a novel move for an English monarch. Admittedly Henry VIII had had some high-powered assistance in composing the *Assertio* (Thomas More described himself as Henry's editor). Yet Wolsey, the Venetian ambassador and Richard Pace all witnessed the king scribbling away at it in April 1521.[55] In dealing with Lollardy, for instance, Henry's royal predecessors had confined themselves to prosecuting offenders who had been identified by the clergy and lavishing gifts on the traditional church in England.[56] With Wolsey's encouragement and co-ordination with Richard Pynson, the royal printer, however, Henry VIII defended his subjects' faith with his own pen.[57] The king acknowledged to Leo X that his project was more

[53] Erasmus, *CWE: Letters 1356 to 1534*, no. 1381, p. 61.

[54] Maria Dowling, *Humanism in the age of Henry VIII* (London, 1986), p. 38; Elton, *Reform and reformation*, pp. 75–6; F. Heal, *Reformation in Britain and Ireland* (Oxford, 2003), pp. 20–1, 117; Scarisbrick, *Henry VIII*, pp. 112–13.

[55] Bernard, 'The piety of Henry VIII'; Carley, '*Rex noster est inconstans*: Henry VIII's reading practices', pp. 17–19; Scarisbrick, *Henry VIII*, pp. 110–11.

[56] Diarmaid MacCulloch, 'Henry VIII and the reform of the church', in Diarmaid MacCulloch (ed.), *The reign of Henry VIII: Politics, policy and piety* (Basingstoke, 1995), pp. 160–1.

[57] Pamela Neville-Sington, 'Press, politics and religion', in L. Hellinga and J. B. Trapp (eds.) *The Cambridge history of the book in Britain*, vol. III: *1400–1557* (Cambridge, 1999), pp. 576–607.

suited to one who 'had given himself totally to letters' than to a prince who had spent his 'adolescence partly on the arts of war and partly on diverse studies pertaining to public matters'.[58] He justified his apparent trespass into clerical territory by drawing on Erasmus' account of the responsibilities of a Christian prince to defend religion in his realm: since 'in the administration of the commonwealth [*administranda republica*] religion always has the greatest power and the greatest weight, we have recognised its immense benefits since the beginning of our reign and studied nothing else'.[59] This was an exaggeration of course, but it confirmed the king's growing readiness to colonise ecclesiastical territory. He had even used Erasmus' description of the true power of a Christian prince – *administranda republica* – in order to do so. In August 1521, when on embassy in Bruges, Wolsey showed Erasmus a copy of Henry's work to acknowledge his master's intellectual debt.[60] Subsequently, the Dutch humanist would boast that the king's rhetorical 'bow and spear' in his treatise against Luther was acquired through study of his own works.[61] In 1520 Henry had recognised that, by wearing the mantle of the Erasmian Christian prince to champion the faith, he could cover himself in glory.

As the decade unfolded, Henry VIII's writings against Luther, which Wolsey shepherded through the press, came to offer a fuller statement of those duties that pertained to the 'offyce of a christen kynge'.[62] Henry and Wolsey devoted particular attention to the issue of the vernacular Bible, a cause that Erasmus had championed and, they believed, Luther had perverted. The king declared that he thought 'it good for sacred scripture to be read in any language' by Christian men and women and promised to provide an authorised English Bible, something Erasmus had urged him

[58] 'Q[ue] eius nunc hominis partes nobis sumpserim[us], qui… aetatem consumpsisset in lit[t]eris', 'Quum partim bellicis, partim aliis longe diuersis studiis, rei publica causa, adolescentiam nostram insueuerimus': Henry VIII, *Assertio septem sacramentorum aduersus Martin Lutheru[m], aedita ab inuictissimo Angliae et Franciae rege, et do. Hyberniae Henrico eius nominis octauo* (London, 1521), STC 13078, sig. a2[r].

[59] 'Postq[uam] enim in administra[n]da republica maximam semper uim, maximumq[ue] momentu[m], religionem habere multo usu aduertimus, ut primum maturiores annos attigimus: coepimus eius contemplationi nonnihil studii impendere': Henry VIII, *Assertio septem sacramentorum*, sig. a2[v].

[60] Erasmus, *CWE: Letters 1252 to 1355*, pp. 368–9, 395.

[61] Erasmus, *CWE: Letters 1252 to 1355*, no. 1275, p. 68 and no. 1313, pp. 181–2; Erasmus, *OEDE*, vol. VIII, no. 2143, p. 129.

[62] Henry VIII, 'Fyrst a preface of our soueraygne lorde the kynge', in *A copy of the letters, wherin the most redouted [and] mighty pri[n]ce, our souerayne lorde kyng Henry the eight, kyng of Englande [and] of Frau[n]ce, defe[n]sor of the faith, and lorde of Irla[n]de: made answere vnto a certayne letter of Martyn Luther* (London, 1527), STC 13086, sig. aii[r].

to supply.[63] Like Erasmus and Thomas More, however, Henry and Wolsey were at pains to distinguish the benefits of reading scripture from Luther's schism.[64] In January 1523 the king urged the princes of Saxony to guard against the reformer's German Bible, since his 'object [was] that that which was well written may be subverted by bad translation'.[65] Temporal rulers 'should not regard [inaccurate translations] lightly, or consider them to be merely academic exercises. Rather, they must understand that the dignity that they carry as Christian princes pertains equally to matters of God and man'.[66] They were protecting their subjects' souls and public order by rooting out Lutheran heresy.[67] Luther seems to have reminded Henry of the false prophets, described in 2 Peter 2:4–10, who led Christians astray. Perhaps it was Wolsey who encouraged the king to read and annotate his copy of Erasmus' *Paraphrases on the two letters of Saint Peter*, which the humanist had dedicated to the cardinal. Henry scored the passages that described the torments visited on those who had been tempted by heresy to give in to their 'outrageous lust' and reject 'public authority'.[68] For the sake of Christian souls and the order of the commonwealth, moreover, Henry and Wolsey lobbied Erasmus to join them in the battle and congratulated Erasmus on his eventual repost to Luther, *Concerning the freedom of the will* (1524). Indeed, Wolsey offered him a benefice – or perhaps a post at his college in Oxford – in late 1525 or early 1526, which he declined.[69] Henry's princely office required him to offer his subjects a spiritual guard against Lutheran heresy.

In 1526 Henry was similarly persuaded that it was his royal responsibility to thwart William Tyndale, the Lutheran biblical translator. In the fifteenth century, the church Convocation had dealt with John Wyclif's

63 'Na[m] ut bonu[m] esse non negem, in quauis lingua legi scriptura[m] sacram': Henry VIII, 'Epistola regia ad illustrissimos Saxoniae duces pie admonitoria', in *Libello huic regio haec insunt* (London, 1523), STC 13083, sig. b2^v. For his promise to consider an authorised translation, see Henry VIII, *A copy of the letters*, sig. Aviii^v; *LP*, vol. IV, no. 6377, p. 2865. He made the promise again in 1530: Scarisbrick, *Henry VIII*, p. 253.

64 Alan Stewart, 'The trouble with English humanism: Tyndale, More and Darling Erasmus', in Jonathan Woolfson (ed.), *Reassessing Tudor humanism* (Basingstoke, 2002).

65 'Id illi studium esse, ut bene scripto male verte[n]do peruertat': Henry VIII, Libello huic regio haec insunt, sig. b2^v.

66 'Si rem pro leui non habeant, nec existiment dum taxa[n]t esse scholasticam: sed quum et dei res agatur et hominum, dignam intelligant, cui Christiani principes admoueant manus': Henry VIII, *Libello huic regio haec insunt*, sig. b1^r.

67 'Priusquam et improbi per maliciam [sic], et simplices per errorem in eum numerum et robur coaluerint': Henry VIII, *Libello huic regio haec insunt*, sig. b1^r.

68 Erasmus (ed.), *Novum Testamentum paraphrases*, BL, 3913 k.4, vol. II, p. 329.

69 Erasmus, *CWE: Letters 1356 to 1534*, pp. 362–3, 417; Dowling, *Humanism in the age of Henry VIII*, p. 40.

English Bible but, with Wolsey's support, Henry VIII claimed to be directing the search for Tyndale's version himself.[70] Henry protested that Tyndale intended to 'abuse the... deuotion' of the English 'towarde the holy scrypture' with his corrupting version of the Bible. The king emphasised in a public letter that he had taken the advice of Cardinal Wolsey 'and other reuerende fathers of the spyritualtye' in arriving at his decision to order a crackdown. Nevertheless his 'especiall te[n]dre zele' to his people had spurred him on personally to ban the import of Tyndale's Bibles, to arrange book-burnings and to ask John Fisher, bishop of Rochester, to deliver a corrective sermon in February 1526.[71] In 1527, Henry VIII translated his specific anxieties about Luther and Tyndale into a general statement regarding the spiritual responsibilities of the Christian prince:

> [It was] the office of a christen kynge, ouer and besides... the prouysyon of worldly welth and quyete for his people... to labour, trauayle and studye, by all the meanes and ways to hym possible, howe he maye surely kepe, establysshe and co[n]fyrme, and spyritually set forthe and forther, the hertes and myndes of his subiectes, in the right religion of god, and trewe faythe of Christ.[72]

Henry VIII parroted Erasmus' language of Christian kingship so convincingly in this letter that one of the humanist's correspondents, Johannes Cochlaeus, suspected that Erasmus had actually ghost-written it.[73] In fact, Henry and Wolsey had found in Erasmus' writings the language to explain his princely duty – and consequently his authority – to set forth 'right religion' for his subjects.

How do we know that it was Erasmus, specifically, who had provided Henry with this royal grammar and rhetoric against Luther and Tyndale? We have the king's word for it. On 18 September 1527, several months after Henry VIII had begun to ruminate on the implications of Leviticus for the state of his marriage,[74] he wrote to Erasmus to thank him for reshaping his understanding of monarchy. The king declared that he had 'nourished an uncommon devotion' towards Erasmus 'since we first met you, at a very tender age'. He noted the 'little books' (*libellis*) that the humanist had presented to him over the years and the honour they had

70 MacCulloch, 'Henry VIII and the reform of the church', p. 160; Richard Rex, *Henry VIII and the English Reformation*, 2nd edn. (Basingstoke, 2006), p. 96.

71 Henry VIII, A copy of the letters, STC 13086, sigs. Av^{v}, Avi^{r}; Dowling, *Humanism in the age of Henry VIII*, pp. 42–3.

72 Henry VIII, *A copy of the letters*, sig. Aii^{r-v}.

73 Erasmus, *OEDE*, vol. VIII, no. 2143, p. 129.

74 Virginia Murphy, 'The literature and propaganda of Henry VIII's first divorce', in Diarmaid MacCulloch (ed.), *The reign of Henry VIII: Politics, policy and piety* (Basingstoke, 1995), pp. 136–8; Rex, *Henry VIII and the English Reformation*, p. 3.

conferred upon him. Henry praised Erasmus' devotion to 'the propagation [*propaganda*] and glorification of the Christian faith'. He had come to realise, he wrote, that it was his duty as a prince to assist and protect this endeavour. 'We have felt for some years now', Henry explained, 'a warm and burning desire within us, undoubtedly inspired by the divine Spirit, to restore Christian faith and religion to their former dignity… to ensure absolute freedom to follow the word of God [*sermo dei*]'.[75] In short, Henry declared that he had undergone the passionate embrace of Christ that Erasmus had advocated and he claimed that it had refigured his kingship. To reassure the humanist that he had digested his writings, Henry parroted Erasmus' vocabulary back to him. '*Sermo dei*' was the phrase Erasmus had used, controversially, to describe God's word (John 1:1) in the 1519 *Novum Testamentum*.[76] When Henry and Erasmus were united, 'the gospel of Christ' would be preserved and glorified, he wrote, echoing the humanist's charge to princes in his *Paraphrases*.[77] Moreover, if Erasmus would come to England, the king promised to pattern his rule in accordance with his prescriptions: 'we are determined to follow now and always' Erasmus' 'most judicious counsel'.[78] From the king's own lips we have it; Henry professed himself committed to applying the moral and spiritual dimensions of his Erasmian education in government.

Of course, the king protested too much. What Henry's letter actually shows is that the king wanted Erasmus to help him fight the opening bouts of his Great Matter and that he was capable of mimicking his diction and arguments in an attempt to win him over.[79] Erasmus was a client of Charles V and a known sympathiser with Catherine of Aragon. In his *Christiani matrimonii institutio* (1526), written at the request of the queen, he had declared that Mosaic law enjoined a man to marry his deceased brother's wife.[80] It was conceivable that his opinion might be changed; Erasmus had previously written in favour of the capacity of ecclesiastical

[75] Henry VIII in Erasmus, *OEDE*, vol. VII, no. 1878, p. 180; modified trans. from Erasmus, *CWE: Letters 1801 to 1925*, pp. 339–41.

[76] C. A. L. Jarrot, 'Erasmus' "*In principio erat sermo*": A controversial translation', *Studies in Philology*, 61:1 (1964). Thomas More took Erasmus' part in the controversy in his 'Letter to a monk', in *The complete works of Saint Thomas More*, vol. XV: *In defense of humanism: Letters to Dorp, Oxford, Lee, and a Monk*, ed. Daniel Kinney (New Haven, 1986). It was probably More who assisted Henry in writing this letter.

[77] Henry VIII in Erasmus, *OEDE*, vol. VII, no. 1878, p. 181; modified trans. from Erasmus, *CWE: Letters 1801 to 1925*, p. 341.

[78] Henry VIII in Erasmus, *OEDE*, vol. VII, no. 1878, p. 181; modified trans. from Erasmus, *CWE: Letters 1801 to 1925*, p. 341.

[79] William Blount, Lord Mountjoy, in Erasmus, *OEDE*, vol. VII, no. 1816, p. 55.

[80] Erasmus, *Institution of Christian matrimony*, in *CWE: Spiritualia and pastoralia IV*, pp. 270–1.

courts to grant divorces.[81] On this occasion, however, Erasmus guessed that Henry's promises of religious reform were empty and he refused the invitation.[82] The humanist, at least, doubted Henry VIII's 'Erasmianism'.[83] Nevertheless, Erasmus had supplied Henry and Thomas Wolsey with a political and religious language that the king could use to extend his authority in the religious sphere. Several years before Thomas Berthelet started disseminating the claim that the king 'hath not onely charge on the bodies, but also on the soules of his subiectes',[84] Henry VIII was using Erasmus' language to proclaim himself the propagator of God's word in his realm.

As the matter of his divorce loomed, however, Henry's opponent in the battle for his subjects' religious allegiance began to change. Rather than continuing to charge at Martin Luther, the English prince began to level his lance against Rome and Pope Clement VII (1478–1534). In 1527 both city and pope had fallen under the power of Catherine's nephew Charles V. Scipture offered the king an uncompromising standard against which to judge contemporary clergy who were loyal to Rome.[85] On 28 November 1529, following the fall of Cardinal Wolsey and the commencement of a parliament that was pointedly anti-clerical, Henry held forth to the imperial ambassador, Eustace Chapuys (1490×92?–1556). His topic was the duty of Christian princes to promote 'the general reformation' of the churches in their realms. He lamented the dependence of the pope and cardinals on 'vain and superfluous ceremonies' and 'magnificence' and deplored their 'inordinate ambition'. 'Had they observed to the letter the precepts of the Gospel, and attended to the traditional sayings and exemplary conduct of the old fathers of the Church', Henry opined piously, the world would have been spared 'wars, discords and heresies'. Luther might be a horrible heretic, Henry continued, but he was right to condemn the church's 'vices, abuses, and errors'. Charles V had signed a peace

[81] Erasmus, *Annotations on the New Testament: Acts, Romans, I and II Corinthians: Facsimile of the final Latin text with all earlier variants*, eds. A. Reeve and M. A. Screech (Leiden, 1990), pp. 467–81. For Erasmus' views on the divorce of Henry and Catherine of Aragon, see the preface to Erasmus, *OEDE*, vol. x, no. 2846, pp. 270–1.

[82] Erasmus, *OEDE*, vol. vii, no. 1998, pp. 402–3, no. 2040, pp. 470–1, and vol. viii, no. 2215, pp. 277–9.

[83] Bernard, *King's Reformation*, pp. 233–47; McConica, *English humanists and Reformation politics*, p. 106.

[84] Christopher Saint German, *Here after foloweth a lytell treatise called the newe addicions* (London, 1531), STC 21563, fol. 14v.

[85] For instance, [William of Ockam or Pierre Dubois], *A dialogue betwene a knyght and a clerke concernynge the power spiritual and temporall*, trans. J. Travisa (London, [1531]), STC 12511a, fols. 14r–15v, 19r–v.

with France on 3 August 1529 and the Ottomans had just begun to retreat from Vienna. Henry was hopeful that, with Charles V having established himself as 'the greatest prince in Christendom', he would now join him in 'imposing law and establishing rules' to restore Charles's church to its pristine condition, presumably at the next imperial diet.[86] The king's public fulminations against Rome echoed Erasmus' complaints about the clergy in his *Handbook of the Christian soldier*, a text that would be printed on multiple occasions in England after Henry's break with Rome.[87] Henry's suggestion to Chapuys was no more an attempt to urge Charles V to reform the church in his empire than Henry's 1527 invitation to Erasmus had been a genuine appeal for counsel. Rather, Henry's self-presentation as a defender of the Gospels was a powerful justification for his support for the House of Commons' anti-clerical bills of 1529 and 1530 and the *praemunire* charges it levelled against churchmen in October 1530 and January 1531.[88] The mask of the Erasmian Christian prince helped Henry to justify asserting his authority over the ecclesiastical realm.

The king also used Erasmus' language to support his assertion that he was preserving divine law by insisting on the binding authority of Leviticus 18:16 and 20:21. Henry's *Glasse of the truth* (September 1532) was probably produced with the editorial assistance of Richard Croke, the former tutor to his illegitimate son Henry, duke of Richmond. There, the king explained to his subjects that Pope Julius II had rolled away that 'firm and stedfaste stone of truth and faithe' when he had granted Henry dispensation to marry Catherine of Aragon in December 1503, against scriptural precepts to the contrary. While the pope ignored the Bible to line his pockets, Henry claimed his case for divorce rested on 'the very worde of god'.[89] The king claimed that he merely wished to conduct his life in accordance with sacred scripture; he was willing to 'take paynes for his co[m]munewelthe' to this end.[90] If he and his parliament were not able to determine the matter of his marriage by considering divine law, the realm was as 'euyll in condition as sclaues [slaves] of Turkes'.[91]

86 *CSP Spain*, vol. IV.i, no. 224, p. 349.

87 Erasmus, *Enchiridion militis christiani, whiche may be called in Englisshe, the hansom weapon of a christen knyght replenysshed with many goodly [and] godly precepts*, trans. [William Tyndale?] (London, 1533), STC 10479, for instance sigs. bviii^{v}, cv^{v}. See also E. J. Devereux, *Renaissance English translations of Erasmus: A bibliography to 1700* (Toronto, 1983), pp. 104–5; J. A. Gee, 'John Byddell and the first publication of Erasmus' *Enchiridion* in English', *English Literary History*, 4:1 (1937).

88 Scarisbrick, *Henry VIII*, pp. 252, 274–5, 288.

89 Henry VIII, *A glasse of the truth* (London, [1532]), STC 11919, sig. E2^{v}, see also sigs. B4^{v}–B5^{r}, C3^{v}–C4^{r}, D6^{v}. See Richard Rex, 'Redating Henry VIII's *A glasse of the truthe*', *The Library*, 7:4 (2003).

90 Henry VIII, *A glasse of the truth*, sig. C4^{r}.

91 Henry VIII, *A glasse of the truth*, sig. F2^{r}.

In *A glasse of the truth*, Henry had presented himself as defending the scriptural prescription and Christian freedom that the pope and his clergy had scorned. Gradually, the king and his advisers turned Erasmus' account of the prince as a loving ruler, a champion of the Gospels and the defender of Christian liberty against the authority of the papacy.

Erasmus' *Education of a Christian prince* and his *Paraphrases* did help to prepare Henry VIII and his government for the break from Rome but not because they kindled the light of reform in the king's soul. Instead, Erasmus had given Henry VIII a language in which he could claim that, by seeking praise, attacking Luther and Tyndale and, ultimately, criticising Rome and its clergy, he was doing his duty as a Christian prince. The king, Wolsey and his literary editors cited and paraphrased Erasmus' account of princes' Christian charity, biblical zeal and care for the commonwealth in order to assert the crown's authority over the spiritual lives of Englishmen and women. By urging Henry to propagate the gospel and emulate Christ's compassionate government on earth, Erasmus had inadvertently handed the king tools to extend, rather than moderate, his imperial power. The territory he conquered would be his subjects' souls. When the time came, England would be well prepared for the royal supremacy. After all, Henry had been the defender of his subjects' faith since 1521.

ERASMUS AND THE ROYAL SUPREMACY

Following the 1534 enactment of the royal supremacy in England, the fixed theological mark for the (otherwise wandering) bark of the Henrician church was subjects' spiritual obedience to the king. Henry VIII, his tame churchmen and humanist propagandists claimed that subjects were obliged to submit to the king because 'the word of God', or *verbum dei*, commanded it.[92] God had apparently spoken his most important words in the commandment to 'honour thy father and thy mother'. According to *The king's book* (1543), this verse applied 'not onely [to] the naturall father and mother… but also princes and all other gouernours, rulers, and pastours, under whom we be nourished and brought up, ordred & guided'.[93] Richard Rex has demonstrated that this justification for obedience was cobbled

[92] Rex, 'Crisis of obedience', pp. 863–94. See also Geoffrey Elton, *Policy and police: The enforcement of the Reformation in the age of Thomas Cromwell* (Cambridge, 1972), pp. 192–4; Ryrie, 'Divine kingship and royal theology', pp. 49–77.

[93] Henry VIII, *A necessary doctrine and erudition for any Christen man sette furthe by the kynges maiestie of Englande* (London, 1543), STC 5168, sig. Si^r.

together by Thomas Cromwell, Henry's counsellor and vice-gerent for spirituals, from the writings of Martin Luther.[94] Yet Rex's account of the intellectual foundations of the royal supremacy leaves historians with a troubling question: why did Henry VIII consent to build his church on ground prepared by a man whose theology he continued to disdain?[95] Cromwell was undoubtedly a persuasive man but Henry (and many of his subjects) could not stomach Lutheranism before or after 1534. Time and time again, the king refused to accept that salvation depended on faith and grace alone, so how could he be persuaded that Luther's justification for magisterial authority was the rock on which he should establish his church?[96] In fact, Cromwell also located argumentative assistance in his print campaign for the supremacy from an unlikely quarter: the works of Erasmus.

I say 'unlikely quarter' because, while Erasmus championed subjects' duty of obedience to magistrates, he never defended the Henrician supremacy. He did not condemn it publically in England. Nevertheless Erasmus counselled against the break from Rome in his exposition on Psalm 83, *On mending the peace of the church* (1533), and described Thomas More and John Fisher as the 'new martyrs' of Christendom shortly after their 1535 executions.[97] In his great work on preaching, the *Ecclesiastes*, printed in August 1535, he lamented the destruction of men of great learning and piety at the hands of 'another Herod', the slayer of John the Baptist. 'Such rulers make a mockery of Christ and his teachings',[98] the ageing theologian spat. Contemporaries knew which ruler he was thinking of.[99] Pope Paul III (1468–1549) gave Erasmus a pension of a thousand gold pieces shortly after the publication of *Ecclesiastes*, a fact that was relayed quickly to Thomas Cromwell.[100] Henry's vice-gerent had no illusions about Erasmus' views on Henry's schism and the blood it shed.

94 Rex, 'Crisis of obedience', pp. 872–6 and *Henry VIII and the English Reformation*, pp. 17–18; Ryrie, 'Divine kingship and royal theology', pp. 65–77.

95 Rex, 'Crisis of obedience', p. 881.

96 See the king's handwritten corrections on his copy of *The institution of a Christen man, conteynynge the exposytion or interpretation of the commune Crede, of the seuen Sacramentes, of the x commandementes, and of the Pater noster, and the Aue Maria, iustyfication [and] purgatory* (London, 1537) in Bodleian, Bodley 4; Bodleian, Rawlinson B 245, fol. 37^{v}; Bernard, *King's Reformation*, pp. 282–5, 482–4, 584–7; Henry VIII, *Necessary doctrine and erudition*, sigs. aiii^{r}, diii^{v}–ei^{r}; Rex, *Henry VIII and the English Reformation*, pp. 127–8, 166.

97 Erasmus, *On mending the peace of the church*, in *CWE: Expositions of the psalms III*, p. 215; 'de nouis matryibus': Erasmus, *OEDE*, vol. XI, no. 3063, p. 238.

98 'Sunt hodie magnates quidam Herodi non dissimiles, qui Christum eiusq[ue] doctrina[m] habent ludibrio': Erasmus, *Ecclesiastae, siue, de ratione concionandi libri quatuor: Opus recens, nec antehac à quoquam excusum* (Basel, 1535), sigs. a2^{v}–a3^{r}, sig. g1^{r} (quotation, sig. i5^{v}).

99 For example Erasmus, *OEDE*, vol. XI, no. 3073, p. 255.

100 BL, Cotton MS Nero B VI, fol. 149^{r}.

Nevertheless Cromwell and his clients, who included John Byddell (d. 1545?), Leonard Cox (*c.* 1495–*c.* 1549), Thomas Starkey and William Marshall (d. 1540?),[101] translated, re-edited and disseminated a number of Erasmus' works to urge subjects to submit to the supremacy. Before 1533, Henry, Croke, and More and Wolsey had plucked phrases and sentiments from Erasmus' writings. After 1533, however, the king's apologists lifted and re-purposed entire treatises to urge subjects to spiritual obedience. This circle of printers and scholars may have been encouraged by Thomas Cranmer (1489–1556), whose 'deep admiration' for Erasmus had survived his awakening as a more radical evangelical.[102]

Indeed Cromwell and Cranmer probably turned to Erasmus' writings in the 1530s because they held doctrinal appeal for a broad range of English Christians. To reformers, Erasmus was a critic of papal and clerical corruption, an advocate of vernacular Bibles and scripture-reading, and a proponent of civil order. Erasmus had even confirmed in *Explanatio symboli apostolorum* (1533), a catechism requested by Thomas Boleyn himself, that the commandment to honour one's parents 'doth not onely appertayneth to fathers and mothers: but also… to byshopes / to teachers / & to offycers and rulers'.[103] The *Explanatio symboli* was quickly submitted to Cranmer and translated into English by William Marshall, a Lutheran lawyer who also published an English version of Marsilius of Padua's *Defensor pacis* (1533) and Lorenzo Valla's *Donation of Constantine* (1534) as part of a print campaign to support the supremacy.[104] Yet Erasmus' writings, indeed the doctrine described in the *Explanatio symboli* itself, still had the potential to speak to traditionalists, including men like the king's cousin, the theologian Reginald Pole (1500–58), whom the regime wanted to win over. Like other loyalists, Erasmus retained belief in the seven sacraments, the essential unity of the church, free will and the necessity of good works.[105] Thus his treatises, paraphrases and commentaries remained viable media for reconciling traditionalists to the supremacy. In the 1530s

101 Gee, 'John Byddell and the first publication', pp. 43–59; McConica, *English humanists and Reformation politics*, pp. 136, 141–2; Neville-Singleton, 'Press, politics and religion', p. 591; William Underwood, 'Thomas Cromwell and William Marshall's Protestant books', *HJ*, 47:3 (2004).

102 Diarmaid MacCulloch, *Thomas Cranmer: A life* (New Haven, 1996), p. 99.

103 Erasmus, *A playne and godly exposytion*, fol. 165^r.

104 SP 1/83, fols. 57^r and 58^r; Underwood, 'Thomas Cromwell and William Marshall's Protestant books', pp. 520–2.

105 Erasmus, *A playne and godly exposytion*, fols. 5^{r-v}, 18^{r-v}, 117^r–119^v. On the persistence of the two readings of Erasmus in England, see Richard Rex, 'The role of English humanists in the Reformation up to 1559', in N. Scott Amos, Andrew Pettegree and Henk Van Nierop (eds.), *The education of a Christian society: Humanism and the Reformation in Britain and the Netherlands* (Aldershot, 1999).

Erasmus' account of the Christian prince was made over into a velvet glove to encase the grasping royal fist.

Some of Erasmus' sharpest anti-clerical satires were put into the service of discrediting papal supremacy.[106] There was a spiky English translation of *The dialoge bytwene Julius the seconde, Genius and Saynt Peter* published with royal privilege by Byddell in 1534 and again in 1535; it coincided with the printer's commission to circulate the royal injunctions that commanded clergy to preach the royal supremacy.[107] The anonymous translator excised the original description of Henry VIII as 'restless and warlike… ambitious and immoderate'.[108] Instead, the vernacular *Dyaloge* cast the youthful prince and his English subjects as the innocent dupes of the bellicose and utterly irreligious character of 'Julius II'. The pope was described as wantonly contravening divine law and demanding that the English fill his coffers and fight his battles. 'Julius' is heard to boast that 'no nacyon… passeth lesse upon the authoyte of [th]e pope of Rome tha[n] [th]e Englysshe nacyon'.[109] Fortunately, the translator concluded in an addendum, Henry VIII had recently reasserted his true and ancient royal supremacy over the church. The 'scourge' of Rome had been banished and it was 'hyghe tyme to submytte and humble our selues unto hym… [who] shall make in us a well of water, [for] leapying in to eternall lyfe'.[110] Erasmus' work was translated and transformed. His strident critique of princely ambition was made over to argue in favour of the greatest extension of royal authority England had witnessed.

This image of the bishop of Rome as the true scourge of Christian peace was reused by the humanist Thomas Starkey, who had secured a royal chaplaincy through Cromwell's patronage in 1535.[111] In February that year, Cromwell commissioned Starkey to attempt to persuade Reginald Pole to write in support of the Boleyn marriage and the royal supremacy. Starkey complied by playing on Pole's well-known anxieties about overbearing papal authority.[112] The papacy, Starkey proposed, had been instituted to defend the 'polytyk unyte' of the Christian church but over

[106] For example Erasmus, *The dyaloge called Funus* (London, 1534), STC 10453.5.

[107] [Erasmus], *The dialoge between Julius the seconde, Genius and saynte Peter* (London, 1534), STC 14841.5 and 14842; Gee, 'John Byddell and the first publication', pp. 44–5, 47; Neville-Singleton, 'Press, politics and religion', p. 591.

[108] [Erasmus], *Julius excluded*, in *CWE: Literary and educational writings V*, pp. 111–12.

[109] [Erasmus], *The dialoge between Julius the seconde, Genius and saynte Peter*, sig. Fiii^r.

[110] Anon., 'The translatour to the reders', in [Erasmus], *The dyaloge bytwene Julius the seconde*, sig. Hiii^v.

[111] SP 1/92, fol. 45^r; BL, Cotton MS Nero B VII, fol. 116^r; BL, Cotton MS Vitellius B XIV, fol. 145^r.

[112] Reginald Pole, *Ad Henricu[m] octauum Britanniae regem, pro ecclesiasticae unitatis defensione, libri quatuor* (Rome, 1539), fol. 48^v; T. F. Mayer, 'Pole, Reginald (1500–1558)', *ODNB*.

time it had become its predator. Otherwise pacific 'chyrstyan princys', he wrote, in echo of Erasmus' treatise, had 'drawen theyr swordis for the mayntenance of [the Bishop of Rome's] authoryte'. Indeed, Starkey concluded, papal supremacy 'hath byn the gretyst brake, that in memory we have, to al Chrystyan cyvylyte'.[113] The royal chaplain developed and elaborated his account in his *Exhortation to the people, instructynge theym to unitie and obedience* (1536). In order to maintain its 'hye pride & cloked tiranny', Starkey wrote, the papacy 'hath amonge christe[n] princes many tymes to the greatte ruine of common quietnes, sette greatte diuision'.[114] His final complaint of peace could have come straight from Erasmus' 1518 treatise of the same name: 'O lord what a blyndnes was this regnynge in princes hartes, and what a superstition [it was for] one christen man to kyll another under the pretext of Christis religion?'[115] Starkey claimed that he did not count Henry's executions of John Fisher, Thomas More and the Carthusian monks as instances of Christians killing Christians; these were legitimate responses to subjects' superstition, disobedience and treason.[116] With the creation of the royal supremacy, Starkey claimed that the king had become the defender of Christian faith and Christ's peace.[117]

Unfortunately for Starkey, Pole remained thoroughly unconvinced. On 27 May 1536 the cardinal despatched a letter rebutting the king's pretensions and the arguments of his apologists, which was printed as *Pro ecclesiasticae unitatis defensione* (1539). Henry had behaved more like a Roman emperor, a 'lord of all', who had treated the church as 'a piece of land captured from the enemy', than a Christian prince.[118] If he must play at being an emperor, Pole recommended that Henry follow the example of Constantine, who had at least 'acknowledged that bishops had the supremacy in God's church'.[119] In addition, Pole thundered, amongst the English, 'Erasmus' name is sufficiently celebrated and taken up' that readers would not tolerate men like Richard Sampson and Thomas Starkey,

[113] BL, Cotton MS Cleopatra E VI, fol. 372^{v}. See also BL, Harleian MS 283, fols. 131^{r}–132^{r}.

[114] Thomas Starkey, *An exhortation to the people, instructynge theym to unitie and obedience* (London, 1536), STC 23236, sig. M1^{v}.

[115] Starkey, *An exhortation*, sig. Mii^{r}.

[116] There are eight drafts composed between February 1535 and 1537 in BL, Cotton MS Cleopatra E VI, fols. 367^{r}–380^{v}. Internal evidence suggests that the letter on fols. 372^{r}–374^{v} was written in May or June 1535. Starkey's attempted defence of the executions is on fol. 373^{r-v} and fol. 379^{v}.

[117] BL, Harleian MS 283, fol. 132^{r}.

[118] 'Ipsam tanq[uam] agrum ex hostibus captum… ac quasi omnium dominus': Pole, *Pro Ecclesiasticae unitatis defensione*, fols. 4^{v}–5^{r}.

[119] 'Agnouit episcopos in ecclesia Dei supremum locum, superiorem omnibus mundi rectoribus, sibi a Deo datu[m] tenere': Pole, *Pro Ecclesiasticae unitatis defensione*, fol. 20^{r}.

who cherry-picked his writings for their own purposes.[120] Pole described the use made of Erasmus' writings by Henry's tame theologians as intellectually shoddy. The king's accession in 1509 may have raised humanists' hopes, Pole argued, but Henry was no Christian prince. Indeed the executions of More and Fisher made the king 'seem to all to be more reckless than Satan himself'.[121]

Starkey tried persuading Pole that the 'most nobul and catholyke pry[n]ce'[122] Henry was using the supremacy to reform the church in the way that men like Erasmus, Fisher, More, Pole's patron Cardinal Gasparo Contarini and, indeed, Pole himself had advocated. Starkey proposed that Henry's church would lie on the golden mean between Roman 'superstition' and Lutheran 'impiety' or 'contempt of religion'.[123] When Cromwell wrote to ask Starkey to define the 'mean' further, Starkey responded that 'obedyence ys more necessary to thinges decred by co[m]my[n] authoryte then scrupulose knowledge'.[124] Nevertheless, insofar as Starkey did define 'true Christian faith' in his *Exhortation*, he claimed that Henry's church was intent on cultivating scripture-reading, personal piety and charitable living. Its doctrine, he claimed, emphasised the role of faith in salvation and the search for reason as a concomitant of the pursuit of revelation. That this programme resembled Erasmus' account of personal religion in the *Enchiridion* was no coincidence.[125] The *Dialogue between Pole and Lupset*, which Starkey revised and presented to Henry in 1534, also recommended having Erasmus' treatise 'put in to our mother tong' alongside the gospels so that 'al me[n] schold know hyt & study to aply to forme thyr lyfys therafter'.[126] In the heat of debate with a reforming Catholic like Pole, Starkey portrayed Henry VIII as an Erasmian Christian prince who

[120] 'Apud quos scires Erasmi nomen satis esse celebre, & acceptum': Pole, *Pro Ecclesiasticae unitatis defensione*, fol. 64^{v}.

[121] 'Secu[n]dum Deum, totius Christiani nominis spes habebatur' and 'audacior, quam ipse Sathanas omnibus videare': Pole, *Pro Ecclesiasticae unitatis defensione*, fols. 16^{v} and 111^{r}.

[122] BL, Cotton MS Cleopatra E VI, fol. 368^{v}.

[123] Starkey, *An exhortation*, sigs. Aiv^{r-v}, Zi^{r-v}. See D. Eppley, *Defending royal supremacy and discerning God's will in Tudor England* (Aldershot, 2007), pp. 41–60; Thomas Mayer, *Thomas Starkey and the commonweal: Humanist politics and religion in the reign of Henry VIII* (Cambridge, 1989), pp. 215–37.

[124] SP 1/89, fol. 152^{v}. See similarly Peter Lake, 'Joseph Hall, Robert Skinner and the rhetoric of moderation at the early Stuart court', in Lori Anne Ferrell and Peter McCullough (eds.), *The English sermon revised: Religion, literature and history, 1600–1750* (Manchester, 2001), pp. 167–87; Ethan Shagan, 'Beyond good and evil: Thinking with moderates in early modern England', *Journal of British Studies*, 49:3 (2010).

[125] Starkey, *An exhortation*, sigs. Eiii^{v}, Kiv^{v}, Qi^{r}, Tiii^{r}, Yi^{r}–ii^{v}.

[126] Thomas Starkey, *A dialogue between Pole and Lupset*, vol. XXXVII, ed. Thomas Mayer (London, 1989), p. 141; SP 1/90, fols. 1^{r}–2^{r}.

took pains to care for his subjects' religion and who was attempting to institute an Erasmian church in England.

In 1535 Starkey would have been well aware that Cromwell and his tame printer John Byddell had been brandishing Erasmus' *Handbook of the Christian soldier* at English subjects for two years. Erasmus' account of personal piety was one of the first translated and most oft reprinted treatises of the Henrician church. Released under royal privilege in 1533 as *Enchiridion... or Manuell of a christen knyght*, it was quickly revised and reprinted under the title of *The handsome [ready] weapon of a Christen knyght* on 12 February 1534 and then reissued by John Byddell on four subsequent occasions before 1547.[127] The *Enchiridion... or Manuell* nominally opened the way to reason and revelation for all English subjects. In addition to potentially appealing to Catholic reformers like Pole, it had also had currency with the young William Tyndale. In fact it may have been Tyndale's translation of the *Enchiridion*, made in the early 1520s, that was used for the 1533 English edition.[128] The translated treatise was presented to urge both evangelical and traditional subjects to acknowledge the spiritual obedience they owed Henry VIII.

As printer, Byddell added marginal notes to the *Enchiridion... or Manuell* to draw readers' attention to salient points. Where Erasmus' text referred to the pretensions of 'popes and bishops' to certain titles of 'power and dominion' that Christ had denied them, the notes in Johann Froben's 1518 edition (on which the translation was based) had pointed neutrally to 'Popes. Bishops. Theologians. Our rulers'. Byddell's 1533 edition, however, was pejorative: 'The clergy is touched of ambicion & vayne tytles of names'.[129] Rather than following Roman usurpers, the marginal notes encouraged readers to look to their temporal rulers, who took 'the maner & forme of bering rule' from Christ for direction.[130] This analogy had potential significance for the extent of royal dominion. If one accepted that 'Chryste is lorde bothe of laymen & also of preestes', it followed that princes who took their 'maner & forme' of rule from Christ also possessed authority over both sorts.[131] As we have seen, Erasmus had originally used

[127] STC 10479, 10480, 10480.5, 10482, 10483, 10484, 10485. Miles Coverdale also produced an abridged translation: STC 10488.

[128] Devereux, *Renaissance English translations of Erasmus*, p. 104 but see Erasmus, *Enchiridion militis Christiani: An English version*, ed. Anne O'Donnell (Oxford, 1981), p. liii.

[129] 'Pontifices. Episcopi. Theologi. Magistri nostri': Erasmus, *A booke called in latyn Enchiridion militis christiani, and in englysshe the manuell of the christen knyght* trans. [William Tyndale] (London, 1533), STC 10479, sig. Oiv[r] and *Enchiridion militis Christiani, saluberrimis praeceptis refertum* (Basel, 1518), fol. 109[r].

[130] Erasmus, *A booke called in latyn Enchiridion militis christiani*, sig. Oiii[r].

[131] Erasmus, *A booke called in latyn Enchiridion militis christiani*, sig. Oi[v].

the parallel between Christ and the Christian prince to urge temporal rulers to champion scripture and care for their subjects' souls and welfare. Byddell's marginal notes, however, excised Erasmus' use of the subjunctive mood. When expressed indicatively, the printed annotation seems to describe the 'maner & forme' of *existing* royal authority, rather than the moral and spiritual qualities that truly Christian governors should aspire to. By the next year Byddell had grown bolder still. In addition to commissioning a new translation of the *Enchiridion* for the 1534 edition, the printer added further printed comments urging subjects' obedience: 'Piety is the reuerent loue & honour which the inferiors haue towarde theyr superiors', he wrote, 'whiche is chefly requyred, & therfore it is that perfytenes of a chrysten man'.[132] Cromwell's print campaign had translated Erasmus' *Enchiridion* into a lesson on subjects' Christian duty to submit to their Christ-like prince in all things. Yet, in this rendering, subjects' obligation to follow their king's spiritual direction did not stem from scriptural prescription. It came from the charitable ethos that Erasmus described as the mark of the 'perfyt' Christian.

Leonard Cox's 1534 translation of Erasmus' *Paraphases on the epistle to Titus* (1519) provided a more detailed justification for why religiously conservative and anti-Lutheran subjects should submit to the royal supremacy.[133] Cox, a schoolmaster and reformist sympathiser, had sent the work to Cromwell through the printer John Toy and offered to follow it with other translations of Erasmus' works.[134] The *Paraphrases… to Titus* was printed under royal privilege in May 1534, the very moment that Englishmen were being rounded up to take the Oath of Succession.[135] Cox's preface got readers in the mood to consider an alternative to Rome by excoriating its lupine clergy, who had preyed on their English flock for too long. The royal supremacy had come about because God himself had run out of patience with the 'bysshop of Romes tyrannye'. 'I shall requyre of the shepherd myne herde out of theyre honde',[136] the Lord had (allegedly) thundered before turning over England to 'our moste redoubted souerayne/ whome he hath made the veray defender of the fayth and an hed shepherd to set such herdes men under hym/ which shall fede us & not deuour us'.[137] Like a second King David, Henry had been divinely

[132] Erasmus, *Enchiridion militis christiani, whiche may be called in Englysshe the hansom weapon of a christen knight*, trans. [William Tyndale] ([London], 1534) STC 10480, sig. Hii^r.

[133] Regrettably Gregory Dodd's *Exploiting Erasmus: The Erasmian legacy and religious change in early modern England* (Toronto, 2009) neglects this early translation of Erasmus' *Paraphrases*.

[134] S. F. Ryle, 'Cox, Leonard (b. *c.* 1495, d. in or after 1549)', *ODNB*.

[135] SP 1/84, fol. 22.

[136] Leonard Cox, letter dedicatory, in Erasmus, *Paraphrase of Erasm[us] Roterdame upon [the] Epistle of sai[n]t Paule unto his discyple Titus* (London, 1534), STC 10503, sig. A5^r.

[137] Cox, in Erasmus, *Paraphrase of Erasm[us]… unto… Titus*, sig. A5^v.

appointed to wield both 'spirituall gouernau[n]ce' and 'erthly domynyon' over God's chosen people.[138] To disobey the king was, in the words of the translation that followed, to 'resysteth agaynst the ordinaunce of god'.[139] Nevertheless, the heart of the case for the supremacy in Cox's translation of the *Paraphrases… to Titus* was not the prescriptive force of the commandment to honour fathers and mothers. Instead, Erasmus is heard to urge subjects to submit in the name of 'Chyrsten charyte'. If subjects obeyed their prince readily in spiritual matters they were performing a 'good worke [*opus bonum*]… of theyr owne fre wyll [*sponte*]'.[140] It was a text well suited to appeal to English readers who could not stomach *sola fideism*. It implied that one could submit to the royal supremacy without going over to Luther. While his subjects obeyed, Cox explained, Henry VIII would be 'diligently labor[ing]' in his turn 'with all his hole entent to haue [make] us the veraye shepe of Chrystes folde'.[141] Erasmus' argument for the duty of a Christian prince to take care of religion in his realm was turned into an argument for subjects' spiritual submission.

Starkey did not convince Reginald Pole but Erasmus' *Paraphrases*, in Cox's rendering and in the original Latin, resonated with other English subjects. In the few short years between the oath and the dissolution of the monasteries, the act of reading Erasmus' *Paraphrases* became firmly associated with submission to the royal supremacy. In April 1537, for instance, Furness Abbey in Cumbria, the second richest Cistertian house in England, was under investigation. One sycophantic friar, Robert Legate, wrote to the king to report against a commissary to the abbey (who was probably an agent of the traditionalist John Kite, bishop of Carlisle) for inappropriately disciplining William Rede, a priest of the locality. According to Legate, Rede had committed two acts that were as pernicious in the commissary's eyes as they were desirable to Henry and Cromwell. The first was that Rede had spoken against the bishop of Rome's usurped authority in England, an act that cost him his pulpit. The second was that Rede had been caught '[con]struyng of Erasmus

[138] Cox, in Erasmus, *Paraphrase of Erasm[us]… unto… Titus*, sig. A6^r^. For Henry's self-presentation as an English David, see John N. King, 'Henry VIII as David: The king's image and Reformation politics', in Mark Rankin, Chris Highley and John N. King (eds.), *Henry VIII and his afterlives: Literature, politics and art* (Cambridge, 2009); Pamela Tudor-Craig, 'Henry VIII and King David', in Daniel Williams (ed.), *Early Tudor England: Proceedings of the 1987 Harlaxton Symposium* (Woodbridge, 1989).

[139] Cox, in Erasmus, *Paraphrase of Erasm[us]… unto… Titus*, sig. B1^r.

[140] Erasmus, *Paraphrase of Erasm[us]… unto… Titus*, sigs. D5^r, D6^v; Erasmus (ed.), *Novum Testamentum paraphrases*, BL, 3913 k.4, vol. II, p. 322.

[141] Cox, in Erasmus, *Paraphrase of Erasm[us]… unto… Titus*, sig. B1^v.

Paraphrase unto his scolers'. This act had cost him his school.[142] Legate was confident that the king would comprehend the force of his accusations immediately: those, like Rede, who read and taught Erasmus' *Paraphrases* were loyal subjects who respected the supremacy; those Englishmen who rejected them, like the commissary, still looked to Rome.

In addition to providing subjects with alternative grounds for obedience, Erasmus' *Paraphrases* offered the Henrician church a non-Lutheran argument for providing vernacular scripture to the realm. Indeed, Erasmus' *Paraphrases* may have been used by an evangelical close to Henry to persuade the king himself that his new religious order required an authorised Bible. Sometime after Henry had marked up his 1524 copy of the *Paraphrases on the New Testament*, a second early sixteenth-century reader annotated the royal copy, undoubtedly with the king's permission.[143] This hand was wider and flatter than the king's script and wrote using a different grade of ink. The purpose of the annotations seems to have been to draw the king's attention to key aspects of Erasmus' argument for the dissemination of scripture. The hand began by pointing to passages that countered Henry's oft-stated fear that Bible-reading would encourage his subjects to engage in contentious disputation and 'mayntayne erronius oppinions'.[144] Here, the hand wrote, was an explanation of 'how he who wishes to read sacred letters should carry himself'; there, Erasmus offered 'laws for how sacred scripture may be read perfectly and pleasantly', even by Turks.[145] The evangelical reader returned Henry's attention to the king's own, earlier marks next to Erasmus' account of Paul's words (2 Timothy 3, Romans 15) and Moses' support (Deuteronomy 12 and 31) for the wide dissemination of scripture. These divine authorities stood, the hand noted, 'against the priests [of Rome] who neither know nor teach the word of God'. Henry acknowledged in the margins that he had, indeed, taken '*nota*' of their lamentable failure.[146] Finally, the evangelical reader drew attention to

[142] SP 1/118, fol. 9^{r}.

[143] I am grateful to James Carley for confirming that a second hand marked this letter. The black ink occasionally covers the brown, indicating that these notes were added later, but the style of the script is similar to the king's, suggesting the writing of a contemporary. Both are visible on Erasmus, 'Pio lectori', in Erasmus (ed.), *Novum Testamentum paraphrases*, BL, 3913 k. 4, vol. 1, sig. a6^{r}.

[144] Henry VIII, annotations (April 1539): BL, Cotton MS Cleopatra E V, fols. 314^{v}–315^{r}.

[145] 'Qualis e oportet qui studet velt legit litteras sacras' and 'hic disce quomodo leges sacra scriptura aditum p[er]fectum ac co[m]modum aie' in black next to the brown Henrician markings on passages: Erasmus, 'Pio lectori', in Erasmus (ed.), *Novum Testamentum paraphrases*, BL, 3913 k. 4, vol. 1, sigs. a3^{v} and a4^{v}, respectively.

[146] 'Co[n]tra sacerdotes qui aut nescient aut nolu[n]t p[re]dicare verbum dei' in black with a brown Henrician 'nota', on Erasmus (ed.), *Novum Testamentum paraphrases*, BL, 3913 k. 4, vol. 1, sig. a7^{r}.

Erasmus' proposal for reformed spiritual leadership at the conclusion of the treatise. 'Take care', Henry had written, alongside Erasmus' argument that princes would only truly be great when their authority served the glory of Christ. The alternative was the descent into civil wars (*intestinae co[n]flictationes*).[147] Rather than inflame dissent, the notes suggest that the dissemination of scripture would stabilise the Henrician church.

Henry VIII claimed that he was eventually persuaded to issue an authorised Bible by 'the instruct of God' himself.[148] Nevertheless he and his counsellors used Erasmus' writings to attempt to shape the reception of the English translation. In 1534 the king granted permission for the printing of a vernacular version of Erasmus' letter *Pio lectori* and his *Paraclesis*. Thus the 'ploughman & husbandeman... the carpe[n]ter, [th]e Smyth, the mason, yea & harlottes also... and to be shorte [th]e Turkes' could read or hear an argument in favour of their study of scripture in the English tongue.[149] They would also learn from Erasmus' letter that scripture would come to them from a 'great and noble' prince who was doing 'servyce unto the honour of Chryste, and to the profet of the Christan flocke' by providing a vernacular Bible. For their part, Erasmus told them, they would 'be happye & in good ease: yf they be obeydynt unto suche prynces and rulers, as unto Chryste hymselfe'.[150] The English Bible was a gift that non-Lutherans could welcome. The English translations of Erasmus' letter *Pio lectori* and his *Paraclesis* were used to argue that the charitable bond between loving ruler and obedient subjects would be strengthened, rather than frayed, by the provision of vernacular scripture.

The Christian duties of the supreme governor of the church and his charitable bond with his subjects lay at the heart of Henry VIII's justification for printing an authorised Latin Bible in 1535. He mimicked Erasmus by composing his own letter, *Pio lectori*, to introduce his *Biblia sacra*, a shortened Latin Vulgate, which has been largely neglected by historians.[151] The king's first-person (plural) letter described the role of scripture in his newly established church. He began with a *sola scriptura*-like argument

[147] 'Caue' in brown on Erasmus (ed.), *Novum Testamentum paraphrases*, BL, 3913 k. 4, vol. 1, sig. a8^{v}.
[148] SP 1/212, fol. 111^{r}.
[149] Erasmus, *An exhortacyon to the study of the Gospell* [trans. William Roy] (London, 1534), STC 10494, sig. eii^{r}. Henry VIII and Wolsey had attempted to have William Roy apprehended in 1528 alongside Tyndale: BL, Cotton MS Vitellius B XXI, fol. 49^{r}.
[150] Erasmus, *Exhortacyon to the study of the Gospell*, sig. iv^{v}.
[151] *Biblia sacra... in quo continentur quinque libri Moysi, libri Josu[a]e, et Iudicum, liber Psalmorum, Prouerbia Salomonis, liber Sapieti[a]e, et Nouum Testamentum Iesus Christi* (London, 1535), STC 2055. BL, C.3.e.19 was the king's copy. It is a rare volume, with only four known surviving copies; however, Thomas Hearne was aware of its existence: *Reliquiae Hernianae: The remains of Thomas Hearne MA of Edmund Hall*, ed. P. Bliss (Oxford, 1857), pp. 17–19.

that those who 'hear and obey the preceptor Christ' would find that 'he beseeches and exhorts them' in John 5:39, amongst other places, to 'search the scriptures, for in them you will find eternal life'.[152] As Richard Rex has argued, the king identified holy writ with God's law and his own: 'As is set forth for all in the Word or scripture, our Lord commanded that the king, once he was seated on the throne of his kingdom, should set down the law of God'.[153] Yet, in addition to the mandate of God's word, Henry insisted that he had a duty, as a Christian prince, to protect God's church and instruct his flock:

> We must guide and defend the Church assiduously in God's stead. And we must restore knowledge of Him, whether this is by increasing learning or consolidating it, since God has consigned [this knowledge] to us. We act in his stead; we bear his image.[154]

Henry described his care for his subjects' spiritual welfare at some length. Since the king had 'embraced God's law to his breast' (as Erasmus had urged him to do in 1517), he had been 'contemplating continuously how the common sort, as well as the spiritual leaders' in his realm 'could make a faithful account of their duties to God and discharge them fully'.[155] While many of Henry's subjects 'had been bound already' to God and their prince by the supremacy, he was authorising a Bible 'to increase [the number] of our people, by whom [God's] law is kept and taught'.[156] Henry's discourse was consistent with his 1527 letter to Erasmus. He protested his embrace of Christ and his fervent desire, as a Christian prince, to spread the gospel throughout his realm as an expression of his love for his subjects.

The greater step in the dissemination of God's word was, of course, the Great Bible (1539) in English, which Thomas Cranmer and Thomas

[152] 'Christum monitorem audiant ac sequa[n]tur, dum serio co[m]monifacit et hortatur, Scrutamini Scripturas [Joan. 5] in quibus vitam habebitis eternam': Henry VIII, 'Pio lectori', in *Biblia sacra*, sig. i^r col. 1.

[153] 'Quemadmodum dominus deus noster, de cuius verbis seu scripturis agitur, imperauerit, ut rex postquem in regni sui solio sederit, legem dei sibi describeret': Henry VIII, in *Biblia sacra*, sig. i^r col. 2. Henry paraphrased Deuteronomy 17:19. See similarly BL, Cotton MS Cleopatra E V, fol. 131^v; Rex, 'Crisis of obedience', pp. 863–94.

[154] 'Ipsam etiam Ecclesiam vice dei sedulo regamus ac tueamur: et disciplina euis sive augeatur aut soluatur, nos ei rationem reddituri simus, quo nobis eam credidit, in eo dei vicem agentes, deiq[ue] habe[n]tes imaginem': Henry VIII, in *Biblia sacra*, sig. i^r col. 2.

[155] 'Quod populi nostri necessitas in spirituale sui regimen expetierit… ut ipsam dei legem ipsi tanquam in sinu gestemus, qua continue peruisuri simus uti tam plebs ipsa q[uam] spirituales patres euis utriq[ue] quod debeant fideliter ac vigilanter adimplea[n]t': Henry VIII, in *Biblia sacra*, sig. i^r col. 2.

[156] 'Unde quamquam complura iamiam contexta sunt, e quibus ea lex haberi doceriq[ue] possit, nostrum tamen hoc adiicere voluimus': Henry VIII, in *Biblia sacra*, sig. i^r col. 2.

Cromwell fathered through the printing press with royal authority. Cranmer's prologue, which first appeared in the July 1540 edition, illustrated his long-standing interest in Erasmus' biblical scholarship.[157] In spite or perhaps because of the Pilgrimage of Grace (1536), he followed Erasmus' letter *Pio lectori* and his *Paraclesis* in emphasising the beneficial civil and Christian order that was enjoined by scripture: there 'prynces learne howe to gouerne their subietes: [and] Subiectes obedie[n]ce, loue and dreade to theyre prynces'.[158] Like Erasmus, Cranmer emphasised that these benefits would accrue to 'al maner of persons of what estate or condicyon soeuer they be… aswell concerning almyghtye God as also concernyne them selues and all others'.[159] These social bonds of obedience and love between hierarchically stratified sorts were depicted on the Holbein-like pictorial frontispiece of the Great Bible. There, the mutuality of Erasmus' account of the benefits and charitable obligations enjoined on all Christians by Christ's sacrifice was transformed into a simple argument that God's word enjoined obedience to the king and his royal supremacy.[160] Nevertheless, the observant reader will still spot a direct reference to Erasmus' letter *Pio lectori* on this frontispiece: a portrait of a Turk who has been saved by reading scripture in the vernacular.[161] The figure hovers in the lower right-hand register of the frame wearing a turban and beard and crying *Vivat Rex* with the rest of Henry's loving and obedient subjects. In the king's own illuminated copy of the Great Bible his skin is coloured brown and his turban is a vivid yellow, which draws the eye to his presence.[162] A prince who had defended the gospel so that even the Turk might read it was Christian indeed.

Even after Henry's church retreated from its commitment to vernacular scripture in 1543, Henry VIII continued to use Erasmus' account of the charitable bonds between Christians as an argument for his subjects' duty of spiritual obedience. For instance, William Petre (1505/6–72) reported that, in his December 1545 speech proroguing Parliament, Henry spoke in 'so Kingly, or rather fatherly' a manner and altered 'his

[157] MacCulloch, *Thomas Cranmer*, p. 34.

[158] Thomas Cranmer, 'The prologue', in *The Byble in Englyshe* (London, 1540), STC 2070, sig. +ii^{r}.

[159] Cranmer, 'The prologue', sig. +ii^{r-v}.

[160] John N. King, *Tudor royal iconography: Literature and art in an age of religious crisis* (Princeton, 1989), pp. 70–4; T. C. String, 'Henry VIII's illuminated *Great Bible*', *Journal of the Warburg and Courtauld Institutes*, 59 (1996).

[161] Erasmus, *CWE*: *Paraphrases on Matthew*, p. 11.

[162] School of Holbein, frontispiece to *The Byble in Englyshe, that is to saye the conte[n]t of al the holy scrypture, both of ye olde, and newe testame[n]t* (London, 1540), STC 2070. The king's illuminated copy is BL, C.18.d.10.

countenance to a weeping sort', that his auditors were in no doubt of his tender, Christian 'Love unto them'. He assured them their grants and subsidies demonstrated 'the zeal and love that his Subjects did beare unto him' in return, 'whereof he thought himself most bounden to Allmighty God'.[163] Having established his *ethos* as a loving prince, learned in rhetoric and his Christian duties alike, the king complained that his subjects' affection to him did not extend to the English church. 'The speciall foundation of our Religion' was 'Charity between Man and Man', Henry said, yet these warm ties had grown 'refrigerate' in his realm. 'There was never more dissention and lack of Love between Men and Men', he lamented. Englishmen called each other papists, Pharisees, Lutherans and Anabaptists, 'names deuised by the Devill… for the seuering of one Mans heart… from the others'. By way of remedy, he insisted on uniformity of teaching from the clergy and the cessation of alehouse disputation. As we will see, Henry VIII was not the last British prince to use a deliberative oration to warn his subjects against indulging in popular rhetoric on religious questions. He echoed Erasmus in reminding his subjects to read the Bible 'reverently, and humbly' rather than contentiously. Rather than name-calling or disputing, the king proposed that 'the Whole Multitude every Man for himself' was to do 'travell' or work 'with him' to live as Christians. Then there would be true 'Unity, Concord, and Charity between themselves'.[164] Henry's object in his oration was to show his subjects that conformity and obedience to the doctrine of *The king's book* was both honourable and useful. Nevertheless, as Alec Ryrie has noted, the king's parliamentary rhetoric justified this appeal on the basis of mutual charity, rather than the scriptural commandment to obey one's parents and magistrates.[165] Further, we might note that Henry described 'Unity, Concord, and Charity' as a 'travell' or work, rather than conduct mandated by holy writ. In this significant speech act, Henry VIII used his Erasmian rhetorical training and the Erasmian language of loving Christian kingship to defend his faith.

CONCLUSION

An Erasmian education had given Henry the rhetorical skills and theological confidence to take charge of his church. Perhaps even more importantly, the humanist's writings also provided the king, his counsellors and

163 SP 1/212, fol. 110^{r-v}. 164 SP 1/212, fol. 111^{r}.
165 Ryrie, 'Divine kingship and royal theology', p. 67.

his apologists with arguments that justified extending his princely care over his subjects' souls. Indeed, despite Erasmus' intention to use princely education to bridle over-mighty monarchy, Henry VIII was able to use the preceptor's treatises to defend enlarging royal authority in England. It would not be the last time that princely pedagogy inadvertently served such a cause in the sixteenth century.

Erasmus' critique of princely vainglory did not deter Henry from war with France. In fact it facilitated other royal ambitions. The humanist attempted to use emotion – an appeal to natural Christian feeling – to goad Henry towards more honourable, moderate conduct. Indeed his account of the charitable bond between a loving Christian ruler and his obedient, affectionate subjects in *The education of a Christian prince* caught the king's attention. Henry marked up his 1522 copy of the *Paraphrases on the New Testament*, where Erasmus argued that princes should demonstrate their passionate embrace of Christian authority by defending the gospel and exerting themselves to improve their subjects' spiritual welfare. Ultimately, however, the king would use his pen and Erasmus' exhortation to moderate, Christian rule to carve out more territory than he ever managed to partition using his sword.

The persona of the Erasmian Christian prince was a mask that Henry donned with increasing comfort and *bravura*, as he began to perform those offices that had previously been the preserve of the clergy. Erasmus' writing gave the king a language with which he could assert that mounting theological arguments against Luther was his royal responsibility. In 1527 and thereafter, the king used Erasmus' diction to support his claim that, by divorcing Catherine of Aragon, he was rooting out papal corruption in England. Following the acts that made the king head of the church in England, Erasmus' letter *Pio lectori* was used by evangelicals and the king himself to argue for the provision of authorised Bibles. Even more critically for Henry, Erasmus' works were translated, re-edited and printed in England to provide his subjects, especially anti-Lutherans, with grounds for submitting to the king's spiritual authority. Reginald Pole did not buy the repackaging of Erasmus as a spokesperson for the supremacy, but he was right to note the English enthusiasm for the humanists' writings. As late as 1545, Henry would turn to Erasmus' account of the 'Charity between Man and Man' to urge his subjects to conform to the doctrine of *The king's book*.

Henry VIII's long-desired son and heir, Prince Edward, was born in 1537, a moment when the regime's use of Erasmus' writings was peaking. When the king planned his son's upbringing, it should not surprise us that he provided Edward with a deluxe Erasmian education. Henry had determined that his successor as supreme head of the church in England would need the grammatical and rhetorical skills, biblical knowledge and Erasmian political arguments that his father had used to defend his faith and spiritual authority in England.

CHAPTER 4

Educating Edward VI: from Erasmus and godly kingship to Machiavelli

'Little one! Imitate your father and be heir to his virtue; the world contains nothing greater', Richard Morison (*c.* 1510–56), the Tudor diplomat and propagandist, had written in Latin verse beneath Hans Holbein's portrait of *Edward VI as a Child* (*c.* 1538). Holbein's image was one of the first northern European portraits of a baby (who was not Christ). On one level, it is a hyper-realistic depiction of infancy. The prince's cheeks are gloriously chubby, and his head, clad in a child's white cap, is proportionally large for his body. Yet, in his New Year's gift for Henry VIII, Holbein also painted Edward VI (1537–53) to appear as his father's political and religious heir. The prince is costumed in a manner that references Henry VIII's garb in Holbein's Whitehall mural (1537/8) – he wears a feathered beret cocked at an angle and a red cape over gold sleeves – and he is depicted in a similarly erect frontal pose. The gold embroidery around the collar of Edward's shirt foretells the golden chain of office he will wear. His right hand opens into the gesture of the blessings he will bestow. His golden rattle is grasped like the sceptre he will wield. When the antiquary John Leland (1503–52) saw the portrait, he got the point immediately: 'I seem to discern the image of your magnanimous father, who shines forth in your face', he wrote to Edward.[1] Holbein portrayed the twelve- or fourteen-month-old prince as born with the capacity to assume Henry VIII's office as supreme head of the church and state in England.

Edward's education was arranged to give the prince the skills and knowledge he would need to govern men's souls as well as their bodies. It succeeded with aplomb, though it is unlikely that Henry VIII would

[1] 'Parvule patrissa, Patriae virtutis et haeres / Esto, nihil maius maximus orbis habet': Richard Morison on Hans Holbein, *Edward VI as a child* (*c.* 1538), oil on panel, Andrew W. Mellon Collection, National Gallery, Washington, DC; FSL, MS Z d 11; 'Expressam toties videor mihi cernere formam / Magnanimi patris, quo nitet ore, tui': John Leland, *Principum, ac illustrium aliquot & eruditorum in Anglia virorum, encomia, trophaea, genethliaca, & epithalamia*, ed. Thomas Newton (London, 1589), STC 15447, p. 96.

have approved of the end result. Before departing for France in 1544, the king had selected Edward's schoolmasters, Richard Cox (*c.* 1500–81) and John Cheke (1514–57) to provide his son with the liberal education that would enable him to govern a church as well as a state. Both men had the scholarly reputations to merit their appointments, yet Henry's choice has puzzled historians. The first section of this chapter will consider the way in which Cheke presented his pedagogical and confessional identity as Erasmian. In fact the schooling of Edward VI, which began in July 1544 and continued until July 1552, represented an apogee of Erasmus' influence in princely education in early modern Britain and, perhaps, Europe.[2] As the second section of this chapter will demonstrate, Edward's tutors adopted the humanist's prescriptions, methods and textbooks with enthusiasm. Indeed Edward's Erasmian education continued and intensified after his accession in 1547. The decision to keep the king in the schoolroom may reflect the rising status of liberal education but some historians have suggested it was a ploy to keep him out of politics. Section three will examine Edward's response to the 1549 rebellions in England's south and west, and ask whether his education had indeed left him a 'king of dust' or made him a precociously fluent political interlocutor.

In fact this chapter will argue that, unlike Henry VIII or the duke of Richmond, Edward was shaped ideologically, as well as intellectually, by his schooling. After 1547, Edward's schoolmasters, counsellors and preachers joined with Edward Seymour, duke of Somerset (*c.* 1500–52) and the newly instituted protector, to form what Diarmaid MacCulloch has called an 'evangelical establishment'.[3] Section four shows how Edward's schoolmaster-servants urged him to overturn the Henrician religious settlement and set a more militantly Protestant version of kingship before his eyes. It also asks how it was that the 'evangelical establishment' succeeded where Erasmus and northern humanists had failed; how did they use liberal education to fashion a genuinely godly king?

By 1551, Edward VI was willing to undergo political hardships, even death, rather than delay religious reform. This commitment permeated his political writing and catalysed his early interventions in government. Despite the praise he garnered for his precocious piety, we will see in section five that the king's determined godliness became something of a political inconvenience to John Dudley, earl of Warwick and later duke of

[2] BL, Additional MS 4724, fol. 155^{r}; SP 1/189, fol. 184^{r}.

[3] Diarmaid MacCulloch, *Tudor church militant: Edward VI and the Protestant Reformation* (London, 1999), p. 8.

Northumberland (1504–53), who became president of his Privy Council in February 1550. Following a particularly frustrating bout of pious intransigence from Edward, Dudley and his client, William Thomas (d. 1554), intervened. The final section of the chapter will examine their attempts to re-educate the king using writings adopted and adapted from a very un-Erasmian sixteenth-century political theorist, Niccolò Machiavelli.

RICHARD COX, JOHN CHEKE AND THE POLITICS OF ROYAL APPOINTMENT

Tower guards celebrated Edward's birth on 12 October 1537 by shooting off two thousand rounds of ammunition. Shortly afterwards, the preacher Hugh Latimer (*c.* 1485–1555) fired off his own volley from the pulpit. He urged Thomas Cromwell to ensure that Edward was surrounded by 'governares, instructores, and offyceres of ryght jugmentes, "lest the best of wits is corrupted by a bad education"'.[4] In fact, historians have claimed that the boy-king was taught to stray from the confessional path set by his father by evangelicals like Latimer himself, who sought to advance the reformed cause through Edward's education.[5] Edward VI recorded that from his sixth year he

> was brought up in learning by Dr. [Richard] Cox, who was after his Almoner, and John Cheke… Master of Arts, two well-learned men, who sought to bring him up in the learning of tongues, of the scripture, of philosophy, and all liberal sciences.[6]

Historians have wondered at these appointments. Richard Cox and John Cheke were almost certainly early and convinced adherents to Protestantism. Their opponents suspected them of evangelicalism in Henry's reign and they were praised by reformers John Leland and John Foxe (1516/17–87) for the godly zeal they exhibited under Edward VI.[7] At

4 'Ne optimum ingenium non optima educatione depravetur': *LP*, vol. XII, no. 947, p. 331, quoting Plato, *Republic*, IV, 491e–d. Latimer's Latin phrase bears some resemblance to Marsilius Ficino's translation, 'ingenio… generoso educatione corrupto procedere': see Plato, *Omnia divini Platonis opera tralatione Marsillii Fincini*, ed. Simon Grynaeus (Basel, 1551), p. 605.

5 A. G. Dickens, *The English Reformation*, 2nd edn. (University Park, PA, 1991), pp. 217–19; Maria Dowling, 'The Gospel and the court: Reformation under Henry VIII', in Peter Lake and Maria Dowling (eds.), *Protestantism and the national church in sixteenth-century England* (London, 1987), pp. 60–7; Geoffrey Elton, *Reform and reformation: England, 1509–1558* (Cambridge, MA, 1977), p. 319; Diarmid MacCulloch, *Thomas Cranmer: A life* (New Haven, 1996), pp. 325–6.

6 BL, Cotton MS Nero C X printed in Edward, *CPP*, p. 3.

7 For Cox, see John Leland, *Principum, ac illustrium aliquot & eruditorum in Anglia virorum*; SP 1/226, fol. 16r. For Cheke, see Foxe, *TAMO* [1563], Book 4, p. 941; Stephen Gardiner, *The letters of Stephen Gardiner*, ed. J. A. Muller (New York, 1933), p. 118; John Strype, *The life of the learned Sir John*

the same moment that Henry VIII's religious policy was becoming more conservative on the issues of Bible-reading and justification, he selected rabid evangelicals to educate his successor.[8] Had the king made a sudden and final turn towards 'a perfect reformation of religion', as John Foxe put it?[9] Was he in the dark about the extent of their evangelicalism?[10] Had he been persuaded to appoint the preceptor by his more radical intimates, perhaps his sixth wife, Katherine Parr (1512–48), or his physician, William Butts (1486–1545)?[11] Or was Henry resigned to appointing reformers since they were more likely to defend his son's supremacy than traditionalists?[12] George Bernard, Jennifer Loach and J. J. Scarisbrick have suggested that Henry VIII chose preceptors such as John Cheke because he thought that they would provide Prince Edward with an Erasmian education.[13] This interpretation has a great deal to recommend it. Henry's study of the *bonae litterae* had given him the discursive skills to defend his faith and, as we have seen, he and his counsellors had found the humanists' writings useful in justifying the royal supremacy. Before 1547, Cox and Cheke's self-presentation would have given Henry VIII every reason to think that he had appointed Erasmus' English successors to educate his son and heir. Rather than being 'a politically uncomplicated academic', Cheke, in particular, played his hand with stealth and guile.[14]

Richard Cox was educated at the Benedictine priory of St Leonard Snelshall near Whaddon, at Eton, and at King's College, Cambridge, where he graduated in 1524.[15] He impressed Cardinal Wolsey sufficiently

Cheke, knight, first instructor, afterwards secretary of state to King Edward VI (Oxford, 1821); Stephen Alford, *Kingship and politics in the reign of Edward VI* (Cambridge, 2002), pp. 60–2, 77–81, 125–7; Alan Bryson, 'Cheke, Sir John (1514–1557)', *ODNB*.

[8] Henry VIII, *A necessary doctrine and erudition of any Christen man, set furth by the kynges maiestie of England* (London, 1543), STC 5168, sigs. Aiii^v–Aiv^r, dii^r, div^r; MacCulloch, *Thomas Cranmer*, pp. 297–322; Glyn Redworth, *In defence of the Catholic church: The life of Stephen Gardiner* (Oxford, 1990), pp. 173–207; Richard Rex, *Henry VIII and the English Reformation*, 2nd edn. (Basingstoke, 2006), pp. 101, 126–8; Alex Ryrie, *The Gospel and Henry VIII: Evangelicals in the early English Reformation* (Cambridge, 2003), p. 254.

[9] Foxe, *TAMO* [1583], p. 1315.

[10] Jennifer Loach, *Edward VI*, eds. George Bernard and Penry Williams (New Haven, 1999), pp. 11–14; John F. McDiarmid, 'John Cheke's preface to *De superstitione*', *Journal of Ecclesiastical History*, 48 (1997), pp. 111–12, 117–18; J. J. Scarisbrick, *Henry VIII* (Berkeley, 1968), pp. 474–5.

[11] Dowling, 'The Gospel and the court', pp. 60–70; MacCulloch, *Thomas Cranmer*, p. 325; Scarisbrick, *Henry VIII*, p. 457.

[12] MacCulloch, *Thomas Cranmer*, pp. 358–69 and *Tudor church militant*, pp. 7–8; Rex, *Henry VIII and the English Reformation*, p. 164.

[13] George Bernard, *The king's Reformation: Henry VIII and the remaking of the English church* (New Haven, 2005), p. 591; Loach, *Edward VI*, p. 14; Scarisbrick, *Henry VIII*, p. 475.

[14] Dale Hoak, *The king's council in the reign of Edward VI* (Cambridge, 1976), p. 80.

[15] Felicity Heal, 'Cox, Richard (c. 1500–1581)', *ODNB*; Scott Wenig, 'The Reformation in the Diocese of Ely during the episcopate of Richard Cox, 1559–77', *SCJ*, 33:1 (2002).

to be invited to join his new college at Oxford as a junior canon, but the appointment was short lived. A brush with heresy accusations in 1525 cost him his office. Subsequently, he trod softly and attached himself to canny patrons, such as Thomas Goodrich, bishop of Ely, and Thomas Cranmer, who facilitated his royal appointments as archdeacon of Ely and the king's chaplain in 1540.[16] Cox sat on the commission that nullified the king's marriage to Anne of Cleves in July 1540.[17] In 1543, he was one of the six theologians charged with preparing the relatively conservative *King's book*. It insisted that faith be joined with works, that human will was free and that the substance of the bread and wine 'turned to the very substance of the body and blood of our Saviour Jesus Christ'.[18] Subsequently, John Foxe records that Cox stuck to the party line and urged Anne Askew, the future martyr, to moderate her reformist view of the Eucharist in 1546.[19] Henry VIII had good reason, then, to regard Cox as a fellow traveller in purging the 'old Mumpsimus' of monasticism and superstition while refraining from too much curiosity about the 'newe Sumpsimus' of reform.[20] As master of Eton, moreover, Cox had shown conviction in pursuing Erasmian reforms to its curriculum and these changes had shaped the statutes of new schools founded in England in Henry's reign.[21] From the king's perspective, Cox must have seemed like a thoroughgoing Erasmian, pedagogically and spiritually.

Cox's supplement, John Cheke, gave Henry VIII apparently fulsome indications of his pedagogical and religious convictions before and after his appointment to Edward's schoolroom. Cheke owed his appointment to the intervention of Henry's physician, Dr William Butts, a great patron of court evangelicals.[22] Yet the humanist also pursued the king's notice independently by presenting Henry with a series of Greek-to-Latin gift translations, much as Erasmus had done with Plutarch and Isocrates between 1505 and 1515. In 1543 Cheke offered the king Latin versions of

16 Heal, 'Cox, Richard (*c.* 1500–1581)'.
17 *LP*, vol. xv, no. 861, p. 429.
18 Henry VIII, *Necessary doctrine and erudition*, sig. Gii^v; *LP*, vol. XVIII, no. 68, p. 34, vol. XIX, no. 80, p. 38.
19 Foxe, *TAMO* [1563], p. 730.
20 Edward Hall, *Hall's chronicle; containing the history of England*, ed. Henry Ellis (London, 1809), pp. 864–5.
21 'Winchester and Eton timetables', in Arthur F. Leach (ed.), *Educational charters and documents 598 to 1909* (Cambridge, 1919), p. 451; T. W. Baldwin, *William Shakespere's smalle Latine and lesse Greek*, 2 vols. (Urbana, 1944), vol. I, pp. 135, 143; Erasmus, *De ratione studii*, in *CWE: Literary and educational writings II*, pp. 669, 673, 677.
22 Old Library, St John's College MS H 18, fol. 6^r, printed in John Chrysostom, *D. Ioannis Chrysostomi homiliae duae*, trans. John Cheke (London, 1543), STC 14634, sig. A4$^{r–v}$; SP 1/189, fol. 184^r.

two homelies of John Chrysostom (d. 407), the church father cited more frequently by Erasmus in his *Annotationes* and *Paraphrases* than any other except Jerome.[23] In the lead up to Henry's campaign against the French and the Turks, Cheke offered him the Byzantine Emperor Leo VI's *Tactics of war* (895–908) on 5 April 1544. In 1545, he gave him a further set of Chrysostom's sermons including his writings *On providence*. Finally, in 1546 and 1547, Cheke presented the king with manuscripts of his translations of Plutarch's *On superstition* and Maximus the Confessor's (580–662) *On the Ascetic life*.[24] As John McDiarmid has pointed out, these literary gifts offer compelling evidence for 'the position [that] Cheke was ready to take up publicly in relation to contemporary religious issues and controversies'.[25] In his innovative studies of Cheke's translation theory and practice, McDiarmid has argued that the royal schoolmaster wrote cautiously but made his 'support for further religious reform unmistakably clear' to the king and court.[26]

When more of Cheke's gift translations to Henry VIII are considered, however, this 'unmistakable' clarity is muddied by footprints that seem to tramp off in different directions. The path most travelled by Cheke in his translations for the king led to flattery fair. His rendering of Chrysostom's homily on 1 Thessalonians 4:13, for instance, attests to his hearty support for the Henrician church's reform of the doctrine of purgatory by urging against elaborate displays of grief during funerals. Yet Cheke was careful not to criticise prayers for the dead, which he stressed were charitable acts. In short, the translations demonstrated the support of a venerable church father for the doctrine set out in the recently printed *King's book*.[27] Even more strikingly, Cheke's translation of Maximus' dialogue *On the Ascetic*

[23] Greta Kroeker, *Erasmus in the footsteps of Paul: A Pauline theologian* (Toronto, 2011), pp. 36–9.

[24] Leo VI, *Leonis imperatoris de bellico apparatus liber*, trans. John Cheke (Basel, 1554); *Beati Maximi Ασκητικός summa Christianae vitae de Graeco conuersus*, trans. John Cheke, BL, Royal MS 16 C IX; Chrysostom, *D. Ioannis Chrysostomi homiliae duae*, sig. A4^{v}; John Chrysostom, *D. Ioannis Chrysostomi de providentia Dei, ac fato, orationes sex*, trans. John Cheke (London, 1545), STC 14630; *Plutarchi Chaeronensis de superstitione liber*, trans. John Cheke, Bodleian, University College MS 171.

[25] McDiarmid, 'John Cheke's preface to *De superstitione*', p. 111.

[26] McDiarmid, 'John Cheke's preface to *De superstitione*', p. 118 and 'Recovering republican eloquence: John Cheke versus Stephen Gardiner on the pronunciation of Greek', *History of European Ideas*, 38:2 (2012). But see Richard Rex, 'The role of English humanists in the Reformation up to 1559', in N. Scott Amos, Andrew Pettegree and Henk Van Nierop (eds.), *The education of a Christian society: Humanism and the Reformation in Britain and the Netherlands* (Aldershot, 1999), p. 30; Ryrie, *The Gospel and Henry VIII*, pp. 183–7.

[27] Chrysostom, *D. Ioannis Chrysostomi homiliae duae*, pp. 33, 40. Cf. Henry VIII, *Necessary doctrine and erudition*, sigs. ev^{v}–evi^{r}.

life seems to praise Henry VIII's refusal to countenance the foundation of Protestant doctrine, *sola fideism*. The older monk in the dialogue quoted James 2:19–20 to his younger brother:

> Perhaps someone will say, 'I have faith, and faith in Him is enough for me for salvation'. But James dismissed this, saying that 'Even demons believe [in God] and shudder' and also 'Faith without works is dead by itself', and so are works without faith.[28]

Cheke's apparent denial of the sufficiency of faith for justification surprised his scribe, who assumed Cheke had meant to write, 'Perhaps someone will say, "I have faith, and yet faith in Him is *not* enough for me for salvation"'. Cheke had to return to the passage to strike out the *non*.[29] Cheke was almost certainly a devout Protestant in 1546 yet he circulated a translation that publically endorsed *The king's book* on the complementary role of faith and works. His willingness to espouse this anti-Lutheran position suggests active dissimulation. Before Henry VIII's death, Cheke bore the person of God's loyal servant, but the king's first.

McDiarmid has acknowledged, with customary candour, that Cheke was careful to avoid the suggestion that Edward 'was being regularly taught Protestant doctrine' in his Latin rendering of Plutarch's *De superstitione*.[30] In fact, the dominant spiritual note of even this preface is Erasmian. Cheke defined superstition as 'the futile fear of God', manifest in religious practices that deserved to be 'totally ejected and eliminated' from demonstrations of true faith. Like Erasmus in the *Handbook of the Christian soldier*, Cheke was perturbed by 'mediocre and minute matters being placed higher than honour or dignity allows', and by the performance of rituals that 'are bent and twisted from the other [meaning] that is proper and for which they have been instituted' by man's invention and custom.[31] Indeed, as Jacques Chomarat has demonstrated, Plutarch's *De superstitione* was the work that Erasmus had drawn on to define and translate δεισιδαιμονια, *superstitio* negatively in his New Testament translation

28 'Sed dicet fortassis aliq[ui]s fidem habeo, fides in illum ~~non~~ mihi satis ad salutem est. Sed reclamat Jacobus. Nam & daemones inquit credunt & contremiscunt. Et rursum. Fides sine operibus mortua per se est, q[ua]m etiam opera sine fide': Maximus, *Asceticus*, Royal MS 16 C IX, fol. 59v.

29 Maximus, *Asceticus*, Royal MS 16 C IX, fol. 59v.

30 McDiarmid, 'John Cheke's Preface to *De superstitione*', p. 119.

31 'Inest inutilis timor dei', 'vel... quod res omnino eiiciendae atque exterminandae ad colendum venerandumque Deum adhibentur, vel mediocres minutaeque res maiori quam par est in honore pretioque collocantur, vel alio quam oportet & institutae sunt, flectuntur atque torquentur': Cheke, prefatory letter to Henry VIII in Plutarch, *De superstitione*, trans. Cheke, Bodleian University College, Oxford, MS 171, fols. 15v, 22v.

of Acts (17:22) and elsewhere.[32] For Cheke, as for Erasmus, Christians were forewarned against superstition by the example of the Jews who so assiduously followed religious laws that they were prepared to 'betray and brand Christ with a crucifixion' to establish their righteousness.[33] Like Erasmus, Cheke advised Henry to 'remove and reject' any ceremony not authorised by 'the word of God and scripture'. Yet Cheke made it clear that he was not pushing a Lutheran principal of *sola scriptura* with this counsel. Rather the schoolmaster cannily evoked Henry VIII's own parliamentary rhetoric from 1545 to recommend a religious *via recta*: 'if nothing is added, and nothing is taken away, if we are not turned to one side or the other but insist on the straight path of His commandments' then God would be the subject of 'pure and sincere worship'.[34] 'God has reserved you and your kingdom', he told Henry, 'for the removal and destruction of superstitious errors, for the extraction of the fibrous roots of impiety, for the propagating [*propaganda*] of the glory of Christ in the broadest way possible'.[35] Henry's care for his church and propagation of the glory of Christ, Cheke declared, had rendered him a true Christian prince. Cheke's gift translations for Henry VIII do not offer windows into the schoolmaster's soul; indeed they suggest his readiness to draw the curtains against prying eyes. In Henry VIII's final years, Cheke did not advertise his eagerness for further reform; he spoke to the king in the placating language of Erasmian Christian kingship.

Henry VIII's decision to appoint Cox and Cheke as Edward's schoolmasters reflected his confidence that these humanists would imitate Erasmus in their pedagogy and that, when it came to their confessional identity, neither would go beyond the Dutch humanist in their desire for reform. They gave the king good reason to believe that they would instruct Edward to attend to scripture and prayer, to live charitably, to weed out popish superstition and corruption while emphasising good

[32] Jacques Chomarat, 'Superstitio, religio et impietas', *Moreana*, 21 (1984), 151–5; Erasmus (ed.), *In Novum Testamentum annotationes* (Basel, 1535), p. 311; *Enchiridion*, in Erasmus, *CWE: Spiritualia and pastoralia I*, pp. 64, 70–9; 'The shipwreck', in Erasmus, *CWE: Colloquies I*, pp. 351–67.

[33] 'Quantum in se est prodere, ac extremae ignominiae cruciq[ue] affigere': Cheke, Bodleian University College, MS 171, fol. 22^r.

[34] 'Quod si ea solum facienda adhibendaque ad cultum Domini sunt, quae ille praeceperit, si nihil adiiciendum, nihil detrahendum sit, si neutram in partem flectendum, sed rectam viam mandatorum eius insistere oportet, ea necessario omnia, quae non habent verbum Dei et scripturam… e medio tollenda sunt ac reiicienda… veneratio pura ac sincera Dei adhibetur': Cheke, Bodleian University College, MS 171, fols. 22^v–23^r. Cf. SP 1/212, fols. 110^r–111^r and Hall, *Hall's chronicle*, pp. 864–5.

[35] 'Deus tuis regnoq[ue] tuo ad religionem quasi expiandam & excolendam, ad superstitionum errores tollendos & delendos, ad impietatis fibras radicitus extrahendas, ad Christi gloriam latissime propagandam reseruauit': Cheke, Bodleian University College, MS 171, fols. 6^v–7^r.

works, the mass and a confessional *via recta*.[36] Cheke, in particular, made it clear to Henry that he was teaching Edward to defend the church of his father. In negotiating the turbulent waters of the late Henrician church and the whims of an increasingly irascible monarch, this course was a prudent one.

During Henry's lifetime, moreover, there is every indication that Cox and Cheke fulfilled their office conscientiously. Prince Edward attended the mass in its traditional form, he offered alms on saints' feast days and he owned a relic of the true cross, enclosed in gold. When the new king, Edward VI, condoled Queen Katherine and Princesses Mary and Elizabeth after Henry VIII's death on 28 January 1547, his obsequies were hardly those of a radical reformer: Henry VIII 'was most surely in heaven', Edward declared, because he had 'made a good life, governed the commonwealth aright… promoted all piety, and expelled all ignorance'.[37] This was not the tribute of a *sola fideist*. Edward's schoolmasters had, until this moment, done their duty by Henry VIII, his mercurial father.

EDWARD VI'S ERASMIAN EDUCATION

Cox and Cheke veiled their confessional identity for Henry VIII's benefit but their belief in the benefits of Erasmian pedagogy was no fiction. At Edward's accession in 1547, the schoolmasters ran their reformed religious colours proudly up the mast of the ship of state, yet they continued to use Erasmus' curriculum and methods to teach the king to rule his church and state. Despite the reformed conviction that man was a depraved and sinful creature, Cheke and Cox kept faith with the humanist commonplace that education would ameliorate (or at least palliate) their prince. Copious evidence of Edward's education survives, including a journal of his activities; a large collection of his letters; notes on his reading of Latin and Greek authors; commonplace books in which he extracted biblical and classical phrases; and Latin and Greek *chreia* and declamations. The volume of these school exercises, their careful preservation and their early seventeenth-century binding show contemporaries' confidence that the prince's education was of political and religious significance. Unlike the uncertainty regarding aims and curricula that attended his half-sisters'

[36] 'Ut nullius in religione partis vel ignorantia, vel simulatio vel deprauatio sit': Cheke, Bodleian University College, MS 171, fol. 32^{r}.

[37] 'Felicem agit vitam, atque rempublicam recte gubernat… promovit omnem pietatem, atque expulit omnem ignorantiam, habet certissimum iter in coelum': Edward, *LR*, vol. 1, p. 38; see also pp. xcii–ci.

schooling, Edward's tutors knew that they were instituting a Christian prince.[38] His exercises show, moreover, that the royal pedagogical pendulum in England had swung from privileging arms to prioritising letters.

Between July and October 1544, Henry VIII's troops had captured Boulogne. On 10 December 1544, Richard Cox captured the triumphal zeitgeist when he reported to William Paget (1505/6–63), secretary of state and privy counsellor, that his new charge, Prince Edward

> hath expunged and utterly conquered an great nu[m]b[er] of the captyans of ignorance. The eight parts of speche he hath made the[m] his subiects and seruants, and can declyn any man[ne]r latyne nowns and coniugate a v[er]be p[er]fectly onlesse it is Anomalus. These parts thus beten downe and conquered, he begynith to buyld them up agayn and frame the[m] after hys purpose w[i]th dew ordre of construction lyke as the kinges M[ajes]ti fframed up [Boulogne] when he had beaten it downe.[39]

Beyond celebrating an English conquest, Cox's imagery reveals the terms in which Henry VIII and his counsellors viewed the purpose and method of Edward's education: the prince was learning to wield his pen as a sword. As we have seen, the schooling of the duke of Richmond was a struggle between the defenders of military training and his humanist schoolmasters. Edward's education would be aggressively liberal. This is not to suggest that his physical development was ignored: the prince describes running at ring, shooting at butts and playing tennis, and observers describe him watching jousts and barriers, playing the lute and the virginal, and performing in court entertainments. In 1551 Giacomo Soranzo, the Venetian ambassador, reported that the king was 'arming and tilting, managing horses, and delighting in every sort of exercise, drawing the bow, playing rackets, hunting, and so forth'. Nevertheless, even Soranzo noted that Edward VI 'never neglected his studies'.[40] In fact, the prince's exercise books show that he plied his books six days a week.[41] Minority rule did not attenuate his liberal education. The crises of his reign, such as the Seymour affair, the rebellions of 1549 and the fall of Protector

[38] Aysha Pollnitz, 'Christian women or sovereign queens? Representing the schooling of Mary I and Elizabeth I', in Anna Whitelock and Alice Hunt (eds.), *Tudor queenship: The reigns of Mary and Elizabeth* (New York, 2010) and 'Humanism and court culture in the education of Tudor royal children', in Tom Betteridge and Anna Riehl (eds.), *Tudor court culture* (Selingrove, PA, 2010).

[39] SP 1/195, fol. 201^{r-v}.

[40] *CSPV*, vol. v, pp. 535–6 (quotation); Edward, *CPP*, pp. 5, 57, 62, 97; Henry Machyn, *The diary of Henry Machyn, citizen and merchant taylor of London, from* AD *1550 to* AD *1563*, ed. John Gough Nichols (London, 1848), p. 7; Loach, *Edward VI*, pp. 14–16; Chris Skidmore, *Edward VI: The lost king of England* (London, 2007), pp. 33–6.

[41] For example BL, Arundel MS 510.

Somerset, did not break his stride. A remarkable political consensus had formed in England: the king had to learn to fight with his pen.

Edward studied alongside other young noblemen and the seriousness with which they took their studies suggests a broad shift in English political culture. They included the sons of the duke of Somerset, Edward (1539?–1621) and Henry (b. 1540) Seymour; Henry Sidney (1529–86), the son of Edward's chamberlain and steward, William, and the future governor of Ireland; and John, Lord Lumley (*c.* 1533–1609), who performed a translation of Erasmus' *Institutio principis Christiani* in 1550 for his father-in-law, the earl of Arundel. Edward's most intimate *socius studiorum* was Barnaby Fitzpatrick, eldest son of the baron of Upper Ossory (*c.* 1535–81), who established a regular correspondence with the king when he went to France as a noble hostage in 1551. Edward made declamations against the sons of the duke of Suffolk, Henry (1535–51) and Charles (1537/8–51) Brandon, who subsequently went up to Cambridge. Their learning was praised by Thomas Wilson in his *Art of rhetoric* (1553) and by fellow scholars in Latin and Greek obituary verses following their deaths from sweating sickness in 1551. The Brandon boys' father, Charles, had won Henry VIII's favour with his exploits in the tiltyard but the brothers demonstrated their nobility with feats of learning.[42] Finally, at least one of battles waged by Erasmus and other northern humanists in the early years of the sixteenth century had been won. Edward's liberal education established the *bonae litterae* as the most honourable and useful training for those who would govern the commonwealth.

Admittedly, Erasmus' strictures against corporal punishment were not always heeded by Edward's tutors. Roger Ascham, Princess Elizabeth's tutor, who stopped by the king's schoolroom to teach him italic handwriting, would out Richard Cox as 'the greatest beater' of his time. Cox admitted to having struck Edward on at least one occasion but there is no record of Cheke following his lead. Indeed Ascham lauds Cheke as his inspiration for the gentle prescriptions of *The scholemaster* (1570).[43] More generally, the fittings of Edward's schoolrooms suggest that he was allured

[42] Dale Hoak, 'Edward VI (1537–1553)', *ODNB*; Maria Dowling, *Humanism in the age of Henry VIII* (London, 1986), pp. 212–13; SP 1/195, fol. 202^{r}; Lord Lumley's translation is in BL, Royal MS 17 A XLIX; Fitzpatrick's correspondence is in BL, Cotton MS Caligula E IV, fols. 296r–301r and Edward, *LR*, vol. 1, pp. 63–92; Edward's declamation against Henry Brandon is in BL, Additional MS 4724, fols. 66^{r}–67^{v}, 113^{r-v}; Thomas Wilson, *Vita et obitus duorum fratrum Suffolciensium* (London, 1551), STC 25816 and *The arte of rhetorique for the vse of all suche as are studious of eloquence, sette forth in English* (London, 1553), STC 25799, fol. 8^{r}.

[43] Roger Ascham, *The scholemaster or a plaine and perfite way of teaching children, to understand, write, and speake the Latin tonge* (London, 1570), STC 832, sig. B1^{v}; SP 1/195, fols. 201^{r}–202^{r}.

to learning with trinkets and devices. The 1547 inventory of Henry VIII's palaces shows that Edward had his own writing desk, covered in black velvet and embroidered with the letter 'E'; a large globe; maps; a set of compasses; a bone hourglass to time his lessons; and astronomical instruments. In 1551 Cheke even designed a handsome brass horary quadrant for his pupil.[44] The student prince had all the tools he would need to become a philosopher-king.

Edward's studies began with Latin grammar. He probably used a compendium of texts printed on vellum: a primer with the alphabet, Lord's Prayer, Creed and Ten Commandments; William Lily's *Introduction of the eyght partes of speche* (1542) and his *Institutio compendiaria totius grammaticae* (1540), enlarged by Cox himself; and a copy of Erasmus' Latin catechism, *Institutio hominis Christianis* (1523).[45] Once he had conquered the basic heads of grammar, Edward began to study the simple sentences attributed to Cato and edited by Erasmus. As Cox noted, they included exhortations 'to feare god… to be obedient to fa[th]er and mother…[and] to be thankfull to him [tha]t telleth hy[m] of hys fawtes'.[46] In keeping with Erasmus' instructions, Edward had also begun to read Aesop's fables, the proverbs of Solomon and Juan Luis Vives's compendium of worthy Latin sentences, *Satellitium animi, sive symbola*, dedicated to Princess Mary, which Edward quoted frequently.[47]

As Erasmus had advised, Edward VI's first compositional genre was the epistle. It offered the prince an opportunity to practice simple grammar, syntax and diction and to season the resulting periods with figures, tropes and sentences culled from his reading. Over forty-three holograph letters and contemporary copies survive from the period between 4 March 1545 and 19 September 1547. The prince cited Erasmus, Vives and the ancient authors they edited frequently in his earliest surviving efforts in Latin.[48] In 1546 he had acquired an octavo copy of Erasmus' *De conscribendis epistolis*, which was small enough to carry around with him as he moved between residences. The next year Edward received a copy of Erasmus' *De copia*, which he also used frequently in compositions. Cheke had complained that Cambridge had been full of slavish imitators of Erasmus' Latin style

44 BL, Harleian MS 1419A, fols. 133^r–135^r; Thomas Gemini, Horary quadrant (1551), brass, British Museum, London, no. 1858,0821.1.

45 BL, C.21.b.4.

46 SP 1/195, fol. 201^v; Richard Taverner (ed.),*Catonis disticha moralia ex castigatione D. Erasmi Roterdami* (London, 1540), STC 4843, sig. Aii^{r-v}.

47 Cox in Edward, *LR*, vol. 1, p. 3.

48 Edward, *LR*, vol. 1, pp. 1–53. For an example of Edward's use of sentences culled from Erasmus' works, cf. SP 1/195, fol. 201^v with Taverner, *Catonis disticha moralia*, sig. $Avii^v$.

but this did not stop him from encouraging his student prince to follow in their footsteps.[49]

The extent to which Erasmus' pedagogical prescriptions and literary models shaped Edward's writing may be seen in two Latin letters from 1546. The first, written on 9 April, is to Cox and the second, written on 8 May, is to Princess Mary. Both epistles consider the relationship between letters and affection. Erasmus had argued in *De conscribendis epistolis* that it would enhance a students' fluency and facility with language if they were required 'to present the same subject a second and a third time… to be treated in different words and with another form of expression'. He also proposed that the second presentation constitute a refutation of the first, since 'arguing against what you have just proposed' would enhance 'skill in invention'.[50] Thus Edward explained to Cox that his regular stream of letters 'is a sign that I love you, and remember you' and he claimed to Mary that his infrequent correspondence with her did not indicate that he was 'ungrateful to [his sister] or had forgotten [her]'.[51] Edward also demonstrated his grasp of argument by comparison, which Erasmus had described in *De conscribendis epistolis* and *De copia*, and which required him to use the subjunctive mood and *[a]ecque* constructions ('equally'). 'I pray that these letters are as sweet [*[a]ecque bene*] to you as others find hunting and hawking, for letters are the more precious treasure', he exhorted Cox, demonstrating that he had memorised the pedagogical priorities of northern humanism as well as this grammar point.[52] Erasmus' textbooks and editions of classical authors dominated the early stages of Edward's foray into Latin grammar and rhetoric. Indeed he quickly began to term his course of studies *bonae litterae*, mimicking Erasmus' preferred phrase for his curriculum.[53]

Edward's education continued in this Erasmian vein after Henry VIII's death and his own accession in 1547. From this point, if not before, it was Cheke, rather than Cox, who directed his studies. Edward began to read Lucian's dialogues and Isocrates' orations, probably in Erasmus'

[49] John Cheke, *De pronuntiatione Graecae potissimum linguae disputationes* (Basel, 1555), p. 262; Erasmus, *De conscribendis epistolis* (Antwerp, 1546), BL, 1083.e.6; Edward cited Erasmus' *De copia* when describing Cicero's eloquence to George Day, 25 January 1547, in Edward, *LR*, vol. 1, p. 37.

[50] Erasmus, *De conscribendis epistolis*, in *CWE: Literary and educational writings III*, p. 43.

[51] 'Cum scribam ad te, est signum me te amare, et tui meminisse' and 'nollem te putare me esse ingratum et tui oblivisci': Edward, *LR*, vol. 1, pp. 7, 8.

[52] 'Hortor te, ut literae sint aeque dulces tibi ac venatio et aucupium delectant alios. Literae enim sunt meliores thesauris': Edward, *LR*, vol. 1, p. 8; Erasmus, *De copia*, in *CWE: Literary and educational writings II*, pp. 641–4 and *De conscribendis epistolis*, in *CWE: Literary and educational writings III*, pp. 43–4, 145–9.

[53] Edward, *LR*, vol. 1, p. 18.

Latin translation.[54] Then on 4 January 1548 he began his intensive study of Cicero's *De officiis*. As Erasmus had recommended, Edward kept a record of 'phrases, and elegant sentences and words' from his reading and used them to amplify his arguments in compositions.[55] From 4 January until 9 July 1548, the young king worked five or six days a week at Cicero's *De officiis*, followed by his *De amicitia, De senectute* and *Paradoxes*.[56] Then, between 21 September and 14 November 1548, Edward continued his introduction to rhetoric with the *Tusculanae quaestiones* in another notebook, completing a lesson every day except Sunday.[57] The king completed most of the works printed in contemporary editions of Cicero's philosophical and oratorical works, as edited by Erasmus, Philip Melanchthon (1497–1560) and Johann Sturm.[58]

Even as Edward's religious studies were turning sharply towards Zurich and Geneva, Erasmus' prescriptions for *bonae litterae* continued to shape Edward's curriculum. Indeed, his studies also reflected the statutes of John Colet's school at St Paul's and Cox's Eton.[59] This should not surprise us. Pupils at English grammar schools in the sixteenth century were frequently destined for holy orders and the break from Rome merely accelerated this trend. In the prince's schoolroom, the effect of the royal supremacy was to render these grammatical and rhetorical skills prerequisite for kingship as well. John Cheke echoed the Dutch humanist when he warned Edward that the main difference in God's eyes between the king and the 'men of base estate, and of low degrees' who served him was that his 'chardge' was greater, and God would punish him more harshly if he failed to execute it well.[60]

From Erasmus' and Cheke's perspective, the study of Greek was critical to the 'chardge' of the princely defender of the New Testament. It might be surmised that it was Henry VIII who had held Edward back

54 Baldwin, *William Shakespere's smalle Latine*, vol. 1, pp. 200–56; Peter Mack, *Elizabethan rhetoric: Theory and practice* (Cambridge, 2002), pp. 27–31, 35; Edward, *LR*, vol. 1, p. 37; Paul S. Needham, 'Sir John Cheke at Cambridge and court', 2 vols. (Ph.D. dissertation, Harvard University, 1971), especially ch. 4.

55 'Phrases, elegantes sententias, et elegantia verba': Edward, *LR*, vol. 1, p. 15.

56 Bodleian, MS Arch F e.26: *De officiis* on fols. 5^r–53^v; *De amicitia* on fols. 54^r–62^v; *De senectute* on fol. 63^r; *De paradoxis* on fols. 63^v–66^v.

57 BL, Arundel MS 510, fols. 3^r–22^r.

58 For instance Cicero, *Ciceronis libri tres De officiis, De amicitia, De senectute, Paradoxa et De somnio Scipionis*, eds. Desiderius Erasmus *et al.* (Lyons, 1536) and *Ciceronis librorum philosophicorum libri*, ed. Johann Sturm, 2 vols. (Strasbourg, 1541); Baldwin, *William Shakespere's small Latine*, vol. 1, p. 230.

59 Alford, *Kingship and politics*, p. 44; Needham, 'Sir John Cheke at Cambridge and court', vol. 1, pp. 175, 226.

60 Cheke, 'Letter to Edward', in Edward, *LR*, vol. 1, p. clx.

from Greek studies, since Edward made rapid progress after 1547. He completed his study of Aristotle's *Dialectic* by the middle of December 1549 and began work on the *Ethics*. To assist his Latin–Greek translations, he began to locate Greek similes for Latin words from Cicero's *De finibus*, followed by the *Tusculanae disputationes* in August and September 1550.[61] Between February and August 1551, Edward read Plato's *Republic* and made notes on its phrases and arguments. Subsequently, he worked through Demosthenes' orations.[62] By this stage in his education, Edward was studying a little more rhetoric and a little less logic than a Cambridge undergraduate.[63]

The capacity to make a persuasive argument was the most important literary skill that Cheke taught Edward. From the first, his Latin and Greek translation exercises were intended to propel him from using language clearly and accurately, like a grammarian, to using it persuasively, as an orator.[64] When Edward translated Cicero's sentences and phrases, for instance, he did not do so word for word. While studying the *De amicitia* on 8 June 1548, for instance, he examined the following passage (XIII.48): 'For when the soul is deprived of emotion, what difference is there, I do not say between man and the beasts of the field, but between man and a tree trunk or a stone, or any such thing?'(*Quid enim interest motu animi sublato non dico inter pecudem et hominem, sed inter hominem et truncum aut saxum aut quidvis generis eiusdem?*) Edward's schoolfellow Barnaby rendered it freely as: 'When the soul is deprived of emotion, there is no difference between a man and a rock or tree trunk' (*Nihil interest inters hominem motu animi sublato & saxum aut truncum*). Edward, who was younger, missed the point of Cicero's gradations: 'When the soul is deprived of emotion, what is the difference between men and beasts?'

61 BL, Arundel MS 510, fols. 37v–38v; Bodleian, MS Bodley 899, fols. 1r–14v; Roger Ascham, *Whole works of Roger Ascham*, ed. J. A. Giles, 3 vols. (London, 1865), vol. I.ii, p. 226; Martin Bucer, *Original letters relative to the English Reformation, written during the reigns of King Henry VIII, King Edward IV and Queen Mary: Chiefly from the archives of Zurich*, ed. Hastings Robinson, 2 vols. (Cambridge, 1847), vol. II, p. 543; Foxe, *TAMO* [1563], p. 940.

62 Bodleian, MS Bodley 899, fols. 15r–19v; Needham, 'Sir John Cheke at Cambridge and court', vol. I, pp. 214–17.

63 BL, Additional MS 4724, fol. 15r; Baldwin, *William Shakespere's small Latine*, vol. I, pp. 234–5, 246–7; Lisa Jardine, 'The place of dialectic teaching in sixteenth-century Cambridge', *Studies in the Renaissance*, 21 (1974); Mack, *Elizabethan rhetoric*, p. 29.

64 For this humanist approach to translation, see Leonardo Bruni, *De interpretatione recta – De la traduction parfait*, trans. Charles Le Blanc (Ottawa, 2008), p. 68 and Etienne Dolet, *La Manière de bien traduire d'une langue en aultre* (Lyon, 1540), pp. 12–13, both citing Pseudo-Cicero, *De optimo genere oratorum*, IV.13–V.15. See too Erasmus, *Ciceronianus*, in *CWE: Literary and educational writings VI*, pp. 399–401.

(*Quid interest motu animi sublato inter hominem et pecudem?*)[65] The error probably occurred because Edward was making a double translation, a grammatical and rhetorical exercise that Cheke had made famous. Having read a passage from Cicero, Edward would have closed his book, translated the passage into English, then sometime later in the day converted his own English words back into Latin. Even if the results were not always perfect, the exercise would teach Edward 'to write… singularlie in bothe tongues'.[66] It would also require the king to internalise the meaning and logic of Cicero's claims in order to rewrite his prose in his own words. From an early age he was learning to assemble material for speech – the technique of *inventio*. In this respect, as we will see, Edward's translation practice differed sharply from Princess Mary's and, more surprisingly given their shared schoolmasters, Princess Elizabeth's.

Inventio would also prove central to the next compositional genre Edward tackled: the *chreia*, a 'brief commentary on something that someone related aptly' in a commonplace or literary example.[67] Edward's *chreia* adopted the traditional structure described in the rhetorical textbook Aphthonius' *Progymnasmata*: they began with praise of the author of the statement and continued with an explanation of the saying, an account of the causes that motivated the sentiment, a contrary point, a comparison or analogy to advance the case, an example of the saying, an antique commonplace supporting the saying and a brief epilogue.[68] Rhetorically, this prepared students for the longer and more demanding genre of the declamation. Politically, this offered the king an opportunity to demonstrate his grasp of Erasmus' account of Christian kingship.

In April 1548, for instance, Edward wrote a *chreia* on the sentence 'it behoves the king to rule with gentleness and mercy'. It was drawn from Isocrates' epideictic oration *Ad Nicocles*, which Erasmus, his pupil Giovanni Boerio and Thomas Elyot had all translated for Henry VIII. Edward interpreted Isocrates' claim in light of Erasmus' injunction to evaluate classical wisdom according to the standard set by Christ. Kings should rule with mildness and gentleness, Edward argued, because they

[65] Bodleian, MS Arch F e. 26, fol. 58r (Edward) and fol. 73v (Barnaby); see Needham, 'Sir John Cheke at Cambridge and court', vol. 1, p. 185.

[66] Quotation from William Cecil in Henry Harrington and Thomas Park (eds.), *Nugae antiquae*, 2 vols. (London, 1804), vol. 1, pp. 133–4; see also Ascham, *Scholemaster*, sigs. C1v–C2r.

[67] 'Chreia est commemoratio brevis ad aliquam personam appositae relationem habens': Aphthonius, *Progymnasmata, idest praeexercitationes rhetorum & Luciani Opusculum de componenda historia*, ed. G. M. Cattaneo (Venice, 1546), sig. Aiir (quotation); Erasmus, *De copia*, in CWE*: Literary and educational writings II*, p. 589; Mack, *Elizabethan rhetoric*, pp. 28–30.

[68] Aphthonius, *Progymnasmata*, sig. Aiiir–v.

were 'appointed and elected by God' to provide 'civil order and laws, by which [His people] might live quietly and tranquilly'.[69] If the king imitated God's just and benevolent government on earth, his subjects would 'imitate and follow the manners of those who rule, govern and lead them… like sheep'. If the king behaved honourably the people would be 'possessed, adorned, and imbued with… all the other virtues' too.[70] Even more critically,

> if the king and administrator of the commonwealth grant and exhibit the highest favour to true and pure religion and to the teachings of God and Christ his son, then that religion and teaching will strengthen and endure for all time.[71]

Otherwise, God would make 'just and righteous censure and correction' of those kings whose 'cruelty' made them 'hostile to all virtue'.[72] This particular *chreia* was undoubtedly set so that Edward could practice certain grammatical constructions, such as 'not only… but also', and learn to render New Testament and classical Greek virtues, such as *πραότης* (*praotēs*) as *clementia* and *mansuetudo* in Latin. The composition also showed that Edward could reproduce Erasmus' argument that the imitation of Christ would encourage princes to moderate their rule and exercise care for their subjects' souls.

The king's proficiency at *chreia* demonstrated his readiness to continue, in 1550, to the ultimate rhetorical exercise in the *Progymnasmata*, the deliberative declamation in Greek and Latin. He would take notes on Thursday and Saturday and deliver an oration on Sunday that showed his capacity to argue *in utramque partem*, 'on both sides' of a moral or political question. If travel or government business had to be undertaken, his studies were not suspended or delayed; he would simply speak a day early.[73] In 1552, Edward moved on to theological topics, arguing that man was not created with free will, that men could not perform God's will without

69 'Est officium et munus eius, qui gerit gubernacula quique constitutus et designates est a Deo… ad designandum et constituendum ordinem civilem et leges quibus vivere possent quiete et tranquille… quod munus qui non recte nec secundum voluntatem Dei': Edward, *LR*, vol. 1, pp. 119–20.

70 'Populus sit (sic)… omnibusque aliis virtutibus praeditus et exornatus imbutusque… Semper sequitur et imitatur mores eius (sic) qui eos regunt et gubernant ducuntque… veluti oves': Edward, *LR*, vol. 1, p. 121.

71 'Si enim rex et administrator reipublicae favorem summum praebeat et ostendat verae et purae religioni et disciplinae Dei Christique eius filii, quae disciplina et religio in omnia secula durabit et manebit': Edward, *LR*, vol. 1, p. 121.

72 'Justa et recta animadversio et castigatio Dei… Sed cum rex non prosequator amore Deum, sed omni crudelitate inimica omnium virtutum': Edward, *LR*, vol. 1, p.123.

73 BL Additional MS 4724, fols. 215^r, 216^r; Needham, 'Sir John Cheke at Cambridge and court', vol. 1, pp. 217–18; Markku Peltonen, *Rhetoric, politics and popularity in pre-revolutionary England* (Cambridge, 2013), pp. 68–70.

the benefit of His grace and that the reformed doctrine of predestination should be openly preached in churches.[74] On these questions, Edward adopted confessional positions that were not Erasmus' any more than they were Henry VIII's. Yet the orations also show that Edward VI had learnt the grammatical and rhetorical skills that his father had employed John Cheke and Richard Cox to teach him. The boy-king was developing the capacity to defend his church, champion its (new) doctrine and maintain the royal supremacy with his pen.

Quentin Skinner has wondered whether teaching boys to argue *in utramque partem* may have encouraged moral relativism in humanist schoolrooms.[75] Cheke argued, however, that in princes the technique cultivated dispassionate reasoning and discouraged prideful decision-making. He told Somerset in 1549 that he was teaching Edward 'to avoide… that self-pleasing that the Greeks do call *φιλαυτια*' (*philautia*, self-love). Making a list of points for and against an action would help Edward to understand that his opinion was not an objective truth, or even the only way. He would learn 'in his youthe, [that] whiche Socrates belived in when he was olde, that he knoweth this onlye thinge, that yet he knew nothing'. Cheke urged Edward that, when he came into his majority, he should 'contynewed to be an Academike', who was 'slow to iudge, gladd to here all men mistrusting his owne reason, taking trouthe to be hidden'.[76] Edward had put this lesson into practice in early 1548 when the Lord Admiral, Thomas Seymour (*c.* 1508–49), pressed him to sign a bill that would remove his brother Somerset as royal governor in favour of Seymour. Despite Edward's affection for his generous, witty uncle, the ten-year-old 'desyred [the Lord Admiral] to lett me alone in that matter'. Later, Cheke confirmed 'ye were not best to wryght' and commended Edward for suspecting Seymour's motives.[77]

Intellectual vanity was particularly dangerous in 'a publique person', Cheke warned, because it was liable to result in arbitrary rule. One who 'delighteth in his own reason' was likely to 'despyseth other mens conseill'. As a minor, Edward was obliged to heed his advisers and his governor, Somerset, above all. Cheke assured the protector that he had prepared the

74 BL, Additional MS 4724, fols. 52^r–57^r, 60^r–61^r, 116^r, 118^r, 146^r–153^r.

75 Quentin Skinner, *Reason and rhetoric in the philosophy of Hobbes* (Cambridge, 1996), pp. 9–10, 15–16; Mack, *Elizabethan rhetoric*, pp. 188–202.

76 Cheke in Edward, *LR*, vol. I, p. ccxlvi. Cheke cites Cicero, *De officiis*, I.18 and Plato, *Republic*, I, 354c. Cicero, *Letters to Atticus*, XIII.13.1 uses *φιλαυτια* to describe the intellectual pride of the author; see also Stephen Alford, *Burghley: William Cecil at the court of Elizabeth I* (New Haven, 2008), p. 192.

77 HHCP, 150/51.

king to confer 'with many wise heads, and... divers good counsells' and take advice from 'men of experience', even when he came into his majority.[78] In May 1552, he reminded Edward to beware flatterers and cherish those counsellors who 'shall francklye admonishe' him.[79] Of course, Cheke's prescriptions were self-interested; his own political future would depend on Edward's willingness to retain him as a secretary. Yet Cheke was also appealing to a humanist discourse, popularised in England by Erasmus and his circle, which posited that good counsel was a critical brake on over-mighty monarchy.[80] According to this mode of thinking, a careful princely education was the bridesmaid to a governor's receptivity to advice and his willingness to rule moderately and wisely.

Cheke also argued that certain antique authors and disciplines were better at cultivating dispassionate, cautious political judgement than others. In December 1550 he explained to Roger Ascham that he thought that moral philosophy, such as Aristotle's *Politics*, and scripture offered the prince the best instruction 'in the universal and infinite precepts and divisions of vice and virtue'. A ruler would develop 'good judgement in singular examples of moral questions' quite naturally if he began with broader, seemingly obtuse cases proposed by philosophers. In contrast, Cheke worried that, if 'the edge of wit' was 'blunted and softened by the sweetness of reading history', it would be harder to move from specific applications discussed by Xenophon and others to general principles of judgement and decision-making.[81]

The particular 'universals' and 'deeper truths' Cheke wanted to impress upon Edward were about matters on which one could not argue *in utramque partem*; they were his duties as a godly monarch. In 1552, when Cheke thought he was dying, he sent Edward a letter in which he urged Edward to 'have before your eyes continuallye the fear of God' and to keep reading the New Testament, the Book of Wisdom and Ecclesiasticus, and the Proverbs, all of which Erasmus had endorsed as particularly suitable for princes. Cheke also echoed Erasmus in recommending Aristotle's

78 Cheke in Edward, *LR*, vol. 1, p. ccxlvi.

79 Edward, *LR*, vol. 1, p. clx.

80 John Guy, 'The rhetoric of counsel in early modern England', in Dale Hoak (ed.), *Tudor political culture* (Cambridge, 1995), pp. 294–6; Jacqueline Rose, 'Kingship and counsel in early modern England', *HJ*, 54:1 (2011).

81 'Respondet, ut mens, inquit, eius prius universis illis et infinitis virtutum vitiorumque praeceptionibus ac partitionibus instructa, firmum iudicium adferat ad singula quotidianorum morum exempla, quae in historiis latissime sese fundunt. Et quia vix fieri potest, ut ingenii acies, in initio, dulcedine historiarum emollita et obtusa, penetret in abstrusas illas et reconditas, sed pernecessarias ad corroborandum iudicium finitae quaestionis comprehensiones: quanquam nullum praeceptum sine appositione insignis exempli tradi cupio': Ascham, *Whole works*, vol. 1.ii, p. 226.

Politics but he was more specific about which bits the prince should focus on, namely chapters ten and eleven in the fifth book, particularly, 'the one *de mutatione regni* and the other *per quae regna servantur*'.[82] These were the parts of the *Politics* in which Aristotle held forth on the causes of the destruction and protection of monarchy. In particular, the Greek philosopher proposed that monarchy was 'preserved by the limitation of its powers'. Indeed, 'the more restricted the functions of kings, the longer their power will last unimpaired'.[83] Like Erasmus, Cheke used moral philosophy and biblical precept to teach his princely student that it was honourable and useful to govern himself, to limit the extent of his authority over others and to replace the instruction of the schoolmaster with the council of advisers.

Edward's pen was to be both his sword and crozier, and it was Erasmus' curriculum of Greek and Latin authors for Christian princes that had showed him the way. Unlike his sisters, he was given the rhetorical skills to fight his corner from the beginning. Cheke used various pedagogical techniques to encourage Edward to moderate the exercise of his authority. It had taken twenty years and the break from Rome, but the priorities of the royal schoolroom had been inverted. In the education of Edward VI at least, northern humanists' appeal to princes to prioritise *bonae litterae* over arms had been heeded.

NO KING OF DUST: LIBERAL EDUCATION AND POLITICAL DISCOURSE

The copiousness of Edward VI's literary exercises, the zeal of his tutors and the prince's apparent failure to rebel against them have puzzled modern historians. Some have gone so far as to describe Edward's education as a hothouse that produced the king's swift bloom and premature demise. T. W. Baldwin lamented that Cheke and Cox had made this docile, uncomplaining boy 'a godly king' but 'a king of dust'.[84] More recent biographies have paid lip service to Edward's academic achievements and proceeded to assume that the king's studies had little impact on real

[82] Cheke in Edward, *LR*, vol. I, p. clx.

[83] Aristotle, *Politics*, V.10, 1312b35–1313a5, 1313a15–20, trans. from Aristotle, *The politics and constitution of Athens*, trans. Jonathan Barnes, ed. Stephen Everson (Cambridge, 1996), pp. 144, 145.

[84] Baldwin, *William Shakespere's small Latine*, vol. I, p. 256. See also Hester Chapman, *The last Tudor king: a study of Edward VI* (London, 1958), p. 50; Anthony Grafton and Lisa Jardine, *From humanism to the humanities: Education and the liberal arts in fifteenth- and sixteenth-century Europe* (Cambridge, MA, 1986), p. 156; W. K. Jordan, 'Introduction', in Edward, *CPP*, p. xxiv.

politics.[85] Without troubling to secure the safety harness of documentary evidence, Geoffrey Elton claimed that 'Edward demonstrably was copying other people's drafts' when he wrote about government. To Dale Hoak, the king was a 'bright, pathetic lad' and his apparent acts of political expression merely parroted existing arrangements.[86] Few historians have been willing to entertain the possibility that Edward's education prepared him to actively engage in the debates of his reign.[87]

Let us not be too hasty to declare Edward's education, and humanist pedagogy more generally, stultifying or entirely removed from the cut and thrust of government. It is true that modern methods for teaching language and the humanities have moved away from Renaissance humanists' emphasis on memorisation and imitation, but this should not blind us to its pedagogical merits. Children are still drawn to activities that require them to imitate, memorise extensively and perform virtually countless repetitions – ballet, spelling bees and playing cricket, baseball and musical instruments. There is pleasure to be had in mimicry, in conquering a skill or piece of knowledge and in error-free performance, particularly when there are cultural rewards for success. In early modern Europe, liberal education channelled this predilection into the study of Latin, Greek and classical authors. Admittedly, Pieter Bruegel the Elder's satirical pen and ink drawing of 'The Ass in School' (1556) suggests that humanist methods could no more turn a hostile child to learning than they could turn a donkey into a horse. Yet Edward's school exercises show us that humanist pedagogy could arrest the attention of a child who had some natural ability and plenty of support and who was motivated to succeed. The prince's schoolbooks show his readiness to use his learning to think about politics.

From May 1549, religious change and the economic woes of enclosure, inflation, poor harvests, food shortages, national debt and devaluation of the coinage were fanning the flames of rebellion in England's south, west and midlands. In addition to demonstrating the limits of government control in the localities and the unpopularity of the new prayer book in the west, the cost of crushing the commotions was over £28,000 (more than £7 million in modern currency).[88]

The revolts had also drawn men, money and mercenaries from Somerset's garrisons in Scotland and mitigated his ability to prosecute the war with

[85] See the treatment in Loach, *Edward VI*, pp. 9–16, 39; Skidmore, *Edward VI*, pp. 6–7, 31–9, 95.

[86] Elton, *Reform and reformation*, p. 372; Hoak, *King's council*, p. 265.

[87] Notable exceptions are Alford, *Kingship and politics*, pp. 55–6, 160–1, 163; MacCulloch, *Tudor church militant*, pp. 20–40.

[88] Andy Wood, *The 1549 rebellions and the making of early modern England* (Cambridge, 2007).

France.[89] When the commons protested religious reform, as they did in Devon and Cornwall, the evangelical establishment presented a unified front, articulated in texts such as John Cheke's *Hurt of sedicion* (1549): 'commotioners' who claimed to be prosecuting 'Goddes causes' had, in fact, broken 'Goddes commaundeme[n]te' that subjects should obey their kings. Similarly commoners who pretended to arise for the 'sake of the commenwelth' were actually 'destroy[ing] the commune welth' with their sedition.[90] Their unlawful, destructive and ungodly conduct warranted a rapid and harsh governmental response.

In Norfolk, however, Robert Kett's (1492–1549) rebellion divided the Privy Council. These rebels loudly proclaimed their love for the gospel and protested that God's word and Somerset's own policies had authorised their complaints against local landowners, enclosure and the high cost of living. Like the Swabian peasants in Germany in 1524 and 1525, they united their religious and economic grievances.[91] In their manifesto, Kett's men appealed to a 'commonwealth language' that had been employed by Somerset and his circle in attempts to compensate for his anomalous claims to political authority. The protector and clients including the preacher Hugh Latimer, the enclosures' commissioner John Hales and his secretary, Thomas Smith, courted popularity by describing economic reforms that favoured the commons (such as the removal of enclosures) as springing from the same font as religious reform.[92] In his 1549 draft instructions to the lord president of the Council of the North, for instance, Somerset required him to 'inculcate' the 'most Godly service' of the new prayer book and simultaneously ensure that 'the poor people be not oppressed' by 'the richest or greatest Lord' in their locality.[93] When Kett's commons began to use the 'language of the commonwealth' to

[89] Susan Doran, *England and Europe in the sixteenth century* (Houndmills, 1999), p. 35.

[90] John Cheke, *The hurt of sedicion howe greueous it is to a commune welth* (London, 1549), STC 5109, sig. Aiii^{v}. See also St John's College, Cambridge, MS D107.3, fols. 235^{r}–257^{r} cited in Richard Rex, 'Lady Margaret Beaufort and her professorships: 1502–1559', in Patrick Collinson, Richard Rex and Graham Stanton (eds.), *Lady Margaret Beaufort and her professors of divinity at Cambridge, 1502–1649* (New York, 2003); see also [Thomas Cranmer], *A message sent by the kynges maiestie, to certain of his people, assembled in Deuonshire* (London, 1549), STC 7506, sigs. Aiii^{r}, Av^{r}, Bvi^{v}, Bvii^{v}.

[91] Diarmaid MacCulloch, 'Kett's rebellion in context', *P&P*, 84 (1979); Nicholas Tyacke, 'Introduction: Re-thinking the "English Reformation"', in Nicholas Tyacke (ed.), *England's long reformation* (London, 1998), pp. 13–19.

[92] Steve Hindle, *The state and social change in early modern England, c. 1550–1640* (Basingstoke, 2002), p. 255; Ethan Shagan, *Popular politics and the English Reformation* (Cambridge, 2003), pp. 275–86 and 'Protector Somerset and the 1549 rebellions: New sources and new perspectives', *EHR*, 114 (1999); Philip Withington, *Society in early modern England: The vernacular origins of some powerful ideas* (Cambridge, 2010), p. 140.

[93] SP 15/3, fols. 99^{r}–101^{r} cited by Shagan, *Popular politics and the English Reformation*, p. 277.

justify their uprising, Somerset's response was mixed. On a number of occasions, however, he wrote letters that acknowledged the validity of the commons' complaints, granted considerable concessions, promised a parliament to address their grievances and pardoned rebels who were still in arms.[94] The protector seemed to hope that maintaining his commonwealth rhetoric would appease and pacify the Norfolk multitude, enabling him to get on with the real business of fighting Scotland and France.

Other privy counsellors disagreed with Somerset's gentle treatment of the commons and the division would ultimately trigger the coup against the protector in October 1549. William Paget, comptroller of the royal household and Somerset's erstwhile ally, had written to the duke on 7 July 1549 to insist that appeasement would only increase the length and severity of the commotions. The German peasants, Paget noted, might have been put down with the loss of twenty men. Yet 'some spiced consciences', who were intent on 'taking pity of the poor' and especially tender towards poor men who were possessed 'of a godly knowledge... suffered the matter to run so far' that it had cost 'a thousand or two thousand men's lives' to put down the rebellion.[95] 'Force and terrour' were what was required against the revolting commoners, a strategy that John Dudley, then earl of Warwick, and his mercenary army eventually employed with success in Norwich. In April Paget had advised the Privy Council that Somerset should abandon his campaigns against Scotland and France and send the troops south for 'the conservacion of the state of the realm here at home'. 'For what availeth yt to seke to wynne foreyne realms, and to lose your owne wherein youe dwell?', he asked.[96] Paget repeated this counsel in July. Somerset had too 'many irons in the fire'. Moreover, Paget alleged that he had brought the commotions on himself by continuing to court popularity with the fickle 'multitude'. Now 'the foot taketh upon him the part of the head, and commyns is become a king'.[97] A motley rabble of French, Scots and commotioners was closing in and the king's councillors were divided as to whether the political language that had shaped the political

[94] See the letters printed by Ethan Shagan, 'Protector Somerset and the 1549 rebellions', pp. 53–63. M. L. Bush, *The government policy of Protector Somerset* (Montreal, 1975), pp. 87–99 also identified a number of instances in which Somerset issued pardons and concessions, though he regarded them as temporary manoeuvres.

[95] BL, Cotton MS Titus B III, fols. 277^r–279^v; SP 10/8/4 as printed in John Strype (ed.), *Ecclesiastical memorials relating chiefly to religion and the reformation of it and the emergencies of the Church of England under King Henry VIII, King Edward VI and Queen Mary I*, 4 vols. (Oxford, 1822), vol. II. ii, pp. 431, 432, 435.

[96] William Paget, 'The letters of William Lord Paget of Beaudesert, 1547–63', in *Camden Miscellany*, vol. xxv, eds. B. L. Beer and S. M. Jack (London, 1974), p. 31.

[97] Strype (ed.), *Ecclesiastical memorials*, vol. II.ii, pp. 430, 431, 432.

culture of the first two years of Edward's reign was the cause of or the solution to their predicament.

In his *Chronicle* and in two declamations written in July 1549, Edward VI grappled with this question using the rhetorical tools of his Erasmian education. The *Chronicle* offers a fast-paced Livy-like account of the summer that integrates the domestic tumults with the French and Scottish campaigns. In his description of the first revolts that had spread from Essex to Somerset, the king noted with approval that his protesting 'people' had been 'appeased' in several instances 'by fair persuasions, partly of honest men among themselves and partly by gentlemen', and by royal commissions 'sent… to pluck down enclosures' that had privatised common land in their districts.[98] He expressed concern for the welfare of the common sort and pleasure that his people's complaints had been answered without violence. The king was significantly less sympathetic to rebels in Cornwall and Devonshire who were complaining about the imposition of the *Book of common prayer* (1549). He had no hesitation in branding these men 'rebels' and recorded the campaign against them, led by John Russell, the Lord Privy Seal, with righteous indignation.[99] By the time of his account of the Norfolk commotions in July and August, Edward recognised that civil disorder was dangerously infectious. Kett's 'rebels' had tainted the Norwich townspeople with their 'mischief'. Nevertheless, the king was still concerned at the viciousness with which John Dudley, earl of Warwick, had slaughtered over two thousand of Kett's men with his mercenary forces and left Norwich's fortifications 'so weak' that 'he could scarcely defend' the town after he had won it.[100] Edward was an avid follower of the Scottish war, launched to enforce the Treaty of Greenwich (1543) and nominally to abolish 'the bishop of Romes usurped iurisdiction' in Scotland.[101] The king recorded that the campaign had begun decisively with around six thousand Scots slaughtered at the Battle of Pinkie. Then thousands of French troops arrived at Leith in June 1548 to support their auld allies. They spirited away the Scottish queen and Somerset began to lose his garrisons, one by one. Edward recorded the English attempts to 'manfully' repulse the French siege of Boulogne in May 1548. Then, on 8 August, Henri II (1519–59) declared war on England proper.[102]

[98] Edward, *CPP*, pp. 12–13. [99] Edward, *CPP*, pp. 12–14.
[100] Edward, *CPP*, pp. 15–16; Wood, *The 1549 Rebellions*, p. 30.
[101] Printed in Marcus Merriman, *The rough wooings: Mary Queen of Scots, 1542–1551* (East Linton, 2000), p. 275.
[102] Bush, *Government policy of Protector Somerset*, pp. 7–39; Edward, *CPP*, pp. 7–8, 12–13, 16.

The king's relatively private thoughts on these conflicts evolved into a more significant piece of political writing in the final weeks of July. Cheke set Edward the task of composing two orations on the theme of war. His declamations constituted an intervention in the debate between Somerset and Paget that had divided his Privy Council. As usual, Edward was required to argue *in utramque partem*; however, his effort from 21 July was relatively perfunctory. It took its prompt from a line in one of Horace's odes, 'It is sweet and honourable to die for one's country' (III.2.13). Edward affirmed that, since death came to all men, it was most glorious to use one's life to defend country, parents and friends against invaders or rebels. He noted, moreover, that, if the cause of the war was religion, 'as it often was these days', then 'what could be more worthy, for pious and godly men, than to suffer to the utmost rather than deny their God, their faith, and their true and correct opinion of the Lord?' This was, however, as long as God's cause and the prince's were aligned.[103] In essence, Edward's first declamation reproduced his council's united opposition to the western uprising.

The next week, however, the king wrote a much longer and more rhetorically sophisticated declamation that took its cue from Erasmus' *Dulce bellum inexpertis* (1515), the very adage that the humanist had used to pour scorn on the bellicose enthusiasms of Henry VIII. Edward began by appealing to some of Erasmus' striking metaphors to describe the destructive forces of war. Then he made it clear that he intended to discuss the humanist's adage in relation to recent struggles 'in England, France, Scotland, Spain, and Germany'. Charles V came under fire for his cruelty against 'our particular neighbours', the German Protestants, and for allowing Rome, the eternal city, to be 'sacked and burnt' in 1527.[104] Yet the Hapsburg emperor was not the only sixteenth-century prince that Edward criticised for unleashing the destructive force of war. 'In the time of my predecessor', Henry VIII, he asked, 'how many people, how many

[103] 'Si enim hostes sint invasuri patriam, quid praeclarius quam eam defendere, protegere, et tueri? Si causa sit religio, ut in hodiernis bellis saepe fit, tum quid dignius piis santisque viris, quam omnia pati potius quam deserere suum Deum, suam fidem, suam veritatem, et rectam opinionem de Deo? Si vero causa sit principis sui…nihil est nobilius, nec praestantius, quam principi suo obedire, parere, inservire': Edward, *LR*, vol. I, p. III.

[104] 'Non solum Anglia, Gallia, Scotia, Hispania, Germaniaque… sed etiam Italia', 'omnes Germani, praecipueque nobis vicini… vastatae erant iam pridem a militibus imperatoris' and 'ille dux Burgoniensis totam Romam spoliauit combussitque; atque antehac illa ipsa urbs a Gothis Vandalisque erat direpta': Edward, *LR*, vol. I, pp. 113, 114; cf. Erasmus, *CWE: Adages III vi 1 to IV ii 100*, pp. 405, 406. Charles V was the duke of Burgundy from 1506. His forces in Rome in 1527 were led by Charles III, duke of Bourbon, whom Edward may have conflated with the emperor in this passage.

towns and homes were burned, razed, and destroyed in Scotland?'[105] Just as Edward had questioned Dudley's brutality towards Norwich in his *Chronicle*, he did not shy away from pointing out that his father's rough wooings had destroyed much of Scotland's value as an imperial possession. Somerset's Scottish campaigns had also cost the English treasury dear. 'Great sums of money have been spent on the fleet, the army, and other munitions against the Scots and the French', Edward complained.[106] In fact the king adopted the protector's rhetoric – the language of the mutual interdependence of the sorts in England – to describe the deleterious economic and political effect of wars on the commonwealth. The princes of nations

> send all their treasure, goods, riches, and properties over that abyss of war; nobles... are shaken from their estates... The fortunes of merchants in war is dire, for when the ships of war scatter and sail over the sea, then the way of trade is not safe from peril... If artisans cannot sell their goods to those from a foreign country who come to buy them... you will see what poverty and penury affects them

Those already poor have 'no hour without hunger' in times of conflict. The culminating effect of such hardship was social disorder.[107] Unlike Paget, Edward did not claim that commonwealth discourse had licensed licentiousness amongst the meaner sorts. Rather he implied that the resources that Henry VIII and Somerset had sunk into their foreign wars had contributed to England's internal disruptions in 1549.

Having argued for war's lack of utility, Edward moved on, in Ciceronian fashion, to claim that fighting was not honourable. The notion of a godly rebel was, for Edward, an oxymoron. It was only when 'we rail at this tumult and follow peace instead... that we may please the Lord our God'.[108] 'Bravery may be shown in rebellion', Edward conceded, 'but neither sedition nor he who moves a subject against his prince is

[105] 'In Scotia vero quot nationes, quot villae domusque combustae, subversae, deletaeque erant... tempus mihi ante': Edward, *LR*, vol. 1, p. 113.

[106] 'Notum est, quanta vis pecuniae in classibus, exercitibus, et aliis munitionibus bellicis contra Scotos Gallosque est impensa': Edward, *LR*, vol. 1, p. 113.

[107] 'Principes... totum suum thesauram, omnia sua bona, omnesque divitias et facultates in illam belli voraginem mittunt. Nobiles... sedibus moveantur...mercatorum in bello est pessima fortuna. Cum enim bellicae naves in mari evagentur et navigent, tum via mercatorem non est tuta a periculo... Artifices vero si sua vendere nec illa quae ex aliena patria veniunt emere possunt, quo tandem incommode, qua paupertate, quaque penuria affici eos putabitis', 'sunt nulla hora... pauperes sine fame': Edward, *LR*, vol. 1, pp. 114–15.

[108] 'Hunc tumultum insectamur, et sequamur pacem... ut domino Deo nostro placere possimus': Edward, *LR*, vol. 1, p. 115; Erasmus, *CWE: Adages III vi 1 to IV ii 100*, pp. 430–3.

honourable'.[109] The king had no wish to appease rebellious subjects, as Somerset had done, but nor did he follow Paget in blaming the commotions on leniency towards the commons. Rather, Edward proposed strengthening the connection between religious reform and the common good. Instead of continuing 'to burn up nations, lay waste to kingdoms, ruin kings and obliterate regions', he thought that the English should redirect their efforts heavenwards, and 'follow and seek out Him, with all our hearts'. Wealth and territorial expansion were 'not really driven by war but affected by the favour and clemency of God'.[110] God would deny the English nothing abroad, Edward suggested, if they attended to the purification of religion at home.

Edward's declamation against war was undoubtedly a school exercise. Yet contemporaries were convinced it relayed his political opinion sincerely. According to John Foxe, who hints that he had his information from Cox, Edward was keenly affected by the plight of the commons and insisted on managing the 'dispatche of poore mennes suites' personally each week.[111] This was probably an exaggeration, but Edward spoke the language of the commonwealth fluently enough that Foxe's praise could stick. His declamation was not the product of a docile mind broken by rote-learning and over-exertion, or a pedantic pedagogy ill-suited to shape its pupil's political outlook. If Edward was a hothouse plant, he rewarded his schoolmasters' care and attention by flowering spectacularly. With their encouragement, Edward used his July 1549 school exercises to ruminate on England's contemporary military and political predicament.

We should not exaggerate Edward's political sophistication but we should give the twelve-year-old credit for composing a response to the tumults that did not parrot either Paget's or Somerset's positions. Indeed he was implicitly critical of both men's perspectives. He complained about the Scottish campaigns of his father and Somerset. Yet he refused to follow Paget in disavowing commonwealth discourse. His conclusion, moreover, was insightful: the revolts that were engulfing the south and east of England in 1549 were not unconnected with the high cost of fighting the 'auld alliance' in the 1540s. The king's liberal education was teaching him

[109] 'Nam audacia monstratur a rebellibus; sed tamen seditio, et ille motus subditorem contra principem, non est honestus': Edward, *LR*, vol. 1, p. 116; Cheke, *Hurt of sedicion*, sig. Avii^{v}.

[110] 'Fortasse bellum prodesse patriae, quia facit latius patere imperium. At illud non bellum, sed favor et clementia Dei affert. Belli enim propria est natura nationes comburere, regna vastare, reges spoliare, et regiones penitus delere. Favor autem et clementia divina iis qui eum sequuntur, et toto corde investigant, donat victoriam et praemium': Edward, *LR*, vol. 1, pp. 116–17.

[111] Foxe, *TAMO* [1563], p. 941.

how to discover and articulate his perspective on contemporary questions using the dominant political language of his reign. Edward's Erasmian education was giving him the capacity to fight with his pen and speak on the world's stage.

DEFENDING THE REFORMED FAITH

The royal supremacy meant that the play at hand was religious and ecclesiastical. As Cranmer explained in his *Homilies* (1547), princes received their 'power & strength, not fro[m] Rome, but immediatly of god highest' so they needed to be 'dilige[n]tely taught, to apply the[m]selfes, to knowledge & wisedom, necessary for the orderynge of Gods people, to their gouernau[n]ce committed'.[112] Henry VIII and Cranmer had seen eye to eye on the significance of the royal supremacy for Edward's education but the boy's father is unlikely to have approved of the religious reforms that Cranmer championed after his demise. After 1547, however, it was critical that Edward VI understand and publically endorse the reforms being carried out in his name. His schoolmasters and French tutor, Jean Belmaine (fl. 1546–59), a follower of Jean Calvin (1509–64) who had been recruited from Princess Elizabeth's household, began to instruct him in evangelical doctrine using a variety of school exercises. We have seen that Henry VIII and the duke of Richmond proved impervious to their teachers' attempts to use liberal education to inculcate ideology. Edward's early compositions, however, suggest that his schoolmasters were considerably more successful.

From February 1547, Cranmer encouraged the clique of churchmen and counsellors who had risen to prominence with Protector Somerset to direct the church towards more coherently reformed doctrine. The process was slow and indirect.[113] As the 1549 revolts in the western counties show, it aroused hostility amongst various sorts, both lay and clerical. One of the weaknesses in the evangelical establishment's case for further reform was Edward's youth. In the last days of Henry VIII's reign, John Feckenham (*c.* 1510–84), who would become Mary I's chaplain and confessor, urged his listeners at St Paul's Cross against allowing anyone under thirty to 'preach or have regiment' in England.[114] He was canny enough not to quote Ecclesiastes 10:16, 'O woe to the land when the king is a

[112] [Thomas Cranmer] *Certayne sermons, or homelies appoynted by the kynges maiestie* (London, 1547), STC 13640, sig. RII^r; see Deuteronomy 17:19.
[113] MacCulloch, *Tudor church militant*, pp. 57–8.
[114] SP 1/228, fol. 54^r.

child', but his meaning was clear enough. Stephen Gardiner, bishop of Winchester, argued that Cranmer and Somerset could not make substantive changes to Henry VIII's ecclesiastical polity during his successor's minority.[115] Between 1547 and 1550, traditionalists from Edmund Bonner (d. 1569), bishop of London, to the Devonshire rebels and Princess Mary reiterated this argument whenever they were exhorted to adopt reformed modes of worship.

By way of retort, Edward's godly preachers turned to Old Testament rulers Joash (2 Kings 11–12) and Josiah to insist on a minor-king's right, indeed his responsibility, to purify God's temple.[116] As Hugh Latimer argued to the court in his *Second sermon* of Lent 1549, these examples proved that 'a kynge in hys childehode is a kynge, as well as in any other age'. Further, England's godly king was supported by 'noble counsaylours' and 'excellent and well learned Scholemasters' who took 'payne… for the settynge forthe of Gods word, and profit of the co[m]mune wealth'. These advisers had also worked to ensure that 'Hys maiestye hath more Godlye wytte and understanding, more lernynge and knowledge at thys age, then xx of hys progenitors… at anye tyme of theyr lyfe'.[117] On a discursive level, Edward's erudition was used to justify the religious reforms carried out in his name. Erasmus had argued that the careful institution of princes would bridle over-mighty monarchy. During the reign of a minor sovereign, however, education and good counsel were used to buttress the authority of a weak ruler to an audience of febrile subjects.

It was politically important, then, to fast-track Edward's evangelical education. In this endeavour reformed preachers joined with Edward's schoolmasters, who were now at liberty to let their confessional flags fly up the mast of the ship of state. Prior to his accession, Edward had not read anything more radical than those books of the Bible that Erasmus recommended for Christian princes. After 1547 scripture became Edward's passport to the study of reformed doctrine. This did not represent a complete break with his previous studies. Edward VI's preachers and polemicists generally celebrated Erasmus as a proponent of scripture-reading, faith and piety; as a critic of corrupt popes, monks and priests; and as a scourge of superstition and idolatrous ritual. They were particularly eager to use

[115] Gardiner, *Letters of Stephen Gardiner*, p. 265.

[116] John Hooper, *Oversight, and deliberacion upon the holy Prophete Jonas* (London, 1550), STC 13763, sigs. +3^v–+5^r; For example Alford, *Kingship and politics*, p. 36.

[117] Hugh Latimer, *Seconde sermon of Maister Hughe Latimer, which he preached before the kynges majestie* (London, 1549), STC 15274.7, sigs. Cii^r, Cii^v–Ciii^r, Ciii^v–Civ^r.

his *Paraphrases* to cultivate religious reform in England.[118] Nevertheless, Bible study took on a new function within Edward's schooling after his accession. Rather than simply reading God's word to learn to live piously, as Erasmus had instructed, Edward was also studying scripture to make arguments. According to Martin Bucer (1491–1551), the Strasburg reformer whom Cranmer invited to be Regius Professor of Theology in Cambridge in 1549, the king was reading ten Bible chapters a day by May 1550.[119] Edward started to make notebooks of *loci* drawn from his biblical reading, much like the compendiums maintained by Cranmer himself, on topics relating ecclesiastical power and theological controversies. The king was laying down a storehouse of biblical authorities that he could use to defend his church in future speeches, letters and treatises.[120]

In December 1548 Edward presented Somerset with a 'compendium of the principal places of Holy Scripture that consider faith in God' that he had translated from the English Bible into French. He explained that these scriptural places would help him to 'fight against the enemies of God, by hunting down all superstition, whether diabolical or papist'. Edward used passages from Genesis, the Gospels and Paul's letters to argue that 'everyone who believes in Jesus Christ, and places all his faith in him, will be saved'.[121] In declaring his *sola fideism* Edward publically distinguished his confessional identity from his father's and demonstrated his knowledge of and support for the religious reform being carried out in England in his name.

This translation exercise had been set by Jean Belmaine, Edward's French tutor. Belmaine had entered royal service in around 1544 through the patronage of John Cheke, whose daughter he would subsequently

[118] Erasmus, *The first tome or volume of the Paraphrases of Erasmus upon the Newe Testament*, ed. Nicholas Udall, trans. Mary I *et al.*, ed. Nicholas Udall (London, 1548), STC 2854 variant; 'Injunctions for religious reform', in *Tudor royal proclamations*, eds. Paul L. Hughes and James F. Larkin, 3 vols. (New Haven, 1964–9), vol. I, pp. 395–6; John Craig, 'Forming a Protestant consciousness? Erasmus' *Paraphrases* in English parishes, 1547–1666', in Hilmar M. Pabel and Mark Vessey (eds.) *Holy Scripture speaks: The production and reception of Erasmus' 'Paraphrases on the New Testament'* (Toronto, 2002).

[119] Bucer, *Original letters relative to the English Reformation*, vol. II, p. 543.

[120] BL, Arundel MS 510, fols. 39^{r}–52^{r}. For Cranmer's commonplace books, see Matthew Parker Library, Corpus Christi College, Cambridge MS 102, fols. 151^{r}–193^{r}. See also MacCulloch, *Thomas Cranmer*, p. 468; K. J. Walsh, 'Cranmer and the fathers, especially in the *Defence*', *Journal of Religious History*, 11 (1980). On the humanist technique of managing information in this form, see Ann M. Blair, *Too much to know: Managing scholarly information before the modern age* (New Haven, 2011), pp. 63, 69–85.

[121] 'Je me puisse defendre, et de mon baston battre les ennemis de Dieu, en dechassant toutes les superstitions diaboliques, ou papistiques', 'chacun qui croit en Jesus Christ, et a mis toute sa fiance en lui, sera sauvé': Edward, *LR*, vol. I, pp. 155, 172.

marry. In September 1546, Belmaine transferred from the Princess Elizabeth's household to become 'schoolmaster to my lord the Princes grace for the French tongue', at a wage of forty marks a year. Edward began his study of French on his ninth birthday and was writing letters in that tongue by December that year. If the imperial ambassador François van der Delft (1500–50) is any guide, though, Edward's speaking and listening skills lagged behind.[122] Belmaine became a gentleman of his privy chamber and continued to instruct Edward after his accession. As his 18 April 1553 gift to Edward of a French translation of the 1552 Book of Common Prayer shows, he remained attached to his royal pupil to the end of his life.[123] From early 1547, moreover, French became a significant medium for Edward's study of reformed theology and Belmaine became an influential spiritual guide.

Closer analysis of the first gift translation that Belmaine set Edward shows how the schoolmaster used what were ostensibly tasks in French grammar and commonplacing to introduce his pupil to reformed dogma. The first purifying measure Edward learnt to defend was the removal of idolatrous images and objects from churches. On 31 July 1547, a royal proclamation had been issued for 'the suppression of Idolatrye, and Supersticio[n]'. In particular, the third injunction ordered clergymen to 'take awaye, utterly extincte, and destroye, all shrines, coueringe of shrines, all tables, candelstickes, tryndelles or rolles of waxe, pictures, payntynges, and all other monuments of fayned miracles, pilgremages, Idolatry, and supersticio[n]: so that there remayn no memory of the same... within their churches' or private homes. This was militant iconoclasm; stained-glass windows had been left intact in Zurich but in England they were an anathema. The measure proved controversial. In April 1548, for instance, up to three thousand yeomen in St Keverne rioted in protest and petitioned for a moratorium on religious innovation until the king's twenty-fourth birthday.[124] It was crucial that Edward both understand and publically endorse his regime's injunctions.

[122] *LP*, vol. XXI, no. 260, p. 124; Edward, *LR*, vol. I, pp. 31–2; Jean Belmaine in Jean Calvin, *Ioannis Calvini opera quae supersunt omnia*, eds. William Baum *et al.*, 59 vols. (Brunswick, 1863–1900), vol. XIV, no. 1626, cols. 324–35; *CSP Spain*, vol. IX, p. 47.

[123] BL, Royal MS 20 A XIV; Gordon Kipling, 'Belmaine, Jean (fl. 1546–1559)', *ODNB*.

[124] [Church of England], *Iniunccions geue[n] by the moste excellent prince, Edward the sixte, by the grace of God, kyng of England, Frau[n]ce and Irelande: Defendor of the faythe, and in earthe vnder Christ, of the churche of Englande and of Ireland, the supreme hedde: To all and singuler his louyng subiectes, aswell of the clergie, as of the laietie* (London, 1547), STC 10090, sigs. aii^{r}, cii^{v}–ciii^{r}; John Strype, *Memorials of the most reverend father in God, Thomas Cranmer*, 3 vols. (Oxford, 1840), vol. I, pp. 206–7; Edward, *CPP*, p. 6; Eamon Duffy, *The stripping of the altars: Traditional religion in England, c. 1400–c. 1580* (New Haven, 1992) pp. 448–51, 457–62.

By early 1548, Belmaine had got Edward up to speed. The king presented Somerset with a collection of 'many Sentences which speak against idolatry'. Edward described the exercise as a grammatical one: he had extracted sentences from the Great Bible and translated these places 'into the French tongue'.[125] In fact, Edward began his search with the Book of Exodus but only got as far as the Prophet Hosea before Belmaine let him off. As Edward explained, 'there were other places in sacred scripture' that spoke against idolatry, but be felt they simply reiterated 'those places' he had already translated.[126] From Belmaine's (and presumably Somerset's) perspective it was less important that Edward complete his translation than that he had grasped the doctrinal point – that English churches needed to be stripped of images.

Nevertheless, the translation exercise that Edward had performed was a demanding one. Indeed it was more rhetorically complex than he acknowledged in his letter. His diction cleaved to his source text, the Great Bible.[127] Nevertheless he rendered Bible sentences very freely. For instance, the Great Bible rendered God's words at 1 Samuel 8:7–8 as, 'For they have not caste ye awaye, but me: that I shuld not rayne over the[m]. And as they have ever done (sence I brought them out of Egypte into this daye and have forsaken me, and serued other gods) even so do they unto the[e].' Edward's version, however, compressed the passage into a neat, powerful parallelism: 'And just as they have cast me out and have served other Gods than me, so they have done the same to you.'[128] Occasionally his tendency to epitomise passages produced a misleading outcome. In Exodus 15:11, it was Moses and the Israelites who sang 'Who is lyke unto the, O Lorde, among Goddes? Who is lyke the so glorious in holynes, fear full in prayses, shewing wonders?' Edward, however, put the passage in God's mouth, so the Lord appeared to be acknowledging the existence of other 'Gods of the Gentiles' and to be boasting that he was pre-eminent amongst them, like a sort of Judeo-Christian Zeus.[129] In his rendering of Old Testament passages against idolatry, Edward took as

[125] 'Avoir noté en ma Bible en Anglois plusieurs sentences qui contre disent a toute ydolatrie': WLTC, MS R 7 31, fol. 3ʳ.

[126] 'Il ya autre Places en le sainte Escriture… qui toutesfois sont correspondentes a celle dont est faite mention par cy deuant': WLTC, MS R 7 31, fols. 20ʳ.

[127] For example, his rendering of 'grauen ymage' as *ymage grauee*, rather than *image taillee*. See *La Bible qui est toute la Sainct escripture. En laquelle sont contenus, le Uieil Testament & le Noueau transltez en Francoys*, trans. Pierre Robert Olivetan, intro. Jean Calvin (Serrières, 1535), sig. diiiiʳ; WLTC, MS R 7 31, fol. 5ᵛ; *The Byble in Englyshe, that is to saye the conte[n]t of al the holy scrypture, both of ye olde, and newe testame[n]t* (London, 1540), STC 2070, sig. dVʳ.

[128] 'Ainsy comme ilz m'ont delaissé, et ont seruy a autres Dieux qu'a moy, ainsy maintenant font ilz a toy': WLTC, MS R 7 31, fol. 12ʳ; *The Byble in Englyshe*, sig. DVIIᵛ.

[129] 'Dieu a aussy dit. Qui est semblable a moy entre les Dieux des Gentilz? Qui est si Glorieux? ou qui est celuy qui monstre si grans Miracles entre les Dieux?': WLTC, MS R 7 31, fol. 7ʳ; *The Byble in Englyshe*, sig. DIVʳ.

many liberties with God's word as he had with Cicero's. As with his study of classical authors, then, the king was not translating scriptural sentences into French from an open English Bible. Belmaine seems to have borrowed Cheke's technique of double translation to teach the king to internalise the essence of the biblical authorities he read.

Edward claimed, however, that the exercise was merely to demonstrate his 'understanding and study' of French grammar and scripture.[130] By understanding the rhetorical work that went into distilling and paraphrasing these passages from the Old Testament, Edward was also making an appeal to reformed traditions of biblical translation. Since Erasmus' *Novum Testamentum* (1519), at least, biblical translators had insisted that they had worked as grammarians rather than orators in converting God's word. While Leonardo Bruni had taught humanists to translate classical texts eloquently, it was generally agreed that converting the Bible called for accuracy, clarity and, above all, fidelity. Whereas rhetoric aimed to persuade, grammar was a conduit to truth.[131] This move was partly defensive. Traditional theologians, such as Noël Béda, alleged that those who introduced 'into a pious and humble doctrine the arrogance and blandishment of pagan letters' were 'approaching sin and sacrilege'. Did the translator think himself more eloquent than God?[132] Yet reformers themselves were eager to ground their understanding of faith and grace in grammar, the correct understanding of words. In 1545 Martin Luther accounted for his own theological revelation in these terms: 'when I understood the matter and learned that the righteousness of God means that righteousness by which he justifies… then I understood the grammar' and consequently the power of grace.[133] In his prefatory letter to Somerset, Edward was similarly eager to insist that his treatise and faith were formed 'by His Words alone'.[134] Through the grammatical study of the Bible, Edward suggested, he was learning to become a theologian-king.

[130] 'À celle fin de m'apprendre et exercer en l'Escriture Françoise': WLTC, MS R 7 31, fol. 3^r.

[131] Bruni, *De interpretatione recta*, pp. 30, 31, 68, 69 drawing on Pseudo-Cicero, *De optimo genere oratorum*, IV.13–V.15; Erasmus, *Capita argumentorum contra morosos quosdam ac indoctos* (1519), in *Opera omnia*, VI, sigs. **^r, ***^v; Erasmus, *CWE: Letters 842 to 992*, no. 843, p. 9.

[132] Cited by Erika Rummel, *Erasmus' annotation on the New Testament: From philologist to theologian* (Toronto, 1986), p. 98.

[133] *D. Martin Luthers Werke, kritische Gesamtausgabe: Tischreden* 5, (Weimar, 1912-) no. 5247 cited by Brian Cummings, *Literary culture of the Reformation: Grammar and grace* (Oxford, 2002), p. 51.

[134] 'Tant de gens ont osé, et osent commettre ydolatrie, en faisant et adorant des ymages', 'il ne peut estre Veu en choses qui soient matérielles, mais Veult ester Veu par ses oeuvres', 'regardant et considerant l'excellence du Firmament et les choses tant parfaites et merueilleuses qui y sont comprises nous pouuons ymaginer quel est le Créateur qui les a formees, seullement par sa Parolle': WLTC, MS R 7 31, fol. 2^{r,v}.

Beyond knowledge of French grammar, the collection of 'many Sentences which speak against idolatry' also required Edward to locate passages in the Old Testament and to order them cogently.[135] As Ann Moss has argued, Erasmus popularised a method in his *De copia* (1512) for extracting sentences (*sententiae*) regarding vice, virtue and human affairs from ancient authors, copying them into books under predetermined headings and reusing them in subsequent compositions.[136] We have seen Edward using such sentences as illustrations and for ornamentation in his letters and, indeed, commonplacing became a standard technique for reading and writing in sixteenth-century European schoolrooms. Philip Melanchthon refined this method for storing and retrieving knowledge to make it a suitable vehicle for reformed theological argument. In his *De rhetorica* (1519) he had proposed that doctrine should be studied by creating heads (*capita*) of relevant knowledge, on topics such as 'faith, ceremonies, sin, law' amongst others. Then students should read scripture, extracting places (*loci*) that related to them. He offered a model for this practice in *De loci communes* (1521), where he showed, moreover, that these places, once collected and arranged, would enable students to conduct an analysis (*iudicium*) of the *capita*, from which they could derive true doctrine. Commonplacing offered theologians and schoolboys alike a dialectical process for 'methodologically secure exegesis'.[137] This is precisely how Belmaine had taught Edward to use biblical *loci*. The king had begun working through the books of the Old Testament systematically, locating places that discussed idolatry. He analysed his repository of biblical knowledge to derive the argument that he offered up to Somerset in his introductory letter. God had spoken clearly and persistently against worshipping other entities, Edward explained. Nevertheless amongst the Israelites, and in the modern world, there were those who 'have dared, and still dare to commit idolatry by making and worshipping images'. They have failed to understand that God 'cannot be seen in material things, but He wants to be seen in his works'. Through contemplating 'the excellencies of the firmament and the perfect and marvellous things upon it', Edward explained, 'one can imagine the Creator who has formed them through his Words alone'. He concluded, therefore, that our 'Spiritual Eye sees much better through these things that are of God, than our Bodily Eye can see in things that a human

[135] 'Avoir noté en ma Bible en Anglois plusieurs sentences qui contre disent a toute ydolatrie': WLTC, MS R 7 31, fol. 3^{r}.

[136] Erasmus, *De copia*, in *CWE: Literary and educational writings II*, pp. 603–36; Ann Moss, *Printed commonplace-books and the structuring of Renaissance thought* (Oxford, 1996), pp. 134–85.

[137] Ann Moss, *Renaissance truth and the Latin language* (Oxford, 2003), pp. 167–77; Skinner, *Reason and rhetoric*, p. 59.

creature has made and formed'.[138] Rather than simply translating phrases from the Great Bible into French, Belmaine had Edward use the technique of commonplacing to derive reformed theology for himself. It gave the king a keen sense of ownership over the evolving doctrines of his church.

Once assembled and analysed, Melanchthon argued that *loci* could be disposed for the construction (*dispositio*) of a theological argument. After his first collection of sentences, Belmaine set Edward progressively more complex argumentative challenges that required the king to derive doctrine through exegesis and then dispose of it to create a defence of further reform in England. At the end of August 1549, for instance, just a few weeks before the coup that would unseat Somerset, Edward sent his uncle a 'Little treatise against the primacy of the pope'. The king used scripture, church history and the writings of church fathers to support his claim that the pope was the 'Antichrist and a tyrant' and the source of the disorder that was plaguing the world. His argument suggested that he had been reading and extracting widely. Diarmaid MacCulloch has pointed to the particular influence of John Ponet's (*c.* 1514–56) translation of Bernardino Ochino's (*c.* 1487–1564/5) *Dialoge of the uniuste usurped primacie of the bishop of Rome* (1549), which had been dedicated to Edward.[139] The king wrote with vigour that occasionally bubbled over into anger. 'Even now in France', Edward fulminated, 'before they burn someone, they cut out his tongue, so he cannot speak at the end' to testify to his faith. As a young man who was increasingly finding his own voice on matters of religion, Edward seemed to have regarded this practice as particularly cruel. Indeed, the writing task had enflamed the king sufficiently that Belmaine felt called to moderate some of Edward's language against Henry VIII's Act of Six Articles (1539) in the treatise.[140] In addition to being circulated amongst reforming theologians in the British isle, Edward's polemic was sent to Jean Calvin as evidence of the king's burgeoning godliness.[141]

[138] 'Tant de gens ont osé, et osent commettre ydolatrie, en faisant et adorant des ymages', 'il ne peut estre Veu en choses qui soient matérielles, mais Veult estre Veu par ses oeuvres', 'regardant et considerant l'excellence du Firmament et les choses tant parfaites et merueilleuses qui y sont comprises nous pouuons ymaginer quel est le Créateur qui les a formees, seullement par sa Parolle, et en telle maniere nostre Oeil Spirituel pourra beaucoup mieux voir quelle chose c'est que de dieu, que nostre oeil corporel ne le pourroit Voir en chose que creature humaine ait faite et formee': WLTC, MS R 7 31, fols. 2^r–2^v.

[139] MacCulloch, *Tudor church militant*, p. 30.

[140] 'Le pape est… un Antichrist, et tiran abominable' and 'Aussy maintenant en France, devant qu'on brule quelqu'un, on luy couppe la lange un peu auparavant, a celle fin qu'il ne parle': Edward VI, 'Petit traité le contre de la primauté du pape', CUL, MS Dd 12 59, fols. 2^v–3^r, 50^v; cf. the tutor's corrections to the draft BL, Additional MS 5464, fol. 26^v to CUL, MS Dd 12 59, fol. 33^{r-v}.

[141] See letters from 1551 to 1552 in Calvin, *Ioannis Calvini opera*, vol. XIV, no. 1499, cols. 130–2; no. 1606, cols. 290–2; no. 1626, cols. 324–35.

The methods of Edward's liberal education – translation, commonplacing, relatively wide reading, note-taking and *dispositio* – meant that, as Edward was learning reformed doctrine, he was also learning to defend it polemically.

Why were these humanist pedagogical techniques so effective in conveying ideology to Edward? One of the significant differences between the duke of Richmond's education and Edward VI's was that the latter grew up in a world that was virtually hermeneutically sealed. At the very least, he was protected from the rival ideologies that had divided his half-brother's household and had shaped his father's upbringing. The 1563 illustration of the king in John Foxe's *Actes and monuments* showed him listening intently to a sermon delivered by Hugh Latimer from the pulpit in the garden at Whitehall.[142] Somerset stands beside him. Cheke may be the figure tucked behind the protector's shoulder. Nobles haunt the galleries and preaching-place, and Edward's bearded ministers and counsellors ring the pulpit. Even a court woman is portrayed with an open Bible in her lap. Jennifer Loach has described the woodcut as reformed propaganda.[143] Nevertheless the scene shows us several things that written testimony of Edward's reign, including the letters of hostile witnesses, confirms. First, it shows that, with the exception of his half-sister Mary, Edward VI had relatively little personal contact with non-evangelicals. Second, it suggests the king's enjoyment of reformed preaching. According to John Hooper, who had spoken before the king on the seven Wednesdays of Lent 1550, Edward received 'with his own hand a copy of every sermon' he heard. The king was no passive listener, either. He took notes with his own hand – extracting *loci*, no doubt – and expressed enthusiasm for the more militantly reformed sort of preaching.[144] Sermons played a key role in radicalising Edward's religious education and in stoking his ardour for further reform.

The reformed clergy in England did not agree on all matters and Edward was encouraged to weigh in on debates from an early age. Following the Lords' debate on the Eucharist in December 1548, he wrote his 'own opinion, with reasons' for rejecting both traditional accounts of transubstantiation and the Lutheran formulation that emphasised the real presence of Christ. Instead, Edward regarded the bread and wine as

142 Foxe, *TAMO* [1563], p. 1422.

143 Loach, *Edward VI*, pp. 180–1 but see MacCulloch, *Tudor church militant*, p. 25.

144 Edward, *CPP*, p. 25; John Hooper in Bucer, *Original letters relative to the English Reformation*, vol. I, p. 82; *CSP Spain*, vol. IX, p. 50, vol. X, p. 63; Edward, *LR*, vol. I, pp. xx, clxxxii; Foxe, *TAMO* [1563], pp. 940, 1353; Gardiner, *Letters of Stephen Gardiner*, pp. 255, 265–7; Strype, *Life of the learned Sir John Cheke*, p. 232; Peter E. McCullough, *Sermons at court: Politics and religion in Elizabethan and Jacobean preaching* (Cambridge, 1998), p. 56.

'symbols… indicating that just as bread and wine nourish the bodies of men, so the grace of God will nourish their souls if they remember the passion of Christ and his death and place all their hope in his goodness and mercy'. It was an opinion in the spirit of the contemporary *Consensus Tigurinus* (1549); the king was ready for the more radical account of the Lord's Supper offered in the second *Book of common prayer* (1552).[145] When Edward gave his opinion on Bishop John Hooper's investiture controversy in 1550, he sided with the radicals once more.[146] Not only had the king's schoolmasters and preachers got him up to speed with reforms but also he was beginning to outflank parts of the evangelical establishment in his zeal for purging and rebuilding the Lord's temple in England.

Edward was no passive sponge, filled with learning to be squeezed dry as occasion demanded. From the outset, Belmaine encouraged him to derive doctrine for himself, to articulate authorities in his own words, to order them as he saw fit, to attend to theological controversy and to make his own cases (though Belmaine reserved the right to correct or moderate them). He used the disciplines of grammar, rhetoric and Melanchthon's humanist dialectic to shape a student prince who felt passionately possessive about the doctrines of the 1552 *Book of common prayer*. Liberal education could affect an ideological turn in a student with the right temperament provided that he was immersed in a cultural environment that honoured those convictions militantly.

INSTRUCTING THE GODLY MONARCH

The object of this preaching and instruction was not merely to teach the king doctrine. English reformers were urging Edward to embrace his identity as a godly monarch. As a godly monarch, Edward would have the divinely instituted power and duty to purify the temple, despite his youth. As Stephen Alford and Jaqueline Rose have shown, however, he would also be required to take counsel from his godly preachers and advisers, and potentially share his spiritual and ecclesiastical authority with them.[147] Indeed,

145 'Ses symbols du pain & vin leur monstrans que comme le pain & vin nourisset le corps des gens aynsy la grace de dieu nourrira seur ames, silz ont sovenance de sa mort et passion de Christ, et mettent toute leur esperance en sa bonté et bénignité': BL, Additional MS 29432, fol. 6v; MacCulloch, *Thomas Cranmer*, pp. 615–16.

146 W. K. Jordan, *Edward VI: The threshold of power and the dominance of the duke of Northumberland* (London, 1970), pp. 294, 371–2.

147 Alford, *Kingship and politics*, pp. 33–43, 49; Jacqueline Rose, *Godly kingship in Restoration England: The politics of the royal supremacy, 1660–1688* (Cambridge, 2011), pp. 52, 59 and 'Kingship and counsel in early modern England', pp. 47–71.

Edward's schoolroom provided a context in which an international circle of reformed clergy could tell a king what to do. They instructed him to become a loving 'nursing father' of the church who was willing to countenance his own destruction before he neglected the reform of religion. Edward's 1551 writings show that he embraced this identity but that his education had also given him the skills and knowledge to distinguish his understanding of his duties from the prescriptions of contemporary theologians.

Edward VI's youth meant that the discourse of counsel frequently merged with that of religious instruction during his reign. Clergymen and theologians including Bucer, Cranmer and Latimer insisted on their duty to speak 'frankelye and frely' to the king, 'without respecte of favoure or displeasure'. More unusually, they expected to be obeyed rather than merely heard out by the king; they tended to address Edward as their pupil rather than their ruler.[148] Simultaneously, Edward's schoolmaster, Cheke, took on political and ecclesiastical duties as a gentleman of the king's Privy Chamber, as an MP for Bletchingley in Surrey, as the provost of King's College, Cambridge, as the Lady Margaret Professor of Divinity in Cambridge (1549) and as principal secretary to the Privy Council (1553).[149] The line between royal schoolmaster and religious adviser was hard to discern in Edwardian England.

These men set out a mirror of godly monarchy before Edward in their letters, treatises and sermons. It conjoined his weighty responsibility to purify and rebuild the church like 'your predecessor Josiah' with the traditional kingly duty to effect justice and peace and to relieve poverty.[150] This account of godly monarchy was theoretically more absolute than Erasmus' description of the Christian prince had been. Where Erasmus urged monarchs to remember that their authority depended on their subjects' consent, Edward's preachers told him that he had been placed on the throne by God alone. Rather than merely defending the Bible for his subjects' benefit, Edward was responsible for instituting the church that would lead them to salvation. In practice, however, the clergymen reassured (and warned) Edward that they would share his burden and his authority.[151]

[148] Bernardino Ochino, *A tragoedie or dialoge of the unjust usurped primacie of the bishop of Rome*, trans. John Ponet (London, 1549), STC 18770, sig. Y2^r.

[149] Bryson, 'Cheke, Sir John (1514–1557)'.

[150] Strype, *Memorials of the most reverend gather in God*, vol. 1, pp. 206–7; Alice Hunt, *The drama of coronation: Medieval ceremony in early modern England* (Cambridge, 2008), pp. 87–8.

[151] Alford, *Kingship and politics*, pp. 33–43, 50–2; Margaret Aston, *The king's bedpost: Reformation and iconography in a Tudor group portrait* (Cambridge, 1993), pp. 26–36; Christopher Bradshaw, 'David or Josiah? Old Testament kings as exemplars in Edwardian religious polemic', in Bruce

In early 1551, Erasmus received prescriptive treatments of this topic from two of the most influential theologians of Reformation Europe. Martin Bucer explicated Edward's duty to 'restore for [his] peoples the blessed Kingdom of the son of God' in a New Year's gift treatise *De regno Christi* (1551). Bucer had coordinated with both Cranmer and Cheke in drafting *De regno*, so the treatise reflected the views of Edward's evangelical establishment in its radical phase.[152] The king was instructed to purge the church of 'dead wood, thorns and brambles' that were liable to entangle subjects' souls and to 'suppress the impiety and injustice of dissipated men' who might corrupt others. Bucer urged Edward to be willing to 'countenance dangers, exile and death itself' to nourish the kingdom of God on earth.[153] In January 1551, Jean Calvin also exhorted Edward to re-establish the purity of God's service in England.[154] Three months later, he dedicated his commentaries on Isaiah to the king, urging him to let 'nothing, howsoever disastrous, turn [him] from his object'. Instead, Edward was to heed the prophet and serve as a 'nursing father' to his church.[155]

Bucer and Calvin differed on the breadth of the godly monarch's pastoral responsibilities. Calvin's concern was primarily the reform of the ministry and clerical education in the universities.[156] In contrast, Bucer's vision for the 'administration and care of the eternal life of God's elect' was 'richly social'.[157] In addition to insisting on ministerial training and discipline, he proposed that the royal 'nursing father' should provide for the liberal, religious and vocational education of parishioners. He should reform marriage law, improve the courts and maintain law and order. Like Erasmus and adherents of commonwealth discourse, Bucer encouraged

Gordon (ed.), *Protestant history and identity in sixteenth-century Europe*, 2 vols. (Aldershot, 1996); MacCulloch, *Tudor church militant*, pp. 62–3.

[152] Martin Bucer, *De regno Christi*, in *Martini Buceri Opera Latina: XV*, ed. François Wendel, 2 vols. (Paris, 1955), vol. II, p. 293; the dedication copy is BL, Royal MS 8 B VII, part I; the letters to Edward and Cheke are Matthew Parker Library, Corpus Christi College, Cambridge, MS 119, pp. 3–6 and 45–50, respectively. See also N. Scott Amos, 'The Alsatian among the Athenians: Martin Bucer, mid-Tudor Cambridge and the Edwardian Reformation', *Reformation and Renaissance Review*, 4:1 (2002); Patrick Collinson, 'The reformer and the archbishop: Martin Bucer and an English Bucerian', in *Godly people: Essays on English Protestantism and Puritanism* (London, 1983), pp. 19–44; MacCulloch, *Thomas Cranmer*, pp. 381–2, 399–403, 426–31.

[153] 'Inutiles arbores, sentes et vepres, oppressa scilicet perditorum hominum impietate et iniusittia', 'quaeuis pericula, exilium et mortem ipsam subire': Bucer, *De regno Christi*, vol. II, pp. 7, 8.

[154] Jean Calvin in Bucer, *Original letters relative to the English Reformation*, pp. 708–10. See also Matthew Parker Library, Corpus Christi College, Cambridge, MS 119, fols. 106a^{r-v}, 156^{r-v}.

[155] 'Nihil quantumvis adversum abducere te ab instituto deberet': Calvin, *Ioannis Calvini opera*, vol. XIV, col. 673. Cf. Isaiah 49:23.

[156] Calvin in Bucer, *Original letters relative to the English Reformation*, p. 710.

[157] 'Administratio est et procuratio salutis aeternae electorum Dei… doctrina et disciplina sua': Bucer, *De regno Christi*, vol. II, p. 54; Collinson, 'Reformer and the archbishop', p. 21.

Edward to strengthen the economic tendons of the body politic. Social reforms would help Christians live 'quiet and tranquil lives in all piety and honour'.[158] Bucer argued that, once the church had been purified, the prince could guarantee these civil benefits by transferring 'full authority' for them 'not only to the public ministers of Christ... but also to the churches in their entirety'.[159] Only then would the elect be ruled by Christ 'on earth and hereafter'.[160] Bucer offered an account of kingship that made reformed ministers more than mere advisers to the supreme head. They were to be Edward VI's active partners in government.

These gift treatises and the event of the parliament from January to April 1551 prompted Edward to set out his own vision for reform in a discourse on the 'gouvernaunce of this realme'. Historians have described it as imitating the writings of Bucer, who had died on 28 February that year.[161] In fact, Edward did not trot out either Bucer's or Calvin's prescriptions unreflectively. The king began his discourse by considering the ecclesiastical regimen. He was cognisant of his duty, described by both Bucer and Calvin, to prepare and appoint learned 'teachers and spiritual officers' to set 'forth the words of God' to his people. In an allusion to the parable of the sower (Matthew 13:23) and the power of the printing press, Edward argued that, just as 'the good husbandman makes his ground good and plentiful, so does the true preacher with doctrine and example... print and [en]grave in the people's mind the word of God'.[162] He blamed the commons' 'swearing, rioting, [and] neglecting of God's word' on the deficit of good clergy in England. 'Some for papistry, some for ignorance, some for age, some for their ill name, [and] some for all these' failed to teach the word of God. Edward's solution – to replace outright these clergymen with 'honest' and 'learned' ministers – was not realistic in 1551. Nevertheless Edward may have been reflecting on the February deposition of Stephen Gardiner and the April installation of John Ponet and imagining a policy of ongoing, gradual substitution.[163] He knew enough about his bench to warn that broad disciplinary powers could not be 'given generally to all

[158] 'Quo quietam et tranquillam uitam degere liceat in omni pietate et honestate [1 Tim. 2:2]': Bucer, *De regno Christi*, vol. II, p. 20; see pp. 299–303 for his proposed reforms. Cf. Erasmus, *CWE: Paraphrases on Timothy, Titus, Philemon, Peter, Jude, James, John, Hebrews*, pp. 13–14.

[159] 'Quamobrem non publicis modo ministris Christi... principes, sed et totis Ecclesiis se penitus mancipant... ut impleant illud Iesaiae': Bucer, *De regno Christi*, vol. II, pp. 16–17.

[160] 'Bene beateque uiuant et hic et in futuro': Bucer, *De regno Christi*, vol. II, p. 54.

[161] Edward VI, 'Discourse on the reform of abuses in church and state', in Edward, *CPP*, pp. 159–6; the relationship between Edward's discourse and Bucer's treatise was first noted by Gilbert Burnet, *The history of the Reformation of the Church of England*, 4 vols. (New York, 1843), vol. II, pp. 249–51.

[162] Edward, *CPP*, p. 159.

[163] Edward, *CPP*, pp. 58, 159–60; Jordan, *Edward VI*, p. 372.

bishops' immediately. Chichester, Durham, Exeter, Gloucester, Lincoln and Worcester were still unreliable. Instead he proposed to commission 'those that be of the best sort' to reform other dioceses.[164] Finally, Edward took Bucer's point about the need for a more thoroughly reformed order of worship, particularly as it touched the Eucharist. He proposed to put statutes for the second *Book of common prayer* to Parliament himself.[165] In short, Edward had engaged closely with Ponet and Calvin's prescriptions but put some thought into the way that he could apply them as 'nursing father' of the church in England.

Nevertheless Edward's 1551 discourse reveals that the king was firmly opposed to Bucer's suggestion that the church, rather than the king and nobility, should take over responsibility for social discipline in England. Edward insisted that lay 'gentlemen' (by which he meant landowners) were still the 'arms' of the body politic and critical to enforcing 'new laws' in the localities, including religious decrees.[166] He was careful enough of the royal supremacy and sufficiently cognisant of the exigencies of ruling the localities in England to reject any movements towards theocracy. Further, Edward diagnosed the most debilitating disease of the body politic in 1551 as economic rather than ecclesiastical. The tendency of each and every 'part of the whole' to attempt to enrich itself and 'eat another up through greediness' was, he argued, at the root of its existing distemper. He regarded his duty, as England's chief physician and 'head... governor... [and] law', as providing for 'well-ordering, enriching, and defending the whole body politic of the commonwealth, and every part of the whole, so one hurt not the other'.[167] In fact, the king continued to use the language of the commonwealth, rather than godly monarchy, to understand his temporal responsibilities.

Ultimately, Edward's discourse suggests that by 1551 Cheke and Belmaine were tasting the fruits of their pedagogical labours. Imitation, variation and translation lay at the heart of humanist teaching of grammar and rhetoric and these literary methods and intellectual processes shaped Edward's response to the image of godly monarch that his counsellors had set before him. At the age of thirteen, he could imitate Bucer's and Calvin's account of the king as a nursing father of the church yet refuse to countenance theocracy. Liberal education had taught Edward to defend the royal supremacy as well as his faith. The result was a prince capable of

[164] Edward, *CPP*, pp. 159–60; Charles Wriothesley, *A chronicle of England*, ed. W. D. Hamilton, 2 vols. (London, 1877), vol. II, pp. 45–6.

[165] Edward, *CPP*, pp. 58, 160; Bucer, *De regno Christi*, vol. II, p. 102; Jordan, *Edward VI*, pp. 372–3.

[166] Edward, *CPP*, pp. 163, 166–7. [167] Edward, *CPP*, pp. 164, 160, 162.

using his pen to redraw the lines on the portrait of godly monarchy and to make it his own. His intellectual investment in delineating the form of his office would encourage him to discharge his spiritual duties zealously.

EDWARD VI: A GODLY INCONVENIENCE?

Historians have objected that Edward's writings were just that: documents that 'went no further than his desk'.[168] Once Edward had clarified his own thinking on paper, however, he was eager to put his ideas into action. During the same months that Edward was composing his discourse against abuses, for instance, he attempted to suppress the idolatry of his sister and heir presumptive, Princess Mary, who had persisted in hearing traditional masses despite the Act of Uniformity (1549). When his counsellors warned him that the course of action he proposed would bring danger to the realm, he insisted that he must forge ahead with the purification of his church. Indeed he adopted the language of his school exercises to make his case. On this occasion, however, Edward's eagerness to convert the lessons of his schoolroom to the council chamber did not win him universal praise. Indeed, it seems to have alerted John Dudley, earl of Warwick, who installed himself as lord president of the Privy Council in February 1550, to the potential inconveniences of serving a second Josiah. Warwick was a long-time supporter of religious reform; indeed, he had advocated distribution of vernacular Bibles in 1543 and for the reform of the Eucharist in 1548, but he was also an able soldier and fiscal manager.[169] With Somerset's wars, the continued debasement of the coinage and the unrest of 1549, England's resources were spent; it was not the time to antagonise Mary's cousin Charles V, who commanded the greatest military machine in Europe.

Somerset's protectorate had tolerated Princess Mary's insistence on worshipping according to the ancient religion. When the Act of Uniformity had imposed the new liturgy and prayer book, Charles V had requested that his cousin be exempted from compliance. William Paulet, earl of Wiltshire, and William Paget, who had been England's ambassadors to Brussels at the time, nominally agreed to give Mary time to accommodate herself to the new law and also to protect the ready trade with Flanders in ammunition, alum and gunpowder that came with the emperor's friendship during England's wars with Scotland and France.[170] Somerset,

[168] Eric Ives, *Lady Jane Grey: A Tudor mystery* (Oxford, 2009), p. 135; see also Hoak, *King's council*, pp. 120–1, 132–6.

[169] Ives, *Lady Jane Grey*, p. 114.

[170] *CSP Spain*, vol. x, pp. 56–7, 205; Edward, *LR*, vol. I, p. ccxxv.

however, was ousted in October 1549 following his failure to quell the revolts of the summer and, according to Warwick, his insistence on ruling 'all by wilfulness'.[171] Early in the new year Warwick won control of the council with support of court evangelicals including Cranmer and Henry Grey (1517–54), marquis of Dorset. The earl ended the protector's costly wars with France and Scotland and pressed ahead with religious reform at home by placing more evangelicals in Edward's privy chamber and promoting godly preachers to bishoprics.[172] In spring 1550, the princess began to suspect that Warwick's Privy Council was reneging on its deal.[173] In April it had prohibited Mary from worshipping with her household or with strangers. In August it indicted her chaplains for celebrating mass. The princess's Christmas visit to court culminated in a tearful confrontation with her brother.[174] At the end of January 1551, however, Mary discovered that the king had not wept away his objection to her masses.

Indeed, it was Edward, rather than Cranmer or Warwick, who led the charge against his half-sister's idolatry and he adopted the language of godly monarchy to make his case. On 28 January Edward wrote to Mary, partly in his own hand, ordering her to cease and desist. The 'ordinances and laws contained in the public book [of Common Prayer]' that Mary had spurned were 'in conformity with the word of God'. 'Knowledge' of God's word 'was offered to you, and you refused it', Edward wrote prissily. 'We might ourselves chide you for this; for we acquire knowledge daily in our schooling.' Next, Edward claimed that, unless he enforced 'the will of God, as my duty binds me to do', he would not be 'a true minister of God' on earth. Bucer and Calvin could not have put it better. In addition to the issue of Mary's own salvation, there was the question of her disobedience. The law had to be applied 'without exception of persons'; it would not be just 'to support some [such as Mary] with favour whilst others are… punished' for their transgressions. In a thinly veiled reference to the unrest of 1549, Edward warned Mary that anyone who incited 'my subjects by their obstinate resistance' would be 'watched and denounced'.[175] Edward used the vocabulary he had acquired from his schoolroom and pulpit to make an active intervention in the government of his realm.

171 *HMC Salisbury*, vol. I, p. 76.

172 Dale Hoak, 'Rehabilitating the duke of Northumberland: Politics and political control, 1549–1553', in Jennifer Loach and Robert Tittler (eds.), *The mid-Tudor polity, c. 1540–1560* (London, 1980), pp. 29–51; David Loades, *John Dudley, duke of Northumberland, 1504–1553* (Oxford, 1996), pp. 142, 146–9.

173 *CSP Spain*, vol. x, pp. 7–9.

174 *CSP Spain*, vol. x, pp. 67–70, 80–4, 150–3.

175 *CSP Spain*, vol. x, pp. 209, 212.

Mary recognised the connection between Edward's speech and his education immediately and blamed his tutors for prejudicing him. 'Both sides of the question are not brought before you', she protested. Mary lamented to the imperial ambassador's secretary, Jehan Dubois, that Edward's counsellors had 'carefully instructed the King what lesson he is to read to her'.[176] The ambassador Van der Delft had no such illusions. As early as April 1550 he had warned the emperor that there was no point in broaching the question of Mary's masses with the king. Edward took 'increasing pleasure in disputing on and upholding the [new] doctrines'. There was 'no hope therefore that I may obtain anything from him'.[177] Even Edward's confessional opponents recognised that the king's education had given him the rhetorical skill and theological knowledge to defend his faith.

When Edward first wrote to Mary in January 1551, the king and his counsellors were still singing from the same hymnal. On 17 March, however, the princess brought pressure to bear on their coalition when she arrived at Westminster with a large retinue and declared melodramatically that 'the King and Council should take away her life rather than the practice of the old religion'.[178] According to Edward, the imperial ambassador then read 'a short message from his master' threatening war if Mary was denied the mass.[179] The calendared letters of the emperor and his new ambassador, Jehan Scheyfve, did not make clear or specific warnings of this nature. Scheyfve had told the Privy Council that Charles V 'would simply not stand' for any disrespectful behaviour towards Mary. The emperor's own communications suggest he was more troubled by the religious wars in Germany and the impertinence of Richard Morison, the English ambassador in Brussels, than Mary's cause.[180] In fact, in a private communication Charles actually urged Mary to moderate her demands. Should the mass be denied her, he soothed, her soul would remain unsullied since she was acting under duress.[181]

One wonders whether the sight of Mary and her retinue had actually raised another visored spectre before the council. She had arrived at Westminster flanked by fifty knights and over four hundred gentlemen and ladies, '[every] one having a peyre of bedes of black' as testament of their faith and political loyalty.[182] Was she threatening religious revolt and civil war, backed with Spanish silver and a trade embargo? England needed a 'vent in Flanders' for their cloth and the arms and seventy-five

176 *CSP Spain*, vol. x, pp. 213, 222. 177 *CSP Spain*, vol. x, p. 70.
178 *CSP Spain*, vol. x, p. 261. 179 Edward, *CPP*, p. 56. 180 *CSP Spain*, vol. x, p. 252.
181 *CSP Spain*, vol. x, pp. 237–43, 248, 251–61, 284–5.
182 Machyn, *Diary of Henry Machyn*, p. 5.

tons of gunpowder then warehoused in the Spanish Netherlands.[183] The battle-weary Warwick started to spook. According to Morison, 'the wholl counsell' took its cue from the lord president and crumbled, conceding that 'the ladi Mary must be allowed her chaplenes to masse it' after all. Edward, however, stood firm and declared he 'neither could [allow the masses] at counselores advises' nor would he 'agree to it at any kinge or kaisor's intreate'.[184] Edward was insistent that, when it came to the purification of the church, it was his duty as a godly monarch to push on.

The three surviving accounts of the ensuing division between king and council were written by Morison, John Foxe and Edward VI himself. All were partisan and two were written after the fact, yet they depict the schism in similar colours. On one side, there was the zealous king, trying to prohibit Mary's mass regardless of the political cost; on the other, there was a council, led by Warwick, who urged caution that 'the realme might be and alredie was in great perrill, like enough to be utterly undon' if Charles V was not appeased.[185] On 20 March, the council sent Cranmer and Nicholas Ridley (*c.* 1502–55) (Edward also reckoned Ponet amongst their number) to the king to soften his opposition. According to Edward, the bishops counselled him that while 'to give licence to sin was sin; to suffer and wink at it for a time might be borne'.[186] Morison claimed that the clerics cited the examples of certain 'good kings in the ould testament, [who] had suffered hill alteres, and yet were praised for good kings'.[187] The king had been taught how to refute such claims; indeed, Cranmer and Ridley had been two of his tutors. Edward explained, in a Cheke-like phrase, that historical examples had to be judged on the basis of the underlying principle they illustrated. Were the bishops suggesting that God condoned the immoral acts of the kings of Israel? 'Solomon did worshipe the idolle Moloch; may wee therefore give preistes our subjects leafe… to make a pece of dough bread for God?' he demanded. The greater danger to the realm was not the emperor's ill will or civil revolt, Edward protested, but God's wrath. He cited a lesson he had heard on Psalm 78 against the rebellious Israelites: kings may 'in vaine require obedience at their subjectes hands yf… they therfore will refuse to obaye God the Kinge'.[188] According to Foxe, the bishops then turned to the 'daungers' that denying Mary's mass

[183] Edward, *LR*, vol. II, p. 309. [184] Morison in Edward, *LR*, vol. I, p. ccxxviii.

[185] Morison in Edward, *LR*, vol. I, p. ccxxvi (quotation); Foxe, *TAMO* [1563], pp. 940–1; Edward, *CPP*, p. 56. On Morison' s account, see MacCulloch, *Tudor church militant*, pp. 38–9 and *Thomas Cranmer*, pp. 496–7.

[186] Edward, *CPP*, p. 56. [187] Morison in Edward, *LR*, vol. I, p. ccxxvii.

[188] Morison in Edward, *LR*, vol. I, pp. ccxxv–ccxxix.

'might brynge to his grace what breach of amitie… what troubles, what unkindnes' his refusal would occasion. Morison and Foxe report that Edward replied that a truly godly monarch must 'contempne any perill' (Morison) or 'spend his life' (Foxe) before neglecting God's charge to nourish his church. Foxe added that, upon leaving Edward's presence, the vanquished Cranmer congratulated Cheke on fashioning 'a scholler' with 'more diuinitie in his little finger, then all we haue in al our bodies'.[189] Edward had learnt to sustain the case for godly reform in the face of considerable theological and political pressure. Arguing may not be the same thing as political thinking, but, at thirteen, Edward had acquired sufficient proficiency to face down his teachers and counsellors.

To Warwick, however, Edward must have seemed frustratingly obdurate. The earl may have been a proponent of reform but he had little appetite for martyrdom, domestic unrest or a trade embargo.[190] He sent Nicholas Wotton, a diplomat of more temperament demeanour, to Charles V in Morison's place 'to win some time'. Mary was left unmolested temporarily.[191] According to Simon Renard, writing to Charles V on 21 March, Edward was enraged by this outcome. He had 'plucked a falcon, which he kept in his private chamber, and torn it into four pieces, saying as he did so… that he likened himself to the falcon, whom every one plucked; but that he would pluck them too, thereafter'.[192] Even if we discount the dismembered falcon as a colourful elaboration, the king was widely believed to resent the compromise that had been foisted upon him. In what may have been a sop to his conscience, the council imprisoned two members of Mary's household for popish practices and sent her chaplain, Francis Mallet (d. 1570), to the Tower for celebrating mass.[193]

Warwick was well informed about the king's state of mind. He had placed loyal clients, including John Gates and his own son-in-law, Henry Sidney, in Edward's privy chamber.[194] He was also in the position to know that Edward's stand on Mary's masses was unlikely to be a one off. The king's priggish efforts to reform the Order of the Garter between 1550 and mid-1551 confirmed his waxing confessional militancy.[195] Nevertheless Warwick's relatively tenuous authority – he had no familial mandate with which to overawe

[189] Foxe, *TAMO* [1563], p. 941 (quotation); Morison in Edward, *LR*, vol. 1, p. ccxxix.

[190] *CSP Spain*, vol. IX, p. 454; Loades, *John Dudley*, pp. 142–4, 147–8; MacCulloch, *Thomas Cranmer*, pp. 446–50.

[191] *CSP Spain*, vol. X, pp. 286–8, 93.

[192] *CSP Spain*, vol. X, p. 249.

[193] Edward, *CPP*, p. 56.

[194] BN, MS Ancien Saint-Germain Français 15888, fols. 214v–15v cited by Hoak, *King's council*, p. 123.

[195] MacCulloch, *Tudor church militant*, pp. 32–5.

Edward or a patented office, such as the protectorship, to evoke – encouraged him to cultivate a relationship with the king that could survive the transition to the royal majority. Inviting Edward to come to the council table 'when great matters were in debating, or when [he] would' may have been Warwick's attempt at a prophylactic against further unmediated royal outbursts.[196] Edward, however, seized the opportunity to return to the question of Mary's religious practices and won support from the council. After the first set of emissaries returned from Mary's household with a slight on Edward's capacity to compel consciences, senior privy counsellors were sent in. On 28 August 1551 Lord Chancellor Richard Rich, Sir Anthony Wingfield and William Petre, a secretary of state, went to Mary's house at Copped Hall, Essex, with the king's letters ordering Mary and her chaplains to conform to reformed rites. When the imperial ambassador objected, Edward replied 'that I had done nothing but according to a king's office herein, in observing the laws that were so godly and in punishing the offenders'.[197] When Mary refused to comply, again, her officers were moved from the Fleet to the Tower.[198] If anything, Edward's understanding of 'a king's office' had been further purified by the fire of opposition.

Of course, the king's adolescent absolutism may have been tempered by time and the gradual drip of governmental exigencies, but Warwick needed Edward's compliance immediately. In 1551 civil disturbances, dressed in commonwealth colours, were on the rise again. On 15 April Edward's *Chronicle* recorded the discovery of a conspiracy of Essex men, set to 'spoil the rich men's houses' in Chelmsford. The next day, the king noted that a threatened May Day riot had been disclosed.[199] The same night, a would-be assassin was apprehended near Warwick's house brandishing a bloody sword. Rumours linked these planned uprisings to Somerset. Was the duke planning to ascend from the political ashes and reclaim his pre-eminence? The evidence built over the summer. On 16 October, Warwick struck. Somerset was arrested for high treason and making threats against the lord president's life.[200] This was not the moment for Edward to decide that it was his godly duty to intervene in the cause of filial piety.

The question, then, was how to manage a king who was increasingly assertive, unwilling to compromise and obdurate about the godly responsibility of his office. Simply ignoring him was out of the question. If

[196] Edward, *CPP*, pp. 76, 86; *CSP Spain*, vol. x, pp. 493, 592.
[197] Edward, *CPP*, pp. 76, 78, 80; SP 10/13, fol. 70[r].
[198] Ives, *Lady Jane Grey*, p. 93. [199] Edward, *CPP*, p. 59.
[200] Loades, *John Dudley*, p. 179; Skidmore, *Edward VI*, pp. 189, 192.

Warwick wanted Edward VI on side, he would have to persuade him. Fortunately, a measure was at hand – the methods of liberal education and the practice of princely counsel. Edward had shown himself an apt pupil of both. Could they be used to turn the king towards a more pragmatic approach to political life?

WILLIAM THOMAS AND NICCOLÒ MACHIAVELLI

In September 1551, shortly after Edward began to sit at council regularly and had renewed his assault on Princess Mary's masses, the king received a secret letter from one William Thomas (d. 1554). Thomas was a clerk of the Privy Council and, more pertinently, one of Warwick's clients. His letter contained a list of eighty-five 'common places of state' and an offer to elaborate on any of them for the king's use. Thomas claimed to rejoice at Edward's 'erudicion', 'studie of the tonges' and 'holie scriptures' yet he noted that the king's education had neglected the knowledge of 'historie or of policie'. Now Edward had 'alreadie gowen to the adminystracion' of the commonwealth, Thomas argued that no study was more important. He claimed to have 'gathered' his corpus of commonplaces from 'divers aucthors'.[201] In fact, the titles of the majority of his proposed 'discourses' had been drawn from Niccolò Machiavelli's *The prince* (written *c.* 1513, printed 1532) and his *Discourses on Titus Livy* (written *c.* 1518, printed 1532). In 1551 Machiavelli had not yet acquired his English reputation as a stage villain but his works were not viewed favourably by members of Cheke's circle. Ascham, for instance, accused him of irreligion.[202] Thomas, however, proposed that the Florentine humanist's works and his historical method would offer insight for godly governors of the English commonwealth.

Thomas's writings for Edward VI have enjoyed scholarly attention yet few readers have taken seriously his claim to be teaching Edward something new. To Sydney Anglo, for instance, Thomas was the first European writer 'to attempt topical political analysis on the basis of Machiavelli's work' but, insofar as Edward was concerned, the discourses were merely 'reminiscent

[201] BL, Cotton MS Titus B II, fol. 84r. This letter is undated but several factors suggest a likely date of September 1551, not least Thomas's account of international politics, which draws on his embassy to France.

[202] Sydney Anglo, *Machiavelli – the first century: Studies in enthusiasm, hostility, and irrelevance* (Oxford, 2005), pp. 325–7; Ascham, *Scholemaster*, fols. 28v–29r. For this reason, I cannot agree with John Guy, *The Children of Henry VIII* (Oxford, 2013), p. 140 that Cheke facilitated Thomas's appointment.

of Castiglione' and traditional mirror-for-princes literature.[203] A penetrating study by Cathy Shrank argued that the clerk was expressing himself in the language of civic humanism. Thomas's 'belief in... the theory that the monarch acted for the nation, and not vice versus, underpinned his prioritization of the commonweal over its ruler'.[204] Once again, Thomas appears to have domesticated the foxy Machiavelli for lion-like pedagogical purposes; as we have seen, Edward was already well versed in commonwealth discourse and his kingly duty to serve the common good. In fact, locating Thomas's discourse in the social practices of Edward's schooling and the ideology it sought to impart suggests the radical nature of his intervention. I argue here that Thomas was actually engaged in a covert attempt to use Machiavelli's political writing to re-educate Edward VI.

William Thomas was a Welsh reformer and humanist, though quite when and how he had acquired his confessional and literary commitments remains something of a mystery.[205] He arrived at court in the early 1540s to serve in the train of Sir Anthony Browne (*c.* 1500–48), Henry VIII's master of the horse. In what an observer would subsequently call the 'frayilte and slipperines of youth', Thomas ran up significant gambling debts and embezzled Browne's money to pay for them. In April 1545 he attempted to elude his pursuers by running off to Venice. He was swiftly apprehended by Edmond Harvel, the English ambassador, with the assistance of the *signoria*.[206] After a chastening stint in prison, Thomas travelled the length of the peninsula. He acquired a facility with Italian, delved into the literary culture of the city-states and sharpened his disdain for Roman Catholic *mores*.[207] He attempted to hook a wealthy patron by writing one of the first English–Italian grammars and dictionaries – it would run to three editions in print – and a defence of Henry VIII's break from Rome.[208] Browne's death in 1548 cleared the way for Thomas to return home, perhaps with some politic assistance from that rising star William Cecil (1520/1–98), who did not share his fellow Cantabrigians' distaste for Machiavelli's political writings.[209]

[203] Anglo, *Machiavelli – the first century*, pp. 102, 108.

[204] Cathy Shrank, *Writing the nation in Reformation England, 1530–1580* (Oxford, 2004), p. 141.

[205] Dakota Hamilton, 'Thomas, William (d. 1554)', *ODNB*.

[206] SP 1/200, fol. 115^{r}; BL, Additional MS 5476, fol. 28^{r}.

[207] William Thomas, *The historie of Italie, a boke excedyng profitable to be rede: Because it intreateth of the astate [sic] of many and divers common weales, how thei have ben & now be governed* (London, 1549), STC 24018, fols. 22^{v}, 39^{v}, 84^{v}, 139^{v} and 162^{r}.

[208] Printed as William Thomas, *Principal rules of the Italian grammar, with a dictionarie for the better understandying of Boccace, Petrarcha, and Dante* (London, 1550), STC 24020; BL, Additional MS 33383 printed as *Il pellegrino Inglese* (Zurich, 1552).

[209] Jordan, *Threshold of power*, p. 416; SP 68/9, fols. 165, 174; HHCP, 273/3.

Once back on English soil, Thomas had the good fortune or good information to present his next literary effort, a *Historie of Italie*, to Warwick on 20 September 1549.[210] Just as the earl joined the first coup to remove Somerset, Thomas offered him a justification for striking against a protector who had encouraged 'division, either amongest the nobilitee or the commons' and thus catalysed the 'subvercion of common wealthes'. Thomas also offered advice for resolving such conflict: the 'alteracion of auncient lawes and customes' was an extreme measure but warranted by the seriousness of the problem. In fact, Warwick would show an unusual appetite for 'alteracion' during his leadership of the council. He effected real change in the management of government business, ended the debasement of the coinage and forged ahead with confessionalisation.[211] The *Historie*'s commendation of Venetian government was also well designed to appeal to the earl, whose professed justification for ousting Somerset was the duke's disregard for his council's advice.[212] Finally, Thomas also claimed that his chief aim in writing was to offer Warwick certain lessons, extracted from Machiavelli's *Florentine histories*, on 'how thei that haue had the power to rule, by usyng their auctoritees well and prudently, haue merited immortall fame'.[213] When Warwick gained the 'power to rule', Thomas rose alongside his new patron. Thomas was appointed clerk of the Privy Council in 19 April 1550 and acquired a number of significant political responsibilities. From 24 April to 12 August 1551, for instance, Thomas had served as the council's emissary to William Parr, marquis of Northampton, in his mission to France to negotiate a marriage between Edward and Henri II's daughter, Elizabeth.[214] He was well rewarded for his efforts and offered the opportunity to acquire property in Sussex, Worcestershire, Gloucestershire, the Welsh Marches and Herefordshire, and a one-off grant of £248 to offset his purchase costs. In February 1551, the Welsh embezzler was even granted a coat of arms.[215] Thomas was the earl's man, through and through.

Shortly after his return from France, Thomas wrote to Edward VI and offered to become his secret counsellor. His first letter made it clear that his advice would challenge Cheke's teaching. More specifically, it

[210] Loades, *John Dudley*, p. 200.

[211] David Loades, 'Dudley, John, duke of Northumberland (1504–1553)', *ODNB*.

[212] Andrew Hadfield, *Literature, travel, and colonial writing in the English Renaissance, 1545–1625* (Oxford, 1998), p. 26.

[213] Thomas, *Historie of Italie*, sig. A2^{r-v}; Shrank, *Writing the nation*, p. 125.

[214] SP 68/7, fol. 166^{r}; PC 2/4, fol. 356^{r};.

[215] Edward, *CPP*, p. 25; NA, PC 2/4, fol. 62^{v}; Hamilton, 'Thomas, William (d. 1554)'; Shrank, *Writing the nation*, p. 127.

countered the pedagogue's claim that it was more important for rulers to understand moral philosophy than history. Thomas argued that there was 'no earthelie thinge more necessarie' for princes 'than the knowledge… of such examples as in this and uther regimentes heretofore have happened'. He urged Edward to study his collection of political questions since they 'concerneth the chief mayntenaunce of yo[u]r high astate and preservac[i]on of yo[u]r com[m]on wealthe'. This was a reiteration of Machiavelli's (and Polybius') claim that it was the comparison of ancient and contemporary political events that provided the best preparation for political action.[216] Cheke might have taught Edward to speak well, to think clearly and live piously but Thomas proposed to provide the king with a guide for ruling effectively.

Thomas urged Edward to keep his advice a secret from others, including Cheke. He nominated Nicholas Throckmorton (1515/16–71), one of Warwick's appointments to Edward's privy chamber, to serve as a go-between. If Throckmorton was unavailable, Thomas proposed to deliver his missives 'unto yo[u]r Ma[jes]tie as it were a thinge from the Counsail'.[217] Ostensibly, this was so that Edward could 'have the greater creadite with [his] Counsaill' for formulating such utterances himself. Scholars have debated whether Thomas's ostentatiously stealthy approach was designed to appeal to 'arcane' or 'Protestant' traditions of counsel, whatever the later might mean.[218] In fact, Thomas had hit on a convenient method of avoiding Cheke's scrutiny and probable opposition to the king's study of Machiavelli. The idea of secrecy also proved tempting to a young king eager for more independence and about to turn fourteen, the age at which his cousin, James V of Scotland, had come into his majority in 1526.[219] Edward accepted the clerk's offer and its terms.

In the months that followed, Thomas elaborated on several Machiavellian commonplaces for the king. He used the Florentine's historical method to challenge the utility of two ideologies that had shaped Edward's education: godly monarchy and commonwealth discourse.

[216] BL, Cotton MS Titus B II, fol. 84^{r-v}; Machiavelli, *The discourses*, trans. Leslie Walker and Brian Richardson, ed. Bernard Crick (London, 1970), pp. 98–9 and *The prince*, eds. Quentin Skinner and Russell Price (Cambridge, 1988), pp. 3, 52, 53; Polybius, *Histories*, IX.1–2. See also Lisa Jardine and Anthony Grafton, '"Studied for action": How Gabriel Harvey read his Livy', *P&P*, 129 (1990).

[217] BL, Cotton MS Vespasian D XVIII, fols. 28^{v}–29^{r}; BL, Cotton MS Titus B II, fol. 90^{r}; Stanford Lehmberg, 'Throckmorton, Sir Nicholas (1515/16–1571)', *ODNB*.

[218] BL, Cotton MS Vespasian D XVIII, fol. 29^{r}; Anglo, *Machiavelli – the first century*, p. 105; Peter Donaldson, *Machiavelli and mystery of state* (Cambridge, 1988), pp. 42–4; Shrank, *Writing the nation*, p. 133.

[219] Jamie Cameron, *James V: The personal rule, 1528–1542* (East Linton, 1998), p. 9.

Thomas tackled the former in his discourses on foreign affairs, the first of which was entitled 'What princes amitie is best' and based on chapter twenty-one of *The prince* and parts of book two of the *Discourses*. The clerk began by urging Edward to set aside his Ciceronian understanding of *amicitia* as 'perfict concorde of all divine and humayne things', as the 'perverse nature of men in this tyme' precluded such friendships between rulers. Nevertheless, the same perversity compelled princes to establish 'politike amitie' with other rulers, what Machiavelli had termed 'ally' (*amico*) and 'alliance' (*amicizia*), if they wished to 'mainteigne their owne'.[220] He drew on Machiavelli's discussion of the Roman conquest of Italy in the *Discourses* (II.22) to argue that small and weak kingdoms like England could neither 'mainteigne peace nor susteigne warre' independently. The ancient Italians' mistake had been a failure to measure 'their forces with their doinges'. In the time of the Danish and Norman invasions, Thomas argued, Anglo-Saxon kings had made a similar miscalculation and failed to seek the 'foreyn frendships' they needed to repel conquest. Thomas argued that Edward's England also needed allies 'to resist [the] enemy', 'to live peaceably without molestation' and to supplement its 'lack of commodities' with imported goods.[221] Indeed, in a subsequent 'opinion toocheng yo[u]r Ma[jest]tes outwares affaires at this present', Thomas made it clear how vulnerable Edward and England were without such politic friends. The break from Rome, military weakness and poverty left them 'both hated and contempned' by neighbours on all sides, which, as Machiavelli has said, was the most dangerous condition for the prince. The only thing in the realm's favour, Thomas argued, was that 'no enemye' currently had 'the swearde in hande' against them.[222] Thomas urged Edward to consider his paltry forces, assess the potential costs of maintaining peace or sustaining war, and avoid giving Charles V or Henri II any pretext to strike.

In determining the ploys likely to open hostilities, Thomas considered a question that Machiavelli had had less reason to ponder: the role of religion in generating conflict. The Florentine had attracted contemporary criticism for treating both popes and sultans as nothing more or less than rulers struggling to maintain their states and win glory. Thomas, however, insisted that the 'tymes' had changed. The division of Christendom

[220] BL, Cotton MS Vespasian D XVIII, fols. 12^{r-v}; Machiavelli, *Discourses*, pp. 257–60 and *The prince*, pp. 77–8.
[221] BL, Cotton MS Vespasian D XVIII, fols. 13^{r-v}, 14^{r}; Machiavelli, *Discourses*, pp. 346–7, on Livy, *Ab urbe condita*, VIII.13.2–3.
[222] BL, Cotton MS Vespasian D XVIII, fol. 37^{r}; Machiavelli, *The prince*, p. 64.

and the fortunes of the Franco-Ottoman alliance suggested that there could be no lasting 'amitie' between princes unless they were 'of one opinion' touching religion.[223] Thomas's embassy to France had given him a front-row seat to the participation of Gabriel de Luetz, Baron et Seigneur d'Aramon, in the Turkish assault on Sicily and Malta and the Turks' capture of Tripoli in 1551. He was scathing about the lack of utility of the alliance for Henri II: 'If by the Turkes means the ffrenche king might have extirped thempor (which was thende of this desired amitie) his owne destruct[i]on must have followed'. 'For with the Turke', Thomas wrote, translating a quotation from Ennius in Cicero's *De officiis* (1.26), '*Nulla sancta societas nec fides est.* No sacred tie or public faith exist.'[224] Edward was a keen enough student of Latin grammar and Cicero to know that the commonplace really meant, 'There is no fellowship or faith where *kingship* is concerned.' Thomas warned Edward in a subsequent discourse, drawn from *The prince* (ch. 25) and *The discourses* (III.40), that he was living in an age when princes 'have lesse confines to their willes and lesse amitie… than in tyme past'. Religious differences offered rulers sufficient pretext to break the delicate threads of a treaty. It was necessary, therefore, that Edward follow the advice of 'Macchiauegli' and 'phrame his proceadinge unto his tyme'. In what may have been a reference to the king's recalcitrance over Mary's masses, Thomas warned him 'not to persever obstinately in one opinion' when he found that circumstances had altered.[225] Indeed, a time in which amities were so easily broken might require him to adopt some extreme measures.

In his discourse touching 'outwardes affaires', Thomas set out the demands of the 'tyme' for a reforming king of England in alarmist terms, much as Machiavelli had attempted to alert Lorenzo de Medici to the difficulties of his position as a newly installed prince of Florence in chapter seven of *The prince*. Thomas warned Edward that confessional differences meant that he could not expect any more 'perfict amitie' from those 'puissant' kings Henri II and Charles V than the French would get from the Turk. Despite the recent peace treaty with England, France remained 'a doubtfull frend'. It has 'don us already displeasure' in war and by its 'possession of Scotlande and practiseth in Ireland… amongst a people… readie to revolte'. As for Charles V, the Spanish king merely wanted the

[223] BL, Cotton MS Vespasian D XVIII, fol. 18^{r}.

[224] BL, Cotton MS Vespasian D XVIII, fol. 18^{r-v}; Christine Isom Verhaaren, *Allies with the infidels: The Ottoman and French alliance in the sixteenth century* (New York, 2011), p. 42.

[225] BL, Cotton MS Vespasian D XVIII, fols. 34^{v}, 4^{r}, 9^{r-v}, 10^{r}; Machiavelli, *Discourses*, pp. 513–14 and *The prince*, pp. 84–5.

right moment to strike at the English heretics. 'For what quarrel hath he to the Germaynes but Religion?' Thomas asked, neglecting the question of the political obedience these minor magistrates arguably owed the Holy Roman Emperor. 'Whan [Charles] shall have overcomen those fewe' rebels that remain, Thomas wondered, 'wheare shall he ende his furie but against us?' England had to hope that the plucky town of Magdeburg would survive the siege of Prince Maurice of Saxony, that the Germans would 'not [be] wonne to the papisticall secte' and that the Turks might come into Hungary.[226] This, he warned, was not sufficient security. Machiavelli had argued in chapter thirteen of *The prince* that the best method of deterring aggression was to arm oneself but Thomas pointed out that Edward currently lacked the time and money to augment his forces. Having used techniques of *amplificatio* to impress the king with the imminence and severity of the threat posed by foreign powers, Thomas revealed his radical conclusion: 'o[u]r extremest shift', he wrote, 'is to worke by policie'.[227] The king would need to adopt expedient stratagems and dissimulation to preserve the commonwealth.

The notion that honesty was not necessarily commensurate with good kingship ran counter to everything Edward had been taught. Thomas was quick to reassure Edward that his godly ends justified, perhaps even mandated, such 'policie': England's difference with France and Spain 'is in God'; thus it was beholden on 'us' not 'to neglect that policie that may helpe us' to preserve His word and 'establishe Religion w[i]thin yo[i]r Realme'. Just as 'wickednesse happened to thelect [sic.] people of Israell' and their kings were required to respond, so England's rulers had a duty to prevail in God's quarrel on earth.[228] Thomas reminded Edward that he, and implicitly Warwick, shared the king's commitment to purifying and rebuilding the church. This was especially critical given the nature of the stratagem that Thomas was about to propose. He recommended that the king insure his recent alliance with Henri II by forming a pact of mutual defence against France with the Emperor. Indeed, in 1551 and 1552 Warwick would pursue an alliance of this kind on the basis suggested by Thomas, that French activities in Scotland and Ireland were a threat to Charles V's holding in the Low Countries and England alike.[229]

226 BL, Cotton MS Vespasian D XVIII, fols. 35^{v}–36^{r}. The end of the siege of Magdeburg suggests a terminal date of 4 November 1551 for this discourse.

227 BL, Cotton MS Vespasian D XVIII, fols. 35^{v}–36^{v}, 37^{r-v}. For a contemporary use of 'policie' in this sense, see Erasmus, *First tome or volume of the Paraphrases*, on *Acts*, XXVII, fol. 87^{r}.

228 BL, Cotton MS Vespasian D XVIII, fols. 37^{r}, 39^{v}.

229 BL, Cotton MS Vespasian D XVIII, fols. 37^{v}–38^{r}; *HMC Salisbury*, vol. I, pp. 82, 100–2.

The clerk warned Edward that Warwick's overtures were effective; 'the principall poinct' of the emperor's response would be to 'demaunde alterac[i]on of Religion'. Thomas anticipated Edward's probable answer to such a request and urged him not to reject Charles's terms outright. The matter, he argued, could 'be dissembled with such practice of delaies as may best serve to the mynneng of tyme'. The king would not need to convert; indeed, he would only need to adopt the guise during Charles V 'lief', which he augured 'can not longe endure'. This would buy Edward time to advance reform at home and ready his subjects to defend the realm with arms. The stratagem would also deter the French from breaking their 'leage' out of fear of further conflict with Spain.[230] In a *refutatio* of possible objections to the scheme, he urged Edward not to fear giving heart to English 'papists' or diminishing his reputation as a second Josiah abroad; 'th'ende' of preserving 'our Religion' and estate would bring Edward glory, obedience and piety in the end.[231] When it came to foreign affairs, Thomas argued, the zealous expressions of godly monarchy that Edward had been exhorted to articulate would be counter-productive, because he could not defend his confessional militancy with arms. To this end, Thomas evoked one of Machiavelli's more notorious departures from classical wisdom: 'Where [a prince] could not plaie the Lyon it was no shame to plaie the Foxe.' 'To establishe Religion w[i]thin [his] Realme', Edward would need to play Nicodemus, rather than Josiah, on the world's stage.[232]

In concluding this discourse on foreign affairs, Thomas suggested that there might be an additional local benefit to mustering troops in preparation for defending England against the emperor. 'Those subiectes which have their heades occupied w[i]th civile com[m]oc[i]onns', Thomas asserted, 'sall the lesse thinke on their mischeif at home' if they understood the threat from abroad.[233] Like Warwick, Thomas had little patience with the febrile 'commonalitie'. Indeed, Thomas adapted Machiavelli's consideration of whether liberty was best safeguarded by the populace or nobility (*Discourses*, I.5) to urge Edward against relying on the language of the commonwealth in ordering his subjects. The clerk began by altering Machiavelli's question. In his discourse, the issue at stake was not liberty but power, more specifically

[230] BL, Cotton MS Vespasian D XVIII, fols. 38^v, 39^r.

[231] BL, Cotton MS Vespasian D XVIII, fol. 41^r; Machiavelli, *The prince*, p. 63.

[232] BL, Cotton MS Vespasian D XVIII, fols. 6^r, 39^v; Machiavelli, *Discourses*, II.13, p. 311 and *The prince*, p. 61.

[233] BL, Cotton MS Vespasian D XVIII, fol. 45^r.

'whether it be better for a com[m]on wealthe that the power be in the nobilitie or in the co[m]monalitie'.[234] Thomas set out the dangers to the realm in allowing the 'commons' to grow into a 'partie' capable of avoiding the impositions of the aristocracy. Unlike Machiavelli, Thomas had little to say in favour of powerful 'moltitudes': they were inconstant, eager to shuck the authority not only of the nobles but 'their civile laws and the orderes of their magistrates' and thoroughly lacking in 'wisdome' about how to reconstitute order once the 'gentelmen' had been overcome. There was 'perill in their frenzy', Thomas wrote, drawing upon Jean Froissart's account of the popular revolt of the Jacquerie in northern France in 1358. Once the commons 'attaigne the power they destroie both the nobilitie and themselfes'.[235] 'Popularitie', by which Thomas meant a democracy or republic like that of 'the Swizzers… Athenes, Fflorence and such other', could not 'longe prosper'. He specifically warned Edward against appearing to encourage 'popularitie'. Though it might seem 'evill' that 'the commons have been oppressed, and that for the disordinate appetites of a few the multitude had suffered', the history of the last 'xxx yeres togither' had made it plain that where magistrates had favoured the commons nothing but 'sectes, sedicion, and commocions' had followed. What was worse, Thomas asked Edward in a clear nod towards 1549, 'the tyrannie of a fewe, or the subversion of thastate?'[236] Warwick's man tried to persuade Edward to re-evaluate his own reliance on commonwealth discourse to understand England's economic and political plight. Unlike his uncle Somerset, Thomas implied, he did not need to depend on the support of the 'moltitude' to maintain his estate. Indeed, to do so would actually put his monarchy and the commonwealth as a whole in constant 'daunger of subversion'.[237]

Rather than trust in the commons to contain the aristocracy, as 'Macchiauegli in his discourses of the libertie of a common wealthe determineth', Thomas argued that Edward should 'bridell' any 'ambicion or tyranny' in amongst the 'magistrates or nobilitie' himself.[238] Could he have been referring to the 'ambicion' of Somerset himself, who had probably

[234] BL, Cotton MS Vespasian D XVIII, fol. 20^{r}.
[235] BL, Cotton MS Vespasian D XVIII, fols. 20^{v}–24^{v}. For the Jacqueries, see George Campbell Macaulay (ed.), *The chronicles of Froissart* (London, 1904), pp. 136–7.
[236] BL, Cotton MS Vespasian D XVIII, fols. 24^{r}–25^{r}.
[237] BL, Cotton MS Vespasian D XVIII, fol. 25$^{r–v}$.
[238] BL, Cotton MS Vespasian D XVIII, fol. 26^{r}.

been arrested shortly before Edward read Thomas's discourse? When the king described the duke's 'device' in his *Chronicle* of October 1551, he stressed that Somerset had attempted 'to raise the people'. If the duke were overthrown in the first stage of his conspiracy against Warwick, he allegedly intended to 'run through London and cry "Liberty, liberty", to raise the [ap]prentices' to his side. The appeal to popularity was coupled with his supposed tyrannical eagerness to subjugate the king by marrying him to his daughter and spying on him 'in all matters of my doings and sayings'.[239] What could be the end of such a plan but the 'subversion' of the state? Thomas concluded his discourse with an implied appeal to Edward to respond to the time and spurn his uncle's example. It was critical that he refrain from offering 'so much libertie' to the commons 'as to talk of the Princes causes and of the reason of the Lawes'. They would co-opt the language of the commonwealth, wax in 'contempte and consequentlie disobedience' and 'shewe their desire not to be ruled'.[240] This had been Somerset's mistake. It was an error that Thomas and Warwick intended that Edward should not repeat.

When Thomas's discourses are located in the social context of Edward's education, it becomes clear that they are no minor Machiavellian moment, reiteration of Castiglione or attempt to tame the Florentine fox. Rather, Thomas was making a strident and 'politike' refutation of the utility of playing the godly monarch in international affairs, and of using commonwealth language at home. He used Machiavelli's historical method to challenge Cheke's preference for moral philosophy and attempted a covert re-education of the king. Probably at the behest of the earl of Warwick, Thomas attempted to fast-track Edward's appreciation of the exigencies of government and the 'tyme', and the importance of acting to secure the survival of his princely 'astate' and commonwealth. The principles of godly monarchy needed to be distinguished from the good of the commonwealth. Commonwealth discourse needed to be jettisoned in favour of using 'education and discipline' with the commons that the 'name of their Prince shulde make them to tremble'.[241] In 1551, as the king turned fourteen and began to take steps towards exercising his authority, Edward's Erasmian education was challenged by its ideological counterpoint, a reading of Machiavelli that emphasised dissimulation and force and attempted to bolster rather than moderate the power of the prince.

[239] Edward, *CPP*, pp. 87, 89, 93.
[240] BL, Cotton MS Vespasian D XVIII, fol. 27^{r-v}.
[241] BL, Cotton MS Vespasian D XVIII, fol. 27^{r}.

CONCLUSION

There was much that was radical about Thomas's discourses but his literary methods were familiar to Edward. Rather than attempting to overawe, bribe or manipulate the king to modify his behaviour, Thomas used techniques derived from liberal education – the elaboration of commonplaces and appeals to history – to persuade him. As such, this Machiavellian counsel did not shatter the lens through which Edward saw the world but its beams did not bounce off his consciousness either. Rather, Thomas's emphasis on maintaining power, working through dissimulation when it was necessary and measuring his doings according to his forces became another political language in Edward's polyglot artillery.

The king did not turn his back on Cheke or Belmaine in the final eighteen months of this life. Both continued to benefit from royal favour. As Edward's 'summary of matters' for his council in October 1552 shows, the king also remained a zealous advocate of religious reform. He continued to refuse the January 1552 pleas of Charles V's ambassador 'that my sister Mary might have mass' with her household.[242] The difference, however, was that after autumn 1551 Edward began to use indirect means and a subtler vocabulary to further his ends. To appease Mary, or persuade her that she had more to gain from his friendship than from his enmity, Edward granted her property in Essex, Hertford, Norfolk and Suffolk alongside a gift of £570 to recompense repairs she had needed to make on her coastal holdings after a storm. The political benefits of his strategy accrued quickly. By June 1552 the princess was prepared to visit Edward at Greenwich. In February 1553 she entered London in state as 'the second person in the kingdom' and was received by the king in the presence chamber.[243] Her threat to public order in England had been neutralised, at least until the king's demise. Edward also thought carefully about how to deal with Charles V. Having monitored the emperor's persecution of Protestants in Germany, and considered pros and cons of action in a discourse, he decided on 19 September 1552 to ally himself to the emperor in a cause against the Turks and, indirectly, the French as long as his participation was 'not to be acknown'. The second Josiah knew he could not play the lion with the emperor and Henri II and was willing to be a fox,

[242] Edward, *CPP*, pp. 179, 104 (quotation).

[243] *Calendar of state papers domestic: Edward, Mary and Elizabeth*, eds. Robert Lemmon and Mary Anne Everett Green, 12 vols. (London, 1856), vol. 1, p. 48; Machyn, *Diary of Henry Machyn*, pp. 30–1; SP 10/15, fol. 133^{r}.

at least temporarily.[244] The king also deemed Somerset and his commonwealth discourse to be at odds with the time. Edward resigned himself to his uncle's execution, merely noting in his *Chronicle* that on 22 January 1552 the duke 'had his head cut off upon Tower Hill between eight and nine o'clock in the morning'.[245] In his written proposals for augmenting the wealth of the realm, he began to turn away from the need to curb enclosures and contain the rapacity of noblemen, in favour of restoring the coinage and, from March 1552, a scheme for establishing an entrepôt in England.[246] Edward still considered it his foremost duty to promote the piety and welfare of his subjects, but he had a new political language, new methods and increasing authority to work with.

The ideological purpose of Edward's education had changed at least three times during his short life and reign. Henry VIII had wanted to fashion his son and heir in his own image, politically and doctrinally. Somerset and Cranmer had attempted to shape a commonwealth king and godly monarch. Warwick and Thomas tried to teach Edward to measure his actions by his forces. In each case, Edward had been a conscientious student. The constant throughout, however, had been the centrality of letters to his performance of kingship. When Edward faced a political or religious problem, he used his pen to tackle it. We should not be surprised, then, that in the brief lull between his penultimate and final illnesses, around April 1553, the young king concocted a plan for the descent of the English crown by drafting, correcting and revising a 'Deuise for the succession'. After Edward's death on 6 July 1553, it was Warwick, by then duke of Northumberland, who attempted to enforce the plan to bypass Mary and Elizabeth in favour of the Suffolk line, 'Lady Jane~~s~~ [inserted above: and her] heires masles'.[247] Yet the device itself had been Edward's.

Once sprung, Edward's will represented the blasted hopes of royal schoolmasters and counsellors. The king's demise rendered their Herculean efforts to use liberal education to fashion the perfect prince null and void. Yet Edward's efforts to manage the succession with his pen, in lieu of heirs of his body, were testaments to their success. The hand in which the multiple corrections and additions were made was the king's, and it bore

244 Edward, *CPP*, pp. 127, 136, 146; *Calendar of state papers foreign series of the reign of Edward VI, 1547–1553*, ed. William B. Turnbull (London, 1861), p. 221.

245 Edward, *CPP*, p. 107.

246 Edward, *CPP*, pp. 82–3, 168–73; BL, Cotton MS Vespasian D XVIII, fols. 28^r–31^v.

247 Inner Temple Library, London, Petyt MS 47, fol. 317^r. For Edward's authorship and instigation, see Alford, *Kingship and politics*, pp. 171–3; Ives, *Lady Jane Grey*, pp. 137–47; Loach, *Edward VI*, pp. 163–7. *CSPV*, vol. v, pp. 535–6 exaggerates Northumberland's role.

the marks of all his teachers. Henry VIII had appointed Cox and Cheke to teach Edward to maintain the royal supremacy with his pen; Edward attempted to preserve his church's independence by bucking the common law of inheritance as violently as Henry VIII had with his Succession Acts, and by upholding Henry's declaration of Mary's and Elizabeth's illegitimacy.[248] After February 1547 Cranmer, Somerset and Belmaine taught Edward to purify the church; in his device, Edward was willing to supplant his own Tudor line in order to ensure an 'evangelical dynasty' via the more thoroughly reformed house of Suffolk in England.[249] Finally, Warwick employed Thomas to counsel Edward to measure his doings by his forces and vary his conduct according to the time; at the last minute, the king modified his plan to introduce an English version of Salic law and added Jane Grey herself, rather than merely her 'heires masles', to the succession. Jane's marriage to Guildford Dudley on 25 May meant that Northumberland was now compelled to provide the forces necessary to bring Edward's scheme to pass.[250] It was an audacious stroke of the princely pen. Edward's Erasmian education had given him the rhetorical artillery to use ink, rather than force of arms or the fruits of his own failing body, to fashion a dynasty. He came remarkably close to pulling it off.

[248] Eric Ives, 'Tudor dynastic problems revisited', *Historical Research*, 81 (2008).
[249] MacCulloch, *Tudor church militant*, p. 39.
[250] Ives, *Lady Jane Grey*, p. 158.

CHAPTER 5

Fortune's wheel and the education of early modern British queens

Edward VI's final, clerkish attempt to protect the royal supremacy and purify the church resulted in the 10 July proclamation of Lady Jane Grey of Suffolk (1537–54), the first woman to claim the English throne since the Empress Matilda (1102–67). Nine days later, however, Princess Mary (1516–58) trumped Edward's device of the pen with her sword. Henry VIII's eldest daughter had won a victory 'more of Herculean than of womanly daring' and made her triumphal entry to London as its warrior queen.[1] Her successor, Elizabeth I (1533–1603), also (perhaps) claimed to have a stomach for battle.[2] More generally, however, England's sovereign queens would rely on their piety and learning to advance their status and authority. As her chaplain, John Angel (d. 1566×8), put it in 1555, Mary I was 'a new Judith', the slayer of Holofernes who wisely brought her people to 'knowledge… of Goddes worde'.[3] In 1562, the Italian humanist Celio Secondo Curione (1503–69) compared the 'most learned Queen Elizabeth' to Deborah the judge of the Israelites, to Judith, their liberator, and to Paula and Eustochium, the Roman followers of St Jerome; 'indeed', he wrote, 'posterity will admire you no less than them'.[4]

Curione's words were prophetic. In the past twenty years, in particular, scholars have studied, edited and generally commended the 'good letters' composed and translated by Mary I (1516–58), Elizabeth I (1533–1603),

[1] Robert Wingfield, *Vita Mariae Angliae Reginae*, ed. Diarmaid MacCulloch, *Camden Miscellany*, vol. XXVIII (London, 1984), p. 252. See also Anna Whitelock, *Mary Tudor: England's first queen* (London, 2009), p. 178 and '"Woman, warrior, queen?": Rethinking Mary and Elizabeth', in Anna Whitelock and Alice Hunt (eds.), *Tudor queenship: The Reigns of Mary and Elizabeth* (Basingstoke, 2010).

[2] On the controversy of the Tilbury oration, see Steven May, 'Queen Elizabeth to her subjects: The Tilbury and Golden speeches', in Donal Stump, Linda Shenk and Carole Levin (eds.), *Elizabeth I and the 'sovereign arts': Essays in literature, history, and culture* (Tempe, 2011).

[3] John Angel, *The agrement of the holye fathers, and doctors of the church, upon the cheifest articles of Christian religion* (London, 1555), STC 634, sig. Aiii^v.

[4] 'Elisabeta Regina lectissima… facis ut posteritas te no[n] minus quam illas sit admiratura': Celio Secondo Curione, Epistle dedicatory, in Olympia Morata, *Orationes, dialogi, epistolae, carmina, tam Latin quam Graeca*, ed. Celio Secondo (Basle, 1562), fols. 1^r, 5^r.

Lady Jane Grey (1537–1554), Mary, Queen of Scots (1542–1587), and Elizabeth Stuart, Queen of Bohemia (1596–1662).[5] The intoxicating pessimism of early investigations, which concluded that early modern women were likely to be vilified as sexual monsters, confined to golden cages for going 'beyond their sex' or rendered 'silent but for the word' by their liberal educations, has been purged.[6] Instead humanism is praised for contributing to 'the emergence of secular women… as cultural protagonists' and the creation of 'women writers' who were 'central to the development of the Protestant literary tradition' and even to 'the birth of feminism' in the sixteenth and seventeenth centuries.[7] At the vanguard of those Renaissance women who succeeded in translating their learning into personal and political authority were the Tudor and Stuart queens.[8]

This is all the more remarkable because, despite some scholars' confidence to the contrary, these women had not been brought up to rule.[9]

[5] For example *Brief confessional writings: Grey, Stubbes, Livingstone and Clarksone*, ed. Mary Ellen Lamb (Aldershot, 2001); Elizabeth, *ACFL*; Elizabeth I, *Elizabeth I: Collected works*, eds. Leah Marcus, Janel Mueller and Mary Beth Rose (Chicago, 2000); Elizabeth, *Translations*; Elizabeth I and Mary I, *Early modern Englishwoman: Elizabeth and Mary Tudor*, ed. Ann Lake Prescott (Aldershot, 2001); Peter J. Herman, *Royal poetrie: Monarchic verse and the political imaginary of early modern England* (Ithaca, 2010); Lisa Hopkins, *Writing Renaissance queens: Texts by and about Elizabeth I and Mary Queen of Scots* (Newark, 2007), pp. 72–87; Elizabeth Stuart, *The correspondence of Elizabeth Stuart, Queen of Bohemia*: vol. II: *1632–42*, ed. Nadine Akkerman (Oxford, 2011).

[6] For example Anthony Grafton and Lisa Jardine, *From humanism to the humanities: Education and the liberal arts in fifteenth- and sixteenth-century Europe* (Cambridge, MA, 1986), pp. 29–57; Margaret P. Hannay (ed.), *Silent but for the word: Tudor women as patrons, translators, and writers of religious works* (Kent, OH, 1985); Patricia H. Labalme (ed.), *Beyond their sex: Learned women of the European past* (New York, 1980); Colette Nativel, *Femmes savantes, savoirs des femmes: Du crépuscule de la Renaissance à l'aube des lumières* (Geneva, 1995).

[7] Respectively Virginia Cox, *Women's writing in Italy, 1400–1650* (Baltimore, 2008), p. xiii; Kimberly Coles, *Religion, reform, and women's writing in early modern England* (Cambridge, 2010), p. 1; Sarah Ross, *The birth of feminism: Woman as intellect in Renaissance Italy and England* (Cambridge, MA, 2009).

[8] For example Rayne Allison, *A monarchy of letters: Royal correspondence and English diplomacy in the reign of Elizabeth I* (New York, 2012); Jacqueline Broad and Karen Green, *A history of women's political thought in Europe, 1400–1700* (Cambridge, 2009), pp. 90–110; Linda Shenk, *Learned queen: The image of Elizabeth I in politics and poetry* (New York, 2010).

[9] Maria Dowling, *Humanism in the age of Henry VIII* (London, 1986), pp. 219–43; Catherine Eskin, 'The reigning of women's tongues in English books of instruction and rhetorics', in Barbara Whitehead (ed.), *Women's education in early modern Europe: A history, 1500–1800* (New York, 1999), p. 120; Jonathan Gibson, 'Katherine Parr, Princess Elizabeth and the crucified Christ', in Victoria Burke and Jonathan Gibson (eds.), *Early modern women's manuscript writing: Selected papers from the Trinity/Trent colloquium* (Aldershot, 2004), pp. 33–50; Elizabeth Mazzola, 'Schooling shrews and grooming queens in the Tudor classroom', *Critical Survey*, 22:1 (2010); Jane Stevenson, *Women Latin poets: Language, gender, and authority from antiquity to the eighteenth century* (Oxford, 2005), pp. 258–9. Andrew Taylor, '"Ad omne virtutum genus"? Mary between piety, pedagogy and praise in early Tudor humanism', in Susan Doran and Thomas Freeman (eds.), *Mary Tudor: Old and new perspectives* (Basingstoke, 2011), pp. 103–22, 296–302 is unusual in questioning the extent and nature of the queen's learning.

Not really. Their families' doubts regarding their princely potential were reflected in the provisions made for their liberal educations, which usually began later than the studies of their male kin and commanded fewer resources. Nevertheless, they had some entry to 'good letters', facilitated by the success of humanists' arguments that the liberal arts and sciences would help royal and aristocratic women to respond honourably to the changing circumstances in their life cycles and 'susteyne fortune at al times paciently'.[10] Scholars have praised those elite, early modern European families who identified this argument with their dynastic self-interest and nurtured their daughters' studies of Latin and occasionally Greek. The family, once thought to shackle women to the domestic sphere, to 'personal' concerns and to child-bearing, is increasingly celebrated as an 'intellectual' circle, a vehicle for 'representative publicity' and a status-rich asset whose value women increased with their writings.[11] The first sections of this chapter will ask whether the reverse side of the coin of filial empowerment was constraint: a well-educated daughter might be better positioned to help her family through marriage or to minimise the cost of a failure of primogeniture, yet the same consideration dictated that she should not be, or appear to be, a threat to the interests of her male kin. These simultaneous and contrary forces may help to explain why learned women concentrated their intellectual efforts on producing good letters in three genres in the early modern period: the familial letter, the prayer and the translation.

The empowering and constraining weights of dynastic strategy certainly shaped the liberal studies of Tudor and Stuart queens, though they affected them in different ways. The second section of this chapter compares the educations of Mary, Queen of Scots, and her granddaughter, Elizabeth, the future queen of Bohemia. Despite their confessional differences, the geographical locations of their schooling and their varying proximities to the throne, the superior claims of Mary's French fiancé and Elizabeth's British brothers meant that both came to Latin late. Indeed, they scrambled to pick it up when, as young women, they were surprised by fortune. From the beginning, Lady Jane Grey's fates were closely allied to her schooling. She was the eldest child of ambitious parents who had no sons. The third part of this chapter asks whether the same forces that propelled the Suffolks to thrust Jane into Thomas Seymour's household,

[10] Thomas Elyot, *The defence of good women* (London, 1540), STC 7657.5, sig. Eiiii^r.

[11] Respectively Ross, *Birth of feminism*, p. 2; Jaime Goodrich, 'Thomas More and Margaret More Roper: A case for rethinking women's participation in the early modern public sphere', *SCJ*, 39:4 (2008); Diane Purkiss (ed.), *Three tragedies by Renaissance women* (Harmondsworth, 1998).

to beat her and to compel her to accept the English crown in 1553 had also led them to provide her with the education that humanists and reformers praised.

Jane Grey had begun to use her liberal education in the captivity of the Tower but her Tudor cousins, Mary and Elizabeth, would brandish their pens as their sceptres. The final sections of this chapter identify ways in which their study of the liberal arts and sciences was delayed, watered down and feminised, even after Henry VIII's daughters were officially returned to the line of succession behind Edward in 1544. Despite their confessional differences, Elizabeth Tudor's schooling resembled Mary's more closely than Edward VI's. When fortune's wheel turned, both Henry VIII's daughters were ill-prepared to rule a church, at least in the conventional sense. For Mary, this did not present a doctrinal or political problem. Yet the way in which Elizabeth's liberal education constrained and facilitated her understanding of 'devynyte till [she] came to the crowne' may shed new light on an old question about the government of her ecclesiastical polity.[12]

FEMALE HUMANISM AND RULING FAMILIES

If few royal men in England or Scotland studied Latin in the fifteenth century, their female kin had even less opportunity.[13] Even Margaret Beaufort, the great educational patron and learned translator of Dionysius the Carthusian's *Speculum aureum* from French, confessed to John Fisher that 'in her youthe she had not gyven her to the understondynge of latyn' and that she still had but 'lytell perceyvnge'.[14] When humanists began to argue that all those who played a role in governing the commonwealth required a liberal education, the existing gap between male and female aristocratic education threatened to expand.[15] Yet the same pedagogues who agitated for princely education in the *bonae litterae* also proposed to overcome royal and aristocratic women's ignorance of ancient authors. Humanists were optimistic that learning would encourage female virtue but they described women's achievements as a sign of the moral health of a collective – a family, a polity, a confession – rather than an agent

[12] Elizabeth in *PPE*, vol. 1, p. 148.

[13] Dowling, *Humanism in the age of Henry VIII*, p. 219.

[14] Michael K. Jones and Malcolm S. Underwood, *The king's mother: Lady Margaret Beaufort, Countess of Richmond and Derby* (Cambridge, 1992), p. 184.

[15] Walter J. Ong, *Rhetoric, roman and technology: Studies in the interaction of expression and culture* (Ithaca, 1971), p. 120.

or catalyst of its reform. In part, humanists' lack of ambition for female pupils stemmed from an assumption that learned early modern European women generally shared: the object of their studies was not to challenge the pre-eminence of their fathers or brothers.

At the same time that they were warning young noblemen off military training and paramilitary exercises such as hunting, northern humanists including Erasmus, Thomas More and Vives criticised the traditional schooling of noblewomen.[16] Instead of learning to dance and read vernacular romances, northern humanists argued that gentlewomen and noblewomen would derive as much moral and intellectual benefit from the study of the *bonae litterae* as their brothers. They, too, would learn to govern their passions with reason and live more virtuously by studying classical languages and literature.[17] Nevertheless, as Ian Maclean has argued, northern humanists tended to follow Aristotle's argument in the *Nicomachean Ethics* that female goodness was different from, indeed dichotomous to, male excellence.[18] Vives's influential *De institutione feminae Christianae* (1523), which the humanist presented to Catherine of Aragon, nominally for the education of her daughter Mary, emphasised obedience, piety and chastity.[19] As Vives explained in his letter, using liberal education to promote these qualities would spare a husband the horror of 'sharing [his] life with a person of no principles'.[20] Whereas male excellence was predicated on responsibility to the *civitas*, female virtue depended on women's successful discharge of their duties to male kin.

Nevertheless, northern humanists recognised that, for royal and aristocratic women, familial responsibilities could have political implications. The French Huguenot Agrippa d'Aubigné (1552–1630) argued that liberal

[16] For example Juan Luis Vives, *De institutione feminae Christianae: Introduction, critical edition, translation and notes*, trans. C. Fantazzi, eds. C. Fantazzi and C. Matheeussen, 2 vols. (Leiden, 1996), vol. I, pp. 38, 39, 46, 47.

[17] For example Thomas More, *The correspondence of Sir Thomas More*, ed. Elizabeth F. Rogers (Princeton, 1947), p. 122; John Guy, *A Daughter's love: Thomas More and his dearest Meg* (Boston, 2009), pp. 61–7.

[18] Ian Maclean, *The Renaissance notion of woman: A study in the fortunes of scholasticism and medical science in European intellectual life* (Cambridge, 1980), pp. 49–51, 54, 56, 59; Aristotle, *Nicomachean ethics*, VIII.12.7, 1162a15–33.

[19] Vives, *De institutione feminae Christianae*, vol. I, pp. 10, 11. In 1529, the treatise was translated into English by Richard Hyrde, one of Thomas More's protégés, and it was reprinted on eight further occasions before 1600: Virginia Walcott Beauchamp, Elizabeth H. Hageman and Margaret Mikesell, 'Introduction', in *The instruction of a Christen woman: Juan Luis Vives*, eds. Virginia Walcott Beauchamp, Elizabeth H. Hageman and Margaret Mikesell (Urbana, 2002), pp. xliii, lxxvii–xciii.

[20] Vives, *De institutione feminae Christianae*, vol. I, pp. 2, 3; see also Aristotle, *Politics*, I.5.12, 1260b14–21.

education was 'almost always useless to ladies of the middling sort' but he conceded that princesses were 'obliged by their condition to assume the care and knowledge of men, and superiority, administration, and authority over [them]', which required knowledge of letters.[21] They argued that a liberal education would prepare such women to meet the vagaries of their dynastic and political fortune. Thomas Elyot's treatise, *The defence of good women* (1540), pointed to the *exemplum* of Zenobia, the ancient Queen of Palmyra. Before her marriage, reading ancient authors had taught Zenobia to live chastely. As a consort queen, her studies had helped her to ornament her husband's court and obey her husband. As a mother, her education had enabled her to attend to the liberal education of her own children. As a widow, her study of rhetoric had enabled her to maintain justice as regent of Palmyra during her son's minority.[22] Zenobia's liberal education had helped her to 'susteyne fortune at al times paciently'.[23] Humanist pedagogues rarely encouraged women to use their learning to seek greatness, but they argued that they could turn to the *bonae litterae* if they were born great or had greatness thrust upon them.

Indeed they argued, quite cannily, that the existence of a learned woman was evidence of the greatness of her collective, be it her family, her confession or her temporal polity. In England Erasmus, Nicholas Harpsfield, William Roper and Thomas Stapleton would all praise the learning and virtue of Margaret More in order to praise her father, Thomas More.[24] When Roger Ascham wished to eulogise the spread of evangelicalism in a 1550 letter to Johann Sturm, he made a point of listing those female proponents of religious reform 'who surpass the daughters of Thomas More in all kinds of learning. Amongst them the shining star… is my Lady Elizabeth'.[25] To educate your daughter was to demonstrate the greatness of your family, your religion and your state.[26] Nevertheless, humanists

[21] 'C'est que je j'ay veu presque toujours inutile aux Damoiselles de moyenne condition, comme vous, car les moins heureuses en ont plus tost abusé… Je ne voudrois aucunement inciter au labeur des lettres autres que les Princesses qui sont par leur condition obligees au soin, à la cognoissance, à la suffisance, aux gestions, et auctoritez des hommes': Théodore Agrippa D'Aubigné, *Oeuvres completes*, eds. E. Réume and F. de Caussade, 6 vols. (Paris, 1873), vol. 1, pp. 449–50.

[22] Elyot, *Defence of good women*, sigs. Ei^r, Eii^v, Div^r–Dv^v.

[23] Elyot, *Defence of good women*, sig. Eiiii^r.

[24] Goodrich, 'Thomas More and Margaret More Roper', p. 1025.

[25] 'Thomae Mori filiabus innumerae nunc honoratae feminae in omni literarum genere praestant. Inter quas tamen universas veluti sidus quoddam… sic eminet illustrissima domina mea, D. Elizabetha': Roger Ascham, *Whole works of Roger Ascham*, ed. J. A. Giles, 3 vols. (London, 1865) I.i, p. 191.

[26] Brenda Hosington, 'Learned ladies: Éloges de l'Anglaise savant (1550–1558)', in Colette Nativel (ed.), *Femmes savantes, savoirs des femmes: Du crépuscule de la Renaissance à l'aube des lumières* (Geneva, 1995).

assumed that, unlike the prince, the learned lady was not an agent of social and political reform.

It is likely that humanists' lower expectations stemmed from their assumption that the liberal education of women would not alter existing power relations between the sexes. Participants in Baldassare Castiglione's influential dialogue *Il Cortegiano* (1528), translated into English by Thomas Hoby in 1561, were eager that court ladies acquire knowledge of 'letters' and 'sweetnesse in language'.[27] Nevertheless, a woman who possessed them merely rendered herself a suitable muse for male courtiers and more appreciative of their conversation, poetry and prose.[28] Castiglione's discussants acknowledged that women might occasionally need to fill a deficit of adult, male authority. The framing conceit in *Il Cortegiano*, for instance, depicted Elisabetta Gonzaga, the duchess of Urbino, and her gentlewoman, Emilia Pia, stepping into the breach left by the incapacitated duke.[29] The liberal education of elite women minimised the political and dynastic costs of failures of primogeniture. Rather than subvert or reform existing gender hierarchies, humanists offered noblewomen and gentlewomen a course of studies that would protect their family and polity in a succession crisis.

As such, the case for schooling early modern royal women in the *bonae litterae* was a strong but conservative one. Well-educated daughters were a dynastic back-up plan. The same filial self-interest that encouraged the liberal education of noblewomen and gentlewomen also discouraged families from teaching their daughters to challenge or surpass their brothers. Even Christine de Pisan (1364–*c.* 1430), who might have been assumed to have some sympathy for her inky-fingered daughter, privileged the schooling of her son. While her daughter wrote 'sweet and pious letters', her son 'mastered the most important branches of knowledge… grammar, rhetoric, [and] poetry'. Christine saved and schemed to place him in noble households in England and France so that he could continue his studies but her daughter remained at home.[30] Pietro Bembo (1470–1547) published letters in which he shamed his son, Torquato for proving less apt in his studies than his daughter Helena; Torquato's inferiority ran against the natural order of things. Yet his son remained his heir, even

[27] Baldesar Castiglione, *The courtyer of Count Baldessar Castilio diuided into foure books*, trans. Thomas Hoby (London, 1561), STC 4778, sigs. Bbiii^{v}, Ccii^{r}.

[28] Castiglione, *Courtyer*, sigs. Hiii^{v}–Hiv^{r}, Iii^{v}.

[29] Castiglione, *Courtyer*, sig. Bbiii^{r}.

[30] 'Elle meismes tu recoups les tres doulces et devotes lettres… il a estudie en noz premieres sciences en gramaire on ne trouveroit ne rethorique et poetique language': Christine de Pisan, *Lavision-Christine*, ed. Mary Louis Towner (Washington, DC, 1932), p. 174.

though providing for his future meant brokering a less illustrious marriage for Helena.[31] The legal and cultural principle of primogeniture encouraged royal and aristocratic parents to maintain their sons' privileged status pedagogically and materially.

For their part, whilst female humanists challenged patriarchal assumptions regarding women's capacity for virtue and asserted agency in their writings, few struck out at their male kin. Indeed, the vast majority of learned women studied, lived and wrote in support of the families that had allowed or even helped them to a liberal education.[32] Filial loyalty was particularly pronounced in female humanists from ruling houses. Ippolita Sforza's (1446–84) one surviving composition after her marriage to the duke of Calabria was a poem lamenting the death of her father, the duke of Milan, in 1466:

> My father-in-law is the king and the glory of the kingdom of Sicily,
> My husband is the next hope of Latium,
> But neither man delights me more
> Than my brothers or mother [then serving as regent in Milan].
> These people, then, are a light to relieve the darkest grief.[33]

A liberally educated royal woman had few allusions about the source of her learning, her status and whatever political authority she possessed. She was prepared to suffer a significant amount of filial abuse before biting the hand that fed her.

In an era of primogeniture, writing in support of one's family could require learned women to bulwark, rather than outshine, the efforts of their male kin. The critical role of Mary Herbert (1561–1621), countess of Pembroke, in refashioning and printing Philip Sidney's (1554–86) *Arcadia* (1593) is a famous example. Her success in creating the 'poetic mythology' of her dead brother's authorship had such an 'enduring influence' on English literature that it actually 'obscured her own decisive role in its development'.[34] More frequently, however, noblewomen pulled off the trick of ornamenting their family's reputation while not threatening the superior learning of male kin by focusing their literary efforts on three key

[31] Ross, *Birth of feminism*, pp. 56–9.

[32] Stevenson, *Women Latin poets*, pp. 172–4, 192–3, 248–9.

[33] 'Est socer ille meus Siculum rex Gloria regum / est meus hic coniux altera spes Latii / Nil socer ipse magis nex coniux deligit eque / Fratribus Ipolite nil genitrice magis / Hiis igitur sevum phar est lenire dolorem': Ippolita Sforza in Stevenson, *Women Latin poets*, pp. 172–3.

[34] Patricia Pender, *Early modern women's writing and the rhetoric of modesty* (Basingstoke, 2012), p. 94.

genres: the familiar epistle, the prayer and the translation of devotional works.[35]

It was not the case that epistles, translations and prayers were necessarily lesser genres in early modern Europe.[36] Indeed, letter-writing and translation were central to the origins of the humanist movement. Collections of correspondence and translations of classical works and scripture were some of the most admired and controversial texts circulated between 1400 and 1700.[37] Printed public prayers may have been even more inflammatory than Erasmus' or Martin Luther's New Testaments. Collections of private prayers were even more popular. Prior to 1600, one hundred distinct works of private prayer were published in England alone.[38] Nevertheless, these genres could still be cast as more elementary than orations or theological treatises. As we have seen in preceding chapters on the educations of the duke of Richmond and Edward VI, letter-writing and translation were two of the earliest exercises performed by schoolboys.[39] If a woman could write a Latin letter, it did not prove that she had progressed to the more advanced literary exercises described in Aphthonius' *Progymnasmata*, or to the reading of Livy, Ovid and Sallust, or to Cicero's, Demosthenes'

[35] Marie-Alice Belle, 'Locating early modern women's translations: Critical and historiographical issues', *Renaissance and Reformation / Renaissance et Réforme*, 35:4 (2012); James Daybell, *Women letter-writers in Tudor England* (Oxford, 2006); Elizabeth Goldsmith and Colette Winn, 'Introduction', in Elizabeth Goldsmith and Colette Winn (eds.), *Lettres de femmes: Textes inédites et oubliés du XVIe au XVIIe siècle* (Paris, 2005), pp. ix–xli; Chris Laoutaris, 'Translation/historical writing', in Caroline Bucks and Jennifer Summit (eds.), *The history of British women's writing 1500–1610* (London, 2010); Jennifer Summit, *Lost property: The woman writer and English literary history, 1380–1589* (Chicago, 2000), p. 111; Micheline White, 'Women, religious communities, prose genres, and textual production', in Micheline White (ed.), *English women, religion, and textual production, 1500–1625* (Aldershot, 2011), pp. 6–8.

[36] Lawrence Venuti, *The translator's invisibility: A history of translation* (London, 1995).

[37] Paul Botley, *Latin translation in the Renaissance: The theory and practice of Leonardo Bruni, Giannozzo Manetti, and Desiderius Erasmus* (Cambridge, 2004); Brian Cummings, *Literary culture of the Reformation: Grammar and grace* (Oxford, 2002), pp. 25, 66–7, 102–10, 192–206, 224–31; Lisa Jardine, *Erasmus, man of letters: The construction of charisma in print* (Princeton, 1993); Ronald G. Witt, *In the footsteps of the ancients: The origins of humanism from Lovato to Bruni* (Boston, 2003), pp. 13–14, 53–8, 224–7, 244, 260, 265, 326–34.

[38] Susan Felch, 'The development of the English prayer book', in Karen Maag and John D. Witvliet (eds.), *Worship in medieval and early modern Europe: Change and continuity in religious practice* (Notre Dame, 2004).

[39] Judith Rice Henderson, 'Humanism and the humanities: Erasmus' *Opus de conscribendis epistolis* in sixteenth-century schools', in Carol Poster and Linda C. Mitchell (eds.), *Letter-writing manuals from antiquity to the present: Historical and bibliographic studies* (Columbia, SC, 2007). In Italy, see similarly Paul F. Grendler, *Schooling in Renaissance Italy: Literacy and learning, 1300–1600* (Baltimore, 1989), pp. 122–35; R. G. G. Mercer, *The teaching of Gasparino Barzizza: With special reference to his place in Paduan humanism* (London, 1979), pp. 1–2, 94–8; Ann Moss, *Printed commonplace-books and the structuring of Renaissance thought* (Oxford, 1996), pp. 56–7, 67–8.

or Isocrates' orations. Such a student had not necessarily learnt to perform a declamation *in utramque partem*.[40] Prayers were traditionally composed not only by learned clergy but also by women and men who were not literate, or only partially so. The medieval practice of not attributing devotions to an individual author, of adapting them to suit a variety of oral and scribal contexts, and of using them to advance the literacy of children and women made them a particularly accessible form.[41] Demonstrating proficiency in these genres, then, left the extent of a woman's liberal education pleasantly vague.

In addition, the prose that classical authors and their humanist imitators deemed suitable, or *apte dicere*, for letter-writing, prayer and religious translations was relatively restrained and familiar.[42] Virginia Cox has shown that most humanists did not prohibit women's study of rhetoric – after all, to readers of Cicero's *De oratore* and Quintilian, any sort of composition involved rhetoric – but they did try to deter female students, particularly, from those forms of speech that required dissimulation or the excessive stimulation of emotion.[43] Letters, translations and prayers employed speech that could be lauded as *elegantia* rather than being combative or meretriciously *eloquentia*. As Roger Ascham wrote, in praise of Princess Elizabeth and other learned aristocratic women of the English court in 1550, 'we often see obscure women striving more skilfully for fame, but truly elegant speech [*elegantia orationis*] prefers to live in the homes of the most eminent families'.[44] 'Elegance of speech is a matter for grammarians', Erasmus wrote, and to be distinguished from eloquence and poetry. Elegance was to be aimed for when translating religious works, particularly, since it demonstrated reverence for the source text.[45] These were genres, then, that women could use to demonstrate their honesty, piety and fidelity in the form of their speech, as well as its contents.

[40] Peter Mack, *Elizabethan rhetoric: Theory and practice* (Cambridge, 2002), pp. 13, 24–46; Quentin Skinner, *Reason and rhetoric in the philosophy of Hobbes* (Cambridge, 1996), pp. 26–34.

[41] Marie Denley, 'Elementary teaching techniques and middle English religious didactic writing', in Helen Phillips (ed.), *Langland, the mystics and the medieval English religious tradition: Essays in honour of S. S. Hussey* (Cambridge, 1990); John C. Hirsh, 'Latin prayers as a lesson in writing and devotion for a lady of standing', *The Chaucer Review*, 41:4 (2007).

[42] Luc Vaillancourt, *La lettre familière au XVIe siècle. Rhétorique humaniste de l'épistolaire* (Paris, 2003), pp. 147–88.

[43] Virginia Cox, 'Leonardo Bruni on women and rhetoric: *De studiis et litteris*', *Rhetorica*, 27:1 (2009).

[44] 'Saepeque ignobiles mulieres nobilibus artificiosius laborare videmus, orationis autem elegantiam in nobilitatis velle domiciliis habitare et praeclaris familiis': Ascham, *Whole works*, vol. II.i, pp. 203–4.

[45] 'Elegantiam sermonis, quae grammaticorum est cum eloquentia cumque poetica, quasi nihil intersit': Erasmus, *OEDE*, vol. II, no. 843, p. 315.

Piety, in particular, was crucial. A persistent oxymoron in pre-modern European notions of gender was that, while women were deemed more sinful and morally weaker than men, they were also expected to be more pious. The female sex 'excelled the male... [in devotion], prayer, and church attendance'.[46] And, though 'the Reformation, with its emphasis on individual salvation and the reading of Scripture' encouraged Protestant and reformed women to engage with the Bible more directly, the emphasis on devotional writing carried across the confessional spectrum.[47] Scholars have shown that pious literature could be a site of agency and even subversion for women.[48] They could use it to intervene in trenchant doctrinal debates, without being censured for immodesty, ambition or lack of expertise.[49] Nevertheless, the extent to which even noblewomen were encouraged to confine their literary activities to devotional writing, rather than other genres of religious composition, suggests the persistence of powerful constraints.

Recent scholarship has emphasised the value of 'intellectual families' in supporting and publicising women's liberal education and social capital in the early modern period.[50] For humanists, the political and religious duties that women from royal and noble families were called on to discharge at times when their male kin were too young, too old, too far away or too ill to rule was a powerful argument in favour of their study of the *bonae litterae*. Yet families' dynastic strategies almost inevitably privileged a viable male line over a female one and this inhibited early modern women's pedagogical opportunities and the ways they used their learning. Demonstrations of filial loyalty and piety formed part of the corpus of writings by men in early modern Europe, but they dominated women's literary output.

[46] Margaret Sommerville, *Sex and subjection: Attitudes to women in early-modern society* (London, 1995), p. 43.

[47] Quotation from Elaine Beilin, *Redeeming Eve: Women writers of the English Renaissance* (Princeton, NJ, 1987), p. xxi but see Brenda Hosington, 'Lady Margaret Beaufort's translation as mirrors of practical piety', in Micheline White (ed.), *English women, religion, and textual production, 1500–1625* (Aldershot, 2011), pp. 189–90.

[48] See Danielle Clarke, *The politics of early modern women's writing* (New York, 2001); Anne Larson, 'Legitimizing the daughter's writing: Catherine des Roches' proverbial good wife', *SCJ*, 21:4 (1990); Diane Wood, *Hélisenne de Crenne: At the crossroads of Renaissance humanism and feminism* (Madison, NJ, 2000).

[49] Coles, *Religion, reform, and women's writing*, pp. 68–70, 100–2; Douglas Robinson, 'Theorizing translation in a woman's voice: Subverting the rhetoric of patronage, courtly love and morality', *The Translator*, 1 (1995).

[50] Goodrich, 'Thomas More and Margaret More Roper', pp. 1021–40; Ross, *Birth of feminism*, p. 2, 29.

DYNASTIC STRATEGY AND THE EDUCATION OF STUART ROYAL WOMEN

Scholars have tended to treat queens as exceptions to general patterns in the history of even elite royal women's schooling, to the point that some allege that they were as well educated as their brothers.[51] In fact twinned forces of capability and constraint shaped the studies of Tudor and Stuart princesses at least as powerfully as their aristocratic contemporaries. Their proximity to the throne certainly facilitated their learning, but the superior political and familial claims of their male kin typically limited their studies. This section will compare the cases of Mary, Queen of Scots, and Princess Elizabeth, daughter of James VI and I and Anne of Denmark (1574–1619).

Mary Stuart became sovereign queen of Scotland a mere six days after her birth on 8 December 1542, yet her classical education started late and was carried out in a fairly superficial manner. The dynastic problem that structured the first six years of her life was Marie de Guise's (1515–60) desire to protect her daughter's person and throne from the English, French and Scottish potentates, who were attempting to capture the child-queen or to marry her off to their advantage.[52] On 29 July 1548, she resolved it by sending her daughter to France as the bride of the dauphin, the future Francis II (1544–60). Thereafter Mary's education was supervised by Diane de Poitiers (1499–1566) and, from 1552, by Charles de Guise, Cardinal of Lorraine (1524–74). Both were cognisant of her sovereignty in Scotland but they trained their eyes on her potential status as a consort queen of France. In September 1548, for instance, de Poitiers explained to Jean de Humières, governor of the royal nursery, that, since Mary was a 'crowned queen' (*royne couronné*) of Scotland, she must walk before all but the dauphin himself in the royal nursery.[53] Yet de Poitiers also surrounded her with thirty-seven other scions of the French nobility to facilitate her assimilation of French language, manners, accomplishments and court protocols. Most of Mary's Scottish attendants were dismissed or temporarily sent away to assist her cultural conversion.[54] From the time of her

[51] Stevenson, *Women Latin Poets*, pp. 258–9. See similarly Dowling, *Humanism in the age of Henry VIII*, pp. 219–43; Eskin, 'Reigning of women's tongues', p. 120.

[52] See for example Mary Piers, Lady Seton in Marie de Guise, *Foreign correspondence with Marie de Lorraine, Queen of Scotland, 1537–1548*, ed. Marguerite Wood (Edinburgh, 1923), pp. 246–7

[53] Diane de Poitiers, *Lettres inédites de Diane de Poytiers*, ed. Georges Guiffrey (Lyon, 1896), p. 34.

[54] Anthoinette de Bourbon in de Guise, *Foreign correspondence with Marie de Lorraine*, Queen of Scotland, 1548–1557, ed. Marguerite Wood (Edinburgh, 1925) p. 25, also pp. 7–8; Jane Stoddart, *Girlhood of Mary Queen of Scots* (London, 1908), p. 41.

arrival, Pierre de Bourdeille (1540–1614), Seigneur de Brantôme, recorded, the young queen of Scots 'always set aside two hours a day for reading and study' of French literature.[55] Mary's language immersion proved successful. By the time Marie de Guise planned her visit in April 1550, her seven-year-old daughter was writing French fluently, if imperfectly.[56] Yet her *francisation* proceeded at the expense of other grammatical skills. She did not learn to write in Scots, English or any classical tongues.[57]

Not only were her studies focused on making her a good and loyal French consort but they were also calibrated to reflect the dauphin's status as the superior royal child. Francis's schoolmasters were titled *précepteur*; Mary's were merely *maistres d'école*. Her first teacher was the little-known Claude Millot but the dauphin studied under Jacques Amyot (1513–93), the learned translator of Plutarch, who was paid some two hundred livres per annum more for his services than Mary's schoolmaster.[58] On Francis's side, Amyot was succeeded by Jacques de Corneillan (d. 1582), the bishop of Vabres, in 1557; in 1559 he was replaced by Pierre Danès (1497–1577), former professor of Greek at the Collège de France.[59] Millot's only surviving letter to Marie de Guise praised Mary's growth in virtue, beauty and grace but said nothing of her progress in learning.[60] His academic expectations for the young Scottish queen do not seem to have been high.

This is not to suggest that Mary was not encouraged to become a very cultured young woman. Indeed, she became an ornament of the French court. She danced, sang, played the harp and harpsichord, embroidered and baked the crystallised quinces known as *cotignac*. She rode and hunted with her own falcon. She began to learn Spanish and Italian and to enjoy the poetry of Pierre de Ronsard (1524–85), who soon became her client, and of Joachim du Bellay.[61] Mary wrote occasional, political and amatory French verse herself that showed the influence of the vernacular poetry of François I and the Pléiade.[62] Her lyrics were not merely decorative. When

55 'Tant qu'elle a esté en France, elle se reservoit tousjours deux heures du jour pour estudier et lire': Pierre de Bourdeille, Seigneur de Brantôme, *Recueil des dames, poésies et tombeaux*, ed. Étienne Vaucheret (Paris, 1991), p. 72.

56 Mary, Queen of Scots, *Lettres, instructions et mémoires de Marie Stuart, reine d'Écosse*, ed. Alexandre Labanoff, 7 vols. (London, 1844), vol. I, pp. 3, 4; Stoddart, *Girlhood*, p. 57.

57 Julian Goodare, 'Mary (1542–1587)', *ODNB*.

58 Alphonse de Ruble, *La Première jeunesse de Marie Stuart* (Paris, 1891), pp. 267, 281.

59 Ruble, *Première jeunesse de Marie Stuart*, p. 267; Stoddart, *Girlhood*, p. 97.

60 NLS, Advocates MS 29 2 4, fol. 67r.

61 Brantôme, *Recueil des dames*, pp. 72–4; John Guy, *My heart is my own: The life of Mary Queen of Scots* (London, 2004), pp. 74–9.

62 Herman, *Royal poetrie*, pp. 52–98; Hopkins, *Writing Renaissance queens*, pp. 72–87; Mary, Queen of Scots, *Lettres*, vol. III, pp. 346–52.

she and Elizabeth I were debating the Treaty of Edinburgh in 1562, the great neo-Latin poet George Buchanan helped the queen of Scots produce French and Italian verses to send to her English cousin to help broker a meeting and an agreement.[63] Mary's study of French literature proved both diplomatically useful and a source of personal pleasure throughout her life. Her *francisation* also secured her loyalty to the Valois, even when members of the family failed to come to her aid in 1567 and thereafter. Her final letter, written the night before her execution in February 1587, expressed to Henri III her desire that her 'body [be] conveyed after my death… to your realm, where I had the honour to be queen, your sister and old ally'.[64]

The Valois were not the only family to attempt to advance their political agenda through Mary's education. Her de Guise kin also yapped and nipped at her ankles in their attempts to herd her out of the nursery and schoolroom. According to the queen's aunt Anne d'Este, duchesse de Guise, by the astonishingly youthful age of nine Mary's mature conduct indicated that she should 'no longer be treated as a child'. It was necessary to seek royal acknowledgement of her princely status, and, by extension, the de Guises' honour.[65] In March 1553, Charles de Guise, the Cardinal of Lorraine, recommended to his sister that she establish an independent household for the queen. Despite the considerable expense involved, he got his way in January 1554, shortly after Mary's eleventh birthday.[66] Thereafter Mary proved sufficiently precocious to play her part in the de Guises' plan to declare her majority in Scotland, enabling her mother to claim the regency in April 1554.[67]

De Guise waited until her political independence and sovereignty were formally recognised to begin Mary's study of classical languages. Despite historians' assertions that she had shared the dauphin's humanist schoolmasters, it was only in October 1554 that Mary's fussy French governess, Françoise d'Estamville, Lady Parois, reported to Marie de Guise that her daughter 'begins to understand Latin'.[68] The queen's new

63 Printed, alongside several more personal poems, in Jane Stevenson and Peter Davidson (eds.), *Early modern women poets (1520–1700)* (Oxford, 2001), pp. 64–70.

64 'Quapres ma mort mon corps fust transporte… en votre royaulme ou iay eu lhonneur destre royne votre soeur & ancienne allyee': NLS, Advocates MS 54 1 1, fol. 1r.

65 'Il ne fault plus peanser d'en faire comme a une enfant': Anne d'Est, in de Guise, *Foreign correspondence with Marie de Lorraine* … 1548–1557, p. 110.

66 'Le Roy y prend tel goust qu'il passe bien son temps a deviser avec elle l'espace d'une heure et elle le scet aussi bien entretenir de bons et saiges propos comme feroit une femme de vingt cinq ans': Charles, Cardinal de Lorraine, in de Guise, *Foreign correspondence with Marie de Lorraine* … 1548–1557, p. 141.

67 Guy, *My heart is my own*, pp. 58–9.

68 'Elle commence d'entendre son latin': Lady Parrois, in de Guise, *Foreign correspondence of Marie de Lorraine* … 1548–1557, p. 253; Guy, *My heart is my own*, p. 69; Ruble, *Première jeunesse de Marie Stuart*, p. 60.

précepteur, Antoine Fouquelin (d. after 1561), was a follower of Petrus Ramus (1515–72) and Omer Talon (1510–62). Both humanists hailed Charles de Guise as their Maecenas, so it seems likely that he, rather than any member of the Valois clan, had provided for Mary's entry to classical languages and literature.[69]

Not only did her liberal education start late but also it seems to have been somewhat superficial. Mary's compositions under Fouquelin have been compared to Edward VI's school exercises but all that survives is a bound set of sixty-four holograph letters and translations, from French into Latin, written between 26 July 1554 and 9 January 1555.[70] Two recurring themes in the translations advertised the nominal object of Mary's liberal education. The first stressed the importance of 'the study of good letters… for we princes'. The second refuted the erroneous view that 'women are never learned'.[71] In practise, her exercises were building to her star turn in 1555 when 'at the age of between thirteen and fourteen years, she declaimed before King Henri, the queen, and all the court in the chamber of the Louvre'. Her 'oration in Latin' argued 'against common opinion that women should not have knowledge of letters and liberal arts'. According to Brantôme, it was greeted with raptures.[72] Fouquelin, her schoolmaster, claimed that she subsequently translated the work into French, and he commended her facility in both tongues.[73] Mary brought the French version of her speech with her when she returned to Scotland, suggesting she had taken some pride in the performance.[74]

Certainly, going from a cold start in 1554 to perform a deliberative oration in 1555 would have required extraordinarily rapid progress in the *artz liberaux*. But there are reasons to suspect some staging was involved. Mary's Latin themes contain *loci* and *exempla* that seem to have been plucked from various ancient Latin and Greek authors, as well as fifteenth- and

[69] Roy E. Leake, 'Antoine Fouquelin and the Pléiade', *Bibliothèque d'Humanisme et Renaissance*, 32:2 (1970), p. 381.

[70] Anatole de Montaiglon, 'Préface', in *Latin themes of Mary Stuart, Queen of Scots*, ed. Anatole de Montaiglon (London, 1855), p. x; BN, MS Latin 8660 printed in *Latin themes of Mary Stuart, Queen of Scots*.

[71] 'De studio bonarum literarum. Quare eadem sunt magis necessariae nobis principibus' and 'possis respondere… qui heri dicebant esse foeminarum nihil sapere': Mary, Queen of Scots, *Latin themes*, pp. 5 and 33 respectively.

[72] 'Estant en l'âge de treize à quatorze ans, elle declama devant le Roy Henry, la Reyne, et toute la Cour, publicquement en la salle du Louvre, une oraison en latin qu'elle avoit faite, soutenant et deffandant, contre l'opinion commune, qu'il estoit bien seant aux femmes de sçavoir les lettres et artz liberaux': Brantôme, *Recueil des dames*, p. 72.

[73] Antoine Fouquelin, *La Rhetorique Françoise* (Paris, 1557), fols. 2^v–3^r.

[74] Julian Sharman, ed., *The library of Mary Queen of Scots* (London, 1889), pp. 31–2.

sixteenth-century humanists, including Aesop's fables, Cato's *Disticbes*, Erasmus' *Colloquia* and *Institutio principis Christiani*, Plautus' comedies, Plutarch's *Moralia* and *Lives* and, later, Cicero's *De oratore* and *De legibus* and Plato's *Phaedo* and *Republic*.[75] In fact, however, the *theses* she worked on in preparation for her court oration and the citations within them were taken from a single source: Angelo Poliziano's letter to the Italian humanist Cassandra Fidele.[76]

Further, unlike Edward VI's compositions, which were the result of the king's own collection and arrangement of materials, Mary's were facing-page translations. They were not, moreover, the sort of advanced literary adaptations that Leonardo Bruni had encouraged adept scholars to perform, but simple substitution exercises.[77] Early on Mary had found even this task challenging. She translated the endearment 'ma seur ma mignonne' (my sister, my dear one), for instance, as 'soror integerrima' (most pure or spotless sister) rather than the more classical 'soror mea desideria'.[78] It seems likely that Mary was performing the sort of introductory single or double translation recommended for beginners in Juan Luis Vives's *De ratione studii puerilis* (printed 1524) and, later, in Ascham's *Scholemaster* (1570).[79] Over the course of the year, her translations became more confident, but she was not on track to deliver a deliberative oration of her own composition in 1555. It seems probable that what Brantôme witnessed in 1555 was a well-memorised performance.

The Valois and de Guise families had every reason to be satisfied with a queen who could put on a good show, but, when fortune's wheel flung Mary back across the channel, she had to learn to use rhetoric and history to construct political arguments. George Buchanan, who returned with her to Holyrood, was quick to diagnose the deficit in her schooling. Of course, his description of the queen and the 'courtly education' that had given her a 'false colouring of virtue' was hardly unbiased.[80] In his *Rerum Scoticarum historia* he was attempting to caricature her as a lustful, tyrannical Julio-Claudian empress. Nevertheless in 1562 he had taken

[75] Mary, Queen of Scots, *Latin themes*, p. 5.

[76] Angelo Poliziano, *Letters*: vol. I, books I–IV, ed. Shane Butler (Cambridge, 2006), pp. 188–93.

[77] Leonardo Bruni, *De interpretatione recta – De la traduction parfait*, ed. Charles Le Blanc (Ottowa, 2008), pp. 68, 69.

[78] Mary, Queen of Scots, *Latin themes*, pp. 8–9. See, for example, Cicero, *Ad familiares*, XIV.2.2.

[79] Roger Ascham, *The scholemaster or a plaine and perfite way of teachyng children, to vnderstand, write, and speake, the Latin tong* (London, 1570), STC 832, fols. 1v–2r; Juan Luis Vives, *Introductio ad sapientiam, Satellitium siue symbola, Epistolae duae de ratione studii puerilis, Tria capita addita initio Suetonii Tranquilli* (Paris, 1527), fol. 53v.

[80] 'Falsis virtutum coloribus, gratiorem fecerat aulica educatio…': George Buchanan, *Rerum Scoticarum historia* (Antwerp, 1583), STC 3992, fol. 176v.

the trouble to work on Livy and Sallust with her each day.[81] Mary made good progress. The English ambassador Thomas Randolph (1525/6–90) was impressed by her speech to open the Scottish parliament in 1563. 'She wrote yt in Frenche', he reported, 'but pronunced it in Englishe with a verie good grace'.[82] When Mary had the time and opportunity to prepare, she invariably put on a good rhetorical and political performance.

When put upon to argue *ex tempore*, moreover, the queen struggled. Certainly, John Knox's (*c.* 1514–72) account of his early September 1561 interview with Mary showed her 'long reasoning' skills to advantage. She accused Knox of raising 'part of her subjects against her mother, and against herself' with his *First blast of the trumpet against the monstrous rule of women* (1558). Knox went on to argue that he had no intent to incite rebellion, merely to promulgate God's word as Moses had in Egypt, the Apostles had in Rome and Daniel had under Nebuchadnezzar. 'Yea', Mary replied, 'but none of those men raised the sword against their princes'. Eventually, of course, Knox bested her and she 'stood as it were amazed, more than the quarter of an hour'.[83] Then Knox drove his advantage home. The queen had no right to appeal to 'conscience' on the matter of her religion, since 'Conscience, Madam… requires knowledge; and I fear that right knowledge ye have none'.[84] On 7 October 1561 he warned William Cecil not to underestimate Mary's cunning and obstinacy. Her 'hole Proceadings do declaryr that the Carinalles lessons ar so deaplie prented in hir Hart, that the Substance and Qualitie ar likelie to perishe together… In communication with her I espied such craft, as I have not found in such Age'.[85] Yet Knox had good reason to present Mary as the self-assured mouthpiece of Gallo–Catholic tyranny; such views were all the better to depose her with.

In fact, it is doubtful that Mary's supposed counter-arguments came trippingly off her tongue. The English ambassador to Scotland, Thomas Randolph, had described her September meeting with Knox quite differently. Mary got few words in before the reformer 'knocked so hashelye upon her harte that he made her weepe'.[86] During their second showdown, precipitated by Knox's sermon to Parliament criticising her proposed marriage to a fellow Catholic, Mary barely spluttered out her horror

[81] *Calendar of state papers foreign series of the reign of Elizabeth*, ed. Joseph Stevenson, 23 vols. (London, 1865), vol. IV, no. 985, p. 584; Mary's copy of Sallust is Trinity College Library, Dublin, Press A 3 18.

[82] *CSP Scotland*, vol. II, no. 9, p. 10.

[83] John Knox, *The History of the Reformation in Scotland*, ed. William Croft Dickinson, 2 vols. (London, 1949), vol. II, pp. 15–17.

[84] Knox, *History of the Reformation*, vol. II, pp. 17–18.

[85] Haynes, *SP*, vol. I, p. 372.

[86] BL, Cotton MS Caligula B X, fol. 160r.

at Knox's 'rigorous manner of speaking' before she was thoroughly overcome. 'Scarcely could [her servant] get napkins to hold her eyes dry for the tears', Knox wrote with satisfaction, 'and the howling, besides womanly weeping, stayed her speech'.[87] Admittedly, many sixteenth-century monarchs would have found themselves confounded by a subject as arrogant as Knox, regardless of their sex or education. Yet Mary reached the limits of her capacity for verbal argument very quickly.

Indeed, Mary's reluctance to 'reason' persisted, even in the face of less formidable opponents. In France she claimed to have enjoyed listening to Cardinal de Guise and his minions debating the relationship between conscience, obedience and kingship in the years following the Peace of Augsburg.[88] Yet she had not been encouraged to take part in their discussions. In late October 1561, when Thomas Randolph and James Stuart, earl of Moray (1531–70), initiated an amicable evening conversation about Théodore de Bèze's (1519–1605) contribution to the recent Colloquy of Poissy, Mary seemed to freeze. Various noblemen present held forth contrary (and theologically confused) opinions on the real presence. When it came time for her to contribute, however, 'the Quene saide that she coulde not reason, but she knewe what she ought to believe'.[89] Mary's education had cultivated her taste for elegant prose and verse in the vernacular and her skill in a variety of courtly arts and exercises, but she had not been taught to 'reason', or make logical and persuasive arguments, a critical skill for princes during the wars of religion. Unlike Thomas Elyot's Zenobia, Mary's studies did not prepare her for the vicissitudes of fortune and she was left to try and pick up knowledge of logic, rhetoric and history on the hop during the tumults of her reign in Scotland and her subsequent captivity in England.

Mary's granddaughter, Princess Elizabeth Stuart, was left in a similar position by her education. Despite James VI and I's own scholarly interests and highly publicised involvement in the education of his sons, the king did not provide his daughter with a tutor for Latin grammar, let alone Greek. The reason for this omission had a great deal to do with family strategy; until just before Elizabeth's marriage in February 1613, James and his wife, Anne of Denmark, had had two sons, Henry and Charles. Their

[87] Knox, *History of the Reformation*, vol. II, p. 82.

[88] Knox, *History of the Reformation*, vol. I, p. 368.

[89] BL, Cotton MS Caligula B X, fol. 190v. With Moray's permission, Randolph seems to have presented Mary with a copy of Théodore de Bèze, *Ce qui a este propose par Theodore de Beze au nom de tous ceux qui desie[n]t la reformatio[n] de l'Eglise selon la pure doctrine de l'Euangile, en la presence du Roy, de la Royne sa mere, du Roy de Nauarre, & des autres Princes, de Messieurs du Conseil, & des Prelats qu'on dit d'Eglise. A Poissy, le neufieme iour de Septembre, 1561* (Geneva, 1561).

daughter Elizabeth was raised to become a consort queen and support for Stuart diplomacy rather than a sovereign in her own right, so her education, like her grandmother's in France, had emphasised the study of vernacular languages and cultivating loyalty to her kin.

Indeed, the first object of Elizabeth Stuart's upbringing was to cultivate filial piety. After coming south with her mother in June 1603, Princess Elizabeth was placed under John Harington of Exton (1539/40–1613), whose own son, also called John (bap. 1592, d. 1614), was installed in Prince Henry's household.[90] The family encouraged Elizabeth to imitate her brother's strict Calvinism and commissioned Robert Peake the Elder (*c.* 1551–1619) to make companion portraits of Elizabeth and Prince Henry with their son, John.[91] In the wake of the Gunpowder Plot, Harington (d. 1613) proudly reported his charge's response to the plan to marry her to a Catholic noble and make her queen of England: 'I had rather have been with my royal father in the Parliament-house, than wear his crown on such condition', she is said to have proclaimed, stoutly.[92] During her years in Warwickshire, Elizabeth was taught to write elegant letters to James and Henry in French and Italian, declaring her devotion to them and demonstrating her progress in vernacular languages and italic script.[93] Henry replied occasionally to her letters. James rarely did. None of this correspondence suggests that Elizabeth possessed any knowledge of Latin.[94]

Indeed, little by way of erudition seems to have been expected of her. Peake's second portrait of Elizabeth, painted in 1606, depicted the princess holding an octavo volume that was a gift from her mother, Queen Anne. It declared itself to be

> A boke not
> big but yet ther
> in Some hidden
> Vertu is.[95]

[90] SP 14/2, fol. 93^{r}; Peter E. McCullough, *Sermons at court: Politics and religion in Elizabethan and Jacobean preaching* (Cambridge, 1998), p. 185.

[91] Karen Hearn, *Dynasties: Painting in Tudor and Jacobean England 1530–1630* (London, 1995), pp. 185–6.

[92] Quoted in Georgianna Ziegler, 'A second phoenix: The rebirth of Elizabeth I in Elizabeth Stuart', in Elizabeth H. Hageman and Katherine Conway (eds.), *Resurrecting Elizabeth I in seventeenth-century England* (Madison, 2007), p. 114.

[93] Jehan de Beauchesne, *A booke containing diuers sortes of hands as well the English as French secretarie with the Italian, Roman, chancelry and court hands. Also the true and iust proportio[n] of the capitall Romae set forth*, engraved by John Baildon (London, 1571), STC 6446 and eight subsequent editions. An early example of Elizabeth's italic hand is HHCP, 147/165.

[94] BL, Harleian MS 6986, fols. 80^{r}–153^{v}; FSL, MS X c 91.

[95] Robert Peake the Elder, *Princess Elizabeth* (*c.* 1606), oil on panel, The Metropolitan Museum, New York, accession 51.194.1.

Modest behaviour, rather than extensive learning, was to be the jewel in her crown. Instead of reading bigger books, Elizabeth spent her youth learning to ride, dance and play musical instruments so that she was well prepared to grace her father's court in 1608 and her husband's, following her marriage to Frederick, Prince of the Palatinate (1596–1632), in 1613.[96]

The princess's education taught her to be a devoted daughter, sister and spouse and an ornamental consort but it seems to have been of rather less use following her ejection from Bohemia in 1618. When she and Frederick V lost their crowns and Frederick's ancestral estates at the outbreak of the Thirty Years' War, Elizabeth proved capable of writing elegantly beseeching letters to her father and brother, Charles, requesting relief but little more. It is certainly true that, over the course of the wars, Elizabeth became adept at diplomacy and learnt to read enough Latin to instruct the secretary who managed her correspondence, though she did not write holograph letters in Latin. She also seems to have picked up a good understanding of military logistics.[97] Yet, like her grandmother, Elizabeth Stuart had to teach herself these critical skills as she went along. Her upbringing betrayed James's confidence that one of his two sons would succeed him in England and Scotland. It also betrayed the princess and she knew it. Despite the trials of exile, Elizabeth Stuart went to some lengths to ensure that her own daughters studied a curriculum that included Latin, mathematics and philosophy.[98]

Both Mary and Elizabeth Stuart were highly cultured but neither was expected to attain much, or in Elizabeth's case any, proficiency in classical languages prior to marriage. Both were close to the throne, indeed Mary was a crowned queen, but the families that brought them up were anxious to ensure that these royal women were filially loyal, conventionally pious and ornaments of the court, rather than intellectual or political forces in their own right. Princess Elizabeth was expected to support, rather than threaten, the government of one of her brothers. Mary, Queen of Scots, was to support rather than threaten the rule of Francis II and the extension of de Guise and Valois authority across the channel. Ultimately both

96 HHCP, 125/8.

97 Emily Benger (ed.), *Memoirs of Elizabeth Stuart: Queen of Bohemia, daughter of King James the first*, 2 vols. (London, 1825); Elizabeth Stuart, *Correspondence of Elizabeth Stuart*.

98 Elisabeth of Bohemia and René Descartes, *The correspondence between Princess Elisabeth of Bohemia and René Descartes*, ed. Lisa Shapiro (Chicago, 2007); Philippe-Joseph Salazar, 'Elizabeth à Descartes: "Êntre mieux intruite de votre bouche" ', in Colette Nativel (ed.), *Femmes savants, savoirs des femmes: Du crépuscule de la Renaissance à l'aube des Lumières*' (Geneva, 1999); Lisa Shapiro, 'Princess Elizabeth and Descartes: The union of soul and body and the practice of philosophy,' *British Journal for the History of Philosophy*, 7:3 (1999).

acquired the literary skills they needed, by hook or by crook, but Stuart royal women were left to grapple with political and religious crises of the Scottish reformation and the Thirty Years' War without adequate preparation in how to make their cases. The reasons for their political downfalls were complex but neither princess had learnt to meet *fortuna* with a pen or a sword.

DYNASTIC AMBITION AND SPIRITUAL EDIFICATION: LADY JANE GREY

Both Stuart princesses were much closer to the throne than Lady Jane Grey, who was born merely the daughter of the marquis of Dorset, but her study of classical grammars and rhetoric and her reading of ancient authors were far more advanced. Jane Grey's much vaunted scholarly aptitude certainly contributed to the extent of her learning, but it is also valuable to consider the political and familial circumstances that gave rise to her educational opportunities. As Eric Ives has argued, the shaping force of Jane's short life was 'what others made, or thought could be made, of her royal potential'.[99] Her parents, Henry Grey and Frances Brandon (1517–59), ultimately the duke and duchess of Suffolk, had no sons so they pushed their eldest daughter instead. The same ambition that led them to beat Jane and to risk her reputation, indeed her life, in various schemes also prompted them to give their daughter a truly princely education that emphasised the study of classical Greek and scripture.

The stars aligned to bless or cross Jane a year before her birth. In 1536, when Henry VIII's second Act for the Succession declared Mary and Elizabeth illegitimate, the common law of collateral descent advanced the position of Frances Grey, then marchioness of Dorset and the daughter of Charles Brandon and Henry's sister Mary Tudor (1496–1533). Her eldest surviving child, Jane, was born in 1537, a few months before Prince Edward. In December 1546, Henry VIII's will bypassed Frances in favour of the heirs of her body.[100] At Edward VI's succession in 1547, then, Jane was third in line to the throne behind Mary and Elizabeth. Her claim, unlike her female cousins', had never been tainted by the bar sinister.[101] Jane was an important piece on the royal chessboard, certainly, but her status was a far cry from the rank of Mary, Queen of Scot. The difference

[99] Eric Ives, *Lady Jane Grey: A Tudor mystery* (Oxford, 2009), p. 24.
[100] Alison Plowden, 'Grey, Lady Jane (1537–1554)', *ODNB*.
[101] Susan James, *Kateryn Parr: The making of a queen* (Aldershot, 1999), p. 315.

between Jane Grey's situation and those of Tudor and Stuart royal women, however, was that the house of Suffolk (as it became after 1551) had no sons. Frances and Henry Grey have been called grasping, brutal, gullible and oafish – allegedly by Jane herself – but they were also unashamed about backing their daughter.[102]

From February 1547 until Jane's imprisonment in the Tower in 1553, the Greys used whatever leverage they had to promote their daughter's potential as a royal consort or even as a sovereign princess. Shortly after the death of Henry VIII, Henry Grey made Jane the ward of Thomas Seymour, brother to Edward's governor and uncle to the king. It was unusual to place a young girl in a bachelor's establishment but by the summer of 1547 news of Seymour's relationship and possible marriage to the former Queen Katherine was on the wing.[103] The Greys' audacious move meant that Jane spent eighteen months in the dowager's cultured and prestigious household, 'term'd a second Court of right'.[104] Katherine proved to be an influential mentor. Janel Mueller has argued that the tiny prayer book, crammed with English translations of devotional works by English Catholic reformers and Protestants, that Jane took to the scaffold in 1553 was a gift from Henry VIII's last queen.[105] Even if this was not the case, Katherine's death in September 1548 was a blow to Jane, who served as chief mourner at Katherine's Protestant funeral rites.[106] Afterwards, Jane's parents took the entirely conventional step of removing her from Seymour's household.[107] Nevertheless, when Seymour revived his ambitious plan to marry Jane to Edward VI, and offered the Greys a bribe of £2,000 with £500 down immediately against his success, they were prepared to risk her return.[108] Seymour's arrest on 17 January 1549 exposed their questionable deal to the court. When Jane returned to Bradgate Park, she allegedly reported to Ascham that her parents treated her with disdain 'some tymes, with

[102] Ascham, *Scholemaster*, fols. 11^v–12^r; Robert Braddock, 'Grey, Henry, duke of Suffolk (1517–1554)', *ODNB*; Hester Chapman, *Lady Jane Grey, October 1537–February 1554* (London, 1962), pp. 19–21; James, *Kateryn Parr*, p. 315; W. K. Jordan, *Edward VI: The threshold of power and the dominance of the duke of Northumberland* (London, 1970), pp. 92, 373; David Loades, *John Dudley, duke of Northumberland, 1504–1553* (Oxford, 1996), pp. 113, 240.

[103] James, *Kateryn Parr*, pp. 302–3.

[104] Nicholas Throckmorton, *Legend of Sir Nicholas Throckmorton*, ed. John Nichols (London, 1874), p. 17.

[105] BL, Harleian MS 2342 in Katherine Parr, *Katherine Parr: Complete works and correspondence*, ed. Janel Mueller (Chicago, 2011), pp. 18, 489–90 but see James Carley's review, *Times Literary Supplement*, no. 5644 (3 June 2011).

[106] James, *Kateryn Parr*, pp. 332–3.

[107] Haynes, *SP*, vol. 1, p. 78.

[108] *Calendar of state papers domestic: Edward, Mary and Elizabeth*, eds. Robert Lemmon and Mary Anne Green Everett, 12 vols. (London, 1856), vol. 1, pp. 12–13; Haynes, *SP*, vol. 1, pp. 76, 83, 84, 106; SP 10/6, no. 7.

pinches, nippes, and bobbes', or blows. Perhaps they blamed her for the failure of the enterprise. Or perhaps they merely feared that their daughter's inability to 'speake, kepe silence, sit, stand, or go, eate, drinke, be merie, or sad, be sawyng, plaiyng, dauncing, or doing anie thing els' with sufficient grace was jeopardising their schemes for her marriage.[109]

Nevertheless, the Greys did not stop plotting. In early 1549, they offered Somerset their daughter as a bride for his son.[110] As soon as the duke seemed likely to be eclipsed by John Dudley, however, Dorset backed Dudley's bid to take control of the Privy Council in the winter of 1549.[111] On 11 October 1551, Dudley became duke of Northumberland and the Greys were created duke and duchess of Suffolk on the same day.[112] Even before Edward wrote the first version of his device for the succession, in or around April 1553, the Suffolks would have seen the advantage in matching their daughter to the son of the only other surviving duke in England, a man who also happened to be president of the council.[113]

According to Guilio Raviglio Rosso, who based his account on the reports of the Venetian ambassador, Giovanni Michele, when Guilford Dudley (*c.* 1535–54) was proposed to Jane as a suitable match, she 'refused the marriage for some time… Nonetheless by both the force of her mother and the threats of her father she was obliged in the end, and so it was concluded' on 25 May 1553.[114] As a member of the Privy Council, Dorset would have been aware from at least 28 May that Edward's device to amend the succession favoured his daughter or her male heirs, and following Edward's death on 6 July they pushed her to accept the crown. In the exculpatory letter that Jane sent Mary from the Tower in August 1553, she avoided blaming her parents directly, merely noting their presence at the meeting in which she had been browbeaten by Northumberland.[115] A visiting papal official, Giovanni Francesco Commedone, was more specific. Jane had been 'unwilling to accept such a burden… but in the end, pressed with many arguments by the Council, the Duke and her Father, she submitted to their will'.[116] A second Italian ambassador added that 'the daughter was

[109] Ascham, *Scholemaster*, fols. 11ᵛ–12ʳ. [110] Haynes, *SP*, vol. 1, p. 79.

[111] Loades, *John Dudley*, pp. 115, 143–4.

[112] Braddock, 'Grey, Henry, duke of Suffolk (1517–1554)'; Ives, *Lady Jane Grey*, pp. 58, 61.

[113] Ives, *Lady Jane Grey*, pp. 153, 184–5.

[114] 'La quale ancora che molto ricusasse il matrimonio… nondimeno & spinta dalla madre, & minacciata dal Padre, fu necessita al fine che si concludesse': Guilio Raviglio Rosso, *I successi d'Inghilterra dopo la morte di Odoardo sesto* (Ferrara, 1560), fol. 4ᵛ; *CSP Spain*, vol. XI, p. 46.

[115] Girolamo Pollini, *L'Historia ecclesiastica della rivoluzion d'Inghilterra* (Rome, 1594), p. 355.

[116] Giovanni Francesco Commendone, 'Events of the Kingdom of England', in C. V. Malfatti (ed), *The accession, coronation and marriage of Mary Tudor, as related in four manuscripts of the Escorial* (Barcelona, 1956), p. 7.

compelled by her father, even with beating'.[117] Bereft of a son, the Greys went to ordinary and extraordinary lengths to promote the political status of their eldest daughter. To make her, they were quite willing to break her.

Amidst these sometimes cruel and unusual measures was their zeal to facilitate and support her liberal education. Despite his reputation for oafishness, Henry Grey patronised a flock of reformers and scholars who praised his generosity and capacity to speak 'Latin with elegance'.[118] The marquis's liberality was not disinterested. He was well placed to appreciate the care being expended on the schooling of Jane's direct contemporary, Prince Edward, and the dynastic advantage in having a daughter who equalled or surpassed the achievements of Henry VIII's and Edward Seymour's daughters. The Protestant refugee Michelangelo Florio reported in his *History of the life and death of the illustrious Jane Grey* (written 1561/2, printed 1607) that he had taught Jane Grey Italian and dedicated his *Regole de la lingua thoscana* to her in return for Dorset's patronage.[119] Dorset's chaplains included advanced students of the *bonae litterae* who probably contributed to her studies, including James Haddon from Trinity College, Cambridge; Thomas Harding (1516–72), the second Regius professor of Hebrew at Oxford; Ralph Skinner from New College, Oxford; and John Willock, who had studied in Cologne and was 'well skilled in Greek and Latin'.[120] According to Dorset, the Zurich reformer Heinrich Bullinger (1504–75) had also played a role in instructing Jane 'to a true faith in Christ, the study of the scriptures, purity of manners, and innocence of life'.[121] Lavish scholarly and religious patronage helped Dorset advance the learning and reputation of his eldest daughter.

Dorset had also supported the education of John Aylmer (1520/1–94), who returned to Bradgate Park after taking his MA in Cambridge in 1545 to serve as 'teacher to my lord marquis children'.[122] As such, Jane was less

[117] '& la figliuola dal padre ui fu constretta etiam con Battiture': Anonymous, *Lettere di principi, le qvali o si scrivono da principi, o à principi, o ragionan di principi, libro primo*, ed. Giordano Ziletti (Venice, 1569), fol. 22[v].

[118] Ellis, *Letters*, vol. II, pp. 400, 406. Dorset's generosity led Bullinger to dedicate one of his *Decades* of sermons to him in March 1551; see Henry Bullinger, *The decades: The fifth decade*, trans. H. I., ed. Thomas Harding (Cambridge, 1852), pp. 529–45. See also Ives, *Lady Jane Grey*, pp. 60–3.

[119] Michaelangelo Florio, *Historia de la vita e de la morte de l'illustrissima Signora Giovanna Graia gia regina eletta e publicata in Inghilterra e de la cose accudute in quell regno dopo la morte del Re Edoardo VI* (Middelburgh, 1607). The dedicated work is BL, Sloane MS 3011. See Ives, *Lady Jane Grey*, pp. 65–6; Michael Wyatt, *The Italian encounter with Tudor England: A cultural politics of translation* (Cambridge, 2005), pp. 98–101.

[120] Ellis, *Letters*, vol. I, pp. 279–88, 309, 313–14; vol. II, pp. 393 (quotation), 397, 399–401.

[121] Ellis, *Letters*, vol. I, p. 4.

[122] Thomas Becon, *The catechism of Thomas Becon… with other pieces written by him in the reign of King Edward the sixth*, ed. John Ayre (Cambridge, 1844), p. 424.

than nine years of age when she commenced her formal study of the liberal arts, younger than the Tudor or Stuart royal women considered here. And she hit the ground running. Jane's first surviving letter was an English missive from 1548 thanking Thomas Seymour for being 'a lovyng and kynd father' to her. While it is in the vernacular (for the benefit of its recipient) it demonstrates apt use of the comparative to create a flattering *syncrisis*; Jane was writing 'rather as a token to shewe howe muche worthyer I thynke youre lorshippes goodness then to gyve worthye thankes for the same'.[123] She had made a quick study of Erasmus' *De conscribendis epistolis* and Cicero's familial letters.

By 1551, Jane was a true adept. The first of the three surviving Latin letters she sent to Heinrich Bullinger was a model of elegant Latin prose, sprinkled with Greek and Hebrew *loci* and written in the narrow, fluid italic hand that suggested the stylistic influence of Ascham.[124] Jane almost certainly had assistance and oversight with her letters; Johannes Ulms, a German reformer who was staying at Bradgate, made copies, which suggests his involvement.[125] Yet there were sufficient infelicities – the repetition of two forms of *gravis* in the same sentence, for instance – to suggest that Jane was the primary author.

The letter began with a gracious opening sentence taken from Plancus' letter to Cicero (*Epistolae ad familiares*, x.11) in which Jane offered her eternal thanks to the reformer for his letter. Her gratitude segued neatly to the second sentence, where, in keeping with Erasmus' advice, Jane praised Bullinger by amplifying the circumstances that made her so grateful for his missive. The specifics accumulated until Jane pronounced that the letter showed its writer to be 'not only a man of exquisite learning and singular erudition, but also a most witty, prudent, and godly counsellor'.[126] At this point, Jane transitioned to what Erasmus had termed a 'conciliatory letter', which sought to recommend the author to its recipient by praising the advice Bullinger offered both her and the 'Christian commonwealth' (*respublica Christiana*). His counsel had 'struck [her] like Blesilla, Paula, and Eustochium, whom, it is known, the divine Jerome taught'.[127] Having

[123] SP 10/5, no. 5.

[124] For Jane's later hand, see Grey, *Ioannae Graiae litterae ad H. Bullingerum* (Zurich, 1840), p. 49; Ives, *Lady Jane Grey*, Plate 24.

[125] Ellis, *Letters*, vol. I, pp. 4–7. For Ulm's copies, see vol. II, p. 436.

[126] 'Non solum te exquisite doctum & singulari eruditione praeditum ostendisti sed etiam ingeniosu[m] prudentem & pium conciliarium': Grey, *Ioannae Graiae litterae*, p. 1; see also Erasmus, *De conscribendis epistolis*, in *CWE: Literary and educational writings III*, pp. 76–8, 80, 90–3.

[127] 'Mihi contingat quod uel Blesillae Paulae & Eustochio quas diuus ille ut fertur Ieronymus instituit': Grey, *Ioannae Graiae litterae*, p. 2.

compared Bullinger to the greatest church father and biblical scholar, she added flattering parallels to St John and Origen, who had also advised women correspondents. She wrote that they, and implicitly she, came to owe 'their praise and commendation not so much to the fact that they united beauty of body, nobility of their birth, and copiousness of wealth' but to their pious correspondence with learned men.[128] This sentence was also a happy instance of *paralipsis*; Jane drew attention to her own nobility by pretending to pass over it. Indeed the force of the letter was to emphasise its author's nobility, filial loyalty and Protestant piety. She presented herself as her father's loyal emissary, expressing his thanks for the dedication of the *Decades*, 'a little book of pure and unadulterated religion' that they were both perusing at every spare moment.[129] To confirm her commitment to purifying religion in England, Jane added a startling request in her conclusion; she was learning, she wrote, the Hebrew of the Old Testament and begged Bullinger to 'show me some way and method to follow this course of studies beneficially'.[130] She had demonstrated the extent of her erudition and showed how it supported the nobility of her family and Protestant faith.

Indeed, like other learned women in early modern Europe, Jane's liberal education had yoked her firmly to her parents and their schemes. In the summer of 1550, Ascham famously came across her at Bradgate Park devouring Plato's *Phaedo* in Greek and discoursing on the true pleasure of study under her kindly schoolmaster, Aylmer. Twenty years later, he would claim that she had also accused her mother and father of regularly beating her. At the time, however, he had written to praise her for bringing joy to her 'most noble parents' (*parentibus tuis nobilissimis*) with her scholarly achievements.[131] Indeed, during her lifetime, Jane used her learning time and time again to demonstrate her filial loyalty. That December, she presented her father with a New Year's gift of the greater part of Bullinger's 1540 treatise on the *Christian state of matrimony* that she had translated into Greek.[132] Even when the Suffolks' ambition placed her in the Tower, even

[128] 'Non tantum sibi laudis & com[m]odi ex corporis forma generis nobilitate & diuitiarum copia compararunt quantum… ex prudentissimorum uiuorum consiliis hauserunt': Grey, *Ioannae Graiae litterae*, p. 2; see, for example, Cicero, *Philippic orations*, VI.7.18.

[129] 'Illustrissimus pater meus… grauissimis Regiae Maiestatis negotiis in ultimos Britanniae fines fuisset auocatus', 'uerae & non fucatae religionis': Grey, *Ioannae Graiae litterae*, pp. 4 and 3 respectively.

[130] 'Si viam & modum aliquem ostenderis quem in hoc studiorum cursu tenere maxima cum utilitate': Grey, *Ioannae Graiae litterae*, p. 4.

[131] Ascham, *Scholemaster*, fols. 11^{v}–12^{r} and *Whole works*, vol. I.ii, p. 239, 241.

[132] Ellis, *Letters*, vol. II, p. 427.

when the duke's involvement in the Wyatt rebellion triggered the decision to execute her, Jane used letters to express her loyalty and affection. She wrote her final epistle to her father in the prayer book that she carried with her to the scaffold on 12 February 1554, saying that, as she had 'honoured youre grace in thys life', so she would 'praye for you in another life'.[133] Like other learned noblewomen, Jane found that her liberal education tightened bonds of filial loyalty and obedience. She was imprisoned, bodily and figuratively, by her family's determination to advance her status.

It was in those works composed during Jane's incarceration, however, that the extent of her learning and the intellectual and spiritual benefits she derived from it may be seen most clearly. Eric Ives has made a strong case for the authenticity of several letters attributed to Jane in the days before her execution, her scaffold speech and her part in a debate with the Benedictine monk John Feckenham, which were collected and printed clandestinely after her death, probably by John Day.[134] They demonstrated that, even when she was deprived of most of her books, she could perform some of the most difficult rhetorical exercises in the *Progymnasmata*. As Ives has shown, Jane's letter to Thomas Harding, a former chaplain of the Grey family who had returned to Catholicism at Mary's accession, used forensic rhetoric in the grand style to devastating effect. The sixteen-year-old Jane proved proficient in the very sort of combative, hyperbolic and destructive form of oratory that Leonardo Bruni had warned noblewomen against.[135]

Jane's subsequent dispute with John Feckenham, who had been sent to convert her, showed her knowledge of Protestant doctrine and her skill in logical reasoning. The sixteen-year-old distilled three key debates of the Edwardian church on salvation by faith alone, the meaning of the Lord's Supper and the status of the Roman church into simple, clear arguments authorised by scripture. Jane must have known that Feckenham had taken part in formal disputations regarding the nature of the Eucharist in 1551 and she had prepared carefully for their encounter.[136] To defend her view that the Lord's Supper was only a 'sure seale and testimoni' of Christ's sacrifice to redeem men, she seems to have drawn on Peter Martyr Vermigli's

133 BL, Harleian MS 2342, fol. 80^{r}.

134 Jane Grey, *An epistle of the Ladye Jane, a righte vertuous woman, to a learned man of late falne from the truth of Gods most holy word, for fear of the worlde read it, to thy consolacion: Vvhereunto is added the communication that she had with Master Feckenham vpon her faith, and belefe of the sacraments: Also another epistle whiche she wrote to her sister, with the words she spake vpon the scaffold befor she suffered, anno. M.D.Liiii* ([London, 1554?]), STC 7279; Ives, *Lady Jane Grey*, pp. 19–22.

135 Grey, *An epistle*, sigs. Ai^{r}–Bii^{r}; Ives, *Lady Jane Grey*, pp. 254–6.

136 C. S. Knighton, 'Feckenham, John (*c*. 1510–1584)', *ODNB*.

(1499–1562) *Tractatio de sacramentio Eucharistae* (1549), which Edward VI also read and used in his compositions. Her choice of biblical authorities and arguments also revealed the influence of Thomas Cranmer's *Defence of the true and catholike doctrine of the sacrament of the body and bloud of our sauiour Christ* (1550).[137] She followed Cranmer in pointing out the inconsistent literalism of those, like Feckenham, who claimed that Christ's words at the Last Supper, 'take, eate, this is my bodi' (Matthew 26:26), demonstrated his real presence in the sacrament. Christ had also said, 'I am the vine, I am the dore', Jane countered, but this did not mean he *was* either in a physical sense. Jane added that St Paul had said that, here and elsewhere in scripture, Christ spoke metaphorically.[138] Then she pulled out her instruments of logic. At the time of the Last Supper, Jane said, Christ was still very much alive. He 'suffred not, til the next daye'. Given this state of affairs, could the disciples really have consumed his blood and flesh during the course of the evening? 'Either [Christ] had. ii. bodies, either els if his bodi wer eaten, it was not broken vpon the crosse, or els if it were broken vpon the crosse, it was not eaten of his disciples'.[139] Scriptural evidence made it very clear which of these possibilities was, in fact, the case. Like Edward, Jane had evidently gained argumentative readiness from the study of humanist dialectic. She concluded that a church that 'altreth the Lordes supper, & both taketh from it, and addeth to it' by denying the congregation communion of both kinds while adding erroneous doctrines to its meaning was 'an euil church, and not the spouse of Christ, but the spouse of the diuel'.[140] Jane's filial obedience had cost her the political case, but she was determined to win the confessional argument against all comers.

Jane may have despised the church of Rome, but she had enjoyed arguing with Feckenham to the extent that she agreed he should accompany her to the scaffold.[141] Perhaps rhythms of theological disputation gave her a sense of liberty and authority despite her physical captivity, or a feeling of intellectual vitality in the face of earthly doom. Indeed, Jane Grey seemed galvanised to really *use* her education in her final days. Her object was no longer to serve her parents but to exhort English subjects against abandoning the true religion. She wanted them to hear her defence of her

137 Thomas Cranmer, *A defence of the true and catholike doctrine of the sacrament of the body and bloud of our sauiour Christ* (London, [1550]), STC 6000; Peter Martyr, *Tractatio de sacramento Eucharistiae* (London, 1549), STC 24673.

138 Grey, *An epistle*, sigs. Biii^v–Biv^r; see similarly Cranmer, *A defence*, fols. 71^v–72^r, 75^r.

139 Grey, *An epistle*, sig. Biv^v. 140 Grey, *An epistle*, sig. Ci^r.

141 Anonymous, *The chronicle of Queen Jane, and of two years of Queen Mary, and especially of the rebellion of Sir Thomas Wyat*, ed. John Nichols (London, 1850), p. 57.

faith. Either she recorded what she remembered of her conversation with Feckenham and smuggled it out, or she made sure that their dialogue was overheard by those who could report it.[142] She wove a declaration of her faith into the fabric of her scaffold speech, a testament she could be sure would be relayed and reproduced. She was, she said, a 'true Christian woman', who asked for prayers only 'while I am now aliue' and who had faith that she would 'be saued by the bloud of Iesus Christ, and bi none other meanes'.[143] In all these speech acts, Jane taught English subjects to refute attempts to lure them away from the true faith as decisively as she had rejected Feckenham's arguments and repudiated Harding's expedient conformism. Like Edward VI, her words were circulated on the eve of the civil wars in Britain and Ireland and during the 1688 revolution to rally anti-Catholic sentiment.[144] Jane was every bit as ready to use her pen to fight for her church as she was to die for it. Her education had left her as well armed to defend the faith as the boy-king who had attempted to make her his successor.

The Greys had given their daughter a superlative liberal education for the same reason they had placed her with Thomas Seymour, forced her to marry Guilford Dudley and pushed her to accept the poisoned chalice of the English crown in July 1553. Without a son to advance, they would go to extreme lengths to drive their daughter up a less travelled path. Jane obeyed their wishes and expressed her loyalty to her father, especially, until the very end of her life. In addition to binding her to their ambitions, however, Jane's liberal education also gave her the skills and knowledge to argue for her faith and defend the church she had come so close to governing. From the prison of the Tower, it became clear that Jane had been taught to rule; when that diamond ring turned to brass, it also became apparent that she had genuinely studied 'to learne to die' well.[145]

The last letter Jane wrote to her sister, Katherine Grey (1540?–68), in her Greek New Testament 'the night before she suffered' suggests that she regretted submitting to her parents' worldly ambitions but that she valued her studies nonetheless. Reading the Greek New Testament, she told Katherine 'shal winne you more, then you should haue gained by the possession of your woful fathers landes'.[146] The family's power was gone but Jane drew on Matthew 6:19 to promise Katherine that, if she applied herself 'diligently [to] this booke' and sought 'to direct your lyfe

[142] Grey, *An epistle*, sig. Ci^{r}; Ives, *Lady Jane Grey*, p. 21.
[143] Grey, *An epistle*, sig. Ciiii^{r}.
[144] For example: STC 7282, Wing C5726.
[145] Grey, *An epistle*, sig. Cii^{r-v}.
[146] Grey, *An epistle*, sig. Cii^{r}.

after it: You shalbe an inheritour of suche ryches, as neither [th]e couvitous shall w[ith]draw fro[m] you / neither the thefe shall steale / neither yet [th]e mothes corrupt'.[147] The corruption, inconstancy and brevity of mortal existence paled against the glorious and eternal life of the faithful. The contrast between the worldly object of Jane's liberal education and its spiritual effects gave gravitas to this traditional *antithesis*. 'Defy the world', Jane counselled her sister.[148]

EDUCATING MARY I

The educations of Mary and Elizabeth lacked the focused ambition that propelled Jane Grey's schooling but both Tudor women came to the throne significantly better prepared to govern than either Mary, Queen of Scots, or Elizabeth Stuart. The final sections of this chapter will explore the dynastic circumstances that simultaneously expanded and contracted Mary and Elizabeth's educational opportunities and the uses to which they put their learning as sovereigns.

Like Elizabeth Stuart, Mary Tudor had brothers. Until Edward's birth in 1537, however, Henry VIII's sons were hoped for, stillborn or illegitimate, so Mary's princely potential was not discounted. Her mother, Catherine of Aragon, had no doubts about her right to rule or the significance of her liberal education to that end. Her father, however, tended to view the point of her schooling as preparing her for marriage to a foreign 'prynce of the greatest honor'.[149] The result was that Mary's education was not 'cutting edge', as some scholars have claimed.[150] Rather her skill in the liberal arts was something she worked at as a young adult. After her disgrace, political resurrection and, finally, political restoration to the succession, a translation project suggested to Mary in 1545 by her final step-mother, Katherine Parr, gave the princess the impetus to return to the *bonae litterae*. It offered her an opportunity to develop her grammatical and rhetorical skills, make a contribution to the devotional lives of English readers and, perhaps, even to think further about the sort of church she wanted to see established in England.

One of Mary I's recent biographers has asserted confidently that Mary was 'heir to the English Crown between 1516 and 1537'.[151] In fact, from birth until Mary forcibly claimed the throne in 1553, her status was in

[147] Grey, *An epistle*, sig. Cii^{v}. [148] Grey, *An epistle*, sig. Cii^{r-v}. [149] SP 1/197, fol. 159^{v}.

[150] Jaime Goodrich, 'Mary Tudor, Lord Morley, and St Thomas Aquinas: The politics of pious translation at the Henrician court', *ANQ*, 24:1–2 (2011), p. 11.

[151] John Edwards, *Mary I: England's Catholic queen* (New Haven, 2011), p. 3.

flux. At best she was an heir presumptive as both her parents prayed for a son and Henry VIII went to considerable trouble to acquire one. As early as 1519 he attempted to distract Catherine's attention from the departure of Mary's nurse, Margaret, Lady Bryan (*c.* 1468–*c.* 1551), to attend the new-born Henry Fitzroy, appointing Margaret Pole, Countess of Salisbury (1473–1541) as Mary's 'lady governess'.[152] Mary was called the king's successor in marriage treaties contracted with France in 1518 and Charles V in August 1520.[153] Yet Henry was gambling on the princess's claim to the English throne remaining untested. On 28 June 1520, when the French sent envoys to check on their dauphin's fiancée, Princess Mary was swiftly relocated to the king's palace at Richmond and a gaggle of additional noblewomen were rounded up to attend her. Salisbury hastily taught Mary to receive the visitors 'w[ith] moost goodly countenence [and] proper commyunycac[i]on' and played enthusiastically on the virginals for their entertainment.[154] Her princely status had to be manufactured for the occasion.[155] The diplomatic fiction that Mary was Henry's heir soon wore thin. By November 1524, the papal envoy, Giovanni Batista Sangi, was reporting that few believed that 'the daughter of the King of England [would] bring that kingdom with her as dower'.[156]

Henry doubted his daughter's princely potential; Catherine of Aragon did not. Catherine's mother, Isabella of Castile (1451–1504), was a sovereign queen praised for her piety, her military prowess and her revival of 'Latin letters' hitherto 'lost in our Castile'.[157] Isabel's own education had not included Latin and she attempted to learn it after her accession to manage state business. As a consequence, she insisted that her daughters, as well as her son, study Latin under Antonio and Alessandro Geraldini and commissioned several Latin grammars and advice books on the subject of royal education.[158] In 1468 Martín de Córdoba had presented Isabel with the *Jardín de nobles donzella* (printed 1500), which recommended that royal woman should 'take some hours of each day to study and digest those works proper

[152] *LP*, vol. III, no. 970, p. 356; John Guy, *The children of Henry VIII* (Oxford, 2013), pp. 23–4; J. L. McIntosh, *From heads of household to heads of state: The pre-accession households of Mary and Elizabeth Tudor, 1516–1558* (New York, 2009), pp. 21–9; Hazel Pierce, *Margaret Pole, Countess of Salisbury, 1473–1541: Loyalty, lineage and leadership* (Cardiff, 2003), pp. 43, 88.

[153] *LP*, vol. II, no. 4468, p. 1372; NA, E 30/868.

[154] BL, Cotton MS Caligula D VII, fols. 238^{v}–239^{r}.

[155] Guy, *Children of Henry VIII*, pp. 32–4. [156] *LP*, vol. IV, no. 843, p. 378.

[157] Juan de Lucena, 'Epistola exhortatoria a las letras', in *Isabel la Católica en la opinión de Españoles y extranjeros: Signlos XV al XX*, ed. Vicente Valencia Rodríguez, 3 vols. (Valladolid, 1970), vol. I, p. 377.

[158] Elizabeth Howe, *Education and women in the early modern Hispanic world* (Aldershot, 2008), p. 47.

for the rule of the kingdom'.[159] Subsequently, Alonso Ortis, humanist and royal chaplain, composed a dialogue *Liber de educatione Johannis Serenissimi principis* (*c.* 1492–7), in which he argued that royal men and women 'must cultivate the custom of exercise, not only for the body, but also in the liberal arts'.[160] As Erasmus would attest, Catherine of Aragon loved the *bonae litterae* 'which she had studied with success since childhood'.[161] As queen of England, Peter Martyr claimed that she had made a 'splendid oration' urging the English captains heading to Scotland in 1512 to 'defend their territory'.[162] Catherine had full confidence in her daughter's princely potential and the honour and utility of the *bonae litterae* for royal women.

Indeed, Catherine attempted to promote Mary's status as Henry's heir through the princess's schooling. Margaret Pole had begun to teach the princess to read, but she was removed temporarily from Mary's household in 1521, following the condemnation of her kinsman Edward Stafford, duke of Buckingham.[163] When no tutor was appointed on Mary's sixth birthday, Catherine seems to have taken Mary's Latin instruction in hand herself, perhaps in conjunction with Mary's chaplain, Henry Rowle.[164] Even when Mary's first schoolmaster was finally appointed in July 1525, Catherine asked her daughter to continue to send her letters 'of yo[u]r owne enditing [composition]' so that she could ensure her daughter was maintaining her 'latten and fayer writing and all'.[165] Catherine was no schemer but her attitude to her daughter's liberal education anticipated that of Frances and Henry Dorset; if Mary was educated as a prince, she had a better chance of becoming one.

Catherine's campaign for Mary's liberal education turned on literary patronage. On 5 April 1523 Catherine's client, Juan Luis Vives, completed his *De institutione feminae Christianae*, which he claimed was a plan for Mary's upbringing.[166] Catherine, however, seems to have required a more

159 'Captar a algunas oras del día en que estudie y oya tales cosas que sean propias al regimiento del reyno': Martín de Córdoba, *Jardín de nobles donzellas*, ed. Harriet Goldberg (Chapel Hill, 1974), p. 244.

160 'Tenemos… que cultivar el hábito del ejercicio, pero no orientado hacia una sola costumbre de los atletas, y más bien dirigidos hacia las obras liberales bien para el hombre, bien para la mujer': Alonso Ortiz, *Diálogo sobre la educación del príncipe don Juan, hijo de los reyes católicos (s. xv–xvi)*, ed. Giovanni Maria Bertini (Madrid, 1983), p. 172.

161 Erasmus, *OEDE*, vol. III, no. 976, p. 602 and Erasmus, *CWE: Letters 842–992*, no. 976, p. 388.

162 *CSP Spain*, vol. II, 17, p. 19.

163 Frederick Madden (ed)., *Privy Purse Expenses of Princess Mary* (London, 1831), p. xxii; Henry Clifford, *Life of Jane Dormer*, eds. E. E. Estcourt and Joseph Stevenson (London, 1887), p. 80.

164 *LP*, vol. II, p. 1473.

165 BL, Cotton MS Vespasian F XIII, fol. 72^{r}.

166 Vives, *De institutione feminae christianae*; James Carley, *The Libraries of King Henry VIII* (London, 2000), p. 68 suggests that the presentation copy was BL, Arch B e 30.

princely curriculum for her daughter. In October that year, at the queen's command (*iussisti*), Vives set out a more challenging course of studies specifically for Mary: *De ratione studii puerilis* (printed 1524).[167] There, Vives offered advice on speaking and writing Latin elegantly and swiftly, encouraging the princess to draw on Thomas Linacre's *Rudimenta grammatices* and Erasmus' *Colloquia* to develop a neo-classical and conversational style, and to study etymologies so as to avoid 'those barbarous words which have usurped [the Latin tongue] through ignorant usage'.[168] She was 'to translate little speeches of increasing difficulty from English into Latin'.[169] The authors he recommended 'cultivated good languages and morals... [they] taught one not only to know rightly, but to live rightly'.[170] Like Erasmus, Vives recommended the New Testament; the works of Cicero, Seneca and Plutarch; and the dialogues of Plato, 'especially those that comment upon the government of the state' for the Christian prince. He encouraged Mary to read his own edition of Augustine; Erasmus' recent version of Jerome's letters, *Education of a Christian prince*, *Paraphrases on the New Testament* and *Handbook of the Christian soldier*; and More's *Utopia*.[171] Like Erasmus, moreover, Vives dedicated two textbooks of moral adages to Mary to help her appreciate the connection between good speech and virtue. The *Satellitium sive symbola* (1524) was a collection of Latin commonplaces that the princess was to commit to memory, to use in compositions and to direct her conduct. We have seen Edward VI's tutors making use of them to this end in his early schooling and Elizabeth I would quote the *Satellitium*'s maxims in her copy of the Geneva New Testament (1578?).[172] Like Erasmus, Vives argued that words could serve as a guard, to protect the princess from falling into vice and to preserve her office. Subjects' loyalty, Vives warned, 'cannot be forced by arms or terror, but enticed through love, faith, diligence, and care of the common good'.[173] By the end of 1524, Catherine had established a road map and plan for her daughter's princely education in the *bonae litterae*. Andrew Taylor has rightly pointed out that Vives was less ambitious for Mary's

167 Vives, *De ratione studii puerilis*, fol. 48^{v}.

168 'Quae usu ineruditirum barbara vocabula usurpantur': Vives, *De ratione studii puerilis*, fol. 53^{v}.

169 'Incipient hoc oratiunculas ex anglico in latinum vertere, faciles initio, paulatim difficiliores': Vives, *De ratione studii puerilis*, fol. 53^{v}.

170 'Qui pariter linguam & mores excolant, quique non modo bene scire doceant, sed bene vivere': Vives, *De ratione studii puerilis*, fol. 56^{r}.

171 'Praesertim qui ad rempublicam gubernandam spectant': Vives, *De ratione studii puerilis*, fol. 56^{r}.

172 Elizabeth, *Translations*, p. 403.

173 'Qui non armis aut terrore extorquetur; amore, fide, diligentia, cura communium commodorum': Vives, *Satellitium sive symbola*, fol. 30^{r}. See similarly his *Introductio ad sapientiam*, fol. 10^{v}, which was also for Mary.

studies than he was in a plan developed for a boy, Charles Blount, the son of Henry VIII's *socius studiorum* Lord Mountjoy. Nevertheless, Vives seems to have provided Catherine with a curriculum that 'gently accommodated the possibility that [Mary] might rule'.[174]

Ultimately, however, it was not Catherine's educational campaign but her failure to carry another child to term that encouraged Henry VIII and Wolsey to promote Mary as Henry's heir in 1525. In August 1525 Mary was sent to Wales to serve as the king's vice-regent in the principality.[175] The princess was accompanied by Margaret Pole, a council led by John Voysey, Bishop of Exeter, and an independent household of up to 304 people.[176] As we have seen, Edward V and Prince Arthur had presided over royal households and councils in Wales as part of their training for kingship. Even at this moment, however, Mary's princely status was not unequivocal. She was not created Prince of Wales before her departure, nor was she typically styled as such during her sojourn in the principality; and, as we have seen, Henry Fitzroy was simultaneously made duke of Richmond and travelled north to be warden general of the Scottish Marches with his own rival royal household and council. The differences between the status and size of the children's households were not so marked as to make it clear which child Henry favoured. The arrangements made for their educations, however, were suggestive.

Before the declaration of the royal supremacy, Henry VIII was less anxious that his children study the *bonae litterae* than he became afterwards. Nevertheless, the resources expended on Mary's schooling were not equal to those consumed in the doomed mission to educate the duke of Richmond.[177] The duke was surrounded by (trouble-making) peers but, despite Vives's advice, no group of 'liberally and piously educated' young women were schooled alongside Mary.[178] Mary was not taught to write in the newly fashionable italic hand that Richmond used. Even more critically, Mary's schoolmaster was not in the same league as her half-brother's. As we have seen, the six-year-old Richmond was accompanied by a humanist schoolmaster, John Palsgrave, who

174 Taylor, '"Ad omne virtutum genus"', pp. 105, 109–11.

175 W. R. B. Robinson, 'Princess Mary's itinerary in the Marches of Wales 1525–1527: A provisional record', *Historical Research*, 71 (1998).

176 *LP*, vol. IV, no. 1577, pp. 707–11; David Loades, *Mary Tudor: A Life* (Oxford, 1989), pp. 39–40; McIntosh, *From heads of household*, pp. 29–37.

177 Aysha Pollnitz, 'Humanism and court culture in the education of Tudor royal children', in Tom Betteridge and Anna Riehl (eds.), *Tudor court culture* (Selingrove, PA, 2010).

178 'Ae puellae, atque etiam selectissimae liberaliter & sanctissime educatae': Vives, *De ratione studii puerilis*, fol. 55^{r}.

had planned his princely education in consultation with Erasmus and Thomas More. Palsgrave was succeeded by the eminent Greek scholar Richard Croke. The nine-year-old Mary, however, was to be taught by Richard Fetherston (d. 1540), archdeacon of St. David's in Brecknock, South Wales.[179] Fetherston graduated from the University of Cambridge in 1499 or 1500 and took an MA degree from Oxford in 1505 but he had no known experience as a schoolmaster at the time of his appointment. He had not circulated works of scholarship. He had no knowledge of Greek nor verifiable connections to northern humanists.[180] Fetherston certainly justified the faith that the queen and princess showed in him; he stayed loyal to Rome, to Catherine and to Mary during and after the divorce and was ultimately executed by Henry VIII for his trouble. In 1525, however, he lacked the humanist pedigree, intellectual vigour, continental experience and prior royal service that distinguished Richmond's schoolmasters.

In July 1526, Henry VIII and Wolsey required Mary's council to report on her progress in Latin at least once a month.[181] Yet the Latin exercises that Mary prepared on Fetherston's watch were more redolent of her grandmother's literary efforts than Vives's humanist prescriptions. In 1504 and 1506, Margaret Beaufort had printed English translations of French devotional works that were becoming popular amongst the English laity.[182] In 1527, Mary translated Thomas Aquinas's prayer for the ordering of life, which appealed to a similar readership. Mary probably worked from a medieval Latin rendering, printed in a 1514 Salisbury book of hours.[183] Yet this traditional prayer remained popular in Tudor England; it would be included in primers authorised by each Tudor monarch regardless of their confessional allegiances.[184] As a literary exercise, it was a rudimentary one that demonstrated Mary's command of basic grammar, syntax and diction rather than a literary work in its own right. Henry Parker, Lord Morley (1480/1–1556), was right to praise

179 *LP*, vol. III, no. 2992, p. 1262, vol. IV, no. 1577, p. 708 and no. 2331, p. 1045, vol. VI, no. 1199, p. 498.

180 Ethan Shagan, 'Fetherston, Richard (d. 1540)', *ODNB*.

181 *LP*, vol. IV, no. 2331, p. 1044; BL, Cotton MS Vitellius C I, fol. 24^v.

182 [Jacques de Gruytrode], *Mirroure of golde for the synfull soule*, trans. Margaret Beaufort (London, 1506), STC 6894.5; Thomas à Kempis, *Full deuoute and gostely treatyse of the imytacion and followynge the blessyd lyfe of our most merciful savyour Cryst*, trans. William Atkinson and Margaret Beaufort (London, [1504] 1517), STC 23957.

183 *Hore beate Marie virgiinis ad usum insignis ac praeclare ecclesiasie Saru[m]* (London, 1514), STC 15919.

184 A. Doyle, 'A prayer attributed to St. Thomas Aquinas', *Dominican Studies*, 1 (1948), p. 233. See, for example, STC 16034–40, 16053, 16079, 16087, 16089, 16090.

the princess for coming 'neare to the laten' of the original.[185] The prayer also articulated sentiments that pedagogues deemed particularly appropriate for Christian women: the penitent expressed 'ardent' devotion to God and begged to be made 'Obedyent w[i]t[h] oute arguyng, Pacient w't oute grutching, And pure wi[t]h oute corrupcion'.[186] While the duke of Richmond's schoolmasters attempted to interest him in Caesar's *Gallic wars*, Mary showed that she had inscribed suitable lessons for a Christian woman on the tablet of her mind.

Alongside Latin, Mary was expected 'to intende to her learning of… French'. She was to walk regularly and to continue to practice the virginals, dancing and decorous deportment.[187] Indeed, like the educations of Mary and Elizabeth Stuart, Mary's schooling in the 1520s privileged vernacular languages and courtly accomplishments over her study of Latin. The princess's avuncular French master, Giles du Wés, had served as the music and language instructor to Henry VII's children and as the royal librarian.[188] He was eminently better qualified for his post than Fetherston.[189] As du Wés's treatise *An introductorie for to lerne to rede, to pronounce, and to speake Frenche trewly* (1533) shows, he introduced the princess to a variety of genres for speaking and writing French in public life: she received messengers from her father and foreign potentates; she responded to letters from her household officers; she commented upon poems in French; and she engaged in learned dialogues on Plato in the manner Castiglione described in *The courtyer*.[190] Did this emphasis on courtly French suggest that Henry VIII was still expecting to use her as a diplomatic asset rather than his heir?

Her betrothal to Francis I in 1527 and recall to the Thames valley in April 1527 is suggestive. At a meeting with the French ambassadors at Greenwich on St George's Day, Mary was called on to speak to the visitors in French, Latin and (allegedly) Italian.[191] The princess's study of languages was useful in ornamenting the ill-fated alliance, as Henry VIII's subsequent gifts of plate to the countess of Salisbury, Fetherston and du Wés imply. All three educators continued in Mary's well-appointed household

185 BL, Royal MS 17 C XVI, fol. 2^{v}. 186 BL, Additional MS 17012, fols. 192^{v}–194^{r}.

187 BL, Cotton MS Vitellius C I, fol. 24^{v}.

188 Giles du Wés, *An introductorie for to lerne to rede, to pronounce, and to speake Frenche trewly* (London, 1533), STC 7377, sigs. Aii^{r}, Aiv^{r}.

189 Gordon Kipling, 'Duwes, Giles [Aegidius de Vadis] (d. 1535)', *ODNB*.

190 du Wés, *An introductorie*, sigs. $Bbii^{r}$–Ddi^{r}; Jeri L. McIntosh, 'A culture of reverence: Princess Mary's household, 1525–27', in Alice Hunt and Anna Whitelock (eds.), *Tudor queenship: The reigns of Mary and Elizabeth* (Basingstoke, 2010).

191 *LP*, vol. IV, no. 3105, p. 1412.

throughout her parents' Great Matter.[192] As Henry VIII moved against Catherine of Aragon, he seems to have decided that Mary's studies posed no challenge to his dynastic plans.

That changed with the birth of Princess Elizabeth, in September 1533. The imperial ambassador, Eustace Chapuys, frothed with indignation as he described the removal of Mary's liveries, the disbanding of her house, the expulsion of her schoolmaster and her incorporation as the cadet royal in Elizabeth's establishment in December that year.[193] The first Act of Succession (1534) confirmed the object of these manoeuvres; the king's heir would be his offspring with Anne Boleyn. During Mary's subsequent years in the political wilderness, the only people who expressed interest in her studies were Catherine and Chapuys, who encouraged Mary to turn to the *bonae litterae* for consolation.[194] Mary's 1536 capitulation, in which she acknowledged her father's royal supremacy, led to a swift improvement in her household and material circumstances. Indeed, by 1542, positions in Mary's chamber were widely sought after.[195] She received an increasing number of literary gifts from well-wishers such as Henry Parker, Lord Morley, but her intellectual life remained largely a private concern.[196]

The third Act for the Succession, passed in January 1544, made Mary's knowledge of Latin a matter of political and religious significance once more. From the king's perspective, the fact that his daughter was 'well educated' and second in line for the throne, if 'ought shuld cum to [Henry's] Son without issue', were still matters he referred to only in the context of marrying her off advantageously.[197] But his last wife, Katherine, saw matters slightly differently. Eustace Chapuys, the imperial ambassador, claimed that Mary owed her restoration to the succession to Katherine's lobbying.[198] The two royal women were certainly very close. Following the death of her second husband in February 1543, Parr obtained a place in Mary's household; it may have been the princess who introduced her to Henry VIII. Together with Edward and Elizabeth, Mary was a guest at their wedding on 12 July 1543.[199] Afterwards, Katherine and Mary continued to lodge together frequently, to exchange gifts, to share servants and

192 *LP*, vol. IV, no. 3748, p. 1672; BL, Cotton MS Cleopatra, E VI, fols. 325r–328r; Loades, *Mary Tudor*, pp. 24–5.

193 *CSP Spain*, vol. IV.ii, pp. 794–5, 800, 820–1, 837, 839, 854, 870–1.

194 BL, Arundel MS 151, fol. 194r; *LP*, vol. VII, no. 121, p. 48.

195 *LP*, vol. X, no. 1187, pp. 1187–8.

196 BL, Additional MS 17012, fols. 192v–194r; BL, Royal MS 17 C XVI, fol. 2v; *LP*, vol. XVI, no. 1253, p. 586.

197 SP 1/197, fols. 159v, 160r.

198 *CSP Spain*, vol. VII, p. 55; *LP*, vol. XIX, no. 118, p. 64.

199 Loades, *Mary Tudor*, pp. 102–5, 116–17; Janel Mueller, 'Introduction', in Parr, *Katherine Parr*, pp. 10–11, 13.

even to write courtesy letters on the same sheet of paper.[200] Mary described herself as Katherine's 'most humble dowghter and seruant' in the queen's copy of Thomas Cranmer's English *Litany*.[201] Despite their increasingly divergent confessional views, they shared a chaplain, Francis Mallet, and books that suggested a mutual interest in Erasmus' spiritual writings.[202]

By September 1545, Katherine had initiated a project for the translation of Erasmus' *Paraphrases on the New Testament* (1522–4) and she roped in Princess Mary to convert Erasmus' explication of John into English.[203] As we have seen, Henry VIII and his apologists hijacked Erasmus' *Paraphrases* to justify the royal supremacy. As Nicholas Udall (1504–56) wrote in September 1545, Katherine, like Cranmer and Cromwell before her, was probably trying to use the humanists' biblical commentaries to promote 'the knowleadge of Goddes holy woorde & gospell' amongst English subjects following the restrictions that had been imposed on Bible-reading.[204] Yet Juan Luis Vives had also encouraged Mary to study the *Paraphrases* in the days when she was still studying Latin with her mother. There was much, too, in Erasmus' account of the gospel of John that would have appealed to traditionalists like Mary, particularly in his account of the Last Supper.[205] Mary agreed to perform what must have been the largest and most sustained translation exercise she had ever contemplated, indeed that any British woman in the sixteenth century had hitherto undertaken. She began working from a 1534 Froben edition of the *Paraphrases* that Erasmus had toned down in an attempt to head off accusations of *sola fideism*.[206]

The translation gave Mary an opportunity to revive those 'most becoming studies' she had undertaken during her years in the political wilderness, perhaps under Mallet's direction.[207] It is difficult to know

[200] *CSP Spain*, vol. VI.ii, p. 459, VIII, p. 2; HHCP, 147/6; James, *Kateryn Parr*, pp. 90, 111, 113, 117, 127–35; *LP*, vol. XVIII, no. 39, p. 19, no. 467, p. 254, no. 501, p. 269, vol. XX, no. 900, p. 438.

[201] In Parr, *Katherine Parr*, p. 625.

[202] NA, LC 2/2, fol. 45^r; NA, E 101/424/12, fol. 15^r; *LP*, vol. XX, no. 909 (47), p. 445 and App. 2, p. 549.

[203] For the date, see Nicholas Udall, 'Letter to Queen Katherine prefacing Luke', in Erasmus, *The first tome or volume of the Paraphrases of Erasmus vpon the Newe Testament*, trans. Mary I *et al.*, ed. Nicholas Udall (London, 1548), STC 2854, sigs. ci^r–cvi^v (Luke is separately paginated).

[204] Udall, 'Letter to Queen Katherine prefacing Luke', in Erasmus, *First tome or volume of the* Paraphases, sig. ci^v.

[205] Richard Rex, 'The role of English humanists in the Reformation up to 1559', in N. Scott Amos, Andrew Pettegree and Henk Van Nierop (eds.), *The education of a Christian society: Humanism and the Reformation in Britain and the Netherlands* (Aldershot, 1999), pp. 30–1. See, for example, Morley's dedicatory letter to Mary accompanying his translation of Erasmus' *Paean virgini matri dicendus*: BL, Royal MS 17A XLVI, fol. 1^v.

[206] See Jane Phillips's note in Erasmus, *CWE: Paraphrases on John*, p. 118n.75.

[207] Loades, *Mary Tudor*, p. 61 and *LP*, vol. XVI, no. 1253, p. 536.

quite how much of the work she completed before illness, feigned or real, discouraged her and she turned it over to her chaplain to finish.[208] But, if she began at the beginning, the early chapters suggest that she stuck fairly closely to the original text and syntax. Like the other (male) translators assigned to the project, Mary strove for verisimilitude. There were a couple of eye-skips and mangled sentences, but, generally, the princess translated Erasmus' prose not merely accurately but sensitively. She managed theological terms and unusual phrases, such as *collybistae* for bankers. Occasionally, she even engaged in some modest rhetorical amplification.[209]

The grammatical and rhetorical skills that Mary must have polished up while working on translating Erasmus' *Paraphrases* served her well in the difficult years of Edward's reign. Her letter to Thomas Seymour on 4 June 1547, for instance, which explained why it was neither honourable nor useful for her to further his 'sewte… to the queen for maryage', was a withering piece of deliberative rhetoric.[210] The princess's capacity to articulate the weaknesses in her opponents' arguments would prove especially valuable in the repeated stand-offs regarding her private masses that were considered in the previous chapter. Mary did not disobey the king, she claimed under examination; rather, she disputed the legal authority of the protector, who was 'no kyng', to alter church services.[211] This was not a particularly original argument but Mary's capacity make it suit various audiences and under considerable pressure from 1549 to 1551, at least, demonstrated some rhetorical sophistication. That 'incomparable oratrix' who won the loyalty of the Guildhall with her speech during the Wyatt rebellion of 1554 was not fashioned in a day.[212] During Henry VIII's last days and Edward VI's reign, Mary used her study of rhetoric to position herself as a viable reversionary interest.

Not only did Mary's translation of Erasmus' *Paraphrases* build her rhetorical skills but it also burnished her reputation for being 'a wise & learned Prince', as Stephen Gardiner had called her following her Guildhall

208 BL, Cotton Vespasian F III, fol. 37^{r}.

209 For example, Erasmus, *Paraphrases of Erasmus vpon John*, transl. Mary Tudor and Francis Mallet, in *First tome or volume of the* Paraphases, sigs. BBb2^{r-v}, BBb4^{r}, CCc7^{r}, DDd1^{ar-v}, Iii6^{r}, KKk2^{v}, LLl1^{r}. See Aysha Pollnitz, 'Religion and translation in the court of Henry VIII: Princess Mary, Katherine Parr and the *Paraphrases* of Erasmus', in Susan Doran and Thomas Freeman (eds.), *Mary Tudor: Old and new perspectives* (Houndmills, 2011), pp. 129–33.

210 Mary in Parr, *Katherine Parr*, pp. 145–6.

211 SP 10/8, fol. 77^{r}.

212 Wingfield, *Vita Mariae Angliae Reginae*, p. 281. Variations of Mary's speech are reported in Foxe, *TAMO* [1570], p. 1618 and Malfatti (ed.), *Accession coronation and marriage of Mary Tudor*, p. 66–8, 132–4.

oration.[213] This was, perhaps, one of the reasons she allowed the translation of Erasmus' *Paraphrases on John* to go into print under her name in 1548, despite her probable anxieties about Somerset's and Cranmer's plans for it. It was Queen Katherine who had alerted her to the desirability of acknowledging her participation in a September 1547 letter that she wrote with secretarial assistance from Princess Elizabeth. Mary had made headway on translating a 'most beautiful and useful work' that demonstrated her care 'for the greatest good of the commonwealth'. Since 'there is no one who does not know how you have sweated in your great labours over this book, I do not see why you would reject the praise that all would heap on your merits', she wrote.[214] Mary was evidently persuaded. In his letter dedicatory to the printed edition, Udall claimed that Mary's efforts put her amongst

> the great noumbre of noble weomen in this our time and countrey of Englande, not onelye geven to the studie of humaine sciences and of straunge tongues, but also so throughlye experte in holy scriptures, that they are hable to compare with the beste wryters as well in endictynge and pennyng of godlye and fruitfull treatises to the enstruccion and edifiynge of whole realmes in the knowleage of god, as also in translating good bokes out of Latine or Greke into Englishe for the use and commoditie of suche as are rude and ignoraunte of the sayd tounges.[215]

Like Margaret Beaufort, and Queen Katherine, herself, who had adapted Robert Whitford's translation of chapters four and sixteen to fifty-four of the third book of Thomas á Kempis's *De imitatione Christi*, in her *Prayers or medytacions* (1545), Mary used her learning to demonstrate her royal care for the souls of English subjects.[216] These were also the terms in which she would be praised most enthusiastically during her own reign. As her chaplain, John Angel, put it in 1555, she was 'a new Judith', the slayer of Holofernes, because she wisely and bravely brought her people

[213] Foxe, *TAMO* [1570], p. 1618.

[214] 'Ut opus hoc Pulcherrimum, atq[ue] utilissimum… summo Reipub[licae] bono suscepisti… cum ergo in hac re abs te laboriose admodum sudatum fuisse nemo non intelligat, cur quam omnes Tibi merito deferant laudem reiiceas non video': BL, Cotton MS Vespasian F III, no. 35, fol. 37r. The letter is dated 20 September. Mueller in Parr, *Katherine Parr*, pp. 126–7 has argued that the year was probably 1545 and that Elizabeth was merely the scribe. As Mueller and Leah Marcus point out in Elizabeth, *ACFL*, pp. xiv–vii, however, Elizabeth's juvenile hand changed with the influence of Roger Ascham. The letter to Mary looks much more like Elizabeth's later, narrow italic than her more bulbous 1545 hand. Additionally, the letter's emphasis on the imminent publication of the *Paraphrases* suggests the 1547 date identified by James, *Kateryn Parr*, p. 32.

[215] Udall, 'To… Quene Katherine', in Erasmus, *Paraphrases of Erasmus vpon John*, in *First tome or volume of the Paraphases*, STC 2854, sig. AAa1r.

[216] Katherine Parr, *Prayers or medytacions wherein the mynd is stirred, paciently to suffre all afflictions here* (London, 1545), STC 4819.

to 'knowledge… of Goddes worde'.[217] Mary's learned translation also shaped her reputation during her siblings' governments. Edwardian and Elizabethan injunctions that installed the vernacular *Paraphrases* alongside the Bible in each parish, chantry and cathedral library ensured that Mary's efforts reached generations of English men and women. She had contributed to a foundational text of the early English church.[218]

Given that the central objective of Mary's reign was to return that church to Rome, this seems a somewhat depressing historical irony. In fact, Mary's close study of Erasmus' *Paraphrases on John* may have encouraged her to think carefully about the sort of church she would cultivate in England, should she succeed her brother. Not only had Mary grown up reading Vives and Erasmus but she also favoured churchmen such as Cardinal Pole, who viewed the Council of Trent as an opportunity for Catholic renewal as well as persecutory counter-reformation in Europe.[219] Mary's partial translation of the *Paraphrases on John* may hint at her desire for certain reforms. For instance Erasmus' commentary on the Pharisees' rebuke at the pool of Bethesda to the paralysed man, who picked up his bed and walked on the Sabbath, read '*Adoriuntur igitur eum… & obiurga[n]t perverse religiosi*' (So the clerics perversely attacked and chided the man). In their punctilious desire to keep a holy day, he suggested, the Pharisees failed to see that the man's recovery was God's work. Mary's English version, however, added a simile to sharpen the criticism and emphasise its contemporary relevance: 'Therefore these [Pharisees], like perverters of true religion, fall in hand and chide with him.'[220] The addition could be read as censuring the empty pedantry of Catholic priests, but it could have been written as a general denunciation of clergymen who preferred doctrinal admonishment to caring for their flock. During her own reign, Mary would take a personal interest in improving clerical education in England.[221]

It is difficult to reconcile the persecutory face of the Marian church with Erasmus' professed horror at violence between Christians and the execution of heretics carried out in the name of the prince of peace. Yet Mary had had plenty of opportunity to study the way earlier Tudor rulers used and abused the Dutch humanist's spiritual and pedagogical writings

[217] Angel, *Agrement of the holye fathers*, sig. Aiii^{v}.

[218] John Craig, 'Forming a Protestant consciousness? Erasmus' *Paraphrases* in English parishes, 1547–1666', in Hilmar M. Pabel and Mark Vessey (eds.), *Holy Scripture speaks: The production and reception of Erasmus' 'Paraphrases on the New Testament'* (Toronto, 2002).

[219] Eamon Duffy, *Fires of faith: Catholic England under Mary Tudor* (New Haven, 2009), pp. 29–56.

[220] Erasmus, *Paraphrases of Erasmus vpon John*, in *First tome or volume of the Paraphases*, sig. EEe4^{v}.

[221] For example, BL, Lansdowne MS 96, fols. 25^{r}–26^{r}.

to advance their own agendas. Some of the queen's churchmen, including Stephen Gardiner and Edmund Bonner, were not fans of the English translation of Erasmus' *Paraphrases* but neither Mary nor Cardinal Pole issued instructions to remove the 1548 edition from churches or to redact her name from its pages.[222] Perhaps they considered the translation useful. After all, Erasmus' *Paraphrases on John* endorsed ideas that historians now argue were central to the doctrinal emphases of the Marian church, such as the importance of faith and charity, the word of God, and the sacrament and sacrifice of the mass.[223] In fact, there was an attempt during Mary's reign to rehabilitate Erasmus' reputation as a member of the one true church. Before Pole's legatine commission to England arrived in 1554, for instance, Erasmus' letter to Conrad Pelicanus testifying to his belief in the real presence was printed in English translation.[224] Where Henry VIII's apologists had once used the humanist to reach out to traditionalists and justify the break with Rome, Mary's regime now used his writings in an attempt to persuade evangelicals to celebrate the mass and return to the Catholic fold. The real irony was that Mary's education turned out to be almost as 'Erasmian' as Henry VIII's.

The queen's study of the liberal arts and sciences had not attracted the resources or cultural energy that Prince Edward's, Lady Jane Grey's or even the duke of Richmond's learning commanded. Nor was she as intoxicated by the spirit of the *bonae litterae* as her half-siblings appear to have been. Her formal schooling was delayed and her Latinate education underserved as Henry VIII hoped and manoeuvred for a legitimate son. Yet Catherine of Aragon and Katherine Parr both had confidence in Mary's princely potential and ensured her early and continued contact with the spiritual and pedagogical writings of northern humanists. Prior to her accession, Mary's circulated 'enditings' were in those seemingly unthreatening genres of female learning – the familial letter, prayer and translation. Yet there are indications that Mary capitalised on these opportunities to advance her command of rhetoric and her reputation for learning and piety, and even to contemplate the shape of a church that no one believed she would

[222] Craig, 'Forming a Protestant consciousness?', p. 317.

[223] Eamon Duffy, *The stripping of the altars: Traditional religion in England, c. 1400–c. 1580* (New Haven, 1992), pp. 524–42; Lucy Wooding, *Rethinking Catholicism in Reformation England* (Oxford, 2000), pp. 152–80. See, for instance, Edmund Bonner, *Profytable and necessarye doctryne, with certayne homilies* (London, 1555), STC 3283.7 and 3285.9; Foxe, *TAMO* [1570], p. 1682; Thomas Watson, *Holsome and Catholyke doctryne concerninge the seven sacramentes* (London, 1558), STC 25114.

[224] Erasmus, *Epistle of Erasmus Roterdamus, sent unto Conradus Pelicanus, concerning his opinion of the blessed Sacrament* (London, 1554), STC 10491.

or should govern. When Stephen Gardiner preached at St Paul's Cross on the first day of Advent, 1554, he described the realm's recent reconciliation with Rome using the language of Romans 13:11. It was time, he wrote, 'that we awake out of our sleepe, who haue slept, or rather dreamed these. xx. yeares past'. That period of spiritual and intellectual unconsciousness had begun, Gardiner said, when 'we desired to haue a supreme head amo[n]g vs' and so it 'came to passe that we had no head at all'. First Edward in his minority and then Mary 'being a woman' could not provide rational direction to the ecclesiastical body.[225] There is no evidence to suggest that the queen disagreed with Gardiner on a doctrinal level but there is plenty to suggest that, while others had slept, she had 'sweated' and toiled quietly and diligently to prepare her pen as well as her sword for 1553.

EDUCATING ELIZABETH I

The birth of Princess Elizabeth had been the catalyst for Mary's political degradation and the expulsion of her schoolmaster but Henry VIII's younger daughter was relegated to share Mary's fate as pawn on their father's dynastic chess board. In other respects, too, Elizabeth's upbringing mirrored her half-sister's education. The 1544 Succession Act, which encouraged Mary to return to her books, also transformed Elizabeth's schooling. She studied Latin and, later, Greek in addition to French and Italian. Nevertheless, historians have been too hasty to declare that 'Elizabeth I certainly enjoyed as good an education as her brother' in the 1540s.[226] In fact, despite their widening confessional differences, Elizabeth's juvenile literary exercises resembled Mary's much more closely than Edward VI's.

At birth Elizabeth may have been proclaimed Henry's heir but in May 1536, before her formal education had commenced, the princess was declared illegitimate. Her political fall triggered the collapse of discipline in her household. Her first governess, Lady Bryan, despaired of providing her charge with regular hours, plain food and garments that fit.[227] Elizabeth's status deteriorated further with Mary's return to favour that year and the birth of Prince Edward in 1537. Neither her father nor his council expressed much concern for her early education. Elizabeth's householders, many of whom were Boleyn kin, attempted to fill the void. She later declared to Edward Seymour that her 'mistress', Katherine Ashley née Champernowne (d. 1565), had taken 'great labor, and paine in

[225] Foxe, *TAMO* [1570], p. 1689. [226] James, *Kateryn Parr*, p. 28.
[227] Ellis, *Letters*, vol. II.ii, pp. 80–2.

brinkinge of me up in lerninge and honestie'.[228] She certainly introduced her charge to needlework, deportment, good manners, music and the rudiments of French and Italian grammar.[229] Then John Picton, a friend of Ashley's brother-in-law, Sir Anthony Denny, seems to have advanced her early studies.[230]

There is no evidence, however, that Elizabeth began Latin, the foundation of the *bonae litterae*, before the middle of 1544. Indeed, there were some signs to the contrary. Ascham rarely missed an opportunity to show off his neo-Roman epistolary style but he wrote to Katherine Ashley in English, suggesting that she could not read Latin.[231] Nor was there any suggestion from the Privy Council that the king's second, bastard daughter required classical tongues. After visiting Elizabeth in December 1539, Thomas Wriothesley reported to Cromwell that the child had enquired after the king's welfare with 'as great a gravitie, as she had been 40 years old. If she be no worse educated than she now appeareth to me', he wrote, 'she will prove of no less honor and womanhood than shall beseem her father's daughter.'[232] When Henry VIII visited her himself in September 1542, he seems to have come to a similar conclusion.[233]

After her return to the line of succession in 1544, however, Elizabeth's liberal education truly began.[234] The princess would later claim she had been 'brought up in a scoole to bide the ferula' rather than to be 'traded in a kingdom to supporte the scepter' as a royal bride.[235] Yet this is not necessarily how her father saw it at the time. As a January 1545 memo by William Paget indicates, the more immediate benefit of acknowledging her as one of the 'next Inheriters of our Realm' and ensuring that she was 'well educated' was that she commanded greater value on the diplomatic marriage market.[236] If Elizabeth was to be a figure in the Tudor family portrait, even the smallest one to the far right of the frame, she would require some sort of liberal education.[237]

[228] Elizabeth, *ACFL*, p. 23.

[229] Ascham, *Whole works*, vol. I.ii, pp. 85–7; *LP*, vol. X, no. 1187, p. 49, vol. XIV, no. 5, p. 5; Dowling, *Humanism in the age of Henry VIII*, p. 63. On householders' links to Boleyn, see McIntosh, *From heads of household*, pp. 91–3.

[230] Guy, *Children of Henry VIII*, pp. 100–1, 108, 110.

[231] Ascham, *Whole works*, I.i, pp. 85–7.

[232] Thomas Wriothesley in Thomas Hearne (ed.), *Titi Livii Foro-Juliensis vita Henrici quinti, Regis Angliae. Accedit Sylloge epistolarum, a variis Angliae principibus scriptorium* (Oxford, 1716), p. 150–1.

[233] *LP*, vol. XVII, no. 364, p. 214.

[234] *CSP Spain*, vol. VI.ii, p. 459, vol. VIII, p. 2; *LP*, vol. XIX, no. 118, p. 64; James, *Kateryn Parr*, pp. 111, 113, 117, 130–44.

[235] Elizabeth in *PPE*, vol. I, p. 472. [236] SP 1/197, fols. 159^v, 160^r.

[237] British School, *The Family of Henry VIII* (*c.* 1545) Royal Collection Trust, no. 405796.

In the summer of 1544, the princess followed her younger brother into the schoolroom, but, from the outset, it was clear that her studies would differ from Prince Edward's. Her schoolmasters were closely connected to his. As we have seen, Jean Belmaine taught Elizabeth French and italic handwriting before he transferred to Edward's household in 1546.[238] Giovanni Battista Castiglione (1516–98), who had fought with Charles V's army in France in 1543 and returned to England with Henry VIII, also taught both royal children Italian.[239] The most important development came in October 1544, however, when Elizabeth began studying Latin under William Grindal (d. 1548), a former student of Ascham's at St John's College, Cambridge, and thus the academic grandson of Edward's schoolmaster, John Cheke. Elizabeth made rapid progress under Grindal and by December 1545 she was writing to her father in Latin rather than French or Italian.[240]

Despite the similarities between Edward's and Elizabeth's schoolmasters, the half-siblings did not study together. Prince Edward's household was formally separated from his sister's when the king returned from France in 1544.[241] And, despite the romantic tales of the faithful bonds between the Protestant princes, Edward spent more time writing to Mary, whose age and superior position in the succession warranted his notice, than to Elizabeth.[242] Moreover, during this period, Edward and Elizabeth were instructed to use their learning in strikingly different ways. Both royal children composed letters to demonstrate their filial piety but, as we have seen, Edward's circulated writings showed him climbing the ladder of the *Progymnasmata* swiftly. After his accession in 1547 he began to use his study of rhetoric, humanist dialectic and logic to compose doctrinal arguments defending the (Protestant) faith. Despite her quick wit, evident bookishness and blossoming literary skills, however, Elizabeth stuck to writing familial letters and making translations of prayers and devotional texts. Edward performed translations too, but, as we have seen in his collection of sentences against idolatry, he was encouraged to work quickly and loosely, epitomising even Bible passages to bring their arguments to

238 *LP*, vol. xix, no. 864, p. 537; Edward, *CPP*, p. 3; Gordon Kipling, 'Belmaine, Jean (fl. 1546–1559)', *ODNB*; for Belmaine's hand, see BL, Royal MS 16 E I.

239 Elizabeth, *ACFL*, pp. 5–7; Anne Overell, *Italian reform and English Reformations, c.1535–c.1585* (Aldershot, 2008), p. 96; Wyatt, *Italian encounter*, p. 125.

240 Ascham, *Whole works*, vol. i.i, pp. 54–5, 57, 62–3, 75–6, 85–7, 92–3, 107–8; Elizabeth, *ACFL*, pp. 8–9; *LP*, vol. xxi, no. 199 (74), p. 86; T. W. Baldwin, *William Shakespere's smalle Latine and lesse Greeke*, 2 vols. (Urbana, 1944), vol. i, pp. 200, 257.

241 Guy, *Children of Henry VIII*, pp. 112–13.

242 Edward, *LR*, vol. i, pp. 2, 8, 9, 27, 29, 32, 39 to Mary versus pp. 31, 32, 40 to Elizabeth.

the surface. Belmaine, however, had Elizabeth 'translate word for word'.[243] These significant differences between the educations of Edward and Elizabeth seem to have had their origins in sex and the children's role in dynastic strategy.

Between 1544 and 1549, Elizabeth's studies were certainly broader than her surviving school exercises from the period suggest. Yet the length, number and nature of her familial letters and translations of prayers and pious works imply that her education, like her half-sister Mary's, had focused on these three traditionally feminine genres. When Elizabeth presented holograph gift translations to her father, step-mother Queen Katherine and Edward VI at New Year, she demonstrated her italic hand and increasingly impressive grasp of Latin, French and Italian, and displayed her filial loyalty, sex-specific virtue and personal piety.[244] These works represented her studies and persona in an unthreateningly feminine manner.

On 31 December 1544, for instance, Elizabeth sent Queen Katherine an English prose version of *Le Miroir de l'âme pécheresse* (1544), a poem composed by another learned royal sister, Marguerite of Navarre (1492–1549).[245] Scholars have been surprised that Belmaine saw fit to set the eleven-year-old daughter of Henry VIII a sexually explicit text that attributed salvation to 'the grace of god' alone and expressed thinly veiled criticisms of primogeniture.[246] In fact the point may have been to demonstrate Elizabeth's capacity to surgically remove these cancers from the body text as she translated it. Despite multiple small errors in her rendering, Elizabeth chastened Marguerite's verse very effectively by excising phrases in which she described God's love as 'a sweet dart' (*ung doulx dard*) and urged her reader to 'let Him alone be enclosed in you' (*Et que luy seul soit enfermé en vous*).[247] Scholars have read a note of familial discontent in Marguerite's account of the figure of Miriam, the sister of Moses, who rebelled against the law-giver in Numbers 12:2: 'Has the Lord indeed spoken only through Moses?', Miriam asked, 'Has he not spoken through us

243 'Translater mot, pour mot': Elizabeth, *Translations*, p. 216; Belmaine reflected on his practice of 'suiuy le texte mot pour mot' in his dedicatory letter to the princess: BL, Royal MS 16 E I.

244 Elizabeth, *Translations*, pp. 40–327; Aysha Pollnitz, 'Christian women or sovereign queens? The Schooling of Mary and Elizabeth', in Anna Whitelock and Alice Hunt (eds.), *Tudor queenship: The reigns of Mary and Elizabeth* (Basingstoke, 2010), pp. 134–6.

245 Bodleian, Cherry MS 36, fols. 2r–63r in Elizabeth, *Translations*, pp. 40–124.

246 Elizabeth, *Translations*, p. 42; Gary Ferguson, *Mirroring belief: Marguerite de Navarre's devotional poetry* (Edinburgh, 1992), p. 27; Anne Lake Prescott, 'The pearl of the Valois and Elizabeth I: Marguerite de Navarre's *Mirroir* and Tudor England', in Margaret P. Hannay (ed.), *Silent but for the word: Tudor women as patrons, translators, and writers of religious works* (Kent, OH, 1985), pp. 68–72.

247 Elizabeth, *Translations*, pp. 66, 88.

also?'[248] Elizabeth quashed any suggestion that she may have been discontented by her cadet role in the English royal family by presenting the gift in a way that emphasised her femininity. Queen Katherine received the holograph manuscript bound between ornate covers of her step-daughter's own embroidery. Elizabeth used virginal blue silk, decorated with braiding and raised-work gold and silver pansies (*pensées* for thoughts). At the centre are the initials KP placed within a cross of knotted strap-work.[249] Elizabeth's December 1545 gifts to Henry VIII and Queen Katherine were similarly bound. Elizabeth displayed her willingness to be a chaste, loyal handmaiden, working with pen and needle alike to support her family.

In 1549 Elizabeth was equally careful to occlude any perceived *sola gratia*-ism in Marguerite's poem. The French princess had included prefatory verses in which she claimed that, since she had received God's free gift of grace herself, she was now

> Moved by a desire that all might see
> The work of God the Creator.[250]

Elizabeth's prefatory letter to Queen Katherine, however, declared her doubts that she was the recipient of such a blessing. Her own faith was like her translation, 'unperfytte and uncorecte'. 'As well spirituall, as manuall', she confessed to her step-mother, 'there is nothinge done as it shulde be'.[251] Doctrinally all that remained in Elizabeth's version was an Augustinian consideration of sin and redemption coupled with a Christocentric, personal meditation 'by the scriptures' of the sort encouraged by Erasmus.[252] Like Mary's translation of Erasmus' *Paraphrases on John*, then, Elizabeth's literary exercises plotted a careful course through the choppy waters of Henrician religious orthodoxy.

Like Mary's translation, moreover, Elizabeth's efforts were published after 1547 to advance religious reform in England. In 1548, John Bale (1495–1563) improved upon her Englishing, added scriptural citations and printed the work

[248] Marguerite de Navarre, *Les Marguerites de la marguerite des princesses: Text de l'édition de 1547 publiés avec introduction, notes et glossaire*, ed. Félix Frank, 4 vols. (Paris, 1873), vol. I, pp. 36–9; Susan Snyder, 'Guilty sisters: Marguerite de Navarre, Elizabeth of England, and the *Miroir de l'âme Pécheresse*', *Renaissance Quarterly*, 50:2 (1997).

[249] The opinions of several experts on early modern embroidery are summarised in Frances Teague, 'Princess Elizabeth's hand in *The glass of the sinful soul*', in Peter Beal and Margaret Ezell (eds.), *Writings by early modern women*, vol. IX: *English manuscript studies, 1100–1700* (London, 2000), pp. 40–3.

[250] 'Fors ung desir, que chascun puisse voir, que fait le don de DIEU le Createur': de Navarre, *Les Marguerites*, vol. I, p. 13.

[251] Elizabeth, *Translations*, pp. 42, 44.

[252] Elizabeth, *Translations*, p. 42; see also Patrick Collinson, *Elizabethan essays* (London, 1994), p. 98.

under a new title: *A godly medytacyon of the christen sowle*. His letter dedicatory made it clear that he wished to claim the princess for the church militant despite the careful calibration of her efforts in 1544. Bale professed, for instance, to have seen her holograph Greek, French and Italian translation from the Vulgate Latin of Psalm 14:1, the 'vnfaythfull reckeneth folyshly in their hartes, there is no God'. 'By thys', Bale claimed hopefully, 'your grace vnto vs sygnyfye, that the baren doctryne & good workes without fayth of the hypocrytes, whych in their vnco[m]maunded latyne ceremonyes serue their [b]ellyes & not Christ'.[253] It was an imaginative bit of exegesis. By allowing her efforts to be thus misrepresented (albeit at a moment when there was political capital to be made from overt protestations of Protestantism), Elizabeth, like her half-sister, secured praise for her learning and virtue. Just as Udall lauded Mary's feminine erudition, so Bale concluded that Elizabeth's translations revealed 'moch vertu, faythe, scyence, & experye[n]ce of la[n]guages & letters, specyally in noble youth & femynyte'.[254] Just as Mary's translation endured, so Bale's version of Elizabeth's *Godly medytacyon* was reprinted by James Cancellar, a former member of Mary's chapel royal, in 1568 and 1580. In 1582, Bale's version also appeared in Thomas Bentley's *Monument of matrones* (1582), a text that may have been intended to celebrate the failure of the French marriage negotiations.[255] Religious translation was a literary genre that enabled elite women to make active contributions to the spiritual lives of English subjects and to receive copious praise for it. Yet, even as sovereign queens, Mary and Elizabeth had limited control over the way others framed their pious efforts.

The princess's 30 December 1545 gift translation for Henry VIII offered further testimony of feminine virtue, conventional piety and filial loyalty. Elizabeth sent her father a trilingual transposition of Queen Katherine's *Prayers or medytacions*.[256] It was an appropriate undertaking for her and a suitable gift for him, Elizabeth claimed, because it demonstrated both Christian and filial devotion. 'It is pious, and has been collected in English by the pious study and great industry of the most illustrious queen', she explained.[257] She was deeply obliged to Katherine, she declared, and eager

[253] John Bale, letter dedicatory in Marguerite de Navarre, *A godly medytacyon of the christen sowle*, trans. Elizabeth I, ed. John Bales ([Marburg], 1548), STC 17320, fol. 7^{v}; see also 41^{v}. The psalm translation is probably by Bale himself: David Scott Kastan, 'An early English metrical psalm: Elizabeth's or John Bale's?', *Notes and Queries*, 21 (1974).

[254] Bale, letter dedicatory in de Navarre, *A godly medytacyon*, fol. 7^{r-v}.

[255] STC 17320.5, 17321 and 1892; Collinson, *Elizabethan essays*, pp. 98–9, 104–8.

[256] BL, Royal MS 7 D X, fols. 11^{r}–117^{v} in Elizabeth, *Translations*, pp. 135–99 and in Parr, *Katherine Parr*, pp. 369–421.

[257] 'Quod quum tam pium sit, et pio studio atque magna industria Reginae illustrissimae fuerit anglice collectum… accommodatissimum mihi visum est, ut hoc, quod argumento suo rege': Elizabeth, *Translations*, p. 138.

to serve her father. The princess amplified her expression of obligation to Henry VIII by identifying the many sources of her duty, as Erasmus had suggested: she was 'bound unto [Henry] as lord by the law of the kingdom, and as lord by the law of nature, and as my father by divine law'.[258] Elizabeth hoped, moreover, that by engaging in the industry and piety of converting the prayers 'into other languages' she 'should be not only the imitator of your virtues, but also the heir of them'.[259] Elizabeth was not presuming with these words to inherit her father's realm. Rather, she was alluding to a passage in Hebrews 6:12 where Paul instructs the Jews to 'imitate those who through faith and patience have inherited [Christ's] promises'. Elizabeth was claiming that she had studied patiently and faithfully to become the true daughter of Henry VIII's true church.[260]

Despite Elizabeth's claim to be studiously following her father's confessional lead, Jean Belmaine took more risks with the texts he had her translate than Edward's English schoolmasters were willing to countenance for him before 1547. Perhaps Belmaine had the courage as well as the conviction of a religious exile. Perhaps he also knew that Elizabeth's literary exercises would excite less attention than her half-brother's. Yet, as with her first translation of Marguerite's *Miroir*, he continued to encourage her to dampen the incendiary material in her exercises. Elizabeth's December 1545 gift to Queen Katherine of an English version of the first chapter of Jean Calvin's *Institution of the Christian religion* (based on the French edition printed in Geneva in 1541) is a case in point.[261] In her dedicatory letter to Katherine, Elizabeth claimed that the treatise explained how we might know 'God by his word', a phrase Henry VIII and his apologists had hijacked to support the royal supremacy.[262] The princess suppressed the name of the work's author and further obscured its origins by claiming she had translated 'a little book' (*un petit liure*) rather than a chapter of a larger one. Finally, Elizabeth plucked the sting out of a reference to predestination in her Englishing of the *Institutes*. In the original, Calvin had argued that God elects only 'those to whom it pleases him to give knowledge of himself for salvation'.[263] As Mueller and Joshua Scodel have

258 'Ego obstricta sum tibi, lege regni ut domino, lege naturae ut domino, et patri meo lege diuina': Elizabeth, *Translations*, p. 138.

259 'A me filia tua il alias linguas conuerteretur: quae non modo virtutum tuarum imitatrix, sed illarum etiam haeres esse debeam': Elizabeth, *Translations*, p. 139.

260 'Hunc internum animi mei laborem': Elizabeth, *Translations*, p. 158.

261 NAS, RH 13/78, fols. 1^r–89^v in Elizabeth, *Translations*, pp. 212–87.

262 'Mon authuer… dieu par sa parolle': Elizabeth, *Translations*, p. 214.

263 'Ausquels il luy plaist se donner à congnoistre en salut': Jean Calvin in Elizabeth, *Translations*, p. 258n.153.

pointed out, however, Elizabeth translated that sentence to read: 'the lord doth sette furthe unto *all men without any exception* the bryghtenes of his maieste' so that they 'may obteyne the true knowledge of him so perfaytely that it preuaileth for their saluation'.[264] Calvin's account of God's horrible decree did not seem so horrible in Elizabeth's italic hand.

After Edward VI's accession, however, Elizabeth found it politic to advertise her belief in the doctrine of election. She presented her half-brother with a Latin translation of *De Christo sermo*, the twelfth sermon of the second part of Bernardino Ochino's *Prediche* (1543?–62) as a New Year's gift. It was a little late and somewhat rushed, in part perhaps because William Grindal died in January 1548.[265] Ochino had arrived in London in the autumn of 1547 at Cranmer's invitation.[266] Like Elizabeth's previous religious translations, this sermon emphasised attending to God's word, the redemptive power of God's grace for true believers and the 'cords and bands of charity, and… force of love alone' by which Christ 'has drawn us to him'.[267] And, like her earlier efforts, the text she was working from resonated with other evangelical women at court. Anne Cooke, for instance, the daughter of Edward's tutor, Anthony Cooke, printed English versions of Ochino's sermons in 1548 and 1551, perhaps with some assistance from Elizabeth's Italian tutor, Giovanni Battista Castiglione.[268] What was new on this occasion, however, was Elizabeth's acknowledgement that 'Christ imprinted love [*amorem*] on the heart of his elect [*suorum electorum*]' alone.[269] Once she had crossed that Rubicon, however, the princess moved quickly to excise the radical implications of a Calvinist account of predestination. She cut Ochino's claim that the elect were 'not justified by observance of the law, for Christ has liberated and redeemed us… we are not damned by non-observance of the law, and we are saved by grace'.[270] Edward's regime

264 Elizabeth, *Translations*, pp. 256, 258.

265 Bodleian, MS Bodley 6, fols. 1^r–35^v in Elizabeth, *Translations*, pp. 291–327; Stephen Wright, 'William Grindal, d. 1548', *ODNB*.

266 Overell, *Italian reform*, pp. 41–80.

267 'Uinculis et lingaminibus charitatis, et solum amoris ui, ad seipsum nos traxit': Elizabeth, *Translations*, pp. 312, 313.

268 Bernardino Ochino, *Certayne sermons of the ryghte famous and excellente clerk master Barnardine Ochine*, trans. [Anne Cook] and Richard Argentine (London, [1551?]), STC 18766, *Fouretene sermons of Barnardine Ochyne, concernyng the predestinacion and eleccion of god*, trans. A[nne] C[ooke] (London, [1551?]), STC 18767 (see 'G. B.', 'To the Christen reader', sig. $A2^{r-v}$) and *Sermons of Barnardine Ochine*, trans. Anne Cooke (London, 1548), STC 18764.

269 Elizabeth, *Translations*, pp. 312, 313.

270 'Non ci giustifichiamo per l'osseruantia sua, ma Christo ci ha liberati… non siamo dannati per l'inosseruantia della legge, & siamo salui per gratia': Ochino, 'De Christo sermo', in Elizabeth, *Translations*, p. 312.

was in the process of using injunctions, proclamations, and laws in an attempt to impose further religious reform in England and made regular appeals to the fifth commandment of Moses' law to command subjects' obedience.[271] Elizabeth evidently had no wish to imply that she encouraged 'non-observance of the law' in England.

Indeed, Elizabeth's religious education moved in perfect step with her brother's regime and became determinedly Protestant. After Grindal's death, Roger Ascham became Elizabeth's schoolmaster, allegedly at the princess's request.[272] Sometime before August 1549 Edmund Allen (1510s–59), the evangelical catechist, had become her chaplain. After Ascham's departure in mid-1550, Allen introduced Johannes Spithovius (d. 1563), a pupil of Philip Melanchthon and client of Martin Bucer, to Elizabeth's schoolroom. Spithovius became her Latin and Greek tutor for five years.[273] It was probably on his watch that Elizabeth began to read and annotate theological treatises, such as Thomas Cranmer's *Defence of the true and catholike doctrine of the sacrament of the body and bloud of our sauiour Christ* (1550), to develop positions on doctrinal controversies.[274] And it was probably Allen's and Spithovius' presence that encouraged John Hooper to assure Henry Bullinger in February 1550 that Elizabeth 'not only knows what the true religion is, but has acquired such proficiency in Greek and Latin, that she is able to defend it by the most able arguments… she encounters few adversaries whom she does not overcome'.[275] Hooper may well have seen evidence of her expertise in classical tongues and heard her demonstrate her understanding of 'true religion' but there is no more evidence of Elizabeth contending with traditional 'adversaries' in Edward's reign than in Mary's.

In November 1566 Elizabeth declared to a delegation from both houses of Parliament that while 'yt is sayde, I am no devyne… I studyed nothynge else but devynytye tyll [she] came to the crowne'.[276] For many of her pre-accession years, however, the centre of her study of 'divinity' was her translation of devotional texts. Some of Elizabeth's translations emphasised the redemptive power of grace for salvation

[271] See for instance John Hooper, *Godly and most necessary annotations in [th]e XIII chaptyer to the Romaynes* ([Worcester, 1551]), STC 13756, sigs. A4^r–5^r.

[272] Ascham, *Whole works*, vol. 1.i, pp. lv–lx; 158–62, 174–6, 191–2.

[273] Simon Adams and David Gehring, 'Elizabeth I's former tutor reports on the parliament of 1559: Johannes Spithovius to the Chancellor of Denmark, 27 February 1559', *EHR*, 128:530 (2013), p. 37.

[274] Cranmer, *A defence*. Elizabeth's copy is in the Royal Library of Windsor Castle and her notations are printed in Elizabeth, *Translations*, pp. 401–2.

[275] Ellis, *Letters*, vol. 1, p. 76.

[276] Elizabeth in *PPE*, vol. 1, p. 148.

and flirted with predestination. More generally, however, she pored over much less radical tracts that encouraged the faithful reader and translator to meditate deeply on the figure of Christ, on her personal relationship with God and on scripture, as Princess Mary had before her. The Christianity of her formative years was sincerely evangelical but certainly not reformed. While Elizabeth was translating, moreover, Prince Edward was learning to defend the faith by arguing cases polemically, assembling biblical *loci* that supported his argument and refuting the claims made by his opponents. In part, the distinction between his education and hers was gendered; Elizabeth's self-presentation in her religious translations within their embroidered covers was pointedly feminine. We have seen, however, that Lady Jane Grey had been taught to argue about doctrine and to take precocious pleasure in theological disputation, so this lacuna in Elizabeth's schooling was probably shaped by her status as a sister, rather than simply as a woman. Edward was expected to become the head of the church in England, and Elizabeth would be a loyal handmaiden of God and the Tudor dynasty. She carefully moderated the doctrinal tone of her gift translations to suit the regime and the confessional expectations of her audience, a mental habit that arguably helped her survive the religious ruptures and psychic violence of the mid-Tudor polity. There was a further lesson, perhaps unintended, that Elizabeth may have derived from her translation practice in the 1540s: the key to managing a doctrinal difference, whether it was *sola fideism* or predestination, was not to contend or argue but to pass over it, divert attention from it, mute its significance and even suppress it from speech acts.

ELIZABETH I AS SUPREME GOVERNOR OF THE CHURCH

In sixteenth-century Europe, the ability of a royal daughter, sister or wife to avoid confessional conflict could be a virtue, even a survival skill. For a prince, however, particularly a prince who ruled a church as well as a state, it was virtually impossible. When fortune made Elizabeth supreme governor of the church in England, she was charged with managing an ecclesiastical polity that was already divided between Marian survivors and returning Protestant exiles. As historians have shown, it became increasingly polarised during Elizabeth's reign. The tensions between the queen and more advanced Protestants and puritans in her realm certainly stemmed from real disagreements about church government, discipline and the management of the Catholic threat.[277] Here, however, I ask whether Elizabeth's education provides any insight into the way that she attempted to govern her church and direct her subjects' spiritual lives.

Elizabethan historians have described the queen's frustration when her subjects agitated for religious reforms beyond the terms of the 1559 church settlement.[278] Part of her ire stemmed from the widening confessional gap between the queen and more advanced Protestants in her realm. The arrangements made for her chapel royal, her views on images of the cross and evidence from her letters suggest that her personal religion was no *more* reformed than the English church as it was established at the commencement of her reign.[279] As her lord chancellor, Christopher Hatton, complained in the parliament of 1589, the queen had 'placed her Reformation as upon a square stone to remain constant', yet 'forward men, I should say forward men' persisted in trying to push it further.[280] Elizabeth was also irked by the presumption of subjects who dared to dictate to a queen's conscience and who showed little respect for the royal prerogative. 'Yt ys monstruous', she declared in her 1567 parliament, 'that the ffeete sholde dyrecte the hed'.[281] Indeed, the queen's 'quintessentially monarchical' view of her inviolable authority seems to have waxed in direct proportion to the vociferousness of her godly citizens.[282] Their 'wicked

[277] Stephen Alford, *The early Elizabethan polity: William Cecil and the British succession crisis, 1558–1569* (Cambridge, 1998); Collinson, *Elizabethan essays*, pp. 31–57 and 'The prophesyings and the downfall and sequestration of Archbishop Edmund Grindal, 1576–1583', in Melanie Barber, Stephen Taylor and Gabriel Sewell (eds.), *From the Reformation to the permissive society: A miscellany in celebration of the 400th anniversary of Lambeth Palace Library* (Woodbridge, 2010), pp. 1–41; Thomas Freeman, 'Providence and prescription: The account of Elizabeth in Foxe's "Book of Martyrs"', in Susan Doran and Thomas Freeman (eds.), *The myth of Elizabeth* (Basingstoke, 2003); John Guy, 'Tudor monarchy and its critiques', in John Guy (ed.), *The Tudor monarchy* (London, 1997); Natalie Mears, *Queenship and political discourse in the Elizabethan realms* (Cambridge, 2005), pp. 19–20, 101, 231–5, 257–9; Alexandra Walsham, '"A very Deborah?" The myth of Elizabeth I as a providential monarch', in Susan Doran and Thomas Freeman (eds.), *The myth of Elizabeth* (Basingstoke, 2003).

[278] See T. E. Hartley, *Elizabeth's parliaments: Queen, Lords and commons, 1559–1601* (Manchester, 1992), p. 87 for a summary.

[279] Margaret Aston, *The king's bedpost: Reformation and iconography in a Tudor group portrait* (Cambridge, 1993), pp. 97–107, 123, 201–2, 207; Roger Bowers, 'The chapel royal, the first Edwardian Prayer Book, and Elizabeth's settlement of religion, 1559', *HJ*, 43 (2000); Collinson, *Elizabethan essays*, pp. 87–118; Susan Doran, 'Elizabeth I's religion: The evidence of her letters', *Journal of Ecclesiastical History*, 51:4 (2000).

[280] Cited by Patrick Collinson, *Richard Bancroft and Elizabethan anti-Puritanism* (Cambridge, 2013) p. 58.

[281] Elizabeth in *PPE*, vol. 1, p. 148.

[282] Peter Lake, 'The monarchical republic of Queen Elizabeth I (and the fall of Archbishop Grindal) revisited', in John McDiarmid (ed.), *The monarchical republic of early modern England: Essays in response to Patrick Collinson* (Aldershot, 2007), p. 145.

and slanderous speeches', as Richard Bancroft (bap. 1544, d. 1610) called them in 1593, intended 'not only the disgrace of our Church' but also to the destruction of public order.[283] Henry VIII and James VI would have agreed with her but these British kings had enjoyed doctrinal discussion and debate. Elizabeth manifestly did not.

As queen and governor of the church, Elizabeth attempted to maintain her youthful practice of muting religious speech she deemed to be unnecessarily controversial or obstreperous. When Alexander Nowell (*c.* 1516/17–1602), Dean of St Paul's, preached too zealously against images and saints from the pulpit in the privy garden in 1565, Elizabeth stuck her head out of the window. 'Do not talk about that', she ordered, 'Leave that, it has nothing to do with your subject, and the matter is now threadbare.'[284] It is little wonder that the practice of prophesying, effectively a preachers' conference, horrified her so thoroughly that she was prepared to sequester and suspend her archbishop of Canterbury, Edmund Grindal (1516x20–83), for failing to repress the practice.[285] Nowell, Grindal and, on another occasion, Matthew Parker (1504–75), all expressed surprise and dismay when Elizabeth attempted to shut them down mid-harangue. They were horrified by the queen's illogical conservatism. Did she not understand that the propagation of God's word required good preachers in parishes? They were also shocked that she had broken with her own customary silence on questions of doctrine and church practice. 'It was an horror to hear such words to come from her mild nature and Christian learned conscience', Parker confessed to William Cecil in 1561.[286] Elizabeth's bishops were not used to hearing the queen tell them what she thought about these questions. Roger Bowers noted that, following the traumatic debates on the 1559 settlement, whenever Elizabeth was under 'pressure to resolve issues, she could avoid the unsettlement of a change of mind if resolutely she possessed no mind made up in the first place'. Yet he and others have noted the queen's quiet persistence in maintaining her crosses, candlesticks and music in her chapel royal, despite the disapproval of a number of bishops.[287] It was not that Elizabeth 'possessed no mind';

283 Quoted by Collinson, *Richard Bancroft*, p. 12; see also Patrick Collinson, *The Elizabethan puritan movement* (Berkeley, 1967).

284 Quoted in McCullough, *Sermons at court*, p. 47.

285 Patrick Collinson, *Archbishop Grindal, 1519–1583: The struggle for a reformed church* (Berkeley, 1979), pp. 239–45.

286 Matthew Parker, *Correspondence of Matthew Parker, D. D. Archbishop of Canterbury, comprising letters written by and to him, from* A.D. *1535, to his death,* A.D. *1575*, eds. John Bruce and Thomas Thomason Perowne (Cambridge, 1853), p. 156.

287 Bowers, 'The chapel royal', pp. 343–4.

it was that on controversial religious issues she was unusually reticent to explain or justify her views. Historians who have attempted to make a window into her soul have realised swiftly how firmly Elizabeth drew the curtains against prying eyes.[288]

If the queen had little appetite for arguing with her clergy, she had none whatsoever for religious debate with the laity. From the beginning of her reign Elizabeth signalled through her lord keeper, Nicholas Bacon, that she would only allow members 'libertie of speech' insofar as it was congruent with their 'reverence and obedience to their soveraigne'.[289] It swiftly became apparent that one of the issues on which free debate would be curtailed was that of religion.[290] Indeed, Elizabeth attempted to seal the lips of her MPs more completely on questions about the church than she did regarding the succession. In 1566 she refused to allow Parliament to consider the 'alphabetical bills' for further reforms of religious abuses, since they brought her 'prerogative in questyon'.[291] When key measures from the bill were revived in 1571, alongside William Strickland's more contentious plans for reform of the prayer book, Elizabeth sent a message via her lord keeper scolding the houses 'for arrogantly and presumptuously they have there reasoned'.[292] In May 1572 she sent word that no bill regarding religion should be debated unless the bishops had been consulted first, a move that an anonymous commentator described as a threat to the Commons' liberty.[293] By the parliament of the spring of 1576, pressure for reform of church discipline had spewed out into a petition. Elizabeth replied on 9 March in a curmudgeonly fashion; she had 'of these thinges consideracion before' and was as likely to address them as if 'this motion had not bene'.[294] When she closed the session a week later, she began the *exordium* of her oration with an unusually indignant *erotema*, or rhetorical question:

Doo I see Gode's most sacred woorde and text of hollie writ drawn to so divers senses bee it never so presiselie taught, and shall I hope that my speech can pas forth thorowe so meanie eares withoute mistaking, wheare so meanie ripe and

[288] Collinson, *Elizabethan essays*, pp. 87–118.

[289] Nicholas Bacon in *PPE*, vol. I, p. 43; on Elizabeth's dislike of 'popular' rhetoric more generally, see Markku Peltonen, *Rhetoric, politics and popularity in pre-revolutionary England* (Cambridge, 2013), pp. 132–4, 227–32.

[290] Norman Jones, 'Religion in Parliament', in David Dean and Norman Jones (eds.), *Parliaments of Elizabethan England* (Oxford, 1990).

[291] *PPE*, vol. 1, p. 171.

[292] Nicholas Bacon in *PPE*, vol. 1, p. 257; Thomas Freeman, '"The Reformation of the church in this parliament": Thomas Norton, John Foxe and the parliament of 1571', *Parliamentary History*, 16:2 (1997).

[293] *PPE*, vol. 1, pp. 263, 330.

[294] Elizabeth in *PPE*, vol. 1, p. 447.

divers wittes doo ofter bende to conster [construe] then attaine the true and perfect understanding?[295]

What was the point, she asked, of attempting to speak with those who were determined to twist even God's word for the sake of an argument?

Elizabeth's attempts to suppress debate may have been counter-productive. The 'culminative momentum' for further reform in the 1570s broke into galloping Presbyterianism in the 1580s.[296] The real threat of Spanish invasion, the persistent presence of Jesuits and seminary priests in England, and the rats' nest of plotters around Mary, Queen of Scots, heightened Protestant anxieties. In March 1584 even William Cecil's and speaker of the house John Puckering's drafts for the keeper's closing speech to Elizabeth stressed the need to remedy abuses.[297] Elizabeth could no longer punt to Convocation or 'ovarskype' disagreements about doctrine and church government, so she tried to obscure her position.

When Elizabeth spoke at the close of her fifth parliament on 29 March 1585, she began by acknowledging the probable accretion of 'faultes and neglygencs' in the church and charged her bishops to amend them 'without heedlesse or open exclamations'. When it came to explaining the form of religion she wished to see established or restored in England, however, she occluded the issue with *perissologia*, or over-elaborate speech. Her *litotes* and double negatives piled up:

I nede not tell yow that I am so symple that I undarstond not, nor so forgetfull that I remembar not… I hope God's Booke hath not bene my seldomest lectures… If I were not perswaded that myne were the trewe way of God's will, God forbyd I shuld lyve to prescribe it to you.

Amidst the understatement, wordiness and appeals to *ethos*, the religion she *did* want to persuade her subjects to follow was unclear. She reassured them that neither was is that of the 'Romanists' nor did she endorse any sort of 'new-fanglenesse' but she would go no further.[298] As a piece of defensive deliberative rhetoric that attempted to explain why religious argument and attempts at further reform were neither useful nor honourable, it is not ineffective. Yet the queen offered no positive vision for the English church, nor a commendation of its existing form, presumably in an attempt to deter a response *in alteram partem*. The result is not dissimilar to her famous *skotison* in November 1586, when Parliament pushed her to execute Mary Queen of Scots; she took refuge in the purposeful

[295] Elizabeth in *PPE*, vol. I, p. 471. [296] Collinson, *Elizabethan essays*, p. 77.
[297] Elizabeth in *PPE*, vol. II, pp. 22–30. [298] Elizabeth in *PPE*, vol. II, pp. 31–2.

obscurity of an 'ausnwere ansWerles' rather than commit to arguing the point.[299] As a child and adolescent, Elizabeth had evaded, obscured and toned down controversial statements in her juvenile religious translations to protect herself from censure. As a queen, she descended into what contemporary rhetoricians would have deemed a catalogue of stylistic vices to avoid doctrinal and ecclesiastical argument. Richard Rex has observed that Elizabeth, 'unlike her father and indeed her brother... was no amateur theologian'. She had 'little time for the polemical theologians of her own day' when they railed at her from their pulpits and even less enthusiasm for lay disputation in Parliament.[300]

Of course, Elizabeth prevaricated on other matters too, but she usually did so by explaining the nub of the political problem at hand – that, while everyone wanted her to marry, no one could agree whom she should wed, or that, while parliamentarians claimed they wanted the succession settled, recent English history had shown how unsettling dynastic decision-making really was. On non-religious questions, moreover, Elizabeth was an extremely effective orator who took evident pleasure in crafting letters and speeches.[301] Steven May has pointed out that she was the first English sovereign to send subjects she knew personal condolence letters when they were bereaved.[302] Amidst the poor harvests, monopolies disputes and Irish revolt of what Collinson called 'the nasty nineties', Elizabeth turned out a 'magnanimous, wise and eloquent answer' in *ex tempore* Latin to a malapert Polish ambassador that Robert Devereux, earl of Essex, described as 'a princely triumph'.[303] She planned not only her 'Golden Speech' but also its wider circulation, authorising a printed version in 1601.[304] Her discomfort arguing about religion, then, did not proceed from an inability to persuade others.

Yet a brief consideration of her early study and use of rhetoric may provide some insight into the signature features of her more reluctant speech acts. Elizabeth's second schoolmaster, Roger Ascham, began boasting of her rhetorical prowess in April 1550. That month, he wrote to the German pedagogue Johann Sturm that '[Elizabeth] speaks French and Italian as

[299] Elizabeth, *ACFL*, p. 77. [300] Richard Rex, *The Tudors* (Stroud, 2002), p. 53.

[301] Mears, *Queenship and political discourse*, pp. 74–8.

[302] Steven May, 'Queen Elizabeth prays for the living and the dead', in Peter Beal and Grace Ioppolo (eds.), *Elizabeth I and the culture of writing* (London, 2007), pp. 208–9.

[303] Patrick Collinson, 'Ecclesiastical vitriol: Religious satire in the 1590s and the invention of puritanism', in John Guy (ed.), *The reign of Elizabeth I: Court and culture in the last decade* (Cambridge, 1995), pp. 153–4; SP 12/264, no. 58, fol. 128v.

[304] Elizabeth I, *Her maiesties most princelie answere, deliuered by her selfe at the court at White-hall, on the last day of Nouember 1601* (London, 1601), STC 7578; *PPE*, vol. III, pp. 289–97, 412–14.

well as she speaks English, and converses in Latin swiftly, correctly, and deliberately. She has even spoken Greek with me frequently, cheerfully, and tolerably well.'[305] In Latin, she liked Cicero and Livy. In Greek, she read Isocrates' orations and the New Testament daily. Elizabeth admired Cyprian's pastoral writings and Melanchthon's *Loci communes* for combining 'pure doctrine with elegant language'. Generally, the princess commended speech that was 'natural, chaste in its correctness, honourable in its perspicuity'.[306] When Ascham returned to Elizabeth's schoolroom in 1555, he claimed that Elizabeth was now deeply engaged in the study of a pair of speeches by Aeschines and Demosthenes, *On the crown*. The humanist praised Elizabeth's grasp of their stylistic and political features. Not only did she understand 'the form of the language and sense of the speech, but also all the charges of the case, the decrees of the people, the customs and manners of their city'.[307] In Ascham's *Scholemaster* (1570), the queen's rhetorical prowess was seized on to prove the effectiveness of Ascham's methods: 'by this double translating of Demosthenes and Isocrates dailie... and likewise som part of Tullie', Queen Elizabeth 'hath atteyned to soch a perfite vnderstanding in both the tonges... as they be fewe in nomber in both the vniuersities, or els where in England, that be... comparable'.[308] Both Ascham and John Alymer, Jane Grey's schoolmaster, argued that Elizabeth's study of rhetoric had enhanced her princely potential.[309]

Ascham was the most self-interested of encomiasts but aspects of his account of Elizabeth's interest in Isocrates may be verified. John Bale recorded that, as a girl, Elizabeth had translated two of Isocrates' orations into Latin, including his epideictic address *Ad Nicocles*. As a queen, Elizabeth's favourite commonplace was, indeed, from that oration: a prince should show that he valued 'truth so highly that [his] word is more to be trusted than the oaths of other men' (II.22). She appealed to the *locus* regularly in parliamentary speeches and letters.[310] Moreover, even

[305] 'Gallice, Italiceque, aeque ac Anglice loquitur; Latine, expedite, proprie, considerate; Graece etiam mediocriter mecum frequenter libenterque colloquuta est.': Ascham, *Whole works*, vol. I.i, pp. 191–2.

[306] 'Pura doctrina cum elegante sermone libari potuerit, adjunxit', 'Orationem ex re natam, proprietate castam, perspicuitate illustrem, libenter probat': Ascham, *Whole works*, vol. I.i, p. 192.

[307] 'Intelligit, non solum proprietatem linguae et oratoris sensum, sed totam caussae contentionem, populi scita, consuetudinem, et mores illius urbis': Ascham, *Whole works*, vol. I.ii, p. 447; see too vol. II, p. 63.

[308] Ascham, *Scholemaster*, sig. Liii^{r}.

[309] John Aylmer, *An harborowe for faithfull and trevve subiectes agaynst the late blowne blaste, concerninge the gouernme[n]t of wemen* ([London, 1559]), STC 1005, sig. N2r.

[310] John Bale, *Index Britanniae scriptorium: John Bale's index of British and other writers*, eds. Reginald Lane Poole *et al.* (Woodbridge, 1990), p. 157. See for example *PPE*, p. 114, 145, 147.

before Ascham started to brag about her eloquence, Elizabeth had actually used her command of epideictic and forensic rhetoric to extricate herself and her householders from the Seymour affair. After Thomas Seymour's arrest on 17 January 1549 for conspiring against his brother, Protector Somerset, Elizabeth's householders Katherine Ashley and Thomas Parry were also taken to the Tower. On the basis of their statements, Elizabeth was suspected of sexual misconduct with the admiral during his marriage to Katherine and complicity in a treasonous negotiation to marry him after the queen's death.[311] As Mueller has argued, in the early winter of 1549, the princess was in 'grave political danger'.[312] Elizabeth's response was a spirited defence of the Isocratian integrity of her 'word'.

Between 28 January and 7 March 1549, Elizabeth wrote four letters to Somerset refuting the allegations made against her. In her first letter, particularly, she employed the structure of the forensic oration to rebut the charge that she had discussed marriage with Thomas Seymour: she identified the issue, 'what I knowe in this matter'; she offered a carefully opaque account of her recent dealings with the admiral that made no reference to the lurid romps in the bed chamber that her servants described; she provided proofs by identifying conversations and letters that consistently showed that she 'neuer consented unto any suche [marriage] without the counsels consent'; she refuted the rumour that she was 'in the tower and with childe by my Lord Admiral'; and, by way of peroration, she asked to 'come to the court… that I may shewe my selfe there as I am' – that is to say, not pregnant.[313] As these final lines suggested, her dominant concern in this letter and those that followed was to re-establish her credibility or *ethos*. She also drew, then, on the topics of epideictic oratory, 'honor' and 'iuel' to make her case. In particular, Elizabeth worried that her 'honor and honesti' had been impugned by the Seymour scandal, which carried the additional risk of undermining her testimony regarding the charges levied against her. In each section of her first letter to Somerset, she identified her word with her integrity – what she knew, what she said, what she did, what she was. All the words she said to her servants she had 'declared to master Tyrwhit', her appointed interrogator, to Somerset, and before God. 'I know I have a soul to save', she insisted.[314] The theme of her

311 David Starkey, *Elizabeth* (London, 2000), pp. 69–80. Ashley's confession is HHCP, 150/85. Elizabeth's confession is HHCP, 150/89.

312 Janel Mueller, 'Elizabeth Tudor: Maidenhood in crisis', in Donald Stump, Linda Shenk and Carole Levin (eds.), *Elizabeth and the 'sovereign arts': Essays in literature, history, and culture* (Tempe, 2011), p. 16.

313 Elizabeth, *ACFL*, pp. 19–20. See Quintilian, *Institutio oratoria*, III.9.i.

314 Elizabeth, *ACFL*, p. 20.

'honor and honesti' carries through Elizabeth's subsequent letters, partly because the protector's answer to her first message alleged that she had not spoken 'plainlie' and seemed rather too 'wel assured of [her] none [own] selfe]' for his liking.[315] In her rebuttals, Elizabeth built a discursive shield of double negatives. On 6 February she declared that she 'wolde not (as I trust you have not) so yuel a oppinion of me that I wolde concile any thinge'.[316] On 21 February, she added *litotes* and alliteration to make a similar point: 'I did assure me of my selfe no more than I trust the trueth shal trie, And to say that wiche I knew of my self I did not thinke shulde haue displeased the counsel or your grace'.[317] In the end, Thomas Seymour's reckless actions condemned him but Elizabeth's defensive rhetoric stayed the executioner's sword. When her life was again imperilled, this time by Thomas Wyatt's rebellion against Mary I in March 1554, Elizabeth had her line of defence prepared. First, she asserted the integrity of her word and appealed to Mary to keep her own promise not to condemn her without a hearing. 'A kings word', Elizabeth protested quoting Isocrates, 'was more than a nother mans othe'. Then she pulled out her favourite defensive devices, double negatives and *litotes*: 'I humbly craue to speke with your highnis wich I wolde not be so bold to desire if I knew not my selfe most clere as I knowe myself most tru… I humbly craue but only one worde of answer from your self'.[318] Elizabeth had not merely studied 'devynyte till [she] came to the crowne'. She had also taken a masterclass in discursive self-defence.

Perhaps we should not be surprised, then, that when Elizabeth found herself under pressure to defend the faith after 1559 she turned to those rhetorical techniques that had served her – saved her, in fact – during the course of her education. She attempted to suppress points of confessional controversy from her own discourse and others' preaching and speaking. When circumstances forced her hand, she turned to *ethos*, leaning especially heavily on Isocrates' claim that 'ther can be no dewar det than princes' word'.[319] She would not prescribe a course for her beloved subjects if she was not persuaded of it herself, she protested, neatly side-stepping why this course was honest or beneficial. And, just as she had used double negatives and *litotes* to avoid incriminating herself in 1549 and 1554, so she used them during her reign to avoid giving her opponents a positive target to aim at. Elizabeth's liberal education had taught her to defend her

315 Elizabeth, *ACFL*, p. 22.
316 Elizabeth, *ACFL*, p. 21.
317 Elizabeth, *ACFL*, p. 22.
318 Elizabeth, *ACFL*, pp. 31–2.
319 *PPE*, vol. 1, p. 114. See similarly her speeches in November 1566: *PPE*, vol. 1, pp. 145, 147.

faith, but she had learnt to use words as a shield rather than a sword. She worked hard to protect her realm from religious 'innovacion' and 'froward' contentiousness of the obstreperous godly citizens, though her tactics of smother and swerve neither extinguished their zeal nor deterred them from firing their arrows.

Elizabeth's education may not have prepared her to dispute doctrine but it did provide her with another mechanism to foster the religious lives of her subjects. William Camden reported that 'shee said & repeated oftentimes, that which she had read of HENRY the third, her Predecessor, that her Maiestie had rather in her Prayers speake to God deuoutly, then heare others speake of Him eloquently'.[320] A miniature prayer book she owned and a collection of French prayers that were probably written by the queen confirm that Elizabeth's faith continued to centre on the devotional life she had developed in the 1540s.[321] In addition, however, Elizabeth I encouraged her subjects to 'speake to God deuoutly' too. Elizabeth defended the faith by sending forth several volumes of private prayers during her reign: the *Precationes priuat[ae] Regiae E.R.* (1563); *Christian prayers and meditations in English French, Italian, Spanish, Greeke, and Latine*, released by the queen's printer John Daye in 1569; and *Variae medications et Preces piae*, produced by Christopher Barker, the royal printer for Latin, Greek and Hebrew, in 1582.[322] There are reasons to doubt the queen's authorship of the 1569 volume particularly: Henry Bull had put his name to most of them in his *Christian prayers and meditations*, printed earlier that year. More generally, prayers ascribed to Elizabeth and written in the first, royal person to ventriloquise the queen's voice were sometimes known to be created and printed by others, including Thomas Bentley.[323]

Nevertheless the circulation of these prayers and meditations under Elizabeth's name and the royal arms and released by the queen's printers demonstrated her authorisation of the collections. Indeed, the verso of Daye's title page carried a woodcut depiction of Elizabeth at prayer in her privy chamber. Thus, subjects overheard Elizabeth own that 'it was

[320] William Camden, *Annales the true and royall history of the famous empresse Elizabeth Queene of England France and Ireland*, trans. Abraham Darcie (London, 1625), STC 4497, pp. 13–14.

[321] BL, MS Facsimile 218, sigs. 3^r–36^r in Elizabeth, *ACFL*, pp. 44–55 but see Henry Woudhuysen, 'The queen's own hand: A preliminary account', in Peter Beal and Grace Ioppolo (eds.), *Elizabeth I and the culture of writing* (London, 2007), pp. 19–22; HHCP, 147, fols. 207^r–212^r in Elizabeth, *ACFL*, pp. 84–94.

[322] *Precationes priuat[ae] Regiae E.R.* (London, 1563), STC 7576.7; Anonymous, *Christian prayers and meditations in English French, Italian, Spanish, Greeke, and Latine* (London, 1569), STC 6428; *Variae meditationes et preces piae variis designatae vsibus, Latino, Italico, Gallico, & Anglico sermone conscriptae* (London, 1582), STC 17774.

[323] Collinson, *Elizabethan essays*, p. 91; May, 'Queen Elizabeth prays', p. 206.

[God's] will' that she was 'born to royal parents and nurtured and educated royally'. Then 'when [she] was surrounded and cast down by the various snares of enemies' God 'liberated [her] with [His] assiduous care from prison and saved [her] from the highest penalty' before granting her 'royal authority and majesty over the earth'. She had been blessed, moreover, by 'a healthy and strong wit, prudence beyond other women' and 'knowledge and use of languages and literature which is highly esteemed'. All of these qualities were God's 'free gift' and entirely unmerited. By way of thanks, Elizabeth begged that 'she may govern [God's] people rightly, and rule for the healthy administration of your state' and 'use [God's] gift for [His] glory'.[324] These devotions and the occasional prayers that Elizabeth probably did write (if not authorise the printing of) in 1588, 1596 and 1597 to celebrate victories in the Anglo–Spanish war expressed Elizabeth's love for her people, established her *ethos* and communicated moderate Protestant doctrines, and encouraged subjects to imagine having a deeply personal relationship with both God and the queen. Elizabeth transformed her early, feminised translations of Marguerite de Navarre's *Le Miroir de l'âme pécheresse* and Queen Katherine's *Prayers or medytacions* into a truly princely attempt to ameliorate and connect to the devotional lives of her subjects.

Elizabeth's liberal education had not prepared her to join her brother, or even her cousin Lady Jane Grey, in the lists as a bellicose champion of religious reform. Like James VI and I, her contemporary in Scotland and successor in England, she distrusted further reform, despised puritans' presumption and was determined to defuse the threat they posed to the royal supremacy. Unlike James, however, she also lacked confidence to debate them on their own terms. Elizabeth was a skilled and charismatic orator, but she tended to fall into obfuscation and circumlocution when she was compelled to deliberate on religion. Like her Catholic half-sister, Mary, much of Elizabeth's liberal education had emphasised the acquisition and demonstration of unthreateningly feminine virtues and skills, yet she did not follow Mary into armed resistance in 1553. Instead she navigated the changing confessional winds of the 1540s and 1550s and survived 1549 and 1554 by using her words defensively. She kept the essentials

[324] 'Sed regiis ortam parentibus regie enutritam atque educatam, regno destinasti: variisque inimicorum insidiis circumuentam atque iactatam, tua assidue protectione tutatus es, et e carcere, atque ultimo discrimine liberatam, regia in terris dominatione, atque maiestate donasti… ingenio et sano et solido, prudentia etiam preter alias foeminas, eximia atque prestante, literarum praeterea atque linguarum cognitione et usu, quum in hoc sexu esse solet, maiore… tuo gratuito murere… ut ad populi tui rectam gubernationem, regni atque reipublicae tuae salutarem administrationem… authoris gloriam illustrandam recte perpetuo utar': Elizabeth, *ACFL*, pp. 121–2.

of her faith few and relatively uncontentious – scripture, faith, grace – and made its expression decorous, Christocentric and reverent. After the settlement of 1559, Elizabeth drew on her juvenile study and translation of prayers and devotional works to discharge her office as supreme governor of the church in a way that reflected her personal religion and intellectual strengths. The result was a monarch who propagated scripture, encouraged her subjects' personal piety and preferred prayer to pedantic disputation. Erasmus had had worse royal students in sixteenth-century Europe.

CONCLUSION

Indeed the education of royal women in early modern Britain generally sustained the revolution of the pen that northern humanists had effected. The future queens all studied vernacular languages and read scripture and devotional literature. All but Elizabeth Stuart were taught some Latin and introduced to classical authors, and Elizabeth I and Lady Jane Grey even had an entry into Greek and, for Jane, Hebrew. All were persuaded of the honour and utility of a liberal education, to the extent that those royal women who survived into adulthood continued their studies or, in the case of Mary I, Mary, Queen of Scots, and Elizabeth Stuart, made adult attempts to overcome what they perceived as early deficits in their curricula. Their families facilitated their education and they, in turn, used their knowledge and skills to praise, support and advance their kin.

Nevertheless royal families' dynastic strategies, which for all but Jane Grey were about advancing sons, imposed limitations on the extent of their daughters' liberal studies and, to some degree, their sense of themselves as Christian princes. Indeed the pedagogical arrangements that Henry VIII, Henri II and James VI and I made for their daughters left it unclear whether they considered them as potential successors. Sadly their schooling was rarely 'cutting edge' or 'equal' to their brothers or even other learned women of the time. The queens' formal schooling started later than their male kins' lessons and commanded fewer resources. It was left to Henry VIII's wives and the de Guise kin of Mary, Queen of Scots, to advance the princesses' liberal educations as part of attempts to promote their statuses. This was the line of political reasoning that Henry and Frances Grey, duke and duchess of Suffolk, took to its logical, pitiless conclusion with the arrangements they made for the education of their daughter, Jane. Moreover the school exercises that the royal women created and circulated when their educations commenced were traditionally feminine, one might even say feminised. Their familial letters, religious translations and prayers displayed their acquisition of unthreatening, sex-specific virtues. Humanists such as Thomas Elyot had argued that 'good letters' would prepare noble and royal women for all fortune, but, when fortune's wheel lurched unexpectedly, the arrangements made for Tudor and Stuart royal women frequently left them clinging on by one hand.

The extent to which gender shaped the educations of royal women in early modern Britain is evident from the continuities of their experience across geographical, chronological and confessional lines. Elizabeth Stuart's education in seventeenth-century England had more in common with her grandmother's schooling in sixteenth-century France than her brothers' upbringings, which will be examined in chapter seven. Elizabeth Tudor's experiences and school exercises resembled her Catholic half-sister's more than her brother Edward's, despite the fact that Elizabeth and Edward shared a number of teachers. None of them rebelled against their teachers' ideological lessons and Mary, alone, resisted the will of her male kin with her pen – when she reversed Henry VIII's and Edward's use of Erasmus – as well as with her sword in 1553. As queens, Mary and Elizabeth capitalised on their early study and composition of prayers and religious translations by circulating printed prayers, meditations and paraphrases that were meant to enhance the piety, scriptural knowledge and devotional lives of their subjects. And, on a personal level, all royal woman derived pleasure and consolation from good letters towards the end of their lives. The most poignant example is, perhaps, that of Lady Jane Grey, who used her liberal education most fulsomely in captivity. Her schooling had been planned to teach her to rule and to advance her family but, when the Suffolks' blind desire of estate brought her low, Jane used her studies to prepare to die.

Jane Grey was, moreover, the only royal woman who seemed prepared (indeed, positively eager) to argue about theology with a hostile cleric. Mary contended with Edward and his council to protect her private masses, yet she, like Mary, Queen of Scots, and Elizabeth, felt much more comfortable discussing the royal prerogative than doctrine or ecclesiastical policy. Despite theologians' persistent doubts about even royal women's right to reason on these issues, the queens' lack of confidence in arguing about religion is surprising. After all this skill was arguably the key reason why the liberal education of princes was taken so seriously in early modern Britain. The lacuna was also, potentially, very dangerous in an era of confessionally motivated warfare. It is hard to judge whether an Elizabeth I who had willingly disputed with puritans or declaimed against

Presbyterians would have released the building pressure for further reform or given already contentious orators additional air time. It can be said, however, that her defensive attempts to smother debate and obfuscate her own position did little to reduce religious tensions in Britain. Her successor would certainly take a different approach to the problem.

CHAPTER 6

Education and royal resistance: George Buchanan and James VI and I

Charles James Stuart (1566–1625) was born on 19 June and crowned king of Scotland a mere thirteen months later at the Kirk of the Holy Rood, Stirling. Like Edward VI, he was a minor at his accession. Like Edward VI, he was to rule a realm that had recently broken with the Roman Catholic church. Unlike Edward, however, James had been placed on the throne by a confederacy of noblemen who had forced his mother, Mary, Queen of Scots (1542–1587), to abdicate in July 1567. Unlike Edward, moreover, James was not supreme head of the church in Scotland, though in 1567 the General Assembly of its godly ministers insisted that he should be a 'comfortable instrument of God' and defender of their Calvinist Kirk.[1] As such James VI's education at Stirling Castle was shaped by a powerful ideological concern. The young king had to be taught to accept the justice of his mother's deposition and learn to rule Scotland on behalf of her political enemies.

Almost three years after his coronation, James came under the tutelage of two men who were meant to secure his compliance to this agenda: George Buchanan, the foremost humanist in the British isle, and his Genevan-educated assistant, Peter Young. James's pedagogues set him on an Erasmian journey through Latin and Greek grammar, rhetoric, poetry, history and moral philosophy, and they gave him a double helping of Bible study and Calvinist commentaries. Buchanan and Young selected and implemented this classical curriculum to cultivate James's reason, reformed piety and capacity for self-government. He was to be his mother's opposite in all things. Intellectually, James thrived, but even from a young age he resisted Buchanan's schoolmasterly authority.

Buchanan raised the stakes on princely obedience in three printed works that in the final years of his life he dedicated to James VI: the verse drama *Baptistes* (1578), the political dialogue *De iure regni apud Scotos*

[1] John Row, *History of the Kirk of Scotland from the year 1558 to August 1639* (Edinburgh: 1842), p. 34.

(1579) and his compendious *Rerum Scoticarum historia* (1582). Not only did these texts insist that the people, or its representatives, possessed the right to forcibly resist an over-mighty monarch but also they prescribed a model of Senecan kingship that circumscribed the ruler's emotional life and civil government even more radically than historians have supposed. Additionally, unlike continental and English reformers, Buchanan explicitly resisted the application of Old Testament princely prototypes to sixteenth-century kingship; the effect was to exclude the implication that James had any spiritual authority in his realm. In short, Buchanan proposed that, as an adult ruler, James VI would have no more lawful power in Scotland than he had wielded as a small boy-king.

What followed the publication of these treatises was one of the more spectacular instances of student rebellion in the early modern world. James VI emerged from the schoolroom of Europe's most radical monarchomach to become a leading proponent of the divine right of kings. J. H. Burns, Rebecca Bushnell, Peter Lake and Roger Mason have demonstrated persuasively that James VI and I repudiated his schoolmaster's views on everything from civil law, the coronation oath and Scottish history to the comparative value of neo-classical and vernacular literature.[2] At the heart of James's account of 'free monarchies', however, was his description of God's role in human affairs, which he authorised using proof-texts from Old Testament accounts of Hebrew kingship. The final section of this chapter will examine James's earliest circulated religious writings and the neglected holograph manuscripts of these meditations, to show how his royal rebellion against Buchanan's pattern of kingship began.

Buchanan was one of the greatest Latin poets and most experienced humanist pedagogues in northern Europe. His failure to teach one small boy to adopt his account of Scottish government stemmed in part from James's early dislike of his schoolmaster and his heavy-handed discipline. Yet this chapter also provides insight into the strengths and weaknesses of the Erasmian model of liberal education, which Buchanan adopted and adapted for James VI. Just as Erasmus had argued that his curriculum would restrain Henry VIII and Charles V from vainglorious warfare

[2] J. H. Burns, *True law of kingship: Concepts of monarchy in early modern Scotland* (Oxford, 1996), pp. 232–4; Rebecca Bushnell, 'George Buchanan, James VI and neo-classicism', in Roger A. Mason (ed.), *Scots and Britons: Scottish political thought and the union of 1603* (Cambridge, 1994); Peter Lake, 'The king (the queen) and the Jesuit: James Stuart's *True law of free monarchies* in context/s', *Transactions of the Royal Historical Society*, 6:14 (2004); Roger A. Mason, 'George Buchanan, James VI and the Presbyterians' and 'James VI, George Buchanan and *The true lawe of free monarchies*', in *Kingship and the commonweal: political thought in Renaissance and Reformation Scotland* (East Lothian, 1998).

and attempts to expand their territorial authority, so Buchanan proposed that the careful study of 'literature and religioun' would deter James from tightening his grasp on the reins of power in Scotland.[3] Buchanan's faith in the moderating effects of liberal education would prove as misplaced as Erasmus' had been. James VI's studies gave the king the intellectual tools and, perhaps, the political will to insist on his 'free' monarchy over church and state.

INSTITUTING KING JAMES VI: MAR, MORAY AND GEORGE BUCHANAN

In March 1567 Mary, Queen of Scots, sent her infant son to Stirling Castle to live under the 'tutill and governance' of John Erskine (d. 1572) and Annabella Murray (d. 1603), earl and countess of Mar.[4] Her decision had been prompted by the political repercussions of the murder of her royal consort, Henry, Lord Darnley, at Kirk o' Field in Edinburgh, six weeks previously. For five years after his installation, James would remain safely in the castle while Mary and her supporters fought a civil war against a largely Protestant, pro-English confederacy who claimed the Scottish throne for James VI. In this struggle, the 'King's Party' held the field in part because the earl of Mar retained James's person. As he grew older, however, they were also concerned that their child-king should endorse the religious and political regime they had established in his name. In March 1570 the Privy Council appointed two humanists and reformers, George Buchanan and Peter Young, to perform this difficult pedagogical office.

By the time of James's birth, the queen and her husband were estranged. Darnley did not attend the lavish festivities that accompanied his son's Catholic baptism at Stirling Castle on 22 December 1566, a move that cast suspicion over his paternity.[5] Early in the new year, two servants of James Beaton, archbishop of Glasgow, warned Mary that Darnley was plotting to abduct Prince James and rule in his name.[6] When Darnley was found dead in Kirk o' Field at around two o'clock in the morning on 10 February 1567, Mary was thought to have had a hand in it. Elizabeth I warned her

[3] Erasmus, *EECP*, p. 5.

[4] NAS, MS RH 2/2/15, fol. $31/1^{r-v}$; *HMC Mar*, vol. I, pp. 18–20.

[5] NAS, MSS E 23/3/45, fols. 1^{r}–10^{v} and E 21/56, fols. 51^{r}–52^{r}; *CSPV*, vol. VII, no. 375, p. 387; Michael Lynch, 'Queen Mary's triumph: The baptismal celebrations at Stirling in December 1566', *Scottish Historical Review*, 69 (1990).

[6] Frank A. Mumby (ed.), *Fall of Mary Stuart: A narrative in contemporary letters* (London, 1921), pp. 154–6.

cousin that Mary could only 'preserve [her] honour' in the matter by prosecuting the murderer.[7] Instead, she married the man widely believed to be Darnley's assassin, James Hepburn, earl of Bothwell (*c.* 1534–78). While rumours and allegations swirled, Mary ordered two noblemen to deliver Prince James to the security of Stirling Castle.[8] The earl of Mar had given the queen 'infallable experience' of his 'trueth and uprychtnes'; he was one of the few lairds who had served her faithfully since her return to Scotland in 1560.[9] In order to assist Mar in his duty to 'conservit' her 'darrest sone', Mary insisted that he 'suffer nor permitt na noble men' to enter James's present 'accompaniet with ony ma persons bot twa or three'.[10] The clause was an attempt to prevent her political opponents from seizing the prince. Mary cannot have expected that Mar would use it against her.

In April, however, news reached Stirling that Mary was considering marriage to Bothwell, a move that threatened Mar's kinsman, James Stuart, earl of Moray, and, potentially, James's welfare.[11] When Mary visited her son on 21 April, Mar prevented her from removing the prince by permitting only two of her ladies to accompany her inside the castle.[12] It was to be the last meeting between mother and son. On 1 May 1567 Mar formed a confederacy with Moray and James Douglas, earl of Morton (*c.* 1516–81), amongst others, to secure Mary's 'liberty' from Bothwell, the safety of the prince and justice for Darnley's killers.[13] In fact, the lairds were declaring war on their queen. The confederacy captured Mary in June and on 24 July 1567 the queen signed her 'voluntary demission' of government to James VI.[14] From this point onwards, the earl and countess of Mar and the four regents of the king's minority had two central objectives regarding James: to keep the child safe in their custody and to teach him to accept the political and religious regime they had established in his name.[15]

7 'M'employre a conseruer v[o]tre honnetur… c'est que bonne regarderez entres voz doigtz sua la revenger': SP 52/13, fol. 17[r].

8 Jane Dawson, *The politics of religion in the age of Mary, Queen of Scots: The earl of Argyll and the struggle for Britain and Ireland* (Cambridge, 2002), p. 149.

9 NAS, MS RH 2/2/15, fol. 31/1[r–v]; *HMC Mar*, vol. I, p. 16; Henry Summerson, 'Erskine, John, seventeenth or first earl of Mar (d. 1572)', *ODNB*.

10 *HMC Mar*, vol. I, p. 16.

11 Jenny Wormald, *Mary Queen of Scots: A study in failure* (London, 1988), p. 162; SP 52/13, fols. 29[r], 35[r]; James Melville, *Memoirs of Sir James Melville of Halhill, 1535–1617*, ed. A. Francis Steuart (New York, 1930), pp. 146, 147. For Mar's perspective, see SP 52/14, fol. 101[r].

12 SP 59/13, fol. 45[r].

13 *CSPV*, vol. VII, no. 390, p. 394. See also Dawson, *Politics of religion*, p. 150; Gordon Donaldson, *All the queen's men: Power and politics in Mary Stewart's Scotland* (London, 1983), p. 81.

14 Melville, *Memoirs*, pp. 158–9; *RPCS*, vol. I: 1549–1569, pp. 538–41; *RPS*, 1567/7/25/1; Wormald, *Mary Queen of Scots*, p. 165.

15 Alan R. McDonald, *The Jacobean kirk, 1567–1625* (Aldershot, 1998), pp. 6–7.

The English queen, Elizabeth I, made it clear to Mar in January 1569 that she would only support the King's Party government in Scotland if the regime looked to the 'surety and benefit of the child', King James.[16] Mar responded by limiting the size of James's Stirling household and taking steps to ensure its loyalty.[17] He continued the lock down of the castle that Mary had established. In fact the second regent, James's paternal grandfather, Matthew, Stewart, earl of Lennox (1516–71), further reduced the number of servants who could be admitted to James's presence. In addition to furnishing the castle with a guard, Mar was charged with directing the inhabitants of the town of Stirling to provide additional security 'at all tymes neidfull'.[18] The parliament that James VI opened at Stirling on 28 August 1571 was one such occasion. On 3 September, the pro-Marian Hamilton clan launched an assault on the castle. They killed Regent Lennox and captured the earl of Morton. James was not spared the sight of his dying grandfather but he remained physically safe.[19] Even the earl of Mar's death in October 1572 did not weaken castle security. James's final regent, the earl of Morton, simply ordered Mar's brother, Alexander Erskine of Gogan, to sign a bond taking responsibility for James's 'sure preservation' in return for the mastership of Stirling.[20] A month later the Marian forces surrendered. Elizabeth I congratulated the countess of Mar for her 'carefulnes and circumspectioun in the bringin up and nourriture of the young King' during the interval and acknowledged her husband's 'hazardouse service'.[21] It is ironic that the Mars' success showed future Jacobean rebels, such as the Ruthven Raiders, the way forward: control of the king's person was critical to control of the realm.

As James VI grew older and the likelihood of him reaching his majority increased, the King's Party showed that they were equally eager to hold on to his heart and mind. The primary players in James's political and religious formation were his pedagogues, George Buchanan and Peter Young.[22] They were appointed in March 1570 by the Privy Council in the wake of the assassination of the first regent, the earl of Moray. Moray had proved himself to be a calculating politician, a steely general, a cautious friend to the English and a godly prince of the Calvinist kirk.[23] Nicholas

16 SP 52/16, fol. 13r.

17 *HMC Mar*, vol. I, p. 21; *ATS*, vol. XII, pp. 117, 134, 149, 166, 170, 282, 347, 353, 354, 356, 378, 337, 362; NAS, GD 124/10/46/1.

18 NAS, GD 124/10/28.

19 Alan Stewart, *The cradle king: A life of James VI and I* (London, 2003), pp. 36–7.

20 NAS, MSS GD 124/10/37, 124/10/39/1, 124/10/41, 124/10/44/1.

21 *HMC Mar*, vol. I, p. 28.

22 *RPCS*, vol. XIV (addenda 1545–1625), p. 40.

23 *RPCS*, vol. I, pp. 673, 675, 680–1, 685–6, vol. II, pp. 40–1; *RPS*, 1567/12/3; Donaldson, *All the queen's men*, pp. 71–4, 78–9; Maurice Lee, *James Stewart, earl of Moray: A political study of the Reformation in Scotland* (New York, 1953), pp. 207–8, 211; McDonald, *Jacobean kirk*, p. 6.

Throckmorton described him as taking the pattern of his regency from the kings who 'led the people of Israell' in the Old Testament.[24] Moray's ideological artillery in office included his own former schoolmaster, George Buchanan, one of the most learned men to be appointed as a royal pedagogue in the sixteenth century.

Buchanan had served as Moray's unofficial director of communications. He moderated the critical meeting of the General Assembly of the Kirk on 25 June 1567, which secured ministerial support for the deposition and the King's Party.[25] He went on to write vernacular pamphlets to justify the Scottish rebellion against Mary and obsequious poems to Elizabeth that were meant to forward Moray's cause in England.[26] The humanist helped to edit the incriminating casket letters and to prosecute Mary at the York and Westminster commissions in 1568 and 1569. Afterwards he wrote scurrilous pamphlets that defamed the Scottish queen to a European-wide audience.[27] In the dark days following Moray's 1570 assassination, a Privy Council dominated by King's Party stalwarts turned to Buchanan, their fallen leader's teacher and mouthpiece, to educate the king.

Despite his advancing years, Buchanan was eager to take on the pedagogical mission. Minister John Row claimed that Buchanan had moderated the General Assembly meeting in July 1567 that had resolved that 'wise, godlie, and learned men' should 'have the charge of the education of the Prince'.[28] Seven years after the break with Rome, the predominately Calvinist General Assembly understood the need to dispense with the model used for James V's education. Horse-riding and vernacular tales of heroism had left James V without great facility in English, French or Latin let alone the knowledge of theology necessary to steer the ship of state through the waves of religious reform.[29] Mary's education in France was another cautionary tale. In 1567, the General Assembly recognised that James VI would need fluency in classical and vernacular tongues and

[24] SP 52/14, fol. 136ʳ.

[25] I. D. McFarlane, *Buchanan* (London, 1981), p. 222.

[26] George Buchanan, 'To Elizabeth, Queen of England', in *George Buchanan: Political poetry*, eds. Paul McGinnis and Arthur Williamson (Edinburgh, 2000), pp. 106–9, 112, 113.

[27] Buchanan's pamphlet, *De Maria Scotorum regina* (London, 1571), STC 3978, was swiftly translated into English, Scots and French. See McFarlane, *Buchanan*, pp. 324–7, 340–52.

[28] Row, *History of the Kirk*, p. 34.

[29] For the General Assembly's high expectations of James VI, see *RPCS*, vol. I, pp. 673, 675, 680–1, 685–6, vol. II, pp. 40–1; *RPS*, 1567/12/3; McDonald, *Jacobean kirk*, p. 6. On James V's low level of literacy, see *State papers: Published under the authority of His Majesty's Commission, King Henry the Eighth*, 11 vols. (London, 1830–52), vol. IV, no. 130, p. 368; 'Entrée du Roi d'Écosse á Paris', in *Relations politiques de la France et del'Espagne avec l'Écosse au XVIe siècle*, ed. Alexandre Teulet (Paris, 1862), vol. I, p. 108; W. Stewart, *The buik of the croniclis of Scotland; Or a metrical version of the history of Hector Boece*, ed. W. B. Turnbull, 3 vols. (London, 1858), vol. I, p. 4, lns. 12–13.

knowledge of scripture and Calvinist doctrine to be 'a comfortable instrument of God' and kirk. As the moderator of the Assembly, Buchanan had written his future job description.

Buchanan had been born near Stirling, 'a Lennox-man' by birth, but he spent much of his youth studying and teaching on the continent.[30] Initially he had worked under the scholastic theologian John Mair. While studying in Paris, however, Buchanan embraced the pedagogical, grammatical and rhetorical methods of Erasmus. He produced a popular Latin translation of Thomas Linacre's schoolboy primer, *Rudimenta grammatices* (1533), then turned his hand to imitating Erasmus' brand of Lucianic wit.[31] Buchanan composed satirical verses, *Somnium* (1537), *Palinode* (1537) and *Franciscanus* (1538), that lampooned clerical greed, drunkenness, hypocrisy and sexual incontinency. The *Franciscanus*, for instance, told the story of a monk whose supposed stigmata had actually been inflicted in self-defence by a girl he had tried to assault.[32] Against this image of false piety, Buchanan held up a true picture of the good Christian that seemed to have been copied straight from Erasmus' *Handbook of the Christian soldier*: 'Religion means becoming accustomed sincerely to right and truthful conduct, / Religion is to follow Christ in both faith and works.'[33] The wrath of the Franciscans in the court of James V was sufficient that, despite his appointment as tutor to the king's illegitimate son, the future earl of Moray, Buchanan was arrested for Lutheranism in 1539 and, after a daring escape through the prison window, he fled to England and then France.[34]

There Buchanan tutored at prestigious schools including the Collège de Guienne in Bordeaux (1539–43, 1545–7) and taught a series of noble pupils, including Gilbert Kennedy, earl of Cassilis; Timoléon de Cossé, son of the Comte de Brissac; and Michel de Montaigne (1533–92).[35] He

[30] Roger A. Mason, 'Introduction', in Buchanan, *De iure regni*, pp. xvii–xviii; Hugh Trevor-Roper, *The invention of Scotland: Myth and history* (New Haven, 2008), p. 35 (quotation).

[31] Thomas Linacre, *Rudimenta grammatices*, trans. George Buchanan (Paris, 1533) and subsequent editions; McFarlane, *Buchanan*, pp. 28, 33–8, 42–7. Erasmus' influence may be seen in George Buchanan, 'To the popes', 'The Graven image speaks to the pilgrims', 'To the worshipper of idols', 'To Pope Pius', 'To Julius [II]', 'To Pope Paul', 'To Rome', 'To the Same Rome', 'To a certain bishop' and 'About the Monks of St. Anthony', in *Political poetry*, pp. 246–55.

[32] George Buchanan, 'The Franciscans', in *Political poetry*, pp. 220, 221; Philip Ford, '*Poeta sui saeculi facile princeps*: George Buchanan's poetic achievement', in Philip Ford and Roger P. H. Green (eds.), *George Buchanan: Poet and dramatist* (Swansea, 2009), pp. 11–12.

[33] 'Vobis relligio est sincero assuescere recto, / Relligio est Christi facta fidemque sequi': George Buchanan, 'Palinode, Part II', trans. modified from *Political poetry*, pp. 178, 179.

[34] Jon Robinson, 'The slippery truth of George Buchanan's autobiography', *SCJ*, 39:1 (2008).

[35] George Buchanan, *Opera omnia*, ed. Thomas Ruddiman, 2 vols. (Leiden, 1725), vol. II, p. 255; McFarlane, *Buchanan*, pp. 42–6, 176–7 and 'Vita', in *The trial of George Buchanan before the Lisbon*

achieved fame as a Latin poet. Between 1544 and 1565, Buchanan created a *Paraphrase of the Psalms of David* in twenty-nine Latin metres, which met with instant and enduring success as a school text in reformed Europe.[36] After a run-in with the Lisbon Inquisition in 1550–2, on charges that referred to his anti-clericism, Buchanan pledged his return to the Gallican church and wrote a series of orthodox poems to adorn French court ceremonies, including the marriage of Mary Stuart and Francis in April 1558.[37] When the widowed queen returned to her Scottish kingdom, Buchanan accepted a pension of £250 Scots per annum to take up a post in her household and as the Privy Council's English, French, Latin and Spanish secretary.[38] As a kinsman of Lord Darnley and the court poet, Buchanan wrote celebratory verses for Mary's second royal wedding in July 1565, and for the baptism of the couple's son James in December 1566.[39]

Buchanan wrote in his *Vita* that he had become a fervent reformer by this time, yet he had really only begun to engage with Luther's and Calvin's theology in the late 1550s. Hugh Trevor-Roper contends that he was simply not 'very spiritual' and was prone to adopting the 'opinions of those around him'.[40] The sincerity of his faith was not doubted by his Calvinist contemporaries in the kirk in the early 1560s any more than it had been doubted by the ultra-Catholic Maréchal de Brissac in Paris in the 1550s.[41] Nevertheless Queen Mary took him for a kirk papist and felt deeply betrayed when he sided with the King's Party in 1567. 'A vile atheist', she spat, upon seeing a Latin version of what was probably his *De Maria Scotorum regina* in 1571.[42] In fact, Buchanan's political and religious allegiances had been shifting since his return to Scotland, perhaps in

Inquisition, James M. Aitken (ed.) (Edinburgh, 1939), pp. xvi, xvii, xxiv, xxv; P. Hume Brown, *George Buchanan, humanist and reformer: A biography* (Edinburgh, 1980), pp. 85, 91, 158–9; Trevor-Roper, *Invention of Scotland*, p. 37.

36 T. W. Baldwin, *William Shakespere's smalle Latine and lesse Greeke*, 2 vols. (Urbana, 1944), vol. 1, p. 351; Roger Green, 'Dry bones of contention? Picking apart Buchanan's *Psalms*', in Philip Ford and Roger Green (eds.), *George Buchanan: Poet and dramatist* (Swansea, 2009), pp. 253–66; McFarlane, *Buchanan*, pp. 500–6.

37 Buchanan, 'Vita', pp. xxii–xxv; Robinson, 'Slippery truth', pp. 71–4, 84–7; Elizabeth Bonner, 'French naturalisation of the Scots in the fifteenth and sixteenth centuries', *HJ*, 40 (1997).

38 SP 52/7, fol. 33^{r}; John Guy, *My heart is my own: The life of Mary Queen of Scots* (London, 2004), p. 159; McFarlane, *Buchanan*, pp. 206–15.

39 Buchanan, 'Genethliacon Jacobi sexti regis Scotorum', in *Political poetry*, pp. 154–63; Hume Brown, *George Buchanan*, p. 185; Mason, 'Introduction', in Buchanan, *De iure regni*, p. xviii; McFarlane, *Buchanan*, pp. 233–4.

40 Buchanan, 'Vita', pp. xxvi, xxvii; Trevor-Roper, *Invention of Scotland*, p. 39.

41 Théodore de Bèze, *Icones, id est verae imagines virorum doctrina simul et pietate illustrium* (Geneva, 1580), sig. *iii^{r}; Bodleian, Smith MS 77, fol. 29^{r}.

42 SP 53/7, fol. 134^{r}. See also fol. 122^{v} (where she calls him an 'Athéo').

anticipation that Mary, too, was about to convert.[43] He had renewed his ties to his former pupil, James, earl of Moray, a leading court Calvinist. In June 1563, the Scottish parliament had appointed both men to a commission for the reform of the three colleges of St Andrews.[44] Buchanan's scheme pleased Moray sufficiently that the earl appointed him principal of the College of St Leonard in 1566.[45] That year, too, Buchanan's *Franciscanus* appeared in print with a letter praising Moray's 'zeal in purging the country of those monsters', the monks, and in upholding 'faith staunchly with the singular virtue of the ancients'. For Buchanan, the earl's civic virtue was measured by his support for religious reform and his readiness to topple those he described as 'tyrants' – here, the Franciscans – to effect it.[46]

Buchanan's subsequent willingness to resist civic tyrants may have been fostered by his involvement in the Scottish General Assembly.[47] The Scottish ambassador, Sir James Melville (1535/6–1617), claimed that Buchanan 'folowed in many thingis the vulgair oppinion; for he was naturally populair' and 'extrem vengeable against any man that had offendit him'.[48] As Buchanan gathered new affinities, a feeling that probably began as an Erasmian distaste for corrupt clerics and over-mighty monarchy sharpened into repugnance for Mary's rule.[49] Ultimately it was the murder of his Lennox kinsman, Darnley, and Mary's emergence from the ashes of Kirk o' Field as Bothwell's wife that turned the poet against the queen.[50] When the King's Party struck in 1567, Buchanan was ready to fight for Mary's deposition and the institution of Moray as regent in her stead using partisan accounts of Scottish law and history. Subsequently, he would glorify Moray's thirty-month governorship as an *exemplum* of virtuous, pious, conciliar and elective monarchy.[51] Following the earl's assassination in early 1570, Buchanan may have hoped to shape James VI in the image of his former student. The humanist arrived in James's schoolroom

[43] Trevor-Roper, *Invention of Scotland*, p. 43. [44] *RPS*, A1563/6/26.

[45] McFarlane, *Buchanan*, p. 222.

[46] Buchanan, 'Jacobe Stuarte… qui in patria ab illis monstris expurganda princeps operam navasti; eam adeo strenuam, ut quae *Graeci*… de *Hercule* suo fabulati sunt, tu rebus praestiteris, & incredibili tua virtute antiquitatis fidem adeo subleuoueris', in *Opera omnia*, vol. II, p. 256, 257 (quotation).

[47] Hume Brown, *George Buchanan*, pp. 226, 237–8; John Knox, *The history of the Reformation in Scotland*, ed. William Croft Dickinson, 2 vols. (New York, 1949), vol. II, p. 132–3; McFarlane, *Buchanan*, pp. 215–17.

[48] Melville, *Memoirs*, pp. 230–1.

[49] Buchanan, prefatory verses, in *Political poetry*, pp. 266, 267.

[50] Hume Brown, *George Buchanan*, pp. 193n., 200, 204, 206–16; McFarlane, *Buchanan*, pp. 320–2.

[51] George Buchanan, *Rerum Scoticarum historia* (Antwerp, 1583), STC 3992, fol. 206r.

as the internationally renowned 'prince of poets',[52] a Calvinist (albeit an odd one), a critic of tyranny and a public proponent of the idea that princely education was critical in securing good government and religion.

For his assistant, Buchanan took Peter Young, a promising scion of Scottish Calvinism. Young was born on 15 August 1544 to a burgess family and educated at Dundee Grammar School and, perhaps, St Andrews University.[53] In 1559 he was admitted to Jean Calvin's Academy in Geneva where he studied under Henry Scrimgeour (1505?–72), a kinsman.[54] In Geneva Young became acquainted with Calvin's successor, Théodore de Bèze, who described him as 'uncommonly learned'.[55] Young started to correspond with de Bèze and Andrew Melville (1545–1622), then a young Scottish poet and Calvinist minister, on his return to Scotland.[56] It was probably Scrimgeour who recommended Young to Buchanan and the Privy Council in 1570.[57] Of the two tutors, Sir James Melville records that 'Mester Peter Yong was gentiller' and 'laith till offend' his pupil-master.[58] Young tended to encourage the king with gifts and games rather than public remonstrations or the birch rod. His early kindness to James was not forgotten and Young remained high in the king's favour throughout his long life.[59]

Together, Buchanan and Young were charged with James's 'instruction and Education... in Literature and religioun'.[60] The preceptors' responsibility to use this office to groom the king confessionally and politically was widely recognised. In June 1574 Buchanan and Young featured on English Privy Council lists of influential men 'fit to be interteyned' north of the border. It was recommended that Peter Young receive £30 and Buchanan £100 for their services; Buchanan's worth was equal to a number of the earls on James's council.[61] Even when the tutors' political prestige in Scotland diminished under James's final regent, the earl of Morton, the English ambassador still proposed entertaining Buchanan, 'a synguler man', and Young, who was 'especially well affected, and redy to p[er]suade

52 'Poetarum nostri...principe': title page of George Buchanan, *Psalmorum Davidis paraphrasis poetica* (Paris, 1565).

53 David Horsburgh, 'Young, Sir Peter (1544–1628)', *ODNB*.

54 Sven and Suzanne Stelling-Michaud (eds.), *Le Livre du recteur de L'Académie de Genève, 1559–1878*, 6 vols. (Geneva, 1959), vol. 1, p. 81.

55 'D. Petro Iunio, eximiae quoque doctrina': Bèze, *Icones*, sig. *iii^{r-v}.

56 Bodleian, Smith MS 77, fols. 27^{r}–28^{v}, 149^{r}–150^{v}, 151^{r}–154^{r}.

57 Bodleian, Smith MS 74, fols. 189^{r}–190^{r}, 191^{r}–194^{r}, 195^{r}–196^{r}.

58 Melville, *Memoirs*, p. 262.

59 BL, Additional MS 32102, fol. 166^{v}; Horsburgh, 'Young, Sir Peter (1544–1628)'.

60 NAS, Edinburgh, GD 124/10/39/1.

61 *HMC Mar*, vol. 1, p. 25; BL, Cotton MS Caligula C V, fol. 119^{r}.

the K[ing] to be in favo[u]r of her Ma[jes]tie'.[62] When Young refused his pension, ambassador Robert Bowes reported that it was of little matter. He trusted Young to 'advance' the king's reformed religion and affinity with the English regardless.[63]

The king's education in 'literature and religioun' was deemed as important as his physical security by his regents, the General Assembly of the Kirk, and the English regime. Neither minority government nor civil war interrupted his lessons. The King's Party must have been anxious to cultivate James's erudition – after all, they had appointed Scotland's most renowned pedagogue and poet as his schoolmaster – yet they also had ideological motivations for educating the prince with such care. Buchanan and Young had to teach James VI to embrace the Kirk, the English and a form of government that had been established in Scotland by his mother's enemies. In chapter four we saw that the appointment of Edward VI's schoolmasters in 1544 was an ideologically loaded affair; Henry VIII needed pedagogues who would teach Edward how to defend his English church. In Scotland in 1570, however, the stakes were even higher.

JAMES'S EDUCATION IN 'LITERATURE AND RELIGIOUN'

Buchanan and Young approached their task at Stirling confident that the study of Latin and Greek grammar, rhetoric, poetry, history, moral philosophy and scripture could shape their pupil's character and political outlook as well as cultivate his literary skills.[64] By 1570, humanist schoolrooms in Europe had graduated many royal disappointments. Yet Buchanan seems to have retained faith in the Erasmian pedagogy he had studied in Paris in the 1520s and 1530s. His success with Moray must have buoyed his confidence. Perhaps, like the scrupulous humanist textual critic he was, he attributed other schoolmasters' failures to their inability to translate Erasmus' pedagogy accurately rather than to any defect in the source text itself. Thus, when it came to securing James's compliance with the King's Party's religious and political agenda, Buchanan determined that a liberal education (*liberalis educatio*) would teach James to reject his mother's lustful, impious, tyrannical example. It would strengthen his mind and character

[62] SP 52/26/1, fol. 52^{v}.

[63] SP 52/28, fol. 183^{v}; BL, Cotton MS Caligula C V, fol. 48^{r}.

[64] Anthony Grafton and Lisa Jardine, *From humanism to the humanities: Education and the liberal arts in fifteenth- and sixteenth-century Europe* (Cambridge, MA, 1986), pp. xii, xix; Peter Mack, *Elizabethan rhetoric: Theory and practice* (Cambridge, 2002), esp. pp. 5, 7, 211–16, 250–1; Quentin Skinner, *Reason and rhetoric in the philosophy of Hobbes* (Cambridge, 1996), pp. 19–26.

against 'moral corruption' and cultivate princely moderation, self-control and piety.[65] Alan Stewart is right to characterise James's schooling as a 'basic (if somewhat outdated) classical humanist education'.[66] Nevertheless, the Presbyterian and republican doctrines that the pedagogues were trying to instil in James VI, and their anxieties about his mother, encouraged them to increase the disciplinary rigour of Erasmus' curriculum.

Buchanan's service at the York–Westminster conference had given him plentiful opportunities to ruminate on the supposed moral inadequacies of Mary, Queen of Scots.[67] In his summary of the case against Mary's readeption, known as *Ane informatioun*, Buchanan alleged that the root cause of her increasingly heinous conduct was her enslavement to her passions, particularly lust. She committed adultery with Bothwell, who 'abusit hyr bodie at his plesr, having passage in at ye bak dur'.[68] He alleged that, while sharing Bothwell's bed, Mary plotted to kill her husband and staged her own abduction to return to her lover.[69] In 1570–1, when Buchanan was establishing James's schoolroom, he was also scribbling furiously to make sure that this representation of the lustful queen reached a wide European audience in his *De Maria Scotorum regina*.[70] The sexual imagery of the *De Maria* was less gratuitous than that of *Ane informatioun* but the tract described Mary as morally unsuitable for rule. The queen lived 'not in accordance with princely honor, but in more than princely, indeed unprincely, licentiousness'.[71] Even in 1582, when Buchanan published his final work, *Rerum Scoticarum historia*, he still claimed that the central impulse of Mary's religious and political tyranny had been lust.[72] To her 'intemperate mind', he wrote, 'the restraint of a lawful government was considered unworthy of kings, and the slavery of others their own liberty'.[73] Thus she attempted to overturn the reformed religious settlement in Scotland. Buchanan blamed Mary's licentiousness partly on her

[65] Buchanan, *De iure regni*, pp. 76, 77.
[66] Stewart, *Cradle king*, p. 38.
[67] George Buchanan in *The indictment of Mary Queen of Scots as derived from a manuscript in the University Library at Cambridge*, ed. Reginald Henry Mahon (Cambridge, 1923), p. 17; William Camden, *Annales rerum Anglicarum, et Hibernicarum, regnante Elizabetha* (London, 1615), STC 4496, p. 144; McFarlane, *Buchanan*, pp. 324–5.
[68] Buchanan in *Indictment of Mary Queen of Scots*, p. 35.
[69] Buchanan in *Indictment of Mary Queen of Scots*, p. 46.
[70] [Buchanan], *De Maria Scotorum regina*, pp. 2, 29; McFarlane, *Buchanan*, pp. 324–7, 340–54.
[71] 'Si non regia honorificentia, certe plus q[uam] regia, aut certe parum regia licentia': [Buchanan], *De Maria Scotorum regina*, p. 6.
[72] Buchanan, *Rerum Scoticarum historia*, fol. 176v and *The history of Scotland*, trans. James Aikman, 4 vols. (Glasgow, 1827), vol. II, p. 440; Roger A. Mason, 'George Buchanan and Mary Queen of Scots', *Records of the Scottish Church History Society*, 30 (2000).
[73] Buchanan, *Rerum Scoticarum historia*, fol. 178v and *History of Scotland*, vol. II, p. 450.

sex, which made her more susceptible to lust, and partly on her 'courtly education' (*aulica educatio*) in France, 'the most corrupt of all courts'.[74] Not only had it left Mary with shoddy Latin but it had also given her a 'specious colouring of virtue' and 'studied anxiety to please' that weakened any 'natural goodness' that may have lain within her.[75] Buchanan's plan was that James's rule would be diametrically opposed to his mother's licentious, papist and over-mighty government.

As such, Buchanan proposed to arrange James's education very differently. It would be liberal rather than 'courtly'. Indeed, Buchanan's prescriptions for the king echoed his proposed curriculum for future ministers of the kirk at St Leonard's College at the University of St Andrews.[76] In his 'Genethliacon', a poem he wrote in celebration of the prince's birth, Buchanan had argued that rigorous schooling in grammar, rhetoric, poetry, history, moral philosophy, religious writings and astronomy would teach James 'self-control, And from the holy fountains [of Greek and Roman literature], / He will learn the true art of ruling a kingdom in peace and war'.[77] In this, Buchanan echoed Erasmus' claim that a liberal education was the only entry to reasonable and just kingship. 'Literature and religioun', Buchanan argued, would teach James to keep 'wayward pleasures in check' and 'the reins loose' on his subjects' bridles. James would learn to 'be king of himself' before he ruled others.[78] Just as Erasmus had proposed that a liberal education could contain Henry VIII's war-mongering, so Buchanan reckoned that it would teach James to reject his mother's supposed licentiousness and tyranny. James VI had begun life under the care of women, led by Annabella, countess of Mar, his 'Lady Minny'.[79] Yet in 1574 Henry Killigrew (1525×8–1603) reported that Buchanan and Young were 'desirous to have him from the handling of women'.[80] The son of Mary, Queen of Scots, required no more effeminising influences in his upbringing! Rather, he was to be taught alongside other young aristocrats, whose presence was supposed to spur him on, as humanists had recommended.[81] One of James's schoolfellows reported that Buchanan was grimly eager to

[74] Buchanan, *Rerum Scoticarum historia*, fols. 176^{v}, 178^{v} and *History of Scotland*, vol. II, pp. 440, 450.
[75] Buchanan, *Rerum Scoticarum historia*, fol. 176^{v} and *History of Scotland*, vol. II, p. 440.
[76] George Buchanan, 'Reformation of the Universitie of St Andros', in *Vernacular writings of George Buchanan*, ed. P. Hume Brown (Edinburgh, 1891–2), pp. 8–11.
[77] Buchanan, 'Genethliacon', in *Political poetry*, pp. 162, 163.
[78] Buchanan, 'Genethliacon', in *Political poetry*, pp. 156–61; similarly Buchanan, *De iure regni*, pp. 76, 77.
[79] NAS, GD 124/10/45. [80] SP 52/26/1, fol. 64^{r}.
[81] They included John Erskine (*c.* 1562–1634), the future earl of Mar; William Murray of Tullibardine; the countess's nephew, Walter Steward, later Lord Blantyre (d. 1617), who was distant kin to

attribute his youthful disobedience to the 'bloody Nest of which [James] was come'.[82] To lessen the supposedly dangerous influence Mary had on her son, he was told that 'he was bound unto [Elizabeth I]... more than to his owne mother'.[83] The virgin queen, at least, had her lusts under control.[84] The ideological priorities of the anti-Marian party encouraged Buchanan to be even stricter than other humanists about making the schoolroom an exclusively male environment.[85]

James probably began speaking (if not writing) Latin before his fourth birthday. He complained that his masters 'gar me speik latin ar I could speik Scotis'.[86] In fact, it seems probable that his first language was actually French, which was useful for speaking at court, for diplomacy, for Calvinist theology and as a pathway to Latin. As an adult king, James VI was proud of the fact that Buchanan had taught him the rudiments of Latin and Greek himself.[87] When these preliminaries were complete, Young's record of James's juvenile library suggests that the king set out on an Erasmian journey through Latin grammar.[88] His first texts were Latin translations of Aesop's fables, Cato's *Distiches* (probably in the volume edited by Erasmus), Erasmus' *Colloquia* and *De civilitate morum puerilium*, and Cicero's epistles (edited by Johann Sturm).[89] These works were composed in clear and colloquial Latin and cultivated stoical virtues. James's notes on the fly-leaves of Young's catalogue of his books show that he extracted *sententiae* from these authors to internalise their moral content and learn their vocabulary and syntax for reproduction in his own writings.[90] James had a number of grammatical primers, including Niccolò Perotti's *Cornucopiae sive linguae Latinae commentarii*, which Erasmus had praised, Lily's grammar and Buchanan's Latin translation of *Rudimenta grammatices*.[91] In accordance with Erasmus' prescriptions, James progressed to the plays of Terence then

the royal house and a youth of some intellectual promise; and George Erskine, Lord Innerteil (*c.* 1567–1646), who was the son of Mar's brother, Alexander: Thomas McCrie, *Life of Andrew Melville, containing illustration of the ecclesiastical and literary history of Scotland*, 2 vols. (Edinburgh, 1819), vol. I, pp. 105–6.

82 George Mackenzie, *Lives and characters of the most eminent writers of the Scots nation*, 3 vols. (Edinburgh, 1711), vol. III, p. 180.

83 SP 52/26/1, fol. 64r.

84 Buchanan, 'To Thomas Randolph, an Englishman', in *Political poetry*, pp. 148, 149.

85 Walter J. Ong, 'Latin language study as a Renaissance puberty rite', *Studies in Philology*, 56 (1959).

86 Warner, p. lxxii.

87 Thomas Craufurd, *History of the University of Edinburgh from 1580 to 1646* (Edinburgh, 1808), p. 86.

88 Baldwin, *William Shakespere's small Latine*, vol. I, pp. 532–3.

89 Warner, pp. lxi, lxii, lxv, lxvi, lxxii.

90 Warner, pp. lxxi, lxxii; Mack, *Elizabethan rhetoric*, p. 18; Ann Moss, *Printed commonplace-books and the structuring of Renaissance thought* (Oxford, 1996), p. 2; Skinner, *Reason and rhetoric*, p. 117.

91 Erasmus, *De ratione studii*, in *Opera omnia*, I.ii, pp. 114–15; Warner, p. lx.

the poetry of Ovid and Virgil.[92] Like Edward VI, James thrived in the hothouse of the royal schoolroom. By October 1574, when the humanist and kirk minister Andrew Melville and his nephew James visited Stirling, they were struck by the king's superior 'ingyne [wit], judgment, memorie' in the Latin tongue.[93]

While many boys found these early stages of grammar stultifyingly dull, the young king seems to have taken precocious pleasure in the performative potential of 'literature and religioun'. James read Terence's *Phormio*, a comedy about a charismatic fixer who rights the love affairs of young men and the deceptions of their fathers with cunning and eloquence.[94] When it came time to practice disputation against one of his schoolmates, Young reported that James had 'prepared well for the debate, so much so that when the young Lord of Mar arrived [the king] said "Come now, come, anyone who wants to challenge Phormio, let him do so." '[95] Phormio's cocky persona gave James a mask for expressing intellectual confidence. Other ancient authors prompted the king to ask moral questions. When Young read Xenophon's account of Gadatas, an Assyrian courtier who had been made a eunuch for 'catching the eye of the king's concubine', James asked why the concubine was not castrated instead. When Young read him the fable of Sisyphus, James asked why the fallen king continued to push the boulder. Why did he not just 'sit down on his rock'?[96] This student prince evidently found the reading and rote learning associated with Latin grammar to be no more 'soulless' than a talented young musician finds scales and arpeggios.[97] For James, exercises in reading, note-taking, memorisation and translation were gateways to supple expression and moral inquiry.

Young's fulsome record of James's childhood 'apophthegmata' suggests that he found the king's lively enjoyment of literature endearing. Buchanan, however, seems to have grown anxious that James's character was not being sufficiently fixed by his education. He worried publically in 1578 that James might be 'turned towards vice' despite his schoolmasters' best efforts.[98] As a first step towards instilling discipline, Buchanan

92 Erasmus, *De ratione studii*, in *Opera Omnia*, I.ii, p. 148; Warner, pp. lviii, lxiii.
93 James Melville, *The autobiography and diary of Mr James Melvill*, ed. Robert Pitcairn (Edinburgh, 1842), p. 38.
94 Warner, p. lix.
95 Peter Young, 'Apophthegmata regis', in Warner, pp. lxxiii–lxxiv.
96 Peter Young, 'Apophthegmata regis', in Warner, p. lxxiii.
97 Grafton and Jardine, *From humanism to the humanities*, p. 155.
98 'Id vitio vertendum esse': George Buchanan, *A critical edition of George Buchanan's Baptistes and of its anonymous seventeenth-century translation 'Tyrannicall-government anatomized'*, ed. Steven Berkowitz (New York, 1992), p. 350.

insisted that the king produce compositions that demonstrated that he could keep his mind and prose style inside the margins. Imitative and formulaic epistle composition was a common feature of Renaissance rhetorical training.[99] Even by this standard, however, James's early Latin letters were closely tailored. The king's surviving letter to Buchanan combined the epistolary sub-types of lamenting sorrow (at his schoolmaster's absence) and making a request (for his return). James saluted Buchanan as his 'father', the title that Erasmus proposed a letter writer might use to address an older man to whom he was indebted.[100] His dignified opening style was sustained by the carefully balanced *antithesis* of the first sentence: 'nothing can be more profitable or more welcome to me than your presence and, on the other hand, nothing can be more unfortunate or more regrettable than your absence'.[101] Alan Stewart has argued that the letter shows James's early alienation from Buchanan – 'the emotions expressed as if by rote' – but his chilly tone may have been the point.[102] A ruler needed to be able to control his emotions and convey moderation.

For Buchanan and Young to fulfil their ideological brief, it was also critical that the king used his grammatical knowledge to study scripture. To assure others of their progress, they taught James a party trick that he performed for Killigrew in October 1574:

> [James] was able *ex tempore* [whi]ch he did before me to read a chapiture of the Bible out of Latin into French, and out of French after into English so well as few men could have added anything to his translation. His scholmasters Mr George Buchanan & Mr Peter Young rare men, conselled me to appoint the K[ing] what chapiter I would whereby I understood it was not studied for.[103]

The English were reassured that James was becoming a good student of God's word and that his grammar was serving as a conduit to grace. James's study of scripture was shaped by Genevan and Zwinglian commentaries, including *L'Institution de la religion Chrestienne* (perhaps Geneva, 1566), Henry Bullinger's *Sermons... avec la Resolution des points de la religion* (perhaps Geneva, 1560) and works by Peter Martyr and de Bèze.[104] The schoolmasters also introduced James to anti-Catholic polemics, perhaps

[99] Peter Mack, *Elizabethan rhetoric*, pp. 24–9, 50–82, 103–4, 115–23 and *A history of Renaissance rhetoric, 1380–1620* (Oxford, 2011), pp. 228–56.
[100] Bodleian, Smith MS 74, fol. 169r; Erasmus, *De conscribendis epistolis*, in *Opera omnia*, I.ii, p. 289.
[101] 'Nihil mihi quicquam utilius aut gratius esse possit, absentia vero contra nihil magis incommodius aut tristius possit accidere': Bodleian, Smith MS 74, fol. 169r.
[102] Stewart, *Cradle king*, pp. 40–1.
[103] SP 52/26/1, fol. 64r.
[104] Cummings, *Literary culture of the Reformation*, pp. 102–17, 232–80; Warner, pp. xlviii, xlix, lii, lxxii.

even before he could read. Young records that James owned a copy of the *Mappe-monde nouvelle papistique* (Geneva, 1566), the largest satirical image printed in the sixteenth century. It depicted horned and cloven-hoofed clerics and monks disporting themselves in the Sea of Hypocrites, Forest of Bandits and Vale of Mandrakes.[105] From a young age, James was taught that his mother's religion was the refuge of the greedy, exploitative and sexually incontinent.

Erasmus had pioneered sixteenth-century approaches to scriptural pedagogy and anti-clerical satire. Yet James learnt that the Dutch humanist did not describe the path to salvation (or Geneva) with sufficient constancy. Young recorded that, upon reading Erasmus' injunction that it was 'occasionally appropriate for us to play the polypus [shellfish]' in our manners and 'adapt ourselves to the customs of the region', the king had retorted that Erasmus was 'a great man in many respects' but that, 'in matters of religion', he himself was 'a polypus', ready to change his colours to suit his audience.[106] Erasmus' recommendations for the study of letters, sacred and profane, had shaped James's schooling, but when it came to his faith Young taught the king to profess himself a true son of the Calvinist kirk in Scotland.

One of James's New Year's gifts in 1576, a copy of Conrad Gesner's *Lexicon sive dictionarium Graecolatinum* (Geneva, 1557), indicated that he was embarking on the next stage of his training in biblical exegesis. Young reported that, after prayers each morning, James had begun to study the Greek of 'the New Testament, or Isocrates, or Plutarch's *Apophthegmata* together with a Greek grammar', probably Nicholas Clenard's *Institutiones absolutissimae in linguam Graecam*.[107] The king made swift progress. Indeed, in April 1577, he 'manfully and clerkly won' a folio edition of de Bèze's Greek Bible (1565) from Young.[108] Jean Meyer has claimed that James was 'one of the very few sovereigns to master Greek'.[109] It is certainly true that very few monarchs had heeded the humanists' call to Attic arms in the early years of the sixteenth century. In the British isle,

[105] Warner, pp. lii, lix; D. Wahrman, 'From imaginary drama to dramatized imagery: The Mappe-Monde Nouvelle Papistique, 1566–67', *Journal of the Warburg and Courtauld Institutes*, 54 (1991).

[106] 'R[ex]... Quamquam interdum nos deceat fieri polypos, Erasmus ipse in religione, alioquin vir magnus, dici potuit polypus': in Warner, p. lxxii; Erasmus, *De civilitate moribus puerilis*, in *CWE: Literary and educational writings III*, p. 274.

[107] 'Ad Graeca se accinget, vel ex *Novo Testamento*, vel *Isocrate*, vel ex *Plutarchi apophthegmatibus* una cum praxi praeceptorum Grammatices': Thomas Smith, *Vitae quorundam eruditissimorum et illustrium vivorum* (London, 1707), p. 6; see also Warner, p. xlv.

[108] Warner, pp. xlvi, xlvii.

[109] Jean Meyer, *L'Éducation des princes en Europe: Du XVe au XIXe siècle* (Paris, 2004) p. 123.

however, James followed Edward IV and Elizabeth I in his readiness to propound upon the New Testament in the original tongue.[110] Indeed, amongst reformed rulers in the sixteenth century, some knowledge of Greek was a badge of prestige. In the 1580s, James and Elizabeth would squabble about the meaning of true kingship by bandying around *sententiae* from Isocrates and Plutarch.[111] Like English rulers, James was educated to be a godly prince. Unlike English rulers, however, the Scottish king's grammatical expertise was not supposed to teach him to exert authority over a national, reformed church.

Indeed James's study of 'literature and religioun' was supposed to discourage him from over-ruling subjects' souls or bodies. In 1577 he read orations by Isocrates that championed limited monarchy, and Demosthenes' attacks on Philip of Macedon's imperial kingship, followed by a dose of Cicero on the virtues of the Roman republic.[112] For many grammar-school boys, this course of study was organised so that the pupil could examine Cicero's rhetorical figures, tropes and techniques in light of the Roman's self-conscious attempt to Latinise Greek oratory.[113] Buchanan, however, insisted that these orations and philosophical treatises should serve as James's 'monitors' or guides to limited – in fact elective – kingship.[114]

James's studies were shaped to impress a certain moral and ideological character upon him. Yet he was also taught to be a probing reader and powerful argumentative interlocutor.[115] Young, in particular, seems to have been eager to cultivate James's capacity for critical thought and debate, despite Buchanan's fears regarding the king's susceptibility to ideological corruption. There was one exercise that he insisted upon. In a letter of 1574 or 1575, Young wrote to the Lord Chief Justice Clerk, Sir John Bellenden, asking him to petition Morton for more funds to buy books. Upon meeting some resistance, Young reiterated that James needed a copy of Caesar's works, printed in Venice 'to conferr him with utheris' editions. He also wanted a copy of 'Caesar correctit' by 'Hotomans'.[116] François Hotman's (1524–90) edition of the *Gallic wars* was duly purchased in November 1575,

[110] Elizabeth, *Translations*, pp. 56–7, 373–7.
[111] Melville, *Memoirs*, pp. 224–5.
[112] Warner, pp. xxxvii–xxxix, xli, xlv, xlvi, li, lii, lix; Smith, *Vitae quorundam eruditissimorum*, p. 6; Baldwin, *William Shakespere's smalle Latine*, vol. 1, pp. 309, 407.
[113] Roger Ascham, *The scholemaster or a plaine and perfite way of teaching children, to understand, write, and speake the Latin tong* (London, 1570), STC 832, sigs. C4^{v}, E4^{r}; Thomas Elyot, *Boke named the gouernour*, ed. H. H. S. Croft, 2 vols. (London, 1883), vol. 1, p. 76.
[114] Buchanan, *De iure regni*, pp. 2, 3 and *Rerum Scoticarum historia*, sig. ∴^{r}.
[115] Mack, *Elizabethan rhetoric*, esp. pp. 5, 7, 211–16, 250–1.
[116] Alexander Macdonald and James Dennistoun (eds.), *The library of Mary Queen of Scots and King James the sixth*, Miscellany of the Maitland Club, 4 vols. (Glasgow, 1834), vol. 1, p. 14.

together with at least twenty-seven other books, including a 'Commentarii Caesaris en francoys' to 'conferr' with Hotman's version.[117] Young constantly pressed James to compare and contrast seemingly similar texts, whether the same work in two different languages, two different parts of the Bible, two editions of an author or two chronicles recording the same event. This philological and rhetorical exercise sharpened the king's ability to test the style, logic, arguments and credibility of texts.

In addition, Treasury accounts and Young's record of James's library show him buying and accepting books liberally.[118] Not all these works reinforced the King's Party's agenda. Indeed, James possessed no fewer than two copies of Jean Bodin's (1529/30–96) defence of indivisible sovereignty, *Les Six livres de la république* (1576).[119] Perhaps the point of keeping such dangerous books around was to teach James to attack their erroneous claims; as an adult, James continued to keep dossiers of his opponents' writings.[120] Yet the physical lockdown at Stirling was not matched by the intellectual gating of the king. Young was also tenacious in reclaiming around 223 volumes of the library of Mary, Queen of Scots, from the men who had pilfered them following her deposition. Young's restoration of the queen's books was more than an attempt to retrieve valuable crown property. The arrival of a collection of Dante, Petrarch, Juan Luis Vives and Ronsard at Stirling, bound with imprints of Mary's arms, offered James a view of his mother and her 'courtly education' that was quite different from Buchanan's portrayal.[121] Ultimately, Buchanan and Young's ideological concerns did not lead them to neglect the development of James's argumentative skills or to restrict his reading material. There was nothing slavish about James's liberal education.

Indeed, it was Young and Buchanan's achievement to cultivate a king who regarded his pen as central to the exercise of monarchy. As James VI and I's folio *Workes* (1616) demonstrates, the king employed the literary genres he had studied at Stirling – epistle, epic poetry, biblical paraphrase and exegesis, deliberative oration, theological disputation and *speculum principis*, amongst others – to make political, religious and literary interventions throughout his reign.[122] He also used reading and writing to

[117] Warner, p. xlviii.
[118] For instance *ATS*, vol. XIII, pp. 46–7, 157, 163, 204, 304, 317.
[119] Jean Bodin, *Les Six livres de la république* (Paris, 1576); Warner, pp. xlii and liii.
[120] Stewart, *Cradle king*, pp. 228–30.
[121] Warner, p. xxxi–xxxii, xxxiv; Julian Sharman (ed.), *The library of Mary Queen of Scots* (London, 1889), pp. 15, 44, 142.
[122] James VI and I, *The workes of the most high and mighty prince, Iames by the grace of God Kinge of Great Brittaine France & Ireland defendor of the faith*, ed. James Montagu (London, 1616), STC 14344.

fashion his monarchical identity. In *The trew law of free monarchies* (1598), James argued that it was the sovereign's office to provide 'discourse and direction' to his people on the basis of his own natural, civil and sacred learning.[123] Tudor sovereigns had used literary skills, acquired during their humanist educations, to great political effect. In addition to possessing this facility, James became a theorist of the honour and utility of the princely pen and, as we will see in the next chapter, wrote his own best-selling prescriptions for the education of princes. More than any other early modern monarch, James regarded authorship as central to his authority.[124] By this measure, his pedagogues had had great success at Stirling.

James VI soaked up classical grammar, rhetoric, history, poetry and scripture but, from the first, observers reported that he almost instinctively resisted Buchanan's schoolmasterly authority and the political implications of his lessons. According to George Mackenzie, who claimed to have got the story from the grandson of James's schoolmate, George Erskine, Lord Innerteil (*c.* 1567–1646), Buchanan had set James a 'theme' on the conspiracy of Lauder Bridge against James III (1452–88). The lead conspirator, Archibald, earl of Angus, attempted to motivate his coevals by likening them to the Council of Mice in Aesop's fable, who tried to hang a bell on a local feline for their common preservation. Angus offered to be the one to begin the tumult by 'belling the cat', first. Presumably Buchanan had set the episode for James as a lesson on the perils of tyranny but James VI understood it differently. That evening, when Buchanan threatened to discipline James for persistent noise-making, James retorted that:

> He would gladly see who would Bell the Cat. Upon this… Buchanan throws the Book from him, and whips the king severely, the Old Countess of Mar… hearing the king cry, ran to him… She asked [Buchanan] how he durst put his Hand on the Lord's Anointed? To which he made this unmannerly Reply, Madam, I have whipt his Arse, you may Kiss it if you please.[125]

The story is so good that one suspects that Lord Innerteil had remembered it with advantages. Yet its lineaments were echoed by other contemporary reports. The boy-king, for instance, supposedly questioned Buchanan's

[123] James, *Trew law*, p. 76.

[124] Daniel Fischlin and Mark Fortier (eds.), *Royal subjects: Essays on the writings of James VI and I* (Detroit, 2002); Jane Rickard, *Authorship and authority: The writings of James VI and I* (Manchester, 2007); Kevin Sharpe, 'The king's writ: Royal authors and royal authority in early modern England', in Kevin Sharpe and Peter Lake (eds.), *Culture and politics in early Stuart England* (Stanford, 1993), pp. 117–38 and *Remapping early modern England: The culture of seventeenth-century politics* (Cambridge, 2000), p. 127.

[125] Mackenzie, *Lives*, vol. III, p. 180.

account of Mary's crimes.[126] He had little truck with the republican themes that ran through his school exercises. From a young age, he had a keen sense of the respect that was due to monarchs. He proved impermeable to his schoolmasters' attempts to beat it out of him.

This was not the only occasion on which Buchanan 'whipt' the 'Lord's Anointed'. James Melville reported that the schoolmaster kept the king in 'gret aw' with regular birchings.[127] In later life James confessed that he still startled when he thought he heard his schoolmaster's footsteps approaching, so fearful had he grown of Buchanan's rod.[128] Buchanan's harsh treatment of James VI was, apparently, uncharacteristic. Other former students had described him as patient and intellectually generous.[129] The northern humanists whose methods he had adopted in other respects decried corporal punishment (particularly for noble pupils).[130] Buchanan's readiness to reject their pedagogical wisdom on this point suggests that he was making a political statement rather than simply letting off steam with the birch rod. Indeed, Buchanan's willingness to beat James was thoroughly in keeping with his eagerness to punish over-mighty monarchs.[131] The master-subject refused to tolerate anything less than absolute obedience from his student prince.

BUCHANAN AND THE *REX STOICUS*

In the final years of his life, Buchanan published three Latin works, which he dedicated to his pupil: the verse drama *Baptistes* (written *c.* 1539–41, printed 1577); the dialogue *De iure regni apud Scotos* (written *c.* 1567, printed 1579); and the weighty *Rerum Scoticarum historia* (1582). They attempted to justify the deposition of Mary, Queen of Scots, to an educated, European audience and achieved it with such success that

126 NLS, Advocates MS 22 2 18, no.7 cited by Guy, *My heart is my own*, p. 383.

127 Melville, *Memoirs*, p. 262.

128 Francis Osborne, *Advice to a son, or, Directions for your better conduct through the various and most important encounters of this life under these generall heads, I. Studies, &c., II. Love and marriage, III. Travell, IV. Government, V. Religion, conclusion* (Oxford, 1656), Wing O512, p. 29.

129 Bodleian, Smith MS 77, fol. 27r–v; Melville, *Autobiography and diary*, p. 120.

130 For instance Ascham, *Scholemaster*, sigs. Biv–Biiv, Cir, Ciiir– Diiv, Eir–Eiiiir; Elyot, *Boke named the gouernour*, vol. I, pp. 32, 36, 50; Erasmus, *De pueris instituendis*, in *CWE: Literary and educational writings IV*, p. 327; Juan Luis Vives, *De tradendis disciplinis*, in *Opera omnia*, ed. Gregorius Majansius, 8 vols. (reprint London, [1745] 1964), vol. VI, p. 282.

131 Rebecca Bushnell, *A culture of teaching: Early modern humanism in theory and practice* (Ithaca, 1996), pp. 63–8; Alan Stewart, 'Boys' buttocks revisited: James VI and the myth of the sovereign schoolmaster', in Thomas Betteridge (ed.), *Sodomy in early modern Europe* (Manchester, 2002), p. 131–47.

Buchanan's historical reputation as a political thinker has exceeded his contemporary fame as a poet.[132] Nevertheless, this was not Buchanan's only object or audience. Compared to contemporary resistance theories printed during the European wars of religion, such as François Hotman's *Francogallia* (1573), Théodore de Bèze's *Du droit des magistrats* (1574) and the anonymous *Vindiciae contra tyrannos* (1579), Buchanan's play, dialogue and history were unusually attentive to the pattern of the good king and his opposite, the tyrant. Buchanan made it clear in his dedicatory letters to James that each of his works was

> a witness to posterity, that if ever [James] should be turned towards vice by bad counsellors or if the license of royalty should overcome [his] morally upright education, the fault should be imputed not to [his] teachers but to [him], who did not obey their virtuous warnings.[133]

They were intended to offer instruction to the prince on discharging his office but they were also meant to encourage other readers – particularly James's subjects – to hold him to the standards that Buchanan had prescribed.

Amongst Roger Mason's compelling studies of Buchanan's political thought is an article that proposes that the humanist's portrayal of kingship in these works was 'imposing' but largely 'conventional'. Mason demonstrated Buchanan's debt to the *speculum principis* tradition, notably to Erasmus' prescriptions in his *Education of a Christian prince.*[134] J. H. Burns has described Buchanan's *imago regis* bluntly, as little more than a 'didactic expansion' of humanist commonplaces.[135] Like other humanists, Buchanan drew on classical *exempla* to urge his royal pupil on to virtue and, like Erasmus, Buchanan regarded Seneca's orations and tragedies as vigilant guards against tyranny.[136] Like Erasmus, Buchanan

[132] Burns, *True law of kingship*, pp. 204–9; Robert M. Kingdon, 'Calvinism and resistance theory, 1550–1580', in J. H. Burns and Mark Goldie (eds.), *The Cambridge history of political thought, 1450–1700* (Cambridge, 1991), pp. 215–18; Quentin Skinner, *The foundations of modern political thought*, 2 vols. (Cambridge, 1978), vol. II, pp. 342–3.

[133] Buchanan, *Critical edition of... Baptistes*, p. 350.

[134] Roger A. Mason, 'Rex stoicus: George Buchanan, James VI and the Scottish polity', in John Dwyer, Roger A. Mason and Alexander Murdoch (eds.), *New perspectives on the politics and culture of early modern Scotland* (Edinburgh, 1982), pp. 11 (quotation), 12, 14 and 'Introduction', in Buchanan, *De iure regni*, pp. li–lxxi. See similarly David Allan, *Philosophy and politics in later Stuart Scotland: Neo-stoicism, culture and ideology in an age of crisis, 1540–1690* (East Linton, 2000), pp. 49–51.

[135] Burns, *True law of kingship*, pp. 202–3; see also 200, 203n.57.

[136] Erasmus, *EECP*, p. 46, as opposed to Peter Stacey's account of the pro-absolutist Senecan tradition in *Roman monarchy and the Renaissance prince* (Cambridge, 2007).

suspected that Israelite kings were unreliable guides for Christian princes.[137] Nevertheless Buchanan's prescriptions for his ideal *rex stoicus* differed from both Erasmian and, indeed, Calvinist *specula* in several important respects. His *imago regis* limited the activity of a hereditary ruler more radically than scholars have supposed.

First, as we have seen, Erasmus adopted a gentle, ironic and probing tone in his *specula principis*. Like Isocrates, he offered praise as precept. Like Lucian, he punctured hypocrisy with wit. He appealed to princely honour and affection and worried in case he was suspected of 'adulation or impertinence' (*vel adulationis vel procacitatis*) by his royal readers.[138] Buchanan, on the other hand, proudly presented 'harsh' (*importunus*) and 'insolent' (*imprudens*) advice to his student-master.[139] Even Buchanan's friend Pierre l'Oyseleur de Villiers, preacher to William of Orange, was struck by the unnecessarily 'hard' (*duro*) tone of his writings. 'I would never have thought that the King of Scotland would have need of such counsel', he wrote.[140] After their time together at Stirling, Buchanan was less sanguine. In 1582, when the humanist's cousin, Thomas Buchanan, questioned the decorum of his portrayal of Mary, Queen of Scots, in book seventeen of the *Rerum Scoticarum historia*, Buchanan retorted that he did not care about offending the king as long as he had 'tauld the treuthe'.[141] The *Historia* was anything but 'treuthe' insofar as that word implies strict adherence to verifiable facts. James later complained that its final chapters were little more than an attempt 'to staine [his mother's] race, and to steal the affection of the people from [her] posteritie'.[142] The tone of Buchanan's dedicatory letters is not as vicious as chapter seventeen would be, yet all three dedicatory epistles assumed that there was no difference between the obedience that a student owed his master and the polite hearing that an adult monarch was obliged to give his advisers. As its title shows, *De iure regni* was not really a 'guide' (*monitor*) for James but an attempt to lay down the 'law' (*ius*) to a king.[143] Buchanan's 'dedications' to James are really a series of public reprimands, one might even say verbal beatings.

Buchanan also used these works to insist on a much stricter standard of princely emotional restraint than Erasmus had recommended to Henry VIII and Charles V in his *Education of a Christian prince*. This is evident from his portrayal of John the Baptist in his play, *Baptistes*, where he serves as a virtuous opposite to drama's tyrant, Herod. Buchanan's John

[137] Erasmus, *EECP*, p. 30. [138] Erasmus, *EECP*, p. 4.
[139] Buchanan, *De iure regni*, pp. 2, 3. [140] SP 83/22, fol. 44^r.
[141] Melville, *Autobiography and diary*, pp. 120–1, quotation from p. 121.
[142] James, *BD*, p. 23. [143] Buchanan, *De iure regni*, pp. 2, 3.

is a pious, self-disciplined, law-abiding leader of men. Buchanan does not make him the sacramental Baptist of the old mystery plays or the fiery preacher of the Protestant tradition. Instead, Buchanan's 'John' separates the time of God's law from the promise of the New Testament and carries 'a' light if not 'the' light of God's word on earth, much like the John of Erasmus' *Paraphrases on the New Testament.*[144] Buchanan described his hero as a 'guard of the truth' who defended 'the religion and laws of the country' and shunned superstitious practices in favour of personal piety and virtue.[145] Unlike Erasmus' ideal Christian prince, however, Buchanan's John was not ostentatiously charitable. His willingness to sacrifice himself stemmed from stoical acceptance of Herod's judgement and God's will, rather than love for his fellow men.[146] Indeed John's lack of emotion in *Baptistes* is striking: he is imprisoned and awaiting death yet he remains infuriatingly reasonable. Probable destruction 'does not strike him with fear'.[147] In his stoical acceptance of death, John the Baptist seems less like Erasmus' all-feeling Christ in the garden of Gethsemane than the stoic philosopher Seneca in Tacitus' description of his death on Nero's orders.[148]

In his political dialogue, *De iure regni apud Scotos,* Buchanan was more insistent in pressing this strictly Senecan model of kingship on James. As the pedagogue hinted in his dedicatory letter, the king was approaching the age when he might embark on his majority. In March 1578 political pressure had prompted the earl of Morton to formally demit his regency to the (reluctant) eleven-year-old. The Stirling household had begun to gather a reversionary interest to Morton's regime and Buchanan was appointed to the council that governed Scotland in the wake of his departure. When Morton returned a few months later, however, Buchanan retained a seat on the Privy Council.[149] The year 1578 proved a false start for James's personal rule. Yet it prompted Buchanan, in his letter to his student-master, to 'submit not only to your teachers but to all those who give you good advice', such as his new council.[150]

144 Berkowitz, 'Sources and parallels', in Buchanan, *Critical edition of... Baptistes,* p. 170; Erasmus, *CWE: Paraphrases on John*, p. 20.

145 'Nam veritatis qui satelles occidit / Pro religione, patriisque legibus': Buchanan, *Critical edition of... Baptistes,* p. 442, lns. 1343–4.

146 'Quem Deus lucis mihi / Concessit usum': Buchanan, *Critical edition of... Baptistes,* p. 422, lns. 1045–6.

147 'Nullo concutitur metu', 'Mortem esse poenam voluit improbis Deus, / Bonisque portum': Buchanan, *Critical edition of... Baptistes,* p. 418, ln. 984 and p. 422, lns. 1057–8.

148 Erasmus, *Disputatiuncula de taedio, pavore, tristicia Iesu,* in *CWE: Spiritualia and pastoralia V,* pp. 65–6; Tacitus, *Annales,* xv.60–5.

149 Mason, 'Introduction', in Buchanan, *De iure regni,* p. xlii.

150 Buchanan, *De iure regni,* pp. 2, 3.

The 'advice' that Buchanan set out for James in *De iure regni* was that the prince needed to master himself and his emotions completely. Rather than have a Platonic philosopher-king who desired at least 'a scholars' retreat', Buchanan claimed he would prefer a 'Stoic king such as Seneca describes in his *Thyestes*'.[151] In Buchanan's original manuscript of the *De iure regni*, probably written in 1567, there was only passing reference to Seneca's *rex stoicus*.[152] When Buchanan was dedicating his work to James VI, however, he prescribed Seneca's stoical *imago regis* more forcefully. This move may have been catalysed by a September 1576 letter from his friend and self-appointed agent, Daniel Rogers, which argued that the dialogue showed 'how very familiar [Buchanan was] with Plato'.[153] To make his Roman expectations clearer, Buchanan concluded the printed edition of *De iure regni* with a passage from Seneca's *Thyestes*:

> A king is one who has laid aside fear and the torments of an evil conscience, who is not moved by uncontrolled ambition and the fickle favour of the reckless mob, or by all the treasure mined in the west… It is a noble mind that masters a kingdom… A king is he who fears nothing.[154]

Seneca concluded that 'a king is he who desires nothing'.[155] Rather than follow Plato, who had acknowledged that self-discipline was a struggle, or Erasmus, who ultimately concluded that 'feeling' (*sensus*) was essential to truly Christian kingship, Buchanan used Seneca to argue that a prince's desires and affections should be set aside completely. What Erasmus had lampooned as Seneca's 'marble statue of a man' Buchanan glorified as his 'portrait of the true king'.[156] Indeed, the model of kingship that Buchanan foisted upon James was more uncompromisingly stoical than anything prescribed by a Renaissance humanist before Justus Lipsius (1547–1606).[157] Buchanan was setting the bar on princely self-discipline vertiginously high for his royal pupil.

There is evidence, moreover, to suggest that Buchanan was making a particular point about stoicism to James. Between 1577 and 1579, Buchanan

[151] Buchanan, *De iure regni*, pp. 38, 39; see also 76, 77.

[152] Mason, 'Introduction', in Buchanan, *De iure regni*, p. xxviii and 'Notes on the text and translation', in Buchanan, *De iure regni*, p. lxxiv; H. R. Trevor-Roper, 'George Buchanan and the ancient Scottish constitution', *EHR*, suppl. 3 (1966), p. 15.

[153] 'Dialogismum de Regno, ab hoc temporis statu non alienum… illud cognoui, quam studiose in Platone versatus esses': Buchanan, *Opera omnia*, vol. II, p. 737.

[154] Seneca, *Thyestes*, 344–89 as cited by Buchanan, *De iure regni*, pp. 162–5.

[155] Seneca, *Thyestes*, 390.

[156] Erasmus, *Moriae encomium*, in *Opera omnia*, IV.iii, p. 106, trans. *CWE: Literary and educational writings V*, p. 104; Buchanan, *De iure regni*, pp. 38, 39.

[157] Jill Kraye, 'Stoicism in the Renaissance from Petrarch to Lipsius', *Grotiana*, 22/23 (2001–2).

presented the king with an edition of Seneca's tragedies and made sure he had a copy of the *Thyestes*. Buchanan also gave him Daniel d'Auge's French translation of the oration of Synesius, bishop of Ptolemais, to Emperor Arcadius in 299 AD, which urged the Christian prince to use reason to rule the passions and submit to the rule of law.[158] In addition Peter Young verbally warned the king about giving in to anger and insisted that indulging the passions was what turned men into beasts. The young king retorted, 'Than I suld not waire ye [emblem of the] lyoun in my armes bot rather a scheip.'[159] Later, of course, James expressed greater affinity with icons of peace. What is significant here is that James's pedagogues used printed books and classroom precept to make sure that the rigid, quixotic figure of the *rex stoicus* remained firmly in his mind's eye.

In addition to urging James VI to cultivate the emotional life of a marble statue, Buchanan proposed to grant him no more political power than a royal effigy. While Erasmus' Christian prince had been encouraged to maintain the customs of his realm and rule with moderation, Buchanan's monarch in *De iure regni* was required to submit to the law and deprived of most legislative and judicial functions. Buchanan argued that criminal cases and judicial interpretation were matters for independent judges, that policy was the responsibility of a council of wise men and that the laws of Scotland were passed by the *populus*, or the people as represented by the estates.[160] Indeed Burns argued that the authority of Buchanan's hereditary monarch was 'far more narrowly prescribed than most contemporaries would have accepted as reasonable, necessary, or practicable'.[161] To make matters worse, Buchanan, who preferred elective to hereditary kingship, made a point of insisting that the powers that James had legally inherited were fewer than those that an elected prince, like Moray, might wield.[162] He argued, in short, that James VI would never possess more lawful authority in Scotland than he wielded during his minority. Buchanan feared that giving a king (even, presumably, a paragon *rex stoicus*) scope for legal or political judgement was tantamount to releasing his inner tyrant.

One might object that Buchanan, like Erasmus and other *speculum* authors, set unrealistically high standards for princely pupils in the hope that they would bestir themselves in that direction, rather than because

[158] Synesius, Bishop of Ptolemais and Philo of Alexandria, *Institution d'un prince chrétien… et Oraison de la vraye noblesse*, trans. Daniel d'Auge (Paris, 1555); Warner, pp. xxxviii, lvii, lxix.

[159] Warner, p. lxxiv. [160] Buchanan, *De iure regni*, pp. 44–7, 54, 55.

[161] Burns, *True law of kingship*, p. 203; see also Erasmus, *EECP*, p. 71.

[162] Buchanan, *De iure regni*, pp. 98, 99.

he had any genuine expectations of royal self-government.[163] Unlike contemporary humanist pedagogues, however, Buchanan insisted that a Scottish ruler who failed to meet his standards could be justly deposed. He threatened James with the 'torments of tyrants' if he failed to repress his passions.[164] In case James thought that these torments were merely psychological, Buchanan showed him the true horrors that had befallen Herod after the action of his play, *Baptistes*, had concluded in his copy of Josephus' *Jewish antiquities*.[165] There, James learnt that, shortly after John's execution, Herod's city was raided by King Aretus IV, the father of Herod's first wife, and the ruler was subsequently exiled to Lyon.[166] For the son of Mary, Queen of Scots, Buchanan's *Baptistes* served as a cautionary tale of deposition and exile following a scandalous marriage and an unlawful killing.

Buchanan's next gift to James, his *De iure regni*, set out the price of royal failure even more explicitly. At Scottish coronations, Buchanan declared (in blithe contradiction of contemporary practice), rulers swore oaths that they would not exceed certain limits on their powers.[167] Specifically, they agreed that 'their speech and actions should conform to the precepts of the law' as it was determined by the estates.[168] If the king failed to respect his oath his subjects might withdraw their obedience, depose him or even assassinate him. One of the most radical claims in *De iure regni* was that 'not only… the people as a whole but also… individuals' could kill a tyrant.[169] In his *Rerum Scoticarum historia*, Buchanan went on to show that the Scots had a proud tradition of removing over-mighty monarchs.[170] Buchanan taught James and his readers more generally that it was the people, rather than the monarch, who had true sovereignty in Scotland.

As James moved towards his majority, then, Buchanan urged his student prince to regard his subjects as his teachers. 'Kindly tell me who in the world will be the law-maker who we will give the king as a sort of schoolmaster?' Buchanan's interlocutor in *De iure regni* asked him. 'The people', Buchanan replied.[171] Just as James's schoolmaster had laid down the law for James and thrashed him when he disobeyed, so the *populus* (or their representatives) would *monitor* an adult monarch and punish him

163 Richard F. Hardin, 'The literary conventions of Erasmus' *Education of a Christian prince*: Advice and aphorism', *Renaissance Quarterly*, 35:2 (1982).
164 'Tyrannorum cruciatus': Buchanan, *Critical edition of… Baptistes*, p. 350, ln. 9.
165 Warner, p. li.
166 Josephus, *Jewish antiquities*, XVIII.5 and 7.
167 Buchanan, *De iure regni*, pp. 186, 187.
168 Buchanan, *De iure regni*, pp. 34, 35.
169 Buchanan, *De iure regni*, pp. 152, 153.
170 Buchanan, *Rerum Scoticarum historia*. See also Buchanan, *De iure regni*, pp. 108–31, 152, 153.
171 Buchanan, *De iure regni*, pp. 52–5.

for his transgressions.[172] Buchanan promised an adult ruler no less scrutiny, no fewer precepts and arguably even harsher correction than he had visited upon his royal pupil at Stirling.

While it was not a typical part of most princely *specula*, the notion that subjects might correct and resist the prince was defended by a number of thinkers during the European wars of religion.[173] Yet Buchanan also distinguished his account of resistance from contemporary Calvinists, who tended to ground their civil disobedience in religious obligations. For instance, John Knox's *Appellation… from the cruell and most iniust sentence pronounced against him* (1558) claimed that God had established the 'publike regiment' in Scotland and required its members to obey divine precepts before the king's.[174] In his *History of the Reformation* (1559–65), Knox described God as ever ready to send a plague or an English army to Scotland when it sinned, or to reward its faithfulness by striking down a tyrant, such as Mary de Guise.[175] Knox's resistance theory, then, drew its strength from what Alexandra Walsham has described as a Calvinist view of God's special providence. God would deal out punishments and rewards as he saw fit and men had a duty to follow and obey him.[176]

Buchanan justified subjects' resistance to monarchy very differently and his position suggests that he meant to add a further, significant limit on James's princely power. Buchanan did not give much credence to the operation of special providence on earth. Since the time of Christ's resurrection, he reckoned that God had been only indirectly and minimally involved in temporal polities.[177] Buchanan agreed that God had authored civil society, but only insofar as His light had enabled men to discern that the most beneficial (*commoda*) and honourable (*honestas*) action they could undertake was to generate a commonwealth.[178] To this Ciceronian account of the formation of the *civitas* Buchanan added a little New Testament gloss. He claimed that

[172] Buchanan, *De iure regni*, pp. 104, 105, 130, 131.

[173] Martin Dzelzainis, 'The Ciceronian theory of tyrannicide from Buchanan to Milton', in Caroline Erskine and Roger A. Mason (eds.), *George Buchanan: Political thought in early modern Britain and Europe* (Aldershot, 2012); J. H. M. Salmon, 'An alternative theory of popular resistance: Buchanan, Rossaeus and Locke', in *Renaissance and revolution: Essays in the intellectual and social history of early modern France* (Cambridge, 1987); Quentin Skinner, 'Humanism, scholasticism and popular sovereignty', in *Visions of politics*, vol. II: *Renaissance virtues* (Cambridge, 2002).

[174] John Knox, *Works of John Knox*, ed. Daniel Laing, 6 vols. (Edinburgh, 1846–64), vol. IV, pp. 441–2, 539–40; vol. V, p. 35.

[175] Knox, *Works*, pp. 89, 220, 270–2; Richard Kyle, 'John Knox's concept of divine providence and its influence on his thought', *Albion*, 18:3 (1986).

[176] Alexandra Walsham, *Providence in early modern England* (Oxford, 1999), pp. 12–15.

[177] J. H. Burns, 'George Buchanan and the anti-monarchomachs', in Nicholas Phillipson and Quentin Skinner (eds.), *Political discourse in early modern Britain* (Cambridge, 1993), p. 4.

[178] Buchanan, *De iure regni*, pp. 18–21; referring to Cicero, *De republica*, VI.13.13.

Paul's letters to Titus, Timothy and the Romans confirmed that God had also established the office of the temporal magistracy, so as to 'hold groups and communities of men together'.[179] Yet it was up to the people themselves to fill these offices. Buchanan's God was like a watchmaker, who created the mechanism of human government and then let it run. Unlike truly Calvinist resistance theorists of the late sixteenth century, Buchanan did not suggest that resistance to a temporal authority was divinely foreseen, let alone mandated.

Rather, the light that led men (and for Buchanan, it was definitely men) to resist a tyrant was their civic virtue. He acknowledged that action inspired by a zeal for the commonwealth might look a great deal *like* providence at work, but he insisted on regarding men as more than God's instruments. Thus, he wrote in the *Historia* that the earl of Moray's pre-eminent reason, piety, Senecan self-discipline and 'zeal in matters of justice' was such that 'divine providence *seemed* to attend all his affairs'.[180] Nevertheless he argued that Moray did not derive his will or right to resist Mary from God but from his own reason and sense of justice. Buchanan drew on Cicero's account of just war in book three of *De officiis* to argue that the definition of a tyrant was one who acted 'in ways which break up the human society that he [or she] was appointed to hold together'. By these actions, the tyrant declared himself an enemy of the 'whole human race' (*totius humani generis hostis*). Anyone might raise a sword against such an enemy. A virtuous citizen, like Moray, would regard it as his duty to do so.[181]

Buchanan was, indeed, an odd sort of Calvinist. Not only did he reject reformed understandings of providence and prefer Ciceronian arguments for resistance to Calvinist ones but he also refused to use the example of Hebrew kings to provide evidence to support his prescriptions for James VI.[182] At the child-king's coronation, John Knox had used 2 Chronicles 23:20–1 to compare the new prince to Joash, the child-king of Judah, and to insist that his government signalled a covenant between God and the king and people of Scotland.[183] Buchanan had no such confidence. In his famed *Paraphrase of the psalms of David*, for instance, the humanist

[179] Buchanan, *De iure regni*, pp. 112, 113; referring to 1 Timothy 2:1–2; Titus, 3:1; Romans 13:3–4.

[180] 'Divina quaedam providentia, in omni negotio affuisse, videatur… in rebus iudicandis, studium': Buchanan, *Rerum Scoticarum historia*, fol. 206^{r}.

[181] Buchanan, *De iure regni*, pp. 152, 153; see also Cicero, *De officiis*, III.32. On the Roman-law phrase 'hostis humani generis', see Martin Dzelzainis, 'Milton and the regicide', in Paul Hammond and Blair Worden (eds), *John Milton: Life, writing, reputation* (Oxford, 2010).

[182] Mason, 'Rex stoicus', p. 11 cites letters from Rodolph Gaulter, Théodore de Bèze, Phillipe du Plessis-Mornay and Thomas Randolph in Buchanan, *Opera omnia*, vol. II, pp. 721–70.

[183] SP 52/14, fol. 81^{v}; Stewart, *Cradle king*, p. 31.

refused to follow contemporary reformers who used Psalm 89 to celebrate 'the messianic hopes' that David's covenant with God raised, both for Christ's rule on earth and the government of subsequent godly kings.[184] Instead, he claimed the psalm described the pact between David and God as a particular, historical covenant that would be broken by David's successors. His royal line would fall and God alone would 'be celebrated for eternity'.[185] For Buchanan, David's kingship did not prefigure Christ's or sixteenth-century Christian rulers' authority. A modern king was neither bound nor protected by a Davidic covenant but established and maintained by the people and their chosen magistrates.[186]

Roger Mason, J. G. A. Pocock and Hugh Trevor-Roper are wise to cast doubt on the extent to which Buchanan's political thinking was shaped by his confessional identity. He had written *De iure regni* 'as a humanist steeped in the literature of classical Greece and Rome' rather than as a Calvinist.[187] Pocock may also be correct that Buchanan did not compose his dialogue 'as a Melvillian' Presbyterian concerned to preserve 'the independence of Christ's people' from the spiritual authority of kings or bishops.[188] Yet, in the decade between the composition of the dialogue and its printing in 1579, the political and religious context in Scotland changed in ways that reshaped the meaning of Buchanan's Ciceronian account of God's minimal and benign involvement in human affairs and his rejection of Davidian kingship.

Buchanan printed *De iure regni* at the height of a trenchant debate about the form of ecclesiastical government in Scotland.[189] From 1574 onwards, the earl of Morton, James's fourth and final regent, had been intervening in bishops' appointments to the extent that he was suspected of trying to 'in[tro]duce into the church of Scotland the lybertye used by the magistrates and byshopes of the church of England which [the ministers of the kirk] like not of'.[190] The General Assembly in Scotland

[184] R. Gerald Hobbs, 'Bucer's use of King David as mirror of the Christian prince', *Reformation and Renaissance Review*, 5:1 (2003).

[185] George Buchanan, *Poetic paraphrase of the Psalms of David*, ed. Roger P. H. Green (Geneva, 2011), pp. 360–7, quotation p. 367.

[186] Arthur Williamson, 'British Israel and Roman Britain: The Jews and Scottish models of polity from George Buchanan to Samuel Rutherford', in R. H. Popkin and G. M. Weiner (eds.), *Jewish Christians and Christian Jews: From the Renaissance to the Enlightenment* (Dordrecht, 1994), pp. 98–9.

[187] Mason, *Kingship and commonweal*, p. 182; see also Trevor-Roper, *Invention of Scotland*, p. 39.

[188] J. G. A. Pocock, 'Two kingdoms and three histories? Political thought in British contexts', in Roger A. Mason (ed.) *Scots and Britons: Scottish political thought and the union of 1603* (Cambridge, 1994), p. 301.

[189] McDonald, *Jacobean irk*, pp. 12–18.

[190] SP 52/261/2, fol. 204v.

responded by establishing a committee that included Andrew Melville, Buchanan's friend and an increasingly vociferous opponent of bishops and proponent of Presbyterianism.[191] Eventually the committee put forward the *Second book of discipline* (1578, printed in 1582), which made a stronger case than the *First book* (1560) for the 'parity' of ministers in the Scottish kirk. Its opening statements reproved Morton's pretensions to supreme authority over the ecclesiastical realm by insisting on its separation from the political kingdom: just 'as the ministers and uthers of the ecclesiasticall estait be subject to the magistrate [in] civill [matters], so ought persons of the magistrat be subject to the Kirk spiritually'.[192] When Morton offered to ratify parts of the *Second book* in June 1578, representatives of the kirk refused to accept his partial support on the grounds that 'it became not the prince to prescribe a policie of the Kirk'.[193] In these years, then, the notion of a Scottish royal supremacy that mirrored the English church was explicitly and forcefully rejected by Buchanan's friends in the kirk.

In this context, Buchanan's refusal to apply Old Testament typologies and proof-texts to the estate of Scottish kingship spoke more loudly than it had in the late 1560s. Since Philip Melanchthon had dedicated his *Loci communes* (1535) to Henry VIII and urged him to be a *nutricius* or 'nursing father' (Isaiah 49:32) of the church, the political function of evoking Old Testament kingship had been to urge English princes to use the royal supremacy to advance religious reform.[194] We have seen how Edward VI was described as Josiah by churchmen who wished him to purify the English temple.[195] Presbyterian ministers in Scotland naturally rejected the notion that princes were ordained by God to 'prescribe a policie' to the kirk. Buchanan's *De iure regni* assumed that a magistrate's election, duties and even the circumstances justifying his deposition were entirely civil concerns. His insistence that kings could not take 'legal principle' from Hebrew kings precluded their right to direct the ecclesiastical polity. Instead, as we have seen, Buchanan directed his royal pupil to imitate

191 McDonald, *Jacobean kirk*, pp. 13, 16.

192 James Kirk (ed.), *The second book of discipline* (Edinburgh, 1980), p. 117.

193 David Calderwood, *The history of the kirk of Scotland*, ed. Thomas Thomson, 8 vols. (Edinburgh, 1842–9), vol. III, p. 413.

194 Margaret P. Hannay, *Philip's phoenix: Mary Sidney, Countess of Pembroke* (New York, 1990), pp. 91–5; John N. King, 'Henry VIII as David: The king's image and Reformation politics', in Mark Rankin, Christopher Highley and John N. King (eds.), *Henry VIII and his afterlives: Literature, politics, and art* (Cambridge, 2009), pp. 34–52 and *Tudor royal iconography: Literature and art in an age of religious crisis* (Princeton, 1989), pp. 34–6, 76–88, 90–3, 254–6; Philip Melanchthon, *Corpus Reformatorum: Philippi Melanchthonis opera quae supersunt omnia*, ed. Karl Gottlieb Bretschneider and Heinrich Ernst Bindseil, 28 vols. (Halle, 1834–1859), vol. II, p. 928.

195 Stephen Alford, *Kingship and politics in the reign of Edward VI* (Cambridge, 2002), pp. 32–64.

Seneca's *rex stoicus*, a king who was 'God-like' in moral reticence and zeal for the commonwealth but who gleaned no 'godly' authority through his institution or pagan proof-texts. In 1567 Buchanan's account of kingship made him an odd Calvinist; in 1579 it made him a good Presbyterian. Not only did Buchanan limit his royal pupil's power over the civil polity but he also excluded him from ecclesiastical government altogether.

At least one of Buchanan's contemporaries regarded the printed *De iure regni* as an intervention in the debate about Scottish bishops – his student prince James VI. The king argued in 1599 and 1603 that the problem with the Reformation in Scotland had been that 'fierie spirited men in the ministrie' had wrought religious change by rebelling against the crown rather than receiving reform through a 'prince's order'. Moreover, these advocates of 'paritie in the Church' were emboldened by the 'fantasie' that they were living under a classically instituted 'popular government'. In James's caricature of Buchanan's account of popular sovereignty, the civil polity was an 'imagined Democracie' or republic in which kirk ministers proclaimed themselves 'Tribuni plebis'.[196] As an adult king, James recognised the sympathy between Buchanan's *rex stoicus* and the Presbyterian usurpation of the ecclesiastical polity in Scotland. J. N. Figgis, Mason and Pocock have all remarked on this passage yet have been puzzled at James's conflation of Buchanan's republicanism and Presbyterianism.[197] By revisiting the context of the 1579 printing of *De iure regni*, however, we can see more clearly why James VI was justified in deeming the dialogue to be a threat to his political *and* ecclesiastical authority from the first.

Buchanan used his published writings to augment and broadcast the disciplinary regime he had established for James at Stirling to a wide audience. His *imago regis* and description of the objects of royal education were not innocuous add-ons to his political theory. Instead, Buchanan ratcheted up the levels of emotional self-control required of a good king from the baseline proposed by Erasmus, drastically limited the legislative and judicial authority of the (hereditary) prince and threatened real and harsh penalties for deviance. At the same time, Buchanan distinguished his description of good government from Calvinist accounts of godly kingship in order to exclude Scottish rulers from the spiritual and ecclesiastical authority of Hebrew kings. Buchanan discharged his pedagogical

[196] James, *BD*, p. 26.

[197] J. N. Figgis, *The theory of the divine right of kings* (Cambridge, 1896), pp. 135–6; Mason, 'George Buchanan, James VI and the Presbyterians'; Pocock, 'Two kingdoms and three histories?', pp. 120–1, 301.

obligations to the King's Party by aggressively curbing James's lawful realm of political and religious activity. Finally, Buchanan urged the king's Scottish subjects to become his new schoolmasters and to enforce the same standard of absolute obedience that Buchanan had required at Stirling.

JAMES VI, THE ROYAL REBEL

As an adult ruler, James VI and I rejected Buchanan's prescriptions with vigour. In his treatise on the nature and extent of kingship, *The trew law of free monarchies*, he claimed that royal power was established by God and was unfettered by human laws or institutions. It was the king, James argued, who was really the 'great Schoole-master of the whole land' and his 'schollers', or subjects, could not displace him 'upon any pretext'.[198] James argued that God had plainly declared 'the obedience that the people owe to their King' in 1 Samuel 8:11–20, a passage Buchanan had claimed was irrelevant to sixteenth-century rulers. Moreover, he insisted that, far from being irrelevant to contemporary Christian government, the 'erection… and the law' of the Hebrew kings 'may, and ought to bee a paterne to all Christian and well founded Monarchies, as being founded by God himself'.[199] In short, Buchanan's attempt to shape James's ideas about kingship had failed; his former pupil emerged from his schoolroom to become one of Europe's leading proponents of the divine right of kings. Roger Mason and Peter Lake have made compelling arguments that, despite the time that elapsed between the *De iure regni* and James's adult political writings, the king intended to refute his schoolmaster's *imago regis* in his treatises.[200] As this section will show, James's rebellion against Buchanan's teaching began rather earlier than historians have suspected. The king discovered his intellectual weapons in the methods and texts of his schoolroom.

In September 1579, nine months after the publication of *De iure regni*, James's nascent desire to evade Buchanan's clutches found a focus and outlet in the arrival of Esmé Stuart (1542–83), sixth Sieur d'Aubigny. D'Aubigny was a French nobleman of charm, wit, liberal means and, if the king's rapidly escalating clothing expenses are indicative, a covetable wardrobe.[201] Following d'Aubigny's dubious conversion to Protestantism,

198 James, *Trew law*, p. 76.

199 James, *Trew law*, pp. 68, 70; see also Buchanan, *De iure regni*, pp. 109–11.

200 Lake, 'The king (the queen) and the Jesuit', pp. 243–60; Mason, 'Rex stoicus', p. 129.

201 Calderwood, *History of the kirk*, vol. III, pp. 456–61; Melville, *Autobiography and diary*, pp. 76–7. For James's new clothes purchased in December 1579, see *ATS*, vol. XIII, pp. 296–301. On Lennox in Scotland, see Caroline Bingham, *James VI of Scotland* (London, 1979), pp. 50–66 and the more positive appraisal in Stewart, *Cradle king*, pp. 51–71.

James promoted him to the earldom then duchy of Lennox. Part of Lennox's attraction for James was that he represented the deferential, luxurious, sensual and courtly life that Buchanan despised. He also offered him the affection that James claimed to have craved and Buchanan never offered.[202] The Frenchman's immediate and extensive influence led to a deterioration in the king's relationship with Elizabeth I, the rise into royal favour of James Stewart, subsequently the earl of Arran (1545–96), and the fall and execution of the earl of Morton in 1581.[203] The kirk's hatred of Lennox and Arran encouraged them to mourn their former foe, Morton, wholeheartedly. One of its self-appointed historians, David Calderwood, wrote that the earl's demise showed 'how absurd it is to commit the reins of government to the hands of a child, who cannot govern himself'.[204] Kirk ministers were convinced that Lennox was in the pay of 'the Pope, the King of France, and the Guisians'.[205] Lennox and Arran's influence loosened Buchanan's iron grip on the king, and the twelve-year-old slipped away forever.

James Melville, the Presbyterian minister, claimed that Lennox and Arran countered Buchanan's ideological teachings with more than the temptations of velvet doublets and silken hose. Between them, they allegedly taught James to refute Buchanan's depiction of the 'Reformation of Religion' in Scotland by claiming that it was 'done by a privie faction, turbulentlie and treasonablie' against the crown, a claim that James certainly echoed in his *Basilicon doron*. Lennox and Arran supposedly described those who had deposed Mary as the king's 'unfrindis' and Lennox facilitated correspondence between the queen of Scots and her son and a short-lived 'Political Association' grew between them in 1582. In addition to breaking with the anti-Marianism of the King's Party, Melville claimed that Lennox and Arran 'put the opinion of absolut powar in his Majestie's head'.[206] Arran found a sympathetic bishop, Patrick Adamson (1537–92), who publically asserted 'that a Christian King should be the chief governour of the Kirk' on James's behalf, while Melville lamented that, having been 'sa weill a brought upe' in his youth by Buchanan and Young, the king was 'miserablie corrupted' by the counsellors of his adolescence.[207]

[202] Maurice Lee, *Great Britain's Solomon: James VI and his three kingdoms* (Urbana, 1990), p. 233.
[203] Stewart, *Cradle king*, pp. 58–62.
[204] Calderwood, *History of the kirk*, vol. III, p. 575.
[205] Calderwood, *History of the kirk*, vol. III, pp. 460–1.
[206] Melville, *Autobiography and diary*, p. 119. For the correspondence, see BL, Cotton MS Caligula C VI, fol. 20^{r-v}; SP 53/11, fol. 44^{r}; SP 53/12, fol. 12^{r-v}.
[207] Melville, *Autobiography and diary*, p. 120.

Despite his failing health, Buchanan was well aware of these unhappy developments. In his last public letter to James, written in 1582, he lamented that 'this regime' – presumably the government of the King's Party and Presbyterian kirk – 'was hastening towards destruction and overthrow in all things'.[208] Buchanan's prayer for its delivery seemed to have been answered when a band of (supposedly) Presbyterian and (certainly) anti-Lennox lairds, known as the Ruthven Raiders, captured the king in August 1582. James only escaped their clutches in June 1583. Thereafter, he pondered the mechanisms by which he could extinguish the rebellious hydra that Buchanan's republican theories had unleashed in Scotland.

In his cogitations, the king rejected the ideology of his schoolroom but he did not ignore its authors or methods. In November 1583 he established himself at Holyrood House, Edinburgh, in readiness for the coming parliamentary convention. He asked Peter Young to send him a chest of forty-six volumes from his library at Stirling, which included Buchanan's works.[209] James requested certain classical texts that he seems to have suspected Buchanan used to authorise his political writings, such as Cicero's *De officiis* and the orations of Demosthenes. James also asked Young to send him chronicles of Scotland other than Buchanan's *Rerum Scoticarum historia*. They included a copy of Hector Boethius' *Historia Scotorum* (Paris, 1574) and John Leslie's *De origine, moribus et rebus gestis Scotorum* (Rome, 1578), which he knew was hostile to Buchanan's perspective.[210] The other telling item on James's list was John Cheke's *Hurt of sedicion*, which fulminated against the supposedly pious and civic motives that had inspired the 1549 rebellions against Edward VI. 'How... do you take in hande to reform [religion]?' Cheke had demanded of the insurgents, since 'Goddes worde teacheth us [tha]t no man should take in hand any office, but [tha]t he is called of God like Aaron. What Moses I praye you, called you? What God?'[211] James was starting to ask similar questions of Buchanan's description of the rebellions against his mother and grandmother. He set out to 'confer' these works against his schoolmaster's writings, much as Peter Young had taught him to do at Stirling.

James's scholarly deliberations resulted in a swift verdict. On 22 May 1584, the king and his three estates declared that Buchanan's *De iure regni* and *Rerum Scoticarum historia* encouraged 'the dishonour and prejudice of

[208] 'Hanc potestatem, in omnium rerum exitium & ruinam properantem': Buchanan, *Rerum Scoticarum historia*, fol. *.*r.

[209] Warner, pp. xxxv–xxxvii. [210] Warner, pp. xxxv–xxxvii.

[211] John Cheke, *The hurt of sedicion howe greueous it is to a commune welth* (London, 1549), STC 5109, sig. Aiv^{r-v}; Warner, p. xxxv.

his hienes, his parentis, progenitouris and estate' and stirred up his 'subjectis thairby to mislyking, seditioun, unquietnes and to cast of thair dew obedience'. Anyone in possession of either volume was required to deliver it up so that 'the offensive and extraordinare materis' could be purged on pain of a £200 fine.[212] In James's first printed work, *Essayes of a prentise in the divine art of poesie* (1584), he issued a blunt prohibition against subjects 'wryting anything of materis of commoun weill'. It was much 'to grave materis', James protested, 'for a Poet to mell in'.[213] In his *Basilicon doron*, he would iterate a slightly more nuanced version of his argument for censoring Buchanan's works: the poet's 'famous inuectives' and libels allowed 'the very spirits of these archbellouses of rebellion' to 'make transition' to later readers and owners, further perpetuating the hurt of sedition to the commonwealth.[214] James implied that he was still fighting its spectre in 1603.

Finally, in May 1584 James and the earl of Arran issued the so-called 'Black Acts'. They asserted James's royal supremacy 'over all statis, alsweill spirituall as temporall' and his plenary legislative and judicial powers.[215] Patrick Adamson leapt to defend the nascent royal supremacy: it was a return to the true form of godly monarchy that had been 'established by the exa[m]ples of the godly gouernouris, Iuges and Kings of the ancient Testament', he declared. Ironically, he credited James's education for making him 'ane Theologue', sufficiently learned in 'the knawledge of the heauenly Philosophie' to divine his office truly.[216] Confronted by this hostile regime, Andrew Melville, Presbyterians ministers and anti-Arran lairds fled south. The exiles swiftly secured Elizabeth I's armed backing and returned to Scotland in October 1585. Arran's authority collapsed and James was compelled to agree that the Black Acts would not be enforced any longer.[217] Yet James's rebellion against Buchanan, the King's Party, the Ruthven Raiders and the Presbyterians in Scotland was not over. The king had set out his political and ecclesiastical agenda and Mason has shown how the king worked towards the reinstatement of the Black Acts – gradually and obliquely at times – for the next twelve years. At the General Assembly of Perth in February 1597, the political 'tide turned for James'.[218] Assemblies after Perth no longer fought to keep Christ's kingdom in

[212] *RPS*, 1584/5/14.
[213] James VI and I, 'Ane schort treatise, conteining some reulis and cautelis to be observit and eschewit in Scottis poesie' (1584), in *James VI and I: Selected writings*, eds. Neil Rhodes, Jennifer Richards and Joseph Marshall (Aldershot, 2003), p. 35.
[214] James, *BD*, p. 46. [215] *RPS*, 1584/5/8.
[216] Patrick Adamson, *A declaratioun of the kings maiesties intentioun and meaning toward the lait actis of Parliament* (Edinburgh [London], 1585), STC 21948.7, sigs. Aii^{v}, Aiv^{r}.
[217] McDonald, *Jacobean kirk*, p. 29. [218] Mason, 'Rex stoicus', p. 135.

'friedom'. Instead, James Melville complained, they pondered 'whow Kirk and Relligioun may be framed to the politic esteat of a frie Monarchie, and to advance and promot the grandour of man, and supream absolut authoritie in all causses, and over all persones, asweill Ecclesiastical as Civill'.[219] It was in 1598, the following year, that James VI laid out *The trew law of free monarchies* in Scotland. James's rebellion against Buchanan was critical in shaping his own understanding of kingship. Between 1582 and 1584, the king had begun to use the methods and texts of his education to transform his instinctive dislike of his pedagogue's strictures into a political rebuttal of Buchanan's account of kingship.

JAMES VI'S *PARAPHRASE* (*c.* 1585) AND *MEDITATIOUNS* (1588, 1589)

Scholarly accounts of James's rejection of Buchanan's teachings and his persistent pursuit of legally unfettered authority offer a persuasive account of the development of James's *political* thought. A problem seems to emerge, however, when James VI's religious writings are admitted into evidence. Indeed, it poses enough of a threat that the king's early biblical exegeses and paraphrases have been omitted from both major modern editions of his writings on statecraft, despite the centrality of religious proof-texts to his account of kingship.[220] Apart from his 1584 *Essayes of a prentice*, these exegetical works constituted James's earliest circulated writings. One might expect to be able to see the royal rebel at work in the *Paraphrase upon the Reuelation* (*c.* 1585, printed 1616), the *Fruitfull meditatioun... of the 20 chapter of the Reuelation* (1588) and *Ane meditatioun upon... the XV chapter of the first buke of the chronicles of the kingis* (1589). Instead, James VI spent the six years following the Black Acts propagating works that appeared to regurgitate the anti-Catholic polemics of his schoolroom and suggested his support for conciliar political culture and a Presbyterian kirk in Scotland. The final sections of this essay will re-examine these problematic exegetical works to argue that they were more significant in shaping James's mature account of kingship than historians have acknowledged.

The context for the circulation of James VI's exegetical writings between 1585 and 1589 was the Anglo–Spanish war (1585–1604).[221] By the

[219] Melville, *Autobiography and diary*, p. 414.

[220] James VI and I, *The political works of James I*, ed. Charles Howard McIlwain (Cambridge, 1918) and *Political writings*, ed. J. P. Sommerville (Cambridge, 1994).

[221] James VI, *Ane fruitfull meditatioun contening ane plane and facill expositioun of ye 7.8.9 and 10 versis of the 20 chap. of the Reuelatioun in forme of ane sermone* (Edinburgh, 1588), STC 14376, sig. Bii^v and *Ane meditatioun vpon the xxv, xxvi, xxvii, xxviii, and xxix verses of the XV chapt[er] of the first buke of the Chronicles of the Kingis* (Edinburgh, 1589), STC 14380, sig. Aiii^v.

terms of the Treaty of Nonsuch, signed in August 1585, Elizabeth I committed troops and a subsidy to support the Protestant revolt against the imperial authority of Philip II in the Netherlands. Facing the probability of a Spanish counter-attack against the British isle, England and Scotland signed a mutual defence accord, the Treaty of Berwick, in July 1586. Following Elizabeth I's execution of Mary, Queen of Scots, in February 1587, the English naval success against the great Spanish Armada in August 1588 and their (sporadically paid) subsidy to the Scots kept the alliance firm.[222] The Spanish posed an ideological threat as well as a military menace in Scotland, where the war exacerbated the General Assembly's anxiety about Catholic nobles and Jesuit missionaries. The king was, by now, unpopular amongst the godly members of the kirk, but the Spanish threat encouraged a temporary cease-fire in the name of unity against a common threat. Presbyterian ministers urged the king to purge the country of papists or at least to make respectable attempts to persecute them.[223]

James's biblical exegeses in this period *appear* to be attempts to affirm the Treaty of Berwick and give heart to kirk ministers. According to James Montagu (1568–1618), bishop of Winchester and James's chaplain and literary editor, in 1616, James's first volley in the conflict, his *Paraphrase on Revelation*, was written before the king turned twenty.[224] It was in circulation by early January 1586, when Elizabeth I claimed to have read and admired it.[225] James may have deemed his description of the final battle against the Antichrist to be a stirring gift for a fellow sovereign who was about to enter into the bloody theatre of the Netherlands. The *Paraphrase* also signalled his readiness to share in the fight against Satan's forces on earth and to fire the 'speciall cannon' of Revelation 'against the Hereticall wall of our common aduersaries the Papists'.[226]

The theological writings that James had studied at Stirling shaped his exegesis. In his introduction, addressed to the 'church militant', James revealed that he had been persuaded of the apostolic authority of Revelation by Théodore de Bèze's defence of it in his New Testament, which Young had given James in April 1577.[227] James followed reformers

[222] Julian Goodare, 'James VI's English subsidy', in Julian Goodare and Michael Lynch (eds.), *The reign of James VI* (East Linton, 2000), pp. 110–25.

[223] McDonald, *Jacobean kirk*, pp. 35–42.

[224] James Montagu, 'Preface to the reader', in James, *Workes of the most high and mighty prince*, sig. d3^{v}.

[225] Elizabeth I, *Elizabeth I: Collected works*, eds. Leah Marcus, Janel Mueller and Mary Beth Rose (Chicago, 2000), p. 268.

[226] James, 'Paraphrase upon the Reuelation', in *Workes of the most high and mighty prince*, p. 2.

[227] Warner, p. xlvii.

since Martin Luther in describing the 'second beast' prophesied by John in Revelation – the Antichrist, the great whore, the 'tyrannicall and hereticall Monarchie' – as the papacy.[228] He echoed the sermons of Zurich reformer Heinrich Bullinger, which he had received in June 1577, in regarding Revelation as a prophesy that the end of the world would occur and the true church would survive.[229] The king also drew his interpretation of a number of John's visions from Bullinger's *Sermons* – that the four horses represented gospel-preaching, war, plague and heresy, and death; that the grasshoppers and locusts were plagues of monks and friars (for James, Jesuits); and that the woman clothed in the sun was the church, pregnant with Christ.[230] However, James departed from Bullinger's interpretation of the first judgement (Revelation 20:4–5) in order to insist that only those 'who were predestinate before all beginnings… ascendeth immediately into heauen'.[231] The king's *Paraphrase on Revelation* was, therefore, conventionally Calvinist. He showed that he had absorbed Young's confessional instruction and could use it to assure Elizabeth, and other English and Scottish readers, that their Spanish enemies were destined to be 'troubled with warres within and without, and with all kinds of plagues' and eventually succumb to Christ's judgement.[232]

In his anti-papal exegesis, he even hinted that he saw the disadvantages of uniting temporal and ecclesiastical authority in the one office. James criticised the pope for combining 'hereticall Tyrannie over the consciences of men' with tyranny in 'ciuill gouernment'.[233] Earlier that year James's erstwhile ally, Patrick Adamson, the bishop of St Andrews, had argued that the ecclesiastical form of Roman Catholicism actually resembled Presbyterianism; both churches claimed to be the sole authority on spirituals but both took to the pulpit to lecture temporal powers on their duties.[234] This was the critique that James VI would return to in his *Basilicon doron*.[235] In the *Paraphrase*, however, James described the powers

[228] James, 'Paraphrase upon the Reuelation', in *Workes of the most high and mighty prince*, p. 44; see also Irene Backus, *Reformation readings of the apocalypse: Geneva, Zurich and Wittenberg* (Oxford, 2000), p. 8.

[229] Heinrich Bullinger, *A hundred sermons vpon the Apocalipse of Iesu Christ*, trans. John Daus (London, 1573), STC 4062, fol. 6r; James, 'Paraphrase upon the Reuelation', in *Workes of the most high and mighty prince*, p. 5; Warner, pp. xli, lxvi.

[230] James, 'Paraphrase upon the Reuelation', in *Workes of the most high and mighty prince*, pp. 24–6, 27, 37; Bullinger, *A hundred sermons upon the Apocalipse*, fols. 86^{r-v}, 115^{v}–116^{r}, 159^{v}–160^{r}.

[231] James, 'Paraphrase upon the Reuelation', in *Workes of the most high and mighty prince*, p. 64, cf. Bullinger, *A hundred sermons upon the Apocalipse*, fols. 273^{r}–275^{v}.

[232] James, 'Paraphrase upon the Reuelation', in *Workes of the most high and mighty prince*, p. 50.

[233] James, 'Paraphrase upon the Reuelation', in *Workes of the most high and mighty prince*, p. 55.

[234] Adamson, *A declaratioun*, sig. Aiv^{r}.

[235] James, *BD*, p. 45.

claimed by the pope as a perverted form of royal supremacy. Satan's power in the world was 'farre greater' because the papal 'monarchie' combined spiritual and political authority.[236] James implied in his *Paraphrase upon Revelation* that the concentration of plenary authority had facilitated the reign of the Antichrist in the world.

The king distilled his exegesis on Revelation for a wider audience in the months following the English success against the Armada. In his *Fruitfull meditatioun on Revelation* (20:7–10), printed in October or November 1588, James focused on the moment when Satan was loosed in the world and assembled his forces against the 'beloued Cittie' of the saints for the final battle. God would save his people, John revealed, by casting the Devil into the lake of fire and brimstone. James pointed to the contemporary persecution of the 'saintis' in France, the Netherlands and the Electorate of Cologne and warned the Scots and English that the 'ciuill Sworde' of the Antichrist had now 'cum fordwart against this Ile'.[237] Spain's first target had been England but James reminded the Scots that they were also 'in ye tentis of ye saintis & belouit citie'.[238] Thus he proposed that the inhabitants of the British isle 'incourage ane another to vse lawfull resistance… as warriouris in ane camp and citizenis of ane belouit citie'. Together, they would defend 'our liberties, natiue countrie, and lyfes' against the 'vsurpit supremacie' of the pope, 'the Iesuitis, his last and maist pernicious vermine' and 'the Princes of the earth his slauis'.[239] This was more than an affirmation of the Treaty of Berwick. James explicitly aligned the civil liberties of the Scots (and, perhaps, the English) with their reformed religion, and he advocated resistance to tyranny. He urged them, moreover, to 'concur ane with another' and form a civil association for their mutual protection.[240] James had learnt enough in his schoolroom to ventriloquise Buchanan's civic humanism with aplomb.

At least one Presbyterian minister, Patrick Galloway (*c.* 1551–1626), was persuaded that exegetical study of Revelation had brought James back to the godly fold after his rebellion in the early 1580s. Galloway was not an easy man to turn. He had been a pestilent preacher against Lennox – indeed, in 1582 the duke had actually tried to attack him in his pulpit.[241] And he was an ally of the Ruthven Raiders. In May 1584, he was exiled from Scotland

[236] James, 'Paraphrase upon the Reuelation', in *Workes of the most high and mighty prince*, p. 39.

[237] James, *Ane fruitfull meditatioun*, sig. Bii^v.

[238] James, *Ane fruitfull meditatioun*, sig. Biii^v.

[239] James, *Ane fruitfull meditatioun*, sigs. Biv^r, Bii^r.

[240] James, *Ane fruitfull meditatioun*, sig. Biv^r.

[241] Calderwood, *History of the kirk*, vol. IV, p. 38.

for refusing to acknowledge the authority of the Black Acts.[242] In February 1588 he was one of a delegation of ministers who lobbied James to root out papists in Scotland.[243] In October 1588, however, Galloway condescended to write the preface to *A fruitefull meditatioun*. There, he lauded his king's 'unfeinzeit loue toward trew religioun' and took his proof-text for James's rule from Isaiah 49:23: the king had been 'appointed be God to be ane nurisner of the [kirk]... in that maist perillous tyme'.[244] The anti-Catholic argument of *A fruitfull meditatioun*, larded with talk of godly 'citizens', had won over at least one doubting minister.

In 1589, Galloway went further still in his praise. As a newly appointed minister of King James's household, he provided an even oilier preface for James's next printed *Meditatioun upon... the XV chapter of the first buke of the Chronicles* (1 Chronicles 15:25–9). Once again Galloway praised James as a 'nursing fatheris' to the kirk. He also hailed him as a second 'Salamon', God's 'lietenandrie' not only in his 'awin boundis' in Scotland but also to 'haill reformed christian Kirkes in the earth'.[245] He was, according to Galloway, the potential leader of the church militant. What had James written to inspire such an encomium? The king took his text from the part of the Chronicles that described King David's establishment of the Ark of the Covenant in Jerusalem, following his great military victory over the Philistines. In his exegesis, James took care to show that King David had sought the 'concurrence of his hail estaitis' in undertaking this great action, indicating that even the great Israelite king had ruled with the active consent of his subjects.[246] Indeed James spent the entire second part of the *Meditatioun upon... the Chronicles* describing the three estates who had participated in the translation of the Ark and who had shared in the government of the Israelites. First were the 'Elderis of Israel', who administered 'iustice and iudgement to the kingis subiectes' in towns and the countryside. They reminded James of 'twa of the estaitis of our kingdome, the Barroun and the Burges'. Second were the 'Captains ouer thousands of men', perhaps the noble lairds, who 'did rewle in tyme of weir'. Their role was to 'subdew the enemies of his kirk'.[247]

Finally, and most critically for ministers such as Galloway, James explained that David had been accompanied in his journey to set up the Ark by the 'Priests and Leuites' in his kingdom.[248] Kevin Sharpe has suggested that, in

[242] Richard L. Greaves, 'Galloway, Patrick (c. 1551–1626)', *ODNB*.
[243] McDonald, *Jacobean kirk*, pp. 26, 41–2.
[244] James, *Ane fruitfull meditatioun*, sig. Aii^{r}.
[245] Patrick Galloway, 'To the Christian reader', in James, *Meditatioun upon... the Chronicles*, sig. Aii^{r}.
[246] James, *Meditatioun upon... the Chronicles*, sig. Aiii^{v}.
[247] James, *Meditatioun upon... the Chronicles*, sig. Aiv^{v}.
[248] James, *Meditatioun upon... the Chronicles*, sig. Bi^{r}.

these lines, James was issuing a 'royal command' to the estates and General Assembly to travel with him in matters of religion.[249] Yet *Ane fruitfull meditatioun* emphasised that it was David, in fact, who had had to back down. James had David acknowledge to his priests that the first time he had attempted to set up the Ark he had neglected to take 'thair counsaill' and so angered 'ye Lord our God... For we socht him not efter dew order'. When David revisited the issue of the Ark, he realised that the Lord required him to act in concert with his priests. Thus, James concluded that it 'is to be market weill of Princes' that 'David dois nothing in matteris appertening to God without ye presence and special concurrence of Goodis Ministeris appointit to be spirituall rewlleris in his Kirk'.[250] No wonder Galloway had come around. In his *Meditatioun* James publically repudiated the divisive Black Acts of 1584 as not reflecting 'dew ordour' of government in Scotland, and lauded the 'spirituall rewlleris' of the presbyteries.

What had possessed James to endorse so many of Buchanan's cherished causes in his religious writings between 1585 and 1589?[251] The most persuasive explanation is that James's exegeses were part of a thick, rhetorical smokescreen.[252] James had begun the stratagem that he pursued in England after 1603 of cultivating the confessional enemies of whichever religious group he was finding most troublesome. In the early 1580s, the threat came from the Presbyterians, so he had begun to consort with Catholics in Scotland. In 1588 and 1589 James continued to protect his new favourite, the Catholic George Gordon, earl of Huntly (1562–1636), despite mounting English intelligence that Huntly was conspiring to support a Spanish invasion of the British isle.[253] Even Huntly's armed insurrection against James in the summer of 1589 – the Brig o' Dee affair – merely earned him a short warding at Borthwick Castle.[254] Other monarchs would have deemed

249 Sharpe, 'King's writ', p. 126. 250 James, *Meditatioun upon... the Chronicles*, sig. Bi^r.

251 Daniel Fischlin, '"To eate the flesh of kings": James VI and I, apocalypse, nation and sovereignty', in Daniel Fischlin and Mark Fortier (eds.), *Royal subjects: Essays on the writings of James VI and I* (Detroit, 2002); W. B. Patterson, *King James VI and I and the reunion of Christendom* (New York, 1997), pp. 17–18; Malcolm Smuts, 'The making of *rex pacificus*: James VI and I and the problem of peace in an age of religious war', in Daniel Fischlin and Mark Fortier (eds.), *Royal subjects: Essays on the writings of James VI and I* (Detroit, 2002), pp. 372–5; Jenny Wormald, '"Tis true I am a cradle king": The view from the throne', in Julian Goodare and Michael Lynch (eds.), *The reign of James VI* (East Linton, 2000), pp. 249–50.

252 Rickard, *Authorship and authority*, pp. 69–95; Stewart, *Cradle king*, p. 96; Astrid Stilma, 'James VI and I as a religious writer', in Crawford Gribben and David G. Mullan (eds.), *Literature and the Scottish Reformation* (Aldershot, 2009), pp. 127–41.

253 SP 52/43, fols. 11^r–13^r.

254 Ruth Grant, 'The Brig o' Dee affair, the sixth earl of Huntly and the politics of the Counter-Reformation', in Julian Goodare and Michael Lynch, *The Reign of James VI* (East Linton, 2000).

this treason. Through the earl of Huntly, moreover, James had been meeting regularly with Jesuits. On 5 February 1588, James cheerfully debated scripture with James Gordon Huntly (1541–1620), his favourite's uncle and the head of the Jesuit ministry in Scotland, in front of courtiers and Presbyterian ministers.[255] There was little chance that the king would be converted, but he seemed to enjoy Gordon's company far too much. All of this enraged the General Assembly, whose ministers were frantic about the possibility that Spanish soldiers would get into the country with the help of Scottish papists.[256] It also jeopardised the potentially lucrative English subsidy that had netted James £5,000 in 1588. One of the terms of its continuance was the expulsion of the Jesuits from Scotland.[257] The English joined the ministers of the kirk in urging James that the honourable and prudent course for a godly king would be to strike against papists.

James VI was not enamoured of the papacy but (at this stage in his life) he felt no animosity towards court Catholics he deemed loyal. Indeed he found men like Lennox and Huntly considerably more congenial than the swarm of godly ministers and English ambassadors that buzzed around the royal ears. The purpose, then, of James's printed and circulated *Paraphrase* and *Meditatiouns* was to placate the kirk and the English embassy with words rather than deeds. James regurgitated the anti-Catholic polemics of his schoolroom and paraphrased his former pedagogue's 'popular' language. His declaration of support for the civic involvement of the estates in government, the 'spirituall rewlleris' of the kirk by its ministers and the prospective triumph of the godly over the tyrannical, heretical and enslaving forces of Spain and Rome was hardly his 'upricht and anefauld [honest] meaning' regarding 'this so greit and weichtie ane caus'.[258]

JAMES VI: 'MONARCHIE IS THE TREW PATERNE OF DIUINITIE'

James VI's printed biblical exegeses were dissimulating pieces of propaganda but a neglected manuscript in the Bodleian Library, Oxford, suggests that they did not start life that way. The holograph drafts of the king's *Meditatiouns* lack the appeals to the 'mutual amitie' of the elect, the civic virtue of resistance or the 'spirituall rewlleris' of the kirk that

[255] BL, Cotton MS Caligula D I, fol. 275r.
[256] Calderwood, *History of the kirk*, vol. v, pp. 2, 7.
[257] BL, Cotton MS Caligula C VII, fol. 274r; Goodare, 'James VI's English subsidy', pp. 114, 116; SP 52/39, fols. 53v–54r.
[258] James, *Meditatioun upon… the Chronicles*, sig. Aiiiv.

mark the printed versions.[259] The manuscripts suggest that, when James was casting around for placating literary gestures in the late 1580s, he revised and re-purposed several biblical exegeses he had been working on privately to serve a new purpose. They suggest, moreover, that James had actually begun his exegeses with the intent to probe Buchanan's account of Scottish kingship.

The two most significant differences between the manuscript and printed versions of James's *Fruitfull meditatioen on Revelation* relate to the status of the elect and their 'lawfull resistance' to incipient tyranny in the text. The printed work contained a substantial passage, absent from the manuscript, that detailed the 'mutuall amitie and freindlie coniunctioun in loue amangis' members of the elect and their 'concurrence to mancene [maintain] the guid caus that thair God hes cled them with'.[260] It had been added, one might suppose, to reaffirm James's public commitment to the 'guid caus' of the Treaty of Berwick, despite his apparent dealings with Jesuits in Scotland. Also absent from James's private draft of the *Fruitfull meditatioen* was his stirring conclusion that all the 'citizenis of ane belouit citie' should 'concur ane with another' for the 'defence of our liberties, natiue countrie, and lyfes'.[261] His apparent enthusiasm for bonds of association amongst subjects pursuing their 'liberties' was a last-minute addition for the benefit of the English and the kirk.

These strategic additions pale in comparison to James's thorough reworking of his *Meditatioun upon… the Chronicles*. The manuscript's structure is entirely different from the printed exegesis and omits the entire 'second part' of the printed discourse, in which James had described David's eagerness to make citizens and priests his partners in setting up the Ark of the Covenant. In his original version of the *Meditatioun*, the Elders, the Captains and the Priests of Israel do not contribute to the establishment of the unified church of Israel. Nor does David rely on the kirk to provide 'spirituall rewlleris' for his people.[262] It was the king alone who 'beildit a house fo the Arke of the lorde' and with 'great solemnitie & glaidness bringis it to the same'.[263] In the version of the *Meditatioun* that James penned, but deemed imprudent to print in 1589,

[259] James, 'A meditation upon the 26, 27, 28 and 29 verses of the 15 chap. of the first of the Chronicles' and 'A meditation upon the 7, 8, 9, 10 verses of the 20 chap. of the Reuelation', in Bodleian, MS Bodley 165, fols. 65r–69r and 70r–74r, respectively. Their existence is noted by Stilma, 'James VI and I as a religious writer', pp. 136–7.

[260] Cf. Bodleian, MS Bodley 165, fol. 71r and James, *Ane fruitfull meditatioun*, sig. Aivv.

[261] Cf. Bodleian, MS Bodley 165, fol. 73v and James, *Ane fruitfull meditatioun*, sig. Bivr.

[262] Cf. Bodleian, MS Bodley 165, fol. 66r and James, *Meditatioun upon… the Chronicles*, sig. Aivv–Bir.

[263] Bodleian, MS Bodley 165, fol. 66v.

David was a monarch raised by God and answerable to him alone. He governed his people temporally and spiritually.

The presence of this biblically derived claim for a royal supremacy in James's papers suggests that the menace of the Armada and the anti-Catholic buzzings of the kirk and the English had not closed his eyes to an outstanding ideological threat to his office in Scotland: the writings of his former schoolmaster, George Buchanan. It is striking that, in his first (surviving) attempts at adult biblical exegesis, James VI selected texts that Buchanan had insisted provided no reliable model for lawful, Christian kingship. In his draft *Meditatioun on Chronicles*, James devoted the concluding section of his exegesis to examining 'hou pertinentlie this place' in the Old Testament 'dois apparteine to us & oure present estaite'. Just as Israel was 'oppugnid by the nationis' of the Philistines who 'hatteris so his holy worde', Scotland was pursued by Spanish papists. If anything, James claimed, 'Scotland's' victory over Spain was 'farr more notable then that of israellis' over their enemies, because it was much more clearly 'wroche by the hande of godd', who had blown the Armada off course.[264] These parallels not only indicated that the Scots were God's 'choosid' people but also that James's kingship over them could be rightly compared to David's.

James would continue to emphasise the relevance of Old Testament kingship to his rule, especially the government of David. In his first speech to the English Parliament in March 1603, the king prayed that God, who had favoured him with victories of peace, as he had favoured David's 'by-past victories of warre… shall also now grant me victory ouer that uncircumcised Philistine'.[265] The English took this comparison fairly well, or at least well enough that James did not hesitate to 'make king David… the foremost scriptural model for Jacobean iconography' in his southern kingdom too.[266] In his *Basilicon doron*, his pedagogical prescriptions for his sons, James contradicted Buchanan directly on the value of studying Hebrew kings: in 'the bookes of the *Kings* [1–2 Samuel and 1–2 Kings] and *Chronicles*… shall yee see your selfe, as in a myrror'; 'the Psalmes of Dauid are the meetest schoole-master that ye can be acquainted with… the composer thereof was a King: and therefore best behoued to know a Kings wants'.[267] Armed with such knowledge, Henry might also 'be called

264 Bodleian, MS Bodley 165, fol. 68r.

265 James, 'A speech, as it was delivered in the upper house of the Parliament… XIX day of March 1603', in *Political writings*, p. 134.

266 John N. King, 'James I and King David: Jacobean iconography and its legacy', in Daniel Fischlin and Mark Fortier (eds.), *Royal subjects: Essays on the writings of James VI and I* (Detroit, 2002), p. 42.

267 James, *BD*, pp. 15, 16.

a louing nourish-father to the Church' – not merely a supporter of the kirk but ready to order his ecclesiastical polity.[268] In the draft of his 1589 *Meditatioun* James established that the general typology for his kingship would not be Buchanan's *rex stoicus* but King David, a divinely appointed royal unifier, despite David's passions and willingness to defy the law.

James's identification of David's persona with his own encouraged him to describe his princely duties differently too. He explained in his draft *Meditatioun upon… Chronicles* that neither he nor the Israelite king had celebrated their military victories by 'banketting [with] princis & being dru[n]kken with thaim'. Instead they 'suffered the quhole praise thairof to re[b]ounde allainirlie [soley]' to God by establishing the covenant in their land.[269] James actually included the same point in his printed *Meditatioun.* Indeed he elaborated upon it by comparing 1 Chronicles 15 with Psalm 132, the verse in which David promised God to establish the Ark and begged him not to turn his face away from David's line. Young's lesson in comparing and contrasting texts had stayed with him. Buchanan, as we have seen, resisted the Christological implications of this psalm in his *Paraphrase*, but James VI emphasised them. 'We may learne' from conferring these texts, James concluded, 'that the cheif vertew quhilk ful be in ane christian Prince, and quhhilk the spirit of God alwayis cheifly praisis in him' was showing 'constant zeale to promove ye glorie of God'.[270] God's will was not to be discerned in earthly things like reason or civic virtue, much less was it to be judged by men. 'Kings are called Gods by the propheticall King David', James would write in his *Trew law of free monarchies*, not because of their stoicism but because 'they sit upon God his Throne in the earth, and have the count of their administration to giue unto him'.[271] In these first *Meditatiouns* James used the methods of biblical exegesis and textual comparison that he had studied at Stirling to reject his pedagogue's prescriptions for emotionally reserved and civically active kingship in favour of divine institution and passionate Christian devotion.

James also used exegesis to refute Buchanan's claim that God did not authorise over-mighty monarchy on earth. Buchanan had evinced little interest in Revelation in his writings, partly because of his conviction that God's involvement in human affairs was generally minimal and benevolent.[272] In his *Paraphrase on Revelation*, however, James insisted that

268 James, *BD*, p. 27. 269 Bodleian, MS Bodley 165, fol. 66^{v}.
270 James, *Meditatioun upon… the Chronicles*, sig. Aiv^{r}.
271 James, *Trew law*, p. 64.
272 The sole reference is Buchanan, *Opera omnia*, vol. II, p. 110.

it was Christ, the Lamb of God, who had opened the seals that released 'heresie and ciuil tyrannie' in the last days.[273] James warned his readers that the faithful would be physically persecuted and excluded from 'ciuill societie' by the agents of the Antichrist.[274] Ultimately, James reassured his reader, God would 'iustly mete to their tyrannie'.[275] Until then, however, Christians simply had to pray, unless their godly ruler commanded them to fight against the forces of Satan. God even made the elect bear the 'croce' occasionally, 'as ane bitter medecine' to 'cureth thair infirmities, sa[t]isfeth them from grosse sinnes, and exerciseth thair faith'.[276] This was a conventional, Calvinist explanation of human suffering but for James it had important political implications. Tyranny, James argued, was not good kingship yet it could teach subjects 'not to resist to Gods ordinance'. In his *Trew law of free monarchies*, James would say that God had 'dited' this very lesson to the Israelites in 1 Samuel 8.[277] Subjects, then, were not demonstrating civic virtue by forcibly resisting a tyrant. Instead, James told his readers, these rebels had cast 'off also rashly that yoke, which God at [their] earnest suite hath laid upon [them]'.[278] Those who had deposed Mary and who continued to threaten his rule were disobeying God's ordinance as well as human law.

As such, James's *Paraphrase* and *Meditatiouns* did not break the flow of the king's swelling resistance against Buchanan's strictures. In fact, the exegeses were significant tributaries to his account of 'free and absolute Monarche' as it emerged in 1598 and 1599.[279] More specifically, in these writings James identified certain key Old Testament examples and proof-texts that he would use to defend his plenary power over church and state in the *Trew law* and thereafter. In addition, James VI began to insist in these works that kings were divinely ordained and responsible to God and that their first and foremost duty was not self-government or civic virtue (though James did not deny the temporal value of such things) but the emotional embrace of divine will and the ordering of their subjects. Like King David, their authority extended over the ecclesiastical life of their realms as well as the civil. As Samuel warned his people, moreover, subjects had a duty to accept 'free and absolute' monarchical rule as godly medicine, however bitter it tasted.[280] James used his schoolroom

273 James, 'Paraphrase upon the Reuelation', in *Workes of the most high and mighty prince*, p. 19.
274 James, 'Paraphrase upon the Reuelation', in *Workes of the most high and mighty prince*, p. 42.
275 James, 'Paraphrase upon the Reuelation', in *Workes of the most high and mighty prince*, p. 41.
276 James, *Meditatioun upon… Chronicles*, sig. Aiv^{r}.
277 James, *Trew law*, p. 67.
278 James, *Trew law*, p. 68.
279 James, *Trew law*, p. 64.
280 James, *Trew law*, p. 64.

methods of biblical exegesis and his reading of Calvinist commentaries to inform his rising levels of resistance to Buchanan's pedagogy and his portrait of the king.

CONCLUSION

Many of James's claims in his biblical exegesis were Calvinist commonplaces. Intellectually it was Buchanan, not the king, who was the true rebel. When charged with the education of a student prince, Buchanan went beyond sixteenth-century humanist prescriptions for cultivating moderate Christian monarchs and rejected contemporary Calvinist models of godly kingship. From the lectern of the royal schoolroom at Stirling, he developed a radical 'law of kingship among the Scots' that would keep the prince a schoolboy forever. Buchanan's ideal monarch would observe, as if he were still a minor, while his council, judiciary and estates determined legislation and discharged justice in his name. The prince would sit respectfully in the pew while godly ministers preached to him on the Presbyterian government of his kirk. All the while, his strict schoolmaster, the people, would be monitoring, birch rod in hand and ready to pounce if he lapsed from the vertiginously high standards of Senecan self-discipline that Buchanan had prescribed. As a sixteenth-century ruler, James would have been surprised by historians' claims that there was anything traditional or commonplace about his pedagogue's *imago regis*.

Buchanan's double portrait of the good king and the tyrant was left hanging in various libraries in early modern Europe; others saw it and used it to justify their attempts to resist over-mighty monarchy. The *De iure regni* and *Baptistes* were translated for the benefit of Dutch rebels against Philip II in the 1590s and used to encourage republican distrust of Spain following the Peace of Vervins (1598) and at the beginning of the Twelve Years' Truce (1612).[281] Buchanan's dialogue and *Historia* were adopted (with extensive Calvinist additions and rewrites) by Scottish Covenanters resisting Charles I and James VII and II (1633–1701) from 1638 to 1688.[282] John Milton (1608–74) drew on Buchanan's account of Mary's deposition to justify the execution of Charles I in his *Tenure of kings and magistrates*

[281] Astrid Stilma, 'Tyrants and translations: Dutch interpretations of George Buchanan's political thought', in Caroline Erskine and Roger A. Mason (eds.), *George Buchanan: Political thought in early modern Britain and Europe* (Ashgate, 2012).

[282] John Coffey, 'George Buchanan and the Scottish Covenanters', in Caroline Erskine and Roger A. Mason, *George Buchanan: Political thought inearly modern Britain and Europe* (Aldershot 2012), pp. 189–203.

(1649).[283] Rye House Plotter Algernon Sidney referred to *De iure regni* regularly in his *Discourses concerning government* (posthumously printed in 1698).[284] John Locke did not acknowledge any formal debt to Buchanan but he read *De iure regni* in the 1660s and endorsed a comparable model of limited kingship, sustained by the threat of resistance, in his *Two treatises of government* (printed 1689).[285] In short, Buchanan's attempt to persuade readers to hold their princes to the *ius* that he had prescribed for James was highly influential.

The schoolmaster's efforts at convincing his royal pupil to limit his authority, however, fell on deaf ears. Buchanan had been appointed to James's schoolroom as part of an effort to maintain the authority of the King's Party in Scotland. Together with Peter Young, he attempted to imprint his severe pattern of self-government on the young king with liberal education and training in biblical exegesis. The pedagogues used a predominately Erasmian curriculum and their efforts bore fruit, though not the sort they hungered for. James VI developed grammatical and rhetorical skills in French, Latin and Greek and derived considerable enjoyment from his studies. Indeed, the king's liberal education did more than cultivate his literary skills; it shaped his understanding of the relationship between authorship and authority, a connection that laid the foundation for his adult exercise of kingship. The efficacy of the king's education in this respect may have contributed to Buchanan's subsequent difficulties with his insubordinate student-master. Far from encouraging 'a properly docile attitude towards authority',[286] James's blossoming skills in verbal argument began to frustrate Buchanan's attempts to indoctrinate his pupil. Simultaneously, moreover, the fear that Buchanan attempted to inspire in James with his regular beatings acted like pressure applied to a steel coil. It was released upon the schoolmaster's death and, in 1583, James VI sprang back.

Buchanan and Young's rigorous education of James VI gave him the skills, the biblical knowledge and the political impulse to claim authority over the Scottish church and state. Even when James was supposedly writing exegetical propaganda pieces to appease the kirk and the English in 1588 and 1589, he was beginning to articulate an account of divine-right

283 John Milton, *Political writings*, ed. Martin Dzelzainis (Cambridge, 1991), pp. 1, 13, 18, 24–5.

284 Algernon Sidney, *Discourses concerning government*, ed. Thomas G. West (Indianapolis, 1990), pp. 9, 11, 292, 339, 398.

285 John Locke, *Two treatises of government*, ed. Peter Laslett (Cambridge, 1988), pp. 420–1, 424–5; John Marshall, *John Locke: Resistance, religion and responsibility* (Cambridge, 1994), pp. 201, 236, 263.

286 Grafton and Jardine, *From humanism to the humanities*, p. xii.

kingship. By the time James began writing his own book on princely education, the *Basilicon doron*, in 1599, he had defined monarchical government in opposition to his schoolmaster's prescriptions. The seed of his critique of Buchanan's *imago regis* may be traced back to those early, draft *Meditatiouns*. Buchanan had taken his model ruler from Seneca; James had chosen the Old Testament King David. Buchanan preached severe legal limitations on kings' civil authority; James taught his son that monarchy was 'free and absolute'. Buchanan explained that the people had come together to form the *civitas* and select their governor; James insisted that the king was divinely instituted and hereditary. Buchanan argued that God's 'divine light' could be observed in the civic virtue of the tyrannicide; James insisted that God had explicitly instructed subjects as to 'the obedience that the people owe to their King in all respects'. Buchanan recused the temporal magistrate from ecclesiastical or spiritual authority; James insisted that God and his coronation oath required the king 'to procure the weale of both soules and bodies… of all of them that are committed to his charge' and order the church in his realm.[287] As we will see in chapter seven, on Prince Henry's and Charles I's schooling, James VI's years under Buchanan's instruction also prompted him to criticise Buchanan's claim that a liberal education provided the best preparation for kingship.

[287] James, *Trew law*, p. 65.

CHAPTER 7

Britain's lost Renaissance? The Stuart princes

When the recovering royal schoolmaster, Thomas Hobbes, set out his *Leviathan* (1651) he did not offer advice about how those who would bear the person of the state should be educated. Having been dismissed from his former position at the Paris court in exile, where he attempted to teach the future Charles II (1630–85) to reason using 'mathematical' proofs, he may have had some interest in the question.[1] Indeed Gilbert Burnet, the historian and Whiggish bishop, alleged that Hobbes had exploited his office in 1646 and 1647 to introduce the prince to 'his schemes, both with relation to religion and politics, which made deep and lasting impressions' of a thoroughly pernicious kind 'on the king's mind'.[2] In *Leviathan* and *Behemoth or the Long Parliament* (*c.* 1668), however, Hobbes did not blame the dissolution of the commonwealth on Charles I (1600–49) or his education but on the grammar schools and universities. There, men had read 'books... of the ancient Grecian and Roman commonwealths', in which 'the popular government was extolled by the glorious name of liberty, and monarchy disgraced by the name of tyranny'. They absorbed dangerous and erroneous 'democratical principles' regarding ecclesiastical and political government as well as 'love of their [own] eloquence' and controversy. They became the 'seditious Presbyterian ministers, and... ambitious ignorant Orators', who contended for liberty in Parliament, the pulpit, and in pamphlets and undermined the unity of the *civitas*.[3] Liberal education was not merely capable of transmitting ('democratical') ideology; sedition was an inevitable consequence of the classical texts and rhetorical

[1] BL, Additional MS 4278, fols. 263r, 265v; Thomas Hobbes, *The elements of law natural and politic*, ed. J. C. A. Gaskin (Oxford, 1994), pp. 19, 75; Noel Malcolm, 'Hobbes, Thomas (1588–1679)', *ODNB*; Timothy Raylor, 'The Anglican attack on Hobbes in Paris, 1651', *HJ*, 53:1 (2010); Quentin Skinner, *Reason and rhetoric in the philosophy of Hobbes* (Cambridge, 1996), pp. 257–93.

[2] Gilbert Burnet, *History of his own time*, 6 vols., 2nd edn. (Oxford, 1833), vol. 1, p. 184.

[3] Thomas Hobbes, *Behemoth or The Long Parliament*, ed. Ferdinand Tönnies (London, 1889), pp. 2–3, 33, 46, 109; see similarly Thomas Hobbes, *The leviathan*, ed. Richard Tuck (Cambridge, 1996), pp. 181, 483–4.

methods of argument that dominated the curriculum. Rather than preparing men to serve and rule the commonwealth, Hobbes accused liberal education of contributing to its dissolution.

Recent research on the ideologically charged uses of the press and the pulpit in the three kingdoms, the English Parliament and developments in political and religious thought in the British isle in the years preceding the wars has suggested that Hobbes may have had a point. Charles I's opponents *were* popular, radical, highly driven and unusually persuasive.[4] They had attended grammar schools and universities in the British isle in unprecedentedly high numbers.[5] Nevertheless it would also be fair to say that Hobbes has not managed to dispel historical speculation as to whether the conflicts would have occurred under a king other than Charles I.

There has been remarkable readiness to argue that 'for Charles, character was destiny'.[6] His education, moreover, has been praised and blamed for forming his personality and political conduct. Samuel R. Gardiner's judgement set the tone for the field: Charles's 'want of imaginative power', particularly his inability to empathise with his subjects, proved fatal.[7] Conrad Russell argued that this failing did not stem from stupidity or the refusal to hear critical council. Rather, Charles's 'low valuation of his powers as a negotiator', a lack of confidence that was 'probably justified', tipped the three kingdoms down the slope to civil war. 'Whatever his virtues', Russell wrote, Charles I was 'unfit to be king'.[8] Gardiner's and Russell's verdicts pick on the same flaw in Charles's education: he had not learnt to identify both sides of a political or religious question, a skill that may have taught him to appreciate his opponents' perspectives or at least to anticipate their arguments and negotiate with them effectively. This was, of course, an aptitude

4 For instance David Cressy, 'Revolutionary England, 1640–42', *P&P*, 181 (2003); Richard Cust, '"Patriots" and "popular" spirits: Narratives of conflict in early Stuart politics', in Nicholas Tyacke (ed.), *The English revolution* c. *1590–1720: Politics, religion, and communities* (Manchester, 2007); John Morrill, 'A liberation theology? Aspects of puritanism in the English revolution', in Laura Lunger Knoppers (ed.), *Puritanism and its discontents* (Newark, DE, 2003); Markku Peltonen, *Rhetoric, politics and popularity in pre-Revolutionary England* (Cambridge, 2013); Quentin Skinner, 'Rethinking political liberty', *History Workshop Journal*, 61:1 (2006).

5 James McConica, *The collegiate university: History of the University of Oxford*, vol. III (Oxford, 1986), pp. 54–5; Victor Morgan, *History of the University of Cambridge, 1546–1750* (Cambridge, 2004), pp. 33–4, 118–20; Rosemary O'Day, *Education and society 1500–1800* (London, 1982), pp. 186–90.

6 Charles Carlton, *Charles I: The personal monarch*, 2nd edn. (London, 1995), p. xviii.

7 S. R. Gardiner, *History of England from the accession of James I to the outbreak of the civil war, 1603–1642*, 10 vols. (London, 1894–6), vol. V, p. 317.

8 Conrad Russell, *The causes of the English civil war* (Oxford, 1990), pp. 206–7. See also Clive Holmes, 'Charles I: A case of mistaken identity', *P&P*, 205 (2009), p. 175; L. J. Reeve, *Charles I and the road to personal rule* (Cambridge, 1989), pp. 172–6.

that was fostered by liberal education, or, more particularly, the study of deliberative rhetoric. More recently, however, Kevin Sharpe has issued a serious challenge to Stuart historians. 'No monarch in English history', he proclaimed, 'succeeded to the throne better briefed in the responsibilities of office than Charles I'.[9] This chapter returns to the surviving sources pertaining to Charles's education – the pedagogical treatises that informed it, records of his household and affinity, contemporaries' accounts of his youth and the prince's schoolroom exercises – to ask whether and how it may have shaped his ideology, discursive skills and political style.

The education of Charles's elder brother, Prince Henry, is relevant to this question. It is often pointed out that Henry was educated as the heir and Charles's upbringing lacked the resources that were lavished on his brother. Henry's robust health, wit, energy and confidence, the breadth of his intellectual interests, the daring of his chivalric pursuits and his accomplishments led Roy Strong to describe his reign-that-never-was as 'England's lost Renaissance'. Prior to his early and much lamented demise, Henry fulfilled the cultural expectations that attended upon primogeniture by thoroughly eclipsing the allegedly sickly, awkward and bad-tempered duke of York. Indeed, even after Henry's death, it has been argued that Charles played second fiddle, this time to his father's favourites at court.[10] Moreover, historians have speculated that Henry's hotter sort of Calvinism would have prevented him from promoting ceremonialists like William Laud (1573–1645) or attempting to impose the unwanted prayer book on Scotland.[11] This chapter revisits the evidence that has been used to buttress these claims and suggests that – up to two critical turning points in 1607–9 and 1622–3 – there were remarkable continuities between the educations of the Stuart princes.

There was a good reason for their cognate experiences and subsequent divergences: their relationships with their father, James VI and I. As James Montagu, bishop of Winchester and editor of James's *Workes* (1616) pointed out, James VI and I drew up a 'Patterne' for both his sons' upbringing in his *Basilicon doron* (1599 and 1603).[12]

[9] Kevin Sharpe, *The personal rule of Charles I* (New Haven, 1992), pp. 179–208 and 'Private conscience and public duty in the writings of Charles I', *HJ*, 40:3 (1997), p. 642; Mark Kishlansky, 'Charles I: A Case of mistaken identity', *P&P*, 189 (2005), p. 50.

[10] Roy Strong, *Henry Prince of Wales and England's lost renaissance* (London, 1986), pp. 15, 52, 71–85.

[11] Christopher Hill, *Intellectual origins of the English revolution revisited* (Oxford, 1997), pp. 13, 195; Malcolm Smuts, 'Prince Henry and his world', in Catherine McLeod (ed.), *The lost prince: The life and death of Henry Stuart* (London, 2012), p. 29; Strong, *Henry Prince of Wales*, p. 219.

[12] James Montagu, 'Epistle dedicatory', in James VI and I, *The workes of the most high and mighty prince, Iames by the grace of God Kinge of Great Brittaine France & Ireland defendor of the faith*, ed. James Montagu (London, 1616), STC 14344, sig. a3^r.

The first section of this chapter examines James VI and I's prescriptions for Henry and Charles's religious education in the context of his ecclesiastical policy. The second considers the way that the king and his counsellors shaped his sons' households and chapels in a manner that cultivated, conformist Calvinism. Section three examines James's prescriptions for his sons' study of the liberal arts and sciences. Despite the extent to which James had fought his own princely battles with his pen, his *Basilicon doron* preceded Thomas Hobbes in claiming that the *ars rhetorica* taught its students to believe that they were living in an 'imagined Democracie'.[13] To protect his sons from contagion, James instructed their schoolmasters to limit their exposure. The final sections will ask whether Henry's and Charles's educations left them bereft of rhetorical expertise at a moment when English and Scottish political culture was becoming more discursive and adversarial. Charles's response to the crisis in the Palatinate and the Spanish marriage, in particular his receptivity to James VI and I's biblical exegesis and Matthew Wren's (1585–1667) private reasoning, were significant in shaping his mature religious and political ideology.

JAMES VI AND I ON THE 'CRAFTE' OF KINGSHIP AND 'ORDER' OF THE CHURCH

We saw in the previous chapter that James VI and I constructed his account of kingship in opposition to the prescriptions of his own schoolmaster, George Buchanan. The ghost of the schoolmaster continued to haunt Holyrood and, later, Whitehall as James fashioned a plan for his sons' educations. James VI and I's *Basilicon doron* and his *Meditation* (1620) on the twenty-seventh chapter of the Book of Matthew have been fruitfully examined as sources for his theory of divine-right kingship.[14] Their pedagogical significance emerges even more clearly, however, when they are contextualised in the king's evolving ecclesiastical policy

[13] James, *BD*, p. 26.

[14] Including by Glenn Burgess, *Absolute monarchy and the Stuart constitution* (New Haven, 1996); Daniel Fischlin and Mark Fortier (eds.), *Royal subjects: Essays on the writings of James VI and I* (Detroit, 2002), pp. 29–37; Roger A. Mason, *Kingship and the commonweal: Political thought in Renaissance and Reformation Scotland* (East Lothian, 1998); Jane Rickard, *Authorship and authority: The writings of James VI and I* (Manchester, 2007); Kevin Sharpe, 'Private conscience and public duty in the writings of James VI and I', in John Morrill, Paul Slack and Daniel Woolf (eds.), *Public duty and private conscience in seventeenth-century England* (Oxford, 1993); J. P. Sommerville, *Royalists and patriots: Politics and ideology in England, 1603–1640*, 2nd edn. (London, 1999); Jenny Wormald, 'James VI and I, *Basilikon doron* and *The trew law of free monarchies*: The Scottish context and the English translation', in Linda Levy Peck (ed.), *The mental world of the Jacobean court* (Cambridge, 1991) and 'King James VI and I: Two kings or one?', *History*, 63 (1983).

and his attempts to quash 'broiling spirits, and rebellious minds' in his kingdoms.[15]

James's rebellion against his own schoolmaster did not dent his optimism that he could shape his sons ideologically. In his *Trew law of free monarchies* James claimed analogously perfect authority over his subjects and sons.[16] A mere schoolmaster like George Buchanan could not command such obedience naturally, nor had he merited it with his conduct. James, on the other hand, claimed to have every reason to expect that his sons would honour the fifth 'command in Gods lawe, *Honour your Father and Mother*'.[17] The *Basilicon doron* would be their 'faithfull Praeceptor and counsellour' as princes and his paternal 'Testament and... will' to his sons.[18] Initially dedicated to Henry, it was redirected in 1616 to Charles, 'who succeeds to it by right'. In 1620, James supplemented it with a *Meditation* on the twenty-seventh chapter of the Book of Matthew for the Prince of Wales, which he deemed 'a good patern to put inheritors to kingdoms in minde of their calling'.[19] In addition to offering instruction to his sons and their schoolmasters, both treatises were widely circulated. In the month that James succeeded to the throne of England, between thirteen and sixteen thousand copies of the *Basilicon doron* alone were printed in London and Edinburgh. At a discursive level, they reminded James's English and Scottish subjects of one of his key attractions: his sons.[20] He had provided for the succession dynastically and now, through these treatises, subjects could overhear him taking pains on their behalf to bring up his heir for the state.

In his 1599 prefatory letter to Prince Henry, James explained that the purpose of the *Basilicon doron* was to instruct him 'in all the points of his calling'. He urged his son to 'study to know well [his] owne craft... which is to rule [his] people'.[21] We have seen that northern humanists and reformers, including Buchanan, had emphasised that the curricula and methods of royal schoolrooms were congruent with those of grammar schools. James, however, argued that princes were distinguished by their 'calling' and that their educations must be specific to their divinely ordained duty. The king did not suppose that this 'calling' spared princes

[15] James, *Trew law*, p. 70.
[16] James, *Trew law*, pp. 65–6, 76–7; Gordon J. Schochet, *Patriarchalism in political thought: The authoritarian family and political speculation and attitudes* (Oxford, 1975), pp. 37–53.
[17] James, *BD*, pp. 47, 23. [18] James, *BD*, pp. 2–3.
[19] James, *BD*, p. 2; James VI and I, 'Meditation upon... the XXVII chapter of Saint Matthew', in *Political writings*, J. P. Sommerville (Cambridge, 1994), p. 229.
[20] Wormald, 'James VI and I, *Basilikon doron* and *The trew law of free monarchies*', p. 51.
[21] James, *BD*, pp. 2, 47.

the obligation to maintain Christian morality at all times, as Niccolò Machiavelli had argued. Nor did it permit a king to put the necessity of the state before his conscience, as continental *raison d'état* theorists advised.[22] On the contrary, James insisted that the prince's exemplary Christian 'behaviour in [his] owne person' was critical to maintaining civil order.[23] He was similarly insistent that his sons reject the *politique* practice of maintaining merely outward conformity to a confession, or even converting to keep the peace. The 'Stoicke insensible stupiditie' of authors such as Justus Lipsius, who advocated such conduct, was belied by 'their inconstant behauiour in their owne liues'.[24] Nevertheless, James did argue that princes' vocations meant that they should focus their attention on the 'science of gouernment'.[25]

For James, the 'science of government' meant expertise in ordering subjects. In particular, he cautioned his sons that they would need 'to containe [their] Church in their calling'.[26] This meant both ensuring that the institution itself did not trespass into civil affairs and curbing subjects rendered 'brain-sicke and headie' by their religious heterodoxy.[27] In the *Trew law*, James worried that the 'very spirits' of Buchanan and other 'archibellouses of rebellion' lived on in their printed writings and were animating further sedition.[28] Between 1596 and 1600, when he was drafting the *Trew law* and *Basilicon doron*, James was struggling to assert his supremacy against Scottish Presbyterians, led by Andrew Melville, whose ecclesiastical arguments reminded him strikingly of his pedagogue's republicanism. Certain 'fierie spiritied men' had 'ofttime calumniated [against him] in their populare Sermons' because he 'was a King, which they thought the highest evill'. They agitated for 'paritie in the Church', which the king deemed 'the mother of confusion, and enemie to Unitie, which is the mother of order'.[29] If parity was 'established in the ecclesiasticall gouernment', James predicted, 'the politicke and civill estate should be drawen to the like'.[30]

[22] Peter Burke, 'Tacitism, scepticism, and reason of state', in J. H. Burns and Mark Goldie (eds.), *The Cambridge history of political thought, 1450–1700* (Cambridge, 1994), pp. 484–91; Chris Brooke, *Philosophic pride: Stoicism and political thought, Lipsius to Rousseau* (Princeton, 2012), pp. 13–36; Christian Lazzari, 'Le government de la raison d'état', in Christian Lazzari and Dominique Reynié (eds.), *Le pouvoir de la raison d'état* (Paris, 1992); Etienne Thuau, *Raison d'état et pensée politique à l'époque de Richelieu* (Paris, 2000); Richard Tuck, *Philosophy and government, 1572–1651* (Cambridge, 1993), pp. 31–64, 79, 89, 117–22; Maurizio Viroli, *From politics to reason of state: The acquisition and transformation of the language of politics, 1250–1600* (Cambridge, 1992), pp. 238–80.

[23] James, *BD*, p. 20. *Pace* Richard Cust, *Charles I: A political life* (Harlow, 2005), pp. 17–18.

[24] James, *BD*, p. 48, in James's 1599 manuscript he named 'that proud inconstance Lipsius' specifically. On the Christian critique of stoicism, see Jill Kraye, 'Stoicism in the Renaissance from Petrarch to Lipsius', *Grotiana*, 22/23 (2001–2).

[25] James, *BD*, p. 61. [26] James, *BD*, p. 45. [27] James, *BD*, pp. 6, 7.

[28] James, *Trew law*, p. 70. [29] James, *BD*, p. 26. [30] James, *BD*, p. 26.

Additionally, however, the fanatics James was objecting to in *Basilicon doron* included the Jesuit Robert Persons, who also used Buchanan's language to oppose the case for James's succession to the English crown.[31] The king used his *Basilicon doron* to counsel his sons on how to maintain the 'free' power of the 'Christian Monarchie' in the British isle against controversialists from either end of the confessional spectrum.[32]

At the time of his 1603 edition of the *Basilicon doron*, James may not yet have decided to attempt to converge the Scottish church towards the English.[33] However, the king was clear on what he did *not* want in either polity: ecclesiastical parity or a liturgy or sermon culture that threatened political obedience and gave 'entry to the Papists by our diuision'.[34] He claimed to have little enthusiasm for the English godly who had troubled Richard Bancroft and John Whitgift in the 1590s.[35] James described these 'Puritanes' as 'verie pestes in the Church and Common-weale, whom no deserts can oblige, neither oaths or promises binde'. They were ambitious 'without measure, railing without reason, and making their owne imaginations (without any warrant of the word) the square of their conscience'.[36] The sins of 'Pride, Ambition, and Auarice' had corrupted 'the Popish Church' and been the 'decay of all Churches, since the beginning of the world'.[37] He urged his sons to channel their energy into supressing the agents of religious disorder in their kingdoms, whether they were Catholics, seditious puritan sermonisers or Presbyterian proponents of ministerial parity.

Historians have debated whether James's ecclesiastical polity is best characterised as an attempt to reconcile various factions within the church of England or as potentially divisive in cracking down on Presbyterianism and ostentatious godliness.[38] It is more fruitful to regard

[31] James, *BD*, p. 46; Peter Lake, 'The king (the queen) and the Jesuit: James Stuart's *True law of free monarchies* in context/s', *Transactions of the Royal Historical Society*, 6:14 (2004).

[32] James, *Trew law*, p. 70.

[33] Alan R. MacDonald, 'James VI and I, the Church of Scotland, and British ecclesiastical convergence', *HJ*, 48:4 (2005); John Morrill, 'A British patriarchy? Ecclesiastical imperialism under the early Stuarts', in A. Fletcher and P. Roberts (eds.), *Religion, culture and society in early modern Britain: Essays in honour of Patrick Collinson* (Cambridge, 1994); David L. Smith, *A history of the modern British Isles, 1603–1707: The double crown* (Oxford, 1998), p. 49; Nicholas Tyacke, 'Puritan politicians and King James VI and I, 1587–1604', in Thomas Cogswell, Richard Cust and Peter Lake (eds.), *Politics, religion and popularity in early Stuart Britain: Essays in honour of Conrad Russell* (Cambridge, 2002).

[34] James, *BD*, p. 7.

[35] Peter Lake, *Anglicans and puritans? Presbyterianism and English conformist thought from Whitgift to Hooker* (London, 1988), pp. 11–13, 59–65, 130–1.

[36] James, *BD*, pp. 26–7. [37] James, *BD*, p. 25.

[38] Ronald Asch, 'Sacred kingship in France and England in the age of the wars of religion: From disenchantment to re-enchantment?', in Charles W. Prior and Glenn Burgess (eds.), *England's*

James's uncompromising language against politicised Presbyterianism and the papal power of dispossession as a critical aspect of his readiness to play down doctrinal differences that did not threaten civic order. James instructed his sons to encompass a relatively wide range of clerical opinion in their churches. 'I doe equally loue and honour the learned and graue men of either of these [English or Scottish] opinions' regarding vestments, James wrote, as long as they were law-abiding, sober and quiet.[39] Loyal and uncontentious men who preferred more ornate rituals and devotions were to be embraced alongside loyal and uncontentious men who preferred plainer forms of worship. In practice, James even incorporated into his chapel and bishops bench clerics such as Lancelot Andrewes (1555–1626), who insisted that 'we are not curiously to enquire and search out of God's secret touching reprobation or election', alongside hard-line Calvinists, such as George Abbot (1562–1633), who was a strict upholder of the doctrine of predestination.[40] Both men, and those they patronised, were expected to conform to the standards of clerical conformity established by the Hampton Court Conference of January 1604. James's ministry were required to recognise episcopacy, the scriptural basis for the prayer book, and the royal supremacy. In July 1604, the king licensed the canons that enabled the non-conformists to this small set of core doctrines to be identified and, if necessary, deprived.[41] A number of historians have described James's general policy of incorporation as a non-inflammatory response to the spectrum of theological emphases in the English and Scottish churches. To this, it is worth adding that the range *itself* proved useful to the king when polemics needed to be articulated. James could rely on high-church conformists, such as Andrewes, to offer voluble support for the sacred nature of monarchy against the depredations of populist

wars of religion revisited (Aldershot, 2011), p. 41; Patrick Collinson, *The birthpangs of Protestant England: Religion and cultural change in the sixteenth and seventeenth centuries* (New York, 1988), pp. 94–126; Lori Ann Ferrell, *Government by polemic: James I, the king's preachers, and the rhetoric of conformity* (Stanford, 1998), pp. 4–6; Kenneth Fincham and Peter Lake, 'The ecclesiastical policy of James I and Charles I', in Kenneth Fincham (ed.), *The early Stuart church* (Stanford, 1993), pp. 27–31.

[39] James, *BD*, p. 7.

[40] Lancelot Andrewes, *Ninety-six sermons*, ed. John Posthumus Parkinson, 5 vols. (Oxford, 1841–3), vol. v, p. 398; Fincham and Lake, 'Ecclesiastical policy', pp. 29–31.

[41] [Church of England], *Constitutions and canons ecclesiasticall treated vpon by the Bishop of London, president of the conuocation for the prouince of Canterbury, and the rest of the bishops and clergie of the said prouince: and agreed vpon with the kings maiesties licence* (London, 1604), STC 10070; Patrick Collinson, 'The Jacobean religious settlement: The Hampton Court Conference', in Howard Tomlinson (ed.), *Before the English Civil War: Essays on early Stuart politics and government* (London, 1983), pp. 27–52; Kenneth Fincham and Peter Lake, 'The ecclesiastical policy of James I', *Journal of British Studies*, 24 (1985).

Presbyterians.[42] When the king decided to chase down the fox of popish conspiracy in the British isle, however, he found conformist Calvinists such as Abbot to be the keenest hounds in his pack. 'I think it all one', James proclaimed to his final parliament, 'to lay down my crown to the pope as to a popular party of puritans'.[43] He cultivated and promoted the churchmen who helped him curb one extreme or the other.

The first and second sections of the *Basilicon doron* prescribed the knowledge, skills and measures that his heir would need to follow in his footsteps. James argued that 'the onely way' to live 'as a Christian, and as a King' was to 'diligently... read [God's] word', especially the Gospels, the acts of the Apostles and the parts of the Old Testament 'where the godly Kings are first made mention of'.[44] The object was to develop sufficient expertise to judge when a 'case' between 'two extremities' was put to him. On the one hand, his sons should not 'beleeue with the Papists' that 'the Churches authority' was 'better then your owne knowledge'. On the other, they should not 'leane with the Anabaptists' or proud Presbyterians in thinking that their 'owne conceits and dreamed reuelations' constituted God's word'.[45] By moderating between the arguments of others, Henry and Charles would learn to serve as 'the Guardian of both Tables' of Moses' law.[46] They would know when a preacher drifted 'from their text in the Pulpit' or when he was misusing scripture 'to meddle... with the estate or policie'. If clergymen attempted to pontificate on civil matters or gather in 'conventions or meetings' to discuss temporal policy or ecclesiastical government, James advocated swift and severe punishment.[47] He was particularly determined that his sons police 'the mysterie of the King's Power', which was 'not to be disputed' lest it 'take away the mysticall reverence, that belongs unto them that sit in the Throne of God'.[48] Later, the king would insist that he was not encouraging his successor 'to usurpe any point of the Priestly office, no more then the Priest should the King's'. It was, however, 'the Kings office to ouersee and compell the church to do her office, to purge all abuses in her' from subjects at large.[49]

Surprisingly, however, James did not insist that princes required theological or doctrinal expertise. We saw in chapter six that James had used his own skills in scriptural exegesis to claim authority for the reforms he

[42] Asch, 'Sacred kingship in France and England', pp. 40–8; Ferrell, *Government by polemic*, pp. 140–66.

[43] BL, Harleian MS 159, fol. 136^{r-v}.

[44] James, *BD*, pp. 13, 15.

[45] James, *BD*, pp. 18–19.

[46] James, *BD*, p. 45.

[47] James, *BD*, p. 45.

[48] James, 'Speech in Star Chamber 1616', in *Political writings*, p. 211.

[49] James, 'Meditation upon... the XXVII chapter of Saint Matthew', in *Political writings*, p. 237.

planned to make to the Scottish ecclesiastical polity. In 1596 he was happy to circulate Théodore de Bèze's praise that he possessed 'so great and exact knowledge of the Christian religion, from the very grounds and principles thereof, that the Lord it seems hath made his majesty both a prince and preacher to his people'.[50] He thrived at the Hampton Court Conference, in the production of the Bible translation that bears his name and as a religious controversialist.[51] Nevertheless James protested that his sons did not need skills in biblical interpretation and that engaging in exegetical debate would diminish their kingship. There was no point trying to reason or debate with ambitious or 'brain-sicke' preachers, he wrote. 'I have over-much surfeited them with that', he confessed to his heir, and had discovered that 'it is not their fashion to yeeld'.[52] Rather, he told the princes to encourage 'good pastors', supply the universities, maintain a 'comelie' hierarchy within the church and use the law to restrain political preaching.[53] It was less important that his sons be scriptural scholars themselves than that they learn to govern the ecclesiastical estate. In his 1620 *Meditation*, James insisted that, by instructing Charles in this vocational manner, he was not urging him to extend 'his royall Prerogatiue' unless 'necessity shall require it'. Nevertheless, the king was certainly not discouraging his heir to moderate or cede his temporal or ecclesiastical authority on earth.[54]

In his desire to distinguish his prescriptions from George Buchanan's and protect his realms from other 'phanaticke spirits', James shifted the focus of princely education from intellectual, moral and spiritual amelioration to practical expertise in the 'crafte' of managing those forces of religious dissent that he depicted as virtually hydraulic. In doing so, he made his theory of princely education more responsive than earlier humanist approaches had been to the political pressures of confessionalisation in the British isle. In this respect at least, he shared common ground with Netherlandish and French *politiques*. Yet the king's pedagogical writings gained urgency, indeed some might say prejudice or even paranoia, from

50 'Tantam Christianae Religionis ex ipsis fundamentis cognitionem adiuxerit, ut in eo pene Dominus, & Regiae Majestatis, & sacri ministerii dignitatem videri possit simul contulisse': Théodore de Bèze in Robert Rollock, *Tractatus de vocatione efficaci* (Edinburgh, 1597), STC 21285, sig. A6^{r} and *A treatise of Gods effectual calling*, trans. Henry Holland (London, 1603), STC 21286, sig. *1^{v}.

51 Alan Cromartie, 'King James and the Hampton Court Conference', in Ralph Houlbrooke (ed.), *James VI and I: Ideas, authority, and government* (Aldershot, 2006); Anthony Grafton and Joanna Weinberg, *'I have always loved the holy tongue': Isaac Casaubon, the Jews, and a forgotten chapter in Renaissance scholarship* (Cambridge, MA, 2011), pp. 178–9.

52 James, *BD*, p. 45. 53 James, *BD*, p. 27.

54 James, 'Meditation upon… the XXVII chapter of Saint Matthew', in *Political writings*, p. 249.

his own early experiences of Presbyterianism and sedition in the British isle. Buchanan and his ilk may well have insisted that a prince's most important duty was to serve as a model of wisdom, erudition and piety for others; he denied that a hereditary monarch had any other powers on earth. James's son, however, would require specific expertise to manage the church and state that God had called him to govern.

THE PRINCES' GODLY HOUSEHOLDS

James's *Basilicon doron* was certainly printed for a wide readership, but there is also evidence that the king meant it to shape the social practices of Henry's and Charles's educations. When the *Basilicon doron* was initially printed in 1599, only seven copies came off the press and two were for Prince Henry and his 'Scoolemaster', Adam Newton (d. 1630).[55] On the eve of James's accession to the throne of England in 1603, he sent his son a copy of the new edition and a letter urging him to 'studdie & profite in it as ye wolde deserue my blessing'.[56] In 1620, James also composed his *Meditation* on Matthew to 'instruct [Prince Charles] in the Controversies of Religion'.[57] It turned out that there was one trick that James VI and I was happy to take from his former schoolmaster: sharing his 'Patterne' for his sons with a wider audience was meant to give them greater motivation to follow his instructions. Charles, at least, found the impression of his father's prescriptions significant enough to offer his son a similar guide, when he sensed his own death approaching in late 1648.[58] Despite James's parallel prescriptions, however, historians have noted that Charles's mature confessional identity diverged sharply from his brother's. From 1606 to 1612, Prince Henry's court supposedly developed the highly politicised godliness that James had decried.[59] Charles I, on the other hand, is accused of becoming the patron of English Arminians, breaking his father's Calvinist consensus in English and Scottish churches and catalysing the kingdoms' descent into civil war.[60] It is certainly true that, from

[55] SP 52/64, fol. 80r; see also SP 52/64, fol. 74r. [56] BL, Harleian MS 6986, fol. 65r.

[57] Peter Heylyn, *A short view of the life and reign of King Charles… from his birth to his burial* (London, 1658), Wing H1735B, p. 18.

[58] Charles I, *Eikon basilike, The pourtraicture of His Sacred Majestie in his solitudes and sufferings* (London, 1648), Wing E268, pp. 232–54.

[59] Thomas Birch, *Life of Henry, Prince of Wales* (London, 1760), pp. 390–1; Hill, *Intellectual origins*, pp. 193–5; Strong, *Henry Prince of Wales*, pp. 155, 223–4.

[60] John Morrill, 'The Religious context of the English civil war', in Richard Cust and Ann Hughes (eds.), *The English civil war* (London, 1997), pp. 165–73; Nicholas Tyacke, 'Puritanism, Arminianism, and counter-revolution', in Richard Cust and Ann Hughes (eds.), *The English civil*

1625 at least, Charles tended to regard public discussions of predestination, popular preaching and preference for plain forms worship as signifying seditious intent.[61] On 8 July 1625, the king even implied his willingness to consider a more liberal account of the doctrine of reprobation when he took Richard Mountague (*c.* 1575–1641), the author of *A gagg for the new gospell?* (1624) and *Appello Caesarem* (1625) and a prominent member of the Durham House group, into his chapel.[62] This section argues, however, that James VI and I's pedagogical prescriptions *were* influential on both his sons' juvenile households and their youthful confessional identities.

After the royal family's arrival in London in 1603 and 1604, James and Robert Cecil established households for the princes.[63] The heir, Prince Henry, was installed in a '*Courtly College* or a *Collegiate Court*'.[64] The institution was originally based in Oatlands and subsequently oscillated between Richmond, Nonsuch and St James. It offered young noblemen an opportunity to be educated alongside the prince and consider themselves part of his chivalric affinity. In the words of James Cleland, tutor to one of Henry's gentle companions, Sir John Harington of Exton (1592–1614), it taught its students to be a '*Privie Counseller*, a *Generall* of an Armie, to rule in peace, & commande in warre'.[65] As mature aristocrats, the collegiate courtiers would serve their monarch and help to stabilise the relationship between the crown and the troublesome commons, something James had encouraged in his *Basilicon doron*.[66] The court was also intended to offer Henry an opportunity to practise governing his household, that microcosm of the commonwealth. Admittedly, order occasionally broke down. In one unfortunate episode, the young scion Robert Sidney stabbed his tutor, Mr Bird.[67] Generally, however, Henry's governor Thomas Chaloner and the other officers helped the young prince

war (London, 1997), p. 138 and *Anti-Calvinists: The Rise of English Arminianism, c. 1590–1640* (Oxford, 1990), pp. 181, 246–7. See also Patrick Collinson, *Religion of Protestants: The church in English society* (Oxford, 1982), p. 90.

61 Tyacke, *Anti-Calvinists*, p. 48, 154, 181, 246.

62 Richard Mountague, *A gagg for the new Gospell? No: a nevv gagg for an old goose* (London, 1624), STC 18038, p. 157 and *Appello Caesarem A iust appeale from two vniust informers* (London, 1625), STC 18031, pp. 30–77, 322; Sharpe, *Personal rule of Charles I*, pp. 293–4.

63 Timothy Wilks, 'The court culture of Prince Henry and his circle, 1603–1613' (D.Phil. dissertation, Oxford University, 1987), pp. 3–4, 6–8, 17–21.

64 Thomas Chaloner in Birch, *Life of Henry*, p. 97.

65 James Cleland, *Hero-paideia or The Institution of a Young Nobleman* (Oxford, 1607), STC 5393, sig. E2^{r-v}. See also Charles Cornwallis, *A discourse of the most illustrious prince, Henry, late Prince of Wales* (London, 1641), Wing C6329, sig. C1^{r}.

66 James, *BD*, p. 37; see also Richard Cust, *Charles I and the aristocracy, 1625–1642* (Cambridge, 2013), pp. 53–5.

67 Cornwallis, *Discourse*, sig. C1^{r}; Wilks, 'Court culture of Prince Henry', p. 79.

to maintain an establishment famed for its moral rectitude, its alms box for cursers and its punctilious attendance at common prayer and sermons.[68] The collegiate court was established to teach Henry to 'contain' the members of the household in their civil, moral and Christian duties, in accordance with James's instructions.

At its centre was Adam Newton, Prince Henry's Scottish schoolmaster. Newton's career shows how thoroughly James's prescriptions in his *Basilicon doron* shaped the social practice of Henry's education. Newton had been born in obscure circumstances in Edinburgh; he may have been the son of a baker.[69] When the king appointed him as Henry's schoolmaster in 1599, he knew that Newton was a humanist with an MA from the University of Glasgow in 1582 and experience teaching Greek and Latin at the prestigious college of St Maixent in Poitou.[70] More significantly, however, he also had expertise in law, which James regarded as a critical subject of royal study. Newton had been elected as the first professor of laws at the new University of Edinburgh in 1595 and his surviving commonplace books include compendiums on the complexities of real property.[71] When the post was dissolved in 1597, Peter Young may have recommended the scholar to King James VI.[72] Like Young, Newton had Presbyterian sympathies.[73] Yet during his years in royal service Newton made his obedience to the king and the royal prerogative articles of faith, and provided valuable support to James during the king's doctrinal disputes. In early February 1612, for instance, Newton translated the king's French *Declaration against Conrad Vorstius* (1612), the Arminian professor of theology at Leiden, into Latin. In this tongue it also served to refute Martin Becanus, a Jesuit controversialist who had argued that James's claim that the vicar of Christ was the Holy Spirit, rather than St Peter and his papal successors, was the same as Vorstius' denial of the ubiquity of God and the Trinity.[74] In short, Newton was not eager to 'contend with Kings and perturb whole kingdomes'.[75]

68 Birch, *Life of Henry*, pp. 85–6; NA, LC 5/179, pp. 9, 26–8, 42–5.

69 John Durkan and James Kirk, *University of Glasgow 1451–1577* (Glasgow, 1977), p. 379.

70 Johannes Henricus Dauber, 'Oratio funebris', in André Rivet, *Operum theologicorum: Quae Latine edidit* (Rotterdam, 1660), sig.**2^{r-v}.

71 W. C. Dickinson, 'The advocates' protest against the institution of a chair of law in the University of Edinburgh', *Scottish Historical Review*, 23:91 (1926), p. 207; James, *BD*, pp. 21, 45; WLTC, MSS R 9 30, R 14 10.

72 Bodleian, Smith MS 77, fols. 49^{r-v}, 51^{r}.

73 James Melville, *The autobiography and diary of Mr James Melvill*, ed. Robert Pitcairn (Edinburgh, 1842), p. lii.

74 James VI and I, *Declaratio… super re Vorstii actum tractatumue sit*, trans. Adam Newton (London, 1612), STC 9232; Frederick Shriver, 'Orthodoxy and diplomacy: James I and the Vorstius affair', *EHR*, 85:336 (1970), p. 454; BL, Harleian MS 7002, fol. 225^{r}.

75 James, *BD*, p. 5.

In return for Newton's staunch support in his controversies, James clasped this obedient (indeed obsequious) Presbyterian to the royal bosom; here was a moderate detached from the dangerous radical minority. Considering inflation, Newton's combined annuity and salary of £250 in 1605 was somewhat higher than the £40 per annum that early sixteenth-century royal schoolmasters received.[76] Yet Newton advanced more quickly than his predecessors, and acquired civic honours, pecuniary rewards and a wealth of ecclesiastical offices (despite his status as a lay man), including the deanery of Durham, in a short space of time. In addition James regularly topped up Newton's salary with generous bonuses.[77] Newton died in 1630 as a baronet, the secretary to Charles I's council, the owner of a substantial estate in Kent and the secretary to the Marches of Wales, an office worth £2,000 per annum.[78] As a schoolmaster, translator, courtier and conforming Calvinist, Newton had proved himself a quick study of the 'crafte' of kingship in Stuart Britain.

There is comparatively little textual evidence of Henry's religious education under Newton. He must have read scripture but his surviving school books and exercises do not suggest he was required to perform regular biblical exegeses or was immersed in the study of theology. Henry was, however, an eager auditor of sermons and the prince's chapel was tremendously important in shaping the confessional tone of his collegiate court. Peter McCullough has made a persuasive case for the 'progressive and politicized Calvinism' of Henry's preachers. Those with strong Calvinist credentials and godly consciences, such as Hugh Broughton, Dr Leonell Sharpe, Daniel Price (1581–1631) and Joseph Hall, gained their places in Henry's circle through the patronage of John Harington of Exton (1539/40–1613), governor to Princess Elizabeth and father to Henry's companion, John, and James's own godly dean of chapel, James Montagu. McCullough suggested, however, that control of the chaplaincy slipped away from James and Cecil and fostered a culture at St James that McCullough claims was dangerously critical of the king's ecclesiastical policy.[79]

In fact, James had good reason to cultivate godly preachers and controversialists in the first decade of his southern rule. After the Gunpowder Plot of 1605, resistance to the Oath of Allegiance (1606) led by Pope Paul

[76] *HMC Salisbury*, vol. XVII, p. 60; Philip Arestis and Peter Howells, 'The 1520–1640 "great inflation": An early case of controversy on the nature of money', *Journal of Post Keynesian Economics*, 24:2 (2001–2), p. 185.

[77] John Gough Nichols, *The progresses, processions and magnificent festivities of King James the first, his royal consort, family and court*, 4 vols. (London, 1828) vol. I, pp. 499, 599.

[78] Stuart Handley, 'Newton, Sir Adam, first baronet (d. 1630)', *ODNB*.

[79] Peter E. McCullough, *Sermons at court: Politics and religion in Elizabethan and Jacobean preaching* (Cambridge, 1998), pp. 141–7, 185–7.

V (1552–1621) and Cardinal Robert Bellarmine, and the assassination of the *politique* Henri IV of France on 14 May 1610 by the Catholic François Ravaillac, James deemed those who believed in the pope's *imperium* and power to depose kings the greatest threat to his authority and his sons' future government.[80] Indeed, during these years, James described his objections to radical, politicised 'papists' in the same terms with which he had previously condemned Presbyterians: they were possessed by 'fanaticall zeale' and 'could not conteine themselves within the bounds of their natural Allegiance' to their divinely appointed rulers.[81] He appointed chaplains to Henry's household who would be eager to protect his son from the popish scourge. During the same years, James promoted their co-confessionalists in other contexts. In 1610 he granted a royal charter to the seventeen fellows of the Chelsea College, led by Matthew Sutcliffe, to defend the English church against Roman Catholic polemicists.[82] In February 1611 he elevated George Abbot, a scourge of papists and popish plots alike and regular preacher on anniversaries of the Gunpowder Plot, to the prelacy of Canterbury.[83] The members of Henry's chapel were part of the king's pack of anti-Catholic controversialists rather than acting as fifth columnists at court. Moreover, James was successful in weeding out non-conformists from their midst. One would-be preacher, John Burgess (1563–1635), had been recommended by Montagu for a post in the prince's household in June 1604. When Burgess auditioned for the place with a sermon criticising James's licensing of the canons of conformity, Burgess not only lost the projected office but also found himself in the Tower.[84] And Montagu refrained from further attempts to place radical non-conformists about the prince.[85] Henry's chapel was an important part of James's ecclesiastical policy of incorporating a wide spectrum of conformists and using those within it to attack outliers.

[80] For instance, Jacques Davy du Perron, *A letter written from Paris by the Lord Cardinall Peron, to Monsieur Casaubon in England* (St. Omer, 1612), STC 6383, pp. 39–45.

[81] James, 'Triplici nodo, triplex cuneus. Or an apologie for the oath of allegiance' (1607/8), in *Political writings*, p. 86.

[82] Anthony Milton, *Catholic and reformed: The Roman and Protestant churches in English Protestant thought, 1600–1640* (Cambridge, 1995), pp. 32–4.

[83] Kenneth Fincham, 'Abbot, George (1562–1633)', *ODNB*.

[84] John Burgess, *A sermon preached before the late King James… with two letters in way of apology* (London, 1642), Wing B5720, p. 29; Birch, *Life of Henry*, pp. 390–1; Peter Lake, 'Moving the goal posts? Modified subscription and the construction of conformity in the early Stuart church', in Peter Lake and Michael Questier (eds.), *Conformity and orthodoxy in the English church, c. 1560–1660* (Woodbridge 2000).

[85] P. E. McCullough, 'Montagu, James (1568–1618)', *ODNB*.

Given that Prince Charles's household was established during the same period, the continuities between the confessional affinities of his officers and Henry's family should not surprise us. Charles's establishment was also characterised by fervent anti-Catholicism and overt loyalty to James. Serious illness had meant that Charles was the last member of the royal family to travel south after James's English accession.[86] According to Robert Carey (1560–1639), who had ridden to Northamptonshire to meet him in 1604, the 'great ladies' of the court recoiled from taking charge of Charles but Carey and his wife, Elizabeth, a lady-in-waiting to Queen Anne, were made of stronger stuff.[87] In fact, after a series of disappointments under Elizabeth I, this godly couple were readier than their peers to pursue high-risk strategies for preferment. It was Robert Carey, of course, who had raced to Edinburgh in March 1603 to announce Elizabeth's death.[88] The Careys demonstrated conspicuous loyalty to the new royal family.

Their household supported puritan divines but they insisted on strict conformity amongst their chaplains. Their own sons were tutored by the godly Henry Burton (bap. 1578, d. 1647/8), who would be maimed and imprisoned for seditious libel during Charles's personal rule. During his less contentious youth, however, the Careys secured Burton's appointment to both princes' households as Prince Henry's and later Prince Charles's clerk of the closet.[89] Between 1604 and *c.* 1618, Burton either played his confessional cards close to his chest or found little to displease him in the Careys' way of life. Robert was fond of fine clothes and gambling but his wife was praised by Daniel Price as an 'Elect lady', who would 'appeare with ioy before God with Sara, Rebecca, Debora, Davids Abigail, Salomons Sulamite, and the Noble Sunamite in the better world'.[90] Charles's religious instruction between 1604 and 1611 was probably managed by one of the Careys' chaplains, so his father's prescriptions regarding scripture-reading would have been followed zealously. The household was not as elaborate or well-funded as his brother's collegiate court, but it shared its confessional tone.

[86] *Letters and state papers during the reign of King James the sixth*, ed. James Maidment (Edinburgh, 1838), pp. 46, 55; NA, E 351/2799; see also John Chamberlain, *The letters of John Chamberlain*, ed. Norman Egbert McClure, 2 vols. (Philadelphia, 1939), vol. I, p. 201.

[87] Robert Carey, *Memoirs of Robert Carey*, ed. F. H. Mares (Oxford, 1972), pp. 67, 68; SP 15/37, fol. 458^{r}.

[88] A. J. Loomie, 'Carey, Robert, first earl of Monmouth (1560–1639)', *ODNB*.

[89] Kenneth Gibson, 'Burton, Henry (bap. 1578, d. 1647/8)', *ODNB*.

[90] Daniel Price, *Spirituall odours to the memory of Prince Henry in foure of the last sermons preached in St James after his Highnesse death* (Oxford, 1613), STC 20304, sig. G4^{r-v}; Chamberlain, *Letters*, vol. I, p. 328.

As McCullough has shown, moreover, after Prince Henry's death in November 1612, conforming Calvinist divines from his household, including Dr George Hakewill (bap. 1578, d. 1649) and Richard Milbourne (d. 1624), were appointed as Charles's chaplains.[91] Hakewill had made valuable intellectual contributions to James's anti-Romanist controversies by authoring and translating treatises against regicide.[92] It was Hakewill, moreover, who prepared Charles for his 'strict and long Examination' of confirmation in 1613, 'yeelded [to] my Lords Grace of Canterburie [George Abbot], and my Lord of Bath and Wels [James Montagu], in the Grounds and Principles of Christian Religion'.[93] To be confirmed by these bishops, the prince must have held strictly Calvinist views regarding predestination.

Hakewill was welcomed in Charles's household by the prince's schoolmaster and secretary, Thomas Murray (1564–1623), who had been appointed in 1606.[94] Two years earlier, James had contemplated installing his own beloved pedagogue, Peter Young, as 'overseer of the household of Prince Charles' with 'special charge of his education'.[95] Ultimately, however, the king offered Murray a salary of £33 per annum and an annuity of £200 for life, for his 'pains and travils' in 'the careful education of our dearly beloved son… instructing him in all kinds of good learning according to the capacity of his tender years' and acting as his secretary and keeper of his signet.[96] Murray brought his nephew, William Murray (d. 1655), to Greenwich to serve as the duke's study mate. Charles I would subsequently make William the first earl of Dysart for his services to the royalist cause.[97] Charles's more modest household did encourage some lasting chivalric affinities.

Historians have either neglected Murray's appointment or been somewhat perplexed by it. After all James's railings against Presbyterians in

[91] McCullough, *Sermons at court*, p. 197.

[92] Pierre du Coignet, *Anti-Coton or A refutation of Cottons letter declaratorie… touching the killing of kings… [and] a supplication of the Vniuersitie of Paris, for the preuenting of the Iesuites opening their schooles among them*, trans. George Hakewill (London, 1611), STC 5861; George Hakewill, *Scutum regium. Id est, Aduersus omnes regicidas et regicidarum patronos* (London, 1612), STC 12618; Emma Rhatigan, 'Preaching to princes: John Burgess and George Hakewill in the royal pulpit', *Journal of Ecclesiastical History*, 62 (2011), p. 276.

[93] George Hakewill, *The auncient ecclesiasticall practise of confirmation confirmed by arguments drawne from scripture, reason, councels, Fathers, and later writers* (London, 1613), STC 12614, sig. A2^r.

[94] Heylyn, *Short view of the life and reign*, p. 9.

[95] SP 14/10A, fol. 15^r.

[96] *HMC Salisbury*, vol. XXIV, no. 177, pp. 62, 63, 66. Murray's salary was topped up shortly afterwards with grants and pensions: *CSPD James*, vol. I, p. 340; *Letters of the kings of England, now first collected from the originals in royal archives, and other authentic sources*, ed. J. O. Halliwell, 2 vols. (London, 1846) vol. II, p. 114.

[97] Malcom Smuts, 'Murray, William, first earl of Dysart (d. 1655)', *ODNB*.

the *Basilicon doron*, why had he appointed a man whom contemporaries described as 'ill Principled in the Rites and Ceremonies' of the English church?[98] As was the case with Adam Newton, however, James had little cause to doubt Murray's conformity prior to or during the first decade of his royal service. First, Murray came with the imprimatur of James's loyal servants in Scotland, the Murrays of Tullibardine, who were probably his kinsmen. John Murray (*c.* 1550–1613), the first earl, was head of the royal household in Scotland from 1578 to 1592 and subsequently appointed to James's Privy Council in Scotland. He seems to have employed Thomas Murray as a tutor to his son, William Murray, the second earl (1574–1627), who was brought up with James at Stirling.[99] The tutor was a known commodity and his family were long-standing supporters of the Stuarts.

Additionally, Thomas Murray recognised the king's authority over the Scottish church directly in a series of literary gifts circulated between 1588 and 1604. He probably penned his prosopopoeic poem 'The tears of Britain' shortly after the execution of Mary, Queen of Scots. In the verse, the divine Britannia urged England and Scotland to resist the call of Mars so that she might 'sleep quietly in the courts of princes, attended by her partners in religion'.[100] It was a well-judged echo of the printed versions of James's biblical exegeses written in support of the Treaty of Berwick (1586). In the late 1590s, when James took action to bring the Presbyterian kirk to heel, Murray kept up the charm offensive, declaring his enthusiasm for James's governorship of the church. In 1599 he wrote epigrams in praise of James's *Trew law of free monarchies*:

> O Defender of Christians, Father of the Country, and Avenger of enemies,
> O Auspicious one, You enlarge Scottish empire,
> Your rule is mild and just.[101]

[98] Heylyn, *Short view of the life and reign*, p. 9; Malcolm Smuts, 'Murray, Thomas (1564–1623)', *ODNB*. The fullest account is McCullough, *Sermons at court*, p. 198. Murray is absent from Cust, *Charles I: A political life* and Sharpe, *Personal rule of Charles I*. His appointment is misdated to 1611 in Charles Carlton, *Charles I, the personal monarch* (London, 1995), p. 15. John Bowle provides no evidence for his claim that the choice of Murray was Lady Carey's: *Charles I: A biography* (London, 1975), p. 22.

[99] Murray wrote a neo-Latin poem in praise of William's new wife, Cecilia Wemyss: William Murray, *Naupactiados, sive Lepantiados Iacobi Magni, Britanniarum, Franciae & Hiberniae Regis, fidei verè Christianae vindicis, & assertoris verè Christianissimi metaphrasis poetica* (London, 1604), STC 14386, p. 45.

[100] 'Diva Britannaea secura quiescit in aula, / Relligio, sociis concomitata suis': Thomas Morauius, 'Lacrima Britanniae', HHCP, 205/43, fol. 46r.

[101] 'Christicolis tutor, patriae Pater, hostibus ultor, / Amplifices Scoticum faustus & Imperium/ Tu clemens, iustusque, regas': Murray, *Naupactiados*, p. 36.

Murray's Ovidian depiction of James as a British Augustus continued in a New Year tribute in 1604, when he praised him (somewhat prematurely) for joining the British isle in an eternal peace. Astraea returned to earth, and justice, the arts and virtue were restored. Most importantly,

> Piety, so long put down, rises again
> The pure and ancient religion is honoured again.[102]

Later that year Murray also celebrated James's peace with Spain by offering the king a Latin verse translation of his poem *Lepanto* (1588). Then he gave John Norton almost the whole collection to print as testimony to his support for the king, even his least popular initiatives.[103] Shortly afterwards, Murray became Charles's schoolmaster. Murray may have been a Presbyterian, but James had every reason to imagine he would be a tame one.

For the next eighteen years, Murray seemed politically domesticated, though he remained firmly Calvinist. In 1622 the anti-puritan John Williams (1582–1650), then bishop of Lincoln, had interviewed Murray and informed George Villiers (1592–1628), soon to become the duke of Buckingham, that he had 'schooled him soundly against puritanism, which he disavows, though somewhat faintly'.[104] Under Murray, we might presume that Charles read scripture daily and worked through his 1587 English edition of Jean Calvin's *The institution of Christian religion*.[105] Murray also exposed his charge to the anti-Catholic controversies of his father's reign. In 1609 he acquired James's *Apologie for the oath of allegiance* (1607/8, 1609); John Barclay's translation of the king's book and perhaps his edition of his father's treatise *De potestate papae*, which denied the civil power of the papacy; a critique by William Barlow, bishop of Lincoln, of the Jesuit Robert Persons' *Answer to a Catholike English-man* (1609); and *Tortura torti*, by Lancelot Andrewes, bishop of Chichester, a four-hundred-page refutation of the papal supremacy and supposed power to dispense Catholics from obedience to civil laws.[106] As James had instructed, Charles seems to have been taught to evaluate, rather

102 'Vindice te, Pietas iam longum afflicta resurget, / Purus & antiquae relligionis honos': Murray, *Naupactiados*, p. 38.

103 Murray, *Naupactiados*; also reprinted in Arthur Johnstoun, *Delitiae poetarum Scotorum: Huius aevi illustrium*, 2 vols. (Amsterdam, 1637) vol. II, sigs. H6^{v}–I4^{v}.

104 [Anonymous], *Cabala, sive Scrinia sacra: Mysteries of state and government, in letters of illustrious persons* (London, 1691), Wing C186, pp. 289–90.

105 Jean Calvin, *The institution of Christian religion*, trans. Thomas Norton (London, 1587), STC 4422, BL, 858.c.24.

106 SP 14/51, fol. 11^{r}.

than participate, in theological discussion. The duke attended sermons at Henry's court, took notes and asked for copies of preachers' texts when he found them particularly arresting. In 1614, for instance, he requested hard copy of two sermons by George Meriton, dean of Peterborough, which testified that 'some are actually saved, others reiected… because God… did purpose and ordain the same'.[107] It was a request that confirms that his successful confirmation had been no one-off. Under Murray's watchful eye, Charles had become a godly youth.

James seems to have been pleased with Murray's service, though the schoolmaster's rewards pale in comparison with the prizes heaped on the bustling, energetic Adam Newton. Murray was naturalised in 1606, enabling him to own property in England, and in 1608 granted mastership of the Hospital of Sherbourne in Durham.[108] After Prince Henry's death, his influence increased, though he seems to have dealt with suitors rather too scrupulously to have skimmed much cream from his master's milk.[109] When Charles's formal education concluded, Murray was considered sufficiently loyal and useful to be kept on as his secretary.[110] He survived a 1615 attempt by the archbishop of St Andrews, George Gledstanes, to have him removed from Charles's household for being 'ill-affected to the estate of the kirk'.[111] Indeed, in his new office he managed to obtain preferment for some godly clients and, in March 1617, acquire a commission for one third of the revenues on the customs duties on certain cloths.[112] Ultimately, the king granted him the reversion to the Provostship of Eton College, an office he would assume, after some controversy, in March 1622.[113] As had been the case with Newton, who joined Charles's household as receiver general in July 1613, Murray was a competent poet and pedagogue. He lacked George Buchanan's pretensions to gentility or his European reputation in the republic of letters, but James may well have regarded this as a good thing: like Newton before him, Murray would owe everything to his royal masters.

That did not mean Murray failed to support Calvinist causes using his office. As secretary to the Prince of Wales, Murray followed the example of Adam Newton, who had used his godly connections to establish an

[107] George Meriton, *The Christian mans assuring house. And a sinners conuersion. Two sermons* (London, 1614), STC 17837, pp. 10–11.

[108] NA, C 89/10/50; SP 15/39. See also *CSPD James*, vol. I, p. 535; *CSPD James*, vol. II, p. 170.

[109] *CSPD James*, vol. II, p. 170.

[110] BL, Harleian MS 7002, fol. 270^{r}.

[111] Smuts, 'Murray, Thomas (1564–1623)'.

[112] *CSPD James*, vol. II, p. 447.

[113] *CSPD James*, vol. II, pp. 484, 490; *CSPD James*, vol. III, pp. 354, 357; SP 14/109, fol. 217$^{r–v}$.

international information network for Henry.[114] Newton exchanged diplomatic knowledge directly with godly men sent to lie abroad, including Sir Thomas Edmondes, the ambassador in Paris; Charles Cornwallis, the ambassador to Spain; Edward Conway, the governor of Brill; and Dudley Carleton (1574–1632) in Venice and the Netherlands.[115] In addition he used the European tours of his former students – Henry's peers in the collegiate court – to gather information pertinent to confessional aspects of international relations.[116] In particular, he had Thomas Lorkin (d. 1625), the tutor of his brother-in-law Thomas Puckering, send him reports of troop movements in France, of the proceedings of the Jesuits and regarding French princes of the blood. In February 1612 Lorkin also obtained an agent in Paris, a mysterious Mr Forboyst, who offered to provide Newton information 'in all mysteries of state… as plenary, as any my Lord Treasurer shall have himself'.[117] As Jacob Soll has demonstrated so formidably, collecting information and storing it systematically was one of the great state-building developments of the seventeenth century.[118] Newton established his diplomatic network to gather confessional data that could be used to persuade the Stuarts to favour Calvinist causes abroad.

After Henry's death, Murray attempted to build a similar information network for Charles. His was more limited. Nevertheless he offered Dudley Carleton, in particular, news of the court, the king's evolving foreign policy and the petitions of the parliament after 1618 in return for information about the estates in the Netherlands, and tokens from figures of international Calvinist standing, such as Prince Maurice of Nassau (1567–1625).[119] The potential military applications of this correspondence were clear from the beginning. The godly soldier Sir Edward Cecil (1572–1638) wrote to Thomas Murray from Utrecht immediately after the death of Prince Henry, promising to help Charles 'inherit the honor of virtue which his brother did possess'. More specifically, he offered the prince 'Modelles of all Instrumentes and Engines necessarie to an Armye, especiallie cummencinge all manner of Artillerie that P[rince] Morys hath by

[114] Newton began writing letters to foreign princes on Prince Henry's behalf in 1600: BL, Harleian MS 6986, fol. 61[r] and Harleian MS 7007. Subsequently, with Salisbury's assistance, he collected incoming diplomatic letters: Harleian MS 7002, fols. 83, 84, 87, 89, 95.

[115] Cornwallis: BL, Harleian MS 7007, fols. 255, 256. In BL, Harleian 7002, see Conway, fols. 69–70, 73–4, 105–106[r], 107–108[r], 109, 133, 142–143[r], 170–171[r], 178–179[r], 184[r–v], 196[r–v], 209–10, 213, 223, 233–234; Edmonds, fols. 182, 185–186[r]; Carleton, fol. 217.

[116] BL, Harleian MS 7007, fols. 215[r], 221[r–v].

[117] BL, Harleian MS 7002, fol. 160[r].

[118] Jacob Soll, *The information master: Jean-Baptiste Colbert's secret state intelligence system* (Ann Arbor, 2009).

[119] *CSPD James*, vol. II, pp. 160, 509, 530, 581; *CSPD James*, vol. III, pp. 53, 224.

longe experience found fitte' in the war between the Dutch republic and Spanish.[120] Negotiations for the models continued for several years before Charles received them in October 1616 and was taught how to use them by the Flemish soldier who delivered them. Murray also asked Carleton for books describing Dutch military techniques in more detail.[121] He was collecting the knowledge that Charles could use to serve the Calvinist cause with arms as well as words.

Only five members of Henry's retinue followed Newton into Charles's household. After the prince's death in November 1612, James had not rushed to increase the size or grandeur of Charles's establishment.[122] In the last three years of his short life, Henry had begun to attract a reversionary interest to his court, and the diplomat Isaac Wake claimed that James wanted his second son 'kept within a streicter compasse then the former, and not to exceed his ordinarie in diet or followers, or any other course of shew or charge'. Nevertheless, it was not the puritans or Presbyterians who were excluded from Charles's affinity. Indeed this was the moment when Hakewill and the equally sober Richard Milbourne were appointed to 'keep [Charles] from popery'.[123] Conformist Calvinists Robert Carey, Sir James Fullerton and Sir Robert Ker of Ancram were to govern the prince's household. Sir David Foulis, Henry's cofferer, who was 'very kind and helpful' to puritans, managed the officers 'below stairs'.[124] James seemed content to allow Charles's court family to become as determinedly Calvinist as Henry's had been, even during the period between 1614 and 1617, when there were diplomatic exchanges regarding a Spanish marriage for his son.[125] In short, there was nothing about Charles I's education in the first eighteen years of his life that pre-disposed him to Arminianism or ceremonialism, or against the strict Calvinism of his household.

It has been suggested that James allowed puritans and Scottish Presbyterians to dominate Charles's household between 1612 and 1618

120 SP 14/71, fol. 32r. The NA has dated the letter to October 1612; however, the references to the death of Henry and to Cecil's role in accompanying Princess Elizabeth to Heidelberg suggest it may have been composed in early 1613.

121 *CSPD James*, vol. II, pp. 383, 385, 398, 415, 420, 473.

122 BL, Additional MS 45142; BL, Harleian MS 7002, fol. 270r; *Manuscripts of His Grace the duke of Portland, preserved at Welbeck Abbey*, ed. James Cartwright, 25 vols. (London, 1891–1919), vol. IX, p. 33; Kevin Sharpe, *Politics and ideas in early Stuart England: Essays and studies* (London, 1989), pp. 288–91.

123 *CSPD James*, vol. II, p. 160; Aysha Pollnitz, 'Humanism and the education of Henry, Prince of Wales', in Timothy Wilks (ed.), *Prince Henry revived: Image and exemplarity in early modern England* (London, 2007), pp. 27–30; Wilks, 'Court culture of Prince Henry', pp. 218–21.

124 SP 14/141, fol. 56r; NA, E 101/434/3, E101/434/2; Chamberlain, *Letters*, vol. II, p. 58 (quotation); Fiona Pogson, 'Foulis, Sir David, first baronet (d. 1642)', *ODNB*.

125 *CSPV*, vol. XIV, p. 484; see also pp. 65, 155, 305, 333, 479, 560.

because he was too caught up with his favourites to exhibit any 'interest in his only surviving son'. Insofar as he did consider Charles, it was to keep him 'under thumb'.[126] In fact, the letters of John Chamberlain (1553–1628), the Jacobean news-hound, show the king bringing his son to public notice and introducing him to a number of his future responsibilities. Charles played a prominent role in dynastic events, serving as chief mourner at his brother's funeral; 'bridesman' to his sister Elizabeth on her February 1613 marriage to Frederick V, count Palatine of the Rhine (1596–1632); host to his new brother-in-law during the remainder of his stay in England; and chief mourner following the death of Queen Anne in 1619.[127] Even more strikingly, James appeared on progress and state occasions with his son. The king took Charles to the opening of the Addled Parliament in April 1614. On the royal visit to the University of Cambridge in March 1615, the university orator, Francis Nethersole, called Charles 'Jacobissime Carole' and 'Jacobule'.[128] From 1616 onwards, the prince accompanied his father to meet with the London aldermen each year and receive their tribute. They inspected the London militia together and the prince stood in for his father at meetings of the Order of the Garter.[129] On 3 November 1616 he was created Prince of Wales in a lavish ceremony, the dignity of which was marred only when Lancelot Andrewes, then bishop of Ely, called on the congregation to 'pray solemnly for Prince Henry' rather than Charles.[130] The following year Charles sat on the council that governed England during James's visit to Scotland.[131] Far from hiding him away, James took every opportunity to introduce his son to the 'science of government'.

During this period, James was undoubtedly besotted with George Villiers and evidence confirms that Charles felt it keenly. Nevertheless, it was James who played 'Dear Dad' and crafted the reconciliation between 'Baby Charles' and his 'sweet boy', George. He castigated both young men for disrespectful behaviour towards the other – a lost ring, a drenching in the fountain, a slight regarding a dinner invitation – until these quasi-sibling rivals became firm friends in 1618.[132] By and large, James treated Charles as he had Prince Henry at the same age: he brought him

[126] Cust, *Charles I: A political life*, pp. 3–4 (quotation); David M. Bergeron, *Royal family, royal lovers: King James of England and Scotland* (Columbia, MI, 1991), p. 155; Carlton, *Charles I*, pp. 12–21.

[127] Chamberlain, *Letters*, vol. I, pp. 423, 427, 430, 434.

[128] Chamberlain, *Letters*, vol. I, pp. 522, 586–9.

[129] Chamberlain, *Letters*, vol. I, p. 611, vol. II, pp. 9, 299; SP 14/88/30.

[130] Chamberlain, *Letters*, vol. II, pp. 31–3.

[131] *CSPV*, vol. XIV, p. 710.

[132] SP 14/86/95; SP 14/87/40; BL, Additional MS 4176, fol. 71^r; *Calendar of the manuscripts of the Marquis of Bath, preserved at Longleat, Wiltshire*, ed. Sophia Crawford Lomas, 5 vols. (London, 1904–80), vol. II, p. 68.

to public notice as long as he was content to play the supporting role of student prince.[133] James VI and I placed his sons 'upon a publike stage, in the sight of all the people' from a young age and asked them to display their princely potential, confessional identities and the fruits of their careful education for a popular audience.[134] In the process of co-ordinating their public appearances and coaching Charles to perform his duty well, the king had ample opportunity to observe his second son closely. If James had misgivings about the direction of Charles's religious education in the years following Henry's death, he was well positioned to intervene.

In his *Basilicon doron* James had insisted that his sons learn to order their ecclesiastical polity and contain both rabid papists and impassioned Presbyterians when they encroached on the civil sphere. In practice, he surrounded them with conformist puritan and Presbyterian tutors and chaplains, who would defend his sons against zealous papists, who seemed the more serious threat after 1605. Under the governorship of these tutors and chaplains, both princes developed a confessional identity that placed them at the strictly predestinarian, sermon-gadding and anti-Catholic end of the Jacobean ecclesiastical spectrum. Both were in contact with continental figures of Calvinist militarism and carried the hopes of the godly in the British isles. How was it, then, that Prince Charles was lured by the siren call of Richard Mountague, bishop of Norwich, and Durham House towards the end of James's reign? What led him to turn against the ideology of the men and women who had raised him, indeed to regard their confessional practices as suspicious and potentially seditious? The key to answering this question lies in his liberal education.

JAMES'S PRESCRIPTIONS FOR HIS SONS' LIBERAL EDUCATION

In addition to instructing his sons on the 'crafte' of managing the churches in their kingdoms, James's *Basilicon doron* also offered his sons prescriptions for studying the 'liberal artes and sciences'. As we have seen, the king's own liberal education had given him the rhetorical skills and experience of biblical exegesis to respond polemically to political, theological and ecclesiastical challenges, to mount persuasive arguments in favour of monarchical government and to lead his subjects to (what he deemed to be) a better understanding of God's law on earth.[135] Learning was the foundation

[133] Pollnitz, 'Humanism and the education of Henry', pp. 29–31.

[134] James, *BD*, p. 4.

[135] Kevin Sharpe, *Remapping early modern England: The culture of seventeenth-century politics* (Cambridge, 2000), p. 135.

of James's princely persona. When Simon van de Passe depicted the king on the frontispiece to the second edition of James's collected *Workes*, he appended the motto 'knowledge makes the KING most like his maker'.[136] Nevertheless, when James drew the patterns for his own sons' course of studies, he claimed to hold the utility of 'the liberall artes and sciences' meanly. His heir, he wrote, should not be 'preassing to bee a passe-master' of these disciplines.[137] Locating James's writings in the context of late humanist pedagogy provides insight into his seeming inconsistency but the king's criticisms went rather further than those of his contemporaries. Much like his prescriptions on Presbyterianism, James's instructions regarding the study of grammar and rhetoric were haunted by the ghost of George Buchanan.

As we have seen, sixteenth-century humanists, including Erasmus and George Buchanan, had argued that a liberal education, above all other aspects of princely learning, would teach future governors to govern themselves and put a brake on over-mighty monarchy. James, however, drew his sons' attention to a passage in Virgil's *Aeneid* in which Anchises described a ruler's 'crafte' to his son: those of Greek nations could 'more pleasingly… draw forth living faces from marble' as artists, or 'better plead cases' as lawyers, 'or mark the movement of the sky' as philosophers and mathematicians. As a 'Roman', however, Aeneas should learn to 'rule [his] peoples by [his] power (for these will be [his] arts), to add law to peace, to spare the humble and to subdue the proud'.[138] James acknowledged some residual similarities between the classically trained orator and the prince; his sons would need to 'delight in reading, and seeking the knowledge of all lawful things' so they could 'controll every one' who performed a profession or craft, yet they must not search for knowledge 'nakedly'. Princes should not be 'like these vaine Astrologians, that studie night and day on the course of the stares… for satisfying their curiositie' alone.[139] James insisted that the first and last object of princely study was to 'order' and 'controll' their subjects; other learning and expertise in the liberal arts and sciences might need to be left behind.

To some extent, James's more vocational account of princely education reflected the prudential turn in late sixteenth-century pedagogical writing.

[136] James VI and I, *The workes of the most high and mightie prince, Iames by the grace of God, King of Great Britaine, France and Ireland, defender of the faith*, ed. James Montagu (London, 1620), STC 14345; Maria Wakely and Graham Rees, 'Folios fit for a king: James I, John Bill, and the king's printers, 1616–1620', *Huntington Library Quarterly*, 68.3 (2005), p. 472.

[137] James, *BD*, p. 46.

[138] Virgil, *Aeneid*, VI, lns. 847–53 in James, *BD*, p. 61, referred to in James, 'Meditation upon… the XXVII chapter of Saint Matthew', in *Political writings*, p. 249.

[139] James, *BD*, p. 44. Marginal annotations in 1603 and 1616 acknowledge Cicero's *De oratore*.

In book 1, chapter 10 of his *Politica* (1589), Justus Lipsius urged rulers to acquire learning 'eagerly, but in order that it may be used' to cultivate civil doctrine. He used Seneca's 106th letter to Lucilius to urge princes against being 'intemperate in study' and acquiring learning 'not for life but the schoolroom'.[140] When Oxford tutor Gabriel Harvey read Livy with Philip Sidney, he tried to leave his noble pupil 'studied for action' on the field or in the council chamber, rather than generally wise and virtuous.[141] In his essay 'On the educating of children', Michel de Montaigne argued that learning should 'deploy her resources for the conducting of a war, the commanding of a nation and the winning of the affection of a prince' instead of just 'drawing up dialectical arguments'.[142] These late sixteenth-century humanists were not just targeting their old pedagogical adversaries, the Aristotelian schoolmen, with their criticisms of the way noble education was being managed. The *bonae litterae* were also on the line. Montaigne claimed that Charles V had attributed his easy conquest of Naples and Tuscany 'to the fact that the Italian princes… spent more time becoming clever and learned' than becoming 'vigorous and soldierly'.[143] When William Shakespeare's eponymous prince Hamlet was 'put upon' by the military, political, moral and dynastic crises afflicting the 'rotten' state of Denmark, everyone from the groundlings to the gods could see that his studies at the University of Wittenberg had not prepared him to act for the commonwealth.[144] As the sixteenth century drew to a close, political writers and dramatists alike were beginning to wonder whether humanist pedagogy was equipped to ready rulers to meet the exigencies of the confessionalised and increasingly militarised state.

James VI and I's contemporaries recognised the *Basilicon doron* as a contribution to this sceptical discourse. Yet one knowledgeable reader, as least, wondered whether he had gone too far. Francis Bacon's (1561–1626) *Advancement of learning* (1605), dedicated to the king, praised James's plan for his heir's education as 'apt for action' and 'Empire'.[145] Yet, even at his most ingratiating, Bacon found the king's emphasis on the 'science of

[140] Justus Lipsius, *Politica: Six books of politics or political instruction*, ed. Jan Waszink (Assen, 2004), pp. 291, 293; see also Harro Höpfl, 'Oxthodoxy and reason of state', *History of Political Thought*, 23:2 (2002).

[141] Lisa Jardine and Anthony Grafton, '"Studied for action": How Gabriel Harvey read his Livy', *P&P*, 129 (1990).

[142] Michel de Montaigne, *The complete essays*, ed. M. A. Screech (London, 1987), p. 168.

[143] Montaigne, *Essays*, p. 162.

[144] Aysha Pollnitz, 'Educating Hamlet and Prince Hal', in David Armitage, Conal Condren and Andrew Fitzmaurice (eds.), *Shakespeare and early modern political thought* (Cambridge, 2009).

[145] Francis Bacon, *Of the proficience and aduancement of learning, diuine and humane* (London, 1605), STC 1164, sig. Vv3^{v}.

government' overly narrow. The lawyer took up James's quotation from Virgil's *Aeneid* to explain his position. Though it had pleased Virgil to attribute only 'the Art of Empire' to the Romans, 'leauing to others the arts of subiects: yet so much is manifest, that the Romanes neuer ascended to that height of Empire, till the time they had ascended to the height of other Arts'.[146] Star-gazing was not necessarily a vain pursuit, even for princes. The 'reformed computation of the year' that Julius Caesar, a master of the 'Art of Empire', had made to the calendar showed that 'he took it to be as great glorie to himself, to obserue and know the law of the heavens, as to give law upon the earth'.[147] James's support for narrowly vocational education for his sons was bad news for Bacon's hopes that the king would augment the study of natural philosophy. It was also at odds with his own persona as a philosopher-king, whom Bacon praised for being 'learned in all literature & erudition, diuine & humane'.[148]

Why would a learned king such as James attempt to cultivate intellectual myopia in his sons? When James's consideration of the study of grammar and rhetoric are examined, it becomes apparent that the spectre of George Buchanan and the seditious preachers of James's youth were plaguing his prescriptions for Henry's and Charles's liberal education as surely as they had inflected his advice for their religious studies. Grammar and rhetoric were the disciplines that James used most frequently in his own political 'crafte'. Nevertheless, in *The trew law of free monarchies*, James had rejected Buchanan's argument, drawn from Cicero's *De inventio* (I.I–II.3), that eloquence was the key to founding and ruling cities, supressing sedition and civilising men.[149] Instead, James insisted that both England and Scotland had been established by the sword of a conqueror; monarchy was better protected by the symbols of the sceptre and the sword than by fluent discourse.[150] In the *Basilicon doron*, he acknowledged that princes should be capable of grammatically correct speech but insisted that their language need only be 'plaine, honest, natural, comely, cleane, short, and sententious'. Determinedly learned or ornate speech, peppered with 'booke-language, and pen and inke-horne terms', was no better than a 'rusticall corrupt leide' for establishing royal clout.[151] Despite

146 Bacon, *Of the proficience and advancement of learning*, sig. C4r.
147 Bacon, *Of the proficience and advancement of learning*, sig. K4r.
148 Bacon, *Of the proficience and advancement of learning*, sig. A3r–v.
149 Markku Peltonen, *Classical humanism and republicanism in English political thought, 1570–1640* (Cambridge, 1995), pp. 7–11, 46–8 and *Rhetoric, politics, and popularity*, pp. 13–20, 23–6; Skinner, *Reason and rhetoric*, pp. 68–74, 78–93; Brian Vickers, '"The power of persuasion": Images of the orator, Elyot to Shakespeare', in James J. Murphy (ed.), *Renaissance eloquence* (Berkeley, 1983).
150 James, *Trew law*, pp. 73–4.
151 James, *BD*, pp. 53–4.

having used the printing press to advance his own vision of kingship and his authority as a ruler, he claimed that taking long writing projects in hand might distract his sons, or make them objects of ridicule. In particular, James urged Henry and Charles to eschew writing in Greek and Latin, largely because 'ynew of poore schollers would match you in these languages'. 'It best becometh a king to… goe before all subiects', which he could do more successfully in his native tongue.[152]

Again, James's ambivalence about royal rhetoricians reflected a sceptical turn in contemporary pedagogical writing. As Markku Peltonen has shown, proponents of strong monarchical government at the turn of the sixteenth century worried that rhetoric was an inherently popular art.[153] Montaigne suggested that overmuch concern for 'fine "colours of rhetoric"' betrayed a vulgar desire 'to entertain the masses who are unable to take [the] heavier solid meat' of reason and matter.[154] In his *Les Six livres de la république*, Jean Bodin had acknowledged that rulers could turn this to their advantage. They could 'charm the most savage and cruel men with the sweetness of eloquence'. In practice, however, Bodin noted that it more frequently came to pass that wily demagogues would use words to ensnare 'the people in sedition' and bring 'commonwealths to utter ruin'. The eloquent preachers 'of our age' were particularly to blame for giving 'chase to kings, and impiety to their states'.[155] In his essay 'On the vanity of words', Montaigne agreed:

> [Rhetoric] is a means invented for manipulating and stirring up the mob and a community fallen into lawlessness… in states such as Athens… and Rome where the populace, or the ignorant, or all men, held all power and where everything was in perpetual turmoil, the orators flooded in…Rhetoric flourished in Rome when their affairs were in their worst state and when they were shattered by the storms of civil war.[156]

In popular estates, the dangers of oratory could hardly be avoided. Montaigne hoped, however, 'that polities which rely on a monarch have less use' for rhetoric.[157] In this context, it seems likely that James was trying

152 James, *BD*, p. 55. 153 Peltonen, *Rhetoric, politics, and popularity*, pp. 218–27.

154 Montaigne, *Essays*, p. 190.

155 'Orateurs charment les plus sauuages et cruels hommes par la douceur d'eloquence… Et n'y a point de moyen plus grand d'appaiser les seditions, & co[n]tenir les sugets en l'obeissance des Princes'; 'qu'ils ont esmeu les peuples à sedition… les Republiques… les ont du tout ruinées… celà par l'exemple des Orateurs d'Athenes ou de Rome, mais bien par ceux de nostre age, qui ont si bien besongné que tout l'Empire… Et s'en est trouué qui par leur eloquence ont donné la chasse aux Rois, & empiété leur estat': Jean Bodin, *Les Six livres de la république* (Paris, 1579), pp. 658–60.

156 Montaigne, *Essays*, p. 342. 157 Montaigne, *Essays*, p. 342.

to provide his sons with a prophylactic against demagoguery by urging them to value only 'clean, shorte, and sententious' words.

More particularly, however, James was attempting to warn Henry and Charles that by engaging in deliberative or judicial rhetoric, as he had done, they would be offering their opponents an opportunity to argue the other side of the case.[158] A prince, James instructed his sons, might explain his political 'reasoning' in private, but, when it came to 'pronouncing of sentences' or declaring his 'wil in judgement', he should not suffer 'of any contradiction'. It lessened 'the maiestie of your authoritie, and maketh the processes endlesse'.[159] The king had to enunciate in a manner 'voyd of all ambiguitie' so that his meaning could not be 'rent asunder in contrary sences'.[160] In 1603, James was thinking of George Buchanan and the Presbyterian clergy who had 'calumniated' against his mother and grandmother in 'their populare Sermons'. Just as they had effected reformation in Scotland 'by popular tumult and rebellion', so they had come 'to fantasie to themselues a Democraticke forme of gouernment'. Arguing with passionate preachers or would-be tribunes merely encouraged them to respond with further 'idle and unreverent speeches'.[161] It was better, surely, to let the waves of popular tumult crash on the empty beach and spend themselves than to attempt to stand against them.[162]

Ultimately, James's experience with a series of English parliaments pushed him to put his theory into practice. In March 1604 James had told the Commons and the Lords that 'it becometh a king… to use no other Eloquence then plainness and sinceritie' with his parliament.[163] Yet denying sophistry was a technique for establishing rhetorical *ethos* as a speaker of 'plainness and sinceritie'.[164] When James did call these early sessions, moreover, he was unusually willing to speak with his Houses in person, at some length and according to the rules of deliberative rhetoric.[165] As Bishop Williams argued, 'that learned King gave too much way to those popular Speeches' by his own willingness to argue.[166] It took the fate of his plans for the Union (1606–7), the rejection of the Great Contract (1610)

158 Peltonen, *Rhetoric, politics, and popularity*, pp. 230–2.
159 James, *BD*, p. 54.
160 James, 'Speech… 19 March 1604', in *Political writings*, p. 146.
161 James, *BD*, p. 26.
162 Peltonen, *Rhetoric, politics, and popularity*, pp. 225–35; Malcolm Smuts, *Court culture and the origins of a royalist tradition in early Stuart England* (Philadelphia, 1987), pp. 258–62.
163 James, *Political writings*, p. 146; see similarly pp. 156, 159, 162.
164 David Colclough, *Freedom of speech in early Stuart England* (Cambridge, 2005), pp. 145–6.
165 Peltonen, *Rhetoric, politics, and popularity*, p. 148.
166 [Anonymous], *Cabala, sive Scrinia sacra*, pp. 255–6.

and the standoff over supply and impositions (1614) to convince him that the idle tongues of MPs could only be stilled by personal rule. As Andrew Thrush has shown, the teenaged Charles watched his 'father's desperate manoeuvrings to avoid a parliament' throughout that period.[167] James had learnt from his own willingness to 'play the linguist' that it could prove counter-productive. He urged his sons to become '*lex loquens*', the speaking law, rather than royal rhetoricians.[168]

In his desire to protect his sons from latter-day Buchanans, James may have gone too far. As Francis Bacon argued in 1605, as long as rulers had to call their increasingly eloquent parliaments for emergency supply, address their counsellors or secure the co-operation of their subjects more generally, they needed to be able to appeal to their people's imaginations and move their wills. He cited Proverbs 16:21; while 'profoundnesse of Wisedome, will helpe a Man to a Name or Admiration' it was 'Eloquence, that preuayleth in an actiue life'.[169] Or, as that arch-critic of rhetoric, Thomas Hobbes, eventually acknowledged in his *Leviathan*, 'if there be not powerfull Eloquence, which procureth attention and Consent,' in political life, 'the effect of Reason will be little'.[170] Bacon encouraged rulers to have 'places… readie handled' to provide matter for the deliberative orations they would be called upon to deliver.[171] In his expanded Latin edition of the *Advancement of learning* in 1623, dedicated to James, Bacon prepared for this eventuality by offering the king a collection of '*Antitheta*' or '*theses* argued *pro* & *contra*' both as a model and a storehouse for his princely usage.[172] Rather than imagining popular passions wearing themselves out like a wave crashing on the beach, Bacon urged his reader to envision the common sort as beasts gathered at Orpheus' theatre to see their ruler perform. The adversarial parliamentary sessions of James's reign had confirmed for the former lord chancellor that a prince had little choice but to keep 'playing his harp' or 'all the birds and beasts' would remember 'their seuerall appetites' and disperse. Some would turn to 'pray, some of game, some of quarrell'. Unless the king kept up his

[167] Andrew Thrush, 'The personal rule of James I, 1611–1620', in Thomas Cogswell, Richard Cust and Peter Lake (eds.), *Politics, religion and popularity in early Stuart Britain: Essays in honour of Conrad Russell* (Cambridge, 2002), p. 102.

[168] James, 'Meditation upon… the XXVII chapter of Saint Matthew', in *Political writings*, p. 238; James, 'Speech… 19 March 1604', in *Political writings*, p. 161.

[169] Bacon, *Of the proficience and advancement of learning*, sig. Rr2[r.]

[170] Hobbes, *The leviathan*, pp. 483–4.

[171] Bacon, *Of the proficience and advancement of learning*, sig. Nn4[r]; see also Brian Vickers, *In defence of rhetoric*, rev. edn. (Oxford, 1989), p. 276.

[172] Francis Bacon, *De dignitate & augmentis scientiarum libros IX*, trans. William Rawley (London, 1623), STC 1108, pp. 314–35.

flow of 'eloquence and perswasion of Bookes, of Sermons, of harangues', Bacon predicted prophetically, 'all thinges' would 'dissolve into Anarchie and Confusion'.[173]

James, however, claimed that, when the monarch was 'set on a stage', Orpheus' most soothing instrument was not eloquent speech but courtly exercises and recreations.[174] He recommended his sons use shows of physical dexterity, like 'running, leaping, wrestling, fencing, dancing, and playing at caitch or tennise, archerie, palle maillé'. Above these 'it becommeth a Prince best… to be a faire and good horse-man', capable of riding dangerous mounts and displaying his ability to 'handle your armes thereon' in 'the tilt, the ring, and low-riding for handling of your sword'. Not only were these good exercise for the body but they also served 'greatly for allurements to the people' and encouraged subjects to 'embrace and follow [the king's] vertue' in more substantial things.[175] At the beginning of the seventeenth century, Erasmus' argument for prioritising letters over courtly recreations and military exercises in princely education had been turned on its head by one of the most learned, pacific princes in Europe.

James's determination to critique the pedagogical practice of George Buchanan resulted in his strident critique of the liberal arts and sciences. He claimed to deny the honour and utility of the studies that had facilitated his royal rebellion and sustained his own art of government. At best, James depicted the liberal arts and sciences as mere distraction from princely duties. At worst, expertise in the *ars rhetorica* could function as a Trojan horse. Subjects who 'fantasie to themselues a Democraticke forme of gouernment' could use the space created by deliberative orations to sneak inside the palace walls and undermine monarchical authority.

THE LIBERAL EDUCATION OF PRINCE HENRY: STUDIED FOR ACTION

James VI and I's polemic against George Buchanan and the liberal arts and sciences was more than discursive. It shaped and constrained the social practice of his sons' education in ways that sporadically frustrated their father and that would ultimately fashion their political and religious outlooks as well as their literary skills. Did the results constitute a 'lost Renaissance' for the humanist turn in royal education in the British isle? Did the king's prescriptions deprive his sons of rhetorical expertise

[173] Bacon, *Of the proficience and advancement of learning*, sig. I1v.
[174] James, *BD*, p. 49. [175] James, *BD*, pp. 55, 59.

at a moment when they needed to make their cases more persuasively than ever?

James had not expunged the liberal arts and sciences completely from his sons' curriculum, so both embarked on the well-trodden path through classical grammar and ancient authors. Adam Newton presented his royal charge with a copy of Hans Holbein's portrait of *Erasmus writing*, which suggests something of his self-image and pedagogical sympathies.[176] Newton started Henry's formal grammatical study of French at the age of five, much as James had done before him.[177] It probably helped Henry make progress with Latin, which he began at six or seven. The prince's earliest compositions in that tongue date from February 1603, his ninth birthday. They confirm that Henry had begun reading ancient authors and had commenced his ascent through the *Progymnasmata* of compositional exercises. The first step was the epistle, as Erasmus had directed.[178] Like Tudor and Stuart royal children before him, Henry also spent considerable time on modern European languages and on perfecting his italic hand.[179]

Nevertheless Henry's schooling departed from the grammar-school curricula and even the educations of his royal predecessors in several telling ways. James's advice in the *Basilicon doron*, that his sons should imagine themselves as set before the world on a 'public stage', was significant in this regard. From the first, Henry was required to play the role of student prince for the edification of his father's subjects. Henry thrived when riding courageous horses, playing tennis, practising with his pike and undertaking other military training.[180] In these respects, he certainly went before all his subjects and developed a chivalric affinity with the other young noblemen of his collegiate court, including his brother Charles, who studied horsemanship and feats of arms with him at Nonsuch.[181] His burgeoning expertise in his princely craft was advertised to foreign potentates, who received Henry's juvenile letters in French and Latin.[182] Domestically, the Stuart prince also accepted an extraordinary number of literary gifts and pedagogical treatises, more even than Edward VI had

[176] Strong, *Henry Prince of Wales*, p.28. [177] BL, Harleian MS 6986, fol. 61^{r}.

[178] Generally, see Pollnitz, 'Humanism and the education of Henry', pp. 32–54. For examples of Henry's early letters, see BL, Harleian MS 7007, fol. 14^{r} and BL, Lansdowne MS 1236, fol. 66^{r}. Henry acquired Cranmer's copy of Erasmus' *De conscribendis epistolis* (Cologne, 1523), BL, 1083.d 1 from the Lumley Library in 1609. On the *progymnasmata* see Peter Mack, *Elizabethan rhetoric: Theory and practice* (Cambridge, 2002), esp. pp. 27–41.

[179] WLTC, MS R 7 23*, I.

[180] Timothy Wilks, 'The pike charged: Henry as militant prince', in Timothy Wilks (ed.), *Prince Henry revived: Image and exemplarity in early modern England* (London, 2007), pp. 196–201.

[181] Strong, *Henry Prince of Wales*, pp. 8, 41–3, 215.

[182] See the index in BL, Harleian MSS 7007, 7008.

accumulated, and many referred to the *Basilicon doron* in some way.[183] James's treatise had made educating Henry a natural part of seeking royal patronage. Eventually, with his father's assistance, Henry established a 'truly princely library' at St James and stocked it with gifts, the remnants of Lord Lumley's library and his own purchases.[184] Managed by the natural philosopher Edward Wright, it was an institution that would complement Newton's information network.[185] Henry's library promised to parlay the enthusiasm that his education had excited into a repository of natural, military and humane knowledge for his royal government. He also became the first British prince to matriculate at university when he entered Magdalen College, Oxford, in August 1605.[186] Henry did not keep Oxford terms or take a degree. Given that the university felt obliged to address him in the vernacular, rather than Latin, when he visited, this may have been for the best.[187] James, moreover, had made it clear in the *Basilicon doron* that Henry should not become a 'passe-master' in the liberal arts and sciences.

There was little risk of that. During the early years of Henry's schooling, Adam Newton took James's caution against over-zealous study seriously. Henry was allowed to move fairly slowly through elementary authors and composition exercises. Antoine le Fevre de la Boderie, the French ambassador, reported in 1606 that Henry studied for two hours a day.[188] To the ambassador, this sounded creditable, but it represented a significant dip from the time that Tudor princes and James VI himself had committed to learning. Unlike other reformed princes in the British isle, including Edward VI, Elizabeth I and James VI and I, Henry had comparatively scant acquaintance with Greek.[189] Furthermore, Newton did not tax Henry to develop his powers of *inventio* in his early compositions. Drafts of Henry's Latin letters often survive in the schoolmaster's

[183] John Buchtel, '"To the most high and excellent prince": Dedicating books to Henry, Prince of Wales', in Timothy Wilks (ed.), *Prince Henry revived: Image and exemplarity in early modern England* (London, 2007), pp. 104–33.

[184] 'In Bibliotheca tua, vere Regia': BL, Royal MS 12 F XI.

[185] T. A. Birrell, *English monarchs and their books: From Henry VII to Charles II* (London, 1987), pp. 32–9.

[186] Isaac Wake, *Rex Platonicus* (Oxford, 1607), STC 24939, sig. A2^{v}. For the visit, see BL, Harleian MS 7044, fols. 100^{r}–107^{r}; CUL Additional MS 34, fols. 28^{r}–45^{v}.

[187] CUL, Additional MS 34, fols. 105^{r}–106^{v}; Anthony Nixon, *Oxfords triumph in the royall entertainement of his moste excellent maiestie, the queene, and the prince* (London, 1605), STC 18589, sig. E3^{r-v}; *pace* Strong, *Henry Prince of Wales*, p. 14.

[188] Birch, *Life of Henry*, p. 76.

[189] Henry used the occasional Greek phrase in BL, Harleian MS 7007, fols. 171^{r}, 231^{r-v} but read authors in Latin or, more typically, a modern language.

hand, suggesting that he dictated the text to his pupil or had him commit the Latin to memory and reproduce it accurately.[190] There is no sign that he expected Henry to undertake double translations, as John Cheke had had Edward VI perform and Roger Ascham had set Elizabeth I. Nor are there surviving exercises from before 1607 that show Henry extracting and ordering his own *loci* from ancient authorities. His education lacked the political and religious urgency that had spurred on Edward's and James's humanist studies.

Despite the fact that Newton had done no more or less than James asked of him, the king grew frustrated by Henry's lack of commitment to his studies. The prince failed to complete a number of his school exercises, including a task that was intended as a New Year gift for his father in 1606. It involved translating Joshua Sylvester's English verse renderings of the French poet Guy du Faur, seigneur de Pibrac's, *Quatrains*, which Sylvester had dedicated to the prince, into Latin. Henry had made this difficult project more manageable by turning the French poetry and English doggerel into Latin prose. Even so, he abandoned the exercise on the thirteenth folio.[191] Admittedly Tudor royal children occasionally struggled to meet their schoolmasters' and parents' academic expectations. Yet Prince Henry seems to have shirked study not because he was ill or pushed beyond his capacities but because he deemed it tedious and unnecessary. A court gossip, who wrote under the pseudonym 'Vincent', reported in 1605 that James had publically 'found fault w[i]th' Henry 'for not following his booke' with sufficient application. Henry allegedly retorted that assiduous study was for clerks rather than princes.[192] The Venetian ambassador, Nicolo Molin, offered up a similar story in his 1607 *relazione*: Henry 'studied chiefly under his father's spur, not of his own desire', and James had chided him and threatened to leave the crowns of England and Scotland to his brother. In Molin's retelling, Henry's self-defence was more specific. 'I know what becomes a prince', he was said to have declared. 'It is not necessary for me to be a professor, but a soldier and a man of the world'.[193] This was a recognisable paraphrase not of early sixteenth-century arguments against letters but of James's instruction to Henry in his *Basilicon doron*. It must have been vexing for James to hear

[190] For example BL, Harleian MS 7007, fol. 22^{r}. For examples of corrections, see BL, Harleian MS 7007, fols. 14^{r}, 17^{r}, 22^{r}.

[191] WLTC, MS R 7 23*, VII, fol. 12^{v}; Guy du Faur, 'Tetrastika; or the Quatrains of Guy de Faur, Lord of Pibrac' in *Bartas his deuine weekes & workes*, trans. Josuah Sylvester (London, 1606), STC 21649a.5, sig. Yy2^{r}.

[192] SP 14/12, fol. 28^{v}.

[193] *CSPV*, vol. x, no. 739, p. 513.

his son using his own words against him. Perhaps there had been a little more polemic and less sincere prescription in the *Basilicon doron* than he wanted to admit.

What really shocked James was Henry's paucity of princely *inventio*. On New Year's Day in 1604 the prince had managed to get his literary tribute off to his father. It was a surprisingly sophisticated Latin poem that contrasted the riches that Zeus expected on feast days to the meagre literary offering Henry was making to James.[194] The verses were intended to compliment the king's Christian charity but James replied with the literary equivalent of a bolt of lightning. The king was pleased to see that Henry's handwriting had improved but he suspected, probably rightly, that his son had copied the poem rather than composed it himself. James longed

to ressave a letter from ye, that maye be… as well formid by youre mynde, as drawin by youre fingers; for ye maye remember, that, in my booke to ye [the *Basilicon doron*], I warne ye to be waire with that kynde of *witte*, that maye flye out the ende of youre fingers.

By copying a poem, Henry had demonstrated a lack of faith in his own princely powers of creation. By analogy, he doubted his authority. 'Trust a little more to youre owin strenth', James implored his son; '*audaces fortuna iuuat timidosque repellit* [fortune favours the brave and spits out the timid]… what ever you are about, *hoc ages* [carry it off]'.[195] James may have warned his heir against becoming a 'passe-master' of the liberal arts in theory, but he eventually discovered that he wanted his son to have the capacity to lead with his pen as well as his sword. Henry's recalcitrance forced James to rearticulate his academic expectations.

During the period 1607 to 1609, James and Newton compelled Prince Henry to take his liberal education seriously. He certainly did not give up on the tilt yard, but he did knuckle down to his books.[196] Newton had Henry work through his copy of Cicero's *De officiis* carefully, underlining unusual words and useful *loci* to transfer into a copybook and reuse in his own writing. He transliterated certain Greek terms and he also numbered the stages in a number of Cicero's arguments, suggesting that he was preparing for more demanding compositional genres of the *Progymnasmata*.[197]

In 1609, at the age of fifteen, Henry produced a sophisticated deliberative oration that made good use of Cicero's oratorical style and his

[194] BL, Harleian MS 7007, fol. 25^r. [195] BL, Harleian MS 6986, fol. 67^r.
[196] Cornwallis, *Discourse*, sigs. C4^r–D1^v.
[197] BL, C.28.a11. See his notations on pp. 9, 11, 17, 18, 105–6. He cited *loci* from *De officiis* in BL, Harleian MS 7007, fol. 229^v, amongst other places.

political philosophy. The prince's *exordium* claimed that he had been pondering what literary genre and subject would be 'most apt to my studies and most acceptable to Your Majesty' as a capstone New Year's gift. It occurred to him that 'amongst [his] school exercises there remained the Oration, the final work of the orator and so far not attempted by me'.[198] Given his facility with the neo-Ciceronian form in the resulting composition, it seems unlikely that this was his first attempt at the genre, but the assertion helped to establish his *ethos* as a dutiful son and prince. The subject matter was also chosen as a compliment to James, whom Henry said had come to him 'like a *Deus ex Machina*' with a suitable topic. He would write on 'the necessity of good letters [*bonae litterae*] for princes'. Henry proposed to support this proposition with 'sentiments that [he] drew from the mouth of Your Majesty and the grounds of reasons that [his] mind and reading supply to [him]'.[199] The prodigal son could not have framed an oration more likely to please his royal audience than one that combined filial piety, intellectual engagement with James's *Basilicon doron*, a readiness to demonstrate his *inventio* and belated gratitude for the Erasmian liberal education (*bonae litterae*) that his father and schoolmaster had foisted upon him.

Henry argued that a liberal education was honourable for and useful to princes. In fact, in the *confirmatio* of his oration, Prince Henry endorsed a much more Erasmian (or, at least, traditionally humanist) account of the liberal arts and sciences than James had offered in the *Basilicon doron*. He used a series of rhetorical questions to describe the ways that four liberal disciplines contributed to a prince's virtue and the 'crafte' of kingship. 'Does the prince wish to enjoy true liberty of the soul'? 'Does he want a mind well-fortified against all fortune' and to 'keep his passions tamed'? 'Would the prince desire to be able to rely on himself in everything that concerns him' and 'not to admire the things that seem marvellous to the crowd'?[200] 'These things… philosophy will supply', he promised. If a ruler

[198] 'Dubita[tio]nem iniiciebat quod vel studiis meis esset accom[m]odatissimum, Vel Ma[jestati] V[estrae] acceptissimum futurum': Henry, BL, Harleian MS 7007, fol. 229^{r}. I have the deepest gratitude to Dr Neil Wright for his advice on the translation of this unpublished and little known oration. Any errors that remain are my own.

[199] 'M[ajestatis] V[estrae] Genius… meis velut Deus ex machina intervenit… orationis meae argu[men]tum… esse putaui; et bonarum l[itte]rarum in Principibus necessitatem, cum iis quae ex Ma[jestatis] V[estrae] ore hausi, tum his quae mens ac lectio mihi suppeditat ra[tio]num firmamentis, astruendam duxi': Henry, BL, Harleian MS 7007, fol. 229^{r}.

[200] 'Vult Princeps vera animi libertate frui? Vult mente esse aduersus omnem fortunam bene composita… domitos habere affectus… Vult Princeps sua Omnia in se positu? Habere, quae vulgo mirabilia videntur non admirari nihil…? Haec… suppeditabit philosophia': Henry, BL, Harleian MS 7007, fol. 229^{v}.

wished 'to set down laws or establish decrees to rule the people with *imperium*', he should study 'politics'.[201] If the prince wished 'to understand how one man rises above the multitude, and takes from the successes of others those things that are healthy and fruitful for himself and his commonwealth, and how he turns away from base beginnings and vile ends', then, as Cicero had said, 'History is the greatest teacher for public life'.[202] Henry even defended the much maligned discipline of rhetoric. If a prince wished 'to urge that which is just, honest, and salutary in deliberations, judgements, in assemblies, or in council, to restrain the inflamed souls of the people from sedition, faction, and internal division', he needed to be eloquent.[203] Like Francis Bacon, Henry acknowledged that, as long as British princes had to negotiate with parliaments and operate with their subjects' consent, they had to be able to persuade them. With this oration he showed that he was willing and able to play Orpheus on the public stage.

In writing his final school exercise, the prince may have conceived of his father as an unreasonable, impassioned animal he needed to soothe and beguile. As Henry was praising his father's political and pedagogical writing, he was simultaneously using his newly won expertise in the liberal arts and sciences to explore intellectual territory that James had forbidden. The prince's interest in the historical writings of Tacitus had begun innocently enough. In 1609, his fellow collegiate courtier, John Harington of Exton (d. 1614), had sent him an excerpt from Tacitus' *Agricola* on the grain tribute in Roman Britain. Henry protested that he could not make it out. Tacitus' Latin was 'too obscure for [his] ability', particularly in that difficult place. Yet true to his desire, as expressed in his oration, to use *historia* to locate examples of virtuous conduct in public life, he asked for Harington's thoughts on two *sententiae* he had also extracted from Tacitus, showing Agricola's moral rectitude and wisdom in discharging his early civic responsibilities. Prince Henry declared that he now proposed to study the historian, since he had heard Tacitus' '*prudentia*... praised by all'.[204] That 'all', however, did not include his father, James VI and I.

[201] 'Vult Princeps leges condere, iura describeret populos imperio regere? Hoc dabit Politica': Henry, BL, Harleian MS 7007, fol. 229v.

[202] 'Vult unus homo quid multis hominibus evenerit intelligere, atque ex aliorum eventis quod sibi suaeque reipublicae salubre et frugi ferum capere, quod foedum inceptu foedum exitu vitare et declinare... Id docebit Historia optima... vitae magistra': Henry, BL, Harleian MS 7007, fol. 230r; Cicero, *De oratore*, II.II.36.

[203] 'In consultationibus, in iudiciis, in Senatu, in Comitiis vult quae iusta, quae honesta, quae salutaria suadere, a seditionibus, a factionibus, ab intestinis dissidiis concitatos populi animos revocare?': Henry, BL, Harleian MS 7007, fol. 229v.

[204] 'Non ausus sum inquam Tacitum inspicere quem prudentia admirabilem, brevibus & acutis sententii refertum, stylo, pro me captu, nimis obscuram, ab omnibus praedicari audiveram': BL,

Justus Lipsius' edition of Tacitus in 1572 and his *Politicorum sive civilis doctrinae libri sex* (1589) and *Monita et exempla politica* (1605), which wove *loci* from the Roman historian into a guide to political conduct, had made Tacitus fashionable amongst those 'whose family or fate calls them to the state'.[205] Tacitus could be seen to offer a cynical commentary on the overweening corruptions of imperial rule. Or he could be used to defend strong monarchy as the best solution to the religiously motivated conflicts of early modern Europe.[206] Members of the Dutch estates and their apologists read him both ways. The French crown gobbled up the feast of Tacitean *exempla* that Lipsius laid before it and used it to fuel centralisation and militarisation.[207] James VI and I, however, had little appetite for either reading. In November 1609 he told Isaac Casaubon that those 'who make Tacitus the great master of political prudence err'. He agreed that neo-Taciteans were bent on either accusing 'our present Princes of Tyranny' or manifestly teaching 'them the Principles of Tyranny'.[208] For James, Tacitus was a gateway to the political culture of inconstancy and dissimulation that he claimed to despise.

Despite James's stance, Prince Henry received a number of works that used Tacitus to instruct him in political prudence, including Samson Lennard's translation of Pierre Charron's *Of wisedome* (1608) and a 1609 manuscript copy of Robert Dallington's *Aphorismes ciuill and militarie*, extracted from Francesco Guicciardini.[209] Moreover he welcomed these

Harleian MS 7007, fol. 226r. Harington cited Tacitus, *Agricola*, 19 and Henry excerpted *loci* from 5 and 9.

205 'Utilissima pars iis, quos genus aut destinatio ad rempublicam vocant': Justus Lipsius, 'Epistola', in *Relectiones hyemales de ratione & methodo legendi utrasque historias, civiles & ecclesiasticas*, ed. Degory Wheare (Cambridge, 1684), Wing W 1596, sig. A7v. See also Ann Moss, '*Monita et exempla politica* as example of a genre', in Erik de Bom *et al.* (eds.), *(Un)masking the realities of power: Justus Lipsius and the dynamics of political writing in early modern Europe* (Leiden, 2011); Jan Waszink, 'Introduction', in Lipsius, *Politica*, pp. 52–5, 84–8.

206 Brooke, *Philosophic pride*, pp. 13–36; Burke, 'Tacitism, scepticism, and reason of state', pp. 479–89; Tuck, *Philosophy and government*, pp. 31–64.

207 J. H. M. Salmon, 'Cicero and Tacitus in sixteenth-century France', *American Historical Review*, 85:2 (1980); Jacob Soll, 'Amelot de la Houssaye (1634–1706) annotates Tacitus', *Journal of the History of Ideas*, 61:2 (2000) and *Information master*, pp. 39–42, 50–66; Martin van Gelderen, *The political thought of the Dutch revolt, 1555–1590* (Cambridge, 1992), pp. 180–96, 254–5.

208 'Quum dixisset Rex errare eos qui Tacitum magistratum civilis prudentiae unicum facerent': Isaac Casaubon, *Epistolae*, ed. Theodor Jansson van Almeloveen (Rotterdam, 1709), p. 53; 'qui ita sentiunt, eos tyrannidis Principes hodiernos tacite accusare; vel palam tyrannidis instituta videri velle eos docere': Isaac Casaubon (ed.), *Polybii Lycortae F. Megalopolitani Historiarum libri* (Paris, 1609), fols. iiv–iiir.

209 Pierre Charron, *Of wisdome three bookes*, trans. Samson Lennard (London, 1608), STC 5051, BL, C.82.b.13; Robert Dallington, *Aphorismes ciuill and militarie* (London, 1613), STC 6197, sig. A3v for the manuscript presentation copy, now in the Norfolk Record Office; see also K. J. Höltgen, 'Sir Robert Dallington', *Huntington Library Quarterly*, 47 (1984).

accounts of *prudentia mixta*. When Charles Cornwallis sent him a set of 'remembrances' in 1609 that included the suggestion that, in order to protect their estates, princes 'may touch upon the Verge of Vice', Henry asked him to send more such advice in the future.[210] At the same time as Henry was composing his *oratio* in praise of his father's wise advice, he was contemplating the utility of Lipsian-style kingship in England.

More dangerously still, there is some evidence that he was also considering the other side of the Tacitean coin, the discourse that used the Roman historian to criticise the corruption of imperial rule. There were wisps of what Richard Tuck called the 'new humanism' of scepticism and reason-of-state theory in at least two manuscripts that Henry received and preserved alongside his own schoolbooks.[211] The first was an incomplete and anonymous treatise, 'An instruction to princes', which included a suspiciously long indictment of rulers who 'heapeth' their 'favour, confidence and grace… upon one onlie', as Tiberius was accused of doing in the *Annales*. When a king had a favourite, the author warned, 'hee dissolveth the unitie of the soveraigntie, hee disbuiteth the counsell hee hath about him, hee weakneth the force of his armes, discordereth the equalitie of iustice, and letteth himself unawares be drawne into a perpetuall nett of wiles'. The cost to the state was significant, but so was the damage to the prince, who was liable 'to be deemed a weak and unwise man' for his partiality.[212] 'Civill warr', the author warned, 'springeth alwaies from the weakenes in the Prince'.[213] James VI and I's sexual proclivities and favourites were not mentioned directly, but their odour clung to the text.

The other manuscript treatise amongst Henry's schoolbooks, Arthur Gorges's (d. 1625) 'Breefer discourse tendinge to the wealth and strength of this kingedome, of Greate Brittayne' (1610), did not pull punches on that score. Gorges lamented the 'English, and Scotts' men, 'on whome the kinge, your father hath bestowed great and bountifull guifts', and who repaid him by seeking 'protections to saue them from arests, or els are readie dailie to begg newe suites'.[214] Gorges claimed to be loyal to James but his meditation on the need for arms and money – two preoccupations of the 'new humanism' – also described the Stuart king as presiding over a peace in which 'our wealth diminish, and forces decaye' as if the realm was in fact suffering 'the calamities of w[ar]'.[215] Gorges urged Henry to take

[210] BL, Egerton MS 3876, fol.3^{v}; Henry's reply is BL, Harleian MS 7007, fol. 266^{r}.
[211] Tuck, *Philosophy and government*, pp. 31–64. [212] WLTC, MS R 7 23* II, fols. 14^{v}, 16^{v}.
[213] WLTC, MS R 7 23* II, fol. 12^{v}. [214] WLTC, MS R 7 23* III, fol. 7^{r-v}.
[215] WLTC, MS R 7 23* III, fol. 3^{r}, evoking Tacitus, *Agricola*, 30; Tuck, *Philosophy and government*, pp. 31–64.

action to remedy these weaknesses and assist those 'whoe by Gods favour, and their noble care still steeare [the ship of state] right', by purging the court of luxury and investing in the navy, amongst other things.[216] British thinkers often met the Tacitean account of court corruption with a Ciceronian call to virtuous action.[217] This hardly made entertaining an appeal like Gorges's less politically contentious for Henry. The poet was rewarded shortly after his presentation with a place in the prince's household.[218] Had Prince Henry begun to imagine he was playing the role of Agricola on the Stuart stage?

The schooling of Henry, Prince of Wales, demonstrates the limits of James's own commitment to the polemically charged criticism of the liberal arts and sciences in the *Basilicon doron*. When Henry pushed back – by being only too willing to abdicate his princely *inventio* and by parroting his father's words to justify his shirking – James felt compelled to concede that Ciceronian eloquence was, in fact, useful for princes and sent his son away to master it. Between 1607 and 1609, Henry made rapid progress. His increased capacity to argue *in utramque partem* did not turn him into a popular opponent of monarchical government, but it did give him the literary skills, knowledge and intellectual independence necessary to strike out in a different political direction on his own. Henry's education was no 'lost Renaissance', even if the humanism he came to favour emphasised *prudentia mixta*. Had Henry lived, Tacitean discourses may have shaped British political culture from the centre. As it was, James's and Charles's public refusal to entertain the politics of necessity and reason of state tended to leave Tacitus as a refuge for those amongst their subjects who would accuse 'our present Princes of Tyranny'.[219]

THE LIBERAL EDUCATION OF PRINCE CHARLES: A RETREAT FROM RHETORIC?

As a duke, prince and king, Charles showed little inclination towards the sort of intellectual independence that characterised Prince Henry's response to his liberal education. He did not resist instruction, like his elder brother, or hijack and repurpose his teachers' writings to suit his own ends, as Henry VIII had done, let alone use his learning to actively resist

[216] WLTC, MS R 7 23*. III, fol. 22v.

[217] Peltonen, *Classical humanism and republicanism*, pp. 124–36.

[218] Colin Burrow, 'Gorges, Sir Arthur (d. 1625)', *ODNB*.

[219] Alan T. Bradford, 'Stuart absolutism and the "utility" of Tacitus', *Huntington Library Quarterly*, 46:2 (1983).

his pedagogue, like James himself. In fact, he seemed 'pathetically eager to please' his father.[220] The result, as Kevin Sharpe has observed, was that James VI effectively 'penned a script for the reign of his second son'. But should we also follow his claim that such an institution left Charles 'better briefed in the responsibilities of office' than any prince before him?[221]

Like Prince Henry, the young duke of York preferred to display his princely potential in martial exercises and courtly recreations. The eagerness with which he rode, ran and danced owed something to his father's *Basilicon doron*, but it was also a response to his infant ill health.[222] Elizabeth Carey had refused to let James put Charles in 'iron boots, to strengthen his sinews and joints' when he proved slow to walk.[223] Instead, her husband took him out to ride every day.[224] What began as rehabilitation became athleticism; even by contemporary standards, Charles became a skilled horseman. He hunted and rode with his brother and undertook military training alongside him.[225] As early as January 1605 he had managed the physical demands of his creation: 'little Charles was made greate D[uke] of Yorke'.[226] Shortly afterwards, Charles took to archery and shooting. Sometime in around 1606 or 1607, he described his favourite possessions as his 'pistolles… my horss… my pieces, and my cross bowes'.[227] On 27 February 1607, he presented himself to the Venetian ambassador, Zorzi Giustinian, brandishing a harquebus and offering to fight for the republic.[228] On 5 June 1610 he danced the role of Zephyrus in Samuel Daniel's *Tethy's festival*, a masque to celebrate Prince Henry's creation.[229] On 24 April 1611, he was elected a Knight of the Garter.[230] The Order played a formative role in his identity. As Charles would tell his son in May 1638, a prince's election represented the Garter Knights' 'joyfull & pregnant hopes of [his] manly virtues' and their 'encrease to your owne honour, both in prowes, wisdome, justice & all princely endowments'.[231] Despite historians' regular comments on his youthful sickliness and lack

[220] Cust, *Charles I: A political life*, p. 4.

[221] Sharpe, 'Private conscience… in the writings of Charles I', p. 642.

[222] James, *BD*, p. 59; *Letters and state papers… of King James the sixth*, pp. 46, 55; SP 14/8, fol. 175^{r}.

[223] Carey, *Memoirs*, p. 69; HHCP, 122/125; HHCP, 194/52; SP 12/16, fol. 69^{r}; Carlton, *Charles I*, p. 4.

[224] SP 14/16, fol. 69^{r}.

[225] HHCP, 125/8; *CSPD James*, vol. I, pp. 582, 592; Strong, *Henry Prince of Wales*, pp. 41–3.

[226] SP 14/12, fols. 8^{r}, 28^{v}.

[227] BL, Harleian MS 6986, fol. 154^{r}.

[228] *CSPV*, vol. x, no. 691, vol. xi, no. 792.

[229] David M. Bergeron, 'Creating Entertainments for Prince Henry's Creation (1610)', *Comparative Drama*, 42:4 (2008), pp. 444, 446.

[230] *CSPV*, vol. xii, no. 236.

[231] Bodleian, Ashmole MS 1108, fol. 117 cited by Richard Cust, 'Charles I and the Order of the Garter', *Journal of British Studies*, 52 (2013), p. 343.

of charisma, contemporaries remarked on Charles's grace in courtly performances and his bravery in chivalric feats at tournaments.[232]

Court gossip also commented favourably on his scholarship.[233] In 1607 Nicolo Molin claimed that Charles was 'far quicker at learning and studied more earnestly' than his brother.[234] He was certainly diligent.[235] Yet Charles was swifter to pick up the handling of a pike than a pen. The duke's liberal education began conventionally enough. His earliest surviving compositions are letters addressed to his father, or more frequently his older brother. In about 1606 he informed James that he was learning 'to decline substantiues and adiectiues' in the Latin tongue.[236] Unlike Henry or James, however, whose earliest missives were in French, almost all of Charles's early efforts were in English with a sprinkling of Scots. Nor was he able to pen the first few with his own hand.[237] Charles did learn French, but in February 1610 the prince's father still had to translate the friendly questions that the Venetian ambassadors put to his second son in that tongue.[238] Moreover, unlike Prince Edward's early compositions or Prince Henry's, Charles's letters were not carefully constructed to demonstrate the prince's copious diction or his mastery of advanced rules of grammar. Nor were they stuffed with commonplaces. Charles and his schoolmaster, Murray, had evidently swallowed neat James's instruction to his sons to adopt 'naturall and plaine' language 'not fairded with artifice'. Charles would simply report 'what sport I haue' and what 'great horses' he had ridden and conclude with a dutiful offer of service.[239] Charles Carlton described the repetitious letters and their author as 'uncertain and insecure… almost to the point of grovelling'.[240] In fact, Charles was articulating the obsequious sentiments decorum obliged him to use when addressing the heir apparent; he merely lacked the *copia* to do it gracefully.

In 1609 Charles began to compose letters in Latin. He was using the same textbooks as his brother and princely predecessors, including Erasmus' *Colloquia*, from which, Charles wrote, 'I trust I will be able to learn pure Latin and elegant manners'.[241] At this stage, however, his

[232] SP 14/80, fol. 40^{v}-41^{r}; Chamberlain, *Letters of John Chamberlain*, I, pp. 423, 431; Sharpe, *Image wars*, p. 112.

[233] SP 14/12, fol. 28^{v}. [234] *CSPV*, vol. x, no. 739.

[235] Heylyn, *Life and reign*, p. 10; William Lily, *Monarchy or no monarchy in England… [with] Passages upon the life and death of the late King Charles* (London, 1651), Wing L2228, p. 75.

[236] Facsimile in *Letters to King James VI*, ed. Alexander MacDonald (Edinburgh, 1835), unpaginated.

[237] BL, Harleian MS 6986, fol. 154^{r}. [238] *CSPV*, vol. xi, no. 792.

[239] BL, Harleian MS 6986, fols. 155^{r}, 156^{r}, 157^{r}. [240] Carlton, *Charles I*, p. 10.

[241] 'Ego iam lego Erasmi colloquia, ex quibus et Latinae linguae puritatem, et morum elegantiam discere posse me consido': BL, Harleian MS 6986, fol. 159^{r}.

grammar was still less sophisticated than his predecessors'. He could conjugate the active indicative and infinitive forms of verbs, but no more. The next twelve months marked a rapid acceleration in his literary skills. A 1610 letter to Henry shows that he had made some headway with Erasmus' *De conscribendis epistolis*, particularly the humanists' advice on addressing absent friends. Charles, who was also writing on behalf of his sister Elizabeth, claimed in well-balanced subjunctives that 'nothing' during the prince's 'long' absence 'can be delightful to me or to my most sweet sister, though your beloved presence is the most delightful remembrance of all'. Then he elaborated using examples: 'whether we refresh ourselves in hunting the deer or the stag, or in another mental diversion thereafter, the only thing we long for is the whole and undivided pleasure of doing it with you'.[242] The subject matter is the same as his earlier missives – his sport in hunting and riding, his filial duty and affection – but Charles had finally learnt to vary his presentation of it.

To write eloquently, according to Erasmus and other humanists, it was necessary to read and imitate ancient authors. As second son, Charles would not be in the market for a 'truly princely library', but in late 1609 Murray began to purchase books for him. He had twelve volumes covered in velvet for Charles and on 12 March 1611 the king's printer, John Norton, was paid £60.2s.8d. for 'sundrie books of diuerse sortes' for the duke and given permission to bill the exchequer for further texts for him, 'from tyme to tyme'.[243] The record of the books Murray ordered has not survived but the authors might be gleaned from the first literary gift that Charles presented to his father, probably in the New Year of 1611. It was a book of commonplaces, or 'flowers, plucked from ancient poets'. At eighty-five folios, it was a considerable intellectual enterprise for a child of his age to attempt and confirms contemporaries' accounts of his diligence. The duke must have spent weeks if not months extracting the quotations. The decision to focus on Latin poets and dramatists meant that verses from the early empire were heavily represented. Horace, Lucan, Martial, Ovid, Seneca and Virgil were quoted most frequently.[244] Nevertheless the poetry of empire sounded more loudly in Charles's education than the political philosophy of the republic.

[242] 'In long hac… absentia; nihil, Princeps Illustrissime, vel Suavissimae Sorori, vel mihi sine iucundissima vestrum omnium recordatione gratum, aut iucundum esse potest. Atque hinc sit, ut si quando cervorum, aut playcerotum venatione, vel quocunque alio oblecta mentia nos subinde recreemus, solidam eam omnem voluptatem vobis unice exoptemus': BL, Harleian MS 6986, fol. 160^{r}.

[243] SP 14/51, fols. 11^{r}, 12^{r}; SP 14/53, fol. 18^{r}.

[244] BL, Royal MS 12 DVIII, fol. 1^{r}.

In addition to revealing the Augustan emphasis in his classical reading, Charles's commonplace book suggests something about his 'wit, memory, and industry' and the way he was learning to write.[245] As we have seen in relation to Edward's collections of Bible sentences, the commonplace book was a critical method of storing and organising knowledge in sixteenth-century schoolrooms. Melanchthon had adapted it to teach reformers skills in theological argument. Lipsius had adapted it to teach prudential political reasoning.[246] Lawyers and natural philosophers, including Bodin and Bacon, used commonplace books to consolidate and organise data in preparation for reasoning and extrapolation.[247] Charles's *Florum flores*, however, did none of these things: his *loci* were collected to illustrate headings (*capita*) copiously and ornamentally. There were some headings that offered the duke an opportunity to dispose places argumentatively, but Charles did not bite. Did he lack the skill? Was he instructed otherwise? Did the notion of making a case simply not occur to him? His heading 'Concerning Christ', for instance, merely contains a single long quotation from Pseudo-Claudian's *Miracula Christi*.[248] If anything, the weight of the collection suggests the duke's desire to retreat from political argument in his literary exercises: Charles collected three *loci* in the collection 'Concerning counsel' but four entire sides of paper were devoted to quotations 'Concerning love'.[249]

Indeed, Charles seemed quite eager to conclude his formal schooling. On 26 November 1611 he declared to his father that he had 'finished my course of studies' and proposed 'to attend always upon Your Majesty, so that I could learn to obey and serve Your Majesty in all things'. After the duty he owed to God, Charles described such service as his 'highest and greatest desire'.[250] He had no hesitations about the life of *negotio*, or learning the 'crafte' of government, but deemed liberal education to have little bearing on his royal responsibilities. He was, perhaps, affirming the knightly service he owed his father as a member of the Order of the Garter, or as the head of his newly independent household.[251] James VI's

[245] 'Ingenii, Memoriae, et Industriae, id est, mei qualiscanq[ue] in studiis progressus, rude specimen exhibeant': BL, Royal MS 12 D VIII, fol. 2^{r}.

[246] Ann Moss, 'The *Politica* of Justus Lipsius and the commonplace-book', *Journal of the History of Ideas*, 59:3 (1998).

[247] Ann Blair, *The Theater of nature: Jean Bodin and renaissance science* (Princeton, 1997).

[248] BL, Royal MS 12 DVIII, fols. 19^{v}–20^{r}.

[249] BL, Royal MS 12 DVIII, fols. 10^{r}-11^{v}, 22^{v}.

[250] 'Iam finissem cur sum studiorum, ut possem semper T[uam] M[ajestatem] adesse, ut etiam discam eidem obedire & seruire in omnibus: quod quidem erit semper mihi post officium Deo debitum summa et maxima uoluptas': BL, Additional MS 19402, fol. 43^{r}.

[251] Carey, *Memoirs*, pp. 70–2; *CSPD James*, vol. 11, pp. 21, 28, 86.

response does not survive, but Charles's readiness to end his education did not provoke his father, as Henry's active disobedience had done.

James was certainly aware that his second son had taken his exhortations to obedience very seriously indeed. Even in a patriarchal age, Prince Charles's zeal in following 'all the movements of his father like a shadow, praiseworthy as it is' startled the Venetian ambassador.[252] The other side of this coin was that Charles became extremely anxious at the prospect of incurring paternal displeasure. In March 1613, Charles wrote to ask forgiveness for being 'so foolish as to sende' a message to James bearing 'anie comment but my owen'.[253] After Queen Anne's death in March 1619, Charles heard that his father blamed him for persuading her to make over her moveable property to him. The prince begged Buckingham to intercede on his behalf. He pleaded to be allowed to return the legacy and 'submit my selfe as wel in this as in all other things'. 'I am verri sorri... I will be content to have anie penance inflicted upon me... I deserve to be punniched for my ill fortune', he concluded miserably.[254] Despite 'Babby' Charles's uneven progress in 1611, James may well have concluded that the prince was doing his best and was likely to be panicked, rather than spurred on, by admonishment.[255]

Thus James was not provoked to anger, but nor did he attempt to accelerate or intensify his son's studies, as he had Henry's. Charles *was* required to stick with his lessons but they did not become more demanding. On 24 April 1612, the exchequer received a warrant to pay Jehan de Beauchesne (*c.* 1538–1620), Princess Elizabeth's former writing master, £60 for his attendance on the duke of York.[256] Between December 1611 and November 1614, Charles continued to send his father dutiful letters that testified to the effectiveness of Beauchesne's instruction in improving his hand, Charles's increasingly rich Latin and French vocabularies, and his proclaimed enthusiasm for 'the liberal arts and exercises of the body'.[257] Yet we lack positive evidence that Charles was moving towards those more difficult exercises in the *progymnasmata* that required extensive *inventio*.

[252] *CSPV*, vol. XVII, p. 85. [253] BL, Harleian MS 6986, fol. 182^r.

[254] BL, Harleian MS 6986, fols. 195^r–196^v; Chamberlain, *Letters*, vol. II, p. 219; SP 14/107, fols. 7^r, 55^r, 59^r.

[255] BL, Cotton MS Titus C VI, fol. 156^r.

[256] HHCP, 129/105. See Jehan de Beauchesne, *A booke containing diuers sortes of hands as well the English as French secretarie with the Italian, Roman, chancelry and court hands. Also the true and iust proportio[n] of the capitall Romae set forth*, engraved by John Baildon (London, 1571), STC 6446 and eight subsequent editions.

[257] 'In bonarum atrium studiis, et liberalibus corporis exercitiis' and several other facsimiles in *Letters to King James VI*, ed. Alexander MacDonald (Edinburgh, 1835), unpaginated.

In fact, Prince Charles's capstone school exercise was not a deliberative oration, as his brother's had been, or indeed as Edward VI and countless grammar-school boys had performed to demonstrate their mastery of rhetoric. Rather, the literary feat with which Charles crowned his liberal education in around 1616 was a scribal manuscript edition 'of the kings short poesis that ar not printed'.[258] A number of hands assisted him with the enterprise and it was eventually presented to James for correction, but Charles was the guiding editorial voice.[259] It was his script, for instance, that divided the poems into 'Amatoria' and 'Miscellanea' and that classified them as sonnets, songs or devotional verses.[260] The fact that the exercise dealt with James's poetry did not make it apolitical. Indeed, the collection included sallies against those who 'imagined Democracie' in the British isle.[261] Charles copied a sonnet James had written 'upon occasion of some great disorders in Scotland' in which the king described the 'cruell' trials of his youth and his betrayal at the hands of those who should have nourished him. His 'miserable Mother' had left him to a callous nurse. His educators were 'wise Pieridaes', an ironic reference to those sisters who failed to equal the Muses and who became twittering birds as punishment for their pretensions. Finally there were the rebellious noblemen, whom he figured as 'shawes [slaves] of Marcellus' (Caesar's republican opponent, who was killed by his servant Magius), who 'made a King of me'.[262] Nevertheless, Charles's role as an editor of the collection was not to defend or oppose this argument but to absorb it, pass judgement on whether it was worthy of inclusion and locate it under a heading. Acting as a textual editor was a literary exercise that Charles continued to enjoy during his reign, as is evident from his annotations on his copy of Shakespeare's second folio.[263] The form of Charles's liberal education encouraged him to think of himself as a judge or arbiter of others rather than a participant in debate or conversation. Moreover, the subject matter suggests that he had little inclination, encouragement or indeed intellectual confidence to do more than tinker with his father's words.

[258] BL, Additional MS 24195. 1616 is the latest date attached to poems contained within: James VI and I, *Poems of James VI of Scotland*, ed. James Craigie, 2 vols. (Edinburgh, 1955–8), vol. II, pp. xxii–xxiii. The poems in the MS are printed pp. 65–160. On the possibility that James co-authored some verses with Sir Thomas Erskine of Gogar, see Curtis Perry, 'Royal authorship and the problems of manuscript attribution in the poems of King James VI and I', *Notes and Queries*, 46:2 (1999).

[259] For James's corrections, see BL, Additional MS 214195, fols. 12^{v}, 49^{v}–50^{v}, 56^{r}–57^{r}.

[260] BL, Additional MS 214195, fols. 2^{v}–3^{r}. [261] James, *BD*, p. 26.

[262] BL, Additional MS 214195, fol. 45^{v}.

[263] William Shakespeare, *Comedies, histories and tragedies* (London, 1632), STC 22274, Royal Library, Windsor, 1080415; see also Birrell, *English monarchs and their books*, p. 45.

There is no positive evidence that Charles spent much time learning to argue *in utramque partem* or that his powers of *inventio* were unduly stretched by his schooling. Peter Heylyn, Charles's first biographer, claimed that the prince was forced into a sort of 'retiredness' by 'the imperfection of his Speech, not fitting him for publick discourse'.[264] We need not go so far: Charles overcame the worst of his physical difficulties at a young age. Elizabeth Carey protected the duke from his father's plan to cut the 'string' under his tongue to correct his speech impediment, and used a gentler regime to encourage Charles to talk.[265] She had sufficient success that, in March 1613, Charles and his new brother-in-law, Frederick, elector Palatinate, were prepared to reply briefly and graciously, and (apparently) simultaneously in Latin, to the welcome offered by the vice-chancellor of the University of Cambridge.[266] In March 1621, moreover, Charles had made a deliberative oration to his father, on behalf of a parliamentary committee against monopolies.[267] Yet the first instance must have been pre-prepared, and probably by a royal secretary, while the second was a carefully stage-managed private performance. The slenderness of Charles's oratorical *oeuvre* prior to his accession suggests that his youthful study of 'publick discourse' had not been extensive or especially successful.

Even after joining the Privy Council in March 1622 and sitting in several parliamentary sessions, Charles confessed to William Laud over dinner on 1 February 1624 that he still lacked confidence arguing *in utramque partem*. He could 'not be a lawyer', he confessed, because 'I cannot… defend a bad, nor yield a good cause'.[268] At the time, Laud was eager to declare this a virtue but, in hindsight, it seems more like a side effect of James's pedagogical proscription of rhetoric and his lower expectations for his second son. And Prince Charles made a point of not challenging his father's prescriptions, or his expectations. During his own reign, Charles was frequently praised for expressing himself well in private conversation.[269] His holograph correspondence during the personal rule

[264] Heylyn, *Short view of the life and reign*, pp. 9, 12; but see Lily, *Monarchy or no monarchy*, p. 75.

[265] Carey, *Memoirs*, p. 69; Chamberlain, *Letters*, vol. I, p. 201; *Letters and state papers… of King James the sixth*, pp. 46, 55; SP 14/8, fol. 175r.

[266] FSL, V a 246; Nichols (ed.), *Progresses… of King James*, vol. II, p. 607, vol. IV, pp. 1086–7.

[267] *Commons debates in 1621*, eds. W. Notestein, F. H. Relf and H. Simpson, 7 vols. (New Haven, 1935), vol. II, p. 231, vol. VI, p. 71.

[268] William Laud, *The works of the most reverend father in God, William Laud*, eds. William Scott and James Bliss, 7 vols. (Oxford, 1847–60), vol. III, p. 147.

[269] For example, *CSPV*, vol. XXIII, p. 23; Laud, *Works*, vol. III, p. 209; *Miscellaneous State Papers: From 1501–1726*, ed. P. Yorke, 2 vols. (London, 1778), vol. II, pp. 186–7.

suggests that he was a conscientious, elegant, even eager letter-writer.[270] We will see, however, that the relative paucity of his upper-level rhetorical training had a legacy for his political and religious ideology. His difficulty in arguing his side of a case or anticipating and parrying an opponent's verbal blows seems to have left him without the confidence to distinguish his course from his father's, as his brother had begun to do. In this respect, Charles's education represents, if not a lost renaissance, a lost opportunity to reap some of the most valuable crops of a liberal education.

RHETORIC, PURITANISM AND PATERNAL OBEDIENCE DURING THE SPANISH MATCH CONTROVERSY

Between 1619 and 1625, a crucible of foreign conflict and domestic dissent forced Prince Charles to weigh his dependence on his father's political prescriptions against his commitment to the anti-popish ideology and international Calvinism of Charles's household. Charles's discomfort with popular rhetoric and his lack of intellectual confidence shaped his evolving response to the marriage that James was negotiating for him with the Spanish Infanta, Maria Anna (1606–46). This section will explore the significance of James's *Meditations* on the twenty-seventh chapter of Matthew and the private reasoning of Matthew Wren (1585–1667) in reshaping the prince's confessional identity and teaching him to adopt and amplify his father's political prejudices.

In the wake of James VI and I's declaration of the Five Articles of Perth in 1618, certain high churchmen around the king grew anxious that this advance for episcopacy in Scotland was liable to be undermined by the aggressive godliness of James's successor, Prince Charles. Peter Heylyn reported that, when the king fell seriously ill in April 1619, Lancelot Andrewes, who was attending on him, had 'bewailed... the sad condition which the Church was like to fall unto' at his death. Prince Charles, Andrewes protested, was 'in the hands of the Scots... and not well principled by those which had tutelage of him, either as to the Government or *Liturgie* of the Church of England'. James was sufficiently persuaded to make 'a solemn vow' to 'take the prince into his own immediate care' so 'there should be no feare of his disaffection either unto the Hierarchy,

[270] Sarah Poynting, '"From his Matie to me with his awin hand": The king's correspondence during the period of personal rule', in Ian Atherton and Julie Sanders (eds.), *The 1630s: Interdisciplinary essays on culture and politics in the Caroline era* (Manchester, 2006).

or the rights and ceremonies of the Church'.[271] He may have even made a speech to Charles from his bed, urging him to respect the 'Bishops as… [the] best companions for princes'.[272] Upon recovery, James made no immediate changes to his son's entourage, but events on the European stage would prompt him to reassess.

In September 1619, Charles's brother-in-law, Frederick, and sister, Elizabeth, accepted the throne of Bohemia, a decision that would put them in conflict with the imperial branch of the Hapsburg dynasty. James explained to the Venetian ambassador, Girolamo Lando, in March 1620 that he was reluctant to intervene militarily on his daughter's behalf, despite 'the inclination and voice of the common people', on account of 'the disadvantages of making such a great war greater, to kindle a universal conflagration'.[273] In August 1620 the Spanish Hapsburgs came to the aid of their kin and Ambrogio Spinola Doria led an army from Flanders into the Lower Palatinate. 'If [the king] was cold' on the idea of military intervention 'before', Lando reported, 'he now seems ice'.[274] Princess Elizabeth and her husband, Frederick V, were the ones frozen out. Having been ejected from Bohemia and Frederick's ancestral estates, the couple would spend the rest of their reign in exile. Their plight at the hands of the Catholic Hapsburgs gave militant Calvinists in the British isle a godly cause.[275]

James tried to gain diplomatic leverage with the Hapsburgs using two mechanisms.[276] He reignited negotiations for the marriage of Prince Charles to the Spanish princess, with the return of the Palatinate as part of the princess's dowry. In 1621 he called a parliament, nominally to raise a subsidy to fight for the Palatinate but mainly to crank up the pressure on the Hapsburgs to make a deal. When the bellicose MPs got wind of the revived marriage strategy in the second session of 1621, they objected strenuously. In the house and the pulpit, puritans proclaimed a popish conspiracy. They pointed to a reversal of Elizabeth's anti-Spanish foreign

[271] Heylyn, *Life and reign*, pp. 17, 18. [272] Chamberlain, *Letters*, vol. II, p. 227.

[273] *CSPV*, vol. XVI, p. 196. [274] *CSPV*, vol. XVII, p. 36.

[275] Brennan Pursell, *The winter king: Frederick V of the Palatinate and the coming of the Thirty Years' War* (Aldershot, 2003), pp. 123–63; Geoffrey Parker, *Europe in crisis 1598–1648* (Brighton, 1980), pp. 164–9.

[276] For this paragraph see Simon Adams, 'Foreign policy and the parliaments of 1621 and 1624', in Kevin Sharpe (ed.), *Faction and Parliament* (London, 1978); Thomas Cogswell, *The blessed revolution: English politics and the coming of war, 1621–1624* (Cambridge, 1989), pp. 12–19; Brennan Pursell, 'James I, Gondomar and the dissolution of the parliament of 1621', *History*, 85 (2000) and 'War or peace? Jacobean politics and the parliament of 1621', in Chris Kyle (ed.), *Parliament, politics and elections 1604–1648* (Cambridge, 2001); Glyn Redworth, *The prince and the infanta: The cultural politics of the Spanish match* (New Haven, 2003), pp. 28–30; Conrad Russell, *Parliaments and English Politics, 1621–1629* (Oxford, 1979), p. 87.

policy, a failure to defend fellow reformers on the continent and a willingness to yoke the heir of the realm to a papist.[277] Despite Prince Charles's attempts to mediate between the king and the houses, the session dissolved into an embittered debate about MPs' freedom of speech.[278] By March 1622, godly ministers were preaching so vociferously against the Spanish match that James began to dream that 'his old tutor Buchanan' had come to visit him and had predicted 'his fate in verse'.[279] With the failure of the parliament, James lost bargaining power with the Spanish.[280] It became even more critical that Charles play the role of besotted suitor, but members of his household were warning him against it.

The anti-Catholic and anti-Spanish rhetoric of a number of Charles's family, and their attempts to stir up popular feeling against the marriage, may well have reminded James of his former pedagogue.[281] From at least June 1619, his secretary, Murray, advised Charles that the marriage was not in the interests of Christendom.[282] Throughout the summer of 1621, Charles's chaplain, George Hakewill, was preaching against the match from the pulpit at St James. Hakewill's series of twelve sermons on Psalm 101, *King Davids vow* (1621), was printed shortly afterwards. He argued that the match would not result in the return of the Palatinate, since it was 'both the doctrine and the practice of the church of Rome, that Faith plighted to Hereticks is not to bee held'. The princess and her adherents would simply ignore the contracts they had made.[283] To twist the knife further, Hakewill incorporated large chunks of John Burgess's famous sermon from 1604 against episcopacy and the terms of Jacobean conformity in his discussion.[284] Finally, he warned Charles that his subjects would hold him to account if he departed from the standard of godly, anti-Catholic kingship he had been brought up in, and now espoused, for 'Princes… act their parts upon an high stage, so… the least errour

[277] Cogswell, *Blessed revolution*, pp. 18–19; Jeanne Shami, *John Donne and conformity in crisis in the late Jacobean pulpit* (Cambridge, 2003), pp. 36–74; Robert Zaller, *The parliament of 1621: A study in constitutional conflict* (London, 1971), pp. 146–7.

[278] Cogswell, *Blessed revolution*, pp. 12–20; Richard Cust, 'Prince Charles and the second session of the 1621 parliament', *EHR*, 122 (2007).

[279] *CSPV*, vol. XVII, p. 444.

[280] If James had sabotaged the parliament he paid a high price for his politicking: Pursell, 'James I, Gondomar and the dissolution', p. 228–45; Michael Questier, 'Introduction', in Michael Questier (ed.), *Stuart dynastic policy and religious politics 1621–1625* (Cambridge, 2009), p. 24.

[281] For one opinion, see George Abbot, *Historical collections*, ed. John Rushworth, 8 vols. (London, 1659–1701), vol. I, p. 12.

[282] SP 14/109, fol. 156r.

[283] George Hakewill, *King Dauids vow for reformation of himselfe, his family, his kingdome deliuered in twelue sermons before the Prince his Highnesse vpon Psalm 101* (London, 1621), STC 12616, p. 259.

[284] Rhatigan, 'Preaching to princes', pp. 283–96.

in their action' would be 'presently discerned'.[285] Then, in July or August 1621, George Hakewill presented Charles with an additional treatise, dissuading him 'from marrying with… an ydolater'.[286] The prince's chapel, which had proved so useful when the threat to James's authority was papal dispensing power, was now at the vanguard of widespread anti-Spanish preaching and barely veiled criticism of Jacobean foreign policy. Not only were Calvinist divines harping on matters of state and encouraging popular dissent but they were also trying to use Charles against his father. To the king, it must have seemed like an unwelcome echo of the 1570s and 1580s in Scotland: passionate puritans were disrupting the realm, limiting the sovereign's activities and attempting to divide royal parent and child.[287] The 'archibellouses of rebellion' lived on in his son's household.

Moreover, they seemed to be having some success in persuading Charles to favour military intervention on the continent over a diplomatic solution.[288] By 1619, Prince Charles was echoing his preachers' aggressive anti-Catholicism. He wrote to James Hay, then Viscount Doncaster (*c.* 1580–1636), to express his pleasure that his brother-in-law, Frederick, was 'of so rype a judgement and of so forward an inclination to the good of Christendome' as to have taken on Ferdinand II (1578–1637). Murray's encouragement to Charles, to see his godly obligations in an international, militarised context, bore fruit when the prince offered to join the fight himself.[289] To signify his bellicose intentions to a wider audience, Charles began to compete aggressively in court tilts in March 1620, 'to the great joy of the people'.[290] His sudden play for popularity was noted by the anti-Spanish courtier Sir Edward Zouche, who wrote to his uncle, Edward, Lord Zouche, that 'the prins… beegyinse to have power'.[291] Charles was flirting with the idea of cultivating a militantly anti-Catholic, anti-Hapsburg interest at St James.

Charles also seems to have contemplated refusing a Spanish match. Even before Frederick and Elizabeth lost their thrones, the Venetian ambassador reported that the proposed marriage 'seemed distasteful to [Charles], owing to the influence of tutors and others with him'.[292] Afterwards, in October 1620, he made it clear to the Spanish ambassador Sarmiento de Acuña, Diego, count of Gondomar (1567–1626), that, whether he went

285 Hakewill, *King Dauids vow*, p. 41.
286 Chamberlain, *Letters*, vol. II, p. 393; *CSPD James*, vol. III, p. 284.
287 Peter Lake, 'Anti-popery: The structure of a prejudice', in Richard Cust and Ann Hughes (eds.), *Conflict in early Stuart England* (London, 1989), p. 87.
288 SP 14/112, fol. 145r.
289 SP 81/16, fols. 126r, 127r.
290 SP 14/113, fols. 87r, 109r.
291 SP 14/113, fol. 78r.
292 *CSPV*, vol. XIV, p. 484; see also pp. 65, 155, 305, 333, 479, 560.

along with it or not, 'at bottom this concerns my sister'.[293] Even as negotiations proceeded, he continued to indicate his preference for a military option. In January 1621, Prince Maurice saluted the prince as a fellow Protestant knight taking on the dragon of the Hapsburgs with the gift of two pieces of artillery.[294] Charles pledged £5,000 of his own revenues to recover the Palatinate. When the parliamentary session opened in 1621, the Venetian ambassador reported that Charles was deeply engaged and eager to promote the interests of 'his sister and religion'.[295] Charles did not go so far as to publically oppose his father's negotiations. Perhaps he lacked confidence in his own powers of argument. Nevertheless, he did little to further the match before the failure of the second session of Parliament. It was only at the end of January 1622, for instance, that he began to learn Spanish. His declarations of love for a princess he had never met began later that year.[296]

For a period between March 1620 and December 1621, Charles seems to have been tempted by the emotionally charged rhetoric of his godly householders to shuck the shell of paternal obedience for the first time in his life. Had he done so, it would certainly have stoked the fire of rebellion that the French and Venetian ambassadors feared was kindling in England.[297] Rather than continuing to be a dutiful son, Prince Charles seemed to be preparing to don Henry's mantle as the country's popular, chivalric defender of the Princess Elizabeth and the Calvinist international.

Neither Charles's plodding academic progress nor Andrewes's accounts of his godliness had perturbed James, but the prince's gestures of support towards a popular, anti-Catholic military policy got his father's attention. In addition to issuing public prohibitions against 'licentious speech of matters of state' and warning preachers, specifically, to keep off politics, he embarked on a campaign to re-educate his son.[298] James began, as usual, with a treatise. With his *Meditation* on the twenty-seventh chapter of Matthew the king returned to biblical exegesis, the literary genre he had used to chart his own political departure from Buchanan, to recall his son to obedience. Historians have remarked on the similarities between

[293] *CSPV*, vol. XVI, p. 433. [294] SP 14/119, fol. 26r.

[295] *CSPV*, vol. XVI, p. 524, vol. XVII, pp. 36, 67–8.

[296] William Bishop in Questier (ed.), *Stuart dynastic policy*, p. 202; Glyn Redworth, 'Of pimps and princes: Three unpublished letters from James I and the Prince of Wales relating to the Spanish match', *HJ*, 37:2 (1994), pp. 405, 408–9.

[297] Cogswell, *Blessed revolution*, p. 50.

[298] James Larkin and Paul Hughes (eds.), *Stuart royal proclamations*, 2 vols. (Oxford, 1973), vol. I, pp. 495–6 (quotation), 519–21; Cogswell, *Blessed revolution*, pp. 32–3; Kenneth Fincham, *Prelate as pastor: The episcopate of James I* (Oxford, 1990), p. 245.

the *Mediation* and the *Basilicon doron*, yet the treatise's attempt to reshape Charles's confessional identity and foreign-policy commitments has gone unremarked.[299]

Matthew 27:27–9 described the taunting of Christ by Roman soldiers, who dressed him in a crown of thorns and hailed him king of the Jews. James's exegesis posited that this seemingly unlikely biblical passage offered a critical account of the 'inauguration of Kings' and an explication of the sacred nature of monarchical government. Each piece of mock regalia presented by the jeering soldiers actually communicated the duties of kingship and its divinely instituted form. In James's exegesis the contemptuous Roman guards and Jewish people emerged as a cipher for the forces of ill-disciplined, popular anti-popery in England. They mocked Christ's pacifism, not comprehending that God had mandated that only a 'King of peace' could be 'the builder of his Church' on earth.[300] They derided his claim to divinely ordained kingship without understanding the thorny and 'stinging cares of Kings'.[301] They lacked knowledge and reverence. Even when Pontius Pilate attempted to 'mooue them, to commiseration', 'the bloudy and malitious Iewes' merely 'mocked him' and urged the judge 'to crucifice' their ruler.[302] Princes should not measure their courses by their popularity with the disobedient and impious mob; the 'popular tribunes' who insisted that royal power came from subjects' consent were simply wrong.[303]

Rather, James argued that 'all good Kings' would see in Christ's response to his humiliation a 'paterne for imitation'. It did not involve pandering to anti-popery, sabre-rattling or establishing a reversionary interest. In fact, in his dedicatory letter to Charles, James emphasised that Henry V had regretted his unseemly haste to assume his father's heavy responsibilities.[304] Instead, Charles should take 'continuall and euer wakeriffe care, of the account he is one day to give to God, of the good gouernment of his people'. Then, just as God had 'wrang [Christ's] glory out of [the soldiers' and Jews'] corruption without their knowledge', so he would turn the jeers of contemporary mockers into the tears and commendation of posterity.[305]

299 Kevin Sharpe, 'The king's writ: Royal authors and royal authority in early modern England', in Kevin Sharpe and Peter Lake (eds.), *Culture and politics in early Stuart England* (Stanford, 1993), p. 117 and *Remapping early modern England*, pp. 149, 166–74.

300 James, 'Meditation upon… the XXVII chapter of Saint Matthew', in *Political writings*, p. 235.

301 James, 'Meditation upon… the XXVII chapter of Saint Matthew', in *Political writings*, p. 240.

302 James, 'Meditation upon… the XXVII chapter of Saint Matthew', in *Political writings*, pp. 242–3.

303 James, 'Meditation upon… the XXVII chapter of Saint Matthew', in *Political writings*, pp. 233, 238–9, 241–2.

304 James, 'Meditation upon… the XXVII chapter of Saint Matthew', in *Political writings*, p. 231.

305 James, 'Meditation upon… the XXVII chapter of Saint Matthew', in *Political writings*, pp. 233, 249.

Finally, in an attempt to inoculate Charles from the blandishments of his puritan preachers, James offered his son a blazon of the insignia of monarchy. It was designed to instruct him in the beauty of Christian symbols and ceremony and their utility in nurturing and communicating the sacred charge of kingship. Charles should be willing to use 'his sword' to procure 'due reverence and obedience' to the devotional activities of his church.[306] On this point, James noted, those '*Puritanes*, that refuse to kneele at the receiuing of the blessed *Sacrament*' required his attention. These men were even worse than the profane soldiers described in Matthew 27, who did such homage, even if in jest.[307] 'God', James emphasised, 'thought it no Idolatry that his sonne should be kneeled unto, even in the time of his greatest humility'.[308] Rather than playing at being 'popular Tribunes', James suggested that British puritans should show due reverence to God in their devotional lives and obey Christian monarchy on earth.

There is plentiful evidence that Charles was profoundly moved by his father's *Meditatioun*. As Kevin Sharpe has shown, the image of the king as a *mixta persona*, half way between heaven and earth, engaged in prayer and reverent devotion, and taking wakeful care to know how he might exchange his earthly crown for a celestial diadem, shaped Charles's public presentation of his kingship, especially in his later years.[309] It would be reflected in the iconography of Peter Paul Rubens's *The Apotheosis of James I* (1636), which Charles commissioned for the ceiling of the Whitehall Banqueting House. The image of James leaving off his worldly cares and becoming a God was, famously, the last thing his son would see before stepping out on the scaffold in January 1649. Similarly, the twenty-seventh chapter of Matthew was the piece of scripture he would hear.[310] Indeed, William Marshall's frontispiece for the *Eikon basilike* (1649) compared Charles's execution to Christ's passion and crucifixion.[311] In prayers printed in the text that followed, Charles beseeched God not to let him 'forget to imitate My crucified Redeemer' nor let his 'bloud be upon them

306 James, 'Meditation upon… the XXVII chapter of Saint Matthew', in *Political writings*, p. 237.

307 James, 'Meditation upon… the XXVII chapter of Saint Matthew', in *Political writings*, pp. 233–4.

308 James, 'Meditation upon… the XXVII chapter of Saint Matthew', in *Political writings*, p. 241.

309 Kevin Sharpe, *Image wars: Promoting kings and commonwealths in England, 1603–1660* (New Haven, 2010), pp. 391–440 and *Reading authority and representing rule in early modern England* (London, 2013), pp. 118, 162, 188, 241.

310 Sharpe, 'Private conscience… in the writings of Charles I', p. 645.

311 Laura Lunger Knoppers, 'Imagining the death of the king: Milton, Charles I, and anamorphic art', in Elizabeth Bellamy, Patrick Cheney and Michael Schoenfeldt (eds.), *Imagining death in Spenser and Milton* (Basingstoke, 2003); John Staines, 'Compassion in the public sphere of Milton and King Charles', in Gail Kern Pastor, Katherine Rose and Mary Floyd-Wilson (eds.), *Reading the early modern passions: Essays in the cultural history of emotion* (Philadelphia, 2004), p. 105.

and their Children, whom… have excited to crucifie Me'.[312] In the king's own *Mediations upon death*, allegedly written while he was imprisoned at Carisbrooke Castle, he wondered if his 'Enemies' would 'seeke to adde (as those did, who Crucified Christ) the mockery of Justice, to the cruelty of Malice'.[313] Finally, James's *Meditation* also shaped Charles's advice to his own son, printed in the *Eikon basilike*, to regard 'the worlds censure' as 'the honour of a kind of Martyrdome'.[314] Charles I would take the script for his final performance as sacralised king and royal martyr from his father's *Meditation* of 1620.

Back in the early 1620s, however, James took additional steps to ensure that Charles digested his prescriptions and retreated from his blooming puritanism. In August 1621, Thomas Murray and Charles's anti-Catholic preacher, Hakewill, were imprisoned and dismissed from their posts.[315] In their stead, James placed Hispanophiles and high-church ceremonialists around his son and his favourite Buckingham, who came under the spiritual guidance of William Laud in 1622.[316] In September, Murray was replaced as Charles's secretary by Francis Cottington (1579?–1652), the former ambassador to Spain, who had been a key player in negotiations for the match from its first mooting in 1614.[317] It was Cottington, together with John, earl of Bristol, the English ambassador to Spain, and Endymion Porter, who persuaded Charles to consider the match seriously.[318] Gondomar also took a key role in reassuring the prince on the subject of religion.[319] Popular ballads and newsletters (and the decidedly anti-popular Edward Hyde, earl of Clarendon) blamed Cottington and Buckingham for encouraging Charles to undertake his daring and foolhardy trip to Spain in February 1623.[320]

James was angered by his son's and lover's unauthorised flight but he rallied swiftly, pleased, perhaps, to find Charles committed to the match and a diplomatic solution to the Palatine crisis. He also recognised that the trip would speed up the tortuous negotiations with Philip IV (1605–65), one way or another: 'If my baby's credit in Spain mend not these things [in the Palatine], I will bid farewell to peace in Christendom', he wrote to his 'boys'

[312] Charles, *Eikon basilike*, pp. 230, 231. [313] Charles, *Eikon basilike*, p. 256.
[314] Charles, *Eikon basilike*, p. 239.
[315] *CSPD James*, vol. III, p. 284; Chamberlain, *Letters*, vol. II, p. 393; SP 14/109, fol. 156r.
[316] Laud, *Works*, vol. III, p. 136. [317] *CSPD James*, vol. III, p. 459.
[318] Redworth, *Prince and the infanta*, p. 44.
[319] Redworth, *Prince and the infanta*, pp. 13, 28.
[320] Cogswell, *Blessed revolution*, p. 47; Edward Hyde, earl of Clarendon, *The history of the rebellion and civil wars in England*, ed. W. Dunn Macray, 6 vols. (Oxford, 1888), vol. I, pp. 14–22; William Farrar in Questier (ed.), *Stuart dynastic policy*, pp. 212, 214.

on 11 March.[321] On 3 April, James sent Charles's new chaplains after him, as much to continue his religious refashioning as to protect him from popery.[322] In January 1622 James had restocked Charles's chapel with men from the Durham House circle, who were supportive of the match and willing to revere the king as well as God: Leonard Maw, then master of Peterhouse College, Cambridge, and Matthew Wren, a graduate of Pembroke College, Cambridge, and protégé of Lancelot Andrewes.[323] They were 'chosen', as the godly gentleman Simonds D'Ewes noted in his diary of 1623, because they were 'altogether free from the suspicion of being Puritans'.[324]

Wren was the only one to make it to Madrid. His ideology may be gleaned from his first published sermon before Charles I. Where Hakewill had warned Charles to fear the judgement of his subjects, Wren exhorted his auditors to 'Fear God, my son, and fear the king' (Proverbs 21:24). He castigated the hypocrites who pretended 'to feare God, but yet feare not the King'.[325] Their dissimulated godliness could be discerned, Wren claimed, in their 'crying out for Sermons… and rayling against Antichrist', 'finding fault with the State and Times' and 'singing… Psalmes, and talking of Scripture' when what God clearly required of Christians was mercy, charity, and reverent obedience to magistrates.[326] Wren's target was clear enough. He made a clear ideological equation between puritanism, popular rhetoric and sedition on earth.

The months Wren spent with Charles in Spain gave him a concentrated opportunity to impress upon him the threat posed by puritanism to the government and liturgy of the church in England, as well as to his relationship with his father. James had given directions that the prince's worship at Philip IV's court was to be 'agreeable to the puritie of the primitive Churche and yett as neare the Romane forme as can lawfullie be done'. It was a ploy to diffuse Spanish apprehensions about the heretics in their midst. Nevertheless the 'altar… palls, lynnen coverings, demy carpet, 4 surplices, candlesticks, tapers, chalices… [and] wafers for the communion' also served to impress Charles with the beauty of worship when 'polemicall preachings' were removed from the equation.[327] In this reverent setting, Wren got to work.

[321] James VI and I, *Letters of King James VI and I*, ed. G. P. V. Akrigg (Berkeley, 1984), p. 394.

[322] Heylyn, *Life and reign*, pp. 18–19. [323] Tyacke, *Anti-Calvinists*, pp. 46, 48–9.

[324] Simonds D'Ewes, *Diary of Sir Simonds D'Ewes (1622–1624)*, trans. and ed. Elizabeth Bourcier (Paris, 1974), p. 185.

[325] Matthew Wren, *A sermon preached before the kings maiestie* (Cambridge, 1628), STC 26015, p. 3.

[326] Wren, *Sermon*, p. 24.

[327] SP 94/26, fol. 80r; Nichols, *Progresses, processions and magnificent festivities of King James*, vol. IV, p. 832.

The godly sort in England were not sure whether Charles's chaplain came to him twice daily or whether he was barred from his presence in Madrid – the possibilities were equally alarming.[328] Wren's first biographer recorded, however, that the chaplain took the opportunity afforded by the trip to 'privately unravel' for Charles 'all those sly and knotty Contrivances, which some of their most eminent Church-men had twisted to entangle the Prince's Affairs'. A critique of their use of popular rhetoric was almost certainly involved. Wren also unfolded the true 'Grounds and Articles of our Religion, with… Perspecuity and Clearness'.[329] He may have gone into the doubts that members of the Durham House circle were expressing regarding the doctrine of reprobation: that, if 'God from all eternity reprobates by far the greater part of mankind to eternal fire, without any eye at all to their sin', then 'the God of all mercies' seems like 'the most fierce and unreasonable tyrant in the world'.[330] Given Charles's support for Richard Mountague in 1625 and his attempts to repress vociferous preaching on predestination thereafter, it seems likely that prince and chaplain had discussed the controversy, at least.

Whatever Charles and Wren discussed, they did so 'privately'. Wren did not attempt to berate the prince from the pulpit, dispute in public or address Charles in print, as his puritan chaplains had done. James would not have countenanced such tactics in Madrid.[331] Yet Wren found contentious speech distasteful anyway. As bishop of Norwich, he tried to clamp down on the fiery sermons and lectures made by roving preachers and university-trained orators in his diocese.[332] It was more efficacious for the individual, and critical for the unity of the church, that men's consciences be moved by private reasoning and prayer rather than by emotive public rhetoric. On this occasion, moreover, Wren's approach gave Charles an opportunity to change his mind without having to argue the case in public.

This was valuable because Charles was almost certainly looking for a way to reconcile with his father. The prince may have been offended by some of James's 'light and familiar ways' but he seems to have been

[328] D'Ewes, *Diary*, pp. 136–7.

[329] Christopher Wren, *Parentalia: Or memoirs of the family of the Wrens* (London, 1750), p. 3.

[330] Laud, *Works*, vol. VI, p. 133. See Alan Cromartie, 'The mind of William Laud', in Charles Prior and Glenn Burgess (eds.), *England's wars of religion, revisited* (Farnham, 2011); Peter Lake, 'Lancelot Andrewes, John Buckeridge, and avant-garde conformity at the court of James I', in Linda Levy Peck (ed.), *The mental world of the Jacobean court* (Cambridge, 1991); Tyacke, *Anti-Calvinists*, pp. 106–24.

[331] Heylyn, *Life and reign*, pp. 18–19.

[332] Peter King, 'Bishop Wren and the suppression of the Norwich Lecturers', *HJ*, 11:2 (1968), p. 242.

extremely discomforted by the defiant position his chaplains and secretary had encouraged him to take regarding the Palatine and Spanish match.[333] For instance, in his 1619 letter to Doncaster, Charles offered to fight the Hapsburgs himself, but only if 'the king, my father will give me leave'.[334] Gondomar reported that, when Charles sat in the Lords in the 1621 parliamentary sessions, he was eager to secure a war chest and 'display his valour against his father's pacifism'.[335] Nevertheless, the prince still felt compelled to defend James's honour, even if it cost him his subsidy. He chastised Sir Henry Yelverton (1566–1630) for comparing Buckingham to Hugh Despencer and James to Edward II. Two days later he demanded Yelverton's imprisonment.[336] In the second session, Richard Cust has shown that Charles was keen to win the favour of the parliamentarians but that he grew increasingly frustrated with the 'seditius fellus' amongst them who criticised his father, pontificated on his marriage and urged war.[337] 'How can they loue you, that hated them whom-of ye are come?' James had asked his sons in the *Basilicon doron*.[338] Charles was no rebel by nature. Not only had his education encouraged him to put a premium on obeying his father and king but it had also not given him the intellectual independence or the argumentative skills to make his own way, even though he was clearly moved by the plight of his sister and had the backing of Buckingham and of a significant cross-section of aristocrats and parliamentarians. Charles's lack of advanced rhetorical training may have made him more susceptible to the emotional exhortations of his chaplains. Yet it also left him unable to sustain a reversionary position. Wren's private conversations and reverent account of faith must have seemed like a life raft, or at least a welcome path whereby the (almost) prodigal son could return to his father's graces and political ideology. For the remainder of his father's reign, and his own, Charles followed James's prescriptions to the point of servility, and he instructed his own sons to conduct themselves similarly.[339]

Consequently, while Prince Charles returned from his Spanish adventure a virulent anti-Hapsburg, more eager for war than ever, Wren ensured

[333] Carlton, *Charles I*, pp. 25–6, 29; Sharpe, *Personal rule of Charles I*, p. 183 and 'Private conscience... in the writings of Charles I', pp. 644–5

[334] SP 81/16, fol. 126^{r}.

[335] Pursell, 'War or peace?', pp. 165.

[336] Chamberlain, *Letters*, vol. II, pp. 357–8; Russell, *Parliaments and English politics*, pp. 85, 107–8, 113–14; Zaller, *Parliament of 1621*, pp. 116–24.

[337] BL, Harleian MS 6987, fol. 205^{r} in Cust, 'Prince Charles and the second session', pp. 431, 436, 440.

[338] James, *BD*, p. 23.

[339] For example Charles in *Letters of the kings of England*, vol. II, pp. 401–2.

that he also returned an obedient son, immune to the godly preachers of his youth. In 1624 Lancelot Andrewes, Richard Neile and William Laud called Wren to Durham House to debrief the chaplain on the prince's confessional identity. Wren declared that Charles's

> learning is not equal to his Father's; yet I know his Judgement to be very right; and as for his Affections in these Particulars, which your Lordships have pointed at, for upholding the Doctrine and Discipline, and the right Estate of the Church, I have more Confidence of him than of his Father, in whom they say… is so much Inconstancy in some particular cases.[340]

In fact, as Archbishop Laud told Elizabeth of Bohemia in 1635, in Wren, Charles had found 'a man who he might trust'.[341] The context of Laud's letter was the king's elevation of his chaplain to the see of Norwich, which had become a hotbed of puritan discontent in the 1630s.[342] Charles's confidence in Wren's capacity to reconcile his flock to more decorous devotions and a less contentious style of faith may well have sprung from the fact that he had performed the same office for the prince himself in 1623.

Charles turned his back firmly on the godly ideology and popular rhetoric that had tempted him between 1619 and 1622 and echoed, indeed amplified, his father's prejudice against 'brain-sicke' preachers and would-be tribunes of the plebs. As Richard Cust, Peter Lake and Malcolm Smuts have demonstrated, Charles I was eager to blame godly popularity for difficulties with his parliaments in 1625, 1626, 1628 and the deadlock and violence of 1629, and for spreading libel during his personal rule.[343] By the late 1630s, the king was limed to blame the outbreak of the Bishops Wars' (1639–40), the allegations that he encouraged the Irish Rebellion of 1641 and 'the events of this black Parliament' and 'those popular clamours and Tumults' more generally on the passionate proponents of 'Presbyterian government' in the three kingdoms.[344] In 1648, he prayed that God would not 'suffer those men long to prosper in their Babel' of adversarial speech, 'who build it with the bones and cement it with the

340 Wren, *Parentalia*, p. 46. 341 SP 16/295/48.

342 King, 'Bishop Wren', p. 237–54.

343 Richard Cust, 'Anti-puritanism and urban politics: Charles I and Great Yarmouth', *HJ*, 35:1 (1992), *Charles I: A political life*, pp. 119–21, 'Charles I and popularity', in Thomas Cogswell, Richard Cust and Peter Lake (eds.), *Politics, religion and popularity in early Stuart Britain: Essays in honour of Conrad Russell* (Cambridge, 2002) and *The forced loan and English politics 1626–1628* (Oxford, 1987), pp. 19–28, 209–12; Peter Lake, 'Puritans, popularity, and petitions: Local politics in national context, Cheshire, 1641', in Thomas Cogswell, Richard Cust and Peter Lake (eds.), *Politics, religion and popularity in early Stuart Britain: Essays in honour of Conrad Russell* (Cambridge, 2002); Smuts, *Court culture*, pp. 253–62.

344 Charles, *Eikon basilike*, pp. 62, 89, 237.

bloud of their Kings'.[345] His readiness to identify popular preaching and parliamentary rhetoric with puritan and Presbyterian religion and rebellion provides a 'key to understanding how Charles's apparently benign aspirations could be transformed into policies that seemed to many to be authoritarian and unconstitutional'.[346] Charles was not incapable of compromise, unable to take counsel or unfit to rule. But, after the Spanish match controversy, he tended to see puritans, Presbyterians and parliamentarians through the lens of his father's anti-Buchanan polemic.

There was an inherited structure to Charles's ideological prejudice, but his readiness to adopt James's bias derived at least in part from his lack of confidence in argument. Twenty-five years later, Charles still seemed to blame Murray and Hakewill for fooling him with their words. In his *Eikon basilike*, Charles explained to his own son that, throughout his childhood, 'Nothing seemed lesse considerable than the Presbyterian Faction in England... so compliant they were to publique order'. Nevertheless, on the first occasion that controversy 'drave men into sidings', they turned on the prince in favour of the 'populacy'. Charles quoted Genesis 27:22 in a particularly revealing manner: 'you may heare from them Iacob's voice, but you shall feele they have Esau's hands'. He implied that Murray, Hakewill and the subsequent Presbyterians he had had dealings with were willing to betray even their brother and father with words, as Esau had. One could not trust their artful language, or 'colours of Piety'. 'Their interest is alwaies made Gods', he wrote.[347] What Charles seemed less willing to remember was that, for a brief period in the early 1620s, he had considered joining his godly householders, Presbyterians and parliamentarians and even leading them. While he had felt ready to fight for the Palatinate with arms and money, however, Prince Charles had found himself unable to maintain his reversionary position against James. The prince's learned deference to patriarchal authority certainly played a role in his capitulation, but, unlike his brother, he had not learnt to plot his own path or fight his corner with words.

CHARLES I IN ORPHEUS' THEATRE

For the first fifteen years of his reign, Charles avoided ostentatiously argumentative speech. He made orations when the occasion demanded it, such as at the opening of parliaments. Like James and Elizabeth before him,

[345] Charles, *Eikon basilike*, p. 257. [346] Cust, *Charles I: A political life*, p. 24.
[347] Charles, *Eikon basilike*, p. 237.

Charles used these speeches to protest against the honour or utility of parliamentary 'eloquence' and establish his own *ethos* as a plain-speaking, trustworthy prince.[348] Like James, moreover, he used the instrument of personal rule to mute the libel, tumult and threatened sedition of his parliaments. Yet Charles's retreat from rhetoric went beyond that of his predecessors. Unlike James, Charles recoiled from making arguments for his policies or his kingship in print. He also avoided arguing in person whenever he could get away with it. When he could not, he revealed his frustration with the exercise. On 11 June 1639, for instance, the Scottish Commissioners came to the English camp to negotiate what became the Pacification of Berwick. Charles used several strategies to attempt to ward off verbal conflict. The English courtier Sir John Burroughs praised his 'demonstrations of reason, Justice, grace'. The anonymous Scottish secretary who was present described the same locutions as interruptions and prevarications.[349] The king refused to hear 'long intended declarations' of the Covenanter cause and insisted that the Scottish Commissioners write down their grievances for him to take away and adjudicate.[350] Eventually, however, the Scots managed to draw Charles into a 'dispute… concerning the validitie of the Assembly at Glasgow', which had continued to sit in November 1638 in defiance of royal instruction.[351] Charles exclaimed in irritation at their exchange, 'When you say one thing, and I another, who shall judge?'[352] The king, in his view, was the arbiter, interpreter and speaker of the laws, not one who had to plead his case before a court, even in a peace negotiation. Did Charles refuse to argue because he continued to lack confidence in his ability to fight his corner or because he had absorbed his father's account of the divine right of kings too thoroughly to see the other side of the question? Was Orpheus giving up his lyre?

Kevin Sharpe and Malcolm Smuts have made compelling cases that, despite Charles's distaste for oratory or argument, he had not relinquished his duty to unite, sooth and stir his audience from the public stage. Historians have identified a variety of 'silent', or at least discursively muted, cultural and literary forms that Charles used to keep the beasts of the three kingdoms at peace. These 'representations of majesty' were conveyed in masques, artwork,

348 Charles I, *The works of King Charles, both civil and sacred* (London, 1735), p. 54; *Proceedings in parliament, 1625*, eds. M. Jansson and W. Bidwell (New Haven, 1987) pp. 28, 647–8; Cust, 'Charles I and popularity', pp. 244–7; Chris Kyle, *Theater of state: Parliament and political culture in early Stuart England* (Stanford, 2012), pp. 22–35; Peltonen, *Rhetoric, politics and popularity*, pp. 187, 228, 230–2, 235–6.

349 SP 16/14/23, fols. 203^{r}, 204^{r-v}.

350 *Miscellaneous state papers*, vol. II, p. 134.

351 SP 16/14/23, fol. 204^{r}; *Miscellaneous state papers*, vol. II, p. 134–5 (quotation).

352 *Miscellaneous state papers*, vol. II, p. 125.

portraiture, architecture and poetry and they were intended to 'reduce the noise of debate and so figure the monarchy as above, not part of, the polemical fray'.[353] Where James had defended his divine-right kingship, royal supremacy and patriarchal authority verbally, Charles presented these ideas in visual and non-adversarial literary forms, to make them seem unassailable truths. To these artistic forms Richard Cust would have us add Charles's reform and promotion of the Order of the Garter and several other institutions that he and his advisers used to cultivate a body of loyalist peers.[354] In addition to modes that spoke exclusively to the court and ancient nobility, Charles published several volumes of official prayers and services, suitable for a variety of occasions, and conciliatory proclamations that were intended to touch all his subjects.[355] Like Charles's early collection of James's poetry, and, indeed, the printed collections of Elizabeth I's prayers, these textual genres could address political and religious questions and move the wills of his audiences without inciting refutation. They were, moreover, derived from the literary, artistic, courtly, devotional and chivalric activities that his education had prepared him to perform with grace and conviction. They played a significant role in shaping the political and religious culture of the royalist party in the British isle.

Nevertheless, Charles ultimately conceded that these supposedly less contentious forms of communication were insufficient to keep his subjects unified. In fact, two of his literary and devotional projects, the *Book of sports* (1633) and the Scottish *Book of Common Prayer* (1637), managed to generate more controversy in two kingdoms than any piece of royal rhetoric hitherto.[356] The rhetorical vehemence and skill of Charles's parliamentary and confessional adversaries amplified Bacon's point about speech: 'the words of a KING' needed to be 'full of power'.[357] Prince Henry had discovered the utility of deliberative rhetoric under his father's spur in 1609. Charles was converted rather later. As the beasts of the three kingdoms recalled 'their seuerall appetites' and 'all thinges' began to 'dissolve into Anarchie and Confusion' in 1640, the king began to try his voice.[358] After many years of taciturnity, over seventy of Charles's speeches were printed between 1641 and 1648.[359] Unlike in 1620, Charles had little

[353] Sharpe, *Image wars*, pp. 141, 143; see also Smuts, *Court culture*, pp. 230–91.

[354] Cust, *Charles I and the aristocracy*, esp. pp. 42–171.

[355] Sharpe, *Image wars*, pp. 144–70.

[356] Alistair Dougall, *The Devil's book: Charles I, the 'Book of Sports' and Puritanism in Tudor and early Stuart England* (Exeter, 2011); Kim Joong-Lak, 'The Scottish-English-Romish book: The character of the Scottish Prayer Book of 1637', in Michael Braddick and David Smith (eds.), *The experience of revolution in Stuart Britain and Ireland: Essays for John Morrill* (Cambridge, 2011).

[357] Charles, *Eikon basilike*, p. 199.

[358] Bacon, *Of the proficience and advancement of learning*, sig. I1^v.

[359] Sharpe, *Image wars*, pp. 144–5.

choice but to fight his corner with his pen and the press as well as his sword and his gun.

Like the conscientious, plodding schoolboy he had been, Charles seems to have attempted a crash course in royal rhetoric to prepare himself for the recall of the English Parliament in 1640. He reviewed his English edition of Bacon's *Advancement of learning*, printed that year, which included the 'prepatory store' of 'Common-places in ready preparation argued...Pro and Contra' for a speaker's use.[360] Charles read the storehouse carefully and enlarged it, as Bacon had recommended. Even then, however, the king seems to have struggled to grasp the point of commonplacing *in utramque partem*. His additions were only ever made to one side of the question: regarding 'On superstition', Charles added, 'if a Man, by eschewing Superstition, grow to be Profane what hath he gotten'; 'On pride', Charles added, 'Pride made Angles Deuils'; 'On knowledge, contemplation', Charles added, 'Knowledge giues lyke Pleasure to the Mynde, wch Venus doth to the Body'; and regarding 'Loquacity', Charles deemed that 'Few great Talkers, are good Doers'.[361] Charles was still trotting out the maxims he had taken from his father's scripts and, more worryingly, he still found it difficult to anticipate the weaknesses in a cause he deemed good or appreciate the reasons why others might support one he reckoned bad. He described his parliamentary opponents as an 'undisciplined rabble' and claimed he had withdrawn from London in 1642 'to give time... for the ebbing of their tumultuous fury'.[362] Charles's difficulty imagining both sides of the case before him led him to underestimate his opponents' strength and constancy.

Nevertheless, Charles gained confidence in his own powers of persuasion during the wars and became an effective leader of the royalist cause.[363] Afterwards his scaffold speech affected even hostile auditors and readers.[364] Charles's greatest rhetorical achievement, however, was undoubtedly the best-selling *Eikon basilike*. He wrote portions of it in 1642 as part of the paper war that preceded the raising of standards and returned to it during his captivity in 1648, in an attempt to strengthen

360 Francis Bacon, *Of the advancement and proficience of learning or the partitions of sciences*, trans. Gilbert Watts (Oxford, 1640), STC 1167; BL, C46.v.i, p. 299.

361 Charles's notes in BL, C46.v.i, pp. 307, 312, 315.

362 Charles, *Eikon basilike*, p. 21.

363 Russell, *Causes of the English civil war*, p. 209; Peter Young, *Edgehill, 1642: The campaign and the battle* (Kineton, 1967), pp. 108, 113.

364 Cust, *Charles I: A political life*, pp. 462–3.

his hand in talks, and during his trial. Charles certainly had assistance from John Gauden and Edward Symmons, but he also intended to send the text forth under his own name.[365] In the *Eikon* Charles adopted and adapted the arguments, *loci*, figures and tropes of his best teachers. We have seen the way the king used the image of Christ's passion, described in James's *Meditations*, to loan pathos to his execution. In imitation of his father's *Basilicon doron*, moreover, Charles claimed to offer his 'Subjects' unmediated 'sight into My most retired thoughts' as they pertained to the education of his own son, Prince Charles.[366] Following Matthew Wren's method and example, he continued to insist that the power of private 'Reason' trumped popular rhetoric.[367] His posthumous interlocutor, John Milton, was grudgingly impressed. 'The book which I have to answer', he complained, 'pretends reason, not authorities'.[368] What is different about the *Eikon Basilike*, however, is that Charles anticipated his opponents' likely responses to his text and acted to defuse them: he did not apportion blame specifically or universally; he avoided detailed references to political events that might give rise to disputes; he acknowledged his opponents' valour; and he rarely expressed bitterness.[369] Charles and his editors did not write contentiously but made their case for his character very persuasively indeed. According to his childhood carers, Charles had learnt to speak late in life. In the end, however, he spoke very powerfully indeed. His words in the *Eikon basilike*, reprinted thirty-five times in 1649 alone, would make a significant contribution to the restoration of monarchical government and royal supremacy in 1659.[370] The royal renaissance may have been lost, but the audience at Orpheus' theatre would demand an encore.

[365] Sean Kelsey, 'The king's book: *Eikon basilike* and the English revolution of 1649', in Nicholas Tyacke (ed.), *The English revolution c. 1590–1720: Politics, religion and communities* (Manchester, 2007); Robert Wilcher, '*Eikon Basilike*: The printing, composition, strategy, and impact of "The King's Book"', in Laura Lunger Knoppers (ed.), *The Oxford handbook of literature and the English revolution* (Oxford, 2012).

[366] Charles, *Eikon basilike*, p. 190. [367] Charles, *Eikon basilike*, p. 199.

[368] John Milton, *Eikonoklastes* (1649), *The complete prose works of John Milton*, ed. M. Hughes, 8 vols. (New Haven, 1962), vol. III, p. 403.

[369] Sharpe, *Image wars*, p. 392–3.

[370] Andrew Lacey, *The cult of King Charles the martyr* (Woodbridge, 2003), pp. 29, 47; Lois Potter, 'The royal martyr in the Restoration: National grief and national sin', in Thomas Corns (ed.), *The royal image: Representations of Charles I* (Cambridge, 1999); Hugh Trevor-Roper, *Historical essays* (London, 1957), pp. 211–12.

Epilogue

In his 1517 presentation copy of his *Education of a Christian prince*, Erasmus had urged Henry VIII to lay down his arms and return to the pattern of moderate, compassionate kingship he had studied during the course of his liberal education:

When a prince is born to office, not elected, which was the custom among some barbarian peoples in the past (according to Aristotle) and is also the practice almost everywhere in our own times, then the main hope of getting a good ruler hangs on his proper education... so that what has been lost with the right to vote is made up for by the care given to his upbringing.[1]

Between 1639 and 1651, many subjects in Britain and Ireland took up their weapons and, subsequently, many others became passionate about the right to vote, petition, campaign and exclude, all in the 'hope of getting a good ruler'. Nevertheless, they had not lost confidence in the power of education to shape a prince's confessional identity or political ideology. The fourth of the parliamentarians' *Nineteen propositions... to the kings maiestie* in June 1642 proposed that both Houses (or, when they were not sitting, the majority of the Privy Council) should have the right to approve 'he or they unto whom the Government and education of the King's Children shall be committed'.[2] During Charles II's reign, measures put to the king by a committee from the Lords in 1673 and set before the Commons in 1676 attempted to ensure that the children of James, duke of Wales, would not be educated as Catholics.[3] Even John Locke, who argued in *Some thoughts concerning education* that a child's education was a matter for his parents, made exceptions in cases where the safety of the commonwealth was at stake.[4] Prior to the passing of the Bill

[1] Erasmus, *EECP*, p. 5.

[2] *Nineteen propositions made by both houses of Parliament, to the kings maiestie, for a reconciliation of the differences between His Majesty and the said houses* (London, 1642), Wing E1675, p. 3.

[3] John Miller, *James II*, 3rd edn. (New Haven, 2000), pp. 76, 83.

[4] John Locke, *Some thoughts concerning education* (London, 1693), Wing L2762, sig. A3^{v} but see John Locke, *Locke on toleration*, ed. Richard Vernon (Cambridge, 2010), pp. 31, 35, 37, 171.

of Rights in 1689, at least, subject-citizens clamoured to exercise some control over royal schoolrooms themselves.

In some ways, this study has suggested that their faith was misplaced. The humanists and reformers in early modern Britain who had used princely education to bridle over-mighty monarchy or to reform a future ruler's personal piety had met with little success. There was no reason to expect that the English Parliament would have any more luck indoctrinating royal children in the seventeenth century than the appointee of the Scottish General Assembly, George Buchanan, had had with James VI and I from 1570 to 1582. Not all acts of royal resistance in early modern Britain were as spectacular as James's rebellion. Many princely responses to education fell into that 'area between mimicry and mockery' that Homi Bhabha described as the inevitable fortune of attempts to impose ideology across a cultural gap.[5] When the school-shy Richmond copied out Richard Croke's encomiums to *bonae litterae* in his painstaking italic hand, it revealed the limits of Erasmian pedagogy to reach an under-motivated student prince without recourse to that most un-Erasmian instrument of corporal punishment. When Lady Jane Grey's parents used the birch rod and deployed considerable resources to promote their daughter's political prospects through her liberal education, the deposed queen spent her last night on earth writing an eloquent letter to her sister in which she urged Katherine Grey to 'deny the world', her stained patrimony and her parents, if necessary, in order to follow Christ faithfully. Jane had been taught to rule but, she wrote, she had really studied 'to learne to die'.[6] When Edward VI's counsellors were trying to persuade him to wink at Princess Mary's masses, the king sincerely and most inconveniently began to parrot the argument made by his preachers and Jean Calvin in a recent letter. He must, he explained, put the purity of the reformed church before all other political considerations, even his own safety.

Other instances of resistance were more knowing. In his final literary gift to James VI and I, Prince Henry composed an oration that mimicked his father's arguments for princely education. While he played the dutiful son in public, he had also begun to read the Tacitean histories that James had condemned and to receive political tracts that critiqued the

5 Homi Bhabha, 'Of mimicry and man: The ambivalence of colonial discourse', *October*, 28 (1984) p.127.

6 Jane Grey, *An epistle of the Ladye Jane, a righte vertuous woman, to a learned man of late falne from the truth of Gods most holy word, for fear of the worlde read it, to thy consolacion: Vvhereunto is added the communication that she had with Master Feckenham vpon her faith, and belefe of the sacraments: Also another epistle whiche she wrote to her sister, with the words she spake vpon the scaffold befor she suffered, anno. M.D.Liiii* ([London, 1554?]), STC 7279, sig. Cii^{r-v}.

corruption of his father's court and his predilection for young male favourites. Even more cynically, Henry VIII had hijacked Erasmus' writings and account of the loving, Christian prince to fabricate a non-Lutheran argument for the royal supremacy in England. These were not simply instances of pedagogues' meanings getting lost in translation. Liberal education had given Tudor and Stuart princes the discursive tools, and occasionally even the political impetus, to repurpose and refute the ideologies of their pedagogues.

Indeed the development of more absolute accounts of monarchical authority in the British isle owes a great deal to these schoolroom confrontations, or in one instance the absence of them. As the family's second daughter, Elizabeth I had been taught to negotiate the confessional changeable winds of her childhood and adolescence by muting controversial statements and passages in the religious texts she translated as New Year gifts for Henry VIII, Queen Katherine and Edward VI. The capacity to smother points of doctrinal dissent certainly helped her to avoid confrontation. Arguably, it helped her to survive under Mary. Yet, as supreme governor of the church, Elizabeth's refusal to hear religious polemics, let alone engage in religious discussion or debate, may have amplified and hardened calls for further doctrinal and ecclesiastical reform. Responding to the increasingly vociferous 'godly citizens' of England certainly encouraged the queen to describe her royal prerogative in more absolute terms. Elizabeth's Stuart successor was even more aggressive in this regard. The ghost of George Buchanan, and other 'archibellouses of rebellion', haunted James VI and I's adult political and religious thought. It shaped his repeated assertions that the prince was answerable to God alone and his instructions to his own sons to perfect the 'crafte' of keeping their subjects in 'order' rather than immersing themselves in the liberal arts and sciences. It prompted James's repeated conflation of popular preaching, Presbyterianism, republicanism and political sedition, and his determination to assert royal supremacy over the 'brain-sicke and headie' clergy of his realms.

Indeed, from Henry VIII until James VI and I, princes had been acquiring the discursive skills and biblical knowledge to declare, maintain and even extend their authority over the church in their realms. Their 'clerkish' expertise was demonstrated in the gutting of treatises; the *inventio* of doctrinal arguments and *dispositio* of scriptural *loci* necessary to support them; the composition of biblical exegeses; and their public engagement in religious controversies. Even Mary I and Elizabeth I, who had not been educated explicitly to govern a church, parlayed their pious translations and composition of private and public prayers into enduring bibliographical and devotional influence. In early modern Britain, the liberal arts and sciences gave sovereigns the knowledge, skill and confidence to be amateur theologians and to shape the idiosyncratic churches of England and Scotland. Their liberal educations had taught them to combine church and state, exactly what later liberals warned sovereign powers against.

Ironically, when parliamentarians articulated their lack of faith in Charles I's plan for the religious and political education of his children in 1642, they were complaining about one of the few early modern British rulers who had not self-consciously set out to resettle the church in his realms. Charles's somewhat leisurely and abbreviated liberal education had left him without the discursive confidence to depart from his father's political and religious prescriptions, even during the Palatinate and Spanish match crises. He claimed to be willing to gather an army in 1620, but he could not find the words to maintain a reversionary position against James. Indeed, it was during this period that Charles came to adopt and augment his father's ideological prejudices and to reject the advice of the Presbyterian schoolmaster and chaplains who had dominated his juvenile household. The king offered his son a *Meditation* (1620) on the dangers of popularity and the martyr-like responsibilities of sacred kingship, and he installed Matthew Wren in his chapel in late 1622. Wren's emphasis on private reasoning over public rhetoric and on reverent devotions over preaching, and his taste for well-ordered churches and ecclesiastical hierarchy, appealed to Charles. The chaplain's mild manners also obscured the readiness of his collaborators at Durham House to break with the Calvinist consensus of the Jacobean church on predestination. In addition to attaching himself to one end of the increasingly polarised confessional spectrum in his realm, Charles also subscribed to a set of paternal prescriptions (rarely followed by James himself) that turned his dislike of oratory into a point of royal principle. Elizabeth may have resented doctrinal disputation but Charles tried to avoid the demands of verbal reasoning and the affray of debate in all contexts, including formal peace negotiations. Charles was willing to make political concessions and compromises and to hear counsel, yet his capacity to see matters from the perspective of an opponent, particularly an 'undisciplined rabble', was limited. A consideration of his education provides some insight into how his relationship with Scottish Covenanters, English Calvinists and parliaments disintegrated into one of mutual fear and incomprehension.

It was Charles, himself, who determined that his education had left him ill prepared for the discursive demands of monarchical government.

Like his sister, Elizabeth, the deposed queen of Bohemia, and his grandmother, the deposed queen of Scots, he attempted to develop his rhetorical skills later in life, as the crisis of his reign unfolded. In the 1640s, the king began to use printed speeches to wrangle his subjects, and he started working on the composition that became the *Eikon basilike*. The British Orpheus took up his lyre and played, first for his throne, then for his life and finally for the future of monarchical government in the three kingdoms. Charles's letters and posthumously printed writings from the war years also suggest that, like his sister, the deficits of his own liberal education encouraged him to take an even keener interest in the schooling of his son, Prince Charles. In the king's official response to the *Nineteen propositions*, he claimed he deserved Parliament's 'present thanks, and the increase of [their] future trusts' for the upbringing that he was providing for his children. And he refused, outright, to countenance their demand to oversee royal schooling in future.[7] The right to determine the education of the prince was at stake. Charles had come to regard it as a power worth fighting for.

[7] [John Colepepper and Lucius Cary, Viscount Falkland] *His majesties answer to the XIX propositions of both houses of Parliament* (London, 1642), Wing C2122, pp. 16–17.

Bibliography

MANUSCRIPTS

Bibliothèque Nationale de France, Paris

Arsenal 360

Bodleian Library, Oxford

Arch F e.26
Ashmole 1108
Bodley 4, 165, 899
Rawlinson B 245, B 274
Smith 74, 77
University College 171

British Library, London

Additional 4176, 4278, 4724, 5464, 5476, 6113, 17012, 19402, 19553, 21404, 24195, 29432, 32102, 33383, 45142, 214195
Arundel 151, 510
Cotton Caligula B III, Caligula B X, Caligula C V, Caligula C VI, Caligula C VII, Caligula C IX, Caligula D I, Caligula D VI, Caligula D VII, Caligula E IV, Cleopatra E V, Cleopatra E VI, Cleopatra F VI, Nero B VI, Nero B VII, Nero C X, Titus B II, Titus B III, Titus C VI, Vespasian D XVIII, Vespasian F III, Vespasian F XIII, Vitellius B XIV, Vitellius B XXI, Vitellius C I
Egerton 616, 1651, 3876
Harleian 159, 252, 283, 433, 1419, 2342, 6986, 6987, 7002, 7007, 7008, 7044
Lansdowne 96, 1236
Royal 8 B VII, 12 D VIII, 12 F XI, 15 E IV, 16 C IX, 16 E I, 16 F II, 17 A XLVI, 17 A XLIX, 17 C XVI, 17 F II, 18 A LXXVII, 18 B XXII, 18 E II, 19 C VIII, 20 A XIV
Sloane 3011

Cambridge University Library

Additional 34
Additional 6858
Dd 12 59

Durham, Ushaw College Library

29

Emmanuel College, Cambridge

5 3 11

Folger Shakespeare Library, Washington, DC

V a 246
X c 91
Z d 11

Hatfield House, Hertfordshire

Cecil Papers 122/125, 125/8, 129/105, 147/6, 147/61, 147/165, 150/51, 150/85, 150/89, 194/52, 205/43, 273/3

Inner Temple Library, London

Petyt 47

Lambeth Palace, London

506

Matthew Parker Library, Corpus Christi College, Cambridge

102, 119

National Archives, Kew

Chancery

C 89/10/50

Exchequer

E 30/868 (diplomatic)
E 101/414/6, 101/414/16, 101/415/3, 101/424/12, 101/434/2, 101/434/3 (wardrobe and household)
E 351/2799 (progresses)
E 404/81 (warrants)

Lord Chamberlain

LC 2/1, 2/2, 2/4 (funerals and mourning)
LC 5/179/9 (household regulations)

Privy Council

PC 2/4 (Registers Edward VI)

Special Collections

SC 6/Henry VII (ministers' and receivers' accounts)

State Papers

SP 1/10, 1/34, 1/37, 1/42, 1/44, 1/49, 1/69, 1/83, 1/84, 1/89, 1/90, 1/92, 1/118, 1/189, 1/195, 1/197, 1/200, 1/212, 1/226, 1/228, 1/235 (Henry VIII: foreign and domestic)
SP 10/5, 10/6, 10/8, 10/13, 10/15 (Edward VI: domestic)
SP 12/264 (Elizabeth: domestic)
SP 14/2, 14/8, 14/10, 14/10A, 14/12, 14/16, 14/51, 14/53, 14/71, 14/80, 14/86/95, 14/87/40, 14/88/30, 14/107, 14/109, 14/112, 14/113, 14/119, 14/141 (James VI and I: domestic)
SP 15/3, 15/37, 15/39 (Secretaries of State: state papers domestic, Edward VI–James I: addenda)
SP 16/14, 16/295 (Charles I: domestic)
SP 52/7, 52/13, 52/14, 52/16, 52/26, 52/28, 52/39, 52/43, 52/64, 52/261 (state papers Scotland: Elizabeth I)
SP 53/7, 53/11, 53/12 (state papers Scotland: Mary, Queen of Scots)
SP 59/13 (state papers Scotland, Border papers)
SP 68/7 (state papers foreign and state papers Calais: Edward VI)
SP 81/16 (state papers foreign: German states)
SP 83/22 (state papers foreign: Holland and Flanders)
SP 94/26 (state papers foreign: Spain)

National Archives of Scotland, Edinburgh

Exchequer
E 21/56 (accounts of the treasurer)
E 23/3/45 (treasury precepts and receipts)

Family Papers
GD 124/10/28, 124/10/37, 124/10/39, 124/10/41, 124/10/44, 124/10/45, 124/10/46 (papers of the Erskine Family, earls of Mar and Kellie)

Register House
RH 2/2/15 (miscellaneous transcripts)

National Library of Scotland, Edinburgh

Advocates: 22 2 18, 29 2 4, 54 1 1

National Library of Wales, Aberystwyth

6620, no. 66

Wren Library, Trinity College, Cambridge

R 7 23* (I–VII)
R 7 31
R 9 30
R 14 10
R 15 19

PRINTED PRIMARY SOURCES OWNED OR ANNOTATED BY BRITISH PRINCES

Anonymous, *The institution of a Christen man, conteynynge the exposytion or interpretation of the commune Crede, of the seuen Sacramentes, of the x commandementes, and of the Pater noster, and the Aue Maria, iustyfication [and] purgatory* (London, 1537), Bodleian, Bodley 4.

Bacon, Francis, *Of the advancement and proficience of learning or the partitions of sciences*, trans. Gilbert Watts (Oxford, 1640), STC 1167, BL, C46.v.i.

Biblia sacra... in quo continentur quinque libri Moysi, libri Josu[a]e, et Iudicum, liber Psalmorum, Prouerbia Salomonis, liber Sapieti[a]e, et Nouum Testamentum Iesus Christi (London, 1535), STC 2055, BL, C.3.e.19.

The Byble in Englyshe, that is to saye the conte[n]t of al the holy scrypture, both of ye olde, and newe testame[n]t (London, 1540), STC 2070, BL, C.18.d.10.

Calvin, Jean, *The institution of Christian religion*, trans. Thomas Norton (London, 1587), BL, 858.c.24.

Charron, Pierre, *Of wisdome three bookes*, trans. Samson Lennard (London, 1608), BL, C.82.b.13.

Cicero, *Commentu[m] familiar in Ciceronis Officia*, ed. Petrus Marsus (Lyon, 1502), FSL, PA 6295 A3 1502 Cage.

De officiis libri tres, collatione optimorum ac vetustissimorum librorum, & recenti emendation (Cologne, 1581), BL, C.28.a11.
Erasmus, *De conscribendis epistolis* (Cologne, 1523), BL, 1083.d 1.
De conscribendis epistolis (Antwerp, 1546), BL, 1083.e.6.
In primum et secundum psalmum exactissimae enarrationes, in tertium paraphrasis (Basel, 1525), BL, 689.a.3.
Institutio hominis Christianis (London, 1523), BL, C.21.b.4.
Paraphrasis in Euangelium Matthaei, Marci, Lucae, Ioannis… Paraphrases in omnes epistolas apostolicas, 2 vols. (Basel, 1522–4), BL, 3913 k. 4.
(ed.), *In Novum Testamentum* (Basel, 1519), BL, D-3225.f.6.
Shakespeare, William, *Comedies, histories and tragedies* (London, 1632), Royal Library, Windsor, 1080415.
Vives, Juan Luis, *De institutione feminae christianae*, BL, Arch B e 30.

PAINTINGS AND MUSEUM OBJECTS

British School, *The Family of Henry VIII* (*c.* 1545), Royal Collection Trust, no. 405796.
Gemini, Thomas, Horary quadrant (1551), brass, British Museum, London, no. 1858,0821.1.
Holbein, Hans, *Edward VI as a Child* (*c.* 1538), oil on panel, Andrew W. Mellon Collection, National Gallery, Washington, DC.
Peake, Robert the Elder, *Princess Elizabeth* (*c.* 1606), oil on panel, The Metropolitan Museum, New York, no. 51.194.1.

CALENDARS AND PRINTED REPORTS

Accounts of the Treasurer of Scotland, ed. C. T. McInnes, vols. XII–XIII (Edinburgh, 1978).
Calendar of the charter rolls preserved in the Public Record Office, 5 Henry VI–8 Henry VIII, vol. v: 1427–1516 (London, 1927).
Calendar of the close rolls preserved in the Public Record Office: Edward IV, Edward V, and Richard III, 1476–1485, ed. K. H. Ledward (London, 1949–54).
Calendar of the close rolls preserved in the Public Record Office for the reign of Henry VII, eds. K. H. Ledward and R. E. Latham, 2 vols. (London, 1955–63).
Calendar of the manuscripts of the Marquis of Bath, preserved at Longleat, Wiltshire, ed. Sophia Crawford Lomas, 5 vols. (London, 1904–80).
Calendar of the manuscripts of the Most Honourable the Marquess of Salisbury, preserved at Hatfield House, Hertfordshire, eds. R. A. Roberts *et al.*, 24 vols. (London, 1883–1976).
Calendar of the patent rolls preserved in the Public Record Office: Henry VI, Edward IV, Edward V, Richard III and Henry VII, 11 vols. (London, 1897–1929).

Calendar of state papers domestic: Edward, Mary and Elizabeth, eds. Robert Lemmon and Mary Anne Everett Green, 12 vols. (London, 1856).

Calendar of state papers, foreign: Edward VI, Mary I, and Elizabeth I, ed. Joseph Stevenson, 23 vols. (London, 1861–1950).

Calendar of state papers foreign series of the reign of Edward VI, 1547–1553, ed. William B. Turnbull (London, 1861).

Calendar of state papers foreign series of the reign of Elizabeth, ed. Joseph Stevenson, 23 vols. (London, 1865).

Calendar of state papers and manuscripts in the archives and collections of Milan: 1385–1618, ed. Allen B. Hinds (London, 1912).

Calendar of state papers of the reigns of Edward VI, Mary, Elizabeth and James I. 1547–[1625] preserved in the state paper department of Her Majesty's Public Record Office. Domestic series, eds. Robert Lemon and Mary Anne Everett Green, 12 vols. (London, 1856–72).

Calendar of state papers relating to English affairs in the archives of Venice, eds. Rawdon Brown *et al.*, 38 vols. (London, 1864–1947).

Calendar of state papers relating to Scotland and Mary Queen of Scots, 1547–1603, ed. J. Bain *et al.*, 13 vols. (Edinburgh, 1898–1969).

Collection of state papers relating to affairs in the reigns of King Henry VIII, King Edward VI, Queen Mary and Queen Elizabeth, left by William Cecil, eds. Samuel Haynes and William Murdin, 2 vols. (London, 1740–59).

Commons debates in 1621, eds. W. Notestein, F. H. Relf and H. Simpson, 7 vols. (New Haven, 1935).

Letters and papers, foreign and domestic, Henry VIII, eds. J. S. Brewer *et al.*, 22 vols. (London, 1864–1932).

Letters and papers illustrative of the reigns of Richard III and Henry VII, ed. James Gairdner, 2 vols. (London, 1861).

Letters and state papers during the reign of King James the sixth, ed. James Maidment (Edinburgh, 1838).

Manuscripts of His Grace the duke of Portland, preserved at Welbeck Abbey, ed. James Cartwright, 25 vols. (London, 1891–1919).

Miscellaneous State Papers: From 1501–1726, ed. P. Yorke, 2 vols. (London, 1778).

Proceedings and ordinances of the Privy Council, ed. Harris Nicolas, 7 vols. (London, 1834–7).

Proceedings in Parliament, 1625, eds. M. Jansson and W. Bidwell (New Haven, 1987).

Proceedings in the Parliaments of Elizabeth I, ed. T. E. Hartley, 3 vols. (London, 1981–95).

Register of the Privy Council of Scotland, eds. J. H. Burton *et al.*, 38 vols. (Edinburgh, 1877–1970).

Relations politiques de la France et de l'Espagne avec l'Écosse au XVIe siècle, ed. Alexandre Teulet (Paris, 1862).

Report on the manuscripts of the Earl of Mar and Kellie preserved at Alloa House, ed. H. Paton, 2 vols. (London, 1904–30).

Rotuli Parliamentorum; ut et petitiones, et placita in Parliamento, ed. John Strachey, 6 vols. (London, 1767–77).

State papers: Published under the authority of His Majesty's Commission, King Henry the Eighth, 11 vols. (London, 1830–52).
Tudor royal proclamations, eds. Paul L. Hughes and James F. Larkin, 3 vols. (New Haven, 1964–9).

PRINTED PRIMARY SOURCES

Abbot, George, *Historical collections*, ed. John Rushworth, 8 vols. (London, 1659–1701).
Adamson, Patrick, *A declaratioun of the kings maiesties intentioun and meaning toward the lait actis of Parliament* (Edinburgh [London], 1585), STC 21948.7.
André, Bernard, 'Annales' and 'Vita Henrici VII', in *Historia regis Henrici septimi, a Bernardo Andrea Tholosate conscripta: Necnon alia quaedam ad eundem regem spectanti*, ed. James Gardiner (London, 1858).
Andrewes, Lancelot, *Ninety-six sermons*, ed. John Posthumus Parkinson, 5 vols. (Oxford, 1841–3).
Angel, John, *The agrement of the holye fathers, and doctors of the church, upon the cheifest articles of Christian religion* (London, 1555), STC 634.
Anonymous, *Cabala, sive Scrinia sacra: Mysteries of state and government, in letters of illustrious persons* (London, 1691), Wing C186.
Christian prayers and meditations in English French, Italian, Spanish, Greeke, and Latine (London, 1569), STC 6428.
The chronicle of Queen Jane, and of two years of Queen Mary, and especially of the rebellion of Sir Thomas Wyat, ed. John Nichols (London, 1850).
Lettere di principi, le qvali o si scrivono o da principi, o à'principi, o ragionan di principi libro primo, ed. Giordano Ziletti (Venice, 1569).
'Proem', in *The first English life of King Henry the fifth written in 1513*, ed. C. L. Kingsford (Oxford, 1911).
Anstis, John (ed.), *The register of the most noble Order of the Garter, from its cover in black velvet, usually called the Black book*, 2 vols. (London, 1724).
Aphthonius, *Progymnasmata, idest praeexercitationes rhetorum & Luciani Opusculum de componenda historia*, ed. G. M. Cattaneo (Venice, 1546).
Aquinas, Thomas, *On kingship to the King of Cyprus*, trans. G. B. Phelan, ed. I. T. Eschmann (Toronto, 1982).
Aristotle, *The politics and constitution of Athens*, trans. Jonathan Barnes, ed. Stephen Everson (Cambridge, 1996).
Ascham, Roger, *The scholemaster or a plaine and perfite way of teaching children, to understand, write, and speake the Latin tong* (London, 1570), STC 832.
Whole works of Roger Ascham, ed. J. A. Giles, 3 vols. (London, 1865).
Aylmer, John, *An harborowe for faithfull and trewe subiectes agaynst the late blowne blaste, concerninge the gouernme[n]t of wemen* ([London], 1559), STC 1005.
Bacon, Francis, *De dignitate & augmentis scientiarum libros IX*, trans. William Rawley (London, 1623), STC 1108.

Of the advancement and proficience of learning or the partitions of sciences, trans. Gilbert Watts (Oxford, 1640), STC 1167.

Of the proficience and aduancement of learning, diuine and humane (London, 1605), STC 1164.

Bale, John, *Index Britanniae scriptorium: John Bale's index of British and other writers*, eds. Reginald Lane Poole *et al.* (Woodbridge, 1990).

Beauchesne, Jehan de, *A booke containing diuers sortes of hands as well the English as French secretarie with the Italian, Roman, chancelry and court hands. Also the true and iust proportio[n] of the capitall Romae set forth*, engraved by John Baildon (London, 1571), STC 6446.

Becon, Thomas, *The catechism of Thomas Becon... with other pieces written by him in the reign of King Edward the sixth*, ed. John Ayre (Cambridge, 1844).

Benger, Emily (ed.), *Memoirs of Elizabeth Stuart: Queen of Bohemia, daughter of King James the first*, 2 vols. (London, 1825).

Bèze, Théodore de, *Icones, id est verae imagines virorum doctrina simul et pietate illustrium* (Geneva, 1580).

La Bible qui est toute la Sainct escripture. En laquelle sont contenus, le Uieil Testament & le Noueau transltez en Francoys, trans. Pierre Robert Olivetan, intro. Jean Calvin (Serrières, 1535).

Bodin, Jean, *Les Six livres de la république* (Paris, 1576).

Bonner, Edmund, *Profytable and necessarye doctryne, with certayne homilies* (London, 1555), STC 3283.7 and 3285.9.

Brantôme, Pierre de Bourdeille, *Seigneur de' Recueil des dames, poésies et tombeaux*, ed. Étienne Vaucheret (Paris, 1991).

Brief confessional writings: Grey, Stubbes, Livingstone and Clarksone, ed. Mary Ellen Lamb (Aldershot, 2001).

British Library Harleian manuscript 433, eds. Rosemary Horrox and P. W. Hammond, 4 vols. (Gloucester, 1978).

Brown, Virginia, James Hankins and Robert A Kaster (eds.), *Catalogus translationum et commentariorum: Mediaeval and Renaissance Latin translations and commentaries* (Washington, DC, 2003).

Bruni, Leonardo, *De interpretatione recta – De la traduction parfait*, ed. Charles Le Blanc (Ottawa, 2008).

'De studiis et litteris', in *Humanist educational treatises*, ed. Craig Kallendorf (Cambridge, MA, 2002).

Bucer, Martin, *De regno Christi*, ed. François Wendel, in *Martini Buceri Opera Latina XV*, 2 parts (Paris, 1955).

Original letters relative to the English Reformation, written during the reigns of King Henry VIII, King Edward IV and Queen Mary: Chiefly from the archives of Zurich, ed. Hastings Robinson, 2 vols. (Cambridge, 1847).

Buchanan, George, *A critical edition of George Buchanan's Baptistes and of its anonymous seventeenth-century translation 'Tyrannicall-government anatomized'*, ed. Steven Berkowitz (New York, 1992).

A dialogue on the law of kingship among the Scots: A critical edition and translation of George Buchanan's 'De iure Regni apud Scotos dialogus', eds. Roger A. Mason and Martin S. Smith (Aldershot, 2004).

George Buchanan: Political poetry, eds. Paul McGinnis and Arthur Williamson (Edinburgh, 2000).
The history of Scotland, ed. James Aikman, 4 vols. (Glasgow, 1827).
Opera omnia, ed. Thomas Ruddiman, 2 vols. (Leiden, 1725).
Poetic paraphrase of the Psalms of David, ed. Roger P. H. Green (Geneva, 2011).
Psalmorum Davidis paraphrasis poetica (Paris, 1565).
'Reformation of the Universitie of St Andros', in *Vernacular writings of George Buchanan*, ed. P. Hume Brown (Edinburgh, 1891–2).
Rerum Scoticarum historia (Antwerp, 1583), STC 3992.
'Vita', in *The trial of George Buchanan before the Lisbon Inquisition* ed. James M. Aitken, (Edinburgh, 1939).
[Buchanan, George], *De Maria Scotorum regina* (London, 1571), STC 3978.
Budé, Guillaume, *De l'institution du prince. Livre contenant plusieurs histoires, enseignments, and saiges dicts des anciens tant Grecs que Latins* (Paris, 1547).
Opera omnia Gulielmi Budaei, 4 vols. (Basle, 1557).
Bullinger, Heinrich, *The decades: The fifth decade*, trans. H. I., ed. Thomas Harding (Cambridge, 1852).
A hundred sermons vpon the Apocalipse of Iesu Christ, trans. John Daus (London, 1573), STC 4062.
Burgess, John, *A sermon preached before the late King James… with two letters in way of apology* (London, 1642), Wing B5720.
Burnet, Gilbert, *History of his own time*, 6 vols., 2nd edn. (Oxford, 1833).
The history of the Reformation of the Church of England, 4 vols. (New York, 1843).
The Byble in Englyshe, that is to saye the conte[n]t of al the holy scrypture, both of ye olde, and newe testame[n]t (London, 1540), STC 2070.
Calderwood, David, *The history of the kirk of Scotland*, ed. Thomas Thomson, 8 vols. (Edinburgh, 1842–9).
Calvin, Jean, *The institution of Christian religion*, trans. Thomas Norton (London, 1587), STC 4422.
Ioannis Calvini opera quae supersunt omnia, eds. William Baum *et al.*, 59 vols. (Brunswick, 1863–1900).
Camden, William, *Annales rerum Anglicarum, et Hibernicarum, regnante Elizabetha* (London, 1615), STC 4496.
Annales the true and royall history of the famous empresse Elizabeth Queene of England France and Ireland, trans. Abraham Darcie (London, 1625), STC 4497.
Carey, Robert, *Memoirs of Robert Carey*, ed. F. H. Mares (Oxford, 1972).
Casaubon, Isaac, *Epistolae*, ed. Theodor Jansson van Almeloveen (Rotterdam, 1709).
(ed.), *Polybii Lycortae F. Megalopolitani Historiarum libri* (Paris, 1609).
Castiglione, Baldassare, *The book of the courtier*, trans. and ed. George Bull (London, 1967).
The courtyer of Count Baldessar Castilio diuided into foure books, trans. Thomas Hoby (London, 1561), STC 4778.
Cavendish, George, *The life and death of Cardinal Wolsey*, ed. Richard S. Sylvester (London, 1959).

Chamberlain, John, *The letters of John Chamberlain*, ed. Norman Egbert McClure, 2 vols. (Philadelphia, 1939).

Charles I, *Eikon basilike, The pourtraicture of His Sacred Majestie in his solitudes and sufferings* (London, 1648), Wing E268.

The works of King Charles, both civil and sacred (London, 1735).

Charron, Pierre, *Of wisdome three bookes*, trans. Samson Lennard (London, 1608), STC 5051.

Chastel, Pierre du, *Deux sermons funebres prononcez es obseques de François premier de ce nom*, ed. Pascale Chiron (Geneva, 1999).

Cheke, John, *The hurt of sedicion howe greueous it is to a commune welth* (London, 1549), STC 5109.

De pronuntiatione Graecae potissimum linguae disputationes (Basel, 1555).

Chrysostom, John, *D. Ioannis Chrysostomi homiliae duae*, trans. John Cheke (London, 1543), STC 14634.

D. Ioannis Chrysostomi de providential Dei, ac fato, orations sex, trans. John Cheke (London, 1545), STC 14630.

[Church of England], *Constitutions and canons ecclesiasticall treated vpon by the bishop of London, president of the conuocation for the prouince of Canterbury, and the rest of the bishops and clergie of the said prouince: and agreed vpon with the kings maiesties licence* (London, 1604), STC 10070.

Iniunccions geue[n] by the moste excellent prince, Edward the sixte, by the grace of God, kyng of England, Frau[n]ce and Irelande: Defendor of the faythe, and in earthe vnder Christ, of the churche of Englande and of Ireland, the supreme hedde: To all and singuler his louyng subiectes, aswell of the clergie, as of the laietie (London, 1547), STC 10090.

Cicero, *Ciceronis libri tres De officiis, De amicitia, De senectute, Paradoxa et De somnio Scipionis*, eds. Desiderius Erasmus *et al.* (Lyons, 1536).

Ciceronis librorum philosophicorum libri, ed. Johann Sturm, 2 vols. (Strasbourg, 1541).

Officia diligenter restituta, eds. Desiderius Erasmus, Philip Melanchthon and Barthow Latomus (Paris, 1541).

The thre bookes of Tyllyes offyces both in latyne tonge [et] in englysshe, trans. Robert Whittington (London, 1534), STC 5278.

Cleland, James, *Hero-paideia or The Institution of a Young Nobleman* (Oxford, 1607), STC 5393.

Clifford, Henry, *Life of Jane Dormer*, eds. E. E. Estcourt and Joseph Stevenson (London, 1887).

Coignet, Pierre du, *Anti-Coton or A refutation of Cottons letter declaratorie... touching the killing of kings... [and] a supplication of the Vniuersitie of Paris, for the preuenting of the Iesuites opening their schooles among them*, trans. George Hakewill (London, 1611), STC 5861.

[Colepepper, John and Lucius Cary, Viscount Falkland], *His majesties answer to the XIX propositions of both houses of Parliament* (London, 1642), Wing C2122.

Córdoba, Martín de, *Jardín de nobles donzellas*, ed. Harriet Goldberg (Chapel Hill, 1974).

Cornwallis, Charles, *A discourse of the most illustrious prince, Henry, late Prince of Wales* (London, 1641), Wing C6329.

Cranmer, Thomas, *A defence of the true and catholike doctrine of the sacrament of the body and bloud of our sauiour Christ* (London, [1550]), STC 6000.

'The prologue', in *The Byble in Englyshe* (London, 1540), STC 2070.

[Cranmer, Thomas], *Certayne sermons, or homelies appoynted by the kynges maiestie* (London, 1547), STC 13640.

A message sent by the kynges maiestie, to certain of his people, assembled in Deuonshire (London, 1549), STC 7506.

Croke, Richard, *Introductiones in rudimenta Graeca* (Cologne, 1520), STC 6044a.5.

Orationes... duae, altera a cura, qua vtilitatem laudem Græcæ linguae tractat, altera a tempore, qua hortatus est Cantabrigiensis, ne desertores essent eiusdem (Paris, 1520).

Dallington, Robert, *Aphorismes ciuill and militarie* (London, 1613), STC 6197.

Dauber, Johannes Henricus, 'Oratio funebris', in André Rivet, *Operum theologicorum: Quae Latine edidit* (Rotterdam, 1660).

D'Aubigné, Théodore Agrippa, *Oeuvres completes*, eds. E. Réume and F. de Caussade, 6 vols. (Paris, 1873).

D'Ewes, Simonds, *Diary of Sir Simonds D'Ewes (1622–1624)*, trans. and ed. Elizabeth Bourcier (Paris, 1974).

De Guise, Marie, *Foreign correspondence with Marie de Lorraine, Queen of Scotland*, 1537–1548, ed. Marguerite Wood (Edinburgh, 1923).

de Guise, Marie, *Foreign correspondence with Marie de Lorraine, Queen of Scotland, 1548–1557*, ed. Marguerite Wood (Edinburgh, 1925).

de Navarre, Marguerite, *A godly medytacyon of the christen sowle*, trans. Elizabeth I, ed. John Bales ([Marburg], 1548), STC 17320.

Les Marguerites de la marguerite des princesses: Text de l'édition de 1547 publiés avec introduction, notes et glossaire, ed. Félix Frank, 4 vols. (Paris, 1873).

Dolet, Etienne, *La Manière de bien traduire d'une langue en aultre* (Lyon, 1540).

du Wés, Giles, *An introductorie for to lerne to rede, to pronounce, and to speake Frenche trewly* (London, 1533), STC 7377.

Edward VI, *Literary remains of King Edward the sixth, edited from his autograph manuscripts with historical notes and a biographical memoir*, ed. John Gough Nichols, 2 vols. (London, 1857).

Elisabeth of Bohemia and René Descartes, *The correspondence between Princess Elisabeth of Bohemia and René Descartes*, ed. Lisa Shapiro (Chicago, 2007).

Elizabeth I, *Her maiesties most princelie answere, deliuered by her selfe at the court at White-hall, on the last day of Nouember 1601* (London, 1601), STC 7578.

Elizabeth I: Autograph compositions and foreign language originals, eds. Janel Mueller and Leah Marcus (Chicago, 2003).

Elizabeth I: Collected works, eds. Leah Marcus, Janel Mueller and Mary Beth Rose (Chicago, 2000).

Elizabeth I: Translations, 1544–1589, eds. Janel Mueller and Joshua Scodel (Chicago, 2009).

Elizabeth I and Mary I, *Early modern Englishwoman: Elizabeth and Mary Tudor*, ed. Ann Lake Prescott (Aldershot, 2001).

Ellis, Henry, ed., *Original letters, illustrative of English history; including numerous royal letters; from autographs in the British Museum, and one or two other collections*, 4 vols. (London, 1824–6).

Elyot, Thomas, *Boke named the gouernour*, ed. H. H. S. Croft, 2 vols. (London, 1883).

The defence of good women (London, 1540), STC 7657.5.

The doctrinall of princis (London, [1533?]), STC 14278, reprinted in 1550, STC 14279.

Erasmus, *Adagiorum collectanea* (Paris, 1500).

Annotations on the New Testament: Acts, Romans, I and II Corinthians: Facsimile of the final Latin text with all earlier variants, eds. A. Reeve and M. A. Screech (Leiden, 1990).

Apophthegmatum sive scite dictorum (Basel, 1531).

A booke called in latyn Enchiridion militis christiani, and in englysshe the manuell of the christen knyght, trans. [William Tyndale?] (London, 1533), STC 10479.

Christiani matrimonii institutio (Basel, 1526).

Collected works of Erasmus, eds. James McConica *et al.*, 52 vols. (Toronto, 1974–).

De conscribendis epistolis (Antwerp, 1546).

Dilucida et pia explanation Symboli quod Apostolorum dicitur, decalogi praeceptorum, & dominicae precationis (Antwerp, 1533).

The dyaloge called Funus (London, 1534), STC 10453.5.

Ecclesiastae, siue, de ratione concionandi libri quatuor: Opus recens, nec antehac a quoquam excusum (Basel, 1535).

The education of a Christian prince, ed. Lester K. Born (New York, 1968).

Education of a Christian prince with the Panegyric for Archduke Philip of Austria, trans. Neil M. Cheshire and Michael J. Heath, ed. Lisa Jardine (Cambridge, 1997).

Enchiridion militis Christiani: An English version, ed. Anne O'Donnell (Oxford, 1981).

Enchiridion militis Christiani, saluberrimis praeceptis refertum (Basel, 1518).

Enchiridion militis christiani, whiche may be called in Englisshe, the hansom weapon of a christen knyght replenysshed with many goodly [and] godly precepts, trans. [William Tyndale?] (London, 1534), STC 10480.

Epistle of Erasmus Roterdamus, sent unto Conradus Pelicanus, concerning his opinion of the blessed Sacrament (London, 1554), STC 10491.

Erasmi opuscula: A supplement to the Opera omnia, ed. W. K. Ferguson (The Hague, 1933).

An exhortacyon to the study of the Gospell, trans. [William Roy] (London, 1534), STC 10494.

The first tome or volume of the Paraphrases of Erasmus vpon the Newe Testament, trans. Mary I *et al.*, ed. Nicholas Udall (London, 1548), STC 2854.

Novum Testamentum paraphrases, 2 vols. (Basel, 1524).

Opera Omnia Desiderii Erasmi Roterdami: Recognita et adnotatione critica instructa notisque illustrata, 9 ordines (Amsterdam, 1969–).

Opus epistolarum Desiderii Erasmi Roterodami: Denuo recognitum et auctum, eds. P. S. Allen *et al.*, 12 vols. (Oxford, 1906–58).

Paraphrase of Erasm[us] Roterdame upon [the] Epistle of sai[n]t Paule unto his discyple Titus, ed. Leonard Cox (London, 1534), STC 10503.

A playne and godly exposytion or declaratio[n] of the co[m]mune crede (which in the Latin tonge is called Symbolum Apostolorum) and of the x co[m] maundementes of goddes law, trans. William Marshall (London, 1534), STC 10504.

Ratio seu methodus compendio perveniendi ad veram theologiam, in *Ausgewählte werke*, eds. A. Holborn and H. Holborn (Munich, 1933).

(ed.), *In Novum Testamentum* (Basel, 1519).

In Novum Testamentum annotationes (Basel, 1535).

[Erasmus], *The dialoge between Julius the seconde, Genius and saynte Peter* (London, 1534), STC 14841.5 and STC 14842.

Faur, Guy du, 'Tetrastika; or the Quatrains of Guy de Faur, Lord of Pibrac', in *Bartas his deuine weekes & workes*, trans. Josuah Sylvester (London, 1606), STC 21649a.5.

Florio, Michelangelo, *Historia de la vita e de la morte de l'illustrissima Signora Giovanna Graia gia regina eletta e publicata in Inghilterra e de la cose accudute in quell regno dopo la morte del Re Edoardo VI* (Middelburgh, 1607).

Fortescue, John, 'In praise of the laws of England', in *On the laws and governance of England*, ed. Shelley Lockwood (Cambridge, 1997).

Fouquelin, Antoine, *La Rhetorique Françoise* (Paris, 1557).

Foxe, John, *The unabridged acts and monuments online* (Sheffield, 2011). Available from: www.johnfoxe.org.

Fuensalida, Gutierre Gómez de, *Correspondencia de Gutierre Gómez de Fuensalida, embajador en Alemania, Flandes é Inglaterra (1496–1509)*, ed. Jacobo Fitz-James Stuart y Falcó (Madrid, 1907).

Fullonius, William, *The comedy of Acolastus by [William] Fullonius*, ed. P. L. Carver (London, 1937).

Fulovisi, Titus Livius de, *Opera hactenus inedita T. Livii de Frulovisiis de Ferraria*, ed. C. W. Previté-Orton (Cambridge, 1932).

Gardiner, Stephen, *The letters of Stephen Gardiner*, ed. J. A. Muller (New York, 1933).

Genêt, Jean-Philippe (ed.), *Four English political tracts of the later middle ages*, vol. XVIII (London, 1977).

Grey, Jane, *An epistle of the Ladye Jane, a righte vertuous woman, to a learned man of late falne from the truth of Gods most holy word, for fear of the worlde read it, to thy consolacion: Vvhereunto is added the communication that she had with Master Feckenham vpon her faith, and belefe of the sacraments: Also another epistle whiche she wrote to her sister, with the words she spake vpon the scaffold befor she suffered, anno. M.D.Liiii* ([London, 1554?]), STC 7279.

Ioannae Graiae litterae ad H. Bullingerum (Zurich, 1840).

[Gruytrode, Jacques de], *Mirroure of golde for the synfull soule*, trans. Margaret Beaufort (London, 1506), STC 6894.5.

Hakewill, George, *The auncient ecclesiasticall practise of confirmation confirmed by arguments drawne from scripture, reason, councels, Fathers, and later writers* (London, 1613), STC 12614.

King Dauids vow for reformation of himselfe, his family, his kingdome deliuered in twelue sermons before the Prince his Highnesse vpon Psalm 101 (London, 1621), STC 12616.

Scutum regium. Id est, Aduersus omnes regicidas et regicidarum patronos (London, 1612), STC 12618.

Hall, Edward, *Hall's chronicle; containing the history of England*, ed. Henry Ellis (London, 1809).

The vnion of the two noble and illustrate famelies of Lancastre [and] Yorke (London, 1548), STC 12721.

Harrington, Henry and Thomas Park (eds.), *Nugae antiquae*, 2 vols. (London, 1804).

[Hawes, Stephen?], *The receyt of the Ladie Kateryne*, ed. Gordon Kipling (Oxford, 1990).

Hearne, Thomas, *Reliquiae Hernianae: The remains of Thomas Hearne MA of Edmund Hall*, ed. P. Bliss (Oxford, 1857).

(ed.), *Titi Livii Foro-Juliensis vita Henrici quinti, Regis Angliae. Accedit Sylloge epistolarum, a variis Angliae principibus scriptorium* (Oxford, 1716).

Henry VIII, *Assertio septem sacramentorum aduersus Martin Lutheru[m], aedita ab inuictissimo Angliae et Franciae rege, et do. Hyberniae Henrico eius nominis octauo* (London, 1521), STC 13078.

A copy of the letters, wherin the most redouted [and] mighty pri[n]ce, our souerayne lorde kyng Henry the eight, kyng of Englande [and] of Frau[n]ce, defe[n]sor of the faith, and lorde of Irla[n]de: made answere vnto a certayne letter of Martyn Luther (London, 1527), STC 13086.

A glasse of the truth (London, [1532]), STC 11919.

Libello huic regio haec insunt (London, 1523), STC 13083.

A necessary doctrine and erudition of any Christen man, set furth by the kynges maiestie of England (London, 1543), STC 5168.

Herbert, Edward of Cherbury, *Life and raigne of King Henry the eighth* (London, 1649), Wing H1504.

Heresbach, Conrad, *De educandis erudiendisque principum liberis, reipublicae gubernandae destinatis, deque republica christiana administranda* (Frankfurt, 1570).

Heylyn, Peter, *A short view of the life and reign of King Charles… from his birth to his burial* (London, 1658), Wing H1735B.

Hobbes, Thomas, *Behemoth or The Long Parliament*, ed. Ferdinand Tönnies (London, 1889).

The elements of law natural and politic, ed. J. C. A. Gaskin (Oxford, 1994).

Leviathan, ed. Richard Tuck (Cambridge, 1996).

Hoccleve, Thomas, *The regiment of princes*, ed. Charles R. Blyth (Kalamazoo, 1999).

Holt, John, *Lac puerorum* (London, 1508), STC 13604.
Hooper, John, *Godly and most necessary annotations in [th]e XIII chaptyer to the Romaynes* ([Worcester, 1551]), STC 13756.
Oversight, and deliberacion upon the holy Prophete Jonas (London, 1550), STC 13763.
Hore beate Marie virgiinis ad usum insignis ac praeclare ecclesiasie Saru[m] (London, 1514), STC 15919.
Howard, Henry, 'So crewell prison', in *Henry Howard, Earl of Surrey: Poems*, ed. E. Jones (Oxford, 1964).
Hume, David, *Inquiry concerning human understanding*, ed. Stephen Buckle (Cambridge, 2007).
Hyde, Edward, earl of Clarendon, *The history of the rebellion and civil wars in England*, ed. W. Dunn Macray, 6 vols. (Oxford, 1888).
James VI and I, *Declaratio… super re Vorstii actum tractatumue sit*, trans. Adam Newton (London, 1612), STC 9232.
Ane fruitfull meditatioun contening ane plane and facill expositioun of ye 7.8.9 and 10 versis of the 20 chap. of the Reuelatioun in forme of ane sermone (Edinburgh, 1588), STC 14376.
James VI and I: Selected writings, eds. Neil Rhodes, Jennifer Richards and Joseph Marshall (Aldershot, 2003).
Letters of King James VI and I, ed. G. P. V. Akrigg (Berkeley, 1984).
Ane meditatioun vpon the xxv, xxvi, xxvii, xxviii, and xxix verses of the XV chapt[er] of the first buke of the Chronicles of the Kingis (Edinburgh, 1589), STC 14380.
Poems of James VI of Scotland, ed. James Craigie, 2 vols. (Edinburgh, 1955–8).
The political works of James I, ed. Charles Howard McIlwain (Cambridge, 1918).
Political writings, ed. J. P. Sommerville (Cambridge, 1994).
The workes of the most high and mighty prince, Iames by the grace of God Kinge of Great Brittaine France & Ireland defendor of the faith, ed. James [Montagu] (London, 1616), STC 14344.
The workes of the most high and mightie prince, Iames by the grace of God, King of Great Britaine, France and Ireland, defender of the faith, ed. James Montagu (London, 1620), STC 14345.
Jayne, Sears R. and Francis R. Johnson (eds.), *The Lumley Library: The catalogue of 1609* (London, 1956).
Johnstoun, Arthur, *Delitiae poetarum Scotorum: Huius aevi illustrium*, 2 vols. (Amsterdam, 1637).
Kempis, Thomas à, *Full deuoute and gostely treatyse of the imytacion and followynge the blessyd lyfe of our most merciful savyour Cryst*, trans. William Atkinson and Margaret Beaufort (London, [1504] 1517), STC 23957.
Kirk, James (ed.), *The second book of discipline* (Edinburgh, 1980).
Knox, John, *The history of the Reformation in Scotland*, ed. William Croft Dickinson, 2 vols. (London, 1949).
Works of John Knox, ed. David Laing, 6 vols. (Edinburgh, 1846–64).

Kraye, Jill (ed.), *Cambridge translations of Renaissance philosophical texts*, vol. II: *Political philosophy* (Cambridge, 1997).

Larkin, James and Paul Hughes (eds.), *Stuart royal proclamations*, 2 vols. (Oxford, 1973).

Latimer, Hugh, *Seconde sermon of Maister Hughe Latimer, which he preached before the kynges majestie* (London, 1549), STC 15274.7.

Laud, William, *The works of the most reverend father in God, William Laud*, eds. William Scott and James Bliss, 7 vols. (Oxford, 1847–60).

Leach, Arthur F. (ed.), *Educational charters and documents 598 to 1909* (Cambridge, 1919).

Lefèvre, Raoul, *The history of Jason (1477)*, trans. William Caxton, ed. John Munro (London, 1913).

Leland, John, *Principum, ac illustrium aliquot & eruditorum in Anglia virorum, encomia, trophaea, genethliaca, & epithalamia*, ed. Thomas Newton (London, 1589), STC 15447.

Leo VI, *Leonis imperatoris de bellico apparatus liber*, trans. John Cheke (Basel, 1554).

Letters of the kings of England, now first collected from the originals in royal archives, and other authentic sources, ed. J. O. Halliwell, 2 vols. (London, 1846).

Letters to King James VI, ed. Alexander Macdonald (Edinburgh, 1835).

Lily, William, *Monarchy or no monarchy in England... [with] passages upon the life and death of the late King Charles* (London, 1651), Wing L2228.

Linacre, Thomas, *Rudimenta grammatices*, trans. George Buchanan (Paris, 1533).

Lipsius, Justus, *Politica: Six books of politics or political instruction*, ed. Jan Waszink (Assen, 2004).

'Epistola', in *Relectiones hyemales de ratione & methodo legendi utrasque historias, civiles & ecclesiasticas*, ed. Degory Wheare (Cambridge, 1684), Wing W 1596.

Locke, John, *Locke on toleration*, ed. Richard Vernon (Cambridge, 2010).

Some thoughts concerning education (London, 1693), Wing L2762.

Two treatises of government, ed. Peter Laslett (Cambridge, 1988).

Lucena, Juan de, 'Epistola exhortatoria a las letras', in *Isabel la Católica en la opinion de Españoles y extranjeros: Signlos XV al XX*, ed. Vicente Valencia Rodríguez, 3 vols. (Valladolid, 1970).

Lull, Ramón, *Here begynneth the table of this present booke intytuled the book of the ordre of chiualry or knyghthode*, trans. William Caxton (London, 1484), STC 3356.7.

Macaulay, George Campbell (ed.), *The chronicles of Froissart* (London, 1904).

Macdonald, Alexander and James Dennistoun (eds.), *The library of Mary Queen of Scots and King James the sixth* (Glasgow, 1834).

Machiavelli, Niccolò, *The discourses*, trans. Leslie Walker and Brian Richardson, ed. Bernard Crick (London, 1970).

The prince, eds. Quentin Skinner and Russell Price (Cambridge, 1988).

Machyn, Henry, *The diary of Henry Machyn, citizen and merchant taylor of London, from AD 1550 to AD 1563*, ed. John Gough Nichols (London, 1848).

Mackenzie, George, *Lives and characters of the most eminent writers of the Scots nation*, 3 vols. (Edinburgh, 1711).

Madden, Frederick (ed.), *Privy purse expenses of Princess Mary* (London, 1831).

Mahon, Reginald Henry (ed.), *The indictment of Mary Queen of Scots as derived from a manuscript in the University Library at Cambridge* (Cambridge, 1923).

Malfatti, C. V. (ed.), *The accession coronation and marriage of Mary Tudor as related in four manuscripts of the Escorial* (Barcelona, 1956).

Mancinus, Dominicus, *The usurpation of Richard the third*, ed. C. A. J. Armstrong, 2nd edn. (Oxford, 1969).

Marck, Robert de la, *Nouvelle collection des mémoires relatifs à l'histoire de France* (Paris, 1854).

Martyr, Peter, *Tractatio de sacramento Eucharistiae* (London, 1549), STC 24673.

Mary, Queen of Scots, *Latin themes of Mary Stuart, Queen of Scots*, ed. Anatole de Montaiglon (London, 1855).

Lettres, instructions et mémoires de Marie Stuart, reine d'Écosse, ed. Alexandre Labanoff, 7 vols. (London, 1844).

McCrie, Thomas, *Life of Andrew Melville, containing illustration of the ecclesiastical and literary history of Scotland*, 2 vols. (Edinburgh, 1819).

Melanchthon, Philip, *Corpus Reformatorum: Philippi Melanchthonis opera quae supersunt omnia*, ed. Karl Gottlieb Bretschneider and Heinrich Ernst Bindseil, 28 vols. (Halle, 1834–59).

Melville, James, *The autobiography and diary of Mr James Melvill*, ed. Robert Pitcairn (Edinburgh, 1842).

Melville, Sir James, *Memoirs of Sir James Melville of Halhill, 1535–1617*, ed. A. Francis Steuart (New York, 1930).

Meriton, George, *The Christian mans assuring house. And a sinners conuersion. Two sermons* (London, 1614), STC 17837.

Milton, John, *The complete prose works of John Milton*, ed. M. Hughes, 8 vols. (New Haven, 1962).

Political writings, ed. Martin Dzelzainis (Cambridge, 1991).

Montaigne, Michel de, *The complete essays*, ed. M. A. Screech (London, 1987).

Morata, Olympia, *Orationes, dialogi, epistolae, carmina, tam Latin quam Graeca*, ed. Celio Secondo (Basel, 1562).

More, Thomas, *The complete works of Saint Thomas More*, vol. III, part 2: *Latin poems*, eds. Clarence H. Miller *et al.* (New Haven, 1984).

The complete works of Saint Thomas More, vol. XV: *In defense of humanism: Letters to Dorp, Oxford, Lee, and a Monk*, ed. Daniel Kinney (New Haven, 1986).

The correspondence of Sir Thomas More, ed. Elizabeth F. Rogers (Princeton, 1947).

Utopia, eds. George M. Logan and Robert M. Adams, rev. edn. (Cambridge, 2003).

Mountague, Richard, *Appello Caesarem A iust appeale from two vniust informers* (London, 1625), STC 18031.

A gagg for the new Gospell? No: a nevv gagg for an old goose (London, 1624), STC 18038.

Mumby, Frank A. (ed.), *Fall of Mary Stuart: A narrative in contemporary letters* (London, 1921).

The youth of Henry VIII: A narrative in contemporary letters (London, 1913).

Murray, William, *Naupactiados, sive Lepantiados Iacobi Magni, Britanniarum, Franciae & Hiberniae Regis, fidei verè Christianae vindicis, & assertoris verè Christianissimi metaphrasis poetica* (London, 1604), STC 14 386.

Myers, A. R. (ed.), *The household of Edward IV: The black book and the ordinance of 1478* (Manchester, 1959).

Nichols, John Gough (ed.), *A collection of ordinances and regulations for the government of the royal household made in divers reigns* (London, 1790).

Inventories of the wardrobes, plate, chapel stuff, etc. of Henry Fitzroy, duke of Richmond, and of the wardrobe stuff at Baynard's Castle of Katharine, Princess Dowager with a memoir and letters of the duke of Richmond (London, 1855).

The progresses, processions and magnificent festivities of King James the first, his royal consort, family and court, 4 vols. (London, 1828).

Nicolas, Nicholas Harris (ed.), *Extracts from the privy purse expenses of King Henry VII, from December 7, 1491, to March 20, 1505* (London, 1831).

Privy purse expenses of Elizabeth of York (London, 1830).

Privy purse expenses of Henry VIII from November 1529 to December 1532 (London, 1827).

Nineteen propositions made by both houses of Parliament, to the kings maiestie, for a reconciliation of the differences between His Majesty and the said houses (London, 1642), Wing E1675.

Nixon, Anthony, *Oxfords triumph in the royall entertainement of his moste excellent maiestie, the queene, and the prince* (London, 1605), STC 18589.

Ochino, Bernardino, *Certayne sermons of the ryghte famous and excellente clerk master Barnardine Ochine*, trans. [Anne Cook] and Richard Argentine (London, [1551?]), STC 18766.

Fouretene sermons of Barnardine Ochyne, concernyng the predestinacion and eleccion of god, trans. A[nne] C[ooke] (London, [1551?]), STC 18767.

Sermons of Barnardine Ochine, trans. Anne Cooke (London, 1548), STC 18764.

A tragoedie or dialoge of the unjust usurped primacie of the bishop of Rome, trans. John Ponet (London, 1549), STC 18770.

Ortiz, Alonso, *Diálogo sobre la educación del príncipe don Juan, hijo de los reyes católicos (s. xv–xvi)*, ed. Giovanni Maria Bertini (Madrid, 1983).

Osborne, Francis, *Advice to a son, or, Directions for your better conduct through the various and most important encounters of this life under these generall heads, I. Studies, &c., II. Love and marriage, III. Travell, IV. Government, V. Religion, conclusion* (Oxford, 1656), Wing O512.

Pace, Richard, *De fructu qui ex doctrina percipitur: The benefit of a liberal education*, trans. and eds. Frank Manley and Richard S. Sylvester (New York, 1967).

Oratio... in pace nuperime composita et foedere percusso: Inter inuictissimum Angliae regem et Francorum regem christianissimum in aede diui Pauli Londini habita (London, 1518), STC 19081a.

Paget, William, 'The letters of William Lord Paget of Beaudesert, 1547–63', in *Camden Miscellany*, vol. xxv, eds. B. L. Beer and S. M. Jack (London, 1974).

Palsgrave, John, *Ecphrasis Anglica in comoediam Acolasti: The comedye of Acolastus translated into oure englysshe tongue* (London, 1540), STC 11470.

Lesclarcissement de la langue francoyse ([London?], 1530), STC 19166.

Parker, Matthew, *Correspondence of Matthew Parker, D. D. Archbishop of Canterbury, comprising letters written by and to him, from* A.D. *1535, to his death,* A.D. *1575*, eds. John Bruce and Thomas Thomason Perowne (Cambridge, 1853).

Parr, Katherine, *Katherine Parr: Complete works and correspondence*, ed. Janel Mueller (Chicago, 2011).

Prayers or medytacions wherein the mynd is stirred, paciently to suffre all afflictions here (London, 1545), STC 4819.

Patrizi, Francesco, *De regno et regis institutione* (Paris, 1567).

Peacham, Henry, *The compleat gentleman fashioning him absolute in the most necessary and commendable qualities concerning minde or bodie* (London, 1622), STC 19502.

Perron, Jacques Davy du, *A letter written from Paris by the Lord Cardinall Peron, to Monsieur Casaubon in England* (St. Omer, 1612), STC 6383.

Piccolomini, Aeneas Silvius, 'The education of boys' (1450), in *Humanist educational treatises*, trans. and ed. Craig Kallendorf (Cambridge, MA, 2002).

Pisan, Christine de, *Lavision-Christine*, ed. Mary Louis Towner (Washington, DC, 1932).

Plato, *Omnia divini Platonis opera tralatione Marsillii Fincini*, ed. Simon Grynaeus (Basel, 1551).

Poitiers, Diane de, *Lettres inédites de Diane de Poytiers*, ed. Georges Guiffrey (Lyon, 1896).

Pole, Reginald, *Ad Henricu[m] octauum Britanniae regem, pro ecclesiasticae unitatis defensione, libri quatuor* (Rome, 1539).

Poliziano, Angelo, *Letters, vol. 1, books I–IV*, ed. Shane Butler (Cambridge, 2006).

Pollini, Girolamo, *L'Historia ecclesiastica della rivoluzion d'Inghilterra* (Rome, 1594).

Pontano, Giovanni, *De principe*, in *Prosatori Latini del quattrocento*, ed. E. Garin (Turin, 1977).

Precationes priuat[ae] Regiae E.R. (London, 1563), STC 7576.7.

Price, Daniel, *Spirituall odours to the memory of Prince Henry in foure of the last sermons preached in St James after his Highnesse death* (Oxford, 1613), STC 20304.

Purkiss, Diane (ed.), *Three tragedies by Renaissance women* (Harmondsworth, 1998).

Rollock, Robert, *Tractatus de vocatione efficaci* (Edinburgh, 1597), STC 21285.

A treatise of Gods effectual calling, trans. Henry Holland (London, 1603), STC 21286.

Rosso, Guilio Raviglio, *I successi d'Inghilterra dopo la morte di Odoardo sesto* (Ferrara, 1560).

Rousseau, Jean-Jacques, *Oeuvres completes*, eds. Bernard Gagnebin and Marcel Raymond, 5 vols. (Paris, 1959–95).

Row, John, *History of the Kirk of Scotland from the year 1558 to August 1639* (Edinburgh: 1842).

Saint German, Christopher, *Here after foloweth a lytell treatise called the newe addicions* (London, 1531), STC 21563.

Sarpi, Paolo, *The historie of the Councel of Trent conteining eight books*, trans. Nathanael Brent (London, 1620), STC 21761.

Searle, William George (ed.), *Grace book gamma: Containing the records of the University of Cambridge for the years 1501–1542* (Cambridge, 1908).

Sessions, W. A., *Henry Howard: The poet earl of Surrey, a life* (Oxford, 1999).

Shakespeare, William, *Comedies, histories and tragedies* (London, 1632), STC 22274.

Sharman, Julian (ed.), *The library of Mary Queen of Scots* (London, 1889).

Sidney, Algernon, *Discourses concerning government*, ed. Thomas G. West (Indianapolis, 1990).

Skelton, John, *The Latin writings of John Skelton*, ed. David R. Carlson (Chapel Hill, 1991).

'The Latin writings of John Skelton', ed. David Carlson, *Studies in Philology*, 88:4 (1991).

Smith, Thomas, *Vitae quorundam eruditissimorum et illustrium vivorum* (London, 1707).

Starkey, Thomas, *A dialogue between Pole and Lupset*, ed. T. F. Mayer (London, 1989).

An exhortation to the people, instructynge theym to unitie and obedience (London, 1536), STC 23236.

Stelling-Michaud, Sven and Suzanne (eds.), *Le livre du recteur de L'Académie de Genève, 1559–1878*, 6 vols. (Geneva, 1959).

Stevenson, Jane and Peter Davidson (eds.), *Early modern women poets (1520–1700)* (Oxford, 2001).

Stewart, W., *The buik of the croniclis of Scotland; Or a metrical version of the history of Hector Boece*, ed. W. B. Turnbull, 3 vols. (London, 1858).

Strype, John, *The life of the learned Sir John Cheke, knight, first instructor, afterwards secretary of state to King Edward VI* (Oxford, 1821).

Memorials of the most reverend father in God, Thomas Cranmer, 3 vols. (Oxford, 1840).

(ed.), *Ecclesiastical memorials relating chiefly to religion and the reformation of it and the emergencies of the Church of England under King Henry VIII, King Edward VI and Queen Mary I*, 4 vols. (Oxford, 1822).

Stuart, Elizabeth, *The correspondence of Elizabeth Stuart, Queen of Bohemia, vol. II: 1632–42*, ed. Nadine Akkerman (Oxford, 2011).

Sturm, Johann, *De educatione principis* (Frankfurt, 1570).

Synesius, Bishop of Ptolemais, and Philo of Alexandria, *Institution d'un prince chrétien… et Oraison de la vraye noblesse*, trans. Daniel d'Auge (Paris, 1555).

Taverner, Richard (ed.), *Catonis disticha moralia ex castigatione D. Erasmi Roterdami* (London, 1540), STC 4843.

Thomas, William, *The historie of Italie, a boke excedyng profitable to be rede: Because it intreateth of the astate [sic] of many and divers common weales, how thei have ben & now be governed* (London, 1549), STC 24018.

Il pellegrino Inglese (Zurich, 1552).

Principal rules of the Italian grammar, with a dictionarie for the better understandying of Boccace, Petrarcha, and Dante (London, 1550), STC 24020.

Throckmorton, Nicholas, *Legend of Sir Nicholas Throckmorton*, ed. John Nichols (London, 1874).

Variae meditationes et preces piae variis designatae vsibus, Latino, Italico, Gallico, & Anglico sermone conscriptae (London, 1582), STC 17774.

Vergil, Polydore, *Anglica historia: The Anglica historia, A.D. 1485–1537*, ed. Denys Hay (London, 1950).

Vives, Juan Luis, *De disciplinis libri XX* (Frankfurt, 1532).

De institutione feminae Christianae: Introduction, critical edition, translation and notes, trans. C. Fantazzi, eds. C. Fantazzi and C. Matheeussen, 2 vols. (Leiden, 1996).

Introductio ad sapientiam, Satellitium siue symbola, Epistolae duae de ratione studii puerilis, Tria capita addita initio Suetonii Tranquilli (Paris, 1527).

Opera omnia, ed. Gregorius Majansius, 8 vols. (London, [1745] 1964).

Wake, Isaac, *Rex Platonicus* (Oxford, 1607), STC 24939.

Warner, George (ed.), 'The library of James VI, 1573–1583: From a manuscript in the hand of Peter Young, his tutor', in *Miscellany of the Scottish History Society* (Edinburgh, 1898).

Watson, Thomas, *Holsome and Catholyke doctryne concerninge the seven sacramentes* (London, 1558), STC 25114.

[William of Ockam or Pierre Dubois], *A dialogue betwene a knyght and a clerke concernynge the power spiritual and temporall*, trans. J. Travisa (London, [1531]), STC 12511a.

Wilson, Thomas, *The arte of rhetorique for the vse of all suche as are studious of eloquence, sette forth in English* (London, 1553), STC 25799.

Vita et obitus duorum fratrum Suffolciensium (London, 1551), STC 25816.

Wingfield, Robert, *Vita Mariae Angliae Reginae*, in *Camden Miscellany*, vol. XXVIII, ed. Diarmaid MacCulloch (London, 1984).

Worcester, William, *The boke of noblesse: Addressed to Edward IV on his invasion of France in 1475*, ed. J. G. Nichols (London, 1860).

Wren, Christopher, *Parentalia: Or memoirs of the family of the Wrens* (London, 1750).

Wren, Matthew, *A sermon preached before the kings maiestie* (Cambridge, 1628), STC 26015.

Wriothesley, Charles, *A chronicle of England*, ed. W. D. Hamilton, 2 vols. (London, 1877).

SECONDARY WORKS

Adams, Simon, 'Foreign policy and the parliaments of 1621 and 1624', in Kevin Sharpe (ed.), *Faction and Parliament* (London, 1978).

Adams, Simon and David Gehring, 'Elizabeth I's former tutor reports on the parliament of 1559: Johannes Spithovius to the Chancellor of Denmark, 27 February 1559', *EHR*, 128:530 (2013).

Alexander, J. J. G., 'Foreign illuminators and illuminated manuscripts', in Lotte Hellinga and J. B. Trapp (eds.), *The Cambridge history of the book in Britain*, vol. III: *1400–1557* (Cambridge, 1999).

Alford, Stephen, *Burghley: William Cecil at the court of Elizabeth I* (New Haven, 2008).

The early Elizabethan polity: William Cecil and the British succession crisis, 1558–1569 (Cambridge, 1998).

Kingship and politics in the reign of Edward VI (Cambridge, 2002).

Allan, David, *Philosophy and politics in later Stuart Scotland: Neo-stoicism, culture and ideology in an age of crisis, 1540–1690* (East Linton, 2000).

Allison, Rayne, *A monarchy of letters: Royal correspondence and English diplomacy in the reign of Elizabeth I* (New York, 2012).

Amos, N. Scott, 'The Alsatian among the Athenians: Martin Bucer, mid-Tudor Cambridge and the Edwardian Reformation', *Reformation and Renaissance Review*, 4:1 (2002).

Anglo, Sydney, *Machiavelli – the first century: Studies in enthusiasm, hostility, and irrelevance* (Oxford, 2005).

Appiah, K. Anthony, 'Liberal education: The United States example', in Kevin McDonough and Walter Feinberg (eds.), *Education and citizenship in liberal-democratic societies: Teaching for cosmopolitan values and collective identities* (Oxford, 2002).

Arestis, Philip and Peter Howells, 'The 1520–1640 "great inflation": An early case of controversy on the nature of money', *Journal of Post Keynesian Economics*, 24:2 (2001–2).

Asch, Ronald, 'Sacred kingship in France and England in the age of the wars of religion: From disenchantment to re-enchantment?', in Charles W. Prior and Glenn Burgess (eds.), *England's wars of religion revisited* (Aldershot, 2011).

Aston, Margaret, *The king's bedpost: Reformation and iconography in a Tudor group portrait* (Cambridge, 1993).

Atwill, Janet M., *Rhetoric reclaimed: Aristotle and the liberal arts tradition* (Ithaca, 1998).

Backhouse, Janet, 'Founders of the royal library: Edward IV and Henry VII as collectors of illuminated manuscripts', in Daniel Williams (ed.), *England in the fifteenth century: Proceedings of the 1986 Harlaxton symposium* (Woodbridge, 1987).

'Illuminated manuscripts associated with Henry VII and members of his immediate family', in Benjamin Thompson (ed.), *The Reign of Henry VII: Proceedings of the 1993 Harlaxton symposium* (Stamford, 1995).

Backus, Irene, *Reformation readings of the apocalypse: Geneva, Zurich and Wittenberg* (Oxford, 2000).

Baker-Smith, Dominic, '"Inglorious glory": 1513 and the humanist attack on chivalry', in Sydney Anglo (ed.), *Chivalry in the Renaissance* (Woodbridge, 1990).

Baldwin, T. W., *William Shakespere's smalle Latine and lesse Greeke*, 2 vols. (Urbana, 1944).

Bataillon, Marcel, *Erasme et l'Espagne*, eds. Charles Amiel and Daniel Devoto, 3 vols. (Geneva, 1991).

Beauchamp, Virginia Walcott, Elizabeth H. Hageman and Margaret Mikesell, 'Introduction', in *The instruction of a Christen woman: Juan Luis Vives*, eds. Virginia Walcott Beauchamp, Elizabeth H. Hageman and Margaret Mikesell (Urbana, 2002).

Beilin, Elaine, *Redeeming Eve: Women writers of the English Renaissance* (Princeton, NJ, 1987).

Belle, Marie-Alice, 'Locating early modern women's translations: Critical and historiographical issues', *Renaissance and Reformation / Renaissance et Réforme*, 35:4 (2012).

Belozerskaya, Marina, *Rethinking the Renaissance: Burgundian arts across Europe* (Cambridge, 2002).

Béné, Charles, 'Erasme et Cicéron', in *Colloquia Erasmiana Turonensis*, 2 vols. (Paris, 1972).

Bergeron, David M., 'Creating entertainments for Prince Henry's Creation (1610)', *Comparative Drama*, 42:4 (2008).

Royal family, royal lovers: King James of England and Scotland (Columbia, MI, 1991).

Bernard, George, *The king's Reformation: Henry VIII and the remaking of the English church* (New Haven, 2005).

'The piety of Henry VIII', in Scott Amos, Andrew Pettegree and Henk van Nierop (eds.), *The education of a Christian society: Humanism and the Reformation in Britain and the Netherlands* (Aldershot, 1999).

War, taxation and rebellion in early Tudor England: Henry VIII, Wolsey and the amicable grant of 1525 (Brighton, 1986).

Bhabha, Homi, 'Of mimicry and man: The ambivalence of colonial discourse', *October*, 28 (1984).

Bietenholz, Peter G. and Thomas B. Deutsche (eds.), *Contemporaries of Erasmus: A biographical register of the Renaissance and Reformation*, 3 vols. (Toronto, 1985–7).

Bingham, Caroline, *James VI of Scotland* (London, 1979).

Birch, Thomas.

Life of Henry, Prince of Wales (London, 1760).

Birrell, T. A., *English monarchs and their books: From Henry VII to Charles II* (London, 1987).

Black, Robert, *Education and society in Florentine Tuscany: Teachers, pupils, and schools, c. 1250–1450* (Leiden, 2007).

'Italian Renaissance education: Changing perspectives and continuing controversies', *Journal of the History of Ideas*, 52:2 (1991), 315–34.

Blackwell, C. W. T, 'Humanism and politics in English royal biography: The use of Cicero, Plutarch and Sallust in the *Vita Henrici quinti* (1438) by Titus Livius de Frulovisi and the *Vita Henrici septimi* (1500–1503) by Bernard André', in I. D. McFarlane (ed.), *Acta conventus neo-Latini sanctandreani: Proceedings of the fifth international congress of neo-Latin studies* (Binghamton, 1986).

Blair, Ann M., *The theater of nature: Jean Bodin and Renaissance science* (Princeton, 1997).

Too much to know: Managing scholarly information before the modern age (New Haven, 2011).

Blockmans, William, *Emperor Charles V, 1500–1558*, trans. Isola van den Hoven-Vardon (New York, 2002).

Bloom, Alan, *The closing of the American mind: How higher education has failed democracy and impoverished the souls of today's students*, 2nd edn. (New York, 2008).

Bloomer, W. Martin, *The school of Rome: Latin studies and the origins of liberal education* (Berkeley, 2011).

Bonner, Elizabeth, 'French naturalisation of the Scots in the fifteenth and sixteenth centuries', *HJ*, 40 (1997).

Born, Lester K., 'Introduction', in *The education of a Christian prince*, ed. Lester K. Born (New York, 1968).

Botley, Paul, *Latin translation in the Renaissance: The theory and practice of Leonardo Bruni, Giannozzo Manetti, and Desiderius Erasmus* (Cambridge, 2004).

Bowers, Roger, 'The chapel royal, the first Edwardian prayer book, and Elizabeth's settlement of religion, 1559', *HJ*, 43 (2000).

'Early Tudor courtly song: An evaluation of the Fayrfax book (BL, Additional MS 5465)', in Benjamin Thompson (ed.), *Reign of Henry VII: Proceedings of the 1993 Harlaxton symposium* (Stamford, 1995).

Bowle, John, *Charles I: A biography* (London, 1975).

Braddock, Robert, 'Grey, Henry, duke of Suffolk (1517–1554)', *ODNB*.

Bradford, Alan T., 'Stuart absolutism and the "utility" of Tacitus', *Huntington Library Quarterly*, 46:2 (1983).

Bradshaw, Brendan, 'The Christian humanism of Erasmus', *Journal of Theological Studies*, 33:2 (1982).

Bradshaw, Christopher, 'David or Josiah? Old Testament kings as exemplars in Edwardian religious polemic', in Bruce Gordon (ed.), *Protestant history and identity in sixteenth-century Europe*, 2 vols. (Aldershot, 1996).

Brandi, Karl, *The emperor Charles V: The growth and destiny of a man and of a world-empire*, trans. C. V. Wedgewood (London, 1939).

Broad, Jacqueline and Karen Green, *A history of women's political thought in Europe, 1400–1700* (Cambridge, 2009).

Brooke, Chris, *Philosophic pride: Stoicism and political thought, Lipsius to Rousseau* (Princeton, 2012).

Bryson, Alan, 'Cheke, Sir John (1514–1557)', *ODNB*.

Buchtel, John, '"To the most high and excellent prince": Dedicating books to Henry, Prince of Wales', in Timothy Wilks (ed.), *Prince Henry revived: Image and exemplarity in early modern England* (London, 2007).

Burgess, Glenn, *Absolute monarchy and the Stuart constitution* (New Haven, 1996).

Burke, Peter, *The Renaissance sense of the past* (New York, 1969).

'Tacitism, scepticism, and reason of state', in J. H. Burns and Mark Goldie (eds.), *The Cambridge history of political thought, 1450–1700* (Cambridge, 1994).

Burns, J. H., 'George Buchanan and the anti-monarchomachs', in Nicholas Phillipson and Quentin Skinner (eds.), *Political discourse in early modern Britain* (Cambridge, 1993).

True law of kingship: Concepts of monarchy in early modern Scotland (Oxford, 1996).

Burrow, Colin, 'Gorges, Sir Arthur (d. 1625)', *ODNB*.

Bush, M. L., *The government policy of Protector Somerset* (Montreal, 1975).

Bushnell, Rebecca, *A culture of teaching: Early modern humanism in theory and practice* (Ithaca, 1996).

'George Buchanan, James VI and neo-classicism', in Roger A. Mason (ed.), *Scots and Britons: Scottish political thought and the union of 1603* (Cambridge, 1994).

Cameron, Jamie, *James V: The personal rule, 1528–1542* (East Linton, 1998).

Carley, James, 'Blount, William, fourth Baron Mountjoy (*c.* 1478–1534)', *ODNB*.

The books of King Henry VIII and his wives (London, 2004).

The libraries of King Henry VIII (London, 2000).

'Marks in the books and the libraries of Henry VIII', *Papers of the Bibliographical Society of America*, 91 (1997).

'Review of *Katherine Parr: Complete works and correspondence*', *Times Literary Supplement*, no. 5644 (3 June 2011).

'*Rex noster est inconstans*: Henry VIII's reading practices', in *King Henry's prayer book*, ed. James Carley (London, 2009).

Carlson, David, 'King Arthur and court poems for the birth of Arthur Tudor in 1486', *Humanistica Lovaniensia*, 36 (1987).

'Reputation and duplicity: The texts and contexts of Thomas More's Epigram on Bernard André', *ELH*, 58:2 (1991).

'Royal tutors in the reign of Henry VII', *SCJ*, 22:2 (1991).

'Writings of Bernard André (*c.* 1450–*c.* 1522)', *Renaissance Studies*, 2:2 (1998).

Carlton, Charles, *Charles I: The personal monarch*, 2nd edn. (London, 1995).

Cavill, P. R., *The English parliaments of Henry VII, 1485–1504* (Oxford, 2009).

Chapman, Hester, *Lady Jane Grey, October 1537–February 1554* (London, 1962).

The last Tudor king: a study of Edward VI (London, 1958).

Charlton, Kenneth, *Education in Renaissance England* (London, 1965).

Chomarat, Jacques, *Grammaire et rhétorique chez Erasme*, 2 vols. (Paris, 1981).

'Superstitio, religio et impietas', *Moreana*, 21 (1984).

Chrimes, S. B., 'The pretension of the duke of Gloucester in 1422', *EHR*, 45 (1930).

Clarke, Danielle, *The politics of early modern women's writing* (New York, 2001).

Clough, C. H., 'A presentation volume for Henry VIII: The Charlecote Park copy of Erasmus's *Institutio principis christiani*', *Journal of the Warburg and Courtauld Institutes*, 44 (1981).

Coffey, John, 'George Buchanan and the Scottish Covenanters', in Caroline Erskine and Roger A. Mason (eds.), *George Buchanan: Political thought in early modern Britain and Europe* (Aldershot, 2012).

Cogswell, Thomas, *The blessed revolution: English politics and the coming of war, 1621–1624* (Cambridge, 1989).

Cogswell, Thomas, Richard Cust and Peter Lake (eds.), *Politics, religion and popularity in early Stuart Britain: Essays in honour of Conrad Russell* (Cambridge, 2002).

Colclough, David, *Freedom of speech in early Stuart England, 1603–1628* (Cambridge, 2005).

Coles, Kimberly, *Religion, reform, and women's writing in early modern England* (Cambridge, 2010).

Collinson, Patrick, *Archbishop Grindal, 1519–1583: The struggle for a reformed church* (Berkeley, 1979).

The birthpangs of Protestant England: Religion and cultural change in the sixteenth and seventeenth centuries (New York, 1988).

'Ecclesiastical vitriol: Religious satire in the 1590s and the invention of puritanism', in John Guy (ed.), *The reign of Elizabeth I: Court and culture in the last decade* (Cambridge, 1995).

Elizabethan essays (London, 1994).

The Elizabethan puritan movement (Berkeley, 1967).

'The Jacobean religious settlement: The Hampton Court Conference', in Howard Tomlinson (ed.), *Before the English Civil War: Essays on early Stuart politics and government* (London, 1983).

'The monarchical republic of Queen Elizabeth I', *Bulletin of the John Rylands Library*, 62 (1987).

'The prophesyings and the downfall and sequestration of Archbishop Edmund Grindal, 1576–1583', in Melanie Barber, Stephen Taylor and Gabriel Sewell (eds.), *From the Reformation to the permissive society: A miscellany in celebration of the 400th anniversary of Lambeth Palace Library* (Woodbridge, 2010).

'The reformer and the archbishop: Martin Bucer and an English Bucerian', in *Godly people: Essays on English Protestantism and Puritanism* (London, 1983).

Religion of Protestants: The church in English society (Oxford, 1982).

De republic Anglorum: Or history with the politics put back (Cambridge, 1990).

Richard Bancroft and Elizabethan anti-Puritanism (Cambridge, 2013).

Corns, Thomas, *Uncloistered virtue: English political literature, 1640–1660* (Oxford, 1992).

Cox, Virginia, 'Leonardo Bruni on women and rhetoric: *De studiis et litteris*', *Rhetorica*, 27:1 (2009).

Women's writing in Italy, 1400–1650 (Baltimore, 2008).

Craig, John, 'Forming a Protestant consciousness? Erasmus' *Paraphrases* in English parishes, 1547–1666', in Hilmar M. Pabel and Mark Vessey (eds.), *Holy Scripture speaks: The production and reception of Erasmus' 'Paraphrases on the New Testament'* (Toronto, 2002).

Craufurd, Thomas, *History of the University of Edinburgh from 1580 to 1646* (Edinburgh, 1808).

Cressy, David, 'Revolutionary England, 1640–42', *P&P*, 181 (2003).

Cromartie, Alan, 'King James and the Hampton Court Conference', in Ralph Houlbrooke (ed.), *James VI and I: Ideas, authority, and government* (Aldershot, 2006).

'The mind of William Laud', in Charles Prior and Glenn Burgess (eds.), *England's wars of religion, revisited* (Farnham, 2011).

Cummings, Brian, *Literary culture of the Reformation: Grammar and grace* (Oxford, 2002).

Cunningham, Sean, *Henry VII* (London, 2007).

Curtis, Catherine, 'The social and political thought of Juan Luis Vives: Concord and counsel in the Christian commonwealth', in Charles Fantazzi (ed.), *A companion to Juan Luis Vives* (Leiden, 2008).

Cust, Richard, 'Anti-puritanism and urban politics: Charles I and Great Yarmouth', *HJ*, 35:1 (1992).

Charles I: A political life (Harlow, 2005).

Charles I and the aristocracy, 1625–1642 (Cambridge, 2013).

'Charles I and the Order of the Garter', *Journal of British Studies*, 52 (2013).

'Charles I and popularity', in Thomas Cogswell, Richard Cust and Peter Lake (eds.), *Politics, religion and popularity in early Stuart Britain: Essays in honour of Conrad Russell* (Cambridge, 2002).

The forced loan and English politics, 1626–1628 (Oxford, 1987).

'News and politics in early seventeenth-century England', *P&P*, 112 (1986).

'"Patriots" and "popular" spirits: Narratives of conflict in early Stuart politics', in Nicholas Tyacke (ed.), *The English revolution c. 1590–1720: Politics, religion, and communities* (Manchester, 2007).

'Prince Charles and the second session of the 1621 parliament', *EHR*, 122 (2007).

'Was there an alternative to the personal rule? Charles I, the Privy Council and the parliament of 1629', *History* 90:299 (2005).

D'Amico, John F., *Renaissance humanism in Papal Rome* (Baltimore, 1983).

Davies, C. S. L., *Peace, print and Protestantism, 1450–1558* (London, 1976).

Dawson, Jane, *The politics of religion in the age of Mary, Queen of Scots: The earl of Argyll and the struggle for Britain and Ireland* (Cambridge, 2002).

Daybell, James, *Women letter-writers in Tudor England* (Oxford, 2006).

De la Mare, A. C., 'Humanistic script: The first ten years', in F. Krafft and D. Wuttke (eds.), *Das Verhältnis der humanisten zum Buch* (Boppard, 1977).

Denley, Marie, 'Elementary teaching techniques and middle English religious didactic writing', in Helen Phillips (ed.), *Langland, the mystics and the medieval English religious tradition: Essays in honour of S. S. Hussey* (Cambridge, 1990).

Devereux, E. J., *Renaissance English translations of Erasmus: A bibliography to 1700* (Toronto, 1983).

Dickens, A. G., *The English Reformation*, 2nd edn. (University Park, PA, 1991).

Dickinson, W. C., 'The advocates' protest against the institution of a Chair of Law in the University of Edinburgh', *Scottish Historical Review*, 23:91 (1926).

Dodd, Gregory, *Exploiting Erasmus: The Erasmian legacy and religious change in early modern England* (Toronto, 2009).

Donaldson, Gordon, *All the queen's men: Power and politics in Mary Stewart's Scotland* (London, 1983).

Donaldson, Peter, *Machiavelli and mystery of state* (Cambridge, 1988).

Doran, Susan, 'Elizabeth I's religion: The evidence of her letters', *Journal of Ecclesiastical History*, 51:4 (2000).

England and Europe in the sixteenth century (Houndmills, 1999).

Dougall, Alistair, *The Devil's book: Charles I, the 'Book of Sports' and Puritanism in Tudor and early Stuart England* (Exeter, 2011).

Dowling, Maria, 'The Gospel and the court: Reformation under Henry VIII', in Peter Lake and Maria Dowling (eds.), *Protestantism and the national church in sixteenth-century England* (London, 1987).

Humanism in the age of Henry VIII (London, 1986).

Doyle, A., 'A prayer attributed to St. Thomas Aquinas', *Dominican Studies*, 1 (1948).

Duffy, Eamon, *Fires of faith: Catholic England under Mary Tudor* (New Haven, 2009).

The stripping of the altars: Traditional religion in England, c. 1400–c. 1580 (New Haven, 1992).

Durkan, John and James Kirk, *University of Glasgow 1451–1577* (Glasgow, 1977).

Dzelzainis, Martin, 'The Ciceronian theory of tyrranicide from Buchanan to Milton', in Caroline Erskine and Roger A. Mason (eds.), *George Buchanan: Political thought in early modern Britain and Europe* (Aldershot, 2012).

'Milton and the regicide', in Paul Hammond and Blair Worden (eds.), *John Milton: Life, writing, reputation* (Oxford, 2010).

Edwards, John, *Mary I: England's Catholic queen* (New Haven, 2011).

Elton, Geoffrey, 'Humanism in England', in A. Goodman and A. MacKay (eds.), *The impact of humanism on western Europe* (London, 1990).

Policy and police: The enforcement of the Reformation in the age of Thomas Cromwell (Cambridge, 1972).

Reform and Reformation: England, 1509–1558 (Cambridge, MA, 1977).

'Review of *English humanists and Reformation politics under Henry VIII and Edward VI* by James K. McConica', *HJ*, 10:1 (1967).

'War and the English in the reign of Henry VIII', in L. Freeman, P. Hayes and R. O'Neill (eds.), *War, strategy and international politics: Essays in honour of Sir Michael Howard* (Oxford, 1992).

Eppley, D., *Defending royal supremacy and discerning God's will in Tudor England* (Aldershot, 2007).

Eskin, Catherine, 'The reigning of women's tongues in English books of instruction and rhetorics', in Barbara Whitehead (ed.), *Women's education in early modern Europe: A history, 1500–1800* (New York, 1999).

Felch, Susan, 'The development of the English prayer book', in Karen Maag and John D. Witvliet (eds.), *Worship in medieval and early modern Europe: Change and continuity in religious practice* (Notre Dame, 2004).

Ferguson, Arthur, *The articulate citizen and the English Renaissance* (Durham, NC, 1965).

Ferguson, Gary, *Mirroring belief: Marguerite de Navarre's devotional poetry* (Edinburgh, 1992).

Ferguson, W. K., *The Renaissance in historical thought: Five centuries of interpretation* (Boston, 1948).

Fernández-Santamaria, J. A., *The state, war and peace: Spanish political thought in the Renaissance, 1516–1559* (Cambridge, 1977).

Ferrell, Lori Ann, *Government by polemic: James I, the king's preachers, and the rhetoric of conformity* (Stanford, 1998).

Figgis, J. N., *The theory of the divine right of kings* (Cambridge, 1896).

Fincham, Kenneth, 'Abbot, George (1562–1633)', *ODNB*.

Prelate as pastor: The episcopate of James I (Oxford, 1990).

Fincham, Kenneth and Peter Lake, 'The ecclesiastical policy of James I', *Journal of British Studies*, 24 (1985).

'The ecclesiastical policy of James I and Charles I', in Kenneth Fincham (ed.), *The early Stuart church* (Stanford, 1993).

Fischlin, Daniel, '"To eate the flesh of kings": James VI and I, apocalypse, nation and sovereignty', in Daniel Fischlin and Mark Fortier (eds.), *Royal subjects: Essays on the writings of James VI and I* (Detroit, 2002).

Ford, Philip, 'Homer in the French Renaissance', *Renaissance Quarterly*, 59:1 (2006).

'*Poeta sui saeculi facile princeps*: George Buchanan's poetic achievement', in Philip Ford and Roger P. H. Green (eds.), *George Buchanan: Poet and dramatist* (Swansea, 2009).

Fox, Alistair and John Guy, *Reassessing the Henrician age: Humanism, politics and reform, 1500–1550* (Oxford, 1986).

Fox, Alistair, 'English humanism and the body politic', in Alistair Fox and John Guy, *Reassessing the Henrician age* (Oxford, 1986).

Freeman, Thomas, 'Providence and prescription: The account of Elizabeth in Foxe's "Book of Martyrs"', in Susan Doran and Thomas Freeman (eds.), *The myth of Elizabeth* (Basingstoke, 2003).

'"The Reformation of the church in this parliament": Thomas Norton, John Foxe and the parliament of 1571', *Parliamentary History*, 16:2 (1997).

Gardiner, S. R., *History of England from the accession of James I to the outbreak of the civil war, 1603–1642*, 10 vols. (London, 1894–6).
Garin, Eugenio, *La disputa delle arti nel quattrocento* (Florence, 1947).
L'educazione in Europa, 1400–1600: Problemi e programmi, rev. edn. (Rome, 1976).
Gee, J. A. 'John Byddell and the first publication of Erasmus' *Enchiridion* in English', *English Literary History*, 4:1 (1937).
Geldner, F., *Die Staatsauffassung und Fürstenlehre des Erasmus von Rotterdam* (Berlin, 1930).
Gibson, Jonathan, 'Katherine Parr, Princess Elizabeth and the crucified Christ', in Victoria Burke and Jonathan Gibson (eds.), *Early modern women's manuscript writing: Selected papers from the Trinity/Trent colloquium* (Aldershot, 2004).
Gibson, Kenneth, 'Burton, Henry (bap. 1578, d. 1647/8)', *ODNB*.
Goldie, Mark, 'The unacknowledged republic: Office-holding in early modern England', in Tim Harris (ed.), *The politics of the excluded, c. 1500–1850* (Basingstoke, 2001).
Goldsmith, Elizabeth and Colette Winn, 'Introduction', in Elizabeth Goldsmith and Colette Winn (eds.), *Lettres de femmes: Textes inédites et oubliés du XVIe au XVIIe siècle* (Paris, 2005).
Goodare, Julian, 'James VI's English subsidy', in Julian Goodare and Michael Lynch (eds.), *The reign of James VI* (East Linton, 2000).
'Mary (1542–1587)', *ODNB*.
Goodrich, Jaime, 'Mary Tudor, Lord Morley, and St Thomas Aquinas: The politics of pious translation at the Henrician court', *ANQ*, 24:1–2 (2011).
'Thomas More and Margaret More Roper: A case for rethinking women's participation in the early modern public sphere', *SCJ*, 39:4 (2008).
Gouwens, Kenneth, 'Perceiving the past: Renaissance humanism after the "cognitive turn"', *American Historical Review*, 103:1 (1998).
Grafton, Anthony, 'On the scholarship of Politian and its context', *Journal of the Warburg and Courtauld Institutes*, 45 (1977).
Grafton, Anthony and Lisa Jardine, *From humanism to the humanities: Education and the liberal arts in fifteenth- and sixteenth-century Europe* (Cambridge, MA, 1986).
Grafton, Anthony and Joanna Weinberg, *'I have always loved the holy tongue': Isaac Casaubon, the Jews, and a forgotten chapter in Renaissance scholarship* (Cambridge, MA, 2011).
Grant, Ruth, 'The Brig o' Dee affair, the sixth earl of Huntly and the politics of the Counter-Reformation', in Julian Goodare and Michael Lynch (eds.), *The Reign of James VI* (East Linton, 2000).
Greaves, Richard L., 'Galloway, Patrick (*c.* 1551–1626)', *ODNB*.
Green, Richard F., *Poets and prince pleasers: Literature and the English court in the late middle ages* (Toronto, 1980).
Green, Roger, 'Dry bones of contention? Picking apart Buchanan's *Psalms*', in Philip Ford and Roger Green (eds.), *George Buchanan: Poet and dramatist* (Swansea, 2009).

Grendler, Paul F., *Schooling in Renaissance Italy: Literacy and learning, 1300–1600* (Baltimore, 1989).

(ed.), 'Forum: Education in the Renaissance and Reformation', *Renaissance Quarterly*, 43:4 (1990).

Griffiths, Ralph A., *The reign of King Henry VI: The exercise of royal authority*, 2nd edn. (Stroud, 1996).

Griffiths, Ralph A. and Roger S. Thomas, *The making of the Tudor dynasty* (New York, 1985).

Gunn, Steven, 'Chivalry and the politics of the early Tudor court', in Sydney Anglo (ed.), *Chivalry in the Renaissance* (Woodbridge, 1990).

'The French wars of Henry VIII', in J. Black (ed.), *The origins of war in early modern Europe* (Edinburgh, 1987).

'Prince Arthur's preparation for kingship', in Steven Gunn and Linda Monckton (eds.), *Arthur Tudor, Prince of Wales: Life, death and commemoration* (Woodbridge, 2009).

'Wolsey's foreign policy and the domestic crisis of 1527–28', in Steven Gunn and Phillip Lindley (eds.), *Cardinal Wolsey: Church, state and art* (Cambridge, 1991).

Guy, John, *The children of Henry VIII* (Oxford, 2013).

A daughter's love: Thomas More and his dearest Meg (Boston, 2009).

'Henry VIII and the *praemunire* manoeuvres of 1530–1531', *EHR*, 97 (1982).

My heart is my own: The life of Mary Queen of Scots (London, 2004).

'The rhetoric of counsel in early modern England', in Dale Hoak (ed.), *Tudor political culture* (Cambridge, 1995).

'Thomas Cromwell and the intellectual origins of the Henrician revolution', in Alistair Fox and John Guy (eds.), *Reassessing the Henrician age: Humanism, politics and reform, 1500–1550* (London, 1986).

Tudor England (Oxford, 1988).

(ed.), *The Tudor monarchy* (London, 1997).

Gwyn, Peter, *The king's cardinal: The rise and fall of Thomas Wolsey* (London, 1990).

'Wolsey's foreign policy: The conferences at Calais and Bruges reconsidered', *HJ*, 23:4 (1980), 755–72.

Habsburg, Otto von, *Charles V*, trans. Michael Ross (New York, 1970).

Hadfield, Andrew, *Literature, travel, and colonial writing in the English Renaissance, 1545–1625* (Oxford, 1998).

Hamilton, Dakota, 'Thomas, William (d. 1554)', *ODNB*.

Handley, Stuart, 'Newton, Sir Adam, first baronet (d. 1630)', *ODNB*.

Hankins, James, 'Rhetoric, history, and ideology: The civic panegyrics of Leonardo Bruni', in James Hankins (ed.), *Renaissance civic humanism: Reappraisals and reflections* (Cambridge, 2000).

Hannay, Margaret P., *Philip's phoenix: Mary Sidney, Countess of Pembroke* (New York, 1990).

(ed.), *Silent but for the word: Tudor women as patrons, translators, and writers of religious works* (Kent, OH, 1985).

Hardin, Richard F., 'The literary conventions of Erasmus' *Education of a Christian prince*: Advice and aphorism', *Renaissance Quarterly*, 35:2 (1982).

Hartley, T. E., *Elizabeth's parliaments: Queen, lords and commons, 1559–1601* (Manchester, 1992).

Hay, Denys, 'England and the humanities in the fifteenth century', in H. A. Oberman and T. A. Brady Jr (eds.), *Itinerarum Italicum: The profile of the Italian Renaissance in the mirror of its European transformations* (Leiden, 1975).

Heal, Felicity, 'Cox, Richard (*c.* 1500–1581)', *ODNB*.

Reformation in Britain and Ireland (Oxford, 2003).

Hearn, Karen, *Dynasties: Painting in Tudor and Jacobean England 1530–1630* (London, 1995).

Heath, Michael, 'The education of a Christian prince: Erasmus, Budé, Rabelais – and Ogier le Danois', in Philip Ford and Gillian Jondorf (eds.), *Humanism and letters in the age of François Ier* (Cambridge, 1996).

Helms, Dietrich, 'Henry VIII's book: Teaching music to royal children', *Musical Quarterly*, 92:1–2 (2009).

Henderson, Judith Rice, 'Despauterius' *Syntaxis* (1509): The earliest publication of Erasmus' *De conscribendis epistolis*', *Humanistica Lovaniensia*, 37 (1988).

'Erasmian Ciceronians: Reformation teachers of letter-writing', *Rhetorica*, 10:3 (1992).

'Humanism and the humanities: Erasmus's *Opus de conscribendis epistolis* in sixteenth-century schools', in Carol Poster and Linda C. Mitchell (eds.), *Letter-writing manuals from antiquity to the present: Historical and bibliographic studies*, (Columbia, SC, 2007).

Herding, Otto, 'Isokrates, Erasmus und die *Institutio principis Christiani*', in Rudolf Vierhaus and Manfred Botzenhart (eds.), *Dauer und wandel der geschichte: Aspekte europäischer vergangenheit, festgabe für Kurt von Raumer* (Munster, 1966).

Herman, Peter J., *Royal poetrie: Monarchic verse and the political imaginary of early modern England* (Ithaca, 2010).

Hexter, J. H., 'The education of the aristocracy in the Renaissance', *Journal of Modern History*, 22:1 (1950).

Hicks, Michael, *Edward V: The prince in the Tower* (Stroud, 2003).

Hill, Christopher, *Intellectual origins of the English revolution revisited* (Oxford, 1997).

Hindle, Steve, *The state and social change in early modern England, c. 1550–1640* (Basingstoke, 2002).

Hirsh, John C., 'Latin prayers as a lesson in writing and devotion for a lady of standing', *The Chaucer Review*, 41:4 (2007).

Hoak, Dale, 'Edward VI (1537–1553)', *ODNB*.

The king's council in the reign of Edward VI (Cambridge, 1976).

'Rehabilitating the duke of Northumberland: Politics and political control, 1549–1553', in Jennifer Loach and Robert Tittler (eds.), *The mid-Tudor polity, c. 1540–1560* (London, 1980).

Hobbins, Daniel, 'Arsenal MS 360 as a witness to the career and writings of Bernard André', *Humanistica Lovaniensia*, 50 (2001).

Hobbs, R. Gerald, 'Bucer's use of King David as mirror of the Christian prince', *Reformation and Renaissance Review*, 5:1 (2003).

Hoffman, Martha, *Raised to rule: Educating royalty at the court of the Spanish Habsburghs, 1601–1634* (Baton Rouge, 2011).

Holmes, Clive, 'Charles I: A case of mistaken identity', *P&P*, 205 (2009).

Höltgen, K. J., 'Sir Robert Dallington', *Huntington Library Quarterly*, 47 (1984).

Höpfl, Harro, 'Oxthodoxy and reason of state', *History of Political Thought*, 23:2 (2002).

Hopkins, Lisa, *Writing Renaissance queens: Texts by and about Elizabeth I and Mary Queen of Scots* (Newark, 2007).

Horsburgh, David, 'Young, Sir Peter (1544–1628)', *ODNB*.

Hosington, Brenda, 'Lady Margaret Beaufort's translation as mirrors of practical piety', in Micheline White (ed.), *English women, religion, and textual production, 1500–1625* (Aldershot, 2011).

'Learned ladies: Éloges de l'Anglaise savant (1550–1558)', in Colette Nativel (ed.), *Femmes savantes, savoirs des femmes: Du crépuscule de la Renaissance à l'aube des Lumières* (Geneva, 1995).

Houlbrooke, Ralph, 'Prince Arthur's funeral', in Steven Gunn and Linda Monckton (eds.), *Arthur Tudor, Prince of Wales: Life, death, and commemoration* (Woodbridge, 2009).

(ed.), *James VI and I: Ideas, authority, and government* (Aldershot, 2006).

Howe, Elizabeth, *Education and women in the early modern Hispanic world* (Aldershot, 2008).

Huizinga, Johan, *Erasmus and the age of the Reformation*, trans. F. Hopman and B. Flower (New York, 1957).

Hume Brown, P., *George Buchanan, humanist and reformer: A biography* (Edinburgh, 1980).

Hunt, Alice, *The drama of coronation: Medieval ceremony in early modern England* (Cambridge, 2008).

Ives, Eric, *Lady Jane Grey: A Tudor mystery* (Oxford, 2009).

'Tudor dynastic problems revisited', *Historical Research*, 81 (2008).

James, Mervyn, 'English politics and the concept of honour, 1485–1642', *P&P*, suppl. 3 (1978).

James, Susan, *Kateryn Parr: The making of a queen* (Aldershot, 1999).

Jardine, Lisa, *Erasmus, man of letters: The construction of charisma in print* (Princeton, 1993).

'The place of dialectic teaching in sixteenth-century Cambridge', *Studies in the Renaissance*, 21 (1974).

Jardine, Lisa and Anthony Grafton, '"Studied for action": How Gabriel Harvey read his Livy', *P&P*, 129 (1990).

Jarrot, C. A. L., 'Erasmus' "*In principio erat sermo*": A controversial translation', *Studies in Philology*, 61:1 (1964).

Jensen, Kristian, 'Humanist reform of Latin and Latin teaching', in Jill Kraye (ed.), *Cambridge translations of Renaissance philosophical texts*, vol. II: *Political philosophy* (Cambridge, 1997).

Jones, Michael K. and Malcolm G. Underwood, *The king's mother: Lady Margaret Beaufort, Countess of Richmond and Derby* (Cambridge, 1992).

Jones, Norman, 'Religion in Parliament', in David Dean and Norman Jones (eds.), *Parliaments of Elizabethan England* (Oxford, 1990).

Joong-Lak, Kim, 'The Scottish–English–Romish book: The character of the Scottish Prayer Book of 1637', in Michael Braddick and David Smith (eds.), *The experience of revolution in Stuart Britain and Ireland: Essays for John Morrill* (Cambridge, 2011).

Jordan, W. K., *Edward VI: The threshold of power and the dominance of the duke of Northumberland* (London, 1970).

Kastan, David Scott, 'An early English metrical psalm: Elizabeth's or John Bale's?', *Notes and Queries*, 21 (1974).

Kekewich, Margaret, 'Edward IV, William Caxton, and literary patronage in Yorkist England', *Modern Language Review*, 66:3 (1971).

Kelsey, Sean, 'The king's book: *Eikon basilike* and the English revolution of 1649', in Nicholas Tyacke (ed.), *The English revolution* c. *1590–1720: Politics, religion and communities* (Manchester, 2007).

Kimball, Bruce, *Orators and philosophers: A history of the idea of liberal education*, rev. edn. (New York, 1995).

King, John N., 'Henry VIII as David: The king's image and Reformation politics', in Mark Rankin, Chris Highley and John N. King (eds.), *Henry VIII and his afterlives: Literature, politics and art* (Cambridge, 2009).

'James I and King David: Jacobean iconography and its legacy', in Daniel Fischlin and Mark Fortier (eds.), *Royal subjects: Essays on the writings of James VI and I* (Detroit, 2002).

Tudor royal iconography: Literature and art in an age of religious crisis (Princeton, 1989).

King, Peter, 'Bishop Wren and the suppression of the Norwich Lecturers', *HJ*, 11:2 (1968).

Kingdon, Robert M., 'Calvinism and resistance theory, 1550–1580', in J. H. Burns and Mark Goldie (eds.), *The Cambridge history of political thought, 1450–1700* (Cambridge, 1991).

Kipling, Gordon, 'Belmaine, Jean (fl. 1546–1559)', *ODNB*.

'Duwes, Giles [Aegidius de Vadis] (d. 1535)', *ODNB*.

'John Skelton and Burgundian letters', in Jan van Dorsten (ed.), *Ten studies in Anglo–Dutch relations* (Leiden, 1974).

The triumph of honour: Burgundian origins of the Elizabethan Renaissance (Leiden, 1977).

Kishlansky, Mark, 'Charles I: A case of mistaken identity', *P&P*, 189 (2005).

Knecht, R. J., *The French Renaissance court, 1483–1589* (New Haven and London, 2008).

Renaissance warrior and patron: The reign of Francis I (Cambridge, 1994).

Knighton, C. S., 'Feckenham, John (*c.* 1510–1584)', *ODNB*.

Knoppers, Laura Lunger, 'Imagining the death of the king: Milton, Charles I, and anamorphic art', in Elizabeth Bellamy, Patrick Cheney and Michael Schoenfeldt (eds.), *Imagining death in Spenser and Milton* (Basingstoke, 2003).

Kohl, B., 'The changing concept of the *studia humanitatis* in the early Renaissance', *Renaissance Studies*, 6 (1992).

Kraye, Jill, 'Stoicism in the Renaissance from Petrarch to Lipsius', *Grotiana*, 22/23 (2001–2).

Kristeller, P. O., 'The European diffusion of Italian humanism', in *Renaissance thought II: Papers on humanism and the arts* (New York, 1965).

Kroeker, Greta, *Erasmus in the footsteps of Paul: A Pauline theologian* (Toronto, 2011).

Kyle, Chris, *Theater of state: Parliament and political culture in early Stuart England* (Stanford, 2012).

Kyle, Richard, 'John Knox's concept of divine providence and its influence on his thought', *Albion*, 18:3 (1986).

Labalme, Patricia H. (ed.), *Beyond their sex: Learned women of the European past* (New York, 1980).

Lacey, Andrew, *The cult of King Charles the martyr* (Woodbridge, 2003).

Lake, Peter, *Anglicans and puritans? Presbyterianism and English conformist thought from Whitgift to Hooker* (London, 1988).

'Anti-popery: The structure of a prejudice', in Richard Cust and Ann Hughes (eds.), *Conflict in early Stuart England* (London, 1989).

'Joseph Hall, Robert Skinner and the rhetoric of moderation at the early Stuart court', in Lori Anne Ferrell and Peter McCullough (eds.), *The English sermon revised: Religion, literature and history, 1600–1750* (Manchester, 2001).

'The king (the queen) and the Jesuit: James Stuart's *True law of free monarchies* in context/s', *Transactions of the Royal Historical Society*, 6:14 (2004).

'Lancelot Andrewes, John Buckeridge, and avant-garde conformity at the court of James I', in Linda Levy Peck (ed.), *The mental world of the Jacobean court* (Cambridge, 1991).

'The monarchical republic of Queen Elizabeth I (and the fall of Archbishop Grindal) revisited', in John McDiarmid (ed.), *The monarchical republic of early modern England: Essays in response to Patrick Collinson* (Aldershot, 2007).

'Moving the goal posts? Modified subscription and the construction of conformity in the early Stuart church', in Peter Lake and Michael Questier (eds.), *Conformity and orthodoxy in the English church, c. 1560–1660* (Woodbridge, 2000).

'The politics of "popularity" and the public sphere: The "monarchical republic" of Elizabeth I defends itself', in Peter Lake and Steven Pincus (eds.), *The politics of the public sphere in early modern England* (Manchester, 2007).

'Puritans, popularity, and petitions: Local politics in national context, Cheshire, 1641', in Thomas Cogswell, Richard Cust and Peter Lake (eds.), *Politics, religion and popularity in early Stuart Britain: Essays in honour of Conrad Russell* (Cambridge, 2002).

Laoutaris, Chris, 'Translation/historical writing', in Caroline Bucks and Jennifer Summit (eds.), *The History of British women's writing 1500–1610* (London, 2010).

Larson, Anne, 'Legitimizing the daughter's writing: Catherine des Roches' proverbial good wife', *SCJ*, 21:4 (1990).

Laynesmith, J. L., *The last medieval queens: English queenship, 1445–1503* (Oxford, 2004).

Lazzari, Christian, 'Le government de la raison d'état', in Christian Lazzari and Dominique Reynié (eds.), *Le pouvoir de la raison d'état* (Paris, 1992).

Leake, Roy E., 'Antoine Fouquelin and the Pléiade', *Bibliothèque d'Humanisme et Renaissance*, 32:2 (1970).

Lee, Maurice, *Great Britain's Solomon: James VI and his three kingdoms* (Urbana, 1990).

James Stewart, earl of Moray: A political study of the Reformation in Scotland (New York, 1953).

Leedham-Green, Elizabeth, *Books in Cambridge inventories: Book-lists from vice-chancellor's court probate inventories in the Tudor and Stuart periods*, 2 vols. (Cambridge, 1986).

Lehmberg, Stanford, 'Elyot, Sir Thomas (*c.* 1490–1546)', *ODNB*.

'Throckmorton, Sir Nicholas (1515/16–1571)', *ODNB*.

Loach, Jennifer, *Edward VI*, eds. George Bernard and Penry Williams (New Haven, 1999).

Loades, David, 'Dudley, John, duke of Northumberland (1504–1553)', *ODNB*.

John Dudley, duke of Northumberland, 1504–1553 (Oxford, 1996).

Mary Tudor: A life (Oxford, 1989).

Princes of Wales: Heirs in waiting (Kew, 2008).

Loomie, A. J., 'Carey, Robert, first earl of Monmouth (1560–1639)', *ODNB*.

Lowe, Ben, 'Peace discourse and mid-Tudor foreign policy', in Paul A. Fideler and Thomas F. Mayer (eds.), *Political thought and the Tudor commonwealth: Deep structure, discourse and disguise* (London, 1992).

Lowe, David E., 'Patronage and politics: Edward IV, the Wydevills and the council of the Prince of Wales, 1471–83', *Bulletin of the Board of Celtic Studies*, 29:3 (1981).

Lynch, Michael, 'Queen Mary's triumph: The baptismal celebrations at Stirling in December 1566', *Scottish Historical Review*, 69 (1990).

MacCulloch, Diarmaid, 'Henry VIII and the reform of the church', in Diarmaid MacCulloch (ed.), *The reign of Henry VIII: Politics, policy and piety* (Basingstoke, 1995).

'Kett's rebellion in context', *P&P*, 84 (1979).

Thomas Cranmer: A life (New Haven, 1996).

Tudor church militant: Edward VI and the Protestant Reformation (London, 1999).

Macdonald, Alan R., 'James VI and I, the Church of Scotland, and British ecclesiastical convergence', *HJ*, 48:4 (2005).

Mack, Peter, *Elizabethan rhetoric: Theory and practice* (Cambridge, 2002).

A history of Renaissance rhetoric, 1380–1620 (Oxford, 2011).

Maclean, Ian, *The Renaissance notion of woman: A study in the fortunes of scholasticism and medical science in European intellectual life* (Cambridge, 1980).
Malcolm, Noel, 'Hobbes, Thomas (1588–1679)', *ODNB*.
Mansfield, Bruce, *Erasmus in the twentieth century: Interpretations* c. *1920–2000* (Toronto, 2003).
Marshall, John, *John Locke: Resistance, religion and responsibility* (Cambridge, 1994).
Marshall, Peter, *Reformation England 1480–1642* (London, 2003).
Martines, Lauro, *Power and imagination: City-states in Renaissance Italy* (New York, 1979).
Mason, Roger A., 'George Buchanan and Mary Queen of Scots', *Records of the Scottish Church History Society*, 30 (2000).
Kingship and the commonweal: Political thought in Renaissance and Reformation Scotland (East Lothian, 1998).
'Rex stoicus: George Buchanan, James VI and the Scottish polity', in John Dwyer, Roger A. Mason and Alexander Murdoch (eds.), *New perspectives on the politics and culture of early modern Scotland* (Edinburgh, 1982).
May, Steven, 'Queen Elizabeth prays for the living and the dead', in Peter Beal and Grace Ioppolo (eds.), *Elizabeth I and the culture of writing* (London, 2007).
'Queen Elizabeth to her subjects: The Tilbury and Golden speeches', in Donal Stump, Linda Shenk and Carole Levin (eds.), *Elizabeth I and the 'sovereign arts': Essays in literature, history, and culture* (Tempe, 2011).
Mayer, T. F., 'Pole, Reginald (1500–1558)', *ODNB*.
Thomas Starkey and the commonweal: Humanist politics and religion in the reign of Henry VIII (Cambridge, 1989).
'Tournai and tyranny: Imperial kingship and critical humanism', *HJ*, 34:2 (1991).
Mazzola, Elizabeth, 'Schooling shrews and grooming queens in the Tudor classroom', *Critical Survey*, 22:1 (2010).
McConica, James K., *The collegiate university: History of the University of Oxford*, vol. III (Oxford, 1986).
English humanists and Reformation politics under Henry VIII and Edward VI (Oxford, 1965).
'The fate of Erasmian humanism', in N. Phillipson (ed.), *Universities, society and the future* (Edinburgh, 1983).
McCullough, Peter E., 'Montagu, James (1568–1618)', *ODNB*.
Sermons at court: Politics and religion in Elizabethan and Jacobean preaching (Cambridge, 1998).
McDiarmid, John F., 'John Cheke's preface to *De superstitione*', *Journal of Ecclesiastical History*, 48:1 (1997).
'Recovering republican eloquence: John Cheke versus Stephen Gardiner on the pronunciation of Greek', *History of European Ideas*, 38:2 (2012).
(ed.), *The monarchical republic of early modern England: Essays in response to Patrick Collinson* (Aldershot, 2007).
McDonald, Alan R., *The Jacobean kirk, 1567–1625* (Aldershot, 1998).

McFarlane, I. D., *Buchanan* (London, 1981).

McIntosh, Jeri L., 'A culture of reverence: Princess Mary's household, 1525–27', in Alice Hunt and Anna Whitelock (eds.), *Tudor queenship: The reigns of Mary and Elizabeth* (Basingstoke, 2010).

From heads of household to heads of state: The pre-accession households of Mary and Elizabeth Tudor, 1516–1558 (New York, 2009).

McKendrick, Scot, '*La Grande Histoire Cesar* and the manuscripts of Edward IV', *English Manuscript Studies*, 2 (1990).

'Lodewijk van Gruuthuse en de Librije van Edward IV', in M. P. J. Marten (ed.), *Lodewijk van Gruuthuse, Mecenas en Europees Diplomaats ca. 1427–1492* (Bruges, 1992).

'The Romuléon and the manuscripts of Edward IV', in Nicholas Rogers (ed.), *England in the fifteenth century: Proceedings of the 1992 Harlaxton Symposium* (Stamford, 1994).

McLaren, Anne, 'Challenging the monarchical republic: James I's articulation of kingship', in John McDiarmid (ed.), *The monarchical republic of early modern England: Essays in response to Patrick Collinson* (Aldershot, 2007).

McManoman, J., *Funeral oratory and the cultural ideals of Italian humanism* (Chapel Hill, 1989).

Meale, Carol M., 'Patrons, buyers and owners: Book production and social status', in J. Griffiths and D. Pearsall (eds.), *Book production and publishing in Britain, 1375–1475* (Cambridge, 1989).

Mears, Natalie, *Queenship and political discourse in the Elizabethan realms* (Cambridge, 2005).

Mercer, R. G. G., *The teaching of Gasparino Barzizza: With special reference to his place in Paduan humanism* (London, 1979).

Merriman, Marcus, *The rough wooings: Mary Queen of Scots, 1542–1551* (East Linton, 2000).

Meyer, Jean, *L'Éducation des princes en Europe: Du XVe au XIXe siècle* (Paris, 2004).

Miller, John, *James II*, 3rd edn. (New Haven, 2000).

Milton, Anthony, *Catholic and reformed: The Roman and Protestant churches in English Protestant thought, 1600–1640* (Cambridge, 1995).

Montaiglon, Anatole de, 'Préface', in *Latin themes of Mary Stuart, Queen of Scots*, ed. Anatole de Montaiglon (London, 1855).

Morgan, Victor, *History of the University of Cambridge, 1546–1750* (Cambridge, 2004).

Morgan-Guy, John, 'Arthur, Harri Tudor and the iconography of loyalty in Wales', in Steven Gunn and Linda Monckton (eds.), *Arthur Tudor, Prince of Wales: Life, death and commemoration* (Woodbridge, 2009).

Morrill, John, 'A British patriarchy? Ecclesiastical imperialism under the early Stuarts', in A. Fletcher and P. Roberts (eds.), *Religion, culture and society in early modern Britain: Essays in honour of Patrick Collinson* (Cambridge, 1994).

'A liberation theology? Aspects of puritanism in the English revolution', in Laura Lunger Knoppers (ed.), *Puritanism and its discontents* (Newark, DE, 2003).

'The religious context of the English civil war', in Richard Cust and Ann Hughes (eds.), *The English civil war* (London, 1997).

Moss, Ann, '*Monita et exempla politica* as example of a genre', in Erik de Bom *et al.* (eds.), *(Un)masking the realities of power: Justus Lipsius and the dynamics of political writing in early modern Europe* (Leiden, 2011).

'The *Politica* of Justus Lipsius and the commonplace-book', *Journal of the History of Ideas*, 59:3 (1998).

Printed commonplace-books and the structuring of Renaissance thought (Oxford, 1996).

Renaissance truth and the Latin language (Oxford, 2003).

Mueller, Janel, 'Elizabeth Tudor: Maidenhood in crisis', in Donald Stump, Linda Shenk and Carole Levin (eds.), *Elizabeth and the 'sovereign arts': Essays in literature, history, and culture* (Tempe, 2011).

Murphy, Beverly A., *Bastard prince: Henry VIII's lost son* (Stroud, 2003).

'Blount, Elizabeth (*c.* 1500–1539×41)', *ODNB.*

'Folbury, George (d. 1540)', *ODNB.*

Murphy, Virginia, 'The literature and propaganda of Henry VIII's first divorce', in Diarmaid MacCulloch (ed.), *The reign of Henry VIII: Politics, policy and piety* (Basingstoke, 1995).

Nativel, Colette, *Femmes savantes, savoirs des femmes: Du crépuscule de la Renaissance à l'aube des lumières* (Geneva, 1995).

Nelson, Eric, *The Greek tradition in republican thought* (Cambridge, 2004).

Neville-Sington, Pamela, 'Press, politics and religion', in L. Hellinga and J. B. Trapp (eds.), *The Cambridge history of the book in Britain*, vol. III: *1400–1557* (Cambridge, 1999).

Newman, John, 'Cardinal Wolsey's collegiate foundations', in Steven Gunn and Phillip Lindley (eds.), *Cardinal Wolsey: Church, state and art* (Cambridge, 1991).

Norbrook, David, 'Rhetoric, ideology and the Elizabethan world picture', in Peter Mack (ed.), *Renaissance rhetoric* (New York, 1994).

Nussbaum, Martha, *Cultivating humanity: A classical defense of reform in liberal education* (Cambridge, MA, 1997).

Not for profit: Why democracy needs the humanities (Princeton, 2010).

Nutton, Vivian, 'Linacre, Thomas (*c.* 1460–1524)', *ODNB.*

O'Day, Rosemary, *Education and society 1500–1800* (London, 1982).

O'Malley, John, *The first Jesuits* (Cambridge, MA, 1993).

Ong, Walter J., 'Latin language study as a Renaissance puberty rite', *Studies in Philology*, 56 (1959).

Rhetoric, roman and technology: Studies in the interaction of expression and culture (Ithaca, 1971).

Orme, Nicholas, *From childhood to chivalry: The education of the English kings and aristocracy, 1066–1530* (London, 1984).

Education in early Tudor England: Magdalen College, Oxford and its school, 1480–1540 (Oxford, 1998).
'The Education of Edward V', *Bulletin of the Institute of Historical Research*, 52:136 (1984).
Education and society in medieval and Renaissance England (London, 1989).
'John Holt (d.1504), Tudor schoolmaster and grammarian', *The Library*, 18:4 (1996).
Medieval schools: From Roman Britain to Renaissance England (New Haven, 2006).
'Schools and school-books', in Lotte Hellinga and J. B. Trapp (eds.), *The Cambridge history of the book in Britain*: vol. III: *1400–1557* (Cambridge, 1999).
Overell, Anne, *Italian reform and English Reformations, c.1535–c.1585* (Aldershot, 2008).
Paris, Paulin, *Études sur François premier roi de France*, 2 vols. (Paris, 1885).
Parker, Geoffrey, *Europe in crisis 1598–1648* (Brighton, 1980).
Patterson, W. B., *King James VI and I and the reunion of Christendom* (New York, 1997).
Peltonen, Markku, *Classical humanism and republicanism in English political thought, 1570–1640* (Cambridge, 1995).
Rhetoric, politics and popularity in pre-revolutionary England (Cambridge, 2013).
Pender, Patricia, *Early modern women's writing and the rhetoric of modesty* (Basingstoke, 2012).
Penn, Thomas, *Winter king: Henry VII and the dawn of Tudor England* (New York, 2012).
Perry, Curtis, 'Royal authorship and the problems of manuscript attribution in the poems of King James VI and I', *Notes and Queries*, 46:2 (1999).
Pierce, Hazel, 'The king's cousin: The life, career and Welsh connection of Sir Richard Pole, 1485–1504', *Welsh History Review*, 19:2 (1998).
Margaret Pole, Countess of Salisbury, 1473–1541: Loyalty, lineage and leadership (Cardiff, 2003).
Plowden, Alison, 'Grey, Lady Jane (1537–1554)', *ODNB*.
Pocock, J. G. A., 'Two kingdoms and three histories? Political thought in British contexts', in Roger A. Mason (ed.), *Scots and Britons: Scottish political thought and the union of 1603* (Cambridge, 1994).
Pogson, Fiona, 'Foulis, Sir David, first baronet (d. 1642)', *ODNB*.
Pollard, A. F., *Wolsey* (London, 1929).
Pollet, Maurice, *John Skelton: Poet of Tudor England*, trans. John Warrington (London, 1971).
Pollnitz, Aysha, 'Christian women or sovereign queens? Representing the schooling of Mary I and Elizabeth I', in Anna Whitelock and Alice Hunt (eds.), *Tudor queenship: The reigns of Mary and Elizabeth* (Basingstoke, 2010).
'Educating Hamlet and Prince Hal', in David Armitage, Conal Condren and Andrew Fitzmaurice (eds.), *Shakespeare and early modern political thought* (Cambridge, 2009).

'Humanism and court culture in the education of Tudor royal children', in Tom Betteridge and Anna Riehl (eds.), *Tudor court culture* (Selingrove, PA, 2010).

'Humanism and the education of Henry, Prince of Wales', in Timothy Wilks (ed.), *Prince Henry revived: Image and exemplarity in early modern England* (London, 2007).

'Religion and translation in the court of Henry VIII: Princess Mary, Katherine Parr and the *Paraphrases* of Erasmus', in Susan Doran and Thomas Freeman (eds.), *Mary Tudor: Old and new perspectives* (Houndmills, 2011).

Potter, Lois, 'The royal martyr in the Restoration: National grief and national sin', in Thomas Corns (ed.), *The royal image: Representations of Charles I* (Cambridge, 1999).

Poynting, Sarah, '"From his Matie to me with his awin hand": The king's correspondence during the period of personal rule', in Ian Atherton and Julie Sanders (eds.), *The 1630s: Interdisciplinary essays on culture and politics in the Caroline era* (Manchester, 2006).

Prescott, Anne Lake, 'The pearl of the Valois and Elizabeth I: Marguerite de Navarre's *Mirroir* and Tudor England', in Margaret P. Hannay (ed.), *Silent but for the word: Tudor women as patrons, translators, and writers of religious works* (Kent, OH, 1985).

Proctor, Robert, *Defining the humanities: How rediscovering a tradition can improve our schools* (Indiana, 1998).

Pursell, Brennan, 'James I, Gondomar and the dissolution of the parliament of 1621', *History*, 85 (2000).

'War or peace? Jacobean politics and the parliament of 1621', in Chris Kyle (ed.), *Parliament, politics and elections 1604–1648* (Cambridge, 2001).

The winter king: Frederick V of the Palatinate and the coming of the Thirty Years' War (Aldershot, 2003).

Questier, Michael (ed.), *Stuart dynastic policy and religious politics, 1621–1625* (Cambridge, 2009).

Rawcliffe, Carol, 'Somerset, John (d. 1454)', *ODNB*.

Raylor, Timothy, 'The Anglican attack on Hobbes in Paris, 1651', *HJ*, 53:1 (2010).

Redworth, Glyn, *In defence of the Catholic church: The life of Stephen Gardiner* (Oxford, 1990).

'Of pimps and princes: Three unpublished letters from James I and the Prince of Wales relating to the Spanish match', *HJ*, 37:2 (1994).

The prince and the infanta: The cultural politics of the Spanish match (New Haven, 2003).

Reeve, L. J., *Charles I and the road to personal rule* (Cambridge, 1989).

Reeve, Michael D., 'Classical scholarship', in Jill Kraye (ed.), *The Cambridge companion to Renaissance humanism* (Cambridge, 1996).

Rex, Richard, 'The crisis of obedience: God's word and Henry's reformation', *HJ*, 39 (1996).

Henry VIII and the English Reformation, 2nd edn. (Basingstoke, 2006).

'Lady Margaret Beaufort and her professorships: 1502–1559', in Patrick Collinson, Richard Rex and Graham Stanton (eds.), *Lady Margaret Beaufort and her professors of divinity at Cambridge, 1502–1649* (New York, 2003).

'Redating Henry VIII's *A glasse of the truthe*', *The Library*, 7:4 (2003).

'The religion of Henry VIII', *HJ*, 57:1 (2014).

'The role of English humanists in the Reformation up to 1559', in N. Scott Amos, Andrew Pettegree and Henk Van Nierop (eds.), *The education of a Christian society: Humanism and the Reformation in Britain and the Netherlands* (Aldershot, 1999).

The Tudors (Stroud, 2002).

Reynolds, I. D. and N. G. Wilson, *Scribes and scholars: A guide to the transmission of Greek and Latin literature*, 3rd edn. (Oxford, 1991).

Rhatigan, Emma, 'Preaching to princes: John Burgess and George Hakewill in the royal pulpit', *Journal of Ecclesiastical History*, 62 (2011).

Richardson, Glen, *Renaissance monarchy: The reigns of Henry VIII, Francis I and Charles V* (London, 2001).

Rickard, Jane, *Authorship and authority: The writings of James VI and I* (Manchester, 2007).

Robinson, Douglas, 'Theorizing translation in a woman's voice: Subverting the rhetoric of patronage, courtly love and morality', *The Translator*, 1 (1995).

Robinson, John, 'The slippery truth of George Buchanan's autobiography', *SCJ*, 39:1 (2008).

Robinson, W. R. B., 'Prince Arthur in the Marches of Wales, 1493–1502', *Studia Celtica*, 36 (2002).

'Princess Mary's itinerary in the Marches of Wales 1525–1527: A provisional record', *Historical Research*, 71 (1998).

Rose, Jacqueline, *Godly kingship in Restoration England: The politics of the royal supremacy, 1660–1688* (Cambridge, 2011).

'Kingship and counsel in early modern England', *HJ*, 54:1 (2011).

Ross, Charles, *Edward IV*, 2nd edn. (New Haven, 1997).

Ross, Sarah, *The birth of feminism: Woman as intellect in Renaissance Italy and England* (Cambridge, MA, 2009).

Rothlatt, Sheldon, *Tradition and change in English liberal education: An essay in history and culture* (London, 1976).

Rubinstein, Nicolai, 'Italian political thought', in J. H. Burns and Mark Goldie (eds.), *Cambridge history of political thought, 1450–1700* (Cambridge, 1991).

Ruble, Alphonse de, *La Première jeunesse de Marie Stuart* (Paris, 1891).

Rummel, Erika, *Erasmus' annotations on the New Testament: From philologist to theologian* (Toronto, 1986).

Erasmus as a translator of the classics (Toronto, 1985).

Rundle, David, 'Filippo Alberici, Henry VII and Richard Fox: The English fortunes of a little-known Italian humanist', *Journal of the Warburg and Courtauld Institutes*, 68 (2005).

'Humanism before the Tudors: On nobility and the reception of the *studia humanitatis* in fifteenth-century England', in Jonathan Woolfson (ed.), *Reassessing Tudor humanism* (London, 2002).

'"Not so much praise as precept": Erasmus, panegyric and the Renaissance art of teaching princes', in Yun Lee Too and Niall Livingstone (eds.), *Pedagogy and power: Rhetorics of classical learning* (Cambridge, 1998).

'Was there a Renaissance style of politics in fifteenth-century England?', in George Bernard and Steven Gunn (eds.), *Authority and consent in Tudor England: Essays presented to C. S. L. Davis* (Aldershot, 2002).

Russell, Conrad, *The causes of the English civil war* (Oxford, 1990).

Parliaments and English politics, 1621–1629 (Oxford, 1979).

Ryle, S. F., 'Cox, Leonard (b. *c.* 1495, d. in or after 1549)', *ODNB*.

Ryrie, Alec, 'Divine kingship and royal theology in Henry VIII's Reformation', *Reformation*, 7 (2002).

The Gospel and Henry VIII: Evangelicals in the early English Reformation (Cambridge, 2003).

Sabbadini, Remigio, *Storia e critica di testi Latini*, 2nd edn. (Padua, 1971).

Salazar, Philippe-Joseph, 'Elizabeth à Descartes: "Êntre mieux intruite de votre bouche"', in Colette Nativel (ed.), *Femmes savants, savoirs des femmes: Du crépuscule de la Renaissance à l'aube des Lumières* (Geneva, 1999).

Salmon, J. H. M., 'An alternative theory of popular resistance: Buchanan, Rossaeus and Locke', in *Renaissance and revolution: Essays in the intellectual and social history of early modern France* (Cambridge, 1987).

'Cicero and Tacitus in sixteenth-century France', *American Historical Review*, 85:2 (1980), 307–31.

Sanchez-Molero, Jose Luis Gonzalo, *Felipe II: La educación de un 'felicísimo princípe' 1527–1545* (Madrid, 2014).

Saygin, Susanne, *Humphrey, duke of Gloucester (1390–1447) and the Italian humanists* (Leiden, 2002).

Scarisbrick, J. J., *Henry VIII* (Berkeley, 1968).

Scattergood, John, 'Skelton, John (*c.* 1460–1529)', *ODNB*.

Schochet, Gordon, *Patriarchalism in political thought: The authoritarian family and political speculation and attitudes* (Oxford, 1975).

Schoeck, Richard, 'Humanism in England', in Albert Rabil Jr (ed.), *Renaissance humanism: Foundations, forms, and legacy* (Philadelphia, 1988).

Shagan, Ethan, 'Beyond good and evil: Thinking with moderates in early modern England', *Journal of British Studies*, 49:3 (2010).

'Fetherston, Richard (d. 1540)', *ODNB*.

Popular politics and the English Reformation (Cambridge, 2003).

'Protector Somerset and the 1549 rebellions: New sources and new perspectives', *EHR*, 114 (1999).

Shami, Jean, *John Donne and conformity in crisis in the late Jacobean pulpit* (Cambridge, 2003).

Shapiro, Lisa, 'Princess Elizabeth and Descartes: The union of soul and body and the practice of philosophy', *British Journal for the History of Philosophy*, 7:3 (1999).

Sharpe, Kevin, *Image wars: Promoting kings and commonwealths in England, 1603–1660* (New Haven, 2010).

'The king's writ: Royal authors and royal authority in early modern England', in Kevin Sharpe and Peter Lake (eds.), *Culture and politics in early Stuart England* (Stanford, 1993).

The personal rule of Charles I (New Haven, 1992).

Politics and ideas in early Stuart England: Essays and studies (London, 1989).

'Private conscience and public duty in the writings of Charles I', *HJ*, 40:3 (1997).

'Private conscience and public duty in the writings of James VI and I', in John Morrill, Paul Slack and Daniel Woolf (eds.), *Public duty and private conscience in seventeenth-century England* (Oxford, 1993).

Reading authority and representing rule in early modern England (London, 2013).

Remapping early modern England: The culture of seventeenth-century politics (Cambridge, 2000).

Shenk, Linda, *Learned queen: The image of Elizabeth I in politics and poetry* (New York, 2010).

Shrank, Cathy, *Writing the nation in Reformation England, 1530–1580* (Oxford, 2004).

Shriver, Frederick, 'Orthodoxy and diplomacy: James I and the Vorstius affair', *EHR*, 85:336 (1970).

Simon, Joan, *Education and society in Tudor England* (Cambridge, 1966).

Skemer, Don C., *Binding words: Textual amulets in the middle ages* (University Park, PA, 2006).

Skidmore, Chris, *Edward VI: The lost king of England* (London, 2007).

Skinner, Quentin, *The foundations of modern political thought*, 2 vols. (Cambridge 1978).

'Humanism, scholasticism and popular sovereignty', in *Visions of politics*, vol. II: *Renaissance virtues* (Cambridge, 2002).

Liberty before liberalism (Cambridge, 1998).

Reason and rhetoric in the philosophy of Hobbes (Cambridge, 1996).

'Rethinking political liberty', *History Workshop Journal*, 61:1 (2006).

Smith, David L., *A history of the modern British Isles, 1603–1707: The double crown* (Oxford, 1998).

Smith, J. Beverley, 'Crown and community in the principality of north Wales in the reign of Henry Tudor', *Welsh History Review*, 3:2 (1966).

Smuts, Malcolm, *Court culture and the origins of a royalist tradition in early Stuart England* (Philadelphia, 1987).

'The making of *rex pacificus*: James VI and I and the problem of peace in an age of religious war', in Daniel Fischlin and Mark Fortier (eds.), *Royal subjects: Essays on the writings of James VI and I* (Detroit, 2002).

'Murray, Thomas (1564–1623)', *ODNB*.

'Murray, William, first earl of Dysart (d. 1655)', *ODNB*.

'Prince Henry and his world', in Catherine McLeod (ed.), *The lost prince: The life and death of Henry Stuart* (London, 2012).

Snyder, Susan, 'Guilty sisters: Marguerite de Navarre, Elizabeth of England, and the *Miroir de l'âme Pécheresse*', *Renaissance Quarterly*, 50:2 (1997).

Soll, Jacob, 'Amelot de la Houssaye (1634–1706) annotates Tacitus', *Journal of the History of Ideas*, 61:2 (2000).

The information master: Jean-Baptiste Colbert's secret state intelligence system (Ann Arbor, 2009).

Sommerville, J. P., *Royalists and patriots: Politics and ideology in England, 1603–1640*, 2nd edn. (London, 1999).

Sommerville, Margaret, *Sex and subjection: Attitudes to women in early-modern society* (London, 1995).

Sowerby, Robin, 'Early humanist failure with Homer (I)', *International Journal of the Classical Tradition*, 4:1 (1997).

'Early humanist failure with Homer (II)', *International Journal of the Classical Tradition*, 4:2 (1997).

Spitz, Lewis W., 'Further lines of enquiry for the study of "Reformation and Pedagogy"', in C. Trinkaus and H. A. Oberman (eds.), *The pursuit of holiness in late medieval and Renaissance religion* (Leiden, 1974).

Stacey, Peter, *Roman monarchy and the Renaissance prince* (Cambridge, 2007).

Staines, John, 'Compassion in the public sphere of Milton and King Charles', in Gail Kern Pastor, Katherine Rose and Mary Floyd-Wilson (eds.), *Reading the early modern passions: Essays in the cultural history of emotion* (Philadelphia, 2004).

Starkey, David, *Elizabeth* (London, 2000).

Henry: Virtuous prince (London, 2008).

Stein, Gabriel, *John Palsgrave as Renaissance linguist: A pioneer in vernacular language description* (Oxford, 1997).

Stevenson, Jane, *Women Latin poets: Language, gender, and authority from antiquity to the eighteenth century* (Oxford, 2005).

Stewart, Alan, 'Boys' buttocks revisited: James VI and the myth of the sovereign schoolmaster', in Thomas Betteridge (ed.), *Sodomy in early modern Europe* (Manchester, 2002).

The cradle king: A life of James VI and I (London, 2003).

'The trouble with English humanism: Tyndale, More and Darling Erasmus', in Jonathan Woolfson (ed.), *Reassessing Tudor humanism* (Basingstoke, 2002).

Stilma, Astrid, 'James VI and I as a religious writer', in Crawford Gribben and David G. Mullan (eds.), *Literature and the Scottish reformation* (Aldershot, 2009).

'Tyrants and translations: Dutch interpretations of George Buchanan's political thought', in Caroline Erskine and Roger A. Mason (eds.), *George Buchanan: Political thought in early modern Britain and Europe* (Ashgate, 2012).

Stoddart, Jane, *Girlhood of Mary Queen of Scots* (London, 1908).

Stone, Lawrence, 'The educational revolution in England, 1560–1640', *P&P*, 28 (1964).

String, T. C., 'Henry VIII's illuminated *Great Bible*', *Journal of the Warburg and Courtauld Institutes*, 59 (1996).

Strong, Patrick and Felicity Strong, 'The last will and codicil of Henry V', *EHR*, 96 (1981).

Strong, Roy, *Henry Prince of Wales and England's lost renaissance* (London, 1986).

Summerson, Henry, 'Erskine, John, seventeenth or first earl of Mar (d. 1572)', *ODNB*.

Summit, Jennifer, *Lost property: The woman writer and English literary history, 1380–1589* (Chicago, 2000).

Taylor, Andrew, '"Ad omne virtutum genus"? Mary between piety, pedagogy and praise in early Tudor humanism', in Susan Doran and Thomas Freeman (eds.), *Mary Tudor: Old and new perspectives* (Basingstoke, 2011).

Teague, Frances, 'Princess Elizabeth's hand in *The glass of the sinful soul*', in Peter Beal and Margaret Ezell (eds.), *Writings by early modern women*, vol. IX: *English manuscript studies, 1100–1700* (London, 2000).

Thomas, A. H. and I. D. Thornley (eds.), *The great chronicle of London* (London, 1938).

Thrush, Andrew, 'The personal rule of James I, 1611–1620', in Thomas Cogswell, Richard Cust and Peter Lake (eds.), *Politics, religion and popularity in early Stuart Britain: Essays in honour of Conrad Russell* (Cambridge, 2002).

Thuau, Etienne, *Raison d'état et pensée politique à l'époque de Richelieu* (Paris, 2000).

Todd, Robert B., 'Geminus Rhodius/ Ps. Proclus', in Virginia Brown (ed.), *Catalogus translationum et commentariorum: Mediaeval and Renaissance Latin translations and commentaries: Annotated lists and guides*, 8 vols., vol. VIII (Washington, DC, 2003).

Too, Yun Lee and Niall Livingston (eds.), *Pedagogy and power: Rhetorics of classical learning* (Cambridge, 2000).

Tracy, James D., *The politics of Erasmus: A pacifist intellectual and his political milieu* (Toronto, 1978).

Trapp, J. B., 'Carmeliano, Pietro (*c*. 1451–1527)', *ODNB*.

'The humanist book', in Lotte Hellinga and J. B. Trapp (eds.), *The Cambridge history of the book in Britain*, vol. III: *1400–1557* (Cambridge, 1999).

Trevor-Roper, Hugh, 'George Buchanan and the ancient Scottish constitution', *EHR*, suppl. 3 (1966).

Historical essays (London, 1957).

The invention of Scotland: Myth and history (New Haven, 2008).

Truman, Ronald, *Spanish treatises on government, society and religion in the time of Philipp II* (Leiden, 1999).

Tuck, Richard, *Philosophy and government, 1572–1651* (Cambridge, 1993).

Tudor-Craig, Pamela, 'Henry VIII and King David', in Daniel Williams (ed.), *Early Tudor England: Proceedings of the 1987 Harlaxton Symposium* (Woodbridge, 1989).

Tyacke, Nicholas, *Anti-Calvinists: The rise of English Arminianism, c. 1590–1640* (Oxford, 1990).

'Puritan politicians and King James VI and I, 1587–1604', in Thomas Cogswell, Richard Cust and Peter Lake (eds.), *Politics, religion and popularity in early Stuart Britain: Essays in honour of Conrad Russell* (Cambridge, 2002).

'Puritanism, Arminianism, and counter-revolution', in Richard Cust and Ann Hughes (eds.), *The English civil war* (London, 1997).

Tyler, Royall, *The emperor Charles the fifth* (Liverpool, 1956).

Ullmann, Walter, 'This realm of England is an empire', *Journal of Ecclesiastical History*, 30 (1979).

Ullmans, B. L., *The origin and development of humanistic script* (Rome, 1960).

Underwood, M., 'John Fisher and the promotion of learning', in Brendan Bradshaw and Eamon Duffy (eds.), *Humanism, reform and Reformation: The career of Bishop John Fisher* (Cambridge, 1989).

Underwood, William, 'Thomas Cromwell and William Marshall's Protestant books', *HJ*, 47:3 (2004).

Vaillancourt, Luc, *La lettre familière au XVIe siècle. Rhétorique humaniste de l'épistolaire* (Paris, 2003).

Van Gelderen, Martin, *The political thought of the Dutch revolt, 1555–1590* (Cambridge, 1992).

Venuti, Lawrence, *The translator's invisibility: A history of translation* (London, 1995).

Verhaaren, Christine Isom, *Allies with the infidels: The Ottoman and French alliance in the sixteenth century* (New York, 2011).

Vickers, Brian, *In defence of rhetoric*, rev. edn. (Oxford, 1989).

'"The power of persuasion": Images of the orator, Elyot to Shakespeare', in James J. Murphy (ed.), *Renaissance eloquence* (Berkeley, 1983).

Viroli, Maurizio, *From politics to reason of state: The acquisition and transformation of the language of politics, 1250–1600* (Cambridge, 1992).

Wahrman, D., 'From imaginary drama to dramatized imagery: The *Mappe-Monde Nouvelle Papistique*, 1566–67', *Journal of the Warburg and Courtauld Institutes*, 54 (1991).

Wakely, Maria and Graham Rees, 'Folios fit for a king: James I, John Bill, and the king's printers, 1616–1620', *Huntington Library Quarterly*, 68.3 (2005).

Walsh, K. J., 'Cranmer and the fathers, especially in the *Defence*', *Journal of Religious History*, 11 (1980).

Walsham, Alexandra, '"A very Deborah?" The myth of Elizabeth I as a providential monarch', in Susan Doran and Thomas Freeman (eds.), *The myth of Elizabeth* (Basingstoke, 2003).

Providence in early modern England (Oxford, 1999).

Watts, John, *Henry VI and the politics of kingship* (Cambridge, 1996).

'The policie in Christen remes: Bishop Russell's parliamentary sermons of 1483–84', in George Bernard and Steven Gunn (eds.), *Authority and consent in Tudor England: Essays presented to C. S. L. Davis* (Aldershot, 2002).

Weiss, Roberto, *Humanism in England during the fifteenth century*, 2nd edn. (Oxford, 1957).

Wenig, Scott, 'The Reformation in the Diocese of Ely during the episcopate of Richard Cox, 1559–77', *SCJ*, 33:1 (2002).

White, Micheline, 'Women, religious communities, prose genres, and textual production', in Micheline White (ed.), *English women, religion, and textual production, 1500–1625* (Aldershot, 2011).

Whitelock, Anna, *Mary Tudor: England's first queen* (London, 2009).

'"Woman, warrior, queen?": Rethinking Mary and Elizabeth', in Anna Whitelock and Alice Hunt (eds.), *Tudor queenship: The reigns of Mary and Elizabeth* (Basingstoke, 2010).

Wilcher, Robert, '*Eikon Basilike*: The printing, composition, strategy, and impact of "The king's book"', in Laura Lunger Knoppers (ed.), *The Oxford handbook of literature and the English revolution* (Oxford, 2012).

Wilks, Timothy, 'The pike charged: Henry as militant prince', in Timothy Wilks (ed.), *Prince Henry revived: Image and exemplarity in early modern England* (London, 2007).

Williamson, Arthur, 'British Israel and Roman Britain: The Jews and Scottish models of polity from George Buchanan to Samuel Rutherford', in R. H. Popkin and G. M. Weiner (eds.), *Jewish Christians and Christian Jews: From the Renaissance to the Enlightenment* (Dordrecht, 1994).

Withington, Philip, 'Public discourse, corporate citizenship, and state formation in early modern England', *American Historical Review*, 112 (2007).

Society in early modern England: The vernacular origins of some powerful ideas (Cambridge, 2010).

Witt, Ronald G., *In the footsteps of the ancients: The origins of humanism from Lovato to Bruni* (Boston, 2003).

Wolffe, Bertram, *Henry VI* (New Haven, 2001).

Wood, Andy, *The 1549 rebellions and the making of early modern England* (Cambridge, 2007).

Wood, Charles T., *Joan of Arc and Richard III: Sex, saints, and government in the middle ages* (New York, 1988).

Wood, Diane, *Hélisenne de Crenne: At the crossroads of Renaissance humanism and feminism* (Madison, NJ, 2000).

Wooding, Lucy, *Rethinking Catholicism in Reformation England* (Oxford, 2000).

Woolfson, Jonathan, 'Croke, Richard (1489–1558)', *ODNB*.

Wormald, Jenny, 'James VI and I, *Basilikon doron* and *The trew law of free monarchies*: The Scottish context and the English translation', in Linda Levy Peck (ed.), *The mental world of the Jacobean court* (Cambridge, 1991).

'King James VI and I: Two kings or one?', *History*, 63 (1983).

Mary Queen of Scots: A study in failure (London, 1988).

'"Tis true I am a cradle king": The view from the throne', in Julian Goodare and Michael Lynch (eds.), *The reign of James VI* (East Linton, 2000).

Woudhuysen, Henry, 'The queen's own hand: A preliminary account', in Peter Beal and Grace Ioppolo (eds.), *Elizabeth I and the culture of writing* (London, 2007).

Wright, Stephen, 'Grindal William, d. 1548', *ODNB*.
Wyatt, Michael, *The Italian encounter with Tudor England: A cultural politics of translation* (Cambridge, 2005).
Young, Peter, *Edgehill, 1642: The campaign and the battle* (Kineton, 1967).
Zaller, Robert, *The parliament of 1621: A study in constitutional conflict* (London, 1971).
Ziegler, Georgianna, 'A second phoenix: The rebirth of Elizabeth I in Elizabeth Stuart', in Elizabeth H. Hageman and Katherine Conway (eds.), *Resurrecting Elizabeth I in seventeenth-century England* (Madison, 2007).

UNPUBLISHED DISSERTATIONS

Curtis, Catherine, 'Richard Pace on pedagogy, counsel and satire' (Ph.D. dissertation, University of Cambridge, 1996).
Needham, Paul S., 'Sir John Cheke at Cambridge and court', 2 vols. (Ph.D. dissertation, Harvard University, 1971).
Wilks, Timothy, 'The court culture of Prince Henry and his circle, 1603–1613' (D.Phil. dissertation, Oxford University, 1987).

Index